Distant Proximities

DYNAMICS BEYOND GLOBALIZATION

James N. Rosenau

PRINCETON UNIVERSITY PRESS

PRINCETON AND OXFORD

Copyright © 2003 by Princeton University Press
Published by Princeton University Press, 41 William Street, Princeton,
New Jersey 08540
In the United Kingdom: Princeton University Press, 3 Market Place,
Woodstock, Oxfordshire OX20 1SY

Library of Congress Cataloging-in-Publication Data

Rosenau, James N.
Distant proximities : dynamics beyond globalization / James N. Rosenau.
p. cm.
Includes bibliographical references and index.
ISBN 0-691-09523-X (alk. paper) — ISBN 0-691-09524-8 (pbk. : alk. paper)
1. International relations. I. Title.
JZ1305 .R67 2003
327.1′01—dc21   2002031741

British Library Cataloging-in-Publication Data is available

This book has been composed in Galliard

Printed on acid-free paper. ∞

www.pupress.princeton.edu

Printed in the United States of America

10 9 8 7 6 5 4 3 2 1

FOR FAN

May the distant proximities of your world be constructive and manageable

Contents

Figures and Tables

Preface

I WAS JUST COMPLETING the fourth revision of this book and getting ready to send it to the publisher when the World Trade Center and the Pentagon were attacked on September 11, 2001. Aside from the numbness induced by these horrendous events, I had to confront the question of what they meant for the book's foci and themes. Was a major rewrite in order, given a widely articulated notion that everything had changed as a result of the attacks—that the world had entered a new era in which long-standing premises and practices were no longer viable? As one analyst put it, "Few veteran foreign policy watchers can remember when a single event has had so instant and so profound an effect on the entire dynamic of world politics."[1]

Further reflection, however, led me to conclude that, shocking as they were, the terrorist attacks did not contradict the basic presumptions of the book: that everywhere people and their societies have entered an emergent epoch, an epoch marked by pervasive uncertainties, perplexing ambiguities, and unending contradictions fostered by a wide range of dynamics, not the least being newly empowered individuals and expanded roles for nongovernmental agents of change. Thus it made sense to interpret the attacks as adding a new dimension to the analysis rather than as upending its central thrusts. Viewed in this way, the attacks were yet another distant proximity—an appalling one that had vast consequences, to be sure, but nevertheless a sequence of events consistent with the underlying patterns set forth in the earlier drafts of the manuscript. Accordingly, what follows (including the remainder of this preface) consists of previously written paragraphs and chapters plus the inclusion, where relevant, of estimates of how the terrorist attacks exemplify and expand the original formulation of a shrinking world in which what is distant is also proximate.

This book has been brewing for a long, long time. For years I have been perplexed and preoccupied by the question of how individuals (alone and in groups) at the micro level and collectivities (states but also any other type of organization) at the macro level shape each other's behavior in world affairs. My conception of where the solution of this micro-macro, or macro-micro, problem lies has never wavered: it has always seemed

---

[1] Serge Schmemann, "A Growing List of Foes Now Suddenly Friends," *New York Times*, October 5, 2001, p. B3.

clear that the two types of agents interactively shape each other, that one is not necessarily more causally powerful than the other. Thus to ignore the impact of either level is to ensure truncated and insufficient analysis. This conviction has been strengthened even further in recent years by the extent to which politics and society have become driven less by long-standing ideologies and more by self-centered preoccupations. As I argue in the ensuing pages, what differentiates people today is not so much their commitment to conservative, liberal, or radical perspectives as it is their orientations toward the near and distant worlds in which their lives are ensconced. Hence the book is organized around twelve worlds that are conceived to be the focus of their orientations toward the course of events.

But to be convinced of where the solution lies is not to overcome perplexity or resolve the micro-macro problem. On the contrary, increasingly the problem has loomed as intractable and insoluble because standard methodologies for unraveling it are scarce and those that do exist lie outside my competence. I do not have the resources to conduct extensive experiments or interviews. Nor do I have the training to employ a methodology that has lately shown promise as a way of addressing the problem, that is, the use of computer simulations to probe agent-based models that allow for observation of how variations at one level are linked to variations at the other level.

So what to do? If the problem will not go away, and if one is unwilling to treat one level as causally predominant, how to proceed? How to dare to take on the problem when it seems virtually certain one is bound to fail?

The chapters that follow are an attempt to answer these questions. They derive from a conviction that the only sure way to fail is not to try, hoping that even if success proves elusive, it will point others to possible solutions of the problem. In retrospect, it seems clear this stubborn conviction has always driven my inquiries, especially after I began to appreciate that profound transformations on a global scale included meaningful and systematic variations at the micro level; that neither individuals nor publics are constants; and that they can vary in systematic ways that have macro consequences. For some time I have contended that micro variations involved change in the skills of people, and here this contention is expanded to include several other micro variables (see chapter 10). This conceptual breakthrough has facilitated a renewed effort to address the micro-macro problem. Now, at least, a plausible basis for linking shifts in the conduct of collectivities to variations in people—in their skills, orientations, interests, and actions—is open to exploration.

Consequently, too, the methodological challenge no longer seems so daunting. Committed to accounting for the influence of ordinary persons at the macro level, one can turn to a form of inquiry—journalism—in which the actions and attitudes of individuals are treated as reflections of larger processes. It takes only a casual reading of today's newspapers to readily imagine editors advising cub reporters to open their accounts with a human interest vignette, with the result that most news stories begin with the plight of a particular person or family and then move on to how one or another macro institution shapes, sustains, ameliorates, or otherwise responds to such individual situations. Such a mode of analysis is not hard—or even soft—science, to be sure, but it does offer a means of more consistently focusing on the micro-macro problem than does virtually any other empirical method. It is thus neither an accident nor a form of laziness that the ensuing pages are pervaded with citations to accounts in the *New York Times* and other news media sources. In effect, reliance on the anecdote becomes a methodology of investigation, allowing for the pursuit of micro-macro linkages that one senses to be crucial to world affairs even though they may not be systematically traceable. Doubtless some readers will deride proceeding in this way, but I make no apology for having done so. It is for me a way to break into an otherwise irresolvable problem. Hopefully the book will provoke further micro-macro inquiries even if it does not vindicate such a seemingly crude methodology.

In a profound sense this book has been greatly helped by an invisible college comprising all those colleagues and students who have heard verbal presentations of one or another of its parts and then sent in relevant suggestions, criticisms, and citations that were incorporated into the manuscript. It is not possible to list all the members of the invisible college to whom I feel so very grateful, but it is a pleasure to acknowledge their contribution and to express the hope that I can reciprocate through membership in their college.

Three dear friends, colleagues, and mentors continued to be influential in framing the intellectual foundations of the book even though they did not live to be present at either its inception or its completion. That is only one of the numerous reason why I continue to miss Harry C. Bredemeier, Richard C. Snyder, and Susan Strange.

Among the many very alive and visible students and colleagues to whom I am indebted for their critical reactions to earlier versions of the various chapters, I am particularly grateful to Richard W. Mansbach, Laura Paler, Gulnaz Sharafutdinova, and an anonymous reviewer for the Princeton University Press, all of whom read the manuscript in its entirety and made a number of useful comments, criticisms, and suggestions. My seminar on the Dynamics of Globalization during the spring semester of 2000 was organized around the original draft of chapters 1 through 7, and I benefited enormously from the vigorous discussions in which the twelve students assessed both the broad conception and the specific details of the emergent manuscript. Among other things, they objected to an early diagrammatic formulation of the twelve-world scheme, and one of the students, Diane Wildsmith, subsequently applied her considerable skills as an architect in helping to design the version that is now figure 2.4. Similarly, at a much later stage, in the summer of 2001, the students in the course on global governance at the Central European University provided critical reactions to tables 3.1, 4.1, 5.1, and 6.1; I am especially indebted to Olivia Rusu-Toderean and Anna Pochylczuk for their specific suggestions on how the tables could be improved. Francis A. Beer, Robert W. Cox, Mary Durfee, David Earnest, W. Michael Fagen, Matthew Hoffmann, David Johnson, Michael LaBelle, and James Liu read one or another part of the manuscript, and their inputs are also gratefully acknowledged. Dawn Moncrief and Sally Montague not only sustained my office while I was preoccupied with the writing of the manuscript but also helped enormously in maintaining its files and preparing the final version. I am also grateful to Katja Gersak for the long hours she put in helping to prepare the indexes.

The feedback and encouragement of Chuck Myers, my editor at the Princeton University Press, were invaluable. He is not only a first-rate editor with a keen understanding of academic publishing but also a fine political scientist.

Finally, I would like to thank Hongying Wang for her many substantive comments on the manuscript and the many ways she has enriched my life.

Notwithstanding the help of so many people, I alone am responsible for the final version of this book. It could not have been completed without their help, but only I can be held to account for the weaknesses that remain.

James N. Rosenau
June 24, 2002

Acknowledgments

ALTHOUGH they have been rewritten a number of times, some sections of several chapters were drawn from parts of previously published papers. I am grateful to the following for allowing me to reproduce the indicated materials in revised form: the University of Michigan Press, for permission to include in chapters 1, 2, and 3 several paragraphs from my article "The Globalization of Globalization," in Michael Brecher and Frank Harvey (eds.), *Millennium Reflections on International Studies* (forthcoming); the Policy Research Institute of Canada, for permission to include in chapter 2 excerpts from my article "Boundaries as Bumps in the Road of a Fragmegrated World," in Robert Roberge and Daniel Wolfish (eds.), *Rethinking the Line: The Canada-US Border* (forthcoming), Chap. 3; I. B. Tauris Publishers, for permission to include in chapter 8 excerpts from my article "Emergent Spaces, New Places, and Old Faces: Proliferating Identities in a Globalizing World," in Jonathan Friedman and Shalini Randeria (eds.), *Worlds on the Move: Globalization, Migration, and Cultural Scarcity* (forthcoming); and to include in chapters 1 and 12 excerpts from my article "The Challenges and Tensions of Globalized Space," in Donald Lamberton (ed.), *Managing the Global: Globalization, Employment and Quality of Life* (2001), pp. 100–17; Rowman and Littlefield Publishers, for permission to use in chapter 9 sections of my article "Normative and Complexity Theories: Complementary Approaches to World Affairs," in P. Wapner and L.E.J. Ruiz (eds.), *Principled World Politics* (2000), pp. 35–49; The State University of New York Press, for permission to use in chapter 10 paragraphs from my article "Information Technologies and Skills, Networks, and Structures That Sustain World Affairs," in James N. Rosenau and J. P. Singh (eds.), *Information Technologies and Global Politics: The Changing Scope of Power and Governance* (2001), pp. 275–87; the coeditors of the *Asian Journal of Political Science*, for permission to include in chapter 12 excerpts from my article "Authority in Crisis: A Global Process and a Hong Kong Reality," *Asian Journal of Political Science*, Vol. 7, No. 2 (December 1999), pp. 1–20; University of California Press, for permission to include in chapter 14 parts of my article "Human Rights in a Turbulent and Globalizing World," in Alison Brysk (ed.), *Globalization and Human Rights: Transnational Problems, Transnational Solutions?* (forthcoming); Lynne Rienner Publishers, for permission to include in chapter 16 parts of my coauthored article with Hongying Wang, "Transparency International and Corruption as an Issue of Global Governance," *Global Governance*,

Vol. 7, No. 1 (January–March 2001), pp. 25–50; Kluwer Academic Publishers, for permission to include in chapter 17 passages from my article "People, Nations, and Credit Cards: Major Variables in an Emergent Epoch," *International Politics*, Vol. 36, No. 3 (September 1999), pp. 291–320; Millennium Publishing Group, for permission to include in chapter 17 paragraphs from my coauthored article with Mary Durfee, "Playing Catch-Up: International Relations Theory and Poverty," *MILLENNIUM*, Vol. 25, No. 3 (winter 1996), pp. 521–45; the University Press of New England, for permission to include in chapter 19 my article "Confessions of a Pre-postmodernist: Or Can an Old-Timer Change Course?" in Neil L. Waters (ed.), *Beyond the Area Studies War: Toward a New International Studies* (2000), pp. 181–89; and Centre Interuniversitaire de Recherche Independent (Brussels), for permission to incorporate into chapter 19 parts of my article "A Transformed Observer in a Transforming World" in C. P. Roosens, M. Helo, and P. Vercauteran (dirs.), *Les Théories des Relations Internationales à l'Épreuve de l'Aprés-Guerre Froide: Défis Théoriques Pluriels, Studia Diplomatica*, Vol. 52, Nos. 1–2 (1999), pp. 5–14.

In addition to using portions of my prior writings, I have reproduced two diagrams designed by others. Hence I am grateful to both Majid Tehranian and his publisher, Lynne Rienner Publications, for permission to use his diagram from page 70 of his book *Global Communications and World Politics: Dependency, Development and Discourse* (1999). Likewise, I am grateful to both Francisco R. Sagasti and his publisher, *Peru Monitor*, for permission to use his diagram from page 50 of "Development Strategies for the 21st Century: The Case of Peru" (May 2001).

PART ONE

Theoretical Perspectives: Recasting Global Life

> A theorist's work is never done . . . ; there is always more thinking, rethinking, and unthinking waiting around the next bend.
> —Ulf Hannerz, *Transnational Connections: Culture, People, Places* (London: Routledge, 1996), p. 45.

> [T]he social sciences today encounter conceptual and methodological difficulty when they face a world of rising uncertainty; when they are confronted on the one hand by constructed futures that outlast their creators by millennia and on the other by information technology operating at the speed of light, which facilitate simultaneous networked responses across the globe. They tend to acknowledge the limitations of traditional theories when they encounter situations where local actions have global effects, when many of the hazards we face today are no longer linked to the time and space of their genesis/inception, and when simultaneity, instantaneity, in/visibility, im/materiality, multiplicity, the loss of "other" and the construction of the future are confronted with the characteristic assumptions of traditional social science. Consequently, there is a widespread consensus amongst social scientists that we need theories that can encompass the contemporary condition and facilitate active engagement with the process.
> —Barbara Adam, "Detraditionalization and the Certainty of Uncertain Futures," in Paul Heelas, Scott Lash, and Paul Morris (eds.), *Detraditionalization: Critical Reflections on Authority and Identity* (Oxford: Blackwell, 1996), p. 134.

CHAPTER ONE

An Emergent Epoch

> [G]lobalization is bringing peoples closer apart and places
> further together.
>
> —John Rennie Short[1]

THE NEWS on the state of the world is both good and bad. Each day
brings word of a world inching slowly toward sanity even as it moves
toward breakdown. And not only do these integrative and disintegrative
events occur simultaneously, but more often than not they are also causally related. More than that, the causal links tend to cumulate and generate a momentum such that every integrative increment tends to give rise
to a disintegrative increment, and vice versa. This intertwining of the
good and the bad, the global and local, the public and the private, the
coherent and incoherent—to mention only a few of the interactive polarities that dominate world affairs—is a central theme of the ensuing
pages. It is a theme captured by the book's title, by the idea that what
seems remote in the present era also seems close-at-hand, thereby compelling individuals and collectivities alike to cope continuously with the
challenge of distant proximities.[2]

The same theme is implicit in the subtitle of the book. It does not refer
to a new world order, an eventual world government, or a colonization
of Mars. Rather, the subtitle highlights the insufficiency of globalization
as a concept with which to organize understanding of world affairs. Not
that the concept is vague or simply a buzzword shorn of meaning by
being applied to too many diverse circumstances. On the contrary, there
are concrete, empirical dynamics at work that can properly be regarded as
processes and structures of globalization. But all the dynamics are extraordinarily complex and require considerable nuance to comprehend
their deeper implications and widespread consequences. Beyond globalization, in other words, lies conceptual equipment that, if used as a supple-

---

[1] *Global Dimensions: Space, Place and the Contemporary World* (London: Reaktion Books,
2001), p. 19.

[2] My first formulation of this concept, now elevated to a book title, can be found in
James N. Rosenau, "Distant Proximities: The Dynamics and Dialectics of Globalization,"
in Björn Hettne (ed.), *International Political Economy: Understanding Global Disorder*
(London: Zed Books, 1995), pp. 46–65.

ment to the analytic tools commonly employed to probe globalization, can substantially clarify, enrich, and expand our grasp of the course of events as the twenty-first century unfolds.[3]

Indeed, a central argument of the book is that the best way to grasp world affairs today requires viewing them as an endless series of distant proximities in which the forces pressing for greater globalization and those inducing greater localization interactively play themselves out. To do otherwise, to focus only on globalizing dynamics, or only on localizing dynamics, is to risk overlooking what makes events unfold as they do. As one cogent observer put it,

> I use the local and the global as prisms for looking at the same thing. . . . [I]t would be wrong to think that you either work at one or the other, that the two are not constantly interpenetrating each other. . . . [W]hat we usually call the global, far from being something which, in a systematic fashion, rolls over everything, creating similarity, in fact works through particularity, negotiates particular spaces, particular ethnicities, works through mobilizing particular identities, and so on.[4]

Other analysts express a similar perspective by contending that

> [g]lobalization and localization unite at all spatial scales. There is little, and maybe nothing, that is global that does not have some sort of a local manifestation. And each local manifestation changes the global context. Place centredness is the amalgam of global change and local identity. Every place reveals itself at a variety of scales. Local perceptions are shaped by global influences, the combinations of which process local actions. These in turn are fuelled by local aspirations, many of which are the product of global images and expectations. All these local activities accumulate to create chaotic but global outcomes.[5]

It follows, then, that a secure grasp of world affairs requires, at the very least, forming a habit of pausing to assess any distant proximities that may underlie or flow from the situations in which one is interested.

In so doing, however, one quickly discovers that distant proximities are not simple interrelationships, readily discernible and easily understood. Distant proximities encompass the tensions between core and periphery, between national and transnational systems, between communitarianism

---

[3] Key dimensions of this additional equipment are analyzed extensively in the remaining chapters of part I and throughout parts II and III.

[4] Stuart Hall, "Old and New Identities, Old and New Ethnicities," in Anthony D. King (ed.), *Culture, Globalization and the World-System: Contemporary Conditions for the Representation of Identity* (Minneapolis: University of Minnesota Press, 1997), pp. 61, 62.

[5] Tim O'Riordan and Chris Church, "Synthesis and Content," in Tim O'Riordan (ed.), *Globalism, Localism and Identity: Fresh Perspectives on the Transition to Sustainability* (London: Earthscan, 2001), p. 3.

and cosmopolitanism, between cultures and subcultures, between states and markets, between urban and rural, between coherence and incoherence, between integration and disintegration, between decentralization and centralization, between universalism and particularism, between pace and space,[6] between the global and the local—to note only the more conspicuous links between opposites that presently underlie the course of events and the development or decline of institutions. And all these tensions are marked by numerous variants; they take different forms in different parts of the world, in different countries, in different markets, in different communities, in different professions, and in different cyberspaces, with the result that there is enormous diversity in the way people experience the distant proximities of which their lives are composed. Whatever the diversity, however, locating distant proximities at the center of our perspectives on politics enables us to avoid the disciplinary trap of maintaining an analytic separation between foreign and domestic politics, as is the case when international politics and comparative politics are treated as different fields of inquiry, with each holding constant the dynamics at work in the other.

To identify a variety of complex tensions and polarities, however, is not to imply that they necessarily involve zero-sum relationships. Many do have this characteristic, as is clearly indicated in the assertion that "the fundamental conflict in the opening decades of the new century . . . will not be between nations or even between trading blocs but between the forces of globalization and the territorially based forces of local survival seeking to preserve and redefine community."[7] Yet, as will be seen, the tensions that sustain other polarities are nonzero-sum in character, with their globalizing dynamics serving to reinforce, or to be reinforced by, their localizing components. That is why distant proximities cannot be treated as simple relationships. They are rooted in complexity, in complementary as well as competitive processes.[8]

---

[6] The reference here is to "an increasingly pervasive and contentious political struggle between a 'discourse of pace' linked, on the one hand, to accelerating transitions, speeding flows, overcoming resistances, eliminating frictions, and engineering the kinematics of globalization, and, on the other hand, a 'discourse of place' centered upon solidifying porous borders, bolstering breached containments, arresting eroded identities, and revitalizing faded essences." Timothy W. Luke and Gearóid Ó Tuathail, "Global Flowmations, Local Fundamentalism, and Fast Geopolitics: 'America' in an Accelerating World Order," in A. Herod, G. Ó Tuathail, and S. M. Roberts (eds.), *An Unruly World? Globalization, Governance and Geography* (London: Routledge, 1998), p. 73.

[7] Richard J. Barnet and John Cavanagh, *Global Dreams: Imperial Corporations and the New World Order* (New York: Simon and Schuster, 1994), p. 22. For a more extended formulation of the conflict between global and local dynamics, see Benjamin R. Barber, *Jihad vs. McWorld*, enlarged edition (New York: Ballantine Books, 2001).

[8] For a useful essay on the distinction between competitive and complementary approaches to the tensions between globalizing and localizing dynamics, see Bob Bahador,

It follows that distant proximities do not revolve around the attentiveness of people to news from abroad. Even if the widespread preoccupation with worldwide terrorism after the attacks on the World Trade Center and the Pentagon proves to be a temporary blip in a long-term pattern,[9] to cite the numerous statistics depicting how little American media cover foreign developments and thereby sustain the parochialism of their audiences is not to negate the concept of distant proximities. Rather, the latter involve the foreign travel experiences of individuals and their friends, the messages they receive from relatives abroad, the ways in which their jobs are linked to or threatened by foreign trade, and a host of other word-of-mouth or electronic inputs that underlie the ever-greater interdependence of life in a shrinking world. Furthermore, while the parochialism of the American people may be considerable in terms of exposure to foreign news, the same cannot be said of counterparts in other countries, all of which have enough adjacent and regional neighbors to be continuously reminded of the proximity of distant events and trends. Nor may the parochialism of Americans return to earlier levels once the shock of the terrorist attacks has worn off. As one analyst put it three days after September 11, "This is the end: the end of an era, the era of our invulnerability. We will recover physically, even psychologically, but nothing will ever be quite the same again. A barrier has been irrevocably breached: a barrier against the world outside."[10]

To comprehend the nature and dynamism of distant proximities, clearly we need to explore both the phenomena viewed as distant and those considered proximate before assessing how the tensions resulting from their interactions play out in diverse contexts. To do so, of course, is to move beyond objective circumstances. Distance is not measured only in miles across land and sea; it can also involve less tangible spaces, more abstract conceptions in which distance is assessed across organizational hierarchies, event sequences, social strata, market relationships, migration patterns, and a host of other nonterritorial spaces. Thus to a large extent distant proximities are subjective appraisals—what people feel or think is remote, and what they think or feel is close-at-hand. There is no self-evident line that divides the distant from the proximate, no established criteria for differentiating among statistics or situations that are reflective

---

"Fragmentation in an Era of Globalization," *ASEN Bulletin*, No. 16 (winter 1999), pp. 9–16.

[9] Evidence that the blip may be more than temporary is suggested by findings that "an eagerness to comprehend the world remains high nearly nine months later." Barbara Crossette, "American Web Browsers Continue a Global Turn," *New York Times*, June 2, 2002, p. 6.

[10] Ronald Steel, "The Weak at War with the Strong," *New York Times*, September 14, 2001, p. A27.

of either the more remote or the close-at-hand environment. In other words, nearness and farness connote scale as well as space. Both are ranges across which people and their thoughts roam; and as they roam, they can be active in both geographic locales and scalar spaces that have been socially constructed.[11] Each is a context, a "habitat of meaning,"[12] a mind-set that may often correspond with spatial distance even as there are other scalar contexts that can make the close-at-hand feel very remote and the faraway seem immediately present.[13]

To ponder the nature and ramifications of distant proximities in a time of vast changes, therefore, is to consider what, when, how, and why people experience some dimensions of their lives and some phenomena in their perceptual space as marvelously or threateningly close. In some cases wide intersubjective agreement prevails as to the appropriate spatial classification; in other cases controversy is intense over where lines between the distant and the proximate should be drawn; and it is both the areas of consensus and the disputes they sustain that underlie the dynamism of distant proximities as they are experienced by both individuals and their collectivities.

CLARIFYING THE POLARITIES

Having already mentioned several polarities, it is important to clarify their relations to each other and the sense in which they differentiate good from bad. Most notably, there is no necessary connection between the good-and-bad dimension of any of the polarities just noted. Some aspects of the several poles are desirable, and some are noxious. Globalization has *both* positive and negative features, as does localization, and much the same can be said about the coherence-incoherence and integration-disintegration polarities.[14] Coherence and integration normally seem

[11] For a pioneering work on socially constructed space, see Henri Lefebvre, *The Production of Space*, trans. by Donald Nicholson-Smith (Malden, Mass.: Blackwell, 1991).

[12] Ulf Hannerz, *Transnational Connections: Culture, People, Places* (London: Routledge, 1996), pp. 22–23.

[13] For a conception that differentiates among gravitational, topological, and attributional distances, see Alan K. Henderson, "Distance and Foreign Policy: The Political Geography Approach" (paper presented at the International Political Science Association Congress, Quebec City, August 1–5, 2000).

[14] Václav Havel, the president of the Czech Republic, has observed that by itself globalization is "morally neutral. It can be good or bad depending on the kind of content we give to it." He cited information about human rights as a good use of the concept, while his negative example was "the spread of silly sitcoms and even more stupid commercials," which he contended conveyed a false picture of human life. Steven Erlanger, "Havel Urges Multinationals to Heed the 'Voices of the People,'" *New York Times*, August 23, 2000, p. A8.

preferable to incoherence and disintegration, but it is not difficult to think of situations—South Africa during the apartheid era comes quickly to mind—with an excess of coherence that could benefit from a period of incoherence and disintegration.

In a like manner, nothing in the pages that follow should be interpreted as implying that the centralizing processes inherent in globalization are preferable to the decentralizing processes that accompany localization. It is all to the good when globalizing dynamics lead international organizations to concert their efforts against corruption or when corporations converge around new, more open attitudes toward environmental problems, but it is surely bad if states collude to ignore corrupt practices and corporations maintain their position that environmental threats have yet to be demonstrated. Similarly, it is all to the good when localizing dynamics lead to decentralizing processes in which opposition voices are encouraged and democratic practices expanded, but it is surely bad if these processes result in a fragmentation that tears communities apart and facilitates the rule of petty tyrants.

In short, more so than in the past because time and space have been so rapidly compressed, we live in an era of pervasive contradictions that give rise to polarities subject to diverse normative judgments. Such evaluations cannot be avoided, but they can be explicated as one works through the contradictions and interprets their implications. In this way there ought be no confusion over the normative stance that underlies any empirical conclusions the analysis yields. Depending on the consequences to which they give rise—whether they elevate or denigrate individuals or groups—distant proximities can be viewed as expressive of a trend that portends future progress or one that points toward retrogression. In the case of some distant proximities, of course, their consequences have still to become fully manifest, and their normative implications thus remain correspondingly obscure.

Since distant proximities encompass polarities that are bound to take inquiry beyond globalization, it would be a mistake to view them as little more than a means of analyzing the processes and dynamics of globalization. Conceived in this larger context, globalization is but one component of the transformative dynamics that underlie the emergence of a new epoch in the human condition. It is, to be sure, a major component, but all too many analyses suffer from treating it as the primary component and thus risk underplaying the complexity of the emergent epoch. There is a need, for example, to recognize that localization is also a powerful force at work throughout the world, that cities, provinces, and other subnational groups are also seeking to realize their goals, that by 2030 some 60 percent of the world's people will live in cities, and that consequently localization is multiplying the range of policy environments as globalization shrinks the world.[15] We live in a messy world, one that is marked by sharp contradictions comprehensible only through nuanced analysis that accords significance to numerous forces that can—and often do—undermine, limit, or otherwise redirect globalizing processes.

Violins offer a useful metaphor for distinguishing between previous epochs in world affairs and the complexities of the one that is presently emerging. Just as a poorly built violin halts and dampens the sound of each note, confining it to its own limited frequency and ceasing as soon as the bow leaves the string, so has the world in earlier epochs tended to retain the effects of events locally, muffling their impact on other systems and restraining their duration. In contrast, the expansionary, enduring character of distant proximities in the present global system is analogous to a good violin. Every note triggers a series of overtones that resonate with the remaining strings through the body of the whole instrument, both amplifying and sustaining the sound. In the case of the violin it is the difference between mere sounds and music; in world affairs it is the difference between international politics and dynamics beyond globalization.[16]

Labeling the Epoch

But how to denote the emergent epoch? "Distant proximities" suggest its ironies, but it is hardly a label that would satisfy the many observers who seek a more descriptive designation of the new historical period that has accompanied the end of the twentieth century and the onset of the twenty-first.[17] For some time attempts to summarize the numerous changes that generated the new period have followed two lines of reasoning and resulted in two main labels for the emergent epoch. The two approaches differ greatly in several respects—one being pragmatic and framed by politicians and journalists, while the other is philosophical and has evolved among intellectuals—but they share a lack of specificity about the essential underpinnings and nature of world affairs at the outset of a new millennium. The pragmatic line of reasoning acknowledges that present-day patterns and institutions are quite different from those of prior eras, but it does not seek to evaluate, much less synthesize, the differences or their long-run implications. Rather, it simply assumes the end of the superpower rivalry between the United States and the Soviet

[15] On the potential ramifications of localizing trends, see Shahid Yusuf, "Balancing Globalization and Localization," *Journal of Commerce*, Vol. 421 (September 24, 1999), p. 9.

[16] I am grateful to Gottlieb J. Duwan, a violinist as well as a keen student of world affairs, for the violin metaphor.

[17] For an extensive example of this felt need, see Symposium, "Naming a New Era," *Foreign Policy*, No. 119 (summer 2000), pp. 29–69.

Union unleashed diverse processes that are altering the practices through which the politics, economics, and social life of communities, nations, and the world are sustained. Lacking specificity, the pragmatic approach tends to treat every development, whether it be familiar or unusual, as expressive of the new historical epoch, and thus it uses a label, the "post–Cold War" era, which hints at changes and differences without indicating what these might be. Indeed, by employing such a label, pragmatists conclude that the present is a congeries of unsystematic, even unrelated, forces that are propelling the world into an uncertain future. In addition, by positing conditions as "post" an earlier era, the pragmatic perspective implies that the present is a transitional period, as if new historical developments have to evolve and generate new global structures before the world can settle once again into stable circumstances such as marked the Cold War era of 1945–90, the interwar period of 1918–39, or the industrial age of the nineteenth century.

The other, more philosophical response to the dynamics that are transforming the present-day world is somewhat more precise in terms of specifying what has changed, but it also is murky about what sustains the changes and where they may be taking the world. And thus it, too, uses the "post" prefix as part of its label for the epoch, thereby also suggesting that a multiplicity of diverse and unstructured forces are at work that offer no hint as to what the world's future may be like. In this case the label is that of "post-modernism," a school of thought that has different meanings for different postmodernists who nonetheless share the conviction that basic changes have moved the world beyond modernity or, at least, into "late modernity." Whether the era is seen as "post" or "late," adherents of the various postmodernisms also share the belief that modernity has run its course because the notions of science and rationality that distinguish it have proven to be ill-founded. After all, many postmodernists assert, two devastating world wars, a deep economic depression, and the hydrogen bomb mark the age of science and rationality— hardly a recommendation for a modernist perspective. For all their criticisms of modernity, however, postmodernists do not offer an understanding of where the world is today and where it is likely to be tomorrow. Indeed, while some of them view the future as an ongoing process of constructed expectations, many postmodernists are inclined to argue that speculation about future developments is wasted effort, that any scenarios depicting paths into the future are hidden political moves designed to advance the particular agendas of the scenarist.

If it is the case that distant proximities have become so pervasive as to serve as the basis for an analytic framework, then the absence of a label suggestive of the nature, processes, and structure of the emergent epoch is especially glaring. Hence, in order to encourage a focus on the dynamics whereby the shrinking of social and geographic distances has rendered the environment of people, organizations, and communities both distant and proximate, here a concocted label will be used to convey the essential nature of the epochal transformation. The label is "fragmegration," which is intended to suggest the pervasive interaction between fragmenting and integrating dynamics unfolding at every level of community.[18] It is admittedly an awkward and grating label,[19] but as such it serves as a constant reminder that the world has moved beyond the condition of being "post" its predecessor to an era in which the foundations of daily life have settled into new and unique rhythms of their own. Equally important, the fragmegration label captures in a single word the large degree to which these rhythms consist of localizing, decentralizing, or fragmenting dynamics that are interactively and causally linked to globalizing, centralizing, and integrating dynamics.

Of course, the fragmegration label can easily lead to oversimplification and misinterpretation. It risks treating localizing and decentralizing processes as forms of fragmentation and equating globalizing and centralizing dynamics with processes of integration. Such a conflation of these polarities would indeed be misleading. Localizing and decentralizing dynamics need not be the same as fragmenting processes, even though all three share a movement away from whole systems and toward less encompassing subsystems. To decentralize, for example, may well be to

[18] One sociologist expresses the same thought by referring to "a massive, twofold process involving *the interpenetration of the universalization of particularism and the particularization of universalism.*" (Roland Robertson, "Social Theory, Cultural Relativity and the Problem of Globality" in A. D. King (ed.), *Culture, Globalization and the World-System* (London: Macmillan, 1991), p. 73; italics in the original. Another stresses the simultaneity of the demand for both "assimilation into the universal . . . [and] adhering to the particular, the reinvention of differences" (Immanuel Wallerstein, cited in ibid., p. 69). Similarly, a political scientist notes that the world now faces two conflicting trends: "On the one hand, a need for collective action; and on the other, a search for closed communities." Stanley Hoffmann, reported in the *World Economic Forum 1993*, p. 39.

[19] Other single-word labels designed to suggest the contradictory tensions that pull systems toward both coherence and collapse are *chaord*, a label that juxtaposes the dynamics of chaos and order; *glocalization*, which points to the simultaneity of globalizing and localizing dynamics; and *regcal*, a term designed to focus attention on the links between regional and local phenomena. The chaord designation is elaborated in Dee W. Hock, *Birth of the Chaordic Age* (San Francisco: Berrett-Koehler, 1999); the glocalization concept is developed in Roland Robertson, "Glocalization: Time-Space and Homogeneity-Heterogeneity," in Mike Featherstone, Scott Lash, and Roland Robertson (eds.), *Global Modernities* (Thousand Oaks, Calif.: Sage, 1995), pp. 25–44; and the regcal formulation can be found in Susan H. C. Tai and Y. H. Wong, "Advertising Decision Making in Asia: 'Glocal' versus 'Regcal' Approach," *Journal of Managerial Issues*, Vol. 10 (fall 1998), pp. 318–39. I prefer the term *fragmegration* because it does not imply a territorial scale, and it broadens the focus to include tensions at work in organizations as well as those that pervade communities.

calculate that advantages can be enjoyed by voluntarily breaking up into smaller units, whereas to fragment is to imply that breakups derive from irresolvable tensions and conflicts. Similarly, globalizing and centralizing processes may not be the equivalent of those that serve to integrate. On the other hand, since the components of the several polarities can be overlapping and interrelated, merging them into a single label is not entirely an oversimplification. If it is viewed as an indicator of complexity, and if the dangers of oversimplification are recognized, the fragmegration label has the virtue of sensitizing us to the contradictory tensions wherein the world is simultaneously moving in opposite directions.

Another virtue of the fragmegration concept is that it inhibits narrow approaches to globalization. Much of the exploding literature on globalization casts its dynamics in strict economic terms—as processes that sustain or advance the power of corporations, that widen the rich-poor gap, that foster the integration of markets, that underlie the flow of investments—but such formulations seem needlessly limited. Diverse economic factors are indeed central to the configurations of the emergent epoch, but so are cultural, social, political, and ecological processes,[20] and their salience is highlighted by focusing on the ways in which local and global forces shape each other.

Fragmegration also serves to underscore the contradictions, ambiguities, complexities, and uncertainties that have replaced the regularities of prior epochs. Consisting of nonlinear processes in which every effect is a cause of yet another outcome in a complex and endless array of feedback loops, these contradictions, ambiguities, complexities, and uncertainties are, in effect, the regularities of our age of fragmegration. And no less important, they are rooted in the decline of ideological belief systems as a consequence of scientific developments and the clusters of values that constitute modernity. In the absence of viable alternative belief systems, many people can experience insecurity about the meaningfulness of life. Even before terrorism came brutally to the United States, the recent generations whose lives had been free of war and marked by high degrees of comfort and not a little affluence felt vulnerable and insecure. Paradoxically, the more risk-free the world seemed, the more risky it felt. In the words of one observer,

> Now, is our world more dangerous? . . . It is. We are asking more of it, more comfort and therefore we are more vulnerable. The more secure we are, the more we feel the danger of losing our security. There are easy ways to inflict major pain with no major effort. People can intrude on our financial and

[20] Philip G. Cerny, "Globalizing the Political and Politicising the Global: Concluding Reflections on International Political Economy as a Vocation," *New Political Economy*, Vol. 4, No. 1 (1999), pp. 147–62.

national-security systems in much easier ways. This is because of the interconnectedness of the world and its infrastructures.[21]

The sense of vulnerability, moreover, can lead to extreme reactions since

> [u]nfortunately change, complexity and information overload are abstract phenomena, which are difficult to grasp. Therefore few people have as yet understood that they are at the root of the anxiety they feel. When trying to rationalize their vague feelings of unease, people will rather look for more easily recognizable causes, such as unemployment, pollution, crime, corruption or immigration. These phenomena, which have become both more visible and less tolerated, play the role of scapegoat: they . . . may lead to backlashes and irrational reactions, such as racism, intolerance and persecution of groups that are held responsible.[22]

Incisive empirical examples of the fragmegrative contradictions that pervade the emergent epoch abound. Quintessentially illustrative of the simultaneity inherent in such situations were the circumstances surrounding the Seattle meeting of the World Trade Organization (WTO) in late 1999: just as the WTO convened in an attempt to extend global integration of trade practices, so did numerous private groups and organizations converge on the city to march in the streets in opposition to the WTO and its policies. Perhaps even more illustrative were the terrorist attacks on the United States in September 2001: just as their disintegrative dimensions were rooted in resentments and hatreds fomented by poverty and challenges to tradition in the underdeveloped world, so were their integrative dimensions manifest in the pervasive sense of unity that the attacks fostered among Americans and their allies. Another contradictory situation is evident in this account of a period in the Israeli-Palestinian conflict:

> What ails the peace process is not just a crisis of confidence. It's a crisis of logic. It's not only that each side doesn't trust the other; it's that nothing makes sense. Opposite causes produce the same effect: There are suicide bombers when the peace process moves ahead and suicide bombers when the process is stuck. And the same causes produce opposite effects: Mr. Netanyahu strikes a Hebron deal one day and undermines it the next by building in Har Homa; Mr. Arafat exposes a cell of Palestinian suicide bombers in Beit Sahur one day and kisses the leader of Hamas the next. Closure of the territories

---

[21] Yacov Y. Haines, president of the Society for Risk Analysis, quoted in Tim Weiner, "Feeling Secure Is a Risky Business," *New York Times*, September 6, 1998, Sec. 4, p. 6.

[22] Francis Heylighen and Jan Bernheim, "Global Progress II: Evolutionary Mechanisms and Their Side-Effects," working paper for CLEA study group "Evolution and Progress, May 24, 2000, p. 45.

increases Israel's security and decreases Israel's security. Everything that happens, for good or ill, seems utterly random. Oslo is no longer a peace process. It's a Tolstoy novel.[23]

Table 1.1 summarizes still other instances of fragmegration currently on the global agenda. Here it can be seen that its dynamics are operative in a wide variety of situations.

Of course, fragmegrative dynamics are not always as obvious as they are in the case of these examples, but the more one gets accustomed to viewing the course of events through fragmegrative lenses, the more will the underlying tensions and contradictions become manifest. There may be situations that are free of fragmegrative contradictions, but one would be hard-pressed to identify them on the current world scene.[24]

Stated more generally, where people came to expect the Soviet-American rivalry to shape the course of events in the Cold War era, and where they became used to the ways in which U.S. hegemony shaped outcomes in the brief post–Cold War period, today they appear to have adjusted to the realization that outcomes stem from multiple sources, that they are transitory and ever subject to reversal, and that what happens at one level of community can rapidly and unexpectedly cascade across other levels. For reasons elaborated in subsequent chapters, in other words, elites, activists, and ordinary persons alike have come to understand intersubjectively that their lives are intertwined in crazy-quilt ways that may often be enhancing and perhaps just as often denigrating.

Awareness of the enhancing and denigrating consequences of distant proximities has the potential of becoming major sources of tension within and among collectivities. People whose life circumstances limit their experience of the distant to global television and prevent them from direct and recurring electronic and physical interactions with remote places may well evolve resentments of those whose movements are less restricted. Not class warfare but spatial-scalar warfare, in other words, may be in the offing. As one observer puts it,

> [R]ather than homogenizing the human condition, the technological annulment of temporal/spatial distances tends to polarize it. It emancipates certain humans from territorial constraints and renders certain community-generating meanings extraterritorial—while denuding the territory, to which other people go on being confined, of its meaning and its identity-endowing capacity. For some people it augurs an unprecedented freedom from physical obstacles and un-

[23] Thomas Friedman, "The Physics of Mideast Peace," *New York Times*, September 15, 1997, p. A15.

[24] For a contrary perspective in which "the effects" of fragmegration "turn out not to be as contradictory, nor even as different, as you might think," see Robert Wright, *Nonzero: The Logic of Human Destiny* (New York: Vintage, 2001), p. 204.

TABLE 1.1.
Instances of Interactive Fragmegrative Dynamics

Globalizing Forces	Localizing Forces
The "free market" (international corporations, international hedge funds, currency exchange)	The dislocation of people and nations attributed to the irresponsible use of U.S. and Western venture capital; the growing gap between rich and poor within and between countries
Global political and economic institutions (the UN, the World Bank, the IMF, the World Trade Organization, etc.)	Resource scarcities caused by global warming, loss of arable land, and the destruction of the natural environment
	Mass migrations, prejudice, ethnocentrism, ethnic and racial hatred
English as the lingua franca	Movements to preserve heritage cultures whose basis is often language and customs
U.S. military, economic, and cultural strength	Resentment of American hegemony, terrorism
Modernists; science and technological innovations in information and transportation	Traditionalists; religious fundamentalism; nationalism

heard-of ability to move and act from a distance. For others, it portends the impossibility of appropriating and domesticating the locality from which they have little chance of cutting themselves free in order to move elsewhere.[25]

In short, it is highly unlikely that the contradictions of the emergent epoch have escaped the attention of individuals. With the fragmenting forces of localization and the integrating dynamics of globalization so interwoven as to be products of each other, people have become increasingly aware of how fragmegrative dynamics have intensified old identities and fostered new ones. However they may articulate their understanding, there are good reasons to presume that people everywhere have come to expect, to take for granted, that the advance of globalization poses threats to long-standing local and national ties, that some groups will contest, even violently fight, the intrusion of global norms even as others will seek to obtain goods, larger market shares, or generalized support

[25] Zygmunt Bauman, *Globalization: The Human Consequences* (New York: Columbia University Press, 1998), p. 18 (italics in the original).

beyond their communities. The forces of fragmentation are rooted in the psychic comfort individuals derive from the familiar, close-at-hand values and practices of their neighborhoods, just as the forces of integration stem from their aspirations to share in the distant products of the global economy, to benefit from the efficiencies of regional unity, to avoid the dangers of environmental degradation, to contribute to coherent communities through policies of inclusion that expand their democratic institutions, and to yield to the implications of the meaning of the pictures taken in outer space that depict the earth as a solitary entity in a huge universe. Stated more succinctly, "There is a constant struggle between the collectivist and individualist elements within each human."[26]

OVERVIEW

The dynamics of fragmegration and globalization, not to mention those of complexity and the methodologies employed to study them, are so pervaded with values that no analyst can be neutral with respect to them. The most that can be achieved is explicitness on the part of each analyst about the underlying values, experiences, and analytic commitments that guide and inform his or her work. I have tried to be faithful to the virtues of explicitness in the postscript to this book (see chapter 19).

The next chapter wrestles with key conceptual challenges that have to be confronted in order to probe the underpinnings of distant proximities. Chapter 3 focuses on some of the prime sources and consequences that drive fragmegration, an analysis that facilitates, in the remaining chapters of part I, a recasting of global life in terms of how diverse individuals experience distant proximities. The chapters of part II set forth additional conceptual equipment that may be useful to comprehend a world that has moved beyond globalization to continuing clashes between integrative and fragmenting forces. The chapters of part III seek to delineate how individuals at the micro level and collectivities at the macro level interact to configure and sustain the structures, processes, and issues that constitute today's global agenda.

Throughout, an effort is made to indicate that while globalization is a central dynamic of our time, it nonetheless needs to be cast in a more encompassing, fragmegrative context if we are to deepen our understanding of how and why events unfold as they do. This effort rests on the premise that the empowerment of individuals in the emergent epoch— their enlarged capacities derived from new technologies; from their greater educational and travel opportunities; from their experience in having

---

[26] Harry C. Triandis, *Individualism and Collectivism* (Boulder, Colo.: Westview Press, 1995), p. xiv.

their collective actions topple or redirect governments, corporations, and other macro institutions; and from the advent of what has come to be called the "me" generation—contributes substantially to where the world is headed. This "triumph of individualism" is not always welcome, but its presence cannot be ignored in any effort to grasp the course of events.[27]

[27] See, for example, James Dale Davison and Lord William Rees-Mogg, *The Sovereign Individual: Mastering the Transition to the Information Age* (New York: Simon and Schuster, 1997); William D. Hitt, *The Global Citizen* (Columbus, Ohio: Battelle Press, 1998); and Richard Tomkins, "We Have Reached Utopia—and It Sucks," *Financial Times*, December 16–17, 2000, Weekend p. I.

CHAPTER TWO

People, Collectivities, and Change

> One can sometimes speak of collectivities as if they were agents, but this is only metaphorical. It presumes certain qualities which they have in the aggregate—firms oriented towards profit, for example, or hospitals concerned with curing people. But the only true agents in history are human individuals.
> —Anthony Giddens[1]

> A theory of global politics that disregards the people that make up the global polity is, at best, an idealized fantasy and, at worst, an impoverished nightmare.
> —Ronnie D. Lipschutz[2]

COGENT ANALYSIS of the crazy-quilt contradictions and uncertainties encompassed by a distant proximities framework is no simple matter. Two theoretical and two methodological problems need to be addressed if the complex nuances of world affairs are to be grasped in a fragmegrative context. There are, of course, a number of other obstacles to nuanced inquiry, but coping with these particular problems is a prerequisite to probing fragmegration with incisive intellectual equipment. One theoretical challenge concerns the concept of change, and the other involves the links between individuals at the micro level and their collectivities at the macro level. One of the methodological dilemmas is posed by the increasingly nonterritorial dimensions of world affairs, and the other focuses on the nonlinearity of many of the processes through which the world gets from day to day.

To focus on these problems is not to imply that inquiries into globalization lack elaborate definitions, theoretical formulations, and sophisticated empirical materials.[3] Analysts differ on the aspects of globalization

---

[1] Anthony Giddens and Christopher Pierson, *Conversations with Anthony Giddens: Making Sense of Modernity* (Cambridge: Polity Press, 1998), pp. 87–88.

[2] "Because People Matter: Studying Global Political Economy," *International Studies Perspective*, Vol. 2 (November 2001), p. 323.

[3] Perhaps the most thorough single coverage of the numerous dynamics that underlie globalization is to be found in David Held, Anthony McGrew, David Goldblatt, and Jonathan Perraton, *Global Transformations: Politics, Economics, Culture* (Stanford, Calif.: Stan-

they emphasize, the values they attach to the various aspects, and the directions in which they anticipate globalizing processes to be moving the world, but such differences are relatively minimal in comparison to the similarities they ascribe to the underpinnings and consequences of the processes. There is wide agreement that profound changes are at work at most levels of most communities. Virtually none contest the proposition that the worldwide turn of countries toward free trade and neoliberal economic policies has had vast consequences. Few dissent from the proposition that advances in transportation and electronic technologies, and especially the Internet, have resulted in a transformation, a compression if not a collapse, of time and distance, as well as altered conceptions of hierarchy, territory, sovereignty, and the state. Yet, despite these broad areas of consensus, and notwithstanding sophisticated models that have been constructed and useful data that have been gathered, the persistence of theoretical and methodological dilemmas undermines any effort to move beyond globalizing processes and probe the distant proximities on which they rest.

TOWARD A THEORY OF CHANGE

More often than not, the concept of change tends to be ignored in studies of world affairs. But if one assumes, as I do, that the world, its societies, and its people, are undergoing transformations so profound as not to be fully appreciated, then this major conceptual challenge needs to be faced more directly than has been the case to date: How do we know change when we see it? How do we differentiate between evolutionary and breakpoint change or between permanent changes and momentary fads? When do changes in degree become changes in kind? At what levels of aggregation are deep and enduring changes most likely? Do changes at micro levels necessitate comparable change at macro levels, and vice versa? Are some forms of change illusory, amounting to no more than brief disruptions of underlying patterns? With few exceptions and in contrast to other disciplines, such questions have not been the focus of con-

---

ford University Press, 1999). For the many other important contributions to an ever-growing literature, see the 713 entries in the bibliography in Jan Aart Scholte, *Globalization: A Critical Introduction* (New York: St. Martin's Press, 2000), pp. 318–48. My contribution to the vast literature is summarized in two books, *Along the Domestic-Foreign Frontier: Exploring Governance in a Turbulent World* (Cambridge: Cambridge University Press, 1997), and *Turbulence in World Politics: A Theory of Change and Continuity* (Princeton, N.J.: Princeton University Press, 1990). For empirical assessments that compare globalizing dynamics across countries, see "Measuring Globalization," *Foreign Policy*, No. 122 (January/February 2001), pp. 56–65, and "Globalization's Last Hurrah," *Foreign Policy*, No. 128 (January/February 2002), pp. 38–51.

ceptual inquiries by international relations (IR) scholars.[4] Some are dubious that change is occurring at all, claiming that history is repetitive, that for every seemingly new aspect of the present one can find comparable developments in the past,[5] that sharp turns in history do not amount to "fundamental" change.[6] Others tend to presume that salient change in the actors and structures of world affairs will somehow be manifest as they unfold. Sure, when regimes collapse, when alliances break up, when markets decline precipitously, when terrorists destroy trade and financial centers, or when communities deteriorate abruptly, we have little difficulty discerning the end of one historical sequence and the onset of another. Ascribing change to such sudden developments is easy, but tracing slow, evolutionary transformations, assessing the durability of rapid changes, and discerning the early indicators of collapsing regimes, alliances, markets, or communities are where our conceptual equipment is rudimentary, if not altogether lacking. This is why all too often we are surprised by the turn of events.

There are, of course, no magic formulas for understanding and anticipating different forms of change.[7] On the other hand, a few helpful formulations that differentiate among types of change have been developed. Perhaps the most useful is one that identifies four concepts of change: "change as replacement, change as addition, dialectical change, and transformation."[8]

In addition to the drawing of conceptual distinctions, two simple mechanisms are available for maximizing our ability to assess when change

[4] Among the exceptions are Barry Buzan and R. J. Barry Jones (eds.), *Change and the Study of International Relations: The Evaded Dimension* (London: Pinter, 1981); K. R. Dark, *The Waves of Time: Long-Term Change and International Relations* (London: Pinter, 1998); Joshua Goldstein, *Long Cycles: Prosperity and War in the Modern Age* (New Haven, Conn.: Yale University Press, 1988); K. J. Holsti, *The Problem of Change in International Relations Theory* (Vancouver: Institute of International Relations, University of British Columbia, Working Paper No. 26, December 1998); Holsti, *Change in the International System: Essays on the Theory and Practice of International Relations* (Brookfield, Vt.: E. Elgar, 1991); and George Modelski, *Long Cycles in World Politics* (Hampshire: Macmillan, 1987). For a work summarizing the extensive preoccupation of other disciplines with the dynamics of change, see Piotr Sztompka, *The Sociology of Social Change* (Cambridge, Mass.: Blackwell, 1994).

[5] The falsity of this perspective is amply demonstrated in the data indicative of accelerated globalization compiled by Jan Aart Scholte; see his *Globalization: A Critical Introduction*, pp. 58, 86.

[6] I have addressed the resistance to "fundamental" change in "Change as Concept and Conversation-Stopper" (paper presented at the annual meeting of the American Political Science Association, San Francisco, August 31, 2001).

[7] For an earlier and more extended effort on my part to probe the concept of change, see Rosenau, *Turbulence in World Politics*, Chap. 7.

[8] Holsti, *The Problem of Change in International Relations Theory*, pp. 11–16; quotation on p. 11.

may ensue. One is to assume that systems are always on the edge of collapse, an assumption that compels us to be sensitive to, even in awe of, the capacity of systems to get from one moment, week, year, or decade in time to the next. To proceed from the opposite assumption—that systems are likely to persist—is to limit our readiness to recognize the formation and early stages of change dynamics. Another way of coping with the challenge of change is to allow our variables to vary—that is, to imagine mentally a wide range of possible shifts in the values of all the variables relevant to our concerns. Many observers, for example, did not allow for the possibility that the Cold War and the Soviet Union would come to abrupt ends. In retrospect, such failures border on the inexcusable.[9] Or at least if we had been more sensitive to the susceptibility of systemic collapse and thus been alert to variations at work in the Cold War and the Soviet Union expressive of such tendencies, it may have been less surprising.

Needless to say, even as the challenges posed by the change and micro-macro problems can be separately probed, so are they also inextricably intertwined. A theory of change is unlikely to evolve unless it includes components that address the micro-macro links in the context of frag-megrative dynamics. Indeed, "[m]uch theory in the social sciences is of limited use because it is macro-macro theory which turns out to be wrong when its implicit micro foundations are false in a specific context."[10] It is for these reasons that the interactions of individuals and collectivities—the micro-macro or agency-structure problem (or, perhaps more accurately, problems)—constitute a central and recurring theme of this volume.[11] Throughout, an effort is made to assess the extent to which such interactions configure distant proximities and shape the phenomena investigated, with the primary argument being that the micro dimensions

[9] For a cogent analysis that explores the failure of observers to anticipate the momentous events of 1989–91, see John Lewis Gaddis, "International Relations Theory and the End of the Cold War," *International Security*, Vol. 17 (winter 1992–93), pp. 3–58. See also Michael Cox, "Rethinking the End of the Cold War," *Review of International Studies*, Vol. 20 (1994), pp. 187–200; Timur Kuran, "The Inevitability of Future Revolutionary Surprises," *American Journal of Sociology*, Vol. 100 (May 1995), pp. 1528–51; and Richard Ned Lebow and Thomas Risse-Kappen (eds.), *International Relations Theory and the End of the Cold War* (New York: Columbia University Press, 1995).

[10] John Braithwaite and Peter Drahos, *Global Business Regulation* (Cambridge: Cambridge University Press, 2000), p. 14.

[11] Although micro-macro interactions can be used as synonymous with the links between agents and structures, I tend to employ the former terminology more extensively. Some would contend that the agent-structure formulation is more suggestive of dynamism in the sense that one cannot think of agents without also being alert to the structures that shape them or that they shape. On the other hand, collectivities are often conceived as agents (as economists do when they talk about the interactions between firms and economies), whereas here any collectivity is regarded as a macro structure, while the micro is confined exclusively to individuals.

of the interactions have been unduly underestimated. Globalization and fragmegration are not inevitable. They are not mystical forces leading the world to a predetermined destiny. Quite to the contrary, they are the result of decisions made continuously by individuals and their collectivities. As a critic of globalization puts it, noting both its micro and macro dimensions, "Human hands and minds have been everywhere in the globalizing process, designing it, guiding it, and taxing the public to pay for it. It has been codified into government policy at almost every level, and the support it receives is deep and systemic."[12]

Of course, at no point are the shared attitudes and actions of individuals conceived to account exclusively for the constant or changing structures operative at the macro level. Likewise, at no point is it presumed that the macro structures of collectivities necessarily shape or produce the agents—ordinary folk, activists, or elites—that constitute them. Rather, the agent-structure relationship is an extraordinarily complex one in which the causal flows are multidirectional and how they interactively impact on each other is often obscure. Analysts do, of course, differ on whether the micro or macro forces are the more powerful in the never-ending interaction between the two,[13] but here no position is taken on their relative strength other than to stress that the empowerment of the individual is a dynamic of the emergent epoch that cannot be ignored. Consequently, as will be seen, there are situations in which the micro dominates and other situations in which the macro is dominant, and thus much depends on the particular circumstances of specific micro-macro linkages.

MICRO-MACRO INTERACTIONS

Whatever may be the locus of the initial input, in other words, it initiates a sequence of interaction between macro and micro dynamics that may continue for long stretches of time. Micro agents and macro structures are endlessly interactive, but the question of which predominates in any particular situation is a matter of perspective, of where one breaks into the interactive cycles. Enduring macro change cannot occur if the individuals it encompasses withhold their support, just as durable micro change is unlikely in the absence of altered and supportive macro struc-

---

[12] Steven Gorlick, "Tipping the Scale: Systemic Support for the Large and Global," *The Ecologist*, Vol. 29 (May/June, 1999), p. 163.

[13] In contrast to the oft-cited notion that all politics is local, for example, one analyst argues that "the history of the latter part of the 20th century is a story of the triumph of the large over the small. Large scale has steadily supplanted small scale, and this scaling-up is closely linked to globalization—shorthand for the relentless expansion of the Western industrial model." Gorlick, "Tipping the Scale," p. 162.

tures. Stated more strongly, change that occurs only at the micro level of people or only at the macro level of collectivities, rather than at both levels, is likely to be more a momentary fad than an enduring transformation.

Different types of micro and macro inputs serve to highlight where the dynamics of change originate and are predominant. The impetus for change can originate or be sustained at either level, but the causal flows between the two are not necessarily balanced. One predominates by initiating, and the other follows even as the two flows become inextricably intertwined in subsequent interaction sequences.

The presumption that people and collectivities shape each other highlights a central problem: while some analysts might agree that the flow between the two levels is central to how collectivities sustain themselves through time and how people shape and are shaped by macro structures, the interactions across the levels have been largely taken for granted and, in one oft-cited case, assessed to be beyond systematic comprehension.[14] Thus probing micro-initiated inputs takes analysis into unexplored territory. We do not have any viable IR theory that anticipates how individuals will vary in response to varying macro inputs or how the structures and policies of macro collectivities might be undermined, redirected, sustained, or otherwise affected by new patterns at the micro level.[15] We tend not to acknowledge, either explicitly or implicitly, that "there is no such thing as a 'state,' an 'economy,' a 'culture,' a 'social class,'" that such entities "are only collections of individual people acting in particular kinds of micro situations" that are recurrent and thus subject to shorthand macro labels.[16]

While such matters are a preoccupation in some of the social sciences,[17]

---

[14] J. David Singer, "The Levels-of-Analysis Problem in International Relations," *World Politics*, Vol. 14 (October 1961), pp. 77–92.

[15] This is not to say the IR literature lacks entries in which the problem is recognized and analyzed. On the contrary, several incisive inquiries are available, but none of them theorize about how the variable conduct of *individuals* shapes and is responsive to macro structures. See, for example, Walter Carlsnaes, "The Agency-Structure Problem in Foreign Policy Analysis," *International Studies Quarterly*, Vol. 36 (September 1992), pp. 245–70; and Alexander Wendt, "The Agency-Structure Problems in International Relations," *International Organization*, Vol. 41 (spring 1987), pp. 335–70.

[16] Randall Collins, "On the Microfoundations of Macrosociology," *American Journal of Sociology*, Vol. 86 (March 1981), p. 988.

[17] Most notably perhaps in the work of Anthony Giddens. See, for example, *The Constitution of Society: Outline of the Theory of Structuration* (Cambridge, Mass.: Polity Press, 1984). A less complex formulation of his agent-structure conceptualization can be found in Anthony Giddens and Christopher Pierson, *Conversations with Anthony Giddens: Making Sense of Modernity* (Cambridge, Mass.: Polity Press, 1998), pp. 75–93. For other inquiries into the micro-macro problem, see Joan Huber (ed.), *Macro-Micro Linkages in Sociology*

those who focus on world affairs have essentially ignored the puzzles posed by the links among these levels of aggregation.[18] Moreover, a major IR paradigm, neorealism, proceeds from the premise that the only relevant action is that of states at the macro level, that individuals at the micro level can be assumed to follow the lead of their states. Nor is the presumption that macro structures are the prime shapers of individual attitudes and actions confined to neorealists. Irrespective of the paradigm to which they subscribe, most analysts see the conduct of individuals as a consequence of the historical, cultural, economic, and political structures in which they live and work. To be sure, at any moment in time people are conceived to possess free will, to be capable of deviating from the norms and expectations imposed by their relevant macro structures, but such deviations are treated as rare, as exceptions that prove the structural rules. Put differently, individuals can be viewed as socially constructed, like organizations or any other units of action. Just as in "many local cultures . . . individual autonomy is highly circumscribed,"[19] for example, so are people in communities conceived as socially constructed in the sense that their loyalties, commitments, and practices relative to their communities are embedded in them early in childhood and continue to guide them throughout their lives.

On the other hand, as distant developments become ever more proximate, the emergent epoch enables people to develop new, more flexible constructions of themselves.[20] Their orientations, practices, and lives are still shaped by macro structures, but the latter are now more numerous

---

(Newbury Park, Calif.: Sage, 1991); Thomas J. Scheff, *Microsociology: Discourse, Emotion, and Social Structure* (Chicago: University of Chicago Press, 1990); Jeffrey C. Alexander, Bernhard Giesen, Richard Münch, and Neil J. Smelser (eds.), *The Micro-Macro Link* (Berkeley and Los Angeles: University of California Press, 1987); H. J. Helle and S. N. Eisenstadt (eds.), *Micro-sociological Theory* (Beverly Hills, Calif.: Sage, 1985); K. D. Knorr-Cetina and A. V. Cicourel (eds.), *Advances in Social Theory and Methodology: Toward an Integration of Micro- and Macro-sociologies* (Boston: Routledge and Kegan Paul, 1981); and Collins, "On the Microfoundations of Macrosociology," pp. 984–1014.

[18] Important exceptions are the work of Philip G. Cerny and Alexander Wendt. See, for example, the former's "Political Agency in a Globalizing World: Toward a Structuration Approach," *European Journal of International Relations*, Vol. 4, No. 4 (2000), pp. 435–63; and the latter's *Social Theory of International Politics* (Cambridge: Cambridge University Press, 1999). For a largely personal history and analysis of micro-macro problems in the discipline of political science, see Heinz Eulau, *Micro-Macro Dilemmas in Political Science: Personal Pathways through Complexity* (Norman: University of Oklahoma Press, 1996), especially Chap. 9 ("The Micro-Macro Reception of Political Science," pp. 119–31).

[19] John Boli and George M. Thomas, "INGOs and the Organization of World Culture," in J. Boli and G. M. Thomas (eds.), *Constructing World Culture* (Stanford, Calif.: Stanford University Press, 1999), p. 37.

[20] See chapters 7 and 8; see also Kenneth J. Gergen, *The Saturated Self: Dilemmas of Identity in Contemporary Life* (New York: Basic Books, 1991), pp. 146–47.

and flexible than in the past, freeing (even forcing) people to shoulder greater autonomy and to evolve new identities and shifting allegiances. The decline of tradition and fixed systems of roles and norms of behavior has led to the imposition of an inescapable and unrelenting autonomy on many people, just as the Internet and other technologies have enabled individuals to greatly expand the range of their interpersonal relationships beyond face-to-face contacts and thus to participate in the formation and enlargement of groups in an ever more networked world. It is no accident that the emergent epoch is often depicted as pervaded by "me-first" orientations.[21] Both singly and collectively, in short, individuals have become increasingly central to the course of events. Observers who seek to make sense of the world scene cannot ignore them: "The question becomes not one of how to integrate agents and structures into one coherent account, but how it could ever be possible to consider methodological individualism or methodological structuralism as viable alternatives."[22]

Accordingly, henceforth the predominance of macro structures is treated as problematic, and the emergent epoch is conceived to provide ample room for individual variation within socially constructed confines imposed by cultural, economic, and political structures. More than that, whatever may be the impact of macro structures on micro actors, several characteristics of individuals can be treated as variables that may shape micro-macro interactions. Here, in the chapters that follow, the values, identities, capacities, strategies, and interests of individuals are posited as pervasive variables that, as they vary or remain constant, can aggregate into substantial consequences for macro structures and the interaction sequences through which they are linked to their collectivities. This elevation of several characteristics of people from constants to variables stems less from my values about the dignity of human beings and more from a presumption that the age of fragmegration has, for better or worse, reduced the reliance of most people on tradition and impelled them to be increasingly independent—increasingly having to innovate and learn in order to cope with the ever-greater complexities of present-day life in large, urban-dominated, technology-driven communities. In short, fragmegrative circumstances constitute "a condition that promotes personal autonomy from socially embedded expectations and opens up the world to exploration and personal experimentation: we can, to an increasing degree, choose who we are. . . . [T]here is no longer any fixed

---

[21] See, for example, the account of the Australian Kindness Movement, which is waging "an uphill battle to get people to be more compassionate," in "Fighting a 'Me-First' Mentality," *Strait Times*, March 19, 2000, p. 47.

[22] Heikki Patomäki and Colin Wight, "After Postpositivism? The Promise of Critical Realism," *International Studies Quarterly*, Vol. 44 (June 2000), p. 231.

system or roles or norms of behaviour."[23] Accordingly, it is reasonable to assert that "[a]gency is now no longer limited to the actions of statesmen or to great revolutionary events, but also takes place in countless daily and often mundane domains"[24] as a consequence of "the self wandering between cultural localization and globalization."[25] In effect, "[t]he concept of the self as an integral, bounded agent is slowly becoming untenable."[26]

The reasons for the downplaying of micro inputs are not difficult to identify. Tracing micro-macro links is extremely difficult theoretically and thus even more challenging empirically. Those who do not subscribe to realist formulations may intuitively sense that the links are endlessly operative, that the actions of collectivities and individuals on the global stage are in part reactions to each other; but faced with the task of tracing their interactions, it tends to be easier to take the predominance of structure for granted than to wrestle with the puzzles their interactions pose. To be sure, structuration theory shares the premise that the course of events is sustained by agent-structure interactions.[27] Promising as this formulation is, however, its advocates have not dug deep into the way individuals as agents shape and are shaped by their structures. One can readily argue that systematic efforts to build this form of micro-macro interactions into premises, hypotheses, and models that focus on globalization are conspicuously scarce. Lacking guidance, therefore, the analysis developed in the ensuing chapters is founded on embryonic and rudimentary reasoning, not to mention empirical observations unsubstantiated by systematic evidence.

While the downplaying of micro inputs can be explained by the difficulties involved in accounting for them, it is nonetheless surprising they have been so fully ignored. For in a profound sense micro-macro sequences are power relationships: people at the micro level want their macro collectivities and institutions to be responsive to their needs and wants, just as macro leaders seek to control—democratically or otherwise—people at the micro level. Even neorealists, for whom power is a

[23] Martin O'Brien, "The Sociology of Anthony Giddens: An Introduction," in Giddens and Pierson, *Conversations with Anthony Giddens*, p. 23.

[24] Roland Bleiker, *Popular Dissent, Human Agency and Global Politics* (Cambridge: Cambridge University Press, 2000), p. 186.

[25] Susantha Goonatilake, "The Self Wandering between Cultural Localization and Globalization," in Jan Nederveen Pieterse and Bhikhu Parekh (eds.), *The Decolonization of Imagination: Culture, Knowledge and Power* (London: Zed Books, 1995), p. 125.

[26] Kenneth J. Gergen, "The Self in the Age of Information," *Washington Quarterly*, Vol. 23 (winter 2000), p. 202.

[27] For an elaborate formulation of structuration theory, see Giddens, *The Constitution of Society*.

central variable, should thus be more ready than they are to build micro-macro interactions into their theories and inquiries.

Types of Micro Actors and Actions

Perhaps a sensitivity to power relationships underlies the fact that while few extant inquiries into micro-macro interactions treat the micro level as consisting exclusively of individuals, many equate micro actors with collective units at the macro level such as firms in the case of economies or countries in the case of international systems. For reasons already indicated, however, the chapters that follow focus mainly on two generic types of actors, namely, individuals at the micro level and collectivities at the macro level. Among individuals, distinctions are drawn among three types of persons. One is the ordinary individual in any walk of life who may not directly participate in micro-macro sequences but whose conduct contributes to the cumulating of unintentional micro inputs. The second is the activist who may contribute to the initiation of intentional micro inputs. The third type consists of the leaders or elites who preside over macro collectivities, by which is meant any impersonal aggregates of people such as societies, economies, states, governments, corporations, international organizations, nongovernmental organizations (NGOs), ethnic minorities, social movements, and so on. The decisions and actions of macro leaders may stem from their own value commitments and readiness to be innovative, but perhaps more often they derive from the particular situations that engulf their collectivity and that generate intentional or unintentional micro inputs from activists or the ordinary individuals who constitute mass publics.

Of course, some micro actors undergo transition to elite status. Most of the time such transitions occur through moving up in organizations, but the ranks of elites also include "idea entrepreneurs"—those individuals who become leaders through the creativity, force, timeliness, or moral authority of their actions. In addition, on occasion some individuals, such as hackers and terrorists, can on their own foster macro outcomes without ever acquiring legitimate leadership status.

In addition to treating the values, identities, capacities, strategies, and interests of individuals as variables, our conceptual toolbox includes mechanisms for tracing how these characteristics are aggregated into dynamics that can shape micro-macro interactions. These mechanisms are seen most clearly in the context of three different processes. One ensues when the values, identities, capacities, strategies, and interests of people are impelled by changing economic, social, or political conditions to alter their attitudes, practices, or behavior in ways that are sufficiently cumulative to arrest the attention of leaders at the macro level as constraints or demands that cannot be ignored and thus initiate sequences of micro-macro interaction. The second unfolds when the elites of collectivities are impelled to pursue a course of action by circumstances in their environments that have consequences for micro actors and initiate sequences of macro-micro interaction. The third occurs when people purposefully engage in protests, demands, or other forms of collective action that leaders at the macro level choose not to ignore. I shall refer to these three sequences, respectively, as *unintentional micro inputs*, as *intentional or unintentional macro inputs*, and as *intentional micro inputs* (see figure 2.1).

When and how do unintentional micro inputs become sufficiently cumulative to generate elite attention and action? While there is no simple answer, two theoretical perspectives are available to probe particular situations.[28] One is the premise of complexity theory that posits the "power of small events,"[29] and the other involves the notion of a "tipping point" that can be brought on by an opinion poll, a calamity, or any number of other developments that indicate to elites the presence of previously unrecognized aggregations occurring in the body politic or specific publics.[30] Tipping points are especially relevant to those situations in which the orientations of mass publics and elites are sharply discrepant and the latter are unresponsive to the former. Opinion polls in the United States, for example, not only have frequently revealed huge differences between the foreign policy preferences of leaders and citizens but also often have found that the differences persist across decades.[31] Whatever such situations might indicate about the limits of democratic theory, they suggest that in and of themselves opinion polls may not bring about tipping points. Why? Because the polls do not necessarily measure the intensity with which the opinions are held.[32] In the absence of intentional inputs initiated by activists or sudden shifts in mass opinion, leaders can ignore consistent poll patterns expressive of values they do not share. But when events induce sharp alterations in the patterns, a tipping point can be said to have occurred that, in turn, gives rise to unintentional micro inputs.

---

[28] Virginia Walsh offers a third theoretical perspective that bears on the cumulation of unintentional micro inputs in "Background Knowledge in World Politics" (manuscript, 2001). Her formulation, however, focuses less on the unintended inputs and more on how they are received and interpreted by macro officials.

[29] See chapter 9.

[30] For a useful discussion of some of the ways unintentional micro inputs undergo transformation into preoccupations at the macro level, see Malcolm Gladwell, *The Tipping Point: How Little Things Can Make a Big Difference* (Boston: Little, Brown, 2000).

[31] Benjamin I. Page and Jason Barabas, "Foreign Policy Gaps between Citizens and Leaders," *International Studies Quarterly*, Vol. 44 (December 2000), pp. 339–64.

[32] James M. Lindsay, "The New Apathy: How an Uninterested Public Is Reshaping Foreign Policy," *Foreign Affairs*, Vol. 79 (September/October 2000), pp. 2–8.

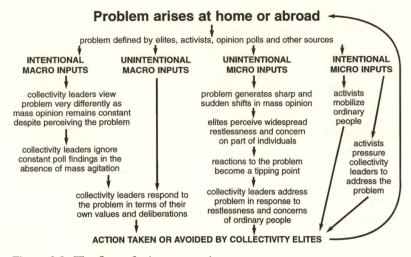

Figure 2.1. The flow of micro-macro inputs.

The advent of e-mail and chat rooms on the Internet has increased the frequency of tipping points, allowing as they do for easy and rapid expressions of opinion on the part of numerous people who have not been mobilized and who may well be unaware that their separate actions may contribute to the development of a tipping point. Consider, for example, the "thousands of calls and e-mail messages" that "streamed" into Kmart with threats to boycott merchandise made in China until the Chinese released the U.S. personnel from the spy plane forced to land on Hainan Island in early April 2001. In Troy, Michigan, the volume of messages was "unprecedented and apparently spontaneous." Indeed, "the company at first suspected that the volume of complaints indicated that an anti-China group had begun an organized campaign, but company officials found no evidence of that."[33] Or consider these remarks by George Tenet, the director of the U.S. Central Intelligence Agency, who explicitly anticipates tipping points facilitated by electronic means of communication. Notwithstanding the attention focused on the Israeli-Palestine conflict, he stresses that

> [p]opulation pressures, growing public access to information and the limited prospects for economic development will have a profound impact on the future of the Middle East. In many places in the Arab world, average citizens are becoming increasingly restive and getting louder. Through access to the Inter-

[33] Joseph Kahn, "Standoff over Plane Brings Calls to Boycott Chinese-Made Goods," *New York Times*, April 11, 2001, p. A1.

net and other communication, a restive public is increasingly capable of taking action without any identifiable leadership or organizational structure.[34]

Perhaps even more frequent are *macro-initiated inputs* that feed back to people at the micro level either when the leaders of collectivities ignore mass opinion and frame policies in line with their values or when they have to respond to sudden and unexpected events—such as the outbreak of war or a major economic downtown—without sufficient time for activist or mass opinion to form and be considered. More often than not, such policies are transformed into macro-initiated inputs when they generate reactions at home or abroad that, in turn, lead activists or mass publics to continue the micro-macro flows.[35] The generic processes whereby both micro and macro inputs initiate and sustain the interactive impacts of publics and collectivities are summarized in figure 2.1.

Of course, instances of intentional micro inputs—collective actions—that alter the behavior of governments and corporations not only are numerous (as happened with the land-mine treaty, disinvestment in apartheid South Africa, human rights in Argentina, the labor practices of the Nike corporation, and the foreign distribution of Nestlé's infant formula)[36] but also reflect the normal practices of politics through which publics are mobilized and around which an ever-growing literature has evolved. The role of pressure groups, the advent of transnational advocacy organizations, the processes of elections—these are but the more conspicuous forms of intentional micro inputs, and, as standard features of political processes, they are well understood and thus not central to the conceptual challenges addressed here. Rather, the prime focus is on how unintentional micro inputs interact with macro collectivities and thereby get embedded in distant proximities.

While a preponderance of micro-initiated inputs involve actual or perceived collective actions, it is useful to note that in addition to Kmart shoppers who resort to e-mail, increasingly a variety of other actions, undertaken by individuals acting alone, can have a discernible impact at the macro level. Terrorists who cause or threaten widespread macro consequences are an obvious example, but there are many others that could be cited. The advent of the Internet, global television, and a wide range of other technological innovations that deepen the world's interdepen-

---

[34] Quoted in Thomas Friedman, "Space Rangers," *New York Times*, February 13, 2001, p. A31.

[35] But this is not to imply macro-initiated inputs consist only of hierarchical, top-down flows. It is entirely possible, even likely, that often some micro actors initiate changes at the macro level that then feed back to shape changes among other micro actors.

[36] See, for example, Margaret E. Keck and Kathryn Sikkink, *Activists beyond Borders: Advocacy Networks in International Politics* (Ithaca, N.Y.: Cornell University Press, 1998).

dence and complexity has made it possible for a single person to initiate micro-macro sequences. Hackers who break into computers can cause at least temporary havoc around the world—as was the case with the ILOVEYOU virus[37]—and acts of vandalism that grab headlines are also illustrative in this regard. A good example of non-computer-initiated inputs is that of José Bové, who gave vent to his antiglobalization attitudes by trashing a McDonald's under construction in southern France and who was then assessed to be "the 12th most popular man in France, ranking just behind the members of the national soccer team."[38] Or consider Brynle Williams, a Welsh farmer distressed about gasoline prices who led a small group of picketers to block exits from refineries and storage deposits in the United Kingdom, with the result that life in Britain was brought to a standstill for a couple of days. In turn, the transportation paralysis tapped into a wellspring of unrecognized public resentments that led to a drop in the fortunes of the Labor Party, polls having revealed that the paralysis diminished Labor's eight-year lead over the Conservatives. Viewed from a micro-macro perspective, this outcome combined inputs that were intentional (Brynle Williams) and unintentional micro (the polls): in the words of the chairman of the House of Commons Trade and Industry Committee, "All of us have been conscious of an undercurrent of opinion on petrol prices, but I don't think we appreciated the combustible character of the issue and the way in which it burst into flames last week."[39] In short, the Williams input is illustrative of a tipping point with widespread consequences.

No less important than the inputs initiated by single individuals is the extent to which collective micro-initiated inputs rest on meaningful variations in the attributes through which people experience distant proximities. As noted, five attributes can be relevant in this respect: the values, identities, capacities, strategies, and interests of people can vary in response to different events or trends, and these variations can impact differently at the macro level. All the attributes are deeply engaged by the dynamics of fragmegration. Values pertaining to human rights, military interventions, terrorism, gasoline shortages, and a host of other newly distant events can vary widely and wildly as such events loom as more or less proximate. Identities are variables in the sense that the emergent

[37] http://www11.cnn.com/2000/TECH/computing/05/04/iloveyou.01/.

[38] Richard Reeves, "Bové Can't Jump Off the Globalizing World, and Neither Can We," *International Herald Tribune*, July 13, 2000, p. 6. See also Emily Eakin, "Questions for José Bové," *New York Times Magazine*, January 6, 2002, p. 13, and Philip H. Gordon and Sophie Meunier, *The French Challenge: Adapting to Globalization* (Washington, D.C.: Brookings Press, 2001), pp. 1–2.

[39] Warren Hoge, "Blair's Disenchanted Kingdom: Strike Takes a Toll," *New York Times*, September 19, 2000, p. A5.

epoch is marked by their proliferation and a greater ability on the part of individuals to shoulder multiple identities and shift back and forth among them. Social unrest and incentives to migrate are illustrative of external stimuli that can lead to the aggregation of identity fluctuations. The capacities variable involves changes in the analytic, emotional, and imaginative skills through which people trace distant events back into their homes and pocketbooks, variations that depend on the access people have to education and information and on a host of other factors.[40] The same factors can also give rise to variation in how people employ different strategies to cope with distant proximities. And clearly, depending on their work, profession, and socioeconomic circumstances, individuals can vary extensively as distant proximities impinge on the interests they hold dear.

It follows that all five attributes can vary in the degree to which an event or trend can serve as micro-initiated inputs or trigger tipping points experienced by macro leaders. Some issues can generate responses largely on the part of elites and activists, while others can also arouse nonelites. And of course, the responses can vary in their intensity from, say, tepid to moderate to extreme. No less relevant, the responses can vary in the degree to which they are widely shared in the ranks of different publics. Terrorism and the threat of war, for example, are likely to evoke extreme reactions widely in every rank, whereas arms control issues are likely to activate mostly elites, and environmental and corruption issues[41] may evoke concern among many elites and activists and only tepid responses within selected segments of the mass public.

While unintentional micro inputs may not be as self-evident as those that are intentional, both types probably occur just as frequently. One recent and obvious example of the former is the widespread resistance in many countries to risking the lives of their young men and women in war. In the case of the United States, for instance, the widely shared perception that people would turn against any military operation that results in soldiers returning home in body bags has led top officials to avoid combat situations or to rely on technologies that do not require sending ground troops into battle. Such a perspective did not prevail during the Vietnam War, but that conflict lay at the root of the changes that resulted in widespread resistance to engaging in subsequent conflicts.[42] Further evidence that unintentional micro inputs are operative with respect to war casualties is provided by the new policies toward press

---

[40] See the discussion of the skill revolution in chapter 10.

[41] Chapter 16 elaborates at length on the response to corruption issues.

[42] However, the polls immediately subsequent to the terrorist attacks in September 2001 indicated a sharp change in this orientation, with high proportions of respondents expressing a readiness to accept body bags as a price paid for an effort to hunt down and prosecute the terrorists as well as to launch an invasion of Iraq.

coverage adopted by militaries. In both the Gulf War and Chechnya, the press was denied access to the battlefield so as to prevent a cumulating of negative micro attitudes toward the conflicts.

But the body-bag example is hardly an exception. Once one becomes sensitive to unintentional micro inputs, the sequences of unorganized aggregations through which they unfold seem pervasive (see figure 2.1). From declining birth rates due to women joining the labor force to political candidates such as Jesse Ventura or Jörg Haider sweeping into office against all conventional expectations; from the rising flow of illegal aliens across borders seeking a better life in the United States to mounting cynicism about politics spurred by scandals; from rising volume on stock markets traceable to investors who had previously kept their money in savings accounts to the overnight collapse of the Soviet Union precipitated by a shared and sudden realization on the part of millions of Russians that an era had ended; from a widespread appreciation that profound changes had occurred with the terrorist destruction of the World Trade Center to the recognition that the Battle of Seattle initiated a new and intense phase of globalizing processes, social and political landscapes are littered with instances of the attitudes and practices of unrelated individuals cumulating into significant micro inputs.[43]

Perhaps the surest indicator that unintentional micro inputs can alter structural constraints is to be found in the conduct of elites. Whatever their field of endeavor, and no matter how authoritarian the structures over which they preside, they devote considerable effort to shoring up the support of their followers because they can never be sure when that support might shift or evaporate. The prime reason that leaders of authoritarian societies prevent their communications media from distributing information that casts negative light on them is that such information might spread and generate opposition to their leadership.

Pervasive as unintentional micro inputs may be, however, they do not necessarily represent swift changes in attitude or practices. Some evolve steadily and incrementally, a few may occur abruptly as the contagion of a shared idea or reaction moves swiftly through publics,[44] but many unfold infinitesimally as people cling to old habits. One might even say that the

---

[43] The Russian case is additionally illustrative because some ten years later, in the summer of 2000, the sinking of the submarine *Kursk* caused immense pain throughout the country, but President Vladimir Putin was slow to recognize the depth of the public reaction and did not return immediately from his vacation to take charge of the crisis. Based on his background as a Soviet official, he apparently interpreted the sinking as a challenge to the Russian state rather than as a tragedy for the Russian people, a misinterpretation of prevailing micro attitudes for which he paid a high political price at the time. See Thomas L. Friedman, "A Russian Dinosaur," *New York Times*, September 5, 2000, p. A31.

[44] Stephen M. Walt, "Fads, Fevers, and Firestorms," *Foreign Policy*, No. 121 (November–December 2000), pp. 34–42.

TABLE 2.1.
Three Paces of Change at Four Levels of Aggregation (intentional change in italics; unintentional change in bold type)

Pace of Change	Levels of Aggregation			
	Micro	*Macro*	*Macro-Macro*	*Micro-Macro*
Infinitesimal change	*tourism* **population size**	*European Union* **global warming**	*NATO expansion* **Africa south of the Sahara**	*Kashmir* **monitored elections**
Incremental change	*opposition to WTO* **spread of AIDS**	*Chechnya* **international financial institutions**	*U.S.-Russian relations* **rich-poor gap**	*land-mine treaty* **spread of democracy**
Abrupt change	*Islamic opposition to the U.S.* **fearful reaction to terrorism**	*East Timor* **collapse of global markets**	*coalition against terrorism* **downing of a U.S. spy plane**	*end of apartheid* **Asian financial crisis**

norm in societies is constancy, that people tend to resist rather than welcome change, and that only as disruptive events or new macro circumstances tap into aspirations or discontent do the prevailing aggregated habits begin to give way to new patterns and clear-cut tipping points. On the other hand, if changes at the macro level fall within the range of micro acceptability, they are likely to occur more readily, since reversals of course by existing or new leaders are often defined as meeting the leadership requirement of being adaptive to altered circumstances.

In sum, a viable theory of micro-macro interactions must take into account the source, pace, and direction of transformative events and patterns that originate at both the micro and macro levels. The sources are multitudinous, the paces can vary greatly, and the directions are hardly less numerous. Using recent examples based on my own analytic judgment, table 2.1 attempts to suggest this variability using two stimuli of change, three paces of change, and four levels of aggregation at which change can occur.

National Boundaries as Illustrative

While micro-macro sequences can vary considerably, all of them share several characteristics. These are perhaps best delineated through an example. Consider the formation and maintenance of national boundaries and the ways in which they reflect the complex processes that link agency and structure to each other. Reduced to its essential quality, a national border is a traditional mental image that can pass through three stages. First, there is the stage whereby elites on either side of the border trace the lines that divide them. Sometimes they do so through long negotiations based on historical commitments and memories; sometimes victory in war enables one side to impose the lines on the other; sometimes agreement is reached on the basis of the configuration of rivers, mountain ranges, and other topological features of nature; and at still other times the lines that are drawn remain controversial for decades and centuries.

Once the borders are established, however, their existence remains precarious as the second stage of the process ensues. This is the stage whereby elites and publics on both sides of the border, whether or not they accept its legitimacy, begin to conduct themselves as if the border was a geographic fact, a line that can be drawn on maps and that is dotted with guard posts and customhouses where one needs a visa or passport to cross into the "foreign" territory. And the more time elapses and people act as if the borders are established facts, the more do they appear "real," and the more do they become a part of the accepted lore and legal traditions of those on either side of the line. The more a people accept the borders as lore and legally binding, the more do the borders serve to bind their country into a cohesive whole. Thus, in effect, maps of the world's political boundaries are no more than either intersubjective agreements that have withstood the test of time or, in some controversial situations, competing intersubjective agreements founded on unresolved tensions over the proper location of the boundaries.

I have cast the border as a tradition because a key feature of modernity—and the fragmegration that has accompanied it—is the large degree to which traditions become problematic as modernity advances. With individuals increasingly skillful, with organizations proliferating, with ideas and pictures being carried swiftly to distant places, with people on the move, with economies being globalized, with authority being questioned, and with states and sovereignty being weaker—see chapter 3 and the rows of table 3.1—long-standing ways of conducting daily routines are no longer satisfying or useful for most people. All the givens of life are undergoing change, and the meaning of boundaries is thus being altered as old traditions yield to the new practices of modernity.[45] Today the

---

[45] On the sources of changing boundary conceptions, see K. J. Holsti, "The Development of Borders as an Institution of the Modern State System" (paper presented at the Conference on the Canada-U.S. Border, Vancouver, October 25, 2000).

intersubjective agreements that sustain the boundaries have become frayed as ideas, people, goods, money, pollution, drugs, crime, and terrorism increasingly pass over and through them with ease.[46] To be sure, since the advent of worldwide terrorist networks, and especially since the attacks on the World Trade Center and the Pentagon, vigilance by border guards has accelerated considerably and greatly heightened awareness of boundaries. However, the use of boundaries to combat terrorism does not negate the conclusion that many national borders can otherwise be viewed as increasingly obsolete traditions. In this sense it is not surprising that communities along both sides of them often have more in common with each other than they do with their home governments.[47] Nor is it surprising that boundaries have become less contested as their salience decreases.[48]

Put differently, in an age of fragmegration the history of borders appears to have entered a third stage. I would not call it a dissolution stage because of the challenge of border-crossing terrorists and also because there remain traditionalists for whom patriotism and historic boundaries are still central to the mental images that guide their conduct. Rather, it is a transition stage, a period in which the competition between alternative intersubjective agreements relative to borders intensifies as those fearful of immigrants vie with those who are open to the values and practices of globalization.[49]

Needless to say, the transition stage is different for different borders that separate countries. The case of the Canadian-U.S. border, for example, has rendered the third stage especially complex.[50] On the one hand,

[46] Cf. Shampa Biswas, "The Production of Boundaries: The Relevance of the Nation-State in the Future of International Relations" (paper presented at the annual meeting of the International Studies Association, Minneapolis, March 1998); Wilfried von Bredow, "The Changing Character of National Borders," *Citizenship Studies*, Vol. 2 (1998), pp. 365–76; Stephen E. Flynn, "Beyond Border Control," *Foreign Affairs*, Vol. 79 (November/December 2000), pp. 1–13; and Patricia M. Goff, "Invisible Borders: Economic Liberalization and National Identity," *International Studies Quarterly*, Vol. 44 (December 2000), pp. 533–62.

[47] James N. Rosenau, "Coherent Connection or Commonplace Contiguity? Theorizing about the California-Mexico Overlap," in Katrina Burgess and Abraham F. Lowenthal (eds.), *The California-Mexico Connection* (Stanford, Calif.: Stanford University Press, 1993), pp. 3–33.

[48] Mark W. Zacher, "The Territorial Integrity Norm: International Boundaries and the Use of Force," *International Organization*, Vol. 55 (spring 2001), pp. 215–50.

[49] One observer describes the transition stage as "an intermediate position" between the presence or absence of borders "that suggests that borders are present but permeable; they are disappearing but still discernible, and the degree to which this is more or less true varies across issue areas." Goff, "Invisible Borders," pp. 533–34.

[50] The advent of transnational terrorist networks that have employed Canada as an entry point into the United States has further complicated the Canadian-U.S. boundary, render-

its long history free of conflict and the similarities of the two countries' cultures have kept differences to a minimum; on the other hand, the asymmetries between the two countries' resources and the ease with which globalizing forces can transgress the border through Canadian satellite dishes that receive American television programs have served to exacerbate tensions. Indeed, since Canadians and Americans have long agreed on the location of their border, the advent of the transition stage has tended to minimize uncertainty. Unlike those borders that have never been intersubjectively agreed upon—say, in Kashmir or Cyprus or between Russia and Japan—the Canadian-U.S. border is marked by precedents for addressing border conflicts or otherwise coping with the transition stage.

Even in the Canadian-U.S. case, however, the boundary continues to challenge understanding and ingenuity.[51] It poses the question of where the transition stage is heading. I think the answer is provided by a fragmegrative perspective, which suggests that the transition is unfolding in a turbulent time when the border is increasingly shorn of content and becomes merely a historic marker, an artifact of an age in which the sovereignty of states was fully in place. And the closer the transition gets to stripping the border of meaning, the greater will be the tensions as localizing reactions to the globalizing dynamics become increasingly defensive, articulate, and resistant.

If a fragmegrative perspective allows for viewing borders as mental images undergoing transition, it also serves to focus attention on the distinctions among the various worlds inhabited by global- and local-oriented elites, activists, and people.[52] Put differently, fragmegrative dynamics can also be a source of new identities as the advance of globalization heightens the sensitivity of people to their relationship with distant events, processes, and structures—to whether they welcome or resist the large extent to which distant developments have become proximate. As indicated by the various reactions to the Battle of Seattle in 1999,

---

ing it a problem for both countries, "given the length of their border and the isolation of many areas." Barbara Crossette, "Canada Pushes Broad Antiterror Measure, Alarming Some Who Fear Erosion of Rights," *New York Times*, October 18, 2001, p. B4. A step toward solving the problem was taken when the two countries signed a thirty-point "action plan" intended to cope with the terrorist challenge. Alison Mitchell, "Ridge and Canadian Sign Antiterror 'Action Plan,' " *New York Times*, December 13, 2001, p. A6. See also Doris Meissner, "After the Attacks: Protecting Borders and Liberties," *Policy Brief No. 8*, Carnegie Endowment for International Peace (November 2001).

[51] For a wide-ranging discussion of the challenges, see Conference Report, "Rethinking the Line: The Canada-US Border," *Horizons*, Vol. 2 (March 2001), pp. 1–56.

[52] See chapters 4 through 7.

many individuals have become Globals or Locals; as such, they care deeply about which side of the divide they are on.

Although the list of fragmegrative issues on political agendas is long and contentious, perhaps none is closer to whom individuals feel they are becoming than the identity that locates them on either side of the border between the remote and the close-at-hand. I do not have in mind the distinction between the nationalist and the internationalist; rather, I am suggesting the evolution of new identities that sum up common reactions to the wide range of issues that crowd high on agendas and that are not always differentiated by the nationalist-internationalist distinction. Borders can also delineate professions, organizational hierarchies, ideological perspectives, social standings, and a host of other salient identities, none of which necessarily coincide with historic geographic boundaries.[53]

Macro Dynamics and Micro Worlds

To probe causal layers that allow for variability among individuals and their links to collectivities, a meaningful theory of micro-macro interactions requires a conceptual scheme that both specifies the prime macro dynamics of the emergent epoch and differentiates among diverse types of micro actors who both shape and respond to the macro dynamics. Here, consistent with the imperatives asserted in the epigraphs to this chapter, a comprehensive scheme is offered in two stages: eight prime macro dynamics are analyzed in chapter 3, while chapters 4 through 7 identify twelve local, global, and private "worlds" individuals can inhabit and the fluidity of their movement among them. These latter chapters rest on the premise that individuals differ in so many respects that a typology of them in relation to fragmegration can help explain the variability of their responses to the same stimuli. More than a few observers have sought to develop a typology for this purpose. Two examples are provided in figures 2.2 and 2.3. They both have the advantage of differentiating between global and local phenomena and treating those at the national level as peripheral. Figure 2.2 stresses the interactive nature of global and local processes, and figure 2.3 also focuses on people at the micro level by distinguishing between four political orientations along a number of dimensions. In contrast to our two-stage scheme, however, neither example allows for the possibility of people changing their orientations or for those who do not maintain orientations toward any level.

---

[53] Languages offer a good example of how borders and geographic boundaries can be discrepant. See, for example, Steven Pearlstein, "Irking Quebec, French-Speaking Arcadians Remain Loyal to Canada," *Washington Post*, September 12, 1999, p. A27.

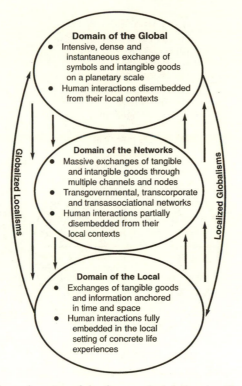

Figure 2.2. The three domains of the fractured global order. Reprinted with permission from Francisco R. Sagasti, "Development Strategies for the 21st Century: The Case of Peru," *Peru Monitor* (May 2001), p. 50.

Nor does either address the interaction of people at the micro level and collectivities at the macro level.

Twelve Micro Worlds

Central to the two-stage scheme developed in the ensuing chapters is the distinction between global and local phenomena. It is not an easy line to draw. Indeed, given the notion of distant proximities linked by frag-megrative processes, it is in many ways a murky line, less an either-or demarcation and more a both-and delineation. People may not be either local or global in their orientations and behavior; rather, they may be both local and global as they confront different circumstances or issues. In other words, since what becomes global is often local in origin, and vice versa, it would be erroneous to treat the "local" as simply the close-at-hand consequences of the "global."

The Greens ☆

(1) communitarian capitalism
(2) socialism
(3) community
(4) intelligentsia
(5) superego
(6) communalism
(7) high integration
(8) tribalization
(9) identity fetishism

The Reds ☆

(1) state capitalism
(2) communism
(3) equality
(4) proletariat
(5) alter ego
(6) Marxism
(7) high mobilization
(8) nationalization
(9) majority fetishism

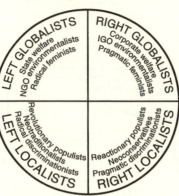

The Blues ☆

(1) capitalism
(2) conservatism
(3) freedom
(4) bourgeoisie
(5) ego
(6) liberalism
(7) high accumulation
(8) transnationalization
(9) commodity fetishism

Any National Color ☆

(1) totalitarian capitalism
(2) nazism, fascism, militarism
(3) order
(4) big and petite bourgeoisie
(5) id
(6) fascism
(7) high repression
(8) totalization
(9) security fetishism

☆ Symbolic Color

(1) indicates social system
(2) indicates political party alignment
(3) indicates axial principle
(4) indicates leadership
(5) indicates psychic energy

(6) indicates ideology
(7) indicates development strategy
(8) indicates process
(9) indicates pathology

Figure 2.3. Remapping the global spectrum. Reprinted from Majid Tehranian, *Global Communications and World Politics: Dependency, Development, and Discourse* (Boulder: Lynne Rienner, 1999), p. 70.

Chapters 4 through 7 undertake to clarify the confusion that can attach to the distinction between global and local phenomena at the micro level. They do so by conceiving of people as populating any one of twelve worlds most of the time even as there may be special occasions when the distinctions among the worlds get obscured and they are inclined to move into one or more of the other worlds. Conceivably, too, some people may occupy more than one world if, say, they are globally oriented in terms of economics and locally oriented with respect to cultural issues. Most people, however, are viewed as residents of only one world on most issues in any given period. In other words, the use of the "worlds" concept is intended to suggest a predominant perspective on life—a worldview—through which people arrange their priorities among the opportunities available to them, the threats they perceive as serious, the values they hold dear, the goals to which they aspire, and the horizons they view as salient.[54] In eleven of the twelve worlds the predominant perspective is not circumscribed by geographic boundaries, albeit their populaces are not lacking in orientations toward territory. Rather, the predominant perspective of persons in each world is marked by a complex of shared attitudes toward the scope of localizing and globalizing processes, toward proximate and distant horizons. Four of the twelve are global worlds (consisting of the Resistant, Specialized, Affirmative, and Territorial Globals), four are local worlds (the Resistant, Exclusionary, Affirmative, and Insular Locals), and four are private worlds (the Alienated Cynics, the Alienated Illegals, the Tuned-Out Passives, and the Circumstantial Passives).

It follows that the distinction between the distant and the proximate, between the global and the local, is founded on the way in which people relate to space and the scale or location of the horizons it encompasses. Those who stress proximate horizons over distant ones are conceived to occupy local worlds, while those who accord greater priority to distant than to proximate horizons are regarded as occupants of global worlds.

---

[54] Geographers have also cast their analysis in terms of local and global worlds, but they do so largely in territorial terms, whereas here the differences among the worlds are not confined to spatial considerations. For a useful but nonetheless geographic formulation based on the "worlds" concept, see John Allen and Doreen Massey (eds.), *Geographical Worlds* (New York: Oxford University Press, 1995). An inquiry similar to the one undertaken here that "seeks to shift the emphasis away from the currently dominant discourse of scalar and territorial relativisation, towards relational processes and network forms of organization that defy a linear distinction between place and space," is developed in Ash Amin, "Spatialities of Globalization," *Environment and Planning* (forthcoming), p. 2. For an early, pathbreaking empirical inquiry that uncovered local-global patterns akin to those developed in the ensuing chapters, see Chap. 12, "Patterns of Influence: Local and Cosmopolitan Influentials," in Robert K. Merton, *Social Theory and Social Structure*, enlarged edition (New York: Free Press, 1968).

Thus, as will be elaborated in subsequent chapters, persons in the four local worlds are ready to accord at least minimal salience to territory as a factor in proximate or distant developments. Individuals in three of the four global worlds contextualize their predominant perspectives in non-linear terms that allow for events and feedback loops to occur in non-geographic spaces, whereas those in the fourth global world retain a territorial orientation toward the course of events. Put differently, the Territorial Globals tend to treat their worlds in terms of landscapes, whereas the other Globals and the Affirmative and Resistant Locals are inclined to view their worlds as a congeries of ethnoscapes, technoscapes, financescapes, mediascapes, and ideoscapes as well as landscapes.[55] As for people in the four private worlds, their orientations are marked by either alienation or passivity and are thus conceived as so disassociated from public affairs that they are not in any local or global world. For them, there are neither distant nor proximate events; rather, except for the Alienated Illegals, everything is simply daily routine that unfolds, as it were, in a vacuum.

An initial effort to systematize the distinctions among these worlds involved locating people on a proximity continuum determined by their orientations toward space and scale, toward the territorial bounds and the scope of the events, issues, and trends that mark their worlds. The more territorial the space and the smaller the scale on which people's worldviews are founded, the more were they regarded as local in their outlooks and practices. Most people were posited as favoring either the local or the global extreme even as allowance was made for some movement along the continuum under certain circumstances.

Further reflection on the utility of the proximity continuum as the basis for differentiating among Locals and Globals led to a realization that it, too, was rooted in linearity, in an either-or context that arrayed the several global and local worlds adjacent to each other on the continuum, thus suggesting that people could only move among the worlds by passing through those adjacent to the one in which they were located at any point in time. But such linear movement is misleading: it needlessly narrows the range of choice available to people as they respond to the course of events. Accordingly, the notion of a proximity continuum was abandoned in favor of the nonlinear conception depicted in figure 2.4. This diagrammatic portrayal is purposely lacking arrows that connect the worlds. Rather, the connections are established through cones of fragmegration. People in each of the three types of worlds are conceived as passing through the cones whenever they are linked or move to either of

[55] Arjun Appadurai, *Modernity at Large: Cultural Dimensions of Globalization* (Minneapolis: University of Minnesota Press, 1996), p. 37.

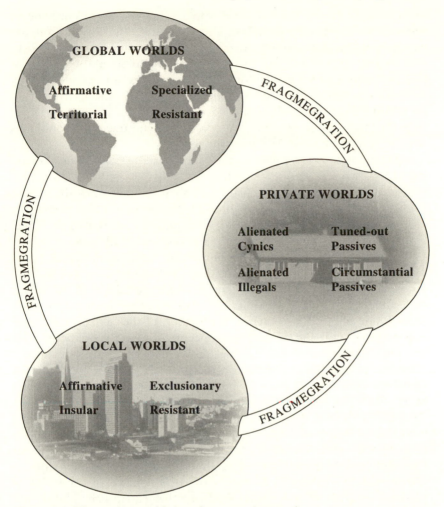

Figure 2.4. The twelve worlds in a fragmegrative epoch.

the other two worlds. The cones of fragmegration represent a fluid space in which passage among the worlds can occur along a variety of routes. They also hint at the complexity of attitudinal and behavioral movement at the micro level and the possibility of new identities forming that may stimulate thought on how one wants to relate to various situations. To be sure, inertia and habit can root some people so fully into the premises of a particular world that they are unlikely to be induced by fragmegrative dynamics to shift to another. And it is also the case that the premises of some of the worlds are so antithetical that movement among them is improbable (a Resistant Local, for example, is unlikely ever to become an Affirmative Global). Nevertheless, and to repeat, the formulation depicted in figure 2.4 presumes that fluidity marks the emergent epoch, that an ever greater number of circumstances and situations now arise that give pause and foster shifting orientations toward the global-local nexus. Thus, while chapters 4 through 6 outline the characteristics and commitments of those who populate each of the worlds, chapter 7 relaxes the presumption of attitudinal consistency and traces the conditions that can lead to movement among the worlds.

But even as figure 2.4 stresses the fluidity of the connections among the various worlds, so does it portray the gulf that separates the global and local worlds on the one hand and these worlds from the private worlds on the other hand. The cones of fragmegration also sustain the many tensions that distant proximities can generate, as well as the limits of fluidity and the barriers to altering predominant worldviews.

To employ a multidirectional, nonlinear formulation, however, is not to dismiss the relevance of space and scale. Some analysts argue that the inclusion of spatial factors as bases for delineating local and global worlds misleadingly downplays the scalar foundations of people's orientations. Indeed, one observer advocates "the abolition of the 'global' and 'local' as conceptual tools and suggest[s] a concentration on the politics of scale and their metaphorical and material production and transformation."[56] Here this perspective is rejected on the grounds that the local and the global are conceived in terms of both space and scale, thereby enabling us to highlight the fluidity of distant proximities. In other words, through combining space and scale "the 'global' can refer to anything from the metropolitan economy at one end, through the national to the international; while the 'local' can refer to the city, the region, the nation, and even particular types of neighborhoods, like the inner city. . . . The consistent element in all this is the maintenance of some sort of relational concept of scale rather than one that equates the global with the international and the local with the sub-national."[57]

It is noteworthy that the formulation summarized in figure 2.4 does not rest on the presence of national worlds.[58] As will be seen, here na-

[56] Erik Styngedouw, "Neither Global nor Local: 'Glocalization' and the Politics of Scale," in Kevin R. Cox (ed.), *Spaces of Globalization: Reasserting the Power of the Local* (New York: Guilford Press, 1997), p. 142.

[57] Kevin R. Cox, "Globalization and the Politics of Distribution: A Critical Assessment," in Cox (ed.), *Spaces of Globalization*, p. 118.

[58] For other inquiries that contest "the usefulness of the nation as a category of analysis," see Ann Cvetkovich and Douglas Kellner (eds.), *Articulating the Global and the Local: Globalization and Cultural Studies* (Boulder, Colo.: Westview Press, 1997), esp. p. 25 (quoted here); and Tim O'Riordan and Chris Church, "Synthesis and Context," in Tim O'Riordan (ed.), *Globalism, Localism and Identity: Fresh Perspectives on the Transition to Sustainability* (London: Earthscan Publications, 2001), p. 11.

tional worlds are regarded as having been largely superseded—as having yielded to fragmegrative pressures that generate orientations toward one or another local or global world. Only one of the twelve worlds encompasses attitudes that may fall between the local and the global, and even in this world—that of Territorial Globals, comprising mostly public officials whose perspectives are cast in terms of the well-being of their states in the interstate system—its occupants are likely to be oriented toward their country as a congeries of local sites.

Another feature of the twelve-worlds, agent-oriented formulation is that it inhibits any inclinations to base the analysis on technological determinism. Technological innovations may be necessary sources of the huge transformations sustaining the emergent epoch, but they are not sufficient sources. The many ways in which people have utilized the new electronic and transportation technologies are no less crucial. Without an active, consumer-oriented response of individuals and societies throughout the world to the availability of rapid means of communication and travel, the technological breakthroughs would have had little consequence. Only because publics and major societal institutions seized upon them have the new technologies served as stimuli to the changes that have ushered in a new epoch in world history. This premise is fully elaborated in chapter 11.

Needless to say, the identities ascribed to those who live in each of these worlds are neither referred to nor consciously recognized by the persons they encompass—nor, indeed, by the literature on identity, culture, or globalization. They refer, rather, to ideal types of persons. Nevertheless, from an analytic perspective I find it helpful to delineate the twelve worlds and the shifts among them as a means of tracing the roles individuals play in the micro-macro interactions that constitute world affairs and thereby clarifying the diversity, nuances, and contradictions inherent in the tensions between the globalizing and localizing forces at work in our emergent epoch. In addition to outlining the orientations and practices of people in each of the twelve worlds, the next four chapters identify some of the conditions under which individuals may either be mobilized to initiate intentional micro inputs or be perceived to evolve new orientations and practices sufficient to foster unintentional micro inputs in response to any distant proximities they experience as meaningful.

METHODOLOGY

By ascribing centrality to macro structures, the ensuing analysis of individuals as micro actors avoids the reductionist flaws inherent in methodological individualism. But two methodological dilemmas are posed by the delicacy and complexity of micro-macro dynamics in a fragmegrative epoch marked by rapid change. One dilemma is that our analytic capacities have long been rooted in methodological territorialism,[59] in a long-standing, virtually unconscious habit of probing problems in a broad geographic or spatial context. This habit poses an acute problem because of the ever-growing porosity of domestic-foreign boundaries[60] that has rendered territoriality much less pervasive than it used to be even as the other social sciences tend to construct their inquiries, develop their concepts, formulate their hypotheses, and frame their evidence-gathering procedures through territorial lenses. Nor are officials free to think in alternative contexts: as one analyst put it, "Trapped by the territoriality of their power, policy makers in traditional settings often have little choice but to address the symptoms rather than the causes of public problems."[61] This first dilemma can be resolved by continuously recalling that distance and territorial boundaries involve subjective appraisals and not objective circumstances.

A second methodological dilemma is that fragmegrative dynamics and micro-macro interactions are pervaded with feedback processes and thus pose the difficult question of how to explore them systematically. In other words, each is rooted in events that unfold virtually simultaneously, making it fruitless to cast analyses in terms of the interaction of independent and dependent variables. Each dependent variable at one moment in time, that is, quickly becomes an independent variable at the next moment, just as every independent variable was a dependent variable in the prior moment. Thus analyses cast in a conventional linear framework seem bound to fall short in terms of capturing the interactive, high-speed nature of the phenomena of interest. How, then, to proceed? What methodologies might be available for probing high-speed and circular sequences of interaction? Are we bound to rely exclusively on case studies that, hopefully, somehow reveal the underlying tendencies that drive the transformative impacts of fragmegration and micro-macro links? Can feedback methodologies drawn from mathematics and statistics be adapted to the needs of IR?

---

[59] See Scholte, *Globalization: A Critical Introduction*, pp. 56–58.

[60] This is the central theme of James N. Rosenau, *Along the Domestic-Foreign Frontier: Exploring Governance in a Turbulent World* (Cambridge: Cambridge University Press, 1997), passim. For a contrary perspective in which "an examination of the ideas, norms, and practices of territoriality leads to the conclusion that it is a venerable and foundational institution of international relations, and one that shows few signs either of obsolescence or of transformation," see K. J. Holsti, "The Changing Norms of International Institutions: The Case of Territoriality" (paper presented at the XVIII World Congress of the International Political Science Association, Quebec City, August 1–5, 2000), p. 20.

[61] Wolfgang H. Reinicke, "The Other World Wide Web: Global Public Policy Networks," *Foreign Policy*, No. 117 (winter 1999–2000), p. 45.

The dilemma of tracing feedback mechanisms marked by simultaneity is not easily resolved. Indeed, never having been very sophisticated as a methodologist, I do not have very precise answers to the foregoing questions. I know they are important and I presume there are analysts who can answer them with some authority. Still, ignorance is no excuse. If the mysteries of a fragmegrative world are to be fathomed, we cannot shy away from methodological questions on grounds of inexperience. Herewith, then, a partial response to the methodological challenge: while case studies can surely be of value, there are also procedures for tracing feedback mechanisms that have become more feasible as a result of advances in computer technologies. As I understand it, there is now the eventual prospect of computer chips that will be ten billion (yes, ten billion) times faster than those in use today.[62] This heightens the potential of using computer simulations based on complexity theory,[63] of building agent-based feedback processes into models that simulate the dynamics of change, fragmegration, and micro-macro interactions. To be sure, and to return to points made earlier, conceptualizations of these three sets of dynamics are in short supply and obviously need to be refined before agent-based computer models can be applied. But if it is assumed that such refinements will eventually be developed, then computer simulations may prove to be a useful methodology in unraveling the mysteries of a fragmegrative world.

As will be seen, moreover, there are substantive dimensions of complexity theory that can help explain the processes of aggregation whereby unintentional micro inputs foster change through having been perceived by macro leaders. In particular, as noted in chapter 9, complexity theory posits self-organization as an emergent property of human populations, a property that is presumably appreciated by leaders sensitive to shifting attitudes and practices among their followers.

CAUSAL LAYERS

Clearly, this book undertakes to juggle a number of powerful dynamics in an attempt to derive a measure of order out of the welter of contradictions and ambiguities on which our fragmegrative epoch rests. The challenge of doing so is further intensified, as indicated in the columns of table 3.1, by the commitment to focusing on the dynamic interactions that operate at four levels of aggregation—the micro level of individuals, the macro level of public and private collectivities, the macro-macro level

---

[62] John Markoff, "Tiniest Circuits Hold Prospect of Explosive Computer Speeds," *New York Times*, July 16, 1999, p. A1. See also Kenneth Chang, "I.B.M. Creates a Tiny Circuit Out of Carbon," *New York Times*, August 27, 2001, p. 1.

[63] The outlines of complexity theory are set forth in chapter 9.

of the interaction among collectivities, and the micro-macro level wherein individuals at the micro level shape and are shaped by their collectivities at the macro level. One cannot adequately grasp the underpinnings of the fragmegration epoch without allowing for the sources and consequences of activities at each of these levels.

Of course, there is a risk in treating the dynamics as causal layers that can be peeled off as one probes deeper into the underpinnings of the global system. The risk is that of conveying the impression of too much order, of causal layers that somehow are systematically linked in a linear array. Such a conclusion is exactly contrary to the essential thrust of the ensuing analysis, and thus it bears repeating that the world today is best understood in the context of feedback loops wherein each major dynamic operates as both cause and effect as it interacts with the others. Technological advances may have at some time preceded changes in individuals, organizations, economies, states, sovereignty, and governments, and in turn these changes may have at some time preceded a number of others to be specified in subsequent chapters; but such simple casual sequences have long since yielded to continuing interaction among all the relevant dynamics. As one astute observer puts it, "[G]lobalization is neither linear nor unidimensional; rather it is a multilayered, asymmetric admixture of international, transnational, domestic, and local processes, the interaction of which *increasingly generates multiple equilibria*."[64]

Some analysts regard micro-macro interactions as dialectically linked. One, for example, insists that "there is always a dialectic, a continuous dialect, between the local and the global,"[65] whereas another perceives the slogan "Think Globally and Act Locally" as a dialectic between micro practice and macro thinking.[66] Still another contends that the "use of the word 'globalization' overshadows and may conceal the dialectical processes which are inherent to it; in particular, globalization inherently carries with it a 'double movement' or dialectic which runs contrary to the integration, convergence, and homogenization it seems to imply."[67] The thrust of the preceding analysis, however, suggests caution in characterizing fragmegrative processes so definitively. Conceivably, they are less dialectical and more cyclical, more an ebb and flow between predominantly globalizing tendencies and predominantly localizing tendencies without

[64] Cerny, "Political Agency in a Globalizing World," p. 439 (italics in the original).

[65] Stuart Hall, "Old and New Identities, Old and New Ethnicities," in Anthony D. King (ed.), *Culture, Globalization and the World-System: Contemporary Conditions for the Representation of Identity* (Minneapolis: University of Minnesota Press, 1997), p. 62.

[66] Chadwick F. Alger, "Perceiving, Analyzing and Coping with the Local-Global Nexus," *International Social Science Journal*, Vol. 117 (August 1988), p. 337.

[67] Claire Turenne Sjolander, "The Rhetoric of Globalization: What's in a Wor(l)d?" *International Journal*, Vol. 51 (autumn 1996), p. 609.

any resolution or (in dialectical terms) synthesis. In any event, whichever they may be, the contradictory and ambiguous fluctuations of the emergent epoch can be traced for what they are.

To facilitate the analysis of elites, activists, and ordinary people in the twelve worlds treated here as the micro level, it is useful to set forth some of the more important macro dynamics to which individuals everywhere have to respond, whatever their degree of autonomy, their material circumstances, and their worldviews. Such is the task of the next chapter.

CHAPTER THREE

Sources and Consequences of Fragmegration

> [T]his backlash, both now and potentially, is very strong.
> Indeed, it could get much stronger, especially when our
> economies begin to turn down and especially if political
> changes . . . make globalization and opposition to it even more
> difficult to manage in light of the role of particular pressure
> groups and political interests.
>   —C. Fred Bergsten[1]

IN A FAST-MOVING, ever more complex world where causes and effects are inextricably linked—where the outcomes of interaction sequences can instantaneously feed back to generate other outcomes—it is fruitless to differentiate the macro sources of fragmegrative dynamics from their consequences. To be sure, there are occasions when localizing responses to globalizing developments take a while to occur or when local events evoke global reactions in due time, but more often than not the interactions are marked by degrees of simultaneity that defy breaking down the sequences in terms of their causes and effects. Hence, in this chapter a diverse array of macro dynamics that seem most central to the emergent fragmegrative epoch are examined without any systematic attempt to delineate where each fits in one or another causal chain. Sometimes they operate as stimuli, and sometimes they follow from other sources; sometimes they initiate forward movements, and sometimes they sustain backlashes; but at all times they are caught up in an endless array of interactive feedback loops. To anticipate a theme of chapter 9, history is not one damn thing after another; it is many damn things all at once!

Not only does the juggling of a number of powerful sources of fragmegration (the rows of table 3.1) pose a huge challenge to any effort to derive a measure of order out of the welter of contradictions and ambiguities on which our fragmegrative epoch rests, but the task is further complicated by the need to focus on the dynamic interactions that may operate at four levels of aggregation (the columns of table 3.1)—the micro level of individuals, the macro level of public and private collectivities, the macro-macro level of the interaction among collectivities, and

---

[1] "The Backlash against Globalization," in *Tokyo 2000* (New York: Trilateral Commission, 2000), p. 51.

the micro-macro level wherein individuals at the micro level shape and are shaped by their collectivities at the macro level. One cannot adequately grasp the underpinnings of the fragmegration epoch without allowing for the sources and consequences of activities at each of these levels. As a means of suggesting how they might underlie distant proximities, eight of the several dynamics examined here are briefly set forth in table 3.1 along with their possible impact on both micro and macro phenomena and the interactions among them. The entries in the cells of the table are by no means exhaustive of the various ways the dynamics can shape micro and macro actors. Rather, they are only intended to highlight the diverse ways in which fragmegration shapes the course of events. The elaboration of the dynamics in the remainder of this chapter amplifies their importance and at the same time facilitates the analysis of ensuing chapters. These dynamics and variants of them are conceived to be so fundamental as to underlie, in varying combinations and to varying degrees, the distant proximities discussed throughout the remainder of the book. Three of the dynamics are also the focus of the chapters of part II, but this is not to imply they are more powerful than the others. It is merely that their relevance and significance are usefully served by additional elaboration.

FRAGMEGRATIVE FLOWS

Anticipating the diversity of fragmegrative dynamics, a communications revolution has facilitated the rapid flow of ideas, information, images, and money across continents; a transportation revolution has hastened the boundary-spanning flow of people and goods; an organizational revolution has shifted the flow of authority, influence, and power beyond traditional boundaries; and an economic revolution has redirected the flow of goods, services, capital, and ownership among countries. Taken together, these flows have fostered a cumulative process that is both the source and the consequence of eroding boundaries, integrating regions, proliferating networks, diminishing territorial attachments, truncated traditions, coalescing social movements, weakening states, contracting sovereignty, dispersing authority, demanding publics, and expanding citizen skills—all of which also serve to generate counterreactions intended to contest, contain, or reverse one or another of the multiple flows and thereby preserve communities and reduce inequities. While each of these dynamics is powerful, none can be listed as primary. Under conditions of high complexity they are all interactive, and each reinforces the others. None are sufficient, but all are necessary to sustain the age of fragmegration. And they all have consequences for people in each of the local, global, and private worlds delineated in subsequent chapters.

TABLE 3.1.
Some Sources of Fragmegration at Four Levels of Aggregation

Sources of Fragmegration	Levels of Aggregation			
	Micro	*Macro*	*Micro-Macro*	*Macro-Macro*
Microelectronic technologies	enable like-minded people to be in touch with each other anywhere in the world	render collectivities more open, connected, and vulnerable; empower them to mobilize support	constrain governments by enabling opposition groups to mobilize more effectively	accelerate diplomatic processes; facilitate electronic surveillance and intelligence work
Skill revolution	expands people's horizons on a global scale; sensitizes them to the relevance of distant events; facilitates a reversion to local concerns	enlarges the capacity of governmental agencies to think "out of the box," seize opportunities, and analyze challenges	constrains policy making through increased capacity of individuals to know when, where, and how to engage in collective action	multiplies quantity and enhances quality of links among states; solidifies their alliances and enmities
Organizational explosion	facilitates multiple identities, subgroupism, and affiliation with transnational networks	increases capacity of opposition groups to form and press for altered policies; divides publics from their elites	contributes to the pluralism and dispersion of authority; heightens the probability of authority crises	renders the global stage ever more transnational and dense with nongovernmental actors
Bifurcation of global structures	adds to role conflicts, divides loyalties, and foments tensions among individuals; orients people toward local spheres of authority	facilitates formation of new spheres of authority and consolidation of existing spheres in the multicentric world	empowers transnational advocacy groups and special interests to pursue influence through diverse channels	generates institutional arrangements for cooperation on major global issues such as trade, human rights, the environment, etc.

TABLE 3.1. (*continued*)

Mobility upheaval	stimulates imaginations and provides more extensive contacts with foreign cultures; heightens salience of the outsider	enlarges the size and relevance of subcultures, diasporas, and ethnic conflicts as people seek new opportunities abroad	increases movement across borders that lessens capacity of governments to control national boundaries	heightens need for international cooperation to control the flow of drugs, money, immigrants, and terrorists
Weakening of territoriality, states, and sovereignty	undermines traditions and national loyalties; increases distrust of governments and other institutions	adds to the porosity of national boundaries and the difficulty of framing national policies	lessens confidence in governments; renders nationwide consensuses difficult to achieve and maintain	increases need for interstate cooperation on global issues; lessens control over cascading events
Authority crises	redirect loyalties; encourage individuals to replace traditional criteria of legitimacy with performance criteria	weaken ability of both governments and other organizations to frame and implement policies	facilitate the capacity of publics to press and/or paralyze their governments, the WTO, and other organizations	enlarge the competence of some IGOs and NGOs; encourage diplomatic wariness in negotiations
Globalization of national economies	swells ranks of consumers; promotes uniform tastes; heightens concerns for jobs; widens gap between winners and losers	complicates tasks of state governments vis-à-vis markets; promotes business alliances	increases efforts to protect local cultures and industries; facilitates vigor of protest movements; polarizes communities	intensifies trade and investment conflicts; generates incentives for building global financial institutions

Microelectronic Technologies

Stunning are the data depicting the ways in which a variety of communications technologies—from the fax machine to the fiber-optic cable, from the cellular phone to the orbiting satellite, from television to the Internet—continue to shrink the world and reduce the relevance of geographic boundaries. Today there are more than one billion telephones in active use throughout the world. In 1964 there was one TV set for every twenty persons, whereas now there is one for every four. Currently more than two hundred functioning satellites orbit the Earth, each capable of carrying tens of thousands of calls and numerous TV signals at once. The number of Internet hosts, or networked computers, grew more than six-fold between 1995 and 1999.[2] More than 1.4 billion e-mail messages are estimated to cross national boundaries every day.[3] It is presumed that the Internet is growing by one million Web pages a day.[4] At the end of 2001 the number of persons on-line throughout the world was 505 million, of which roughly 43 percent used English, 32 percent used a European language, and 25 percent used an Asian language; by 2003 the number of persons on-line was projected to grow to 793 million.[5] It is also noteworthy that the proportion of women in the user population is growing. During the first six months of 2001, for example, the number of women on-line in Great Britain jumped by 10 percent.[6]

Translating such data into day-to-day terms, so voluminous is the flow of e-mail that it has led to a crisis in the U.S. Congress, which received 80 million messages in 2000, with House offices getting as many as 8,000 messages a month and Senate offices as many as 55,000 a month.[7] A historical perspective provides an even more impressive picture of the Internet's ubiquitous growth: it took the telephone forty years to reach its first ten million customers, the fax machine roughly twenty years, personal computers about ten years, and e-mail little more than one year.[8]

Quite possibly, moreover, these dynamics are poised for another step-level leap forward with the advent of new computer technologies, which

---

[2] These data are from the National Geographic Society, *Millennium in Maps: Cultures* (Washington, D.C.: National Geographic Society, June 1999).

[3] Office of the Press Secretary, "Remarks by President Clinton at University of Chicago Convocation Ceremonies" (http://www.whitehouse.gov/WH/New/html/19990612.html: June 12, 1999), p. 2.

[4] Ibid., 1.

[5] http://www.glreach.com/globstats/index.php3.

[6] "Women Lead UK Online Growth" (December 11, 2001); http://news.bbc.co.uk/1/hi/sci/tech/1704063.stm.

[7] "Congress Struggles with Flood of E-Mail," *New York Times*, March 19, 2001, p. A16.

[8] Michael Specter, "Your Mail Has Vanished," *New Yorker*, December 6, 1999, p. 96.

include the prospect of the aforementioned chip ten billion (repeat again, ten billion) times faster than those available today. Future generations might look back to the latter part of the 1990s and the widening scope of the Internet as the historical starting point for a new phase of modern globalization. It is not difficult to extrapolate from these data the conclusion that increasingly people have close encounters with foreign cultures through global networks that offer the potential for both a multiplicity of identities and a continuing proliferation of distant proximities.

To be sure, the benefits of the information revolution have been enjoyed by only a small proportion of the world's population, thus resulting in a huge gap between those who are rich and poor with respect to their access to information. As will be seen in chapter 10, however, there are reasons to anticipate that the gap will slowly narrow with the passage of time. New technologies will enable poorer countries to leapfrog some of the communications stages experienced by more advanced societies.[9] To cite but one example, in 1999 China had nine million Internet addresses, and by 2000 the figure had grown roughly to twenty million.[10]

The Skill Revolution

All too many observers of world affairs are inclined to treat individuals at the micro level as constants on the (often implicit) grounds that collectivities at the macro level, especially states, either ignore their publics or are able to mobilize their support when needed. As stressed in chapter 2, however, it now seems clear that people everywhere need to be regarded as variables in the sense that several of their attributes can, if they vary in similar ways, make a difference in the conduct of states and other collectivities.[11] This is perhaps especially the case with their analytic, emotional, and imaginative capacities, all of which have undergone sufficient expansion to loom large as dynamics to which macro actors must be sensitive.[12]

---

[9] J. P. Singh, *Leapfrogging Development? The Political Economy of Telecommunications Restructuring* (Albany: State University of New York Press, 1999).

[10] William Jefferson Clinton, "China's Opportunities, and Ours," *New York Times*, September 24, 2000, Sec. 4, p. 15.

[11] An example of how macro collectivities have come to appreciate the growing relevance of individuals is provided by a change in the advertising themes of the U.S. Army. In a new commercial a corporal asserts, "Even though there are 1,045,000 soldiers just like me, I am my own force. . . . And I'll be the first to tell you, the might of the U.S. Army doesn't lie in numbers. It lies in me. I am an Army of one." James Dao, "Ads Now Seek Recruits for an 'Army of One,' " *New York Times*, January 10, 2001, p. A1.

[12] Indeed, there is a large literature on the links between individual emotions and social structures. See Steven L. Gordon, "Micro-sociological Theories of Emotion," in H. J. Helle and S. N. Eisenstadt (eds.), *Micro-sociological Theory* (Beverly Hills, Calif.: Sage, 1985), pp. 133–47.

Indeed, the variations in their talents are great enough to warrant referring to them as the "skill revolution."[13] Taken together, the several dimensions of this revolution are pivotal to all the other sources of fragmegrative dynamics noted in the following pages. The data descriptive of enlarged skills are hardly voluminous, and many are anecdotal, but those that have been systematically collected all point in the same direction:[14] the skill revolution enables people to trace more readily the course of distant events back into their own homes, to know more precisely what they favor and oppose as situations unfold, to imagine more fully other cultures, to appreciate more explicitly the possibility that the identity and bases of their citizenship may be changing, and to engage more effectively in collective action. Of course, the skills of people have expanded at different rates, depending on the varying sources, amounts, and types of information and education they receive. To posit a worldwide skill revolution is not to say that everywhere people are becoming equally skillful.

Given the contradictions that underlie the emergent epoch, the enhanced analytic skills of many people serve to expand their horizons to include transnational foci, while for others the skill revolution has facilitated a continuing commitment, even a retreat, to local concerns. It is surely a factor in encouraging some Insular Locals to move beyond their insularity and stimulating some Resistant and Affirmative Locals to move into comparable global worlds. Conceivably, too, it may contribute to some persons becoming Alienated Cynics or Exclusionary Locals.

The Organizational Explosion

Hardly less so than the population explosion, recent years have witnessed a veritable explosion in the number of voluntary associations that have crowded onto the global stage. In all parts of the world and at every level of community, people—ordinary folk as well as elites and activists—are coming together to concert their efforts on behalf of shared needs and goals. Exact statistics on the extent of this pattern do not exist (largely because so much of it occurs at local levels and goes unreported), but few would argue with the proposition that the pace at which new associations are formed and old ones enlarged is startling, so much so that to call it an explosion is almost to understate the scale of growth.[15] It has been calcu-

---

[13] For an initial discussion of the skill revolution as a micro dynamic, see James N. Rosenau, *Turbulence in World Politics: A Theory of Change and Continuity* (Princeton, N.J.: Princeton University Press, 1990), Chaps. 9 and 13. For an updated elaboration of the concept, see chapter 10.

[14] Chapter 10 summarizes both the anecdotal and systematic data on the skill revolution.

[15] For a counterargument with data interpreted as tracing a decline in organizational life in the United States, see Robert D. Putnam, *Bowling Alone: The Collapse and Revival of American Community* (New York: Simon and Schuster, 2000).

lated, for example, that twenty years ago Indonesia had only a single independent environmental organization, whereas now there are more than 2,000 linked to an environmental network based in Jakarta. Likewise, registered nonprofit organizations in the Philippines grew from 18,000 to 58,000 between 1989 and 1996; in Slovakia the figure went from a handful in the 1980s to more than 10,000 today; and in the United States 70 percent of the nonprofit organizations—not counting religious groups and private foundations—filing tax returns with the Treasury Department are less than thirty years old, and a third are less than fifteen years old.[16] "By one estimate, there are now two million [NGOs] in America alone. . . . In Russia, where almost none existed before the fall of communism, there are at least 65,000. Dozens are created daily; in Kenya alone, some 240 NGOs are now created every year."[17] Much the same can be said about international organizations. Where NGOs were involved in some 50 percent of the World Bank projects in 1997, for example, by 2002 the proportion had grown to 70 percent.[18]

Whether these dramatic increases in the organizations of developing societies stem from individuals who shifted from private to local and global worlds, or whether they represent locally or globally oriented people for whom the organizations offer an opportunity to accord active meaning to their value convictions, is difficult to determine. Perhaps both interpretations are valid. But whatever the most accurate interpretation, it seems unquestionable that the organizational explosion has provided people at the micro level new opportunities to infuse intentional inputs into macro processes.

Nor are these opportunities confined to large associations. While the latter have continued to increase their ranks, so are there an ever-growing number of small organizations. This is perhaps particularly the case for religious organizations. A study of forty-one denominations and faith groups in the United States, for example, uncovered one conspicuous finding: "Half of all congregations . . . contain fewer than 100 adults who regularly participate in those congregations."[19]

There are several reasons for the organizational explosion. One is the continuing proliferation of distant proximities that fosters a sense of remoteness from the centers of decision and thus energizes people to come together. Another is the skill revolution, which, as already mentioned, has increased the capacity of people to know when, where, and how to en-

[16] David Bornstein, "A Force Now in the World, Citizens Flex Social Muscle," *New York Times*, July 10, 1999, p. B7.

[17] "Sins of the Secular Missionaries," *The Economist*, January 29, 2000.

[18] Norimitsu Onishi, "Nongovernmental Organizations Show Their Growing Power," *New York Times*, March 22, 2001, p. A10.

[19] Gustav Niebuhr, "Harnessing the Power of Small Congregations," *New York Times*, March 17, 2001, p. A9.

gage in collective action. Given the contradictions and uncertainties inherent in the emergent epoch, all the incentives are in place to implement this greater appreciation of the virtues of collective action. Still another source of the organizational explosion involves the declining competence of states and the greater opportunities thereby opened up for those who organize to press their demands. In important ways, therefore, the organizational explosion serves as a powerful impetus toward empowerment for previously disempowered people. A fourth source concerns the pervasive cynicism toward politics and government throughout the world that encourages people to want to act on their own and in concert with others to remedy their problems. Fifth and perhaps most important, the deepening complexity of world affairs has led to more and more specialization, which, in turn, has fostered greater reliance on coordinating with like-minded others to pursue common goals. A goodly proportion of the organizational explosion, for example, derives from the world's growing preoccupation with environmental concerns, human rights, and resource issues, a preoccupation that has stirred organizational activities at the grass roots in innumerable communities.

Finally, the microelectronic revolution has facilitated the formation of groups, alliances between them, and networks among them. By mobilizing support through e-mail messages, activists can provide those who tend to be apathetic with channels through which to articulate their values and press them on elites.[20] Furthermore, the capacity to network deriving from the use of teleconferencing, the Internet, and the fax machine has profoundly altered the nature of modern-day organizations. Not only is the emergent epoch marked by ever more numerous and diverse organizations, but increasingly the organizations that populate global and local spaces are less vertically and more horizontally structured, less sustained by hierarchy and more enmeshed in networks. Put more emphatically, hastened by the greater complexity of world and community affairs and the lessened ability of states to manage the complexity, the proliferation of organizational networks is a major characteristic of the emergent age of fragmegration—a trend so pervasive that

[20] Consider, for example, this message from Global Youth Connect designed to enlarge its influence through soliciting young people to be active in the Student Action Network (SAN) and thereby "increase the power of our voices by taking collective action": SAN "is an easy way to take action on pressing human rights and environmental issues using the power of the Internet and the ease of e-mail. . . . So, for example, the next time we need a note of support for Bhutanese refugees languishing in camps in Nepal, we will send you an e-mail action through the SAN. When you receive the e-mail, all you will need to do is click on the link to read the action, click on another link to instantly send a fax or e-mail expressing your support for the action." From Jennifer@globalyouthconnect.org, March 23, 2001.

many networks are linked to each other and thus add further to the density of nongovernmental collectivities. Some of the better-known organizational networks—those that focus on human rights and environmental issues—have properly been designated as "advocacy networks,"[21] but there are many other kinds with a variety of purposes and structures.

In short, with boundaries more porous and the need to cooperate across them increasingly imperative, "connectivity is exploding"[22] as organizations are reaching out to—and subsequently getting informally, even formally, linked to—like-minded counterparts. Business mergers, NGO alliances, expert communities, labor coalitions, and social movements are but the more obvious examples of salient organizational networks. Less obvious, but incisively illustrative of the extent to which connectivity is exploding, is the founding of the Professional Car Lifters' Union in Pakistan, a network organization with officers, dues, and regular meetings.[23]

Although many networks are marked by the high degree of informality that accompanies horizontal links, they nonetheless have structure—regularized patterns of interaction through which their memberships sustain a sufficient degree of coherence to move toward their goals—and can readily be regarded as organizations.[24] An organizational network, no less than a hierarchical organization, is a macro agent, a source of actions through which distant proximities are shaped and sustained. In the case of social movements, moreover, their structured networks may further obscure the territorial distinctions that separate local and global worlds. As one observer noted, "It is often difficult to define the traditional

---

[21] Margaret E. Keck and Kathryn Sikkink, *Activists beyond Borders: Advocacy Networks in International Politics* (Ithaca, N.Y.: Cornell University Press, 1998). See also Thomas Olesen, *Long Distance Zapatismo: Globalization and the Construction of Solidarity* (Ph.D. dissertation, University of Aarhus, 2002), and Howard Rheingold, *Smart Mobs: The Next Social Revolution* (Cambridge: Perseus Books Group, 2002).

[22] Jessica Lipnack and Jeffrey Stamps, *The Age of the Network: Organizing Principles for the 21st Century* (New York: Wiley, 1994), p. 48.

[23] At one meeting the president of the union announced how he would sustain the network: "After lifting a car, you should inform me by telephone, so that we can negotiate a deal with the car's owner." *Far Eastern Economic Review*, Vol. 161 (March 19, 1998), p. 34.

[24] "Networking can be defined as a set of organizational arrangements midway between horizontal coordination (markets) and vertical coordination (hierarchies)." Thomas J. Courchene, "Celebrating Flexibility: An Interpretive Essay on the Evolution of Canadian Federalism" (Montreal: C. D. Howe Institute, October 16, 1995), p. 29. Viewed in this way, the proliferation of organizational networks is not the equivalent of the numerous acquaintanceships and contacts to which widespread travel and an ever more wired world have given rise. Such contacts may lead to enduring friendships and professional ties, and thereby contribute to deterritorializing processes, but they are hardly organizational in nature. They lack the minimal requirement of structured networks, namely, shared and articulated goals on behalf of which memberships can be mobilized.

boundaries of a domestic social movement—the domestic and the international have emerged together."[25]

Given their horizontal structures, organizational networks tend to have open rather than restrictive memberships. People can join easily, often simply by declaring themselves to be members and getting on the (e-mail) lists that serve as the communications channels whereby a network's actions are concerted and directed toward remote situations. In some conspicuous cases—such as feminist or environmental organizations—networks take on the characteristics of large and vigorous advocacy groups. In other cases their memberships are smaller, their purposes narrower, and their forms of advocacy less public and more technical. Whatever their size and goals, however, organizational networks offer opportunities for people in both local and global worlds to pursue their interests, serve their values, and become engaged in one or another aspect of public affairs. And the more the world becomes crisscrossed by networks and the more access to them becomes available through electronic channels, the more will horizontal organizations become salient features of the global scene. Put more strongly, the advent of innumerable network organizations has substantially added to the density and complexity of world affairs, thereby rendering the tasks of states and other hierarchical organizations ever more difficult. Viewed from a micro perspective, moreover, the vast network of networks facilitates movement among the local, global, and private worlds through which people cope with distant proximities.

But, it might be asked, is not the proliferation of network organizations misleading? Given the looseness of the ties that bind them, how can they have much consequence for the course of events? Are not cohesive networks, not to mention cohesive networks of networks, required for such forms of organization to mobilize effectively clusters of like-minded persons in any of the local or global worlds? The answers to these questions are paradoxical and not self-evident. It is precisely the weakness of their ties to distant networks that enables people to join them and participate in their organizations' activities. If networks required individuals to develop strong ties and commitments to them, their memberships would be smaller and their influence diminished accordingly. Unless they are network leaders, those in neither local nor global worlds have the time or energy to develop strong ties; instead, most feel compelled to limit their ties to those networks that allow for minimal involvement. Many may have a multiplicity of such memberships, but their contribution to shared network goals lies more in their swelling the numbers for whom a network can claim to speak than in the actual time they give to working on

---

[25] Alison Brysk, *From Tribal Village to Global Village: Indian Rights and International Relations in Latin America* (Stanford, Calif.: Stanford University Press, 2000), p. 86.

behalf of its goals. Thus, one could say that the world of organized networks is marked by "the strength of weak ties."[26] Nor is this the only paradox inherent in the networked world. Close analysis yields the insight that the looser the ties that sustain a network, the more does it have the flexibility to integrate with other networks, whereas strong ties heighten network boundaries and thereby foster fragmentation.[27] In this sense the dynamics of fragmegration are as clearly manifested in the proliferation of organizational networks as they are in the other salient dimensions of the emergent epoch.

An illustration of the potential of emergent networks is provided by their role in ending the Cold War: "Some of the strategic prescriptions that informed the reconceptualization of Soviet security interests originated in the Western liberal internationalist community, which formed transnational networks with 'new thinkers' in the former USSR. These new ideas became causally consequential for the turnaround in Soviet foreign policy."[28] In sum, the importance of networks can hardly be understated:

> The rise of network forms of organization—particularly "all channel networks," in which every node can communicate with every other node—is one of the single most important effects of the information revolution for all realms: political, economic, social, and military. It means that power is migrating to small, nonstate actors who can organize into sprawling networks more readily than can traditionally hierarchical nation-state actors. It means that conflicts will increasingly be waged by "networks," rather than by "hierarchies." It means that whoever masters the network form stands to gain major advantages in the new epoch. Some actors, such as various terrorists and criminals, may have little difficulty forming highly networked, largely nonhierarchical organizations; but for other actors, such as professional militaries that must continue to uphold hierarchies at their core, the challenge will be to discover how to combine hierarchical and networked designs to increase their agility and flexibility for field operations.[29]

Stated differently, the global stage has become ever more dense with actors. In earlier epochs it was occupied mainly by states and their intergovernmental organizations, but in the emergent epoch the cast of char-

---

[26] Note the difference between my use of the phrase and that by Mark S. Granovetter, in "The Strength of Weak Ties," *American Journal of Sociology*, Vol. 78 (1973), pp. 1360–80.

[27] Ibid.

[28] Thomas Risse-Kappen, abstract for "Ideas Do Not Float Freely: Transnational Coalitions, Domestic Structures, and the End of the Cold War," *International Organization*, Vol. 48 (spring 1994), pp. 185–214.

[29] John Arquilla and David Ronfeldt, "A New Epoch—and Spectrum—of Conflict," in J. Arquilla and D. Ronfeldt (eds.), *In Athena's Camp: Preparing for Conflict in the Information Age* (Santa Monica, Calif.: RAND, 1997), p. 5.

acters has multiplied time and time again. States still occupy important roles in the routines of world affairs, but their ranks have become thin relative to all the organizations that now reach across boundaries to conduct their affairs. In addition, the extensive density of the global stage has served to narrow the gap between the global and the local. As people are increasingly either members of or familiar with the many diverse organizations active in world affairs, so are they ever more susceptible to fragmegrative dynamics.

In sum, the proliferation of organizational networks contributes to bridging the gap between people at the micro level and their collectivities at the macro level. It offers a vast array of routes through which individuals can move among the local, global, and private worlds. It also sustains the dynamics of deterritorialization, the spread of the skill revolution, and the continued salience of distant proximities. If hierarchically structured states still dominated the course of events and were thereby able to contain and control the vibrant spread of horizontal networks, it is doubtful whether a new epoch would be emerging. For better or worse—and given the vitality of the drug trade and crime syndicates, sometimes it is for the worse—the ever-greater salience of organizational networks is serving to restructure the underpinnings of world affairs.

The Bifurcation of Global Structures

As the density of the global stage has increased with the proliferation of organizations, the structures of world politics have undergone a profound and pronounced bifurcation in which a multi-centric macro world composed of a wide variety of nongovernmental, transnational, and subnational actors—from the multinational corporation to the ethnic group, from the NGO to the social movement, from the professional society to the epistemic community, from the advocacy network to the humanitarian organization, from the drug cartel to the terrorist group, from the local government to the regional association, and so on across a vast range of collective endeavors—has evolved to cooperate, compete, or otherwise interact with a state-centric world that consists of collectivities increasingly active on local stages.[30] As such, states may still be central to the course of events, but their international system is no longer as predominant as it once was. Now there are two worlds of world politics, a bifurcation that has heightened the relevance and intensity of fragmegra-

---

[30] Given the diversity and multiplicity of collectivities in the multi-centric world, it would be logical to describe the emergent structure as an *n*-furcation rather than a bifurcation (with the *n* representing any number). However, I continue to use the bifurcation label in order not to unduly downplay the importance of the state-centric world.

tive dynamics.[31] These two worlds are still working out their respective domains as the emergent epoch unfolds. While in some instances the actors in the two worlds go their separate ways, most of the time they interact even as the boundaries separating them are maintained. Their interactions turned violent in Seattle in late 1999 and at subsequent meetings of international financial institutions, but prior to that, starting in 1992 in Rio de Janeiro, they interacted peacefully whenever the United Nations sponsored meetings of the state-centric world to negotiate global issues and organizations in the multi-centric world converged on them to press policy positions. In Rio 160 of the former were "watched, bullied, cajoled and lectured" by more than 1,200 of the latter on the environment,[32] and similar interactions occurred the following years on human rights in Vienna, on population problems in Cairo, on the human habitat in Copenhagen, and on women's rights in Beijing. In effect, the bifurcation of global structures has become institutionalized and, as a result, contributes to the weakening of states (noted later) by creating spaces for the formation or consolidation of collectivities in the multi-centric world and, thus, for the activation of individuals who have not previously had an outlet for their global or local orientations.

The Mobility Upheaval

Hardly less central as a transformative dynamic underlying the advent of fragmegration is the vast movement of people around the world. Using the notion of "mobility" in the broadest possible sense so as to include any movement for any length of time and for any purpose—from business to professional travel, from tourism to terrorism, from political asylum to the search for jobs, from legal to illegal migration—the boundary-spanning activities of people in recent decades have been so astounding as to justify regarding them as a veritable upheaval. Statistics for every form of travel reveal sharp and continuous growth, and the trend shows no sign of letting up. Not only is tourism among the world's largest industries, but the data on business travel also portray a continuing and growing flow of people around the world. And then there are the migratory flows that are driven largely by a search for employment and involve mostly people from the developing world moving into the industrial and financial centers of the developed world. All of these flows have been facilitated by transportation technologies, particularly the jet aircraft that

[31] For an extended discussion of the bifurcation of global structures, see Rosenau, *Turbulence in World Politics*, Chap. 10.

[32] Paul Lewis, "Fixing World Crises Isn't Just a Job for Diplomats," *New York Times*, May 4, 1992, Sec. 4, p. 4.

have—through reduced travel time and lowered airfares—had a profound impact on diverse institutions throughout the world.

The vastness of the mobility upheaval can be readily depicted. The movement of people has been so extensive that around 5 percent of the individuals alive today are estimated to be living in a country other than the one where they were born.[33] Every day half a million airline passengers cross national boundaries.[34] In 1997 a total of 220.7 million people (a 4.6 percent increase over the previous year) went abroad by airplane.[35] Nor are the figures for travel within countries any less impressive. While the population of the United States grew 20 percent between 1977 and 1997, for example, the number of miles traveled long-distance (journeys of 100 miles or more) increased by 116 percent.[36] Indeed, in 1969 "the total number of people carried on planes in the United States was less than the country's population, [whereas in 2000] the number of passengers is more than double the population."[37] Even more stunning, it is estimated that by 2020 every year 1.56 billion tourists will be moving around the world, a figure more than double the roughly 668 million foreign tourists in 2000.[38]

It would be an error, however, to assume that the pattern of extensive travel is confined to Western countries. On the contrary, eight of the ten most traveled air routes are in Asia.[39] Perhaps also indicative of the mobility upheaval is the pattern whereby "personal international calls have burgeoned, fed by immigrants talking to relatives or friends. The number of calls from the U.S. to other countries in 1997 was 21 times that in 1980."[40] In 1965, on a worldwide basis 75 million people were migrants from another country, whereas the figure for 1999 was 125 million.[41] Then there are the rising number of refugees and internally displaced people of concern to the United Nations High Commissioner for Refu-

---

[33] Shashi Tharoor, "The Future of Civil Conflict," *World Policy Journal*, Vol. 16 (spring 1999), p. 7.

[34] Office of the Press Secretary, "Remarks by President Clinton at University of Chicago Convocation Ceremonies," p. 2.

[35] National Geographic Society, *Millennium in Maps* (1999).

[36] The total number of domestic miles traveled on such journeys in 1996 was 827 billion. Cf. Nicholas Timmins, "Long-Distance Travel in U.S. 'Has Doubled,'" *Financial Times*, November 11, 1997, p. 7.

[37] Matthew L. Wald, "The Plane That Time Passed By," *New York Times*, July 30, 2000, Sec. 4, p. 6.

[38] "Boom in World Tourism Called Threat to Culture and Ecology," *International Herald Tribune*, July 12, 2000, p. 2.

[39] Edward Neilan, "Air-Travel Rankings Reflect Global Changes," *Journal of Commerce*, Vol. 421 (August 25, 1999), p. 6.

[40] National Geographic Society, *Millennium in Maps* (1999).

[41] *New York Times*, September 19, 1999, Sec. 4, p. 4.

gees (UNHCR): from 17 million in 1991 to 27 million at the beginning of 1995.[42]

Despite the positive benefits that follow from people being exposed to greater economic opportunities, new cultural premises, and alternative lifestyles as they move around the world, the mobility upheaval can also foster negative consequences. As noted in chapter 7, the vast movement of people from the developing into the developed world has generated a backlash against "strangers" (i.e., migrants) and thereby precipitated a rise of immigration issues, not to mention right-wing politicians, to salience on political agendas in a number of countries. In short, while the distinction between the global and the local has been further obscured by the mobility upheaval, in some communities it has become increasingly salient.

The Weakening of States and Territoriality

Although some analysts insist states are as viable and competent as ever,[43] many (myself included) contend that they are in decline. For a variety of reasons, this main institution for serving as a bulwark against fragmegration by maintaining the boundaries between foreign and domestic affairs—between the global and the local—has lately undergone a diminution of its competence. Many (though not all) states continue to be viable. Yes, most states and their central banks still play a primary role in their national economies. Yes, they still maintain legitimate monopoly over the use of force. Yes, they have undergone transformation into managerial entities and thereby "retained [their] capacity for surveillance and social control."[44] And yes, the aspiration to statehood is still shared widely in many parts of the world. Yet for all its continuing authority and legitimacy, key dimensions of the power of modern states have undergone considerable diminution, and states' ability to cope with the dynamics of change has lessened as the complexities and contradictions of fragmegration have become more pervasive. In the words of one analyst, "As wealth and power are increasingly generated by private transactions that take place across the borders of states rather than within them, it has become harder to sustain the image of states as the preeminent actors at

---

[42] UNHCR, *The State of the World's Refugees: In Search of Solutions* (New York: Oxford University Press, 1995), p. 19.

[43] See, for example, G. John Ikenberry, "The Myth of Post–Cold War Chaos," *Foreign Affairs*, Vol. 75 (May/June 1996), pp. 79–91.

[44] Raimo Väyrynen, "Enforcement of International Norms: Why, How and By Whom?" (paper presented at the forty-first annual meeting of the International Studies Association, Los Angeles, March 14–18, 2000).

the global level."[45] A metaphor captures well the extent of the weakening: where states used to be like museum curators, planning, arranging, and funding the exhibits, today they resemble museum guards, guiding the flow of visitors through the exhibits, protecting against vandalism, and ensuring that all the rules are obeyed.

In other words, while state institutions still have a modicum of authority and are not about to disappear from the global stage, their state-centric world is, as already noted, in continuous competition with collectivities in the multi-centric world, an indication of the degree to which their capacity to exercise their authority has lessened. States cannot prevent ideas from moving across their borders. Many cannot control the flow of money, jobs, and production facilities in and out of their country. With few exceptions, they have only minimal control over the flow of people and negligible control over the flow of drugs or the drift of polluted air and water. At best they have difficulty controlling the flow of terrorists across their boundaries. In short, the obstacles to containing or redirecting the flow of distant proximities are considerable, and often states lack the will to exercise the full range of controls available to them. Furthermore, cynicism toward politicians and major institutions is widespread, and people increasingly perceive no connection between their own welfare and that of their communities. Selfishness and greed have tended to replace more encompassing loyalties as attachments to territory have diminished. Thus many states are unable to enforce laws, prevent widespread corruption, collect taxes, reduce crime, lessen ethnic tensions, mobilize their armed forces for battle, or otherwise promote and maintain effective cohesion among their diverse societal groups. They cannot collectively bring order to war-torn societies. A terrorist attack may temporarily induce a shared sense of loss, but it is questionable how long such feelings can endure. It is perhaps a measure of the fragmegrative constraints that in 1992 a number of states collectively agreed to take a number of steps to exert control over pollution and numerous other environmental challenges, but at a follow-up conference five years later they were obliged to concede that these steps had yet to be taken.

As the capacities of states have eroded, so has territoriality lost some of its organizing focus. The history of states is a history of territorial division, of clear-cut links to geographically bound spaces, but in the emergent fragmegrative epoch these links have become frayed, and deterritorialization has become a prime consequence of all the boundary-spanning flows noted previously. The arrival of the Internet and other electronic mechanisms for transgressing—better, ignoring—territorial units

---

[45] Peter B. Evans, "The Eclipse of the State? Reflections on Stateness in an Era of Globalization," *World Politics*, Vol. 50 (October 1997), p. 65.

is illustrative in this respect, but it is only one of many ways in which technological innovations have rendered long-standing national boundaries porous and, in some cases, obsolete. As one observer put it, "The very epoch of the nation-state is near its end. . . . It may well be that the emergent postnational order proves not to be a system of homogeneous units (as with the current system of nation-states) but a system based on relations between heterogeneous units (some social movements, some interest groups, some professional bodies, some nongovernmental organizations, some armed constabularies, some judicial bodies)."[46]

Traces of deterritorialization can be discerned everywhere. In the field of education, for example, U.S. business schools are tapping into new pools of students by establishing branches throughout the world. From Hong Kong to Hyderabad, from Singapore to Frankfurt, from Barcelona to Bangkok, local students are taking U.S.-designed courses under American professors.[47] Similarly, in sports conventional boundaries are increasingly being spanned, with athletes playing for teams in other than their own countries. In 2001, for instance, 25.3 percent of all major-league baseball players were born outside the United States, and in the case of a Japanese star playing in Seattle, attendance rates at home games were noticeably increased by Japanese fans who crossed the ocean to watch their hero in action.[48] Much the same can be said about basketball: the National Basketball Association had some fifty foreign-born players in 2000, and its final play-offs could be seen on television in "205 nations [sic]".[49]

It should be added that the mobility upheaval has added further momentum to the processes of deterritorialization. Those who move across borders, as well as those who move their belongings for a more permanent stay abroad, often not only loosen their ties to the homeland of their birth but also serve as conduits for the transmission of values and practices back and forth from one culture to another. And the diminished sense of geographic space on a worldwide scale adds to the momentum with which deterritorialization occurs. At the same time deterritorialization also involves what might be called "reterritorialization"—those processes whereby migrants converge in neighborhoods, publish their own newspapers, run their own schools, maintain their own television pro-

[46] Arjun Appadurai, *Modernity at Large: Cultural Dimensions of Globalization* (Minneapolis: University of Minnesota Press, 1996), pp. 19, 23.

[47] David Leonhardt, "All the World's a Campus," *New York Times*, September 20, 2000, p. C1.

[48] Sam Howe Verhovek, "Japan's Baseball Idol Wins Fans in Seattle," *New York Times*, April 24, 2001, p. A1.

[49] George Vecsey, "Nations Being United by Large Round Ball," *New York Times*, June 18, 2000, Sec. 8, p. 4.

grams, found their own churches, and open their own restaurants, thereby creating homes away from home, diasporas that through generational time become combinations of old and new homelands, subcultures in increasingly multicultural societies.

There are, of course, many factors that account for the diminished capabilities of states, but some part of the causal trail can be traced to technological breakthroughs and the ways in which these have interacted with the skill revolution, the organizational explosion, and the mobility upheaval. Fueled by greater awareness of where they fit in the course of events, more ready to voice their demands through collective action, and increasingly able to imagine alternative futures, people have used their greater skills to make demands, set limits, or otherwise constrict the policies and actions of states. The organizational explosion has added to these constraints by virtue of the much greater density of actors in the multi-centric world. The crowds in the museum, in other words, have grown much larger, and the guards have all they can do to maintain a modicum of order. And the mobility upheaval has added further to these burdens. State controls at borders have been insufficient to monitor the flow of goods and people across them, thus enabling drug money to be easily laundered and many illegal immigrants to circumvent immigration officials and make their way through national boundaries.[50]

While there is considerable variability in the degree to which different states have been weakened in recent decades, one is hard-pressed to think of any wherein the pattern is one of strengthened capabilities. Authoritarian states such as North Korea or Myanmar (Burma) can still exercise rigid controls over their peoples, but even these states are discovering that their limited involvement in world affairs is serving to constrain their conduct (North Korea because of severe food shortages, and Myanmar because of sanctions and boycotts designed to ameliorate its treatment of dissidents). Likewise, China has revealed its vulnerabilities in its attempts to modernize with the help of foreign investments, and its weaknesses are further demonstrated by a persistent pattern in which its provincial and city governments routinely ignore directives from Beijing. Democratic states, too, have had to accommodate the complexities and contradictions of fragmegrative dynamics. The closing down of the U.S. government twice in late 1995 is indicative of the ways in which the skill revolution had hardened attitudes and intensified collective pressures that conduce to stalemate.

It is noteworthy that the diminution of state capacity has not been lost on activists at the micro level. This is especially the case for some Resistant Globals, who have come to justify the street protests directed at

---

[50] For an astute analysis of the control states exercise over their borders, see Peter Andreas, *Border Games* (Ithaca, N.Y.: Cornell University Press, 2000).

international economic institutions on the grounds that states are no longer as able to shape the course of events as are these institutions. In the words of Annie-Christine Hubbard, the secretary-general of the International Federation of Human Rights, one of those who protested during annual meetings of the International Monetary Fund (IMF) and the World Bank in Prague, "Ours is a new planetary citizenship, reflecting the fact that decisions have migrated from [the] state level. Voting for national representatives, an old expression of citizenship, achieves nothing because they have scant power. We have to be here to fight the political battles that will ensure globalization does not continue to accentuate inequities."[51] Closely related to the weakened capabilities of states is a decline in their sovereignty, their ability to claim the final word at home or speak exclusively for the country abroad and, if necessary, to use force in support of their actions at home or abroad that is widely considered legitimate. Indeed, in some ways sovereignty claims have long been a major source of state capabilities. Strictly speaking, sovereignty is a legal fiction and not a capability, but as a legal fiction it accords legitimacy to states and is thus a source of their capacities.[52] Historically sovereignty was conceived in dichotomous terms—either states do or do not meet certain formal requirements such as having a specified territory and a functioning government. Although most states have not been able to exercise full sovereignty at all times, the myth of states as sovereign has long remained intact. But in the emergent epoch the new uncertainties and contradictions over where, when, and how states can exercise their sovereign rights under particular circumstances are posing serious challenges to this myth.

At some basic level sovereignty is thus a form of authority, an intersubjective state of mind in which the pressures for decisions to be made above or below the level of states are routinely rejected when the sovereignty myth is fully in place, but which are evaluated and sometimes accommodated, if not outright accepted, when the myth has eroded and become problematic. Accordingly, as the posture that state officials take toward challenges to their authority, sovereignty is susceptible to the many fragmegrative dynamics whereby state boundaries are readily circumvented by electronic commerce, polluted air, drug traffickers, exchanges on the Internet, and the subnational or international organizations that undertake collective efforts to initiate or cope with boundary-spanning activities.

The erosion of sovereignty is also evident in the lessening readiness of

[51] Quoted in Roger Cohen, "Growing Up and Getting Practical since Seattle," *New York Times*, September 24, 2000, Sec. 4, p. 1.

[52] An extensive elaboration of this perspective can be found in Stephen D. Krasner, *Sovereignty: Organized Hypocrisy* (Princeton, N.J.: Princeton University Press, 1999).

people to view their states as the object of their highest loyalty. In the absence of threatening enemies, people in many parts of the world experience lessened concern about the preeminence of their state as their expanded skills and ties to a proliferating array of organizations enable them to evolve new commitments or otherwise reorganize their hierarchy of loyalties. In addition, national loyalties have been further undermined by the mobility upheaval that has spawned multicultural societies. Put differently, with the distinction between domestic and foreign affairs increasingly confounded, the sovereignty of states can seem increasingly peripheral. Two recent developments highlight the extent to which such a change has occurred. The intrusion of the North Atlantic Treaty Organization (NATO) into the Kosovo conflict and the intrusion of the European Union into domestic Austrian politics are quintessentially illustrative of the growing public acceptance of the lessened protection sovereignty affords states from outside interference.

The Decentralization of Governments

Partly because of the weakness of the states they serve, but equally because of micro intentional and unintentional inputs pressed on behalf of local autonomy, national governments in many parts of the world are decentralizing some of their operations and, indeed, their authority. This process has been speeded up by a growing sense that national governments are unnecessarily cumbersome and that in many ways local or regional needs can best be served by governments at the local or regional levels. The trend has accelerated further as national economies have become increasingly globalized and as provincial and local governments experienced a need to attract foreign investments and establish diverse relationships abroad. The worldwide turn to a neoclassical economic philosophy—to a lesser reliance on governmental policies and a greater reliance on the marketplace—is still another source of the decentralizing momentum.

France, the United Kingdom, and United States offer good examples of national governments that explicitly sought to decentralize. In France constitutional revisions during the 1980s transferred powers from the government in Paris to the various provinces. The new Labor government in the United Kingdom acted in 1997 to create an independent Parliament for Scotland and to give considerably greater autonomy to Wales. Likewise, welfare programs in the United States have been progressively devolved from the federal to the state level.

But these obvious examples tell only the formal side of the decentralization story. In addition to the explicit, policy-driven efforts, numerous informal, even unrecognized, dynamics have been stimulating the downsizing of national governments. The aforementioned cynicism toward politics and government not only has become a worldwide phenomenon but also has tended to focus on national governments, thereby fostering a greater readiness to encourage and accept policies adopted at provincial or local levels. And increasingly such policies are adopted without the knowledge of, or even against the policies of, national governments. Networks of officials of local governments and NGOs along the U.S.-Mexican border, for example, have developed joint programs undertaken to solve environmental problems without either the U.S. or the Mexican national government being informed of the steps taken.[53]

Stated more generally, the long-term and worldwide process whereby authority is undergoing relocation in response to the skill revolution, the organizational explosion, and the mobility upheaval has hastened the decline and decentralization of national governments. In some instances this trend has resulted in vacuums of authority filled by criminal organizations or by uncertainties regarding where the rule-making power lies, but more often than not local, provincial, or private authorities move into the vacuums and sustain the processes of governance.[54]

One may wonder why and how decentralizing processes manage to unfold in the face of the microelectronic and transportation technologies that are shrinking social and geographic distances. If technological advances are having integrative consequences, how is it possible that the processes of governance are simultaneously undergoing decentralization? The answer is both simple and complex: it is simple in the sense that this is one of the major contradictions presently driving the processes of fragmegration, and it is complex because comprehending it requires a grasp of how global phenomena get converted into local processes of governance. These conversions are considered in chapter 13, but here it is useful to note that often effective integration clarifies lines of authority that, in turn, create opportunities to decentralize a community's or an organization's operations.

Authority Crises

With people increasingly skillful, with states weakened, and with other types of organizations proliferating, governments everywhere are undergoing authority crises in which traditional conceptions of legitimacy are being replaced by performance criteria of legitimacy, thus fostering bureaucratic disarray, executive-legislative stalemate, and decisional paralysis

[53] Cathryn L. Thorup, "Redefining Governance in North America: Citizen Diplomacy and Cross-Border Coalitions," *Enfoque* (University of California, San Diego), spring 1993.
[54] These processes of proliferating spheres of authority are probed at length in chapter 13.

that, in turn, enhance the readiness of individuals to employ their newly acquired skills on behalf of their perceived self-interests. There is hardly a national government today that is not caught up in one or another form of crisis that severely restricts its capacity to frame innovative policies and move toward its goals. To view most states as deep in crisis, in other words, is not to have in mind only street riots and the violence that can accompany them; it is also to refer to crosscutting conflicts that paralyze policy-making processes and result in stasis, in the avoidance of decisions that would at least address the challenges posed by a fragmegrative world undergoing vast and continuous changes.

Nor are these crises confined just to governments and states. The fragmenting tendencies are also operative within other institutions and organizations. Political parties are in disrepute in many parts of the world, with the long-standing dominant parties of Mexico and Japan having undergone major setbacks in recent years. Some churches have also experienced rifts that lessen their authority, and so, even more conspicuously, has the Mafia. Likewise, increasingly shareholders are challenging the decisions of corporate boards and, in a few cases, bringing about resignations and changes in their memberships. Given fragmegrative dynamics, it follows that some authority crises have enlarged the jurisdiction of intergovernmental organizations and NGOs, while others have contracted the range of national jurisdictions and extended that of local institutions.

Equally important, the onset of certain kinds of authority crises has the potential of inducing people to redirect their loyalties and legitimacy sentiments, which, in turn, may alter the allegiances collectivities can command and lead to the emergence of new spheres of authority. How could it be otherwise if it is the case that, as one Territorial Global put it, "There's a feeling in the population that nobody's in charge. People are afraid of losing jobs to the whims of multinationals."[55] Whether the losses in authority suffered by diverse collectivities involve a relocation of authority or the onset of authority vacuums is an issue explored in chapters 12 and 13.

Subgroupism

Although they represent an aspect of authority crises, there are at least two good reasons to take separate note of those groups that form and are active at subnational levels. One is that since many of them come into being by breaking away from more encompassing entities, they are closely linked to the fragmenting side of fragmegration. Second, since many such groups tend to adopt exclusionary policies toward others and,

---

[55] Cohen, "Growing Up and Getting Practical since Seattle," Sec. 4, p. 16.

in so doing, to highlight their sense of "us" confronting "them," it is useful to allow for the sense of coherence to which authority crises can give rise. This is especially the case because of a widespread inclination to refer loosely to "nationalism" as a source of the fragmenting forces at work in the world, whereas it is possible to be more precise about the collective nature of those decentralizing tendencies wherein individuals and groups are predisposed to challenge authority and reorient their loyalties. The authority crises that result from such challenges can be of either an "upward" or a "downward" kind, depending on whether the aspiration is to relocate authority in more or less encompassing jurisdictions than those that operate at the national level. In a number of instances of both kinds of relocation, the motivation that sustains the change is not so deeply emotional to qualify as an "ism." As already noted, the creation of subnational administrative divisions can stem from detached efforts to rationalize the work of a governmental agency or private organization in the context of reasoned dialogue and calm decision making. Often, however, intense concerns and powerful attachments can accompany the press for new arrangements. Accordingly, it seems preferable to label the decentralizing tendencies of fragmegration as those of "subgroupism" and to reserve the concept of nationalism for those subgroup expressions that revolve around nations and feelings of ethnicity.

Subgroupism arises out of the deep affinities that people develop toward the associations, organizations, and subcultures with which they have been historically, professionally, economically, socially, or politically linked and to which they attach high priority. Subgroupism values the ingroup over the out-group. It can derive from and be sustained by a variety of sources, not the least being disappointment with—and alienation from—the performances of the whole system in which the subgroup is located. Its intensities are the product of long-standing historical roots that span generations and get reinforced by an accumulated lore surrounding past events in which the subgroup survived trying circumstances. Moreover, subgroupism tends to beget subgroupism as new splits occur in subgroups after they achieve their autonomy. Just as some people in Quebec want out of Canada, for example, so do the Mohawks want out of Quebec. Indeed, it can be said that the proliferation of many identities is mirrored in the processes of subgroupism.

That subgroupism can be deeply implanted in the consciousness of peoples was manifestly apparent in the resurfacing of strong ethnic identities throughout Eastern Europe and the former Soviet Union when, after decades, the authoritarian domination of communist parties came to an end. In those cases, the subgroups were historic nations, and the accompanying feelings can thus be readily regarded as expressions of nationalism. Likewise, to cite an even more recent example, when viewed from the regional perspective of Europe, the efforts of factions in Great Britain and Denmark to avoid commitments to the European Union can readily be viewed as a form of subgroupism.[56]

Not all, or even a preponderance, of decentralizing tendencies attach to nations, however. Governmental subdivisions, NGOs, political parties, labor unions, professional societies, corporate headquarters, and a host of other types of subgroups can also evoke intense attachments, and it would grossly understate the relevance of the decentralizing tendencies at work in world politics to ignore these other forms of close-at-hand ties.

Especially relevant to a focus on distant proximities are the processes whereby the relocation of authority in diverse directions has been accompanied by—and contributed further to—a surge in the politics of identity, in people redefining who they believe themselves to be in such a way that their commitments to the state, their national loyalties, are lessening. Prior to the war on terrorism, for example, serious proposals were being voiced in the United States that questioned the virtues of patriotism.[57] A thoughtful proposal to rewrite the national anthem even found its way into the public domain.[58] In Europe there are some signs that a sense of regional identity has begun to supersede national identity with the advent of a common currency and a widening body of regional law that takes precedence over national law. A young German woman's right to join the German army, for example, was upheld by the European Court of Justice, leading her to observe, "I used to think of myself as German. Now I feel a little European, too."[59] Thus it would seem that as the proliferation of identities and the values of multiculturalism thereby generated become increasingly ascendant throughout the world, states are bound to weaken, with their capacity to sustain broad consensuses around shared goals di-

---

[56] In Denmark, for example, "the last two decades witnessed a virtual explosion of the political as governance networks with both a local and a global orientation. . . . Many Danes experience this explosion, as if 'Systems-Denmark' has finally turned its back on ordinary Danes and made a joke of their national political identity or sentiments. A neopopulist rebellion 'from below' against the 'anti-Danishism' and arrogance of cosmopolitan elites is arising in the shape of 'The Danish People Party' which is today attracting about 12–20% of the voters in the polls, and which has had considerable successes in changing the social democratic/liberal left government towards a more hostile practice towards 'foreigners.'" Henrik P. Bang, "Excellent Ordinarity: Connecting Elites with a Politics of the Ordinary" (paper presented at the XVIII World Congress of the International Political Science Association, Quebec City, August 2, 2000), p. 3. See also Roger Cohen, "A Danish Identity Crisis: Are We Europeans?" New York Times, September 10, 2000, p. 1.

[57] Joshua Cohen (ed.), For Love of Country: Debating the Limits of Patriotism (Boston: Beacon Press, 1996).

[58] Hendrik Hertzberg, "Star-Spangled Banter," New Yorker, July 21, 1997, pp. 4–5.

[59] Roger Cohen, "European Identity: Nation-State Losing Ground," New York Times, January 14, 2000, p. A3.

minished and their ability to concert the energies of citizens in support of policies reduced.

In short, subgroupism amounts to a decentralizing tendency; as such, it is inherent in the dynamics of fragmegration. Traces of it can be found in any of the local, global, or private worlds previously noted. In addition, as will be seen in chapters 12 and 13, it has resulted in rule-setting authority being dispersed widely throughout the world's neighborhoods, communities, and provinces, as well as among transnational cyberspaces and other nonterritorial entities. As one observer aptly notes, the current scene is marked by "a pluralism of authority."[60]

The Globalization of National Economies

In contrast to the tendencies toward decentralization and subgroupism, the dynamics at work in the realm of economics are powerful sources of centralizing tendencies. A few states may be able to exercise their power to disrupt or divert these tendencies on occasion, but for the most part economic globalization in the last few decades has resulted in financiers, entrepreneurs, workers, and consumers now being deeply enmeshed in transnational networks that have superseded the traditional political jurisdictions of national scope. Such a transformation has served to loosen the ties of producers to their states and workers to their firms, to expand the horizons within which citizens ponder their self-interests, and to contribute to the proliferation of organizations that can operate on a global scale to protect and advance the economic interests of their members. The rapid growth and maturation of the multi-centric world can in good part be traced to the extraordinary dynamism and expansion of the global economy. No less important, as will be seen in chapter 17, the global economy has also accentuated the identity of most people as consumers and, in so doing, possibly weakened their sense of affiliation with national communities.

Put differently, the transformations wrought by economic globalization have lessened national controls, and today most (though, of course, not all) of the world's producers, consumers, traders, investors, makers, and all the other actors who sustain economies tend to conduct themselves in terms of global rather than national markets. Just as corporations, for example, now decentralize their operations and maintain production facilities in diverse countries, so do currency transactions move around the world's financial centers in milliseconds, just as business executives seek

---

[60] Zygmunt Bauman, "A Sociological Theory of Postmodernity," in Peter Beilharz, Gillian Robinson, and John Rundell (eds.), *Between Totalitarianism and Postmodernity: A Thesis Eleven Reader* (Cambridge, Mass.: MIT Press, 1992), p. 160.

to close their deals or maintain their worldwide operations by hopping aboard planes that carry them quickly across oceans. In a like manner, producers move or build their plants where labor costs are cheapest, develop products to cater to regional and local tastes far removed from corporate headquarters, and disperse their research, advertising, accounting, and legal staffs to service corporate needs in far-flung markets.

Clearly, then, economic globalization is a key dynamic of fragmegration. Since it is virtually impossible for any national or local economy to be self-contained and independent of global economic processes, the lives of people everywhere are affected in one way or another by these processes. This intrusion may vary from community to community or from occupation to occupation, but no communities and few occupations are immune to the global forces of supply and demand. Consider, for example, workers whose jobs are enhanced or threatened by productivity abroad and consumers whose tastes and purchases are shaped by foreign-made goods. For them distant proximities can be very salient indeed, with workers and factory owners whose interests are threatened likely to be among the Resistant Globals, while contrary reactions are likely to lead workers, factory owners, and consumers whose needs are served by productivity abroad to become Affirmative Globals. Much the same can be said about politicians whose careers are at least somewhat dependent on global developments with local consequences, such as city mayors eager to get foreign companies to build plants in their communities. Of course, the vulnerabilities of workers, business executives, and politicians to economic developments abroad are not new and have been observed in earlier centuries. In the past, however, neither the scale nor the pace of foreign economic consequences was nearly as great as is the case now that national economies are increasingly absorbed into the vast global market.

The Proliferation of Interdependence Issues

The evolution of the world economy is not the only source of centralizing tendencies at work in global life. In addition to the growing relevance of supranational actors such as the European Union that have increased their authority relative to its member states,[61] there are also a number of new, transnational problems that are crowding high on the world's agenda and sustaining fragmegration. Whereas the political agenda used to consist of issues that governments could cope with on

---

[61] For a recent example of this trend, see Donald G. McNeil Jr., "Europeans Move against Austrians on Nativist Party," *New York Times*, February 1, 2000, p. A1.

their own or through interstate bargaining, conventional issues are now being joined by challenges that by their very nature do not fall exclusively within the jurisdiction of states and intergovernmental institutions. Six current challenges are illustrative: environmental pollution, currency crises, the drug trade, terrorism, AIDS, and the flow of refugees. Each of these issues embraces processes that involve participation by substantial numbers of citizens, that inherently and inescapably transgress national boundaries, and that offer causes with which to identify and thereby evolve into distant proximities. Several of the six issues are the foci of transnational social movements forged to ameliorate, if not to resolve, the challenges they present. To be an environmentalist today, for example, is to have an identity that for the most part did not exist in earlier epochs. Conceivably, in other words, such issues give some citizens pause about their states as the ultimate problem solvers, and in the case of those who join social movements, the issues may reorient people to ponder a restructuring of their loyalties.

CONCLUSION

The foregoing discussion of major fragmegrative dynamics does not fully explore their implications for micro-macro interactions. Much of this exploration pervades the ensuing chapters, but here it is perhaps useful to note that, as indicated in table 3.1, the dynamism of each dynamic is such that it is likely that similar reactions at the micro level will be sufficiently salient to foster responses by leaders of macro collectivities. The latter can hardly be unaware of the expanding skills of those over whom they preside and from whom they derive their legitimacy. They can hardly be oblivious to the potential challenges to their authority stemming from the growing cynicism toward politics of their followers. They can hardly ignore the intensified readiness of many people to organize on behalf of their shared values and interests. They can hardly be insensitive to the challenges inherent in unplanned and spontaneous migrations. They can hardly be ignorant of the spread of negative reactions to pervasive corporate greed and the widening gap between the rich and the poor within and among countries. And they can hardly be unresponsive to a host of other consequences that have accompanied the onset of the fragmegrative epoch.

Nor does it matter, given the underlying premises of the approach used here, whether individuals at the micro level have any inkling that their attitudes and behaviors are shared widely enough to underlie unintentional inputs into the policy-making processes of their macro collectivities. What counts is that they conduct themselves in ways that, consistent with their cultures, enrich, reinforce, or otherwise sustain the dynamics that configure the ways in which people and their collectivities interact.

It bears repeating, moreover, that none of the foregoing sources and consequences of the dynamics that lie beyond globalization are more powerful than any of the others. Or if one or more are, the effort to demonstrate their primacy seems bound to fail inasmuch as they all are caught up in the vast feedback loops that are the hallmark of a fragmegrative epoch. Several of the dynamics are subjected to further examination in part II because their operation involves conceptual formulations that pose especially complex and troublesome issues. The relevance of the various dynamics to particular issue areas is probed in part III. Before turning to these macro situations, however, we need to examine more closely the twelve micro worlds. The next five chapters undertake this complex task.

Local Worlds

> The world during the next century will be less colorful and picturesque than the one we have left behind. Local fêtes, dress, customs, ceremonies, rites and beliefs that in the past have contributed to the rich panoply of human folkloric and ethnological variety are fading away or becoming the preserve of minority and isolated groups, whilst the bulk of society abandons them, adopting more practical habits better suited to our times.
>
> —Mario Vargas Llosa[1]

> Localisation, above all else, is about *place*, it is about living and producing locally as far as possible. It is about knowing and understanding your local area and community, whether it be a hill village in Bhutan or a London postal district. And it is about a *sense* of place—that which, most of all, makes human beings feel that they genuinely *belong*. The word local comes from the Latin locus, meaning "place," and it is this sense of belonging to a community rooted in a particular area, with distinctive environmental and cultural characteristics—and the sense of community with nature, with the stars above us and the soil under our feet—that has been lost in many areas of the "developed" world. Localisation is about reweaving those relationships.
>
> —Helena Norberg-Hodge[2]

As INDICATED in these epigraphs, local worlds are undergoing enormous transformation and are, in many ways, in decline. The epigraphs also share the premise developed in this chapter that there are many local worlds, depending on how the term is conceived and the contexts in which localities are differentiated from distant global worlds. In the succinct words of one analyst, "Places . . . are not so much bounded areas as

---

[1] "Local Cultures and Globalization," in *Tokyo 2000* (New York: Trilateral Commission, 2000), p. 40.

[2] "Bringing the Economy Back Home: Towards a Culture of Place," *The Ecologist*, Vol. 29 (March/April 1999), p. 215 (italics in the original).

open and porous networks of social relations,"[3] a formulation elaborated by another observer who describes boundaries as "increasingly opaque," as "many kinds of kinship, friendship, collegiality, business, pursuits of pleasure, or struggles for security [that] now engage people in transnational contacts."[4]

Just as it is impossible to draw clear-cut lines between the local and the global, since these concepts embrace mental constructs as well as geographic spaces, so is it difficult to delineate unmistakable boundaries that separate the various locals worlds. The emergent epoch, being pervaded with feedback loops, cannot be neatly divided up into firm, much less mutually exclusive, categories. Rather, spillovers and overlaps often becloud any distinctions that may be used. To depict the emergent epoch as consisting of four local, four global, and four private worlds is to draw a picture that is, as Huntington observed in explaining his effort to conceptualize the world in terms of eight civilizations, "highly simplified. It omits many things, distorts some things, and obscures others. Yet if we are to think seriously about the world, and act effectively in it, some sort of simplified map of reality, some theory, concept, model, paradigm is necessary. Without such intellectual constructs, there is, as William James said, only 'a bloomin' buzzin' confusion.' "[5]

An acknowledgment of the confusion embedded in spillovers and overlaps, however, need not prevent drawing a map with distinctions that capture the prime characteristics of the emergent epoch. Differences among the local worlds and among them and their global counterparts can be delineated even if the boundaries that divide them are less than precise. As long as note is taken of such spillovers and overlaps, it is possible to apply some broad brush strokes that depict the variety of local worlds people can inhabit. Such is the task of this chapter. It posits the "local" in broad and varied terms. Even "national" space is treated as a local site.

Equally important, the chapter is concerned not so much with macro collectivities such as neighborhoods, cities, states, or nongovernmental organizations as it is with individuals at the micro level, both elites and ordinary folk, whose horizons are delineated by local space. As indicated in figure 2.4, these consist of four worlds: the Insular Locals—those individuals who are traditional in the sense that they have never altered their ties to geography—and the Resistant Locals, the Exclusionary Locals,

---

[3] Doreen Massey, *Space, Place, and Gender* (Minneapolis: University of Minnesota Press, 1994), p. 121.

[4] Ulf Hannerz, *Transnational Connections: Culture, People, Places* (London: Routledge, 1996), p. 29.

[5] Samuel P. Huntington, *The Clash of Civilization and the Remaking of World Order* (New York: Simon and Schuster, 1996), p. 29.

and the Affirmative Locals, all three of whom are "modern" in the sense that they treat space in contextual as well as territorial terms.

The chapter also focuses on people fixed in time (a snapshot, as it were), with the circumstances and conditions under which they may move into or among other local or global worlds (videotapes) being explored in chapter 7. Distinguishing between the snapshot and the videotape is necessitated by the fact that in the emergent epoch individuals occupy a multiplicity of roles and live in a variety of spaces: "We are connected to all sorts of places, causally if not always consciously, including many that we have never traveled to, that we have perhaps seen only on television."[6] Accordingly, it seems the better part of analytic wisdom to locate people first in one world before assessing their movements among the worlds.

NATIONAL WORLDS AS LOCAL PHENOMENA

A question immediately arises: Would it not be better to minimize spillovers and overlaps by differentiating a group of people, those who are oriented toward national worlds, for separate analysis between those with local and global orientations? Why cling to dichotomization, in other words, when so much variety marks humankind? The answer is severalfold. First, in a time when globalizing dynamics are reconfiguring conceptions of territory, time, and space, clarity is served by remaining focused on the way people experience the two central and opposing tendencies that underlie the emergence of the epoch of fragmegration—namely, the tendency that treats distant proximities as movements toward integration, centralization, and/or globalization, and the countertrend that posits them as movements toward fragmentation, decentralization, and/or localization—and to do so by viewing those persons oriented toward national matters as responsive to the latter tendency, as inclined to treat national problems more as proximate than as distant challenges, more as close-at-hand problems than as remote issues. Put differently, globalizing dynamics are boundary-blurring, while localizing dynamics tend to be boundary-preserving, as do national orientations.

A second reason for leaving national worlds out of the formulation stems from how unfamiliar aspects of the emergent epoch have begun to supersede the relevance of national worlds. Indigenous social movements, for example, "initially developed from local to international (or vice versa) before a corresponding national level of organization was estab-

---

[6] Bruce Robbins, "Actually Existing Cosmopolitanism," in Pheng Cheah and Bruce Robbins (eds.), *Cosmopolitics: Thinking and Feeling beyond the Nation* (Minneapolis: University of Minnesota Press, 1998), p. 3.

lished."[7] To a significant extent, in other words, "the idea of the culturally cohesive national society has blinded us to the various ways in which
the world as a whole has been increasingly 'organized' around sets of
shifting definitions of the global circumstance."[8] Stated more precisely,
"The nation-state, in effect, having been shaped into an 'imagined community' of coherent modern identity through warfare, religion, blood,
patriotism, symbology, and language, is being undone by this fast im-
ploding . . . interface of the global with the local: what we would here
diversely theorize as the *global/local* nexus."[9] Stated in micro terms, "Individuals are less likely to have their life-paths determined by their territory of origin; their identity as individuals becomes more significant than
their position within a national group."[10]

Third, it follows that to locate the national between the local and the
global would be to dilute the concept of fragmegration, to imply that in
the clash between the distant and the proximate intervening actors can
independently ameliorate the dynamics of fragmegration. The stresses
and strains that beset states and societies in the emergent epoch are so
great that states can hardly resolve the powerful tensions that sustain
fragmegrative processes. Policies designed to resolve them are prime
items on national agendas, but their implementation seems bound to
favor either local or global interests. Indeed, it could be argued that "a
framework for relating the global, the national, and the local has yet to
emerge"[11] precisely because of a felt need—or is it a habit?—to maintain
the national level as a central focus superior to the other two foci. By
collapsing the national into the local, it can be argued further, the framework is both more manageable and more empirically accurate. That the
salience of national worlds is much less than rhetoric about them often
implies is also readily discernible in systematic data. For example, while
one survey of 20,000 citizens in twenty countries representing 65 percent

[7] Alison Brysk, *From Tribal Village to Global Village: Indian Rights and International Relations in Latin America* (Stanford, Calif.: Stanford University Press, 2000), p. 86.

[8] Roland Robertson, "Social Theory, Cultural Relativity and the Problem of Globality," in Anthony D. King (ed.), *Culture, Globalization and the World-System: Contemporary Conditions for the Representation of Identity* (Minneapolis: University of Minnesota Press, 1997), p. 89.

[9] Rob Wilson and Wimal Dissanayake, "Introduction: Tracking the Global/Local," in Rob Wilson and Wimal Dissanayake (eds.), *Global/Local: Cultural Production and the Transnational Imaginary* (Durham, N.C.: Duke University Press, 1996), p. 3.

[10] David H. Kaplan, "Territorial Identities and Geographic Scale," in Guntram H. Herb and David H. Kaplan, *Nested Identities: Nationalism, Territory, and Scale* (Lanham, Md.: Rowman and Littlefield, 1999), p. 43.

[11] Arjun Appadurai, *Modernity at Large: Cultural Dimensions of Globalization* (Minneapolis: University of Minnesota Press), p. 188.

of the world's population found that less than half (45 percent) lack trust in their national government to advance society's best interests,[12] in a telephone interview poll of 1,830 Americans conducted in October 2000, the federal government ranked fourteenth on a list of fifteen possible problem solvers in communities (only labor unions ranked lower).[13]

It may seem absurd to treat national concerns as local phenomena at this time (late September 2001) marked by extensive flag-waving and patriotism generated by the terrorist attacks on the Pentagon and the World Trade Center. Such a development, it could be argued, was profoundly global in scope and thus superseded all local orientations. However, more than anything else, such reactions stemmed from attachment to community, from feelings shared widely by Americans (and many non-Americans, too) that their home had been shattered, that the collapsed towers were just around the corner, that the rubble evoked a sense of intimacy rather than a far-off catastrophe. Conceived in this way, in all likelihood the disaster fostered movement toward local as well as global worlds. As one journalist put it, "Flags are everywhere. . . . They are a wondrous expression of communal grief."[14]

To treat national structures and processes as local phenomena is not, of course, to presume that states, their governments and societies, are irrelevant to the course of world affairs. Such a presumption is erroneous. National structures, processes, and values do matter. They are not headed toward oblivion. They continue to be powerful foci and organizers of thought, imagination, and activity, and there are no reasons to believe that their roles in this regard are nearing extinction. Indeed, one observer casts the key local-global and affirmative-resistant distinctions drawn here as the difference between positive and negative nationalism. The two types are seen as differing sharply in a number of ways, but nonetheless they are both conceived to "give priority to 'us' inside the borders over 'them' out there. Both believe that America should come first. Both depend for their force on a nation's sense of common purpose."[15] The same

[12] Environics International, "Poll Findings Suggest Trouble Ahead for the Globalization Agenda," media release, April 30, 2001, p. 3.

[13] Pew Partnership for Civic Change, "New Survey Dispels Myths on Citizen Engagement," January 31, 2001, p. 17 (www.pew-partnership.org.new.../new—survey/detailed—findings.html).

[14] Clyde Haberman, "60's Lessons on How Not to Wave Flag," New York Times, September 19, 2001, p. A20. For an analysis of the downside of flag-waving impulses, see Blaine Harden, "Flag Fever: The Paradox of Patriotism," New York Times, September 30, 2001, Sec. 4, p. 1.

[15] Robert B. Reich, "The Nationalism We Need," The American Prospect, December 6, 1999, p. 64.

observer views only a small minority of persons as having orientations that ignore the borders of states:

> If you look hard, you might be able to find a few globalists who deny that America should come first. They perceive no moral difference between a flood in North Carolina and one in Bangladesh, a sweatshop in Los Angeles and a sweatshop in Ecuador, hungry kids in Alabama and hungry kids in Burundi. To the pure globalist, all are equally worthy of concern. . . . [But f]or most of us, it's easier to empathize with compatriots than with humanity as a whole, and easier to think we can do something to help those within our borders than those outside.[16]

Compelling as such an approach may be, it does not allow for the epochal transformations that are rendering the distant ever more proximate. To posit everybody but a few "pure globalists" as still rooted in a territorial perspective is to oversimplify the complexities and changes wrought by the various dynamics summarized in chapter 3. It is to forgo the opportunity of discerning the nuances that differentiate the several local and global worlds identified here. It overlooks growing tendencies for individuals either to take refuge in their immediate community or to identify themselves with humanity or the world as whole. The former tendency, possibly accelerated by the worldwide spread of neoclassical economic policies and philosophies, has led some people to retreat to private enclaves and become more self-centered, more concerned about their own income and status, with the result that their focus tends to shift away from their responsibilities toward their fellow citizens and toward their own individual privileges and well-being, a shift that substantially diminishes their concern for their national communities.[17] The latter tendency can be discerned in a poll of Americans, for example, that uncovered 77 percent of the respondents agreeing with the statement "I regard myself as a citizen of the world as well as a citizen of the United States."[18] Stated much more strongly, to organize analysis around national phenomena is to give voice to "the same old myth—that the default position has been independent societies following their own course on their own respective territories. . . . historically the default position has been more or less exactly the contrary: intense interaction, and the existence of tradi-

---

[16] Ibid.

[17] This shift is to a large extent worldwide in scope, or at least it is operative wherever public policies are rooted in neoclassical economic premises. For a cogent tracing of these shifts in the United States, see Alan Wolfe, *One Nation, After All: What Middle-Class Americans Really Think about God, Country, Family, Racism, Welfare, Immigration, Homosexuality, Work, the Right, the Left, and Each Other* (New York: Viking, 1998), Chap. 4.

[18] Steven Kull and I. M. Destler, *Misreading the Public: The Myth of a New Isolationism* (Washington, D.C.: Brookings Institution Press, 1999), p. 52.

tions, cultures and institutions of interaction, among all societies when-ever interaction is a possibility. Societies that can interact do."[19]

This is another way of asserting that, in comparison with the more encompassing global processes that have become so central to daily life, national phenomena are local in their scope. Television and other re-cently perfected communications technologies have shrunk countries into local communities. When we turn to national governments for services and support, we are, in effect, going around the corner, reaching out to a neighbor. If the corner and the neighbor may be difficult to contact or persuade, it is not because they are far away but because so many others are turning to them, and they must perforce develop bureaucracies to cope with our requests.

The implications of the shift away from national conceptions are con-siderable. In the cogent words of one observer:

> These are dramatic times. We have entered the era of global politics but have grown up in an age of national politics. Globalization generates anxiety be-cause it places people within the reach of forces which are or seem to be out-side the range of conventional forms of political control. Along with the sense of powerlessness comes the cognitive and emotional anxiety of conventional frames of reference losing their relevance, without new, hospitable and wel-coming images being available. Political conventions, analytical frameworks, mental habits, all are under pressure.[20]

In short, the global is best seen in contrast to the local. Just as there can be no "them" without "us" or no "other" without "self," so there can be no global without the local. More than that, the inextricable links between the two are such that "[t]he global is in the local in the very process of the formation of the local."[21] If "globalization is a matter of increasing long-distance interconnectedness, at least across national boundaries, preferably between continents as well,"[22] then localization involves processes wherein connections within countries are either re-duced to, preserved by, or confined to existing or smaller jurisdictions, preferably within subnational or even subprovincial spaces but not ex-cluding national spaces.

Stated more broadly, it may well be that in the emergent epoch na-tional states and societies are no longer *the* terminal entities around which

---

[19] Jeremy Waldron, "Actually-Existing Cosmopolitanism," from an unfinished (and un-numbered) December 2000 draft of a chapter of a book manuscript entitled *Cosmopolitan Right* (Oxford University Press, forthcoming).

[20] Jan Nederveen Pieterse, "Globalization and Emancipation: From Local Empowerment to Global Reform," *New Political Economy*, Vol. 2 (March 1997), p. 79.

[21] Massey, *Space, Place, and Gender*, p. 120.

[22] Hannerz, *Transnational Connections*, p. 17.

people and their institutions are organized. Conceivably fragmegrative processes may in the long run lead to a proliferation of authority structures above and below the national level that undermines the authority states and societies can wield.[23] If so, "there is no intrinsic reason why actions at local level should reinforce national consciousness, and many reasons why they might run counter both to nation-state requirements and to each other. Indeed, the exercise of citizenship, a sense of responsibility for events in the world, is expressed as much now through support for global movements and their initiatives at local level as it is in working through representative democracy."[24] Another strong indication of the decline of national orientations is to be found among those in the corporate world whose activities are worldwide in scope. Germany's experience in planning for a world's fair, Expo 2000, is illustrative in this regard: a two-year effort to raise money for an American pavilion ended in failure mainly because "many American corporations now see themselves as 'global players'; they do not wish to be associated with a national pavilion. So in the age of globalization, the country that has held world's fairs in New York, San Francisco, and Chicago, among other cities, views an American pavilion as a waste of time, even potentially counterproductive for global movers and shakers."[25]

It might be argued that the surge of patriotism, expressed verbally as well as through widespread display of the American flag, following the terrorist demolition of the World Trade Center in New York demonstrates a continuing preoccupation with the national community and thus argues for maintaining the national level as a conceptual focus. Such reasoning, however, ignores the extent to which the terrorist bombings proved to be a worldwide experience. Not only were people from some sixty countries killed in the attacks, but everywhere abroad people expressed intense feelings indicating that this distant event was extremely proximate, that it was an attack on civilization and not just the United States. Indeed, it could well be that the terrorist attacks gave rise to an upsurge of locally oriented individuals toward one or another of the global worlds, that they just did not have a flag to wave on behalf of this orientation.

In sum, there are good reasons to presume that the inroads that both globalization and localization have made into national states and societies

[23] This possibility is a central theme of James N. Rosenau, *Along the Domestic-Foreign Frontier: Exploring Governance in a Turbulent World* (Cambridge: Cambridge University Press, 1997). Also see chapter 12.

[24] Martin Albrow, *The Global Age: State and Security beyond Modernity* (Stanford, Calif.: Stanford University Press, 1997), p. 181.

[25] Roger Cohen, "A Madcap Germany? Haphazard Expo Cultivates New Image," *International Herald Tribune*, May 30, 2000, p. 1.

are sufficient to justify downgrading the analytic relevance of national phenomena. Put simply, if national states and societies have become "too small for the big problems of life, and too big for the small problems of life,"[26] then at the very least they need to be treated as problematic variables rather than viewed, following the present practice, as certain constants.

FOUR LOCAL WORLDS

Before differentiating among the various local worlds, note needs to be taken of several characteristics they have in common. First, it is useful to reiterate the formulation set forth in figure 2.4 in which all the local worlds are treated as populated by persons whose orientations are toward proximate horizons. They may well be aware of remote events and places that can have consequences for them—that the dynamics of globalization can significantly shape their lives—but they nonetheless interpret distant proximities through local lenses, as readily absorbable into their long-standing practices and worldviews. For them "place and rootedness are as important as ever. Their very identity is tied to place, and they cannot conceive of living anywhere else, for they are dependent on a piece of ground for their livelihood and on a particular culture and language for their sense of well-being."[27]

Second, the notion of the local, of locality, has undergone more than a few changes of meaning as globalizing worlds have steadily encroached on local spaces throughout history. From rural crossroads to small villages, from small communities to urban sprawls, from national societies to sites in cyberspace, locality has both shrunk and grown in contrast to the global. Third, and as will be seen at greater length, it follows that local worlds are not constants. They do undergo transformations. Variations occur in the way globalizing dynamics impinge upon their processes and structures. Such changes may not be as rapid or sweeping as those that occur in global worlds, but it is a mistake to take them for granted or assume they are irrelevant.

An insightful example into the variability that can beset local worlds is provided by Pendleton, a town of seventeen thousand in eastern Oregon that "is as close to nowhere as it is far from somewhere." The town's insularity was abruptly upended when the war against terrorism began following the attacks on the World Trade Center and the Pentagon: "Beneath the brave front of flags and tight-jawed rituals, people are scared by

[26] Daniel Bell, quoted in *The Economist*, July 26, 1997, p. 13.
[27] Richard J. Barnet and John Cavanagh, *Global Dreams: Imperial Corporations and the New World Order* (New York: Simon and Schuster, 1994), p. 21.

an enemy they cannot see and a conflict that should seem so far away."
As a psychiatric counselor, Mike Thompson, at the mental health clinic in
Pendleton put it, "I tell people we are so remote we're not on the map,
that nobody would ever want to bomb us. But people are not sleeping,
they have these big fears, and you can see how this thing has had a real
ripple effect all the way down to some isolated little farm."[28]

Fourth, whatever their bases for being linked to a particular local
world, people are deeply attached to its premises and practices. Unlike
their global counterparts, their local ties and "local habit of mind"[29] are
deep-seated and not easily undone. Diverse circumstances may moderate
their connections or move some into one or another global world, but
most will retain their original affiliations even as distant phenomena become more proximate.[30] People may no longer have "the idea that the
local is autonomous, that it has an integrity of its own," but for many the
local nevertheless

> tends to be a special kind of sensual experience. People often make a distinc-
> tion between "real" experience and what they have read about or seen on
> television. So what is "unreal" about these latter kinds of experience? Of
> course, we can consider this only a figure of speech, but another way of look-
> ing at it is that people are in the local setting bodily, with all their senses, ready
> not only to look and listen but to touch, smell, and taste, without having their
> fields of attention restricted, prestructured for them. There is a feeling of im-
> mediacy, even of immersion, of being surrounded.[31]

Insightful as this observation is, however, it is only partially descriptive
of the inhabitants of three of the four local worlds discussed here. In
some circumstances locally oriented people may not necessarily be
bounded by what they can see, touch, or otherwise directly encounter.
To speak or think of direct encounters is to have in mind the spatially
close and the small in scale, but proximities based on contextual con-

---

[28] Timothy Egan, "Faraway Events Hit Home for Town in Eastern Oregon," *New York
Times*, October 10, 2001, p. A1.

[29] James Dale Davidson and Lord William Rees-Mogg, *The Sovereign Individual: Mastering the Transition to the Information Age* (New York: Simon and Schuster, 1997), p. 199.

[30] For an account of a local community, Portsmouth, New Hampshire, that is bound
together by a pervasive sense of shared affiliations, see Tamar Lewin, "One State Finds
Secret to Strong Civic Bonds," *New York Times*, August 26, 2001, p. 1. More quantita-
tively, the aforementioned telephone survey of a representative sample of 1,830 U.S. adults
found that 77 percent felt either fairly connected or very connected to the communities in
which they live, a proportion that is somewhat less (67 percent) for respondents between
eighteen and twenty-nine years old and somewhat more (86 percent) for those 65 years old
and older. Pew Partnership for Civic Change, "New Survey Dispels Myths on Citizen Engagement," January 31, 2001, p. 1 (www.pew-partnership.org/whatsnew.html).

[31] Hannerz, *Transnational Connections*, p. 27.

straints can lie well outside the easily encountered. Accordingly, so as to maintain clarity with respect to the important distinction between spatial and contextual proximities, henceforth I shall refer to the former as *local phenomena* and to the latter as *localized phenomena* (suggesting they have to be contextually redefined in order to become proximate). To speak of localization is thus to conjure up processes whereby either or both local and localized phenomena become increasingly salient as sources or goals of the attitudes, behavior, or policies of individuals and collectivities. It follows that neither local nor localized phenomena are fixed in time or space, that their salience is subject to variation as circumstances change. Indeed, it is a prime premise of this book that the circumstances of the emergent epoch are such that even as globalizing dynamics are intruding ever more fully into daily routines, so, too, are an ever greater number and diversity of phenomena being localized by an ever greater number of people in every part of the world.

Irrespective of the characteristics they may have in common, individuals in the four local worlds are likely to differentially experience the macro dynamics of fragmegration analyzed in the previous chapter. Indeed, as is evident in table 4.1, the eight dynamics may have sharply different consequences for life in the several worlds.

The diverse macro links are perhaps most discernible in the differences fostered by the fragmenting dimensions of fragmegration. These tend to encourage entrenchment in or movement toward the local through either indifference to, aversion to, or avoidance of globalizing dynamics. There are huge and significant differences among these three paths to localism, the first being traversed by the Insular Locals, the second by the Resistant Locals, and the third by the Exclusionary Locals. The Insular Locals are distinguished by an exclusive concern with spatial proximities, with the geographically near-at-hand, with circumstances that can be directly encountered; the Resistant Locals and Exclusionary Locals contextualize proximity and allow for the spatially remote to be near-at-hand, but the Resistant Locals perceive the spatially remote as so threateningly close as to necessitate opposition, whereas the Exclusionary Locals are inclined to avoid the distant proximities they view as becoming too close. Put differently, Insular Locals work and think in terms of their immediate geographic space and, as such, are essentially isolated from the rest of the world. They do not experience the distant interconnectedness that can attach to proximity. Resistant Locals work and think in response to globalizing dynamics they regard as threatening and thus worthy of opposing. Their interconnectivities to one or more of the ethnoscapes, financescapes, technoscapes, and mediascapes that constitute globalized space are considered so threatening as to generate a need to ward off and overcome them. Exclusionary Locals are not unaware of the interconnec-

TABLE 4.1.
Interaction between Macro Dynamics and Micro Agents in Four Local Worlds

| Macro Dynamics | Local Worlds | | | |
	Insular Locals	Resistant Locals	Exclusionary Locals	Affirmative Locals
Skill revolution	erodes ranks	enlarges ranks	facilitates greater solidarity	increases readiness to move to ranks of Affirmative Globals
Authority crises	ignored	intensify resistance	intensify siege mentality	give pause
Bifurcation of global structures	irrelevant	facilitates opposition of elites, activists, and ordinary people	facilitates cohesion and emphasis on civilizational differences	welcomed as offering mor avenues of influence
Organizational explosion	increases civic-mindedness	fosters coherence and networks	intensifies hierarchy within groups	proliferates net works
Mobility upheaval	diminishes ranks	allows for larger and frequent protests	perceived as threatening	complicates leadership capacities
Microelectronic technologies	disturb territorial links	facilitate member mobilization and expansion	highlight need to control flow of ideas	enhance coordination
Weakening of territoriality, states, and sovereignty	oblivious of changes	strengthens cohesion within and between groups	increases wariness of potential threats	increases auton omy of elites and activists
Globalization of national economies	occasionally experienced as offering wider consumer choice	perceived as noxious, as enhancing power of corporations	perceived as intrusive and as undermining membership	welcomed as furthering wealth and opportunitie

tivities, but they work and think more in terms of avoiding rather than resisting any links to globalized space. Their inclination is to limit their horizons and draw boundaries between themselves and the distant proximities viewed as ominous.

But there is a fourth local world. It is occupied by persons who are neither isolated nor inclined to retreat in the face of globalizing dynamics. They are, rather, capable of absorbing external encroachments on their own terms without fearing their local world will lose its integrity. Indeed, by adapting the external inputs to local practices and norms without diminishing the distinctive features of their world, the Affirmative Locals—as I shall call them—can contribute to the integrative dimensions of fragmegration as much as they do to its divisive dimensions. In other words, Affirmative Locals cannot in any way be regarded as Insular, Resistant, or Exclusionary Locals because they are not disruptive with respect to globalizing patterns. They work and think in a world that has imported foreign practices without substantially altering their small-scale orientations.

The differences among the four types of Locals, in short, stem from several sources. The Insular Locals are distinguished by historic ties to land that has been secluded from globalizng dynamics. For the Resistant Locals the distinction lies in long-standing patterns of life and power balances other than ethnicity that are felt to be threatened; they have long put up with the nonlinear "scapes" of the modern world but see them as fomenting changes that need to be contested. The Exclusionary Locals are moved by their historic ties to an ethnicity that is felt to be under siege; they have lived in a more encompassing world but feel it has become so encroaching that they seek isolation from it. The Affirmative Locals accept their changing ties to the world; they have learned to live with distant proximities that are regarded as acceptable. Stated in another way, the Insular Locals tend to live in closed communities; the Resistant Locals tend to live in political arenas; the Exclusionary Locals tend to live in enclaves; and the Affirmative Locals tend to live in open communities.

The World of Insular Locals

With the possible exception of peasants in remote rural areas of the developing world—and even these exceptions are increasingly rare—the ranks of the Insular Locals are diminishing. Some observers contend this is not so, that many rural peoples remain as isolated from global developments as was the case for their forebears centuries ago, that the struggle to feed and house themselves is too difficult and time-consuming to allow for an awareness of distant proximities. It has been reported, for example, that "huge numbers of Russians outside media centers like Moscow and St.

Petersburg are too consumed by the rigors of daily life to follow politics and current affairs," a reality that led one observer to claim that "'a great number of Russians, more than 80 percent, feel they don't need any kind of information. . . . In many regions of Russia, people don't even buy newspapers because they think they're expensive.'"[32] However, this line of reasoning can easily be exaggerated, ignoring as it does the widespread availability of television and the impact of the mobility upheaval. More accurately, if there still are rural people oblivious to events and trends beyond their small communities, here they are treated as Circumstantial Passives (see chapter 6). Otherwise it seems likely that even in remote rural areas the spread of the global economy, the reach of the micro-electronic revolution, and the vast movement of peoples have made it close to impossible for local communities and their residents to remain self-contained, unaffected by what may be transpiring elsewhere in the world. In the words of two analysts, "Given that there has been centuries of colonization, there is no pure or 'authentic' local that is untouched by global developments. . . . This is especially true today when there are few corners of the world immune from the viral forces of a global consumer and media culture and when global forces offer resources for local con-stellations."[33] Another analyst goes further, arguing that "it is possible to think and act globally and locally at the same time. The spatial differen-tiation of global and local has gone. We are all global beings, acting out our consumerism and citizenship at a local level. As we move about we carry our locality with us."[34] Yet, if only to trace nuance within the local worlds, it seems preferable not to abandon the concept of insularity. Some people are still much less affected by global forces—still much more authentically local—than others, and it is these less globally touched who are here treated as Insular Locals,[35] the premise being that to com-prehend their orientations is to begin to appreciate the scope and limita-tions of the changes ushered in by the emergent epoch.

The spatially proximate community of the Insular Local includes the neighborhood as a specific territory, the family as a hearth, the church as

[32] Michael Wines, "Russia's Media Variety Survives Network's Travail," *New York Times*, April 28, 2001, p. A3. The quoted observer is Oleg Panfilov, the director of the Moscow Center for Journalism in Extreme Situations.

[33] Ann Cvetkovich and Douglas Kellner, "Introduction: Thinking Global and Local," in Ann Cvetkovich and Douglas Kellner (eds.), *Articulating the Global and the Local: Global-ization and Cultural Studies* (Boulder, Colo.: Westview Press, 1997), p. 15.

[34] Tim O'Riordan, "Taking the Transition Forward," in Tim O'Riordan (ed.), *Globalism, Localism and Identity: Fresh Perspectives on the Transition to Sustainability* (Sterling, Va.: Earthscan Publications, 2001), p. 237.

[35] For an analysis of several groups that have purposefully opted for insularity, see Mat-thew Yeomans, "Unplugged," *Wired*, Vol. 10 (February 20002), pp. 81–87.

a haven, the school as a place of learning, the job as a place of employment, and the nearby store as a place to shop and socialize. They are all, as it were, located at a particular addresses. They can be encountered and interacted with directly. All of them are nearby; they have clear-cut boundaries; they can be visited easily; their meaning is normally clear and uncomplicated; they help people define who they are and what they want. But these proximities are not the full measure of the identity of Insular Locals. Some of the close-at-hand spaces they enter and occupy are mental or contextual rather than territorially specific, and the former are just as powerful sources of their identity as are the latter. The friend as a cherished person, the foe as a feared individual, the minority group as a source of emotional comfort, the professional affiliation as a link to like-minded others, and the underprivileged as a matter of deep concern are but a few of the connections that can also foster feelings of proximity even though they may involve spatially remote phenomena.

For the most part, however, there is little variation in the phenomena Insular Locals consider salient. Family, friends, neighbors, school, church, local shops, and job are part of their long-standing daily routines. They are salient precisely because they are always close-at-hand, and, being such, they are usually comforting. In times of difficulty or crisis one knows one can retreat to these resources. Disputes with family and friends may occur, and they may even be enduring, but usually they yield to more encompassing loyalties when the need for support turns desperate. In other words, their salience can be readily revived or restored if the need arises.

While various aspects of daily routines tend to be the most salient of local phenomena, there are other, contextual features of the immediate community that can be equally important for many Insular Locals as part of, say, their weekly or monthly routines. Local elections, sports teams, charity drives, business failures, scandals at city hall, and a host of other issues that constitute a community's life and agenda may periodically be preoccupying as close-at-hand matters. Whether it be civic pride or fervor for the town's sports teams, many people identify closely with their community, gaining satisfaction from its accomplishments and experiencing pain over its setbacks.

As previously indicated, for Insular Locals the immediate community traces the limits of their horizons. Beyond the horizons little is considered salient. Their lives are inextricably tied up with and fully sustained by events and trends in the community, and their orientations toward developments elsewhere in the world are minimal, if they exist at all. They are Insular Locals in the sense that the boundaries of their horizons are defined by what they directly experience through face-to-face contacts and the immediacy of local media. Put differently, proximity for

Insular Locals does not extend across a broad scale or encompass a wide variety of contextual constructs. These individuals localize few situations. They may be attentive to a scandal at city hall, a charity drive, or an issue involving the community's homeless, but for the most part they attach salience to territorially specific aspects of their lives. They may be aware of a larger world beyond their immediate neighborhoods, but they do not contextualize—and thus localize—phenomena in this more encompassing world. The erosion of sovereignty, the weakening of states, the dynamics of globalization, and the other structural transformations that mark the emergent epoch are of little import for Insular Locals.

This is not to say that Insular Locals are apathetic members of their community. On the contrary, both their elites and their nonelites may well be deeply committed to the community's well-being, imbued with its history, ready to defend its institutions, and active in its affairs. Insular Locals, in other words, are neither apathetic nor alienated; rather, they tend to be positively oriented toward their most proximate community, but these orientations extend no further in territorial or contextual space. The ways in which their community is affected by the larger world do not lead them to expand their horizons to that larger world. They may appreciate that outside influences are impacting on their community, but in so doing they are not inclined to focus on the sources of the influences or how pressure might be brought to bear in the outside world to ameliorate any unwelcome influences. Rather, they leave such tasks to the elites among them and concern themselves only with how their community copes with its problems.

Yet Insular Locals are not so fixed in their ways that their world never changes. Families can split up, friends can disappoint and be abandoned, schools can be seen as having lost their élan, jobs can be lost or promotions won—to mention only the more obvious ways in which Insular Locals can experience and accommodate to change. Again, however, such changes all occur within the confines of the immediate community. The more encompassing transformations elsewhere are not salient for an Insular Local; or, if they are, he or she will, by definition, begin to move toward new orientations.[36] Likewise, such movements can occur if developments within the physically close-at-hand lead people to doubt their local orientations, to see their community as a place to escape rather than one to preserve.

Finally, the foregoing portrait of Insular Locals should not be interpreted as suggesting that the skill revolution has passed them by. There is

---

[36] Consider, for example, how a mandatory fee on hog sales in Iowa "transformed the formerly taciturn farmers . . . into angry activists." Elizabeth Becker, "Unpopular Fee Makes Activists of Hog Farmers," *New York Times*, June 11, 2001, p. A13.

no direct correlation between expanded skills and expanded horizons. Insular Locals may be just as exposed to the sources of the skill revolution as anyone else, but for various reasons their exposure results neither in an expansion of their concerns beyond their immediate community nor in a greater receptivity to the feedback loops that pervade nonterritorial space. Rather, any new skills they acquire continue to be focused on their communities, rendering them more effective in any efforts they may undertake to assist or resist changes at work in their neighborhoods.

In some respects, however, the world of the Insular Locals is a myth. Or at least the notion of a neighborhood community wherein people know each other, attend the same meetings, share occupational concerns, talk across fences, and subscribe to the same values can readily be exaggerated. An endless number of people have never greeted their neighbors, much less shared their problems and perspectives. To live with others in the same apartment building is no guarantee of familiarity or friendship in today's urban community. Instead, most people have longstanding friendships or professional ties with people who either have left the community or were never part of it. Even old people, who might be expected "to be the real guardians of [local] continuity, as migrants from the past," may be exiting the world of Insular Locals: "Left to themselves, some of them turn out to become intensely involved with the media, rather than with the people next door."[37] In the United States and probably elsewhere, for example, "Americans old enough to be the typical hacker's grandparents are clamoring for computer instruction at community centers, colleges and libraries across America. . . . Web sites for the elderly proliferate, with chat rooms where they discuss health, travel and finances."[38]

The same can be said of rural areas, which are decreasingly populated by farmers and increasingly made up of urbanites seeking to remove themselves from the difficulties of city life by moving to the country and becoming "lone eagles"—a term given to those who use telecommunications technologies to work out of their homes, thereby "reducing the tyranny of distance, making it possible for knowledge workers (from writers, analysts, brokers, and attorneys to financial planners and manufacturers' reps) to live almost anywhere and stay connected with the outside world."[39] Indeed, in the United States, the population of small towns and rural places is growing at a rapid and accelerating rate, increas-

[37] Hannerz, *Transnational Connections*, p. 29.

[38] Jane Gross, "Wielding Mouse and Modem, Elderly Remain in the Loop," *New York Times*, June 15, 1998, p. 1.

[39] Philip M. Burgess, "Boonies Are Booming—Credit Technology," *Cleveland Plain Dealer*, January 30, 1998, p. 11-B. Burgess coined the term *lone eagles* for such persons a number of years ago.

ing by nearly three million people since 1990 to a total of some fifty-four million in 1998.[40] Little wonder, then, that one observer concludes: "The image of the close-knit working-class urban community, sharing leisure time, intimately connected through marriage, with a common experience passing from parents to children of employment and motherhood, is now as much part of the mythology of modernity as the village community, with its shared customs and rooted experience of the soil, was to pre-modernity. In each case the image is at variance with reality."[41]

Some elites and activists among the Insular Locals move into non-geographic spaces in order to exercise their leadership responsibilities. Mayors of rural towns invited to participate in a sister-city program, local business leaders whose stores are threatened by the possible arrival of franchises owned by multinational corporations, school principals who need to cope with fallout from a heavy influx of immigrant students, police officials who are alerted to the dangers of foreign terrorists, environmental activists who recognize that their community's pollution problems originate across a border—these are Insular Locals who move into nongeographic spaces at particular moments in time. Such activities reflect a profound oxymoron. For in feeling obliged to move beyond their local boundaries so as to enhance the well-being of persons who have long been isolated from and oblivious to developments beyond their immediate neighborhoods and communities, such leaders among the Insular Locals are bound to be sensitive to distant proximities. Consequently, once they undertake to advance the well-being of their constituents by mediating or offsetting the intrusion of globalizing dynamics, they are themselves no longer Insular Locals. Despite its contradiction, however, the notion of an Insular Local active in the outside world has an inner logic. If there still are communities whose people remain insensitive to globalization's repercussions—and this possibility seems, as noted, increasingly unlikely—then clearly their elites may be inclined to represent their interests by moving into the local-global nexus and confronting potentially relevant distant proximities. They remain deeply ensconced in local norms, but their occupations may take them ever deeper into the interstices of globalizing processes.

THREE OTHER LOCAL WORLDS

As one's analytic gaze moves beyond the Insular Locals, another cluster of local worlds comes into focus. These are populated by persons whose

---

[40] Ibid.
[41] Martin Albrow, *The Global Age: State and Society beyond Modernity* (Stanford, Calif.: Stanford University Press, 1997), p. 156.

predominant worldviews lead them to think and act in terms of nonterritorial space and small scale, who remain committed to their near-at-hand communities but for whom this proximity can be as far away as the reach of the Internet and the wide-bodied jet aircraft. Yet, even though their messages and travels may take them widely around the world, these other Locals are not in any sense global in their orientations. Under certain circumstances they may be induced to adopt the worldview of counterparts in one or another global world, but for the most part their local orientations and commitments predominate. Being a Local is for them, so to speak, the default perspective. They are as deeply attached to their family, friends, and communities of residence, as intensely concerned about its well-being, as are Insular Locals. They differ from the latter only in that their personal and primary ties are not confined by geographic limits. For the Affirmative Locals among them, moreover, distant proximities do not pose fragmegrative challenges or impulses to resist or retreat from globalizing dynamics. On the contrary, many hold jobs or otherwise seize opportunities that would not have arisen in the absence of globalization. Their localizing reactions to globalization may involve efforts to achieve greater compatibility with, even to reform, its repercussions and thereby enhance the integrative dimensions of fragmegrative processes. At the very least these Affirmative Locals accept the repercussions of globalizing dynamics without fear of damage to their cherished values and practices.

Persons in the remaining two local worlds, however, are much less sanguine about the emergent epoch. Their criticisms and reservations relative to the emergent epoch are extensive, with the elites and activists among them ever ready to confront, bargain, or otherwise directly engage the ramifications of globalization on behalf of one or another local constituency. They make the "leap out of the local"[42] in order to protect and preserve their small-scale communities, and, in so doing, they conduct themselves as either Resistant or Exclusionary Locals. Since such individuals are major contributors to fragmegrative dynamics, they are a prime focus of this chapter.

The World of Resistant Locals

Diverse types of people reside in this world: workers threatened by a loss of their jobs to foreign competitors; citizens convinced that local cultures are being overwhelmed by Westernization and its corollary, Americanization, and thus fearful that globalizing dynamics are generating an undesirable degree of homogeneity; environmentalists who worry that rapid

[42] This apt phrase comes from Hannerz, *Transnational Connection*, p. 20.

industrialization in the developing world will undermine the ecobalance of their small segment of the developed world; archconservatives who decry the movement of immigrants into their community; intellectuals preoccupied with negative effects of communications technologies for social and political life; and social democrats concerned that neoclassical economic policies underlying globalization are widening the gap between the rich and the poor—these are among the more conspicuous individuals who seek to preserve the meaning of local space by resisting the encroachment of global forces. Whatever their particular concerns, however, they tend to share a conviction that globalization "has led to a way of life in which the nearby is treated with contempt. Many people know what is happening in China but not next-door: at the touch of a TV button, modern consumers have access to all the wildlife of Africa but don't know what birds live in their local park."[43]

In short, Resistant Locals do not live in isolation from the processes of globalization. Nor are they normally tempted to carry on their resistance by elevating their horizons from the local to the global level. On the contrary, while they may be keenly aware of what they regard as detrimental globalizing dynamics, the combination of utter disdain for the dynamics and their commitment to their local values and affiliations enables them to keep their local worldviews intact. Thus, for either ideological or job-exposure reasons, Resistant Locals may be inclined to become deeply engaged in global processes in order to prevent harm to their values or well-being. Indeed, while nonelites among the Resistant Locals confine themselves to limited actions expressive of their worries about the damage globalizing dynamics may unleash, the activists and elites among them participate in transnational and global affairs whenever action at these levels has the potential of preserving those aspects of globalization they find acceptable. For Resistant Locals, the scalar boundaries of the local are variable as they strive to prevent the impact of unwanted distant proximities.

But neither the worries nor the limited actions of the nonelites among the Resistant Locals are inconsequential. At its simplest level the worries focus on globalization as a noxious symbol, a word that "wraps up all the fears of somehow losing control to foreigners, felt as much by Americans who hate the United Nations and immigrants as it is by Indians or Filipinos who feel threatened by the International Monetary Fund, Kentucky Fried Chicken, Joe Camel or Time Warner."[44] As many nonelite Resistant Locals have experienced the skill revolution, they have developed a wide

[43] Norberg-Hodge, "Bringing the Economy Back Home," p. 218.

[44] Barbara Crossette, "Un-American Ugly Americans," *New York Times*, April 11, 1997, Sec. 4, p. 5.

repertoire of activities that are designed to offset the globalizing dynamics that have become part of their everyday routines. Buyers who boycott goods made in prisons or sweatshops; immigrant parents who insist on speaking in their native tongue with their children; fundamentalists who demand compliance to their ways of life from their moderate counterparts; workers who seek protection from foreign imports; individuals who resent the presence of foreigners in their community and do not hesitate to act on their prejudices against them—these are but a few of the myriad practices through which distant proximities are resisted and fragmegrative processes sustained.

In addition to such private acts of resistance, of course, a number of persons among the Resistant Locals stand ready to respond to the mobilizing efforts of their leaders by signing petitions, attending rallies, and joining protest marches. Among the thousands of protesters who converged in downtown Seattle during the 1999 meeting of the WTO were people mobilized by trade unions and environmental organizations; a number of smaller, specialized NGOs, such as Southeast Asian human rights associations concerned about Taiwan and Tibet; a group of one hundred individuals seeking to help indigenous people in southern Colombia who felt threatened by Occidental Petroleum's oil explorations; and students from local universities responding to the activating efforts of their campus organizations. Some self-motivated persons were also moved by one or another issue (and their relative proximity to Seattle) to participate in the marches. For example, "Larry Alexander, who grows potatoes on an 80-acre farm near Kennewick, Wash., says he's tired of relentless pressure to be more productive and efficient. Globalization is crushing the mom-and-pop store and the small farmer, he says. 'They want me to compete with the world. I'm too small.'" Likewise, "Herb Green, a self-described displaced marijuana farmer, felt strongly enough to leave the mountain home where he lives without electricity. 'The [sea] turtles [endangered by WTO pressure on the United States to weaken a law designed to enable them to escape from fishing nets] speak to me. I'm a voice for the critters—the four-legged ones and one-legged ones, the trees,' he says." Little wonder, then, that more than a few observers were impressed by "the astonishing array of causes, costumes, and voices in the Seattle streets."[45]

Another negative reaction to globalization needs to be noted. For some people the inclination to resist stems not so much from opposition to the consequences of globalizing dynamics as from a valuing of the diversity embedded in cultural differences. Such persons are likely to fa-

[45] James Cox and Del Jones, "'This Weird Jamboree': Teamsters and Turtle Protectors on Same Side," *USA Today*, December 2, 1999, p. 2A.

vor localizing processes because they serve the goal of warding off uniformities fostered by the distant proximities and thereby sustain the aesthetic and intellectual pleasures to be derived from the preservation of differences among communities and cultures.[46]

While the ranks of the Resistant Locals include numerous elites who express their resistance through mass media or leaders who devote their energies to activating mass protests, it is important to reiterate that the skill revolution has increasingly enabled workers and other nonelites both to discern the challenges that globalizing dynamics pose for them and to know where and when to respond to their leaders' calls for collective action—to think globally and act locally, to cite an oft-repeated slogan. Such was the case when the WTO convened in Seattle in 1999, for example, and it was perhaps even more evident when the North American Free Trade Agreement (NAFTA) was submitted for approval in the United States. While the White House and other political proponents of the agreement sought to mobilize the support of labor leaders and other elites, it was "the people in the hinterlands"—including "workers, farmers, small-business people, the clergy, civil rights groups, and environmentalists"—who drove the opposition. NAFTA thus proved to be a "bottom-up" issue, with Resistant Locals seeing it "very much about whether they're going to have control over their communities or leave it to corporate board rooms," a perspective that resulted in "stirring local passions as never before."[47] Apart from these rare grassroots issues, however, the cacophony of resistance derives from the efforts of diverse elites to call attention to the dangers of allowing the processes of globalization to undermine their local worlds.

Whatever the direction of the causal arrows between leaders and followers, mass uprisings against the consequences of globalization offer quintessential examples of fragmegration, of how individuals can be caught up in integrative developments that foster fragmenting consequences. More specifically, when mass uprisings turn to violence the inextricable links between globalizing and localizing processes become unmistakably manifest. Two recent examples come to mind. In one, Indonesia, the violence, appears to have had its origins in the streets in the absence of coordinated leadership. The downturn of the Indonesian economy in 1997–98 led the International Monetary Fund to impose stringent reform measures in exchange for needed loans (the integrative stimulus), the imposition of which served as a major source of widespread rioting

---

[46] The aesthetic and intellectual pleasures attached to diversity are among seven cultural arguments in favor of maintaining differences in the face of spreading homogeneity identified by Hannerz, *Transnational Connections*, pp. 56–64.

[47] Peter T. Kilborn, "Little Voices Roar in the Chorus of Trade-Pact Foes," *New York Times*, November 13, 1993, p. 10.

and societal breakdown (the fragmenting response).[48] In the other example, Chiapas, Mexico, the uprising appears to have been planned and mobilized by elites. The Zapatista leadership in Chiapas mobilized its following to resort to violent actions in response to the adoption of NAFTA. To be sure, this upheaval also had deep roots in local Mexican circumstances, but apparently it was not a coincidence that the uprising broke out on the very day that NAFTA went into effect.

The Indonesian and Chiapas cases also illustrate how the changing circumstances that underlie fragmegration can foster the movement of Insular Locals into other forms of localism. Presumably many Indonesians and residents of Chiapas were previously too poor and too deeply rooted in their local communities to be sensitive to the larger world in which the processes of globalization were unfolding. But the intrusion of the outside world, as represented by, say, the IMF, NAFTA, and the WTO, brought an abrupt halt to their isolation and moved them, at least temporarily (and quite possibly permanently), into the ranks of the Resistant Locals. A closer analysis of the various sources that can encourage people to move among the various worlds is undertaken in chapter 7.

If it is reasonable to view the protests of Resistant Locals mentioned thus far as rational actions based on perceived threats to cherished interests and values, it is apparently also the case that some of the resistance derives from habit and other extraneous considerations. Some of those who joined protest marches in Seattle, Washington, D.C., and Melbourne, for example, were seen by journalists either as "counter-culture rebels standing squarely against modern consumerism and liberal economics" or as local people attracted to an unusual event in their hometown for lack of anything better to do. During the September 2000 protests in Melbourne at a World Economic Forum (WEF) meeting, a slogan spray-painted on a statue read, "It's because we're bored," though conceivably this was another way of expressing a "growing sense of powerlessness as people face closing schools, unemployment from corporate downsizing and being forced to work increased hours of unpaid overtime."[49]

In any event, whatever the array of motives that underlie the orientations of nonelite Resistant Lobals, it seems clear that they (and their counterparts among the Exclusionary Locals, too) can be a source of unintentional as well as intentional micro inputs. The occasions when activists undertake protest marches not only are inescapably recognized by leaders among the Affirmative Globals who convene to discuss trade

[48] Ann Marie Murphy, "Indonesia and Globalization," in Samuel. S. Kim (ed.), *East Asia and Globalization* (Lanham, Md.: Rowman and Littlefield, 2000), pp. 209–32.

[49] Simon Pritchard, "The Global Business of Protest," *South China Morning Post* (Internet edition, posted September 15, 2000).

and financial liberalization; such demonstrations also convey a message that more encompassing publics may be restless and ought not be ignored. Such leaders may not fully grasp the backlash against global capitalism, viewing it as unreasonable and counter to the interests of ordinary people; but, as will be seen, there are more than a few indications that they sense the protests are only the surface manifestations of a widely shared unease over the inequities embedded in the course of globalization. To the extent that such perceptions prevail among business and political leaders who preside over macro institutions, then to that extent unintentional micro inputs supplement intentional ones as central features of fragmegrative dynamics.

Turning to the elites and activists among the Resistant Locals, they move in both nonterritorial and territorial spaces in order to act on their antagonism toward globalizing processes and their need to represent the interests and concerns of their followers. Since antagonism to globalization stems from numerous sources, the ranks of Resistant Local elites are as diverse as their counterparts in the mass public, and they often work at cross-purposes on behalf of different constituencies and have little in common other than a shared distaste for the ways in which the distant proximities of the emergent epoch are altering some of the long-standing premises and practices on which their localities were founded in prior epochs.

Nevertheless, despite the numerous disparities among them and depending on what is meant by a social movement, Resistant Locals can be viewed as members of a social movement. As will be seen in the next chapter, opposition to globalization is more likely to form an inchoate than a coherent social movement, but the regularity of street protests since Seattle whenever elites among the Affirmative Globals gather anywhere in the world to deliberate in the boardrooms of international economic institutions suggests that fragmegrative dynamics are stirring the evolution of a vast and significant movement.[50] It may not be an "anti-globalization" movement because many protesters vigorously complain about only selected aspects of the emergent epoch, but its incipient and disparate character ought not be the basis for underestimating its potential. More accurately, perhaps, several "antiglobalization" movements may be forming, one focused on human rights, another on the environment, and so on across a variety of issues.[51]

---

[50] The prospects of such a movement evolving are cautiously affirmed in Michael Massing, "From Protest to Program," *The American Prospect* (Special Report, summer 2001), pp. 2–7.

[51] In the case of environmental issues, for example, see Nancy Dunne, "NGOs Take to Tools of Globalisation to Mobilise Resistance," *Financial Times*, February 21, 2001, p. 8.

In other words, not all the leaders and activists among the Resistant Locals want to roll back the clock to an earlier era in which local or national communities were isolated from the rest of the world. Rather, while they share an unalterable opposition to particular aspects of globalization, many of them converge around values and policies that would moderate, redirect, and control the consequences of globalizing dynamics. Indeed, some are persuaded—or at least hopeful—that the neoliberal policies underlying the dynamism of economic globalization are destined to fail, that sooner or later the unwanted homogenizing and integrating processes fostered by these policies will give rise to extensive counterpolicies, even to reversions to strengthened states and reinstated controls over business and communications practices that have eroded national boundaries.[52] The orientations of these Resistant Locals, however, are clearly different from their counterparts among the Affirmative Locals discussed below;[53] whereas the latter are willing to accept that some good derives from the processes of globalization, those Resistant Locals who promote reversion policies are reluctant to concede that benefits may flow from the economic dynamics presently dominating the processes of globalization. In other words, one group is committed to the politics of reform, while the other engages in the politics of resistance.

Since their concerns and fears are highly differentiated, the various Resistant Locals often employ diverse means to offset globalizing consequences. There is a vast difference, for example, between populists who undertake to mobilize workers, activists who "seek to re-articulate state

[52] Reasoning along these lines underlies the unusual surge of renewed interest in a book published many decades ago. Numerous analyses have recently been added to the globalization literature that focus on the "double movement" thesis advanced in Karl Polanyi, *The Great Transformation: The Political and Economic Origins of Our Time* (Boston: Beacon Press, 1944). See, for example, Robert Latham, "Globalization and Democratic Provisionism: Re-reading Polanyi," *New Political Economy*, Vol. 2 (March 1997), pp. 53–64; Christine B. N. Chin and James H. Mittelman, "Conceptualising Resistance to Globalization," *New Political Economy*, Vol. 2 (March 1997), pp. 29–31; and Stephen Gill, "Theorizing the Interregnum: The Double Movement and Global Politics in the 1990s," in Björn Hettne (ed.), *International Political Economy: Understanding Global Disorder* (London: Zed Books, 1995), pp. 65–99.

[53] But a commitment to tracing nuance requires recognizing that while the Resistant and Affirmative Locals are clearly different, they are not necessarily mutually exclusive. There can be a middle ground between them, as these observations indicate: "Going local does not mean walling off the outside world. It means nurturing locally owned businesses which use local resources sustainably, employ local workers at decent wages, and serve primarily local consumers. It means becoming more self-sufficient, and less dependent on imports. Control moves from the boardrooms of distant corporations and back to the community, where it belongs." Michael H. Shuman, *Going Local: Creating Self-Reliant Communities in a Global Age* (New York: Routledge, 2000), p. 6.

power" in opposition to neoliberal policies,[54] intellectuals who try to expose through writing and other media the undesirable effects of globalization, and militants who are ready to withhold tax payments.

Stated differently, an important distinction can be drawn between forms of resistance that are rooted in advocacy—in persistent lobbying, in mobilizing letter-writing campaigns and street rallies, in generating boycotts and strikes—and those that derive their strength from the power of ideas. The latter can amount to simple condemnations of the policies of the IMF and the World Bank, or they can be based on an extensive agenda: "Among the 'litany of sins' of globalization discourse that we most seek to expose and react to are: its economism; its economic reductionism; its technological determinism; its political cynicism, defeatism and immobilization, its de-socialization of the subject and re-socialization of risk; its teleological subtext of inexorable global 'logic' driven exclusively by capital accumulation and the market; and its ritual exclusion of factors, causes or goals other than capital accumulation and the market from the priority of values to be pursued by social action."[55]

A distinguishing feature of Resistant Locals is that more often than not their ventures out of strict localism are undertaken through the Internet and other communications technologies, both in search of support for their activities and in order to mobilize their followers. Lacking the financial and political clout of those in the global worlds they are contesting, leaders among the Resistant Locals often rely on the Internet to form networks of like-minded others with whom to concert their efforts and pool their resources. Thus it is not far-fetched to describe the world of Resistant Locals as crisscrossed by a vast array of transnational networks that are functionally equivalent to the conferences and airport gatherings where those in the global world converge to frame their strategies, strike their bargains, and implement their policies (see chapter 5). Their activities are functionally and not actually equivalent to those of Resistant Globals, however, in the sense that their immediate communities remain the focus of their concerns, while the horizons of the Resistant Globals are worldwide in scope. The image of Marcos, the leader of the Zapatistas, huddled over a laptop deep in the Chiapas jungle informing a vast network of supporters and appealing for their help captures well both the success of Resistant Locals in using modern communications technologies and their dependence on these means of mobilization. Indeed, Marcos and his followers managed to attract sufficient support to hold in **1996**

---

[54] Barry K. Gills, "Editorial: 'Globalisation' and the 'Politics of Resistance,'" *New Political Economy*, Vol. 2 (March 1997), p. 11.

[55] Ibid., p. 12.

a convention in the jungles of southern Mexico, entitled "The Intercontinental Forum in Favor of Humanity and Against Neo-Liberalism." The closing session met in a steamy, mudhole amphitheater. . . . The session ended with the Zapatistas doing a kind of drum roll and announcing the most evil, dangerous institution in the world today. To a standing ovation, the Zapatistas declared the biggest enemy of mankind to be the W.T.O. . . . [and its promotion] of global free trade.[56]

As indicated, not all the Resistant Locals occupy leadership positions. Many are activists who either independently or in response to leaders move beyond their traditional worlds to pursue their goals. Consider as an example persons deeply committed to environmentalism and concerned that toxic wastes are ruining their community. Such individuals may have been Insular Locals who later became Resistant Locals upon being persuaded that distant sources underlie their proximate concerns and were thus led to undertake, either alone or through participation in a transnational network, to address the problem at its roots. Indeed, with the world having become ever smaller and boundaries ever more readily spanned, activists in local communities who do not extend their horizons on behalf of their local concerns are probably dwindling in number.[57] Chances are that many local activists today are regularly on the Internet and thereby active in the world of Resistant Locals, irrespective of whether they do so to resist globalization or promote other causes.

The World of Exclusionary Locals

For people in this world the near-at-hand—or what some call "localism"—is a refuge, a space to which to retreat because the accelerated impact of globalization is considered to have become too deleterious to tolerate and too powerful to reverse. Once either isolated from or involved in world affairs, the Exclusionary Locals are characterized by an inclination to retreat from the globalizing tide as the latter becomes more encroaching and to do so by withdrawing to their own intellectual haven or emotional (usually ethnic) heritage. Those who retreat for intellectual reasons tend to see themselves as members of a counterculture in which localism is viewed as a solution to multifaceted challenges, as a place "where anti-globalization, anti-development, anti-modernity, anti-science, only-small-is-beautiful come together in an 'island' politics—seeking liberated zones 'outside the system,' enclaves that provide shelter from the

---

[56] Thomas L. Friedman, "Roll Over Hawks and Doves," *New York Times*, February 2, 1997, Sec. 4, p. 15.

[57] See the several essays in Jonathan Barker (ed.), *Street-Level Democracy: Political Settings at the Margins of Global Power* (West Hartford, Conn.: Kumarian Press, 1999).

storm, usually in the hope that the system will somehow atrophy or collapse."[58]

However, these intellectually driven Exclusionary Locals are small in number compared with those whose emotional needs for identity with and support from others sharing the same heritage lead them to seek exclusion behind the walls of ethnicity, nationality, religion, language, or whatever common links to others may bring psychic security. Not all shared heritages, of course, generate exclusionary orientations. Numerous individuals are tied together by common values without a concomitant need to ward off globalization or otherwise build barriers between themselves and the larger world. Yet pronounced patterns of movement in an exclusionary direction are central dynamics of fragmegration. It is not far-fetched to observe that the post–Cold War evolution of intense—and sometimes virulent—ethnic ties has been a major trend in the emergent epoch and perhaps its most pervasive fragmegrative dynamic. The ethnically driven Exclusionary Locals view their shared ties not as a counter-culture but as *the* culture, as a source of comfort and constancy in an ever more intrusive world. At one time their ethnicity may have seemed relatively compatible with the larger world, but in the present era, with its many uncertainties and its emphasis on individual and group identity, the salience of ethnicity looms large—for the Tamils of Sri Lanka, the Basques of Spain, the Kurds of Iran, Iraq, and Turkey, the Chechnians of Russia, the Hawaiians of Hawaii, the Serbs, Croats, or Muslims of Bosnia, and the Albanians of Kosovo, to note only a few of the groups that find wisdom in the aphorism that "it is never too late to revive your origins"[59] and have thus aspired to create or maintain, even to fight for, their own ethnic homes.

The notion of "ethnicity" is used here in the broad sense of any deeply felt bonds of kinship with unknown others of the same background and history. The literature is filled with efforts to differentiate among ethnic, linguistic, religious, national, cultural, tribal, and other historic bonds, some of which are occasionally posited as primordial but all of which are seen as linking people to an idea of who they are and with whom they share deep commonalties. Rather than attempting to draw fine lines among these bonds, it is sufficient for our purposes to lump them together as ethnic ties and to stress that whatever the historic bases of the kinship sentiments toward unknown others, they all have the potential of evolving toward exclusionary orientations. In this sense nationalist movements and the impulses of nationalism can be just as much a form of

---

[58] Pieterse, "Globalization and Emancipation," p. 81.

[59] Jean Baudrillard, quoted in Robertson, "Social Theory, Cultural Relativity and the Problem of Globality," p. 77.

exclusionary localism as can tribal orientations. They offer ethnic homes that appear to serve three important needs:

> There is an answer to the problem of personal oblivion; your destiny is with the nation's future generations. There is also a sense of a national restoration of dignity. If there was a glorious past, there must be a glorious future, and a personal share in that coming renewal. Thirdly, the nation offers the possibility of fraternity. Those living are of one large family [which is identified] through shared symbolic references to the past, to the ancestors held in common.[60]

It may seem odd to treat nationalism as a form of exclusionary localism. In earlier times, during the formation of states in the Western world, nationalism was a key source of how societal coherence evolved and effective states were brought into being. In the case of the United States, to cite an obvious example, nationalism served not as a mechanism for exclusion but as one of inclusion, as a means of welding together into a "melting pot" people with different ethnic, religious, and linguistic backgrounds.[61] In the emergent epoch, however, the notion of nationalism has undergone revision. Today it emphasizes boundaries and the distinction between us and them, with the result that even in the United States the idea of a melting pot has tended to give way to what some regard as a multicultural regime in which different minorities stress their ethnic and racial ties even as they downplay the relevance of an inclusive identity that links them to the varied groups that reside in their country. Viewed in this fragmegrative context, nationalism becomes a form of localism and more a fragmenting dimension of fragmegration than an integrative dimension. Wherever nationalism is highly salient in states today, or wherever nations aspire to being states, exclusionary localism can be readily discerned, with the ethnic cleansing policies of Serbia in the 1990s the most notorious recent example that can be cited in this regard.

It follows that the Exclusionary Locals are not unmindful of the dynamics of globalization. They are not like the Insular Locals who are oblivious to the world outside their immediate community or the Resistant Locals who accept the reality of globalization but try to alter its dynamics so as minimize its perceived consequences. Rather, Exclusionary Locals seek to render inconsequential the dynamics of globalization by closing themselves off from the intrusions of a globalizing world. Nor is there more than a superficial resemblance between the Exclusionary Locals who resort to violence and those Alienated Illegals discussed in chapter 6 who occupy a private world and resort to violence as a means

[60] Hannerz, *Transnational Connections*, p. 83.

[61] For a cogent historical account of how the melting-pot notion became a foundation of an imagined U.S. community, see Joyce Appleby, Lynn Hunt, and Margaret Jacob, *Telling the Truth about History* (New York: Norton, 1994).

of expressing their alienation. The latter perceive globalization as a generalized evil and form militia or engage in terrorism so as to contest its
diverse manifestations, whereas the former are concerned only with those
manifestations that are seen to threaten their group coherence. Thus, for
some residents of both worlds globalization "is a context in which the
moral foundations are shaken and countervailing, fundamentalist tendencies develop in the hope that they may protect against the excessive con-
tingencies, the uncertainties, and the potential destruction of the future."[62]

Of course, ethnic identities need not lead to exclusionary orientations
and, as will be seen, can instead be relevant for persons who live in other
local worlds or may even be located in one of the global worlds. Mutual
exclusivity is not a necessary characteristic of strong ethnic ties. Such ties
also sustain diasporas, peoples with the same ethnic background who live
in and accept another culture outside their ethnic homelands while re-
taining their shared sense of ethnicity with their origins. Many Jews,
Irish, Greeks, and Armenians in the United States, Chinese in Southeast
Asia, and Turks in Germany are illustrative of diasporas in which people
regard themselves as closely tied to both their original heritage and their
adopted homelands.[63] On the other hand, when their homelands are
threatened, such people may well enter the world of Exclusionary Locals
and seek to assist their ethnic compatriots however they can.

For leaders and activists among the Exclusionary Locals, however, mutual exclusivity is a pervasive concern. For them, intruding globalizing
dynamics are unacceptable and always to be contested. They generate
support by remaining unqualified in their commitment to the politics and
policies of constructing and maintaining ethnic boundaries. Whether the
basis for exclusion stems from a desire to protect against the contamina-
tion of a fundamentalist religion by the modern values and practices inherent in globalization or from a political aspiration to maintain a power
base by positing ethnic identity as under siege, leaders of such groups do
not hesitate to appeal to the primordial impulses of their followers and to
emphasize how their integrity is threatened by the infidels in the globalized world who seek to undermine their coherence and alter their identity. But even as they condemn the technologies of globalization and the
values they perceive to be fostered by the technologies, so do they use
the same techniques to pursue their exclusionary goals. The audiotapes
smuggled into Iran by the Ayatollah Khomeini, in which he preached the

---

[62] Barbara Adam, "Detraditionalization and the Certainty of Uncertain Futures," in Paul
Helas, Scott Lash, and Paul Morris (eds.), *Detraditionalization: Critical Reflections on Authority and Identity* (Oxford: Blackwell, 1996), p. 138.

[63] For a general discussion of five major diasporas, see Joel Kotkin, *Tribes: How Race,
Religion, and Identity Determine Success in the New Global Economy* (New York: Random
House, 1993).

virtues of exclusionary policies, are a quintessential example in this regard. Even more recently, Osama bin Laden's use of videotapes to disseminate his message and to recruit jihad fighters for Al Qaeida was designed to serve similar purposes.

Aware that modern "improvements in transportation and communication and global interdependence increased tremendously the costs of exclusion,"[64] and thus faced with knowledge that their followers are often tempted by the fruits of globalization, leaders among the Exclusionary Locals tend to be shrill in their calls for adherence to the values they espouse. And the less these shrill demands are countered by more moderate and sober voices, the higher the probability they will prevail and transform the many Insular Locals among their followers into Exclusionary Locals. Such was the case in the former Yugoslavia, for example. Where Serbs, Croats, and Muslims had lived side by side peacefully, even intermarrying, the turn of their leaders, especially Slobodan Milosevic, to exclusionary and inciting language resulted in the tightening of ethnic groupings and, eventually, in a tragic, prolonged, and violent struggle, one that is likely to leave traces for decades and possibly centuries even though the perniciousness of exclusionary localism may seem self-evident to others.[65]

Is this to say the skill revolution has yet to take hold among fundamentalist groups, that they are insufficiently skilled analytically and emotionally to envision the consequences of the actions they are incited to undertake? Not at all. It means only that the skills have enabled the members of such groups to be more sensitive and competent on behalf of their shared goals, much as others may view such goals as an anathema. Furthermore, as indicated by present tensions in Iran, there is more than a little evidence pointing to the conclusion that neither the followers of Exclusionary Local leaders nor their opponents lack a capacity to discern the downsides of exclusionary policies.[66]

That Exclusionary Locals are able to cope with the pressures upon them to drop their resistance to other local worlds has been plainly evident in Afghanistan since the end of Taliban rule. Some of the members of various Afghan tribes have made clear their unwillingness to shift their loyalties to a nationwide Afghan identity. Indeed, a group of tribesmen "bristled when asked about the role of the Afghan government. 'We don't have anything to do with them,' said Abdul Zahir, a tribesman with rotting teeth." His local tribal chief said "he thought of himself as a

---

[64] Huntington, *The Clash of Civilization and the Remaking of World Order*, p. 73.

[65] For a discussion of the durability of exclusionary localism, see chapter 15.

[66] Amy Waldman, "In Iran, an Angry Generation Longs for Jobs, More Freedom and Power," *New York Times*, December 7, 2001, p. 8.

Stanekzai first, then as a Pashtun. Being an Afghan is a distant third. 'We are loyal to our tribe,' he said. 'We support them.' "[67]

The World of Affirmative Locals

Despite the differences among them, the populations of the resistant and exclusionary worlds share in the central tendencies whereby the fragmenting dimensions of fragmegration are sustained. But there is another local world composed of persons who are disposed neither to resist nor to retreat from the processes of globalization even as their worldview remains organized around their immediate community. Unlike the Insular Locals or their Resistant and Exclusionary counterparts, the occupants of this fourth local world do not seek to lessen the impact of globalizing dynamics. Rather, the nonelites who live in this world are sufficiently open to distant proximities to integrate them into their own patterns of life. They may even regard themselves as beneficiaries of globalization, as able to travel more widely, purchase a greater variety of consumer goods, reach out to unknown others on the Internet, and have satellite dishes that receive foreign programming. In effect, they absorb what globalization has to offer without giving up the fundamental premises and practices of their long-standing routines. Through their consumerism they may contribute to globalizing processes, but the commodities they consume or the distant developments they render proximate are transformed into their own local customs, a characteristic that leads to their being designated as Affirmative Locals.

In other words, Affirmative Locals are not inclined to contest the consequences of globalization. Other things being equal, they simply accept that the world has shrunk, and, in so doing, they see this shrinkage as offering opportunities to enrich their own local ways without undue compromises. Two very different examples, one involving a centuries-long process and the other spanning relatively few years, illustrate the conduct of nonelites in this fourth local world. The former is exemplified by the role that cricket has come to play in India, while the latter pertains to the diverse ways in which eating at McDonald's has undergone localization in East Asia.

In the case of the indigenization of cricket in India, the processes of absorption unfolded across a lengthy and complex history consisting of several transformations from a sport played by upper classes in Victorian England to a stimulus of religious and communal identities in India, from a passion expressive of postcolonial nationalism to a "deeply vernacu-

---

[67] David Bohde with Barbara Crossette, "Loyalty in Rural Afghanistan Places Tribe before Country," *New York Times*, December 17, 2001, p. A1.

larized" game that has special significance for different Indian localities.[68] A number of interactive sources of these transformations—including the nature of the game, the role of language, the activities of corporations, the coverage of the mass media that underlay "the domestication of the vocabulary of cricket,"[69] the dynamics of class, and the evolution of post-colonial male spectatorship—have been identified, and together they account for a "profoundly Indianized"[70] sport that occupies a "central place . . . in the Indian imagination" and that "is the very symbol of a . . . practice that seems to embody India."[71]

Of course, the absorption of cricket into Indian life has varied somewhat in pace and degree in different sections of the country. The sport has taken on different meanings for rural folk, urban workers, lumpen youth, upper-middle-class people, technocrats, media specialists, and public officials[72]—with the result that some of the participants in the indigenization process are more characteristic of elites among the Affirmative Locals than among the masses—as local or national teams compile winning or losing records. For some less affluent groups, cricket offers a sense of group cohesion that can culminate in violent riots, as has happened in "soccer wars" elsewhere in the world. It also enables more affluent political and economic elites to play on nationalist sentiments. Whatever the differences among the various classes and groups, however, the sport has come to represent "a confluence of lived interests, where the producers and consumers of cricket can share the excitement of Indianness without its many, divisive scars. . . . [It] gives all these groups and actors the sense of having hijacked the game from its English habitus into the colonies, at the level of language, body, and agency as well as competition, finance, and spectacle."[73] The local absorption of globalizing dynamics, in short, can be thoroughgoing without being expressive of either resistant or exclusionary localization.

It is noteworthy that cricket and soccer may not be the only sports involved in the absorptive processes fostered by globalization. Spurred partly by the televising of the Olympics and World Cup matches and partly by the aspiration of sports franchises to develop global markets,

---

[68] An extended, incisive, and compelling account of how cricket became de-Victorianized and incorporated into Indian culture can be found in Arjun Appadurai, *Modernity at Large: Cultural Dimensions of Globalization* (Minneapolis: University of Minnesota Press, 1996), Chap. 5; quotation on p. 105.

[69] Ibid., p. 102.

[70] Ibid., p. 111.

[71] Ibid., p. 110.

[72] An interesting analysis of the various meanings these different groups attach to cricket can be found in ibid., p. 112.

[73] Ibid., pp. 112–13.

American baseball, basketball, and football are increasingly watched and followed throughout the world even as the playing of them has increasingly undergone adaptation to local norms and practices. When an American became the first non-Japanese umpire to work in Japan's professional baseball leagues, for example, he quickly generated animosity among players and fans by applying American interpretations of the rules of the game, not knowing that the Japanese version of baseball is "as different as sushi and a McDonald's fish sandwich: the same basic ingredients but adapted to suit two extremely different cultures."[74] To be sure, with professional and college teams increasingly composed of players from different parts of the world, with the players ever ready to move from a team in one country to one that offers better opportunities abroad, with some golf, tennis, sailing, and hockey matches pitting regional teams against each other, and with the worldwide merchandising of sweatshirts, caps, T-shirts, and other logo-embossed wear, sports have become a major vehicle for globalizing processes that have undermined local affiliations.[75] At the same time, and as was noted with respect to Insular Locals, hometown pride (or dejection) in the accomplishments (or failures) of local teams continues to serve as a stimulus for Affirmative Locals who tailor a sport to their own cultural premises.

In contrast to the centuries-long integration of cricket into Indian culture, the absorption of McDonald's into the habits and routines of people everywhere has been remarkably swift and in many instances impressively thorough. The first McDonald's outside of North America opened in 1971, but in the several subsequent decades the franchise has spread throughout the world to the point where every day a total of forty-five million customers at twenty-eight thousand restaurants in 120 countries make a purchase at McDonald's.[76] In the countries of East Asia, where the processes of "McDonaldization" have been subjected to especially intense scrutiny,[77] the number of franchises more than doubled in the five-year span between 1990 and 1995.[78] But the quantitative figures do

[74] Kevin Sullivan, "American Ump Shakes Japan's Major Leagues," *Washington Post*, April 10, 1997, p. A1.

[75] For an analysis along this line, see David L. Andrews, "The (Trans)National Basketball Association: American Commodity-Sign Culture and Global-Local Conjuncturalism," in Ann Cvetkovich and Douglas Kellner (eds.), *Articulating the Global and the Local: Globalization and Cultural Studies* (Boulder, Colo.: Westview Press, 1997), pp. 72–101.

[76] Interview with Jack Greenberg, CEO of McDonald's, "McAtlas Shrugged," *Foreign Policy*, No. 124 (May–June 2001), p. 29. A year later the number of customers had risen to 46 million a day, and the number of restaurants to 30,000 worldwide, with 13,100 of these located in the United States (*Globe and Mail*, May 29, 2002), p. B7.

[77] James L. Watson (ed.), *Golden Arches East: McDonald's in East Asia* (Stanford, Calif.: Stanford University Press, 1997).

[78] James L. Watson, "Introduction: Transnationalism, Localization, and Fast Foods in Asia," in Watson (ed.), *Golden Arches East*, p. 3.

not begin to tell the whole story. The qualitative evidence, though not identical for all of the countries, points clearly to the conclusion that McDonald's has had a large impact on the dietary, family, and communal life of East Asia's major cities. Equally important, in each case it was found that the impact was as much one of localization as of globalization. Yes, some of the popularity of McDonald's is linked to its American standards and a desire on the part of middle- and upper-class people to encounter Western practices, but these globalizing dynamics seem rather minimal compared with the various ways in which eating at McDonald's has been redefined in Asian terms. Whereas Americans use the fast-food chain as a place to get a quick meal in a busy schedule, for example, East Asians treat McDonald's as a place to linger, to celebrate birthdays, and to engage in conversation long after the food has been consumed. Indeed, a considerable "percentage of young people in Tokyo, Taipei, and Hong Kong have grown up with McDonald's as their favorite venue for entertaining family and friends."[79]

The reasons for these localizing dynamics are several. At more abstract levels the chain's popularity is linked to the consequences of industrialization in the region, to the greater number of working women, to changing family structures and values, to a new generation whose members knew little of the hardships endured by their parents. In the words of one observer, "Children are driving the localization process."[80] At more practical levels McDonald's offers clean rest rooms, orderly procedures, and friendly service, all of which have often been in short supply in East Asia's traditional eating establishments.

Needless to say, the localizing dynamics initiated and sustained by McDonald's are not simply a matter of Asian customs prevailing over Western practices. The company early recognized the need to adapt to local customs and adopted policies designed to facilitate acceptance of its products without compromising its worldwide standards. Perhaps most notably, it has not been averse to modifying its dishes to suit Asian tastes while at the same time keeping on its menu the same hamburgers, french fries, and drinks for which its franchises are everywhere known. In Singapore, for instance, a pepper burger was introduced to cater to local preferences for spicy foods, while in India McDonald's sells lamb and vegetarian burgers so as not to offend Hindus.[81] To summarize, "The process of localization is a two-way street: It implies changes in the local culture as well as modification in the company's standard operating procedures. Key elements of McDonald's industrialized system—queuing,

[79] Ibid., pp. 22–23.
[80] Ibid., p. 20.
[81] Jonathan Holburt, "Global Tastes, Local Trimmings," *Far Eastern Economic Review*, Vol. 160, (December 26, 1996–January 2, 1997), p. 24.

self-provisioning, self-seating—have been accepted by consumers through-out East Asia. Other aspects of the industrial model have been rejected, notably those relating to time and space."[82]

Even as McDonald's has been a source of affirmative localization, so has it provoked the ire of Resistant Locals throughout the world. For such persons the enormous worldwide success of McDonald's serves as a quintessential example of the evils of globalization, the transplantation of American "junk culture" on unsuspecting peoples. The fast-food chain is seen as having served to hasten yet another dimension of homogeneity and thereby undercut local cultures. As a French newspaper, *Le Monde*, observed, "Resistance to the hegemonic pretenses of hamburgers is, above, all, a cultural imperative."[83] More than that, the ranks of the Re-sistant Locals include "a loose international network of self-proclaimed libertarians, union organizers, vegetarians, environmentalists and animal rights campaigners who have seen the enemy and decided that it is McDonald's itself."[84] Several activists in the network issued a pamphlet in 1989 accusing the company of a long list of misdeeds such as promoting poor nutrition, using advertising to exploit children, encouraging litter, mistreating animals, and destroying rain forests, all of which led McDon-ald's to sue them for libel and resulted in "the longest trial in British history."[85]

Whatever the veracity of the charges of Resistant Locals—and there is much to suggest they are exaggerated, even wrong in many instances—their number is considerably less than that of the Affirmative Locals. In all parts of the world McDonald's has become an aspect of daily rou-tines—routines that have common dimensions even as they also vary from culture to culture. Like cricket in India, and like many other prod-ucts in the global marketplace, its offerings have become staples with local twists. While the rapid and continued spread of its franchises might be viewed as global saturation, so has the spread contributed to a global maturation wherein local cultures have synthesized the external inputs in such a way as to make them their own.[86]

Elites among the Affirmative Locals—those media, business, and sports leaders, for example, who facilitated the absorption of cricket in India—sustain globalizing dynamics at the local level, as do the ordinary citizens

---

[82] Watson, "Introduction: Transnationalism, Localization, and Fast Foods in Asia," p. 37.

[83] Quoted in Geneva Overholser, "Anti-globalist France Doesn't Practice What It Preaches," *International Herald Tribune*, July 15–16, 2000, p. 6.

[84] Sarah Lyall, "Britain's Big 'McLibel Trial' (It's McEndless, Too)," *New York Times*, November 29, 1996, p. A4.

[85] Ibid.

[86] For a discussion of the saturation-maturation distinction, see Ulf Hannerz, "Scenarios for Peripheral Cultures," in King (ed.), *Culture, Globalization and the World-System*, pp. 122–27.

who consume goods from abroad. An obvious example is provided by the concern among intellectuals, politicians, and journalists to integrate the benefits of globalization into the civic life of their communities. Such elites are wedded to a communitarian philosophy that emphasizes the need for Insular Locals and those in other local worlds to take responsibility for the well-being of their geographic spaces; in pursuing these concerns, inevitably they seek to channel globalizing dynamics such that they enhance rather than undermine their communities. They practice, in effect, the politics of reform rather than the politics of resistance, an orientation that is a prime characteristic of Affirmative Locals. Stated more generally, Affirmative Locals undertake to harness globalization on behalf of "local citizens movements and alternative institutions [that] are springing up all over the world to meet basic economic needs, to preserve local traditions, religious life, cultural life, biological species, and other treasures of the natural world, and to struggle for human dignity."[87]

In sum, with the possible exception of those occasions when their involvement in local sports teams turns intensely nationalistic, Affirmative Locals are not parties to the fragmenting side of fragmegration. They do not initiate or sustain fragmenting processes, but their activities can be the basis for integrative processes in the emergent epoch. Their contributions in this regard are not nearly so extensive as the contributions of those who move in global worlds, as will be seen in the next chapter, but neither are they inconsequential insofar as the contradictory dimensions of fragmegration balance each other off. At the same time, while globalization has substantially influenced the lives of Affirmative Locals, it has not been a wholesale replacement for long-standing traditions and practices.

CONCLUSION

Although it should be clear from the foregoing analysis, it is useful to reiterate that this account of the several local worlds involves snapshots at a moment in time, that the boundaries separating the worlds are not rigid, and that under certain circumstances people can move from one local world to another (though it would be extremely difficult to move back to the life of an Insular Local). Equally clear, and far more important, this summary of four local worlds highlights the large extent to which the dynamics of localization are very much a part of the emergent epoch, that they are highly variable, that they provide a context within which globalization advances, falters, or sustains the course of events. It could not be otherwise. The local is where people are born and (with few exceptions, such as the children of military and foreign service personnel)

---

[87] Barnet and Cavanagh, *Global Dreams*, p. 429.

grow up, and while the traces of early experience may eventually give way to new and expanded horizons, for many individuals local values, practices, and memories retain a hold on their perspectives and emotions. Such persons are rarely the movers and shakers of history, but without them the pace of globalizing processes would be quite different, and so would the structures of the emergent epoch. Indeed, as will be seen in subsequent chapters, the various local worlds are never far removed from the consciousness and concerns of those located in one or another of the global worlds.

The variability of localizing processes also serves as a useful reminder of the dangers of generalizing about the impact of globalization. Yes, there are numerous ways in which consumer tastes, organizational structures, and cultural practices are undergoing homogenization; and yes, the sources of many of the universalizing tendencies can be ascribed to Americanization and Westernization; but no, the emergent epoch is not confined to such dynamics. The activities of Resistant, Exclusionary, and Affirmative Locals all make clear, each in their own way, that it is a vast oversimplification to equate the deterritorialization and shrinking of the world with the spread of pervasive uniformities.

This is not to downplay the powerful ways in which globalization is generating commonalties around the world. To repeat for purposes of emphasis, consumer tastes are certainly converging more extensively than in earlier epochs. Cultural differences are surely narrower than in the past. The economic policies of states are certainly more uniform than ever. Still, such dynamics are more complex than the intellectual criticisms of some Resistant Locals acknowledge. Indeed, their critique that the United States is the prime culprit in the processes that are fostering worldwide homogeneity may have once been sound, but it now appears increasingly ill-founded as the products and processes of Japan, China, and India (to mention only the more obvious countries) have entered the stream of globalizing dynamics, such that today "in cities, towns and satellite-dished villages across Asia—and in other parts of the world where rising incomes and greater access to goods and information are breeding consumerism and speeding modernization—it is getting much harder to hold the West, particularly the United States, responsible for assaults on local cultures."[88] It is even questionable whether American movies have made such deep inroads into cultures elsewhere as critics allege. Forty-four percent of all feature-length films are produced in neither Hollywood nor any other Western country.[89]

[88] Crossette, "Un-American Ugly Americans," p. 1.
[89] Bernard Wasow, "Globalization Has Two Sides," *Financial Times*, November 23, 2001, p. 13.

One can even assert that the dynamics of globalization have undergone high degrees of localization, or at least that the stimuli they sustain undergo refinement and transformation as they work their way into the life of diverse individuals in local settings. In the cogent words of two analysts, "The geographic origin of imported culture has become increasingly less relevant; what matters is its local consequences,"[90] which is to say that "localization is not a unilinear process that ends the same everywhere."[91] More specifically, it is to say that under fragmegrative conditions the global-local nexus derives from a multiplicity of sources that are bound to be as much bases for differences as for similarities. As still another observer concluded, "The consequences of globalization are substantial, but by no means uniform or homogenizing. Rather globalization can strengthen local differences through access to information, audiences, markets, foreign policy processes, and transnational pressure points."[92]

[90] Yunxiang Yan, "McDonald's in Beijing: The Localization of Americana," in Watson (ed.), *Golden Arches East*, p. 75.

[91] Watson, "Introduction: Transnationalism, Localization, and Fast Foods in Asia," p. 37.

[92] Brysk, *From Tribal Village to Global Village*, p. 284.

CHAPTER FIVE

Global Worlds

> If we wish to understand the local character of our lives, the
> changing nature of the places in which we live, we have to
> grasp both the wider global context of which we are a part and
> what it is that makes us distinctly local. . . . [W]e are part of
> more than one world. We live local versions of the world and in
> so doing we have to locate ourselves within a wider *global*
> context.
>
> —John Allen and Doreen Massey[1]

> [I]n the modern world, which I take to be an International
> Empire, the sense of home is not just divided, but scattered
> across the planet, and in the absence of any center at all, people
> find themselves at sea. . . . Reflecting on this, I began to
> wonder whether a new kind of being might not be coming to
> light—a citizen of this International Empire—made up of
> fusions (and confusions) we had not seen before: a "Global
> Soul." . . . This creature could be a person who had grown up
> in many cultures at once—and so lived in the cracks between
> them—or might be one who, though rooted in background,
> lived and worked on a globe that propelled him from tropic to
> snowstorm in three hours.
>
> —Pico Iyer[2]

JUST AS there are several local worlds, so are there at least four global
worlds that are sufficiently different from each other to be worthy of
separate analysis. All of them are populated by individuals described by
the epigraphs, by people who share tendencies to think and act on a scale
that exceeds a local context; but at the same time each of the global
worlds is differentiated by the ways in which large scale is conceived and
nonterritorial dynamics contextualized.[3]

[1] "Introduction," in J. Allen and D. Massey (eds.), *Geographical Worlds* (Oxford: Oxford
University Press, 1995), p. 1 (italics in original).

[2] *The Global Soul: Jet Lag, Shopping Malls, and the Search for Home* (New York: Knopf,
2000), p. 18.

[3] As was the case in the previous chapter, the ensuing discussion captures people at a
specific moment in time; I postpone until chapter 7 tracing how they might move among

FOUR GLOBAL WORLDS

Three of the global worlds consist of persons whose thoughts and actions are worldwide in scale and not confined to any territorially bounded space. One of these is populated by the Affirmative Globals, by elites, activists, and ordinary people who share positive inclinations toward the processes of globalization—especially toward those dynamics that foster and sustain a global marketplace—seeing them as moving humankind toward greater integration and prosperity. In contrast, the Resistant Globals are no less worldwide in the scale of their orientations, but they, like their Local counterparts, regard one or more of the prevailing dynamics that sustain globalization as detrimental to the well-being of peoples. Similarly, the Specialized Globals are persons whose territorial orientations are not locally bounded but who are oriented toward only limited issues on the global agenda.

Finally, as indicated in figure 2.4, a fourth global world consists of the Territorial Globals, whose scale of thought and action is large but territorially bounded. Foreign policy officials are quintessential (though not the only) examples of Territorial Globals inasmuch as they are concerned about problems that arise anywhere abroad even as their concerns are framed in terms of their country's interests and are thus necessarily territorially specific.

It follows that, taken as a whole, persons in the several global worlds contribute to both the fragmenting and the integrative dynamics of fragmegration. They share a relative indifference to the dynamics of localization, but they can conflict intensely over whether the world is better off as a result of a globalizing economy, technologies that shrink distance, and a vast movement of people that renders long-standing boundaries ever more porous. Clashes between Affirmative and Resistant Globals are thus very much the substance of politics and power in the emergent epoch, with leaders in each group often seeking to garner support from like-minded counterparts in local worlds. Table 5.1 summarizes some of the different reactions of people in the four global worlds to the prime macro dynamics set forth in chapter 3.

Unlike Insular Locals, the ranks of the several global worlds are not diminishing. Quite to the contrary, the macro dynamics of fragmegration are swelling their ranks continuously, a process that seems likely to continue for the foreseeable future. This growth pattern is perhaps especially discernible for nonelites who, with their skills enhanced by greater education and new communications technologies, are exposed to diverse stim-

---

the various worlds with the elapse of time. Those in each of the global worlds can be seen as snapshots and not as videotapes; as such, the overlaps among them are minimized here for the sake of analytic clarity.

Table 5.1.
Interaction between Macro Dynamics and Micro Agents in Four Global Worlds

Macro Dynamics	Global Worlds			
	Affirmative Globals	Resistant Globals	Specialized Globals	Territorial Globals
Skill revolution	expands horizons	enlarges ranks	enhances authority	strengthens policy-making process
Authority crises	contested or ignored	often promoted and welcomed	promoted by some, ignored by others	contested
Bifurcation of global structures	not seen as relevant	facilitates opposition of elites, activists, and ordinary people	facilitates cohesion	reluctantly accepted
Organizational explosion	enlarges ranks	fosters coherence and networks	facilitates recruitment of like-minded	seen as posing new challenges
Mobility upheaval	expands contacts, facilitates networks	allows for larger and frequent protests	perceived as threatening	complicates leadership capacities
Microelectronic technologies	allow for coordinated networks	facilitate mobilization and expansion	reinforce specialized foci	enhance coordination
Weakening of territoriality, states, and sovereignty	viewed as inevitable and desirable	strengthens cohesion within and between groups	increases autonomy of elites and activists	regretted and contested
Globalization of national economies	promoted and welcomed	perceived as noxious, as enhancing power of corporations	welcomed by some, opposed by others	welcomed if appropriately controlled

uli conducive to orienting them toward global events and trends. The pattern for elites in the four global worlds involves, virtually by definition, slower growth, but even their ranks are expanding as the complexities of urban life and the global economy proliferate organizations and the leaders required to manage them. The number of such elites is probably more in the hundreds of thousands than in the millions, but it is reasonable to presume that the trend line traces an upward slope.

The World of Affirmative Globals

Needless to say, to label some individuals as the "Affirmative" Globals is to run the risk of considerable misunderstanding. Such a designation implies that their values are superior to and more pure than the Resistant, Specialized, or Territorial Globals; or that distant proximities are conceived in hierarchical terms, with the Affirmative Globals presiding over the pace and direction of globalizing dynamics. Such implications are not intended. Distant proximities are more often circuitous than direct links sustained by a multiplicity of diverse actors with a multiplicity of conflicting interests and orientations. In other words, the label "Affirmative" is not used in a value-laden way. It does not necessarily refer either to a controlling, consensual, and coordinated business/government/military elite or to idealists who envision a world government. Rather, the label is used strictly to designate persons who contextualize globalizing dynamics in both positive and nonterritorial terms. (Indeed, the world-government idealists are more in the nature of Territorial Globals, since their orientations are toward a specific geographic space.) At the same time, as will be seen, both the elites and the nonelites among the Affirmative Globals are far from uniform in their outlook toward global affairs even though they share a perspective in which globalization, for all its drawbacks, is seen as essentially an irreversible and desirable set of processes with which humankind must contend.

Nor are the labels used here intended to imply that the orientations of the Affirmative Globals are invariably right and those of the Resistant Globals invariably wrong. Just as one can applaud the motives and actions of some Affirmative Globals and decry those of others among them—a humanitarian aid worker who seeks to minimize the evils of genocide is surely more admirable than a self-serving business tycoon who seeks only to maximize corporate profits—so is it possible to approve of the actions of Resistant Globals who contest the effort of some Affirmative Globals to exploit the world's resources irrespective of any ecological damage they may cause.

Risky as it is, a prime reason for using the "Affirmative" designation is the lack of a suitable alternative designation. The most likely candidate, "cosmopolitans," has become increasingly ambiguous and is often loosely used "to describe just about anybody who moves about in the world."[4] More than that, this alternative label is marked by a long history that has recently become controversial because the dynamics of globalization have undermined its traditional meaning, so much so that "what was cosmopolitan in the early 1940s may be counted as a moderate form of localism by now."[5] Stated more generally, while cosmopolitanism was once regarded as referring to wealthy aristocrats and elite intellectuals who had a "devotion to the interests of humanity as a whole," who "often seemed to claim universality by virtue of [their] independence, [their] detachment from the bonds, commitments, and affiliations that constrain ordinary nation-bound lives,"[6] today it has become a "tarnished term"[7] because it has been variously extended to refer to broadly diverse people, non-European as well as European, underprivileged as well as rich, who, far from being detached, have a variety of ties and goals that link them inextricably into one or another aspect of life beyond the nation. In effect, the term, "separated from its (European) universalist moorings, quickly becomes a traveling signifier, a term always in danger of breaking up into partial equivalences, exile, immigration, migrancy, diaspora, border crossing, pilgrimage, tourism."[8] Among others, for example, "North American merchant sailors, Caribbean au pairs in the United States, Egyptian guest workers in Iraq, [and] Japanese women who take *gaijin* lovers"[9] have been posited as practicing a form of cosmopolitanism, and this list can be extensively elaborated if a cosmopolitan is viewed as anyone whose life is not bound to a single country. In short, the concept of a cosmopolitan has been altered to encompass persons in all four of the global worlds discussed here, thus reinforcing the ensuing formulation that confines the label of Affirmative Globals to those elites, activists, and ordinary people whose thoughts and actions, for better or worse, roam widely across continents in support of globalizing dynamics, while treating those with narrower or resistant orientations as members of one of the other three global worlds.

The ranks of elites among the Affirmative Globals consist mainly of persons whose organizational positions, intellectual achievements, artistic

---

[4] Ulf Hannerz, *Transnational Connections: Culture, People, Places* (London: Routledge, 1996), p. 102.

[5] Ibid.

[6] Bruce Robbins, "Actually Existing Cosmopolitanism," in Pheng Cheah and Bruce Robbins (eds.), *Cosmopolitics: Thinking and Feeling beyond the Nation* (Minneapolis: University of Minnesota Press, 1998), p. 1.

[7] Cheah and Robbins (eds.), *Cosmopolitics*, p. vii.

[8] James Clifford, "Mixed Feelings," in Cheah and Robbins (eds.), *Cosmopolitics*, p. 363.

[9] Robbins, "Actually Existing Cosmopolitanism," p. 1.

accomplishments, or other professional successes cumulate and usually lead to extensive influence, wealth, and respect—even to an unaccustomed celebrity status for heads of corporations[10]—that accord them access to many corridors of power. They are "the jet-setters, the ones sending and receiving the faxes and the e-mail, holding the international conference calls, the ones distributing the films, controlling the news, organizing the investments and the international currency transactions. These are the groups who are really in . . . charge of time-space compression, who can really use it and turn it to advantage, whose power and influence it very definitely increases."[11] As a result, whatever particular position or success paves the route for individuals to enter into the ranks of the Affirmative Globals, they tend toward perceiving untold benefits for people everywhere in free flows of trade and investment. More than that, they are likely to become broad-gauged in their orientations, to care about a wide range of matters beyond their specific area of expertise, to be, in effect, concerned about the world as a whole, its economic, political, cultural, and social processes. Unlike the Specialized Globals, in other words, elite Affirmative Globals tend not to think in terms of narrow issue clusters but instead become preoccupied with the entire range of problems on the global agenda in a context that presumes deep interdependence among all areas of human endeavor.[12] Top officials of the World Bank, the International Monetary Fund, and the United Nations are quintessential examples in this regard. Perforce they must be attentive to the diverse global sources and consequences of the situations in and among different countries that they seek to alter or preserve.

Of course, some Affirmative Globals may not have any influence over

[10] G. Pascal Zachary, "CEO's Are Stars Now, But Why?" *Wall Street Journal*, September 3, 1997, p. A1. For one answer to the question posed in the title of this article—in which it is argued that business leaders in the United States felt they lost public confidence in the 1970s and launched a "five-prong" campaign to foster a favorable, celebrity-like image— see P. Dreier, "Capitalists vs. the Media: An Analysis of an Ideological Mobilization among Business Leaders," *Media, Culture and Society*, Vol. 4 (1982), pp. 111–32. Since 2001, however, in the wake of scandals involving the Enron Corporation and other companies in the United States, the celebrity status of CEOs has been severly undermined. In the words of the head of a major investment bank, Goldman Sachs, "I cannot think of a time when business over all has been held in less repute." See Henry M. Paulson Jr., quoted in Patrick McGeehan, "Goldman Chief Urges Reforms in Corporations," *New York Times*, June 6, 2002, p. A1. For an extensive analysis of the extent to which business executives have "undergone siege," see David Leonhardt, "The Imperial Chief Executive Is Suddenly in the Cross Hairs," *New York Times*, June 24, 2002, p. A1.

[11] Doreen Massey, *Space, Place, and Gender* (Minneapolis: University of Minnesota Press, 1994), p. 149.

[12] For an argument that the evolution of broad perspectives has not occurred as quickly and fully among business leaders as circumstances seem to warrant, see Jeffrey E. Garten, *The Mind of the C.E.O.* (New York: Basic Books, 2001), pp. 10, 17–18.

the course of events. The nonelites among them consist, so to speak, of ordinary folk who, for reasons of family background, early experience, education, or economic circumstances respond favorably to the incentives to develop and maintain the orientations of Affirmative Globals even though they lack access to the corridors of political power and must restrict their involvement to intentional micro inputs such as giving money, writing letters, attending rallies, or otherwise lending support on behalf of distant causes they believe to be highly proximate. A capacity to exercise power, in other words, is by no means a requirement for entry into the ranks of the Affirmative Globals.

Whatever the extent to which Affirmative Global elites are a coordinated, consensual network—and chances are that many of their paths cross on numerous occasions[13]—they do share certain characteristics that derive from their readiness to move, personally or electronically, widely around the ethnoscapes, mediascapes, financescapes, ideoscapes, and technoscapes that constitute their world. Perhaps most notably, except for family and friends, Affirmative Global elites are less likely to be concerned about their local communities than about trends transpiring beyond their immediate neighborhoods. Thus rarely do they encounter or interact directly with salient phenomena in their communities of residence. They live, instead, in a world of contextual constructs, of scenarios conceived to begin, unfold, and cascade across horizons considerably removed from where they are physically located—a lifestyle that has been designated as "high-tech nomadism."[14] In the words of a well-traveled banker, "I can live anywhere in the world, but it must be near an airport."[15] Even less territorial is the consultant who says, with not a little pride, "My cell phone is my house."[16]

As already indicated, it follows that unlike the Affirmative Locals, whose values and ties orient them to developments relevant to their immediate locales, Affirmative Globals may be challenged by, involved in, or otherwise affected by what transpires anywhere in the world. They care about distant events; they follow them, judge them, react to them. Their world is spatially remote but contextually close. For them, developments anywhere are potentially proximate.

---

[13] For questionnaire data supporting this point, provided by 187 persons defined as active on the cutting edge of globalization, see James N. Rosenau, David C. Earnest, Yale F. Ferguson, and Ole R. Holsti, "On the Cutting Edge of Globalization" (Washington, D.C.: Foreign Policy Leadership Project, George Washington University, 2000), forthcoming.

[14] Joel Garreau, "Home Is Where the Phone Is," *Washington Post*, October 17, 2000, p. A1.

[15] Aihwa Ong, "Flexible Citizenship among Chinese Cosmopolitans," in Cheah and Robbins (eds.), *Cosmopolitics*, p. 157.

[16] Garreau, "Home Is Where the Phone Is," p. A1.

This is not to imply, of course, that everything that unfolds beyond their communities of residence is salient for Affirmative Globals. No one can follow or be preoccupied with all the situations that constitute the global agenda at any one time. The point is, rather, that the numerous matters of concern that are salient for Affirmative Globals are all located at distances they have to contextualize to follow and comprehend.

Nor do their common concerns imply that these elites have similar reactions as they attend to developments anywhere. They may share a feeling that the world is troubled and that it can be well served by expanded globalization. Many may feel some obligation to use their influence on behalf of lessening or resolving the troubles. But at the same time, as indicated in the previous chapter, large numbers are unlikely "to exchange an old commitment to the nation for a new global citizenship, with an even more extended sense of social responsibility. There are no strong attachments here, but more likely a sense of resignation,"[17] a sensitivity "to the problems that plague the world [even as] these dilemmas may seem so intractable and overpowering in their global dimension that any attempt to remedy them appears futile."[18]

Given the scope of their concerns, elite Affirmative Globals are especially likely to take advantage of the skill revolution, to expand their analytic talents, enlarge their emotional capacities, and refine their imaginations through their reliance on the products of new microelectronic technologies and through the opportunities offered by the considerable extent to which their professions lead them to travel frequently, in person or electronically, across and around the world's political and economic boundaries. A measure of their global movements is provided by the 1996 figure for individuals who belong to the United Airlines 1K Club (those who travel one hundred thousand miles a year): while it is far from clear that a large proportion of the club's membership would meet the criteria for Affirmative Globals used here, it is indicative that the members for that year numbered 25,131, of which 23,638 resided in the United States and the remainder lived in thirty-six different countries.[19] Or consider the figures for the Star Alliance (of which United Airlines is a member): it "has more than 32 million frequent fliers, with just under a million achieving elite status, and more than 40,000 traveling on average

[17] Hannerz, *Transnational Connections*, p. 84.

[18] Robert Reich, *The Work of Nations: Preparing Ourselves for 21st Century Capitalism* (New York: Knopf, 1991), p. 310.

[19] Letter dated May 23, 1996, from Stephanie Burnham, manager of market research for the airline. For an insightful discussion of how United Airlines divides its client base into eight categories, with the "Road Runners" and the "Global Travelers" exhibiting behavior that most closely approximates that of Global elites, see Don Phillips, "Plane Favorites," *Washington Post*, December 7, 1997, p. H1.

2,000 miles a week, year in and year out, on that one airline group alone."[20] To be even more specific, one businessman, the CEO of a worldwide advertising agency, during a recent twelve-month period flew "over 360,000 miles on 128 flights," which involved being "in the air for almost 34 days [and] took him to 40 cities in 24 countries."[21]

It goes without saying that there is no necessary connection between being an Affirmative Global and having one's horizons expanded by the skill revolution. As noted, some Affirmative Globals may be reluctant to change despite their large-scale and nonterritorial orientations. Business travelers who would prefer to stay at home are illustrative in this regard and might even be labeled anti–Affirmative Globals. On balance, however, it seems reasonable to presume that the outward-looking orientations of most Affirmative Globals encourage them to remain open to new stimuli and capable of expanding both their skills and their horizons.

While many elites are surely specialists in whatever field of endeavor through which they entered the ranks of the Affirmative Globals, neither their orientations nor their activities are confined to a particular line of work. They are, by definition, generalists—else they would be among the Specialized Globals discussed later—capable of contextualizing a variety of the issues and problems that constitute the global agenda at any moment in time. Or at least it is a reasonable presumption that their refined skills, worldwide travel, and extensive movement in leadership circles, along with the orientations they may have acquired earlier in their lives, have served to broaden their concerns beyond whatever may be their narrow professional responsibilities as corporate executives, heads of NGOs, academic and scientific researchers, artistic leaders, and the many other types of elites to be found among their ranks.

The Identities and Loyalties of Affirmative Globals

Given their broad orientations toward diverse issues on the global agenda, the important question arises as to whether Affirmative Global elites have been led by their expanded horizons to experience transformations in their loyalties to and attitudes toward their countries and communities of origin as well as toward themselves. If they are active in a world not pervaded with territorial boundaries, for example, do they alter their sense of identity and become more attached to that world than to the earlier ones in which they resided? Have many or most Affirmative

---

[20] Garreau, "Home Is Where the Phone Is," p. A1.

[21] Gillian Upton, "Surviving Four Weeks Every Year in the Air," *Financial Times*, May 7, 1998, p. vii. For another account of a businesswoman who flies four or five times a week, see John Schwartz, "Swashbucklers Buckle Down," *New York Times*, October 22, 2001, p. B1.

Global elites become so acclimated to their worldwide concerns, interests, and responsibilities, and thus so cut off from local stimuli, that their community and national commitments undergo progressive attenuation? With an unbounded world as their field of play, and with an ability to move readily from one cultural setting to another, might not Affirmative Globals begin to lose touch with their home country or, alternatively, begin to supplement their national values with commitments to a more encompassing set of concerns? Whether they are corporate executives, entertainers, or leaders of transnational NGOs, have elites among the Affirmative Globals become much less wedded to territoriality than are those located in one or another local or private world? Have they lost a sense of identity with any territorial spaces? What new identities do they develop, and what old ones do they abandon?

The answers to such questions must perforce be speculative. Little is known about the loyalty and orientation shifts that may be occurring among individuals in any of the global worlds. History tells us that loyalties neither build up nor decline quickly, that they evolve out of diverse sources and are path-dependent experiences that culminate slowly into new commitments; but in the emergent epoch such processes may be truncated by the pace of cascading events, by the speed with which ideas move across increasingly obsolete conventional boundaries, by the advent of new and vigorous social movements, and by the seemingly endless transformation of long-standing institutions. Hence speculation that loyalties and patriotism may be shifting is not surprising. More than a few analysts allow for the possibility that the responsibilities and activities of elite Affirmative Globals may indeed be reshaping long-standing commitments and loyalties that have previously been directed toward the state-centered world. In so doing, they tend to come up with diverse and opposing estimates of what may be happening to the orientations of Affirmative Global elites. Consider, for example, these observations:

> Patriotism, certainly, does not rank very high in their hierarchy of virtues. . . . Their loyalties . . . are international rather than regional, national, or local. They have more in common with their counterparts in Brussels or Hong Kong than with the masses of Americans not yet plugged into the network of global communications. . . . Without national attachments . . . people have little inclination to make sacrifices or to accept responsibility for their actions. . . . The new elites are at home only in transit, en route to a high-level conference, to the grand opening of a new franchise, to an international film festival, or to an undiscovered resort. Theirs is essentially a tourist's view of the world—not a perspective likely to encourage a passionate devotion to democracy. . . . To an alarming extent the privileged classes . . . have made themselves independent not only of crumbling industrial cities but of public services in general. . . . In

effect, they have removed themselves from the common life. . . . Many of them have ceased to think of themselves as Americans in any important sense, implicated in America's destiny for better or worse. Their ties to an international culture of work and leisure . . . make many of them deeply indifferent to the prospect of American national decline.[22]

Another observer puts the same thought more succinctly, noting that the new elites, "[l]acking a sense of 'we,' . . . might nonetheless remain fiercely loyal to a single airline."[23]

While allowing for possible loyalty transformations, still another observer is less certain of the answer and leaves open the question of whether such changes are occurring:

> The question is whether the habits of citizenship are sufficiently strong to withstand the centrifugal forces of the new global economy. Is there enough of simple loyalty to place—of civic obligation, even when unadorned by enlightened self-interest—to elicit sacrifice nonetheless? We are, after all, citizens as well as economic actors; we may work in markets, but we live in societies. How tight is the social and political bond when the economic bond unravels?[24]

Put differently, there are probably several contradictory tendencies at work among Affirmative Globals. In some cases they involve "a jet-set searching for roots";[25] in others their orientations give way to magnanimity, to "a willingness to engage with the Other, . . . an intellectual and esthetic openness toward divergent cultural experiences, a search for contrasts rather than uniformity";[26] and in some instances the changes may lead to self-centered and selfish perspectives that are anything but magnanimous, flexible, or worldly. While one observer, for example, writes of "border-running executives with no state loyalty but flexible citizenships and cultural identities in the service of maximal profit to family and self,"[27] an Indian author stresses that the latter kind of orientation is even worldwide in scope: "The super-rich are seceding from their nations. So what you have is not a Western or East Asian or Southeast Asian or Chinese model. We are building enclaves of super-privilege. What you're having is not a global village but a series of global ghettoes. The Western elite is not the sole villain."[28]

---

[22] Christopher Lasch, *The Revolt of the Elites and the Betrayal of Democracy* (New York: Norton, 1995), pp. 6, 35, 45, 47.

[23] Iyer, *The Global Soul*, p. 19.

[24] Reich, *The Work of Nations*, p. 304.

[25] Hannerz, *Transnational Connections*, p. 75.

[26] Ibid., p. 103.

[27] Rob Wilson, "A New Cosmopolitanism Is in the Air: Some Dialectical Twists and Turns," in Cheah and Robbins (eds.), *Cosmopolitics*, p. 356.

[28] Palagummi Sainath, quoted in Barbara Crossette, "Un-American Ugly Americans," *New York Times*, April 11, 1997, Sec. 4, p. 5.

Similarly, using the label "symbolic analysts" for some of those here called Affirmative Globals—individuals who "are problem-identifiers, problem solvers, strategic brokers, highly skilled people whose continuously cumulative, varied experience . . . makes them relatively autonomous *vis-à-vis* particular places and organizations"—another observer also posits altered loyalties by describing such persons as " 'seceding from the rest of the nation,' " a process that has been "taking place gradually and without fanfare. The symbolic analysts may pledge allegiance to the flag with as much sincerity as ever, yet 'the new global sources of their economic well-being have subtly altered how they understand their economic roles and responsibilities in society.' " The result is that "[t]hey build their own monuments—the convention centers, the research parks, the international airports—and withdraw into their own private habitats, enclaves with security guards if need be."[29] In a slightly more generous interpretation of business elites among the Affirmative Globals, two other analysts summarize their "interviews with top executives" by noting that a sense of limits rather than selfishness underlies their conduct:

[W]e encountered executives of broad vision and understanding of global issues that affect their markets. Their capacity for global thinking struck us as far more developed than that exhibited by most officials of national governments. But they do not appear to dwell much on the long-term social or political consequences of what their companies make or what they do. The combined negative impact of corporate activities on the job market or the environment or education or family life is regarded as beyond their power to address and therefore not within their province.[30]

Still another conception of the loyalties and identities of Affirmative Globals involves a neo-Marxist class perspective. It is a "neo" perspective in the sense that it makes "the extraordinarily difficult decisive break with state-centrism" and posits the existence not of a capitalist class, but of a transnational capitalist class (TCC) that rules the global system. The TCC is seen as transnational in three respects:

First, its members tend to have outward-oriented global rather than inward-oriented national perspectives on a variety of issues. . . . *Second*, members of the TCC tend to be people from many countries, more and more of whom begin to consider themselves "citizens of the world" as well as of their places of birth. . . . *Third*, they tend to share similar lifestyles, particularly patterns of

---

[29] This formulation is from a summary by Hannerz, *Transnational Connections*, p. 84, of Reich, *The Work of Nations*. The internal quotes are taken directly from Reich, pp. 252–53.

[30] Richard J. Barnet and John Cavanagh, *Global Dreams: Imperial Corporations and the New World Order* (New York: Simon and Schuster, 1994), p. 18.

higher education (increasingly) in business schools . . . and consumption of luxury goods and services.[31]

Like the symbolic analysts, members of the TCC are seen as having evolved their own unique subculture, which consists of "exclusive clubs and restaurants, ultra-expensive resorts in all continents, 'the right places to be seen,' private as opposed to mass forms of travel and entertainment and, ominously, increasing residential segregation of the very rich secured by armed guards and electronic surveillance, from Los Angeles, to Moscow and from Manila to Beijing."[32]

A similar but less elaborate conception of the loyalties of Affirmative Globals qua capitalists is ascribed to

[t]he triumph of capitalism [which] will lead to the emergence of a new global, or extranational, consciousness among the capitalists, many of whom will become Sovereign Individuals. Far from depending upon the state to discipline workers, as the Marxists imagined, the ablest, wealthiest persons were net losers from the actions of the nation-state. It is clearly they who have the most to gain by transcending nationalism as markets triumph over compulsion.[33]

Whether the daily routines of Affirmative Globals encourage magnanimous, class, or self-serving orientations toward their work and the world, it seems likely that they are unlike their counterparts in earlier epochs in at least one important respect, namely, they lack clarity with respect to their own identity. Indeed, one observer even suggests that some individuals who move widely around the world may in fact share the orientations of Resistant Locals: "[O]n the one hand, the dominant global elites inhabiting the space of flows tend to consist of identity-less individuals ('citizens of the world'); while on the other hand, people resisting economic, cultural, and political disenfranchisement tend to be attracted to communal identity."[34] At the very least some of the Affirmative Globals who are business travelers appear to fit this description of identity-less individuals:

[T]hey are something more than just supersonic versions of the Phoenician traders or Bedouin merchants of old, and are separated from Willy Loman by differences of kind as much as of degree. For one thing, these new ungrounded bodies operate in a world where many companies are richer than most countries, and this very notion of the nation-state—like loyalty—has been privatized. In a

[31] Leslie Sklair, "Social Movements for Global Capitalism: The Transnational Capitalist Class in Action," *Review of International Political Economy*, Vol. 4 (autumn 1997), pp. 521–22 (italics in original).

[32] Ibid., p. 522.

[33] James Dale Davidson and Lord William Rees-Mogg, *The Sovereign Individual: Mastering the Transition to the Information Age* (New York: Simon and Schuster, 1999), p. 297.

[34] Manuel Castells, *The Power of Identity* (Malden, Mass.: Blackwell, 1967), p. 356.

post-ideological world, they cannot know, as easily as the encyclopedia salesman surely did, exactly where they stand. And flying from winter to summer in an afternoon—or waking up alone in 14th-century Nepal and sitting down for dinner that night with the family in Century City—they face, and are forced to find new answers for, the most basic human questions: Where do they belong, what is their community and to whom are they most responsible?[35]

By way of contrast, other analysts suggest that social movements concerned about, say, the environment, human rights, or women's rights may encourage their elites (Specialized Globals) to refocus their loyalties in ways comparable to those long enjoyed by nation-states, including a readiness on the part of their adherents to make extensive sacrifices, perhaps even risking their lives (as members of Greenpeace have done).[36]

While many Affirmative Global elites may undergo confusion over their identities and loyalties, some manage to resolve any ambiguity in favor of their worldwide orientations. Charitable donations are a good indicator in this regard. By posing the question of whether one favors causes in one's community of residence or those devoted to ameliorating more worldwide problems, contributions to charities serve as a measure of the extent to which Affirmative Globals can become disassociated from their local ties. The pattern of giving recorded by four Americans is illustrative. At the most global extreme is Ted Turner, the wealthy founder of Cable News Network (CNN): "For all of his philanthropy, crowned by his $1 billion pledge to the United Nations [in 1997], relatively little of his largess has landed in Atlanta, where he lives and where his company and sports teams are based."[37] Indeed, even though both CNN and Turner's Atlanta Braves benefited enormously from the construction that facilitated the 1992 Olympics, his contribution to the building of Centennial Olympic Park ($150,000) was meager compared with his UN gift. "A call was made to get him to put in a lot of money and it just wasn't on his radar scope," a member of the Atlanta Olympic Committee observed; another analyst commented, "Turner's personality explains his lack of focus on Atlanta, suggesting that his U.N. donation stemmed from 'a heroic self-conception.'"[38] A much simpler explanation has been offered by Turner himself: "I consider myself a citizen of the world before I'm anything else."[39]

Some three years after announcing his gift to the United Nations,

---

[35] Pico Iyer, "The New Business Class," *New York Times Magazine*, March 8, 1998, p. 38.

[36] See, for example, Appadurai, *Modernity at Large*, p. 176.

[37] Kevin Sack, "Turner's Charity Blind Spot," *New York Times*, September 28, 1997, Sec. 4, p. 4.

[38] Ibid.

[39] Quoted in Claudia Dreifus, "Noble Tycoon: Magnate Ted Turner Likes to Put His Money Where His Heart Is," *Modern Maturity*, September–October 2000, p. 18.

Turner paid $34 million in dues the United States owed the United Nations when the Congress refused to meet the American commitment. This action, the gifts of Bill Gates's foundation to improve global public health (which included $100 million to the fund for AIDS, tuberculosis, and malaria), and the extensive agenda of George Soros to expend his wealth creating open societies in some ninety countries (in 2000 his foundation allocated $470 million to projects in Indonesia and South Africa) amount to "miniature foreign policies" that "often bump shoulders with Washington's version."[40]

Contrariwise, some wealthy Americans give predominantly to institutions within their own communities. Brooke Astor, for example, was an Affirmative Local "because she had the idea that her husband's wealth was made in New York and she would give it in New York, and she did not give it abstractly: she has visited every project she has funded."[41] In Los Angeles, on the other hand, "[t]here is no Brooke Astor . . . [because] there is, unlike New York, no sense of civic pride that obliges one to give in a sustained or systematic way."[42] George Soros and Bill Gates fall between Ted Turner and Brooke Astor in their pattern of charitable giving: both have funded major projects at home as well as abroad. In the case of Soros, for example, he not only has funded several foundations in the former Soviet Union committed to maintaining the skills of scientists in the region but also has devoted considerable resources to alleviating drug and other problems in the United States.[43]

Notwithstanding traces of evidence and an underlying logic that loyalties among elite Affirmative Globals are changing, some observers are skeptical that the changes are meaningful or will prove to be enduring. The skeptics perceive, in effect, that a localism lurks in all elites, that under certain conditions global elites will be unable to sustain their transnational ties to each other. In the succinct words of one analyst, "The tougher things get, the more ties of loyalty to those near at hand tighten, and the more those to everyone else slacken."[44] Another skeptic goes even further and expresses doubt that fundamental loyalties are subject to alteration by globalizing dynamics: "[A]lthough globalization creates a

[40] Tina Rosenberg, "Building Their Own Private State Departments," *New York Times*, August 12, 2001, Sec. 4, p. 12.

[41] Claudia Dreifus, "It *Is* Better to Give Than to Receive," *New York Times Magazine*, December 14, 1997, p. 54.

[42] Judith Miller, "In Los Angeles, a New Generation Discovers Philanthropy," *New York Times*, December 8, 1997, p. 12.

[43] For Soros's own account of the basis of his charitable contributions, see George Soros, "The Capitalist Threat," *Atlantic Monthly*, February 1997, pp. 45–58.

[44] Richard Rorty, "Justice as a Larger Loyalty," in Cheah and Robbins (eds.), *Cosmopolitics*, p. 45.

greater sense of belonging-to-a-world insofar as it makes individual lives globally interdependent, it has not, thus far, resulted in a significant sense of political allegiance or loyalty to the world."[45]

One cannot help but wonder, however, how the long-terms effects of the terrorist attacks on New York and Washington will impact on the loyalties of elites among the Affirmative Globals. Two themes, a flag-waving sense of patriotism and a sense that humanity as a whole was attacked, may vie for their hearts and minds. Certainly non-American elites have good reasons to stress the common humanity involved, while those in the United States may not view the two themes as mutually contradictory. But with the passage of time and the onset of new issues that pit patriotism against more encompassing loyalties, U.S. elites may have difficulty balancing the conflicting tugs on their priorities. While patriotism may prevail for many of them, it is far from clear that this priority will be extensively shared.[46]

A Coordinated Elite?

Like the loyalty issue, whether the shared attributes of the Affirmative Global elites underlie the formation of a social class or a coordinated group is a question about which not much is known. Leadership ranks at the global level have not been systematically studied, and one can only conjecture that just as the formation of national societies tended to coincide with the coalescence of national elites, so might the unique experiences of those for whom the world is their arena of action underlie the emergence of interconnected global elites. Signs of such a development can be discerned in the annual six-day meetings of the World Economic Forum, where Affirmative Global elites (mainly business executives, but also a smattering of distinguished intellectuals, scientists, journalists, and governmental leaders) from around the world convene in the luxury resort of Davos, Switzerland, to discuss (in panels and through an interactive computer communications and videoconference system) common

[45] Pheng Cheah, "Given Culture: Rethinking Cosmopolitical Freedom in Transition," in Cheah and Robbins (eds.), *Cosmopolitics*, p. 315.

[46] For a compelling set of essays in which intellectuals located in the affirmative, resistant, and specialized global worlds contest and contrast these priorities through comparisons of the virtues of cosmopolitanism and patriotism, with some of the essayists espousing world citizenship and others casting doubt on this aspiration and arguing instead that only through the localism embodied in patriotism can life, education and human relationships become meaningful, see Joshua Cohen (ed.), *For Love of Country: Debating the Limits of Patriotism* (Boston: Beacon Press, 1996). A penetrating critique of the essays can be found in Bruce Robbins, "Root, Root, Root: Martha Nussbaum Meets the Home Team," in Bruce Robbins, *Feeling Global: Internationalism in Distress*, (New York: New York University Press, 1999), Chap. 8.

problems that undermine the forces of a free global market. In 1997 some one thousand companies paid an annual membership fee of more than $13,000—partnership status cost $100,000—which entitled them to attend the Davos meeting, as well as smaller regional forums held in various parts of the world throughout the year. To be a member a corporation has to have an annual volume of a billion Swiss francs (roughly $700 million), a figure that is expressive of what the WEF's recruiting director describes as its "philosophy—we call it the global one thousand. Once we determine that a company has a global presence in sales or sourcing, we go after it."[47] It is hardly surprising, therefore, that a "Davos culture" has been said to emerge:

> Participants in this culture know how to deal with computers, cellular phones, airline schedules, currency exchange, and the like. But they also dress alike, exhibit the same amicable informality, relieve tensions by similar attempts at humor, and of course most of them interact in English. Since most of these cultural traits are of Western (and mostly American) provenance, individuals coming from different backgrounds must go through a process of socialization that will allow them to engage in this behavior with seemingly effortless spontaneity. . . . But it would be a mistake to think that the "Davos culture" operates only in the offices, boardrooms, and hotel suites in which international business is transacted. It carries over into the lifestyles and presumably also the values of those who participate in it. Thus, for example, the frenetic pace of contemporary business is carried over into the leisure activities and the family life of business people. There is a yuppie style in the corporation, but also in the body-building studio and in the bedroom. And notions of costs, benefits, and maximization spill over from work into private life. The "Davos culture" is a culture of the elite and . . . of those aspiring to join the elite. Its principal social location is in the business world, but since elites intermingle, it also affects at least the political elites. There is, as it were, a yuppie internationale.[48]

It seems doubtful, however, that this intimacy of the Davos culture was maintained in 2002, when the WEF convened in New York City rather than the Swiss ski resort. Impelled in part by wanting to help New York recover symbolically and economically from the September 2001 terrorist attack and in part by the cost of security incurred in 2000 as a consequence of antiglobalization protests, moving the locale of the annual conference may have altered the ambiance of the occasion even if it did not diminish the elite interconnections sustained by the WEF.[49]

---

[47] Craig R. Whitney, "Hobnobbing at Very High Levels," *New York Times*, January 28, 1997, p. D1.

[48] Peter L. Berger, "Four Faces of Global Culture," *National Interest*, No. 49 (fall 1997), p. 24.

[49] Presumably the ambiance will not be maintained by calling the New York meeting

Another indicator of elite coordination among Affirmative Globals, or at least those in the United States, is provided by newspaper advertisements that many of them signed in an effort to steer the country in directions that preserve the viability and integrity of the global marketplace. When the financial crisis of Asian economies accelerated in 1998, for example, a distinguished array of nineteen founding members, thirty-one former public officials, and eighty-eight corporate leaders signed and placed a full two-page message in which they identified themselves as coming together with diverse political and professional affiliations to express their concern about "a dangerous drift toward disengagement from the responsibilities of global leadership."[50]

On the other hand, competitive drives for larger market shares, greater influence, and sympathetic government policies also mark life among Affirmative Global elites and limit the extent to which they can coalesce as a coordinated and dominant force. It is not unusual, for example, for corporations to spy on each other, lure each other's executives, and otherwise conduct themselves as participants in zero-sum rather than nonzero-sum games.[51] While the Davos meetings suggest that such tactics have their limits and that Affirmative Globals do experience incentives to share information, merge enterprises, and otherwise coalesce,[52] it would be erroneous to posit their ranks as comparable to a large, happy family.

Much the same obtains for analysts who posit a transnational capitalist class. They, too, see the TCC as composed of diverse elements, with four groups as the core members: transnational corporate executives, globalizing bureaucrats, globalizing politicians and professionals, and consumerist elites (merchants and media). Communication and coordination among these four elements of the TCC are perceived as "facilitated in a variety of ways, notably interlocking directorates, cross-memberships of groups in different spheres (business, government, politics, professions, media, etc.) and leadership roles of business notables in non-business activities, think tanks, charities, universities, medical, arts and sports foundations

---

"Davos" and renaming some meeting rooms at the Waldorf after the mountains towering over the Swiss conference center. Jay Newton-Small, "From Davos to New York: Where Has the Spirit of Davos Gone?" *Earth Times*, December 3, 2001, pp. 5–8.

[50] Advertisement, "A Time for American Leadership on Key Global Issues," *New York Times*, February 11, 1998, pp. A14–A15.

[51] A clear-cut instance of such practices occurred when former executives of the General Motors Corporation took some of its confidential documents with them to their new positions in the Volkswagen Company. See Thomas C. Hayes, "G.M. Is Seeking Criminal Action against Officer Who Joined VW," *New York Times*, May 22, 1993, p. A1.

[52] For a cogent discussion of the diverse incentives that foster coalescence in the business world, see John H. Dunning, "The Advent of Alliance Capitalism," in John H. Dunning and Khalil A. Hamdani (eds.), *The New Globalism and Developing Countries* (Tokyo: United Nations University Press, 1997), pp. 12–50.

and the like."[53] Nor is the TCC's underlying consensus viewed as frayed by the existence of cleavages and factionalism: "Despite real geographical and sectoral conflicts the whole of the transnational capitalist class shares a fundamental interest in the continued accumulation of private profit."[54] Indeed, while "struggles within the ruling class structures at all levels" are persistent and not trivial, "the balance of power is swinging decisively from the localizers (inner-oriented economic nationalists) to the globalizers (outward-oriented neoliberals)."[55]

It follows that while those in the world of Affirmative Globals have overlapping interests and more than a few shared values, it is doubtful whether either the elites or the nonelites among them are sufficiently organized to register a coherent voice on behalf of the positive features of globalization. They may agree on the virtues of free trade, and they may be responsive to appeals for money on behalf of common goals, but it is hard to imagine them openly coordinating messages designed to counter the protests in the streets of Seattle during the 1999 WTO talks. Bill Gates of Microsoft did rise to the occasion with an op-ed piece supportive of WTO.[56] Yet this was an isolated act, and in fact the Affirmative Globals were conspicuously absent from the scene in Seattle.[57]

In sum, Affirmative Globals are positive about the benefits of a globalizing world and not deterred by its potential for negative consequences. They tend to believe that, on balance, the detrimental, fragmenting dimensions of globalization are temporary, and that in the long run everyone will benefit. They may grant that the excesses of neoliberal economic policies need to be contained, and many probably perceive the need for greater transparency in the decisions and activities of corporations and NGOs, but rightly or wrongly, their optimism is so extensive that they tend not to see any need to engage in widespread public efforts to defend their ideas and interests. Put in a micro-macro context, the Affirmative Globals avoid the public arena and confine their intentional micro inputs into globalizing processes to individual actions within the IMF, WTO, and other policy-making circles. Their unintentional inputs—the orientations they convey through pursuing their interests—tend to suggest an all-will-benefit attitude that can readily be interpreted as disdain for the concerns of their critics.

However, note should be taken of some indications that the Battle of

[53] Sklair, "Social Movements for Global Capitalism," p. 533.

[54] Ibid., p. 523.

[55] Ibid.

[56] Bill Gates, "Shaping the Future in Seattle," *New York Times*, November 29, 1999, p. A29.

[57] "Where Have All the Seattle-Based CEOs Gone?" *Wall Street Journal*, December 3, 1999, p. A6.

Seattle and subsequent protests have generated a modification of some of the Affirmative Globals' more unqualifiedly positive attitudes. More than a few elites among them, for example, have acknowledged the desirability of relieving some developing countries of their international debts. Still others, such as the Dalai Lama and numerous other religious leaders, have begun to seek to bring the moral authority of religion into the globalization debate, an effort that gathered momentum when some one thousand of them convened in New York just prior to the UN's Millennium Summit to frame a statement on world peace and serve as a bridge to international economic institutions.[58]

The World of Resistant Globals

Despite their basic orientations, in other words, Affirmative Global elites are not as free of fragmegrative dynamics as they might like to be. As protests against the WTO, IMF, and World Bank accelerate, they can hardly avoid facing other leaders and publics who share their large-scale nonterritorial orientations but who perceive global capitalism as being out of control and needing reform, if not resisted. More accurately, activists and elites among the Resistant Globals seek to reform those features of globalization they view as creating undesirable equilibria. Most of them oppose the globalizing processes not in the hope of reverting to a form of localism but in an effort to bring them more fully under the jurisdiction of national governments, thereby rendering them more transparent and democratic. Although they are moved to resistance by particular issues, their diverse concerns have undergone transformation into generalized opposition, a convergence that was quickly interpreted as the globalization of resistance: "It is only relatively recently, perhaps in the last five or ten years, that activists around the world have begun to put their local struggles—against environmental damage, social decay, the destruction of local economies and cultures, the exploitation of labour and so forth—into a global context. Only in the 1990s has resistance, like capital itself, begun to become truly globalized."[59] Indeed, it can be readily argued that "the activists have globalised faster than the firms they target."[60]

While activists among the Resistant Globals have led the way in escalating specific issues into intentional micro inputs based on general opposition, the elites in their ranks seem more inclined to focus on selective

---

[58] Guest interview, "Recasting Globalization," *Newsletter*, Boston Research Center for the 21st Century, No. 17 (spring/summer 2001), pp. 6–7, 14–15.

[59] Paul Kingsnorth, "The Heads of the Hydra," *The Ecologist*, Vol. 29 (May/June 1999), p. 203.

[60] "Anti-capitalist Protests," *The Economist*, December 23, 2000, p. 86.

issues. George Soros is illustrative in this respect. A leading financier, he was persuaded by the excesses of globalization to shift from being an Affirmative to a Resistant Global. Convinced that the global economy needed reform, he warned in various media that "the spread of market values into all areas of life" poses a prime threat to "our open and democratic society," that an "uninhibited pursuit" of laissez-faire ideology can lead to a slighting of education and other pillars of a civilized society that do not provide a quick return on investment, and that being obsessed with competitiveness leads to an unwillingness "to make any sacrifices for the common good."[61] A more specific echo of Soros's concerns was voiced by John J. Sweeney, the president of the AFL and CIO and the only American labor leader to attend the WEF in its first twenty-seven years. In his public talk at the Davos meeting in 1997, Sweeney contended that the onset of the global economy rendered workers vulnerable to lower-wage labor and economic crises abroad, leading him to demand "coordinated efforts to stimulate growth, to regulate currency and capital speculation, to extend labor and democratic rights as part of the response to the Asian collapse." Dissenting from the idea that strong economic growth would raise worker incomes, Sweeney "drew no applause."[62]

Spurred by the Asian financial crisis and the Battle of Seattle, elites and activists among the Resistant Globals have become more numerous and outspoken. More than sixty nonprofit organizations in the United States, for example, formed a coalition favoring "democratic, localized, ecologically sound alternatives to current practices and policies." Prior to the 1999 Seattle meeting on the WTO, some twenty of these NGOs, most of them in the environmental field, placed a series of three full-page advertisements in major U.S. newspapers highlighting a variety of dangers posed by globalization and especially the WTO, which was posited as "emerging as the world's first global government. . . . elected by no-one, it operates in secrecy, and its mandate is this: To undermine the constitutional rights of sovereign nations." The advertisement then proceeded to ask, "How could this happen? What can we do?"[63]

More recently, elites and activists among the Resistant Globals estab-

---

[61] See, for example, Soros, "The Capitalist Threat," pp. 45–58. For a severe critique of this theme in the article, see Robert J. Samuelson, "George Soros, Don't Give Up Your Day Job," *Washington Post*, March 5, 1997, p. A21. A subsequent and more elaborate statement of Soros's views can be found in his *George Soros on Globalization* (New York: PublicAffairs, 2002).

[62] Louis Uchitelle, "Rare Bird in Davos: Labor Chief Makes His Points," *New York Times*, February 5, 1998, p. D4.

[63] The quotations are from an advertisement headlined "Invisible Government," *New York Times*, November 29, 1999, p. A15. The first advertisement in the series, which covered two full pages and was headlined "Global Monoculture," can be found in the *New York Times*, November 15, 1999, pp. A8–A9. The second was titled "Globalization vs. Nature," *New York Times*, November 22, 1999, p. A15.

lished the World Social Forum (WSF), which is explicitly designed to counter the World Economic Forum and plans to hold annual meetings in Porto Alegre, Brazil, at the same time of the year as the Davos meetings of the WEF. Committed to providing "a space for building economic alternatives, exchanging experiences, and strengthening North/South alliances between NGOs, unions, and social movements," the first meeting of the WSF was held in 2001 and attended by some ten thousand participants.[64] A year later the second meeting of the WSF drew forty thousand people and was marked by more than a little contention. Indeed, "by the time this meeting concluded . . . it was clear that the refrain, 'Politics is local,' won out."[65]

Harsh criticisms of the IMF and the WTO are an especially persistent theme of those Resistant Globals who reject the dominant neoliberal assumptions of the global business community. They see the IMF's conditionalities as hurting the poor and favoring the wealthy, as part of the problem rather than as bases for solutions to the dislocations that periodically beset the different countries or regions. More than that, the IMF is viewed as having "awesome power," as "a surrogate government in financial matters . . . [that] is insinuated into the inner sanctums of nearly 75 developing country governments around the world—countries with a combined population of some 1.4 billion."[66]

Another way of framing the clash between Affirmative and Resistant Globals in the economic realm is to distinguish between "Separatists" who oppose globalization and the integration it fosters and "Integrationists" who champion globalization and favor free trade on a worldwide basis on the one hand, and between the "Safety-Netters" who want to protect the losers in the globalization process and the "Let-them-Eat-Cakers" who argue that the winners in the process should take all on the other hand.[67] Cast in terms of distant proximities, the Separatists favor the proximate over the distant, the Integrationists favor the distant over the proximate, the Safety-Netters favor both the distant and the proximate, and the Let-Them-Eat-Cakers favor neither the distant nor the proximate, preferring instead to let distant proximities unfold without any interference or regulation. Table 5.2 presents the matrix that results from the two pairs of polar opposites and in each cell offers current groups that exemplify the four poles of the debate.

A less elaborate conception of the conflict between Affirmative and

---

[64] http://www.forumsocialmundial.org.br.

[65] Simon Romero, "Brazil Forum More Local Than Worldly," *New York Times*, February 7, 2002, p. A9.

[66] Jeffrey Sachs, "The IMF and the Asian Flu," *The American Prospect*, No. 37 (March–April 1998), pp. 16–17.

[67] This formulation, including the labels, has been adapted from Thomas L. Friedman, "Roll Over Hawks and Doves," *New York Times*, February 2, 1997, Sec. 4, p. 15.

TABLE 5.2.
Alternative Perspectives on the Consequences of Economic Globalization

Let-Them-Eat-Cakers	
libertarians	republicans
Separatists_____**Integrationists**	
economic nationalists	social democrats
Safety-Netters	

Resistant Globals posits a dichotomous split between them by recourse to the global-local nexus:

> A new political scheme of opposed parties . . . is beginning to take form. This is essentially a two-party system, and it divides over the fundamental issue of community. One of these parties holds that community has no value, the other holds that it does. One is the party of the global economy; the other I would call simply the party of local community. The global party is large, though not populous, immensely powerful and wealthy, self-aware, purposeful and tightly organized. The community party is only now becoming aware of itself; it is widely scattered, highly diverse, small though potentially immense, weak though latently powerful, and poor though by no means without resources.[68]

For many Affirmative Globals, however, this dichotomy is oversimplified. They do not perceive their resistant counterparts as converging on a common outlook. On the contrary, only some of the protesters are seen as an antiglobalization faction opposed to capitalism or the lowering of trade barriers. Others are viewed as accepting that technology is shrinking the world, thus rendering globalization inevitable and leading them to support globalization if its excesses can be brought under control.[69] Still others are regarded as unsure of what they oppose or, at least, as ranged against different and often contradictory challenges. While some Affirmative Globals are not "sure how to even label" the protesters and settle for seeing them as "an organized network of troublemakers,"[70]

---

[68] Wendell Berry, "The New Politics of Community," *The Ecologist*, Vol. 29 (March/April 1999), pp. 229–30.

[69] For analyses that acknowledge not all Resistant Globals are opposed to all globalizing processes, see Edward Wong, "A Quiet Forum at Town Hall Opposes the East River Forum," *New York Times*, September 6, 2000, p. A13; Thomas L. Friedman, "Time for Globalization Protesters to Get Their Act Together," *International Herald Tribune*, July 21–22, 2001, p. 6; and Michael Hardt and Antonio Negri, "The New Faces in Genoa Want a Different Future," *International Herald Tribune*, July 25, 2001, p. 6.

[70] Romesh Ratnesar, "Chaos Incorporated," *Time*, July 23, 2001, pp. 17, 18.

others assert they "deserve credit for highlighting" serious problems even though their solutions are considered erroneous and misguided,[71] and still others perceive them as "mainly advertisements for the strength of the capitalist democracies that provoke them. These ardent young people, who plan their trips to these conferences on the Internet, carry cell phones and arrive by jet, often without having to stop at customs because of relaxed rules in the new Europe. They are symbols for the wonders of the very system they're so worked up about."[72]

However the diverse and divisive perspectives on globalization may be categorized, it seems clear that the series of protests initiated in Seattle by the Resistant Globals have registered with elites among the Affirmative Globals. The latter remain unwavering in their belief that "globalization is overwhelmingly, though not entirely, a good thing . . . a huge force for good"; and that while "driven not by human goodness but by the profit motive, [it] has done far more good for far more people than all the foreign aid and soft loans ever provided by well-intentioned governments and international agencies." At the same time such elites have come to recognize "just how serious a public relations problem now faces the global economy in which Davos Man flourishes."[73] Evidence of this recognition is plentiful. In the words of Caio Koch-Weser, a senior German economic official, "If we do not succeed in making clear to citizens that globalization is to their benefit, we run a big political risk. There's a feeling in the population that nobody's in charge. People are afraid of losing jobs to the whims of multinationals. We need to bring Wall Street to Main Street."[74] Even more telling, international financial institutions have begun to recognize the public relations problem. John Sweeney, for example, has attended every Davos meeting since he was snubbed there in 1997, and, more indicative, the WEF now "invites its enemies and critics to participate and mingle with the chief executives of the 1,000 companies whose dues and fees pay almost all of the forum's $37 million annual budget." At the 2000 meeting "some of the Seattle protesters got invitations and found that their street demonstrations added weight to their words at Davos."[75] Likewise, beginning with their 2000 annual meetings in Prague, the World Bank and the IMF have given "entry

[71] Fareed Zakaria, "Real Street Smarts for G-8 Protesters," *International Herald Tribune*, July 24, 2001, p. 7.

[72] Daniel Akst, "In Genoa's Noise, a Trumpet for Capitalism," *New York Times*, August 5, 2001, Sec. 3, p. 4.

[73] Paul Krugman, "The Magic Mountain," *New York Times*, January 23, 2000, Sec. 4, p. 15.

[74] Quoted in Roger Cohen, "Growing Up and Getting Practical since Seattle," *New York Times*, September 24, 2000, Sec. 4, p. 16.

[75] Louis Uchitelle, "From the Streets of Seattle to the Table at Davos," *New York Times*, January 30, 2000, Sec. 3, p. 4.

passes to some charity and watchdog groups so that they could attend the annual meetings, and the outreach seems to be working. Many protesters now call the two lending agencies potential friends or, at worst, ciphers." As a consequence of this greater responsiveness to their critics, "[t]he bank and the fund are, by the standards of huge bureaucracies, changing quickly. . . . [I]ncreasingly the protesters are aiming at moving targets."[76]

The World of Specialized Globals

But the economics of globalization are not the only dynamics that serve as the focus of elites with large scalar orientations and nonterritorial spatial perspectives. Myriad people in a variety of walks of life other than business are concerned about particular dimensions of the global scene. Many of the elites among the Specialized Globals are intellectuals, NGO leaders, foundation officials, and spokespersons for broad transnational social movements, while the nonelites include teachers, social workers, and others who see themselves as participants in one or another social movement. Taken together, the elites among these Globals have been viewed as forming a " 'faculty club culture.' Essentially, this is the internationalization of the Western intelligentsia, its values and ideologies. To put it graphically, if the 'Davos culture' tries to sell computer systems in India, the 'faculty club culture' tries to promote feminism or environmentalism there—a rather different agenda."[77]

Another analyst not only posits the Specialized Globals in broader terms by including non-Westerners but also implies that they share values that enable "an increasing number of scientists, academics, artists and other elites (and perhaps also a less privileged population) of widely different nationalities, languages, ethnicities and races to communicate more easily with each other than with others of their own ethnic or national background in the less globalized regions of their society."[78] Still another observer highlights even more emphatically the large degree to which the intellectuals among these Globals form an integrated, if not coordinated, culture:

> The global flow of information proceeds on many different technical and institutional levels, but on all levels the intellectuals are the ones who know most about one another across the frontiers, who keep in touch with one another,

[76] Joseph Kahn, "International Lenders' New Image: A Human Face," *New York Times*, September 26, 2000, p. A5. See also Joseph Kahn and Tim Weiner, "World Leaders Rethinking Strategy on Aid to Poor," *New York Times*, March 18, 2002, p. A3.

[77] Berger, "Four Faces of Global Culture," p. 25.

[78] Anthony King, "The Global, the Urban, and the World," in Anthony D. King (ed.), *Culture, Globalization and the World-System: Contemporary Conditions for the Representation of Identity* (Minneapolis: University of Minnesota Press, 1997), p. 152.

and who feel that they are one another's allies. . . . We may describe as trans-national those intellectuals who are at home in the cultures of other peoples as well as their own. They keep track of what is happening in various places. They have special ties to those countries where they have lived, they have friends all over the world, they hop across the sea to discuss something with their col-leagues; they fly to visit one another as easily as their counterparts two hundred years ago rode over to the next town to exchange ideas.[79]

This is not to suggest, however, that the Specialized Globals are a harmonious cluster of elites. They, too, experience fragmegrative dy-namics that derive from diverse values that divide them and that separate them from the Affirmative Globals. Conspicuous, for example, are the tensions between Western leaders and those of various indigenous move-ments who stress the need for cultural revitalization, or between Western feminists and Islamicists or the Vatican, or between environmentalists and developers among the business elite, or between leaders of Green-peace and other NGOs that support a resort to coercive force on behalf of their specialized goals and those elites who approve of the goals but abhor the means used. And perhaps "[a]t this time, the most visible con-flict is between the 'ecumenism of human rights,' carried out by a multi-tude of nongovernmental organizations, and the belief of the 'Davos Culture' that all good things, including human rights, will eventually re-sult from the global establishment of successful market economies."[80]

While many Specialized Globals, for all their differences, tend to find common cause when opportunities arise to take their objections into the streets—as happened during the Seattle protests against the WTO—for the most part they occupy a world of their own that is narrower than that in which Resistant Globals are active. It is a world that includes both elites and nonelites, some of whom may favor the ways in which global-ization impacts on their specialized concerns even as others remain firmly opposed to it and thereby sustain the dynamics of fragmegration. The difference between the Resistant and Specialized Globals is thus more than one of degree. It is the difference between single-issue and multi-issue orientations, as well as between singular opposition and mixed pro-and-con attitudes.

A Coordinated Opposition?

Given the many differences among Resistant and Specialized Globals (as well as among action-oriented Resistant and Exclusionary Locals), the question arises as to whether opposition to globalization has the poten-

[79] George Konrad, *Antipolitics* (New York: Harcourt Brace Jovanovich, 1984), pp. 208–9.
[80] Berger, "Four Faces of Global Culture," p. 26.

tial to become an enduring social movement. Yes, these groups' differences can be bridged during the brief period of protest marches. And yes, the protest marches appear to have become a regular occurrence whenever board meetings of the IMF, WTO, World Bank, or WEF are convened: the battle of Seattle in November 1999, for example, was followed by similar protests in Washington, D.C., in April 2000; Melbourne, Australia, in September 2000; and Prague, Czechoslovakia; Quebec City; and Genoa in subsequent months. But the question remains: Can the common cause achieved at these moments be sustained across time and thereby acquire the coherence that marks social movements? Can right-wing nationalists and left-wing union members come together on an enduring basis? Can otherwise opposed people be lumped together in a set of shared aspirations? Can the antiglobalization movement be summarized as "largely the well intentioned but ill informed being led around by the ill intentioned and well informed"?[81] And while this summary may be exaggerated, have the terrorist attacks on the United States so altered the climate of opinion that the antiglobalization coalition will feel obliged to alter its strategies and tactics and avoid protest marches susceptible to collapsing into violence?[82]

The answers depend on what is meant by a social movement. If it refers to an integrated and coordinated political force organized around shared values and concerns, then a negative answer seems appropriate. Those who join the protests do so for such a variety of unrelated reasons—from concerns about trade and the environment to animal rights and a host of other issues—that it can hardly be said they are unified around any common values other than a shared belief that globalization is a symbol of what they find objectionable in their lives.[83] Certainly, they are not held together in the same way that the goals of the more narrowly framed human rights, environmental, and nuclear disarmament movements foster internal cohesiveness. Indeed, the concept of a social movement is conspicuously absent from a lengthy inquiry into the various bases for opposition to globalization.[84]

On the other hand, if by a social movement is meant people with separate and diverse concerns who converge around common symbols,

---

[81] Thomas L. Friedman, quoted in Michael Kelly, "Globalization: No Pain, No Gain," *Washington Post*, April 25, 20001, p. A31.

[82] For cogent analyses of this question, see Leslie Wayne, "For Trade Protesters, 'Slower, Sadder Songs,'" *New York Times*, October 28, 2001, Sec. 3, p. 1; and John Micklethwait and Adrian Woolbridge, "Globalism under Siege," *Wall Street Journal*, November 9, 2001, p. A14.

[83] For an elaboration of this interpretation, see "Anti-capitalist Protests," pp. 85–87.

[84] See Robin Broad (ed.), *Global Backlash: Citizen Initiatives for a Just World Economy* (Lanham, Md.: Roman and Littlefield, 2002).

then the spate of protests that began in Seattle can be readily treated as a major social movement—an inchoate movement, to be sure, but none-theless a movement in the sense of galvanizing a lot of people into action at relevant moments in various parts of the world.[85] It is indicative, for example, that a brief survey of the letters to the editor of Australian news-papers following the Melbourne protest suggests that most of the marchers were not members of the lunatic fringe; rather, they were quite ordinary folk, ranging from young professionals to mothers accompanied by their children, from pensioners to trade union members, virtually all of whom were not so much against globalization as they were against cer-tain of its consequences. The Australian press described the occasion as "mobbed by thousands of anti-globalization demonstrators,"[86] but a more careful inquiry led to the conclusion that this characterization of the demonstrators was exaggerated, that people were "participating in the protest because they feel it's the only way of effectively expressing their concern: they feel isolated from government, powerless in the face of corporate interests and are cynical about the democratic process. As one letter-writer put it, 'Were the world leaders of WEF elected demo-cratically, the people planning to protest would happily turn up at the ballot box to express their concern for the environment and social justice in an economic context.' "[87]

In other words, in the absence of procedures that serve to democratize the world's economic institutions, the protest marches provoked by their board meetings seem destined to be part of the political landscape for a long time to come, drawing upon diverse people distressed by the uncer-tainties inherent in globalizing processes. That being the case, it matters little whether the periodic protests amount to a coordinated social move-ment. The varied interests and issues that attract people to march, along with the philosophical and ideological differences between the Resistant and Specialized Globals and their counterparts among the Resistant and Exclusionary Locals, are not so considerable as to prevent them from converging around a common symbol and converting their disparate concerns into shared activities that generate intentional micro inputs suf-ficient to maintain a meaningful campaign against the excesses of global-

---

[85] Incisive inquiries into the various segments of the nascent but still inchoate social movement can be found in Michael Edwards and John Gaventa (eds.), *Global Citizen Action* (Boulder, Colo.: Lynne Rienner, 2001).

[86] Virginia Marsh, "Protesters Mob Melbourne Summit," *Financial Times*, Septem-ber 11, 2000 (http://globalarchive.ft.com/globalarchive/articles.html?print=true&id=000911008169).

[87] I am grateful to Mark Beavis for an e-mail, dated September 8, 2000, containing this summary account of the letters to editors of the Australian press.

ization.[88] Indeed, activists among the Resistant Globals are inclined to contend that such a convergence is rapidly maturing: in the words of one of them, "All over the world, there are signs that this resistance is co-alescing. Activists from the political left and right, from North and South, rich and poor, peaceful and militant, are beginning to work together to oppose globalisation."[89]

Furthermore, as previously indicated, there are reasons to presume that the intentional micro inputs represented by the continuing protests are only the tip of the iceberg, that they reflect a much wider unease—unintentional micro inputs—that elites among the Affirmative Globals perceive and feel they cannot simply dismiss. Indeed, both the intentional and the unintentional micro inputs have already led to the modification of certain practices at the macro level: it is noteworthy, for example, that in early 1999, at Davos, the secretary-general of the United Nations warned international business leaders that "globalization might be more fragile than they realized" and proposed a Global Compact "based on nine key principles drawn from the Universal Declaration of Human Rights, the International Labor Organization's fundamental principles on rights at work, and the Rio Principles on environment and development."[90] Sensitive to the secretary-general's implicit warning about the adverse publicity inherent in the burgeoning protests against them, more than a few multinational corporations signed the Global Compact and, in doing so, agreed (1) to "become public advocates for the compact and its nine principles in the corporate mission statements, annual reports and similar venues"; (2) "At least once a year they will post on our [UN] web site examples of progress they have made, or lessons learned, in putting the principles into practice in their own corporate domains"; and (3) "They will join with the United Nations in partnership projects, either at the policy level (for instance, a dialogue on the role of corporations in zones of conflict) or at the operational level, such as helping African or South Asian villagers link up to the Internet, or strengthening small and medium-sized firms in developing countries."[91]

Of course, to modify the excesses of globalization is not to bring them

---

[88] For a cogent assessment that discerns a long-run potential in an antiglobalization movement, see Stephen J. Kobrin, "'Our Resistance Is as Global as Your Oppression': Multinational Corporations, the Protest Movement and the Future of Global Governance" (paper presented at the annual meeting of the International Studies Association, Chicago, February 2001).

[89] Helena Norberg-Hodge, "Turning the Globalization Tide," *The Ecologist*, Vol. 29 (May/June 1999), p. 200.

[90] Kofi A. Annan, "A Deal with Business to Support Universal Values," *International Herald Tribune*, July 26, 2000, p. 7.

[91] Ibid.

to a halt. Even assuming the Global Compact holds and is adhered to as it gains an ever greater number of signatories, and assuming that the sensitivities of Affirmative Globals lead to the introduction of other modifications of globalization's economic excesses—and the jury remains out on whether these assumptions will prove sound[92]—it remains questionable whether the antiglobalization movement will achieve the coherence necessary to redirect the course of globalization. In the first place, it is unlikely that the modifications will be sufficient to meet the multiplicity of demands of the Resistant and Specialized Globals and those of counterparts among the Resistant and Exclusionary Locals, thereby consolidating their diverse preoccupations into a unified social movement that can successfully press for additional modifications. Second, neither the intentional nor the unintentional micro inputs are likely to lead to the adoption by Affirmative Global elites of genuinely democratic procedures. Their acceptance of the Global Compact may result in greater transparency in the process of implementing the compact's principles, but in the words of the secretary-general of the International Chamber of Commerce, "Business would look askance at any suggestion involving external assessment of corporate performance, whether by special interest groups or by UN agencies."[93] A severe and worldwide economic recession might create the conditions for a unified social movement and a major reversal of the present fragmegrative balance, but such a reversal is unlikely to stem from the activities of Resistant or Specialized Globals. To repeat, they appear too divided among themselves to have a coherent impact on the present structures of the global economy. They may convene "counter-Davos conferences . . . to fight the idea that global free-market forces will inevitably triumph over government attempts to regulate, or that the elite who gather here [in Davos] have any claim to set the world economic agenda. But with companies represented here doing an estimated $4.5 trillion a year of business, [and with heads of states in attendance,] the opposition view can seem like a cry in the wilderness."[94]

In sum, many activists among the Specialized and Resistant Globals appear to have been sufficiently emboldened by the Battle of Seattle to hold protest rallies whenever the leaders of the world's financial institutions gather to frame policies, but in the absence of severe economic downturns, their ranks are not sufficiently coherent to generate policies

[92] For an early but upbeat appraisal of the Global Compact, see John Gerard Ruggie, "Taking Embedded Liberalism Global: The Corporate Connection" (keynote address at the "Workshop on Global Governance: Towards a New Grand Compromise," (Canadian Congress of the Social Sciences, Toronto, May 29, 2002).

[93] Maria Livanos Attaui, "Yes to Annan's 'Global Compact' If It Isn't a License to Meddle," *International Herald Tribune*, July 26, 2000, p. 7.

[94] Whitney, "Hobnobbing at Very High Levels," p. D1.

that meet their demands. The leaders of financial institutions have heard their demands, but to hear is not to heed, and the latter response is much more problematic. Severe downturns in the global economy, on the other hand, might well substantially enlarge the ranks of the Specialized and Resistant Globals and Locals, thus possibly altering the prevailing balance that favors neoliberal economic policies.[95]

As for the less broad, more coherent conception of a social movement composed of those in an issue area who, stimulated and mobilized by activists, band together on behalf of the issues it encompasses, the environmental movement is a case in point. The NGOs devoted to various environmental issues, for example, have formed alliances to exert pressure through disinvestment campaigns and shareholder resolutions against projects deemed harmful to the environment. In 2000 an alliance of Project Underground, Amazon Watch, and the Rainforest Action Network mounted seventy-five protests against Fidelity Investments, the largest shareholder in Occidental Petroleum, which was drilling in Colombia. When Fidelity dumped more than 60 percent of its Occidental holdings, the alliance switched its focus to pressure the company that then became the largest shareholder of Occidental Petroleum. Steve Kretzmann, an NGO consultant, said, "Anyone who doesn't see the power of this movement wasn't paying attention to Seattle last year."[96]

That the environmental movement should register successes is hardly surprising, given the energy of some of its activists, as the following account illustrates:

> With her backpack and duffle bag, she struggled aboard the aircraft, heading toward the cheaper seats in the rear. She inched past business travelers, who were settling in with drinks.
>
> Among them, she noted, were several World Bank staffers working on the deal she hoped to delay—the $3.7 billion Chad-Cameroon pipeline.
>
> Korinna Horta of Environmental Defense has become a frequent flier. With cell phone in hand, she travels from capital to capital, mobilizing opposition to projects she fears will damage the environment or people who have lived in harmony with it for centuries. . . .
>
> Ms. Horta learned about the proposed Chad-Cameroon pipeline from a Swiss human rights activist with contacts on the diplomatic circuit.[97]

In short, the picture is mixed insofar as the extent to which distant proximities have generated the evolution of social movements. On the

---

[95] A more extensive examination of these issues in undertaken in chapter 17.

[96] Quoted in Nancy Dunne, "NGOs Take to Tools of Globalization to Mobilise Resistance," *Financial Times*, February 21, 2001, p. 8.

[97] Ibid. For an extensive analysis of Specialized Globals who focus on environmental issues, see Mitchell Thomashow, *Ecological Identity: Becoming a Reflective Environmentalist* (Cambridge: M.I.T. Press, 1995).

large question of general opposition to globalization, the picture is murky and may not include an effective social movement. In narrower, more specialized issue areas, on the other hand, there are signs that nascent movements are maturing and becoming salient features of the world scene.

The World of Territorial Globals

To have thus far made little mention of public officials; but to have dichotomized the local-global nexus such that the level of the national state is downplayed is not to say that governmental leaders are peripheral to the dynamics of fragmegration. The inordinate complexities of the emergent epoch—the continuing privatization of economies; the widening porosity of traditional boundaries, the endless proliferation of organizations; and the mounting flow of people, ideas, networks, goods, currencies, and technologies across borders—may have diminished the extent to which state, provincial, city, or other territorial leaders can control the course of events, but they can still play key roles by seeking to offset or channel the repercussions of change and the continuity of their collectivities. Obviously, those who hold positions at every level of the political world are bound to be keenly aware that what is distant is also proximate and that thus they can be key players in the processes that mark the emergent epoch. Since most of the jurisdictions over which they preside are vulnerable to remote events cascading into their backyards, public officials are likely to think and act in terms of the territorial spaces for which they are responsible, with their scalar orientations being a consequence of whether those spaces are large or small. That is, a preponderance of the world's individuals who occupy or aspire to governmental positions are, by definition, Territorial Globals or Insular Locals, depending on whether their political responsibilities incline them to think and act with reference to worldwide developments that may circuitously cross into their jurisdiction's boundaries (the Territorial Globals) or only to those developments that may directly impact on the people of their community (the Insular Locals). This distinction is most conspicuous in terms of the difference between foreign policy officials who are ever sensitive to how developments anywhere in the world may feed back and shape their country's institutions and those officials who are responsible for a limited aspect of the domestic scene but recognize that it may be an aspect seriously affected by any repercussions that flow from distant events.

Put differently, public officials at all levels of politics are located at the vortex of fragmegration, at those points where the forces pressing for integration and those demanding fragmentation converge and confront each other, where a decision favoring one direction is likely to have negative consequences for the other direction. Thus officials are bound to be highly sensitive to fragmegrative dynamics; they are often caught up in them even as they try mightily to avoid them, knowing that in such situations they can only lose support when forced to choose between integrating and fragmenting alternatives. Virtually by definition, in short, fragmegrative circumstances confront governmental leaders with their worst nightmare, with mutually exclusive alternatives in which they either serve distant needs and negate close-at-hand wants or vice versa. Indeed, it can readily be asserted that fragmegrative situations lie at the very core of politics in the sense that they unmistakably reveal the priorities and philosophies of governance that public officials bring to their work.

Two recent situations provide a clear-cut insight into the ways in which fragmegrative dynamics sometimes overtake public officials despite their efforts to avoid them. One is the recent testing of nuclear devices by both India and Pakistan. In each case domestic pressures—unintentional as well as intentional micro inputs—in support of tests proved much greater than those deriving from the sanctions and opprobrium of the international community, with the result that officials of both countries carried out the tests despite any private reservations they may have had about the wisdom of doing so. Similarly, the decision to press for the adoption of the North American Free Trade Agreement by U.S. officials was seen as promoting open markets and serving the goals of neoliberal economic policies even as the officials acknowledged that there would be losers as well as winners among companies and workers at home. These two situations also illustrate that the handling of fragmegrative dynamics can vary greatly: in the first case domestic pressures prevailed,[98] while in the second their fragmenting domestic consequences were deemed less important by the White House than the integrative accomplishments to be gained through freer trade.

Of course, governmental leaders do not alone make up the ranks of the Territorial Globals. Their ranks may include heads of NGOs, labor unions, professional societies, chambers of commerce, and others whose responsibilities are geographically bounded.[99] Some Territorial Globals

[98] For an analysis of how domestic pressures prevailed in the tensions between India and Pakistan over nuclear proliferation, see James N. Rosenau and Mary Durfee, *Thinking Theory Thoroughly: Coherent Approaches to an Incoherent World*, 2nd ed. (Boulder, Colo.: Westview Press, 2000), pp. 104–11.

[99] In a limited sense even elites, activists, and ordinary people preoccupied with environmental issues could be regarded as Territorial Globals—limited in the sense that the integrity of particular places or, indeed, of the whole planet may be their central concern, an orientation that has been aptly labeled as "planetary topophila" by Daniel Deudney. See his "Global Village Sovereignty: Intergenerational Sovereign Publics, Federal-Republican Earth Constitutions, and Planetary Identities," in Karen Litfin (ed.), *The Greening of Sovereignty in World Politics* (Cambridge, Mass.: The MIT Press, 1998), p. 448.

may collaborate with Affirmative Globals, and others may work closely with Resistant Globals, but they engage in such interactions only to serve their territorially based interests. It is noteworthy, however, that as jurisdictional boundaries become more porous and spatiality more complex, so are both governmental and other leaders among the Territorial Globals likely to experience an expansion of their horizons to include "scapes" other than those linked to land.

While the ranks of Territorial Globals are diverse and substantial, it is perhaps useful to note that in the long run their numbers may be dwindling. Or at least it may be indicative that attrition is occurring among personnel in the diplomatic arm of the U.S. government, not least because the world of Affirmative Globals is luring them away and creating

> what experts say is a crippling problem at the State Department: talented diplomats are leaving for careers that they believe have more power and prestige in the new global economy. And college graduates who used to rush to take the Foreign Service exam no longer bother. The State Department . . . is finding it hard to adjust to an era in which financial markets pack more punch than a Washington-Moscow summit meeting. It is losing recruits to investment banks, dot.com companies and the Treasury and Commerce Departments, which have magnified their foreign policy roles. Some are turning to idealistic private organizations that work in risky environments abroad, a far cry from the days of the cold war, when the State Department was the only place to be.[100]

OVERLAPS AND SPILLOVERS

As the previous paragraph suggests yet again, taking a snapshot of individuals in a fragmegrated world can be misleading. If Territorial Globals are increasingly capable of expanding their horizons and revising their notions of geography's relevance, clearly an assessment of their activities at a single moment in time understates the ways in which they overlap with counterparts in other global worlds. If George Soros can publicly warn against the excesses of neoliberal economic policies even as he severely criticizes an Asian prime minister's proposal to ban currency trading,[101] plainly the distinctions set forth in figure 2.4 do not allow for possible ways in which the orientations of individuals can spill over the categorical lines drawn to differentiate among the several local and global worlds.

[100] Jane Perlez, "As Diplomacy Loses Luster, Young Stars Flee State Dept.," *New York Times*, September 5, 2000, p. A1. For an analysis that depicts a similar pattern among governmental scientists, see Katie Hafner, "Technology Boom Too Tempting for Many Government Scientists," *New York Times*, September 19, 2000, p. A1.

[101] John Ridding and James Kynge, "Soros Hits at Mahatir's Currency Trade Proposal," *Financial Times*, September 22, 1997, p. 1.

Indeed, conceivably some people can be oriented toward both local and global worlds within the same time frame. Possibly the foci of some Globals are not so preoccupying that they are unconcerned about developments in their own immediate communities. They may not be able to give much time and energy to local matters, but they may be sufficiently broad in their interests that on occasion their attention can be drawn to close-at-hand problems or opportunities. In the words of one observer, "[O]ur loyalty to humankind—so vast, so abstract, a unity—does *not* deprive us of the capacity to care for lives nearer by."[102] Contrariwise, possibly some Locals are not so narrow in their orientations as to ignore transnational developments even as such distant concerns are secondary to their involvement in nearby events and trends. It may even be that there is a Local and a Global in everyone today as the dynamics of fragmegration tug at us from both directions.

But the notation of ambiguous overlaps and spillovers should not be interpreted as a backing away from the multiworld formulation elaborated in this and the previous chapter. The several local and global worlds represent the central tendencies through which individual agents sustain fragmegrative processes in the emergent epoch. The ways in which they manage to balance any overlaps between the local and global worlds are explored in chapter 7, which undertakes to assess the sources of movement among the worlds. First, however, it is useful to take note of those persons whose thoughts and actions occur in such private worlds that they cannot be agents of fragmegration in any meaningful sense. They are either too passive or too alienated to be the subject of either snapshots or videos because they do not participate in any local or global world. They are the focus of the next chapter.

[102] Kwame Anthony Appiah, "Cosmopolitan Patriots," in Cheah and Robbins (eds.), *Cosmopolitics*, p. 95 (italics in the original).

CHAPTER SIX

Private Worlds

> We are in danger of becoming a people distinguished by what
> we consume, rather than what we believe. As more and more
> people tune out, our noblest beliefs and value systems begin to
> atrophy. Social and political dialogue is impoverished. The
> problems grow larger as the number of the truly committed
> grows smaller. The uncommitted seek the uncomplicated and
> become numb to the unconscionable.
>
> —Robert F. Erburu[1]

> The world is getting more and more out of reach of simple
> people who have only religion. And the more they depend on
> religion, which of course solves nothing, the more the world
> gets out of reach.
>
> —V. S. Naipaul[2]

EARLIER IT was noted that numerous dynamics of globalization have
made it extremely difficult for individuals to be insensitive to distant
proximities. The number of the "truly committed" may have shrunk, as
the first epigraph asserts, but the ranks of ordinary people in the various
local and global worlds remain huge and continue to expand. Yet, for
some individuals this sensitivity to the course of events is also a source of
discontent, a fear that the world is out of control and that it cannot
readily get back on track. And the more people feel they have lost control
over their lives, the more they distrust the leaders and institutions that
appear to be taking their communities in the wrong direction. Consequently, "the 90's is a world where people are searching for connections.
But there's a feeling of disconnection from all the old things people were
born feeling they were supposed to feel connected to, like the church,
God, institutions, school, and parental figures."[3] Indeed, to the extent
the sense of disconnection stems from the tensions inherent in distant
proximities, it is a world that seems "schizophrenic, calling for theories of

---

[1] "Commitments in Common," commencement address reproduced in *Transcript* (Los
Angeles: University of Southern California, June 4, 1990), p. 8.

[2] Quoted in Adam Shatz, "Literary Criticism," *New York Times Magazine*, October 28,
2001, p. 19.

[3] Amy M. Spindler, "Tracing the Look of Alienation," *New York Times*, March 24, 1998,
p. A25.

rootlessness, alienation, and psychological distance between individuals and groups on the one hand, and fantasies (or nightmares) of electronic propinquity on the other."[4]

To be sure, most people who feel disconnected have not been dissuaded from experiencing distant proximities, but some have either tuned out or become deeply alienated from any world other than their own private one. Consequently, although relatively few in number, there are people in every community who are so remote from the course of events anywhere that they are not occupants of any of the local or global worlds. Some of these are oblivious to what happens in any of the worlds, and others are purposeful in their remoteness, but all of them live in one or another private world and do not experience fragmegrative tensions. For them there is no nearness and no farness, but only daily routine, precedent, avoidance, or disdain. Events at neither the local nor the global level are of interest to them, either because prior developments have alienated them or because for any number of reasons they have never evolved community concerns of any sort. Since we are interested in movement among the worlds, these two groups can usefully be labeled the Alienated and the Passives,[5] both of which engage in behavior and adhere to perspectives that, despite their relative scarcity, help us explore what attracts people to and deters them from local or global involvement.

While the Passives consist mainly of people who have never been caught up in local or global affairs, a preponderance of the Alienated are likely to have moved among one or another of the local or global worlds at some prior time and then subsequently rejected all of them. For any number of reasons—such as cynicism about politics, disdain for the affairs of any community, or pessimism over humankind's ability to control either distant or close-at-hand developments—they have been led to opt out of the public arena. Indeed, the Alienated explicitly and self-consciously want no part of any distant proximity. They are intensely alienated rather than being routinely passive. They may know there are alternatives to alienation but have grounds for denying their viability. Being alienated, in other words, they are sufficiently engaged to return to a local or global world if changes occur in any of the stimuli (enumerated in chapter 3) that encourage their involvement in one or another community. As will be seen, it is an open question whether they are likely to return in large numbers. Given a worldwide decline in the respect for politicians, gov-

---

[4] Arjun Appadurai, *Modernity at Large: Cultural Dimensions of Globalization* (Minneapolis: University of Minnesota Press, 1996), p. 29.

[5] While there are other terms that capture the notion of alienation and passivity—such as *apathy, indifference, nonparticipation, disconnected,* and *apolitical*—these seem most appropriate as labels for those who do not live in any of the local or global worlds described in chapters 4 and 5.

ernments, the media, and other public institutions, it may well be that increasing numbers of people will enter the ranks of the Alienated by passing through the cones of fragmegration that set them apart from the local and global worlds (see figure 2.4).

Quite different attributes and likelihoods can be ascribed to the Passives. They have never consciously experienced any distant proximities. For diverse reasons the paths of their lives have not led to local or global concerns. In effect, the dynamics of fragmegration have passed them by—or at least this is the case until such time as either events in the external world intrude so rudely as to jolt them out of their passivity or their surroundings are wired and the words and pictures of communities invade their perceptual space and allow for a broadening of their concerns. As previously implied, one of the long-term impacts of the microelectronic revolution and the mobility upheaval may be a steady diminution in the ranks of the Passives.

But qualifications are in order. Two distinct groupings can be identified within both the Alienated and the Passives. In the former case it is helpful to differentiate between the Cynics, whose alienation is such that they refrain from engagement with any political world, and the Illegals, who are so self-conscious about their own alienation that they resort to illegal, even violent, behavior to express their contempt for the political mainstream that sustains localizing and globalizing processes. Similarly, in the case of the Passives, it is plausible to distinguish between the Tuned-Out Passives, who may be fully aware of their apathy but do not avail themselves of ample opportunities afforded by time, energy, and resources to locate themselves in a local or global world, and the Circumstantial Passives, whose daily conditions are such as to leave them no time, energy, or resources to care about anything beyond their daily efforts to maintain their subsistence. Their life situations are marked by a lack of education and a hand-to-mouth existence that compels them to focus so intensely on the daily needs of food, clothing, and shelter that no larger community is of relevance.

Of course, there is more than a little variety among those who populate the private worlds of the Alienated and the Passives. In both cases degrees of alienation and passivity can readily be discerned, but no attempt is made here to trace the various distinctions and shades of difference among either the Alienated or the Passives. Accordingly, by dichotomizing the degree of their alienation or apathy on the one hand and their relative self-consciousness about their location apart from the local and global worlds on the other, table 6.1 treats the distinctions among the four types as being mutually exclusive even as their presence in the same matrix indicates they share a remoteness from world affairs. The goal is to assess how the pushes and pulls of fragmegration may impact

TABLE 6.1.
Four Private Worlds

Relative Self-Consciousness of Their Own Alienation/Apathy	Relative Degree of Alienation/Apathy	
	Low	High
Low	Circumstantial Passives	Alienated Cynics
High	Tuned-Out Passives	Alienated Illegals

on those who are not oriented toward public arenas, whatever may be the degree of their disdain for or indifference to any of the local and global worlds.

Put differently, presumably persons in all the private worlds depicted in table 6.1 get unintentionally caught up in fragmegrative processes. They may prefer to have nothing to do with the mainstreams of political life, but more often than not their alienation or passivity results in unintentional micro inputs that contribute to the interaction of localizing and globalizing dynamics. As a consequence, as can be seen in table 6.2, the impact of the various fragmegrative dynamics is likely to be somewhat different in the several private worlds.

TWO ALIENATED WORLDS

The difference between cynicism that leads to disengagement and apathy on the one hand and to breaking the law and violence on the other is, of course, huge. But those who populate these two alienated worlds do have some tendencies in common. Both share a distaste for the institutions that constitute and sustain the local and global worlds. As a consequence, neither contributes social capital to any mainstream communities. Quite to the contrary, both groups are a drain on the worlds they physically inhabit: the Alienated Cynics through an abstention from politics that inhibits the generation of the support needed for effective authority, the Alienated Illegals through the resources that are required to offset their illegal conduct or the measures that are necessitated to prevent or minimize any damage that may result from their illicit or violent actions. Indeed, while the difference between deep cynicism and illegal opposition is usually considerable, in some instances the cynicism can become so intense as to foster a turn either toward a pattern of illegality or toward a pervasive and studied passivity. Cynicism, alienation, violence, and passivity, in other words, draw upon some common sources,

TABLE 6.2.
Interaction between Macro Dynamics and Agents in Four Private Worlds

| Macro Dynamics | Private Worlds | | | |
	Alienated Cynics	Alienated Illegals	Circumstantial Passives	Tuned-Out Passives
Skill revolution	sustains cynicism	facilitates doubt	minimal impact	minimal impact
Authority crises	ignored	encourage action	irrelevant	give pause
Bifurcation of global structures	irrelevant	highlights enemies	irrelevant	irrelevant
Organizational explosion	not experienced	fosters recruitment and coherence	irrelevant	minimal impact
Mobility upheaval	irrelevant	facilitates networking	irrelevant	minimal impact
Microelectronic technologies	reinforce cynicism	facilitate networking	minimal impact	reinforce passivity
Weakening of territoriality, states, and sovereignty	denied	strengthens cohesion of subversive groups	irrelevant	minimal impact
Globalization of national economies	reinforces cynicism	intensifies alienation; heightens impact of terrorism	increases the ranks of losers and widens the gap between them and winners	minimal impact

even though they are also sufficiently different in form to allow for the delineation of the separate worlds identified here.

The World of the Alienated Cynics

For a variety of reasons ranging from childhood experiences to adult disillusions, those who populate this world are marked by a profound distrust, a sense that the larger forces and organizations to which their well-being is linked are not reliable, that their pronouncements ought not be believed, and that their actions stem from unacknowledged and corrupt purposes. The lack of trust may be especially focused on a workplace or social institution, but such alienation is not ordinarily confined to particular issues. Rather, it tends to be enlarged and directed toward any authorities, including those quite removed from the original sources of distrust. Hence governments, media, corporations, and international agencies—to mention only some of the more conspicuous institutions with which people are linked—can become foci of alienation, even though their policies may not be directly experienced. Irrespective of the foci of their alienation, however, Alienated Cynics are keenly self-conscious of their disdain for the public arena. In its most extreme form their cynicism can become a way of life, a worldview that colors reactions to both the public and the private arenas in which people live and work, a set of behavioral predispositions that is pervaded with incentives to remain aloof from local and global processes. In effect, "cynicism is a reaction to and barrier against culturally induced and socially reinforced hopes that have been dashed."[6]

There is more than a little evidence that the cynical worldview is spreading on all continents, thereby generating deep concern about the capacity of communities to maintain, much less extend, the social capital they require to mobilize their resources and preserve their viability. In recent years this concern has escalated into a pervasive preoccupation among thoughtful observers with respect to the United States, Russia, China, and other major countries. In the United States and other Western countries observers fear that the spread of a cynical worldview portends nothing less than the decline of civil society, a decline that becomes ever more worrisome as the dynamics of globalization intensify and appear to threaten democratic institutions. In the developing world that is turning to free-market economic policies, the fear focuses on how an extensive self-centered stress on profits may foster a degree of selfishness that diffuses the cynical worldview and thereby inhibits, if it does not prevent, the evolution of democratic institutions.[7]

---

[6] Donald L. Kanter and Philip H. Mirvis, *The Cynical Americans: Living and Working in an Age of Discontent and Disillusion* (San Francisco: Jossey-Bass, 1989), p. 3.

[7] Whether the cynicism evolves in the Western or non-Western world, it is useful to note that "there are three ingredients in the development of the cynical outlook. One is the formulation of unrealistically high expectations, of oneself and/or other people, which generalize to expectations of society, institutions, authorities, and the future. A second is the experience of disappointment, in oneself and in others, and consequent feelings of frustration and defeat. Finally, there is disillusion, the sense of being let down or of letting oneself down and, more darkly, the sense of being deceived, betrayed, or used by others." Kanter and Mirvis, *The Cynical Americans*, p. 3.

The evidence for this concern is both diverse and controversial. Those most concerned about the West cite statistics on declining voter turnout, reduced associational activities, shrinking organizational memberships, and other indicators of a loss of social capital, as well as those expressive of increased private activities such as television viewing,[8] whereas those who worry about developing societies point to data indicative of flourishing black markets, increasing corruption, and the absence of a growing private sector committed to volunteerism.[9] Although the accuracy of such data may not be contested, their sufficiency and meaning are, with some observers contending that the patterns are not new, that comparable data for earlier centuries can be cited, and that it is wishful thinking to believe that social capital has ever been abundant anywhere. Others stress that Western societies continue to function with a fair degree of effectiveness, that widespread apathy can be a "virtue" (in the sense that an agitated public can undermine stability and democracy),[10] and that developing societies are going through processes of adjustment that are part and parcel of the history wherein democratic practices eventually evolve.[11] Viewed from a fragmegrative perspective, the deepening controversy over the nature of social capital and the meaning of relevant data can be seen as an acknowledgment of the large extent to which global and local dynamics are causally intertwined, a recognition that social capital at local levels can ebb and flow as dynamics at global levels unfold.

Nor is the concern about social capital confined to the impact of Alienated Cynics. As noted later, it also focuses on the consequences of widespread apathy and a possible growth in the ranks of the Tuned-Out Passives. For not only does pervasive passivity undermine the control ordinary people have over their own lives and open the way for authoritarian rule, but it is also viewed with concern because the more endemic passivity becomes in communities, the more it is subject to transformation into alienation. Passivity toward the local or global worlds can be said to evolve into alienation when the apathetic are required to act, or choose to act, and their actions express opposition to established norms

---

[8] Robert D. Putnam, *Bowling Alone: The Collapse and Revival of American Community* (New York: Simon and Schuster, 2000).

[9] Robert D. Kaplan, "The Coming Anarchy," *Atlantic Monthly*, February 1994, pp. 44–76.

[10] Tom DeLuca, *The Two Faces of Political Apathy* (Philadelphia: Temple University Press, 1995), Chap. 5.

[11] For inquiries that cast such processes in a historical and comparative context, see Francis Fukuyama, *Trust: The Social Virtues and the Creation of Prosperity* (New York: Free Press, 1995); and Robert D. Putnam, with Robert Leonardi and Raffaella Y. Nanetti, *Making Democracy Work: Civic Traditions in Modern Italy* (Princeton, N.J.: Princeton University Press, 1993).

legally (such as purposefully not voting or actively campaigning against the system), illegally (such as nonpayment of taxes), or violently (as is the case of suicide bombers or when impoverished masses are provoked to riot in the streets). In other words, while the line between alienation and passivity can be murky, basically it involves the difference between contempt and indifference, between opposition and quiescence.[12]

But alienation and cynicism are worlds apart from skepticism. Skeptics are likely to be found in any of the local or global worlds,[13] whereas the Alienated Cynics are by definition so alienated as to locate themselves outside the interplay of local and global dynamics. To be sure, the Alienated Cynics may also be profoundly skeptical of authorities, but not all—and perhaps not even many—skeptics are driven by cynicism. Rather, skeptics have

> a tendency to disbelieve but a willingness to be convinced . . . [a readiness to be] hard-nosed but open-minded, realistic in real time but ever mindful of timeless ideals. By contrast, cynics are closed-minded and disillusioned. They cast aspersions upon those they deal with and believe that people are self-centered and self-serving. America is sliding into widespread cynicism today. Some 43 percent of the American populace fit the profile of the cynic, who sees selfishness and fakery at the core of human nature.[14]

Likewise, anger is not an exclusive preserve of the Alienated Cynics. One does not have to be alienated to be angry with a particular official, policy, or situation. Indeed, an antigovernment mood that is often ac-

---

[12] To the extent that alienation turns into anger, moreover, it can become a "precursor to revolution." Susan J. Tolchin, *The Angry American: How Voter Rage Is Changing the Nation* (Boulder, Colo.: Westview Press, 1999), p. 45.

[13] For a discussion of how skepticism is inescapable and thus ever present in politics, see Aryeh Botwinick, *Scepticism and Political Participation* (Philadelphia: Temple University Press, 1990).

[14] Kanter and Mirvis, *The Cynical Americans*, p. 1. The calculation of the proportion of cynics in the United States was based on a four-point scale derived from the responses of a national probability sample consisting of 850 persons who chose among four alternatives (ranging from "strongly agree" to "strongly disagree") for each of eight questions that dealt with various dimensions of cynicism. In addition to the Cynics, the authors classified 41 percent as the Upbeat and 16 percent of the respondents as the Wary. Of course, their conception of cynicism is much broader than the one used here, so that their 41 percent figure is misleadingly high in the sense that it includes people in the various local and global worlds as well the Alienated Cynics. It should be noted, moreover, that the terrorist attack on the United States in 2001 may have served to diminish the degree of cynicism, that Americans may have been shocked into a greater appreciation of public institutions. See Robin Toner, "Now, Government Is the Solution, Not the Problem," *New York Times*, September 30, 2001, Sec. 4, p. 14; and John D. Donahue, "Is Government the Good Guy?" *New York Times*, December 13, 2001, p. A39.

companied by anger prevails in many countries,[15] and it can stiffen the stand of both Affirmative and Resistant Locals and Globals toward officials and policies. But anger can also serve as an integral part of political contestation and, as such, can be as much an expression of a body politic passing through a period of self-correction as an indicator of deep-seated and pervasive alienation. In short, the mistrust of public institutions that has accelerated in recent decades stems from diverse sources.

Whatever their level of anger and distrust, and no matter how unconcerned about distant proximities they may be, the Alienated Cynics often contribute, intentionally or otherwise, to the onset and persistence of fragmegration. Angry at the mainstream, suspicious that its leaders are manipulative and its publics thereby exploited, and unwilling or unable to accept information that might modify their sense of alienation, Alienated Cynics are likely to agitate the tensions at work in the local and global worlds. This is perhaps especially the case in the United States, where the "country's cynicism about politics is not the aged, mellow European variety. It is more like the outrage that turns away from its object because it feels helpless to take effective action."[16] Still, wherever it may be pervasive, the expression of cynicism is such that it will further roil the waters of controversy and make it more difficult for conciliators to bring disputing factions together in efforts to address problems. By their very nature the Cynics can foster doubts where none existed before, thereby adding to the polarization inherent in distant proximities.

To be sure, many Alienated Cynics may not give voice to their alienation, preferring instead to express their disdain for public affairs through withdrawal and isolation. Yet the more vocal among them are sufficiently numerous and persistent in loudly voicing their antagonism to render more complex and intractable the problems posed by fragmegrative processes. At the very least they constitute a large entry on the debit side of the ledger of social capital. In the words of two management specialists, their "corrosive attitude diminishes country and community and, in business, shrinks the fabric of organization life."[17]

The World of the Alienated Illegals

Although persons who enter this world share a disdain for legal orders and often a readiness to engage in violent acts, the differences among them are considerable. Some are money launderers; some are tax evaders; some are militia who engage in illegal acts to "guard" local interests.

---

[15] This is the main theme of Tolchin, *The Angry American*.

[16] Leonard Garment, "Perhaps Washington Needs a Shot Clock," *New York Times*, June 23, 1998, p. A25.

[17] Kanter and Mirvis, *The Cynical Americans*, p. 2.

Among those whose alienation involves a resort to violence, some are loners—like Theodore Kaczynski, the Unabomber, and Timothy McVeigh, who bombed and destroyed the Alfred P. Murrah Federal Building in Oklahoma City—while others are joiners and serve as the base for terrorist organizations such as Hamas in Palestine and Al Qaeda in Afghanistan. The illegal and violent actions of the loners are not consequential insofar as the interplay of localizing and globalizing dynamics is concerned, but those implemented by the joiners, being meticulously planned, well organized, and worldwide in scope, are profoundly fragmegrative, both when they succeed and when they fail. The actions of loners are not consequential in the sense that they tend to pose threats to individuals rather than to societies or communities. Joiners, on the other hand, form terrorist organizations that are a major preoccupation of publics and governments throughout the world, irrespective of whether their well-planned actions succeed or fail. The September 11, 2001, attacks on the World Trade Center and the Pentagon, along with the societal unity and counterterror actions they generated, are quintessential examples of successful fragmegration initiated by terrorists, just as are terrorist efforts that fail because they lead to fragmegration when regulations pertaining to civil liberties are stiffened in order to prevent their success.

Alienated Illegals are not conceived to be psychotics who simply thrill at taking lives. Rather, their actions are undertaken for explicit purposes, warped as these may seem from the perspective of those who reject behavior that exceeds what is considered morally and lawfully permissible. Some explicate the purposes and rationale for their actions at length; others do so briefly; and still others do so piecemeal, interview by interview or article by article. Yet, however they may articulate their goals, the Alienated Illegals are not lacking in convictions regarding what is wrong with the world and how it can be righted. In the case of Al Qaeda, the goals are cast in elaborate religious terms, a formulation that is alleged to have its roots in Islamic teachings but that for most Islamicists amounts to grave distortions even as they enumerate grievances against the West and American capitalism.[18] Indeed, it is such teachings, along with organizational skills, that enable terrorists to maintain their coherence across many countries and avoid police efforts to track them down. More than that, the distorted teachings underlie the effectiveness of their organizations and motivate them to frame and implement their horrific goals. In addition, their goals are so explicit that they readily and easily circulate among the various national components of their terrorist networks. They

---

[18] For an extended and excellent analysis of the history, goals, structure, and operations of Al Qaeda, see the series entitled "Holy Warriors," *New York Times*, January 14, 15, and 16, 2001.

do not need the sponsorship of a state to undertake their attacks. As an intelligence official in the Middle East put it, Osama bin Laden "is his own state, a global state."[19]

There is no need to add to all that has been written about terrorism since the attack on the United States, but a question that is relevant to the concerns of this book is whether the commitments and activities of Al Qaeda are likely to foster increases in the ranks of the Alienated Illegals or the Alienated Cynics, or possibly even those in the various local and global worlds. The scenes of angry, young Pakistanis marching in support of the attack suggest that the pool from which Alienated Illegals seek recruits may have been enlarged, that the success of the attack may have heightened the self-consciousness of some Alienated Cynics in the Middle East and elsewhere to their own alienation and thus encouraged a move from cynicism to terrorism. Or at least it seems likely that such a move may be more easily accomplished than was previously the case. A similar line of reasoning may also lead some Tuned-Out Passives in the region to join the ranks of Alienated Cynics. Contrariwise, as indicated by the pervasive sense of unity among publics throughout the West provoked by the terrorist attack, the televised pictures of the crumbling trade towers may have stimulated some Tuned-Out Passives in the West to become Resistant or Affirmative Globals. The September 11 tragedy may have changed the world in many ways, but one of the most important is likely to be its impact on the way individuals respond to the local-global nexus.

Can the same be said about the impact of the loners? Are their actions and statements likely to evoke shifts among the several worlds? Will an earlier trend toward decreases in the ranks of Allienated Illegals be reversed?[20] Negative answers to these questions would seem to be in order. To be sure, while the lengthy statement of Unabomber Theodore Kaczynski, in which he detailed what he conceived to be the evils of technology and the industrial revolution,[21] led to his undoing, it also contained, for all its flaws, an intellectual position that might well have resonated among some of the more seriously estranged Alienated Cynics and perhaps also among the more restless Tuned-Out Passives. In most cases, however, the actions of Alienated Illegals either are not accompanied by elaborate justification (Timothy McVeigh's explanation of why he bombed the Alfred P. Murrah Federal Building in Oklahoma City, for

[19] Quoted in Raymond Bonner, "Experts Doubt Iraq Had Role in Latest Terror Attack," *New York Times*, October 11, 2001, p. B7.

[20] For indicators of this trend, see "The Rise and Decline of the 'Patriots,'" *Intelligence Report*, No. 102 (summer 2001), pp. 6–38.

[21] The statement was reproduced in a supplement to the *Washington Post*, September 19, 1995, pp. 1–8.

example, was simple and succinct)[22] or their published justifications are so extreme, so pervaded with implausible conspiracy theories, as to be viewed by most people as absurd ranting. To argue, for example, that globalization is "TREASON" or that the two main political parties in the United States "are controlled by the David Rockefeller crowd—the global greedsters and world industrial overlords who love slave labor and big profits"[23] is to describe a world most Americans neither recognize nor can conjure up in their imaginations.[24]

Perhaps more so than the Alienated Cynics, whose cynicism tends to thrive on an intellectual understanding of what is wrong about mainstream goals and policies, the Alienated Illegals can be subdivided into elites and ordinary folk, into leaders and followers, with the latter normally lacking an elaborate grasp of why the world seems so deleterious. This hierarchical, often authoritarian structure of the Alienated Illegals is perhaps best illustrated by the militia groups in the United States or the skinheads in Germany. In both cases the leaders of the groups frame the issues, specify the threats, and articulate the conspiracies that lead the rank and file to follow them in their illegal or violent endeavors. Their worldview can thus be viewed as "functional and adaptive: It guides [how they] acclimate to culture, society, and workplace and relate to their peers, subordinates, and superiors."[25]

Two Passive Worlds

The line between alienation and passivity is not easily drawn at the point where the two come close to overlapping. Some Alienated Cynics are inclined to implement their cynicism by fully tuning out distant events, and some Tuned-Out Passives may be one pernicious situation away from turning to a cynical view of public affairs. Indeed, as indicated in the next chapter, it may well be that people fluctuate between these private worlds as circumstances and situations change. For the present, however, we

---

[22] http://cbsnews.com/now/story/0,1597,171231-412,00.shtml.

[23] The comments are those of Chuck Harder, a right-wing radio host in the United States whose programs are a combination of conspiratorial ideologies and populist rhetoric. Quoted in Mark Rupert, "Globalization and American Common Sense: Struggling to Make Sense of a Post-hegemonic World," *New Political Economy*, Vol. 2 (March 1997), p. 113.

[24] I am indebted to David Johnson for pointing out that I may be underestimating the imagination of Americans, that the popularity of *X-Files* and other programming on broadcast TV in the United States these days is awash with such ideas, that "'conspiracy' is the hottest form of action entertainment going."

[25] Kanter and Mirvis, *The Cynical Americans*, p. 3. For a cogent analysis of how "the lure of conspiracy theories . . . defines a common bond between Islamic and Western societies," see Erica Goode, "Finding Answers in Secret Plots," *New York Times*, March 10, 2002, Sec. 4, p. 3.

shall presume that passivity stems from apathy, self-preoccupation, bore-dom, and any of a number of sources other than cynicism and anger that lead some people to tune out—or never to tune in—to world affairs even though they have the time and resources to respond to distant prox-imities. As already noted, it is the availability of time and resources for participation in local or global issues that differentiates the Tuned-Out Passives from their Circumstantial counterparts. Both groups are marked by apathy, but the Circumstantial Passives are more easily understood in that their passivity derives from the burdens of surviving from day to day and thus having neither the time nor the resources to become involved in the public sphere. Despite this important difference, on the other hand, both groups also contribute, perhaps unwittingly on some occasions, to fragmegrative processes even as their orientations are also partly shaped by the processes.

The World of Tuned-Out Passives

It seems clear that most of the concern of thoughtful observers about people who eschew participation in either local or global worlds focuses on the Tuned-Out Passives. There is a sense that not much can be done about those who live in alienated private worlds other than containing their illegal actions. The sources of their alienation appear too personal, too closed to consider alternative perspectives, to be responsive to ap-peals to return to the mainstream. But the apolitical orientations of Tuned-Out Passives seem puzzling and worrisome precisely because, other things being equal, these individuals ought not be immune to ap-peals that seek to mobilize their involvement in distant proximities. If their passivity springs from mistrust of the public arena, how to generate bases for a resurgence of trust? If it stems from a sense that they have lost control over their own destinies, how to restore confidence in their abil-ity to influence the course of events? If it springs from a self-centered preoccupation with consumption and money, how to develop a civil soci-ety that increases concern for the welfare of others? These are the ques-tions that concern increasing numbers of analysts who fear the decline of civil society and the breakdown of societal ties.

The literature expressing such concerns seems to be expanding expo-nentially, enlarged by skepticism in Europe about further integration,[26] as well as by a concern about the orientations of persons in the former Soviet Union and other parts of the world where corrupt and authori-tarian rule is fueling malaise and a sense that the individual citizen can do

[26] Barry James, "The EU Poll Finds Public Skeptical and Indifferent," *International Her-ald Tribune*, July 20, 2001, p. 1.

nothing to exercise any control over the course of events. As implied earlier, it is also a controversial literature insofar as the United States is concerned, with some analysts interpreting findings on patterns of citizen affiliation as indicative of a decline in civil society,[27] while others generate alternative data and interpret the patterns in a much less apprehensive way.[28] Whatever the proper explanation, the question remains as to why the ranks of the Tuned-Out Passives in the United States—which is not founded on authoritarian rule and where corruption is considerably less widespread than in countries that have yet to develop fully a system ruled by law—are seemingly so conspicuous. With a skill revolution still accelerating, how can—to cite again from the chapter's first epigraph—"the number of the truly committed grows smaller" even as "the uncommitted seek the uncomplicated and become numb to the unconscionable"? The answers are complex and need not detain us for long,[29] inasmuch as our concern focuses less on the sources of apathy and more on its fragmegrative consequences. Suffice it to note that apathy has been heightened partly by a mistrust of politicians and their world that has been mushrooming in the United States for several decades, spurred by a series of such high-level deceptions as the Gulf of Tonkin incident, Watergate, and Irangate,[30] partly by the ascendancy of a liberal economic philosophy that has led to an increased preoccupation with personal wealth at the expense of community orientations, partly by the advent of postmaterial values that embrace criticism of all authority,[31] and partly by changing standards of reporting on the part of the mass media, all of which have reduced people's trust in government and stimulated apathy toward public affairs.

In other words, it is misleading to imply that the failure of political

[27] Robert D. Putnam, "Tuning In, Tuning Out: The Strange Disappearance of Social Capital in America," *P.S.: Political Science and Politics*, Vol. 28 (December 1995), pp. 1–20; and Alan Wolfe, "Is Civil Society Obsolete?" *Brookings Review*, Vol. 15 (fall 1997), pp. 9–12.

[28] Everett C. Ladd, "The Data Just Don't Show Erosion of America's 'Social Capital,'" *Public Perspective*, Vol. 7 (June/July, 1996), pp. 5–22; and Nicholas Lehmann, "Kicking in Groups: Alleged Decline of America's Communal Capital," *Atlantic Monthly*, April 1996, pp. 22–27.

[29] For efforts to comprehend the scope and explain the underpinnings of political disengagement by citizens, especially in the United States, see Symposium, "Civil Society," *Brookings Review*, Vol. 15 (fall 1997), 2–41; as well as the citations by Dionne, Fukuyama, Inglehart, Kanter and Mirvis, Ladd, Lehmann, Nye, and Putnam in this chapter.

[30] For a historical overview of such events, see E. J. Dionne Jr., *Why Americans Hate Politics* (New York: Simon and Schuster, 1991).

[31] Ronald Inglehart, "Postmaterialist Values and the Erosion of Institutional Authority," in Joseph S. Nye Jr., Philip D. Zelikow, and David C. King (eds.), *Why People Don't Trust Government* (Cambridge, Mass.: Harvard University Press, 1997), pp. 217–36.

leaders to live up to the trust placed in them is the only, or even the primary, reason why some people tune out the political world. Socio-economic changes have also induced civic disengagement. Recent trans-formations in such institutions as marriage, family, and work have fos-tered new patterns that tend to facilitate tuning out public affairs.[32] For example, with husbands and wives both needing to work, or with women no longer being content in the role of housewife, two-career marriages may leave little time for following public affairs. No less important, it seems likely that in some cases people have redirected their activist im-pulses away from the political to the social world, away from participating in the work of political parties to involving themselves in a variety of forms of volunteer activities, away from a concern about political issues to an interest in church or community affairs.[33] In effect, "social activ-ism may be increasing as political activism declines,"[34] a pattern that, if pervasive, could have substantial consequences for the processes of frag-megration in that it signifies a potential for a wider range of public reac-tions to globalizing dynamics that affect cultural, religious, and societal institutions.[35]

And if this pattern is pervasive, it suggests that some Tuned-Out Pas-sives have many characteristics in common with the Insular Locals dis-cussed in chapter 4. But there is an important difference between them. The latter are concerned about political issues that may arise in their community, whereas Tuned-Out Passives turn to charitable work and other forms of nonpolitical social activism while remaining aloof from matters that require political involvement. Developments that affect the well-being of the community are meaningful to Insular Locals, but the Tuned-Out Passives, having disengaged from public affairs, could not care less about such developments. To be sure, the border between these two groups may sometimes be thin and ambiguous—especially when the social activism encompasses public issues around which social movements have formed—but the difference is quite relevant when it comes to trac-

[32] For an incisive discussion of the possible impact of lifestyle issues, see Robert D. Put-nam and Steven Yonish, "New Evidence on Trends in American Social Capital and Civic Engagement: Are We Really 'Bowling Alone?'" (unpublished manuscript, 1998).

[33] It is noteworthy, for example, that a national telephone survey of eight hundred college students in the United States found that 85 percent preferred community volunteerism to political engagement as a better way to solve important issues facing their communities and that 60 percent preferred community volunteerism to political engagement as a better way to solve important issues facing the country. Institute of Politics, Harvard University, "Atti-tudes toward Politics and Public Service: A National Survey of College Undergraduates" (http://ksgwww.harvard.edu/~iop/findings.html), September 12, 2000, pp. 6–7.

[34] E. J. Dionne Jr., "Why Civil Society? Why Now?" *Brookings Review*, Vol. 15 (fall 1997), p. 6.

[35] This potential is explored further in chapters 7, 8, and 10.

ing (in part III) macro fragmegrative processes and (in chapter 7) the vulnerability of each group to the dynamics of change.

The World of Circumstantial Passives

Although the number of people in the world below the poverty line is substantial, they are a matter of concern because of their circumstances rather than their passivity.[36] It is assumed that many of them would become involved in distant proximities if they did not have to spend their days and nights eking out a living under dire conditions. Observers worry about the Alienated Cynics and the Tuned-Out Passives because of the losses in social capital they represent, but the situation of the Circumstantial Passives is distressing because the conditions of their lives are so horrendous and unacceptable, so increasingly removed from distant developments (as this chapter's second epigraph poignantly notes). Hence the Circumstantial Passives are the focus of programs to alleviate their plight rather than to activate their involvement in public affairs. Those who preside over such programs tend to assume that an improvement in the situation of Circumstantial Passives would lead to their becoming more conscious of roles they might play in the distant proximities in which they and their communities are caught up. Alternatively, if their plight worsens as a consequence of external events—such as was the case for numerous Circumstantial Passives in Indonesia and Argentina when their countries' economies collapsed—many in their ranks are likely to be stirred by the changes to forgo their passivity and resort to action on the streets as Resistant Locals.

While it is difficult to estimate the number of Circumstantial Passives, in all probability they are not especially numerous. Their lives may be fully devoted to feeding, clothing, and housing themselves, but as previously noted, in a shrinking world marked by global television, it is not easy to be oblivious to the course of events. It is indicative, for example, that often the poorest of urban families seek to acquire a television set before a refrigerator or any other convenience, thus enhancing their ability to maintain a modicum of contact with the local and global worlds in which their lives are ensconced. In the case of poor peasants, moreover, it is all too easy to exaggerate the extent to which they are cut off from the worlds around them; or at least there is evidence that their plight is such as to foster sensitivity to the local worlds in which they are situated: systematic data on rural peasants in Central America, for example, suggest that "[l]iving on the edge of disaster makes peasants constantly

---

[36] Cf. Mary Durfee and James N. Rosenau, "Playing Catch-Up: IR Theory and Poverty," *Millennium*, Vol. 25, No. 3 (1996), pp. 521–45.

aware of their own vulnerability and of the extent to which they depend on community support for survival. This reality makes individual and community interests blend and become one and the same. The individual depends on the community for protection from disaster, but the community support system depends equally on individual input in order to survive."[37]

It may be, in short, that the ranks of the Circumstantial Passives are not very extensive, that they are more a theoretical possibility than a reality. Tuned-Out Passives and the two Alienated groups are likely to be sufficiently numerous to contribute noticeably to the dynamics of fragmegration, but for qualitative as well as quantitative reasons, the contribution of the Circumstantial Passives is likely to be minimal.

CONCLUSION

It is useful to recall that the separate analyses of different kinds of Passive or Alienated citizens in this chapter—as well as the different types of Locals and Globals in the previous two chapters—amount to snapshots captured at a moment in time. Clearly, holding everything else constant in this fashion can be highly misleading. Most notably, some people move from one type to another as circumstances change and provide incentives to shift orientations. Indeed, because such movement is possible, some people can occupy different worlds on the same day, depending on the stimuli from external events that may be operative on that day. Thus to repeat yet again, the typology developed in this and the previous two chapters is a static picture of micro actors who participate in fragmegrative processes. The next two chapters are devoted to identifying the conditions under which internal or external changes can move people among the several worlds, thereby intensifying, diminishing, or otherwise sustaining the interaction of localizing and globalizing dynamics.

[37] Leslie Anderson, *The Political Ecology of the Modern Peasant: Calculation and Community* (Baltimore: Johns Hopkins University Press, 1994), p. 3.

CHAPTER SEVEN

Movement among Twelve Worlds

> All of us are, willy-nilly, by design or by default, on the move.
> We are on the move even if, physically, we stay put: immobility
> is not a realistic option in a world of permanent change.
>
> —Zygmunt Bauman[1]

> [T]he urgency of the problem of structure and agency is . . .
> one which imposes itself on . . . every human being. For it is
> part and parcel of daily experience to feel both free and
> enchained, capable of shaping our own future and yet
> confronted by towering, seemingly impersonal constraints.
> Those whose reflection leads them to reject the grandiose
> delusion of being puppet-masters but also to resist the supine
> conclusion that they are mere marionettes then have the . . .
> task of reconciling this experiential bivalance, and must do so if
> their moral choice is not to become inert or their "political
> action" ineffectual.
>
> —Margaret S. Archer[2]

HAVING FRAMED a picture of people in fixed positions in relation to their distant proximities, now we need to relax the presumption of constancy and allow for video images, for how individuals may shift—or decide not to shift—their position with respect to the dynamics of fragmegration. The previous three chapters identify those who populate four local, four global, and four private worlds. The abandonment of this presumption of constancy allows for the theoretical possibility of 132 changes from one of the worlds to any of the other eleven.[3]

As the epigraphs imply, the present era is not only one in which large numbers of people are vulnerable to distant proximities that encourage

---

[1] *Globalization: The Human Consequences* (New York: Columbia University Press, 1998), p. 2.

[2] *Culture and Agency: The Place of Culture in Social Theory*, rev. ed. (Cambridge: Cambridge University Press, 1996), p. xii.

[3] An initial assessment of the probability of the 132 shifts occurring resulted in 11 considered as likely to happen if circumstances are conducive to change, 57 viewed as plausible if the circumstances were especially jolting, 51 as unlikely under any circumstances, and 13 as logically improbable. Such assessments, however, seem too crude and unwieldy to present here.

movement among the several worlds; it also impels them to choose how to articulate their micro orientations in terms of macro structures. Unlikely, implausible, and difficult as many of the 132 shifts may be, the skill revolution, organizational explosion, mobility upheaval, and other dynamics of fragmegration outlined in chapter 3 are often sufficiently powerful to overcome the statics of continuity. Responsive to societal and global changes, people at all levels of community tend to be more restless than content, more eager to stay ahead of the curve than fall behind. Consequently, as the capacities and impulses of people to shoulder multiple identities expand, the twelve worlds are sites of continual fluctuation.

The purpose of this chapter is to assess these fluctuations or, more accurately, to trace various sources of movement among the several worlds. Often the sources interactively combine to constrain change, but here we focus on four sources that, taken together, account for much of both the constancies and the changes that underlie what might be called the psychology of fragmegration:[4] that is, movement among the worlds depends on the challenges to the orientations and worldviews of people generated by the circumstances of their lives, as well as by the salience they attach to territory, issues, and identity. In assessing these four dynamics, hopefully we will begin to meet the "urgent need for new conceptualizations and representations of spatial scale to grasp these sites of simultaneous globalization and reterritorialization."[5]

CHANGE AND CONTINUITY

Movement among the worlds can result from attitude changes induced by the intensification of issues without corresponding alterations in a person's roles or identities, or it can stem from the occupancy of new roles, from the evolution of new identities, or from all these sources. Except when issue intensification is involved, none of these changes is likely to occur abruptly. Most people are deeply ensconced in long-standing ways of thinking and acting that tend to be habitual and continuously reinforcing. People are normally comfortable in their roles, identities, and the attitudes that support their location in a particular world. It is a comfort marked by inertia, by an inclination to sustain continuity in their lives.

---

[4] James H. Liu and James N. Rosenau, "The Psychology of Fragmegration: On the Uses of a Simultaneity of Consciousness in the 'New World Order'" (paper presented at the Third Conference of the Asian Association of Social Psychology, Taipei, Taiwan: August 4–7, 1999).

[5] Neil Brunner, "Global Cities, Glocal States: Global City Formation and State Territorial Restructuring in Contemporary Europe," *Review of International Political Economy*, Vol. 5 (spring 1998), p. 27.

Yet whenever a remote situation is discrepant with close-at-hand necessities, which is the case for numerous distant proximities, anxiety and ambivalence are likely to arise. Such discrepancies can give rise to considerable anguish and soul-searching, as none of the worlds are easily abandoned and none of the shifts among them, even the most logical and likely, are easily made.

Nor are any of the shifts necessarily enduring. As circumstances vary, so may people, and it may well be that some individuals are able to overcome inertia and are thus endlessly in motion among the several worlds. Conceivably, too, some persons live in a global world on particular issues but shift to a local world on other issues. In short, to note specific changes among the worlds does not begin to convey the degree to which such shifts may be wrenching, as may also be the case when people ponder the desirability of changing and conclude they ought not do so.

While some conditions can encourage some individuals to alter their outlook and lead them to shift readily from one of the twelve worlds to another, exceptionally dire circumstances may be required to induce altered orientations on the part of many people. If the intensity of fragmegration accelerates dramatically or rapidly enough to break down pervasive resistance to change, the inertia and habits that sustain continuity may give way to new or revised orientations toward the several worlds. Severe economic downturns caused by distant currency crises or huge refugee inflows caused by distant wars and poverty are illustrative of the conditions under which the implausible and the unlikely become the probable. Under such extreme circumstances it seems likely that the dynamics of change will, on balance, predominate over those of continuity as the dynamics of fragmegration quicken and people become increasingly aware of their vulnerability to distant events and trends that once seemed too remote to be of consequence. Most of the movement will then be toward new local or global worlds as people are induced for diverse reasons to appreciate, or at least to accept, the pervasiveness of distant proximities.

To refer to the psychology of fragmegration, however, is not to highlight the personality traits that differentiate individuals. On the contrary, people occupy one or another of the twelve worlds and shift among them largely on the basis of their positions in society or their role in organizations and their psychological reactions to how these may be affected by the unfolding world scene. To be sure, personality traits might predispose a person to react in particular ways to fragmegrative dynamics, but such reactions are filtered through the circumstances, positions, and roles of his or her life rather than stemming from some quintessential personal attribute. As one observer puts it, "Who among us would not become an

Affirmative Global if someone gave us a Lear Jet, a million-dollar expense account, and a multinational corporation to run?"[6]

Life Circumstances

One obvious determinant of how people respond to the world around them is their life circumstances. Whether they remain in one of the twelve worlds or move to a new one is either stimulated or restrained by the cultural, generational, educational, occupational, financial, skill level, and numerous other attributes that derive from their situations at any moment in time. Clearly, for example, their experience of the near and the far is shaped by their families, schooling, and jobs, as well as by the course of events at home and abroad. One's parents or school may have fostered a sense of the world as offering opportunities to be seized or as presenting hostile forces to be repelled. Thus some people are inclined to volunteer for humanitarian work in distant places, while others grow up distrustful of distant unknowns and keep close to home. Similarly, the orientations of individuals toward their immediate community and toward the world at large tend to be circumscribed by their socioeconomic statuses. Because exposure to distant events is likely to be greater the more wealth and education people have, it seems probable that in most societies these traits will be among those that lead to occupancy in one of the four global worlds.[7] (In inward-looking societies with cultures that tend to view the rest of the world with disdain, this correlation is unlikely to prevail.)

This is not to imply the absence of diversity among those who occupy the same world. The greater exposure to distant proximities of those in a global world is likely to stem from a variety of occupations—those mid-level business executives, entertainers, academics, and officials whose responsibilities require a familiarity with situations abroad. Some recent converts to a global world may even remain tied in important ways to their local origins, but through education and occupational mobility their horizons are broadened beyond their home communities.

In many instances, moreover, Affirmative and Specialized Globals are likely to be young—in their late twenties or thirties—inasmuch as many of their entry-level jobs in business, law, information services, engineer-

---

[6] James H. Liu, personal communication, November 3, 1998.

[7] For a discussion of five additional types of "structural conditions in everyday life [that] promote . . . world-citizen engagement," see John Boli, Thomas A. Loya, and Teresa Loftin, "National Participation in World-Polity Organization," in John Boli and George M. Thomas (eds.), *Constructing World Culture: International Governmental Organizations since 1875* (Stanford, Calif.: Stanford University Press, 1999), pp. 74–75.

ing, and government encompass responsibilities with global dimensions. Indeed, many of these Globals (though by no means all) become less and less likely to shift to different worlds as they progress up their occupational ladders. In contrast, individuals in one or another local world, being less occupationally mobile, are likely to be somewhat older than their global counterparts and less likely to have jobs that involve a multiplicity of direct contacts outside their local community. At the same time, there is no lack of diversity among the Locals. They, too, engage in a variety of pursuits in various walks of life.

Generational differences are another dimension of life's circumstances that can powerfully affect which local or global world a person occupies and his or her openness to moving to another world. In all likelihood, for example, those who grew up as members of what is called "Generation X" under the influence of global television, American movies, and computer networks are more sensitive to global developments than older generations whose youth was not so subject to electronic-delivered messages from around the world. Indeed, it could be argued that educated young adults who grew up, say, in New York City and Beijing are more likely to be located in the same world than are their elders in the United States and China. Or consider Cuban exiles in Miami. The generational differences between those who joined the Cuban American National Foundation when Castro came to power more than four decades ago and those who recently joined led to a philosophical rift that resulted in the resignation of two dozen of its board members on the grounds that the organization had strayed from its goals and softened its line on Cuban issues.[8]

There is no reason to presume that random clusters of those in any of the several worlds have enough in common to form coordinated political movements. They tend to be differentiated in their reactions to the dynamics of globalization and the issues thereby generated, but within each world divisions along national, religious, ethnic, generational, and occupational lines are so extensive as to preclude their mobilization on behalf of particular policies. Accordingly, while the twelve-world formulation facilitates understanding of the attitudes and behavior of individuals, its utility in clarifying the collective attitudes and behavior of groups and organizations is best saved for the macro chapters of part III.

While the inertia of daily routines can constrain movement among the worlds, life's circumstances also provide numerous inducements to change. In an age of fragmegration, with remote developments seeming ever more close-at-hand, with substantial increases in education and skill levels, and with imaginations unleashed by global media and the mobility

[8] Dana Canedy, "Cuban Eile Group Fractured as Hard-Liners Quit Board," *New York Times*, August 8, 2001, p. A1.

upheaval, the tendency to move away from local and toward global orientations derives from more than occupational aspirations. Even though they may not have the income or job-supported obligations to travel extensively, the horizons for those in local worlds can also undergo considerable expansion. These individuals' jobs may be improved or jeopardized by shifting patterns of international trade, their investments may be vulnerable to the fluctuation of foreign currencies, their children may study abroad or have friends who do, their access to global television and the Internet may provoke a concern for distant situations, and so on across a wide range of activities that can bring remote developments closer to home.

Of course, more than one reaction to the way the world impinges is possible among those with local orientations. What some see as opportunities opened up by broadened horizons, others may view as sufficiently threatening to intensify their attachments to one or another local world. The debate over the "Fast Track" legislation in the United States is instructive in this regard. In addition to the deep cleavages it revealed among the various Globals, the Fast Track divided the Affirmative Locals on the one hand from the Resistant and Exclusionary Locals on the other. While the former perceived a host of benefits stemming from lowered trade barriers, the latter feared their jobs might be lost to cheaper foreign labor or superior products. As will be seen, however, such divisions within the local worlds may not be enduring.

Life's circumstances can also stimulate shifts to new worlds as a result of promotions in an organization or of movement into new roles induced by fragmegrative dynamics. A clear-cut example of the latter kind of shift is provided by the aforementioned José Bové, who moved from being a Resistant Local to a Resistant Global as a result of becoming a national hero in France after leading an attack on a McDonald's restaurant. Before the attack he "was a local activist and union official living in a small stone farm tucked in the craggy hills of the Larzac region. His activism involved local issues, like opposing use of nearby land for an army base. Nowadays, Mr. Bové . . . trots the globe. He said he would be in Bangalore, India, at the end of the month to take part in a protest against genetically modified grain."[9]

The Salience of Territory

To refer to territory is to suggest several dimensions of geography and, in some instances, human relationships. Governments seek to protect their

[9] Suzanne Daley, "French Farmer Is Sentenced to Jail for Attack on McDonald's," *New York Times*, September 14, 2000, p. A13.

airspaces and territorial waters; business firms divide their sales staffs into territorial jurisdictions; friends, enemies, and families often speak of delineating or staking out their territories in relation to each other. For the most part, however, it is land that the image of territory calls to mind—land where one's ancestors dwelt, soil where one's forebears are buried, terrain that one's compatriots fought to defend, buildings in which one grew up or worked, and so on across a wide range of concrete spaces and structures.

Historic and deeply rooted as such attachments have been, the emergent epoch of fragmegration has witnessed a decline in the salience of this form of territory—what might be called a process of "deterritorialization." With satellite dishes allowing pictures to ignore airspaces easily, with the Internet enabling messages to bypass borders readily, with computer linkups facilitating the swift, unhindered transfer of money around the world, with jet aircraft making it possible for people to move speedily across boundaries, the conception of territory as a bounded land mass is undergoing diminution and revision as new spatial entities—such as off-shore banks, global factories, ethnic diaspora, and transnational organizations—evolve that cannot be linked to a singular geographic locale and that enable people to overcome the obstacles to movement among the twelve worlds.

In short, just as globalization has fostered a proliferation of identities, so have the concepts of territory and territoriality taken on a multitude of new meanings, thereby further intensifying and confounding the dynamics of fragmegration. It is not easy to relax one's notion of landscapes and expand one's understanding to include ethnoscapes, ideoscapes, technoscapes, mediascapes, and financescapes as well.[10] Such "scapes" are increasingly pervading our horizons, but for older generations accustomed to thinking only in terms of landscapes, the diversity of scapes in the emergent epoch is likely to be puzzling and disorienting as they ponder their territorial ties.

Needless to say, the processes of deterritorialization have had differential consequences for the identities people hold dear. They have encouraged those in global worlds to link themselves to organizations, groups, and professions that have little connection to land masses, whereas the very same processes have tended to reinforce the sensitivities of those in local worlds to the neighborhoods, communities, or nations they consider to be their territorial homelands. Thus, whereas the former have experienced a lessening of the salience of their historic links to territory

---

[10] For an extended notion of the various types of scapes, see Arjun Appadurai, *Modernity at Large: Cultural Dimensions of Globalization* (Minneapolis: University of Minnesota Press, 1996).

and, instead, have evolved business alliances, social movements, and a host of other transborder networks, the latter are inclined to experience deterritorializing processes as threatening and, accordingly, to tighten their most salient land-based ties. For them "territory is more than just a physical and measurable entity. It is also something of the mind because people impute meaning to and *gain meaning* from territory. Indeed, many people fully believe in the landscape of 'their' territory as a living entity that is filled with meaning."[11]

In some cases, such as Kosovo, these tightened ties to land have led to a virulent form of localization,[12] while in others they have fostered peaceful efforts to decentralize and deregulate in localizing directions. And as these contradictory responses to deterritorialization accelerate, so do the dynamics of fragmegration become increasingly intense and pervasive, sometimes solidifying individual orientations and at other times inducing doubt and transformation.

The Salience of Issues

At least for those in the local and global worlds, and perhaps for all persons, issues and their evolution matter. People can become involved in one or more of the problems that arise in their worlds. They care about potential outcomes and the ways in which one or another issue might affect their lives. More accurately, they tend to care about clusters of issues—say, territorial clusters such as local issues or functional clusters such as the environment, education, animal rights, or foreign affairs—and not the full array that makes up any community's agenda. Perhaps only politicians and editors have the obligation to dabble in all the issues that constitute an agenda. But whatever their contents and diversity, the issues that people regard as important, as salient to their lives, can operate as the basis for shifts among the various worlds. If the scope of an issue cluster expands or narrows, if the issue becomes more or less controversial, if its technical dimensions are clarified by new scientific findings, people may shift to another world in response to the shifting salience of matters they care about.

Examples abound. Workers who fear that their jobs are in jeopardy because of the factory's poor production record and then come to appreciate that the threat lies in foreign competition or the transfer of production facilities abroad might well be induced to move from being Resistant

[11] David B. Knight, "People Together, Yet Apart: Rethinking Territory, Sovereignty, and Identities," in Goerge J. Demko and William B. Wood (eds.), *Reordering the World: Geopolitical Perspectives on the 21st Century* (Boulder, Colo.: Westview, 1994), p. 77.

[12] An analysis of how this virulence gets perpetuated across generations is presented in chapter 15.

Locals to Resistant Globals or, if the threat takes the form of migrants replacing them for lower wages, to Exclusionary Locals. Contrariwise, as trade patterns and production facilities foster new employment opportunities, Resistant Locals could become Affirmative Locals or Globals. Similarly, as people become increasingly sensitive to global warming, they could shift from being Tuned-Out Passives to Resistant Locals or even Specialized Globals. Virtually every issue on local or global agendas, in other words, has the potential to stimulate revised worldviews and shifts among the twelve worlds.

Furthermore, movement among the worlds can be either fast- or slow-paced, either spasmodic or continuous. In the case of issue-induced changes, the pace and direction are shaped by the ways in which distant events and issues become increasingly proximate. As the scope of a set of issues expands or contracts, corresponding incremental shifts to other worlds may be generated. But in some instances an issue can be so intrusive as to be sudden and jolting for individuals, so much so that the attitudinal reversal is virtually instantaneous as the new developments render the long-standing orientations no longer tenable. A cogent example of issue shock that induced implausible movement—at least a momentary move from Resistant Global to Affirmative Global—is evident in the response of Arundhati Roy, a novelist of renown in India, to her country's announced possession of a nuclear bomb: "If protesting against having a nuclear bomb implanted in my brain is anti-Hindu and anti-national, then I secede. I hereby declare myself an independent, mobile republic. I am a citizen of the earth. I own no territory. I have no flag."[13]

Then there is the issue of terrorism, which for Americans at least was severely jolting when the World Trade Center and the Pentagon were attacked and distant developments became immediately and painfully proximate and, in all likelihood, constituted issue-induced shock that led to extensive movement among the worlds. Most of the movement probably involved people abandoning local orientations and becoming Specialized Globals, but it is also conceivable that some individuals were shocked into retreating into the world of Insular Locals or even becoming Tuned-Out Passives.

An example of shock induced by the terrorist attack is provided by the reaction of Todd Gitlin, a distinguished sociologist who indicated he could never imagine displaying the American flag on the balcony of his New York apartment. After the attack, however, he did exactly that, add-

---

[13] Quoted in Barry Bearak, "Trying to Wreck India's Romance with the Bomb," *New York Times*, August 27, 1998, p. A4. For a post–September 11, 2001 interview with her, see "Arundhati Roy: Activist in an Angry World," *Mother Jones*, January–February 2002, pp. 74–76.

ing a comment suggesting that he moved, at least briefly, from being a Resistant Global to an Affirmative Local: "It's very complicated," he was quoted as saying. "For me this week, the flag affirms that you belong to a nation that has been grievously hurt, and you want to show solidarity. But it's an affirmation that carries absolutely no connotation of support for a particular policy."[14]

Such sharp attitudinal changes, however, are likely to be relatively rare, if only because distant events usually do not clash so abruptly with one's values. Instead, most issue-induced change is incremental and evolutionary, as people adjust slowly to events and trends that are incremental in their transformation. A telling instance of slow attitudinal movement can be seen in this assessment of peasants in two Central American countries:

> [I]n the real world, peasants normally do not move swiftly from quiescence to rebellion. They move incrementally, first trying that, now trying this, depending on whom they are addressing with such action. . . . [W]e come to realize how uncommon peasant revolution really is and to grasp the reasons for its infrequency. We begin to understand that from the peasant perspective, nonviolent behavior is always preferable if it is effective, and it often is. . . . Peasant politics is increasingly moving beyond the village to address wider issues and distant authorities.[15]

Indeed, the inertia embedded in attitudes generated by long-standing issues can lead to backing off of an impulse to move to another world and deciding not to move. Consider, for example, Dejair Birschner, the mayor of Una, a small town on the edge of the rain forest in Brazil. He knows that logging in the rain forest will eventually cause serious environmental problems on a global scale and therefore that he needs to create the circumstances that will give the people of his town alternative lines of work and income. But such circumstances are elusive, and so he does not make decisions that will prevent, or even inhibit, the logging from continuing. In effect,

> Mayor Birschner represents a whole generation of people around the world today who are trapped in a no man's land, between the computer generation that their kids, if they're lucky, might get up to speed for and their parents' generation that enjoyed a stable existence from logging and farming. I knew what he was saying in his question ["Do we have any future?"]: "My villagers

---

[14] Clyde Haberman, "60's Lessons on How Not to Wave Flag," *New York Times*, September 19, 2001, p. A20.

[15] Leslie E. Anderson, *The Political Ecology of the Modern Peasant: Calculation and Community* (Baltimore: Johns Hopkins University Press, 1994), pp. xiii–xiv.

can't live off the forest anymore and we're not equipped to live off computers. What are we supposed to do?"[16]

The salience of issues at the micro level can also change in response to shifts in the values and policies that sustain macro-level, economic, and political institutions. As previously indicated, for example, severe economic downturns generated by distant currency crises can create a climate in which people move from the orientations of Tuned-Out Passives or Affirmative Locals or Globals to those of Resistant Locals or Globals, just as sharp and prolonged economic upturns can lead to shifts out of passivity and resistance to affirmative orientations. Perhaps even more indicative of how changing macro climates can induce micro reorientations are shifts that occurred in the United States among Alienated Illegals— the Patriots—subsequent to the execution of Oklahoma City bomber Timothy McVeigh:

> People have left the militia movement for a variety of reasons. They have gone home disillusioned and tired of waiting for the revolution that never seems to come. They have been scared off, frightened by the arrests of thousands of comrades for engaging in illegal "common-law" court tactics, weapons violations and even terrorist plots. And they have, in great numbers, left the relatively non-racist Patriot world for the harder-line groups that now make up most of the radical right.[17]

The Salience of Identity

Perhaps in part due to their particular circumstances, the identities people regard as salient to their lives also underlie the worlds in which they are comfortable. As the distant becomes ever more proximate, it seems likely that people will be confronted with taking on an ever greater number of identities, many of which may be configured by one or another global world. Put differently, the more individuals define themselves in terms of roles they occupy in aggregates larger than their family or neighborhood, the more are they likely to shift their orientations toward distant proximities. Indeed, if they regard themselves as linked to a social movement, their identity might continue to evolve: "Movements do not merely define identities but also develop them. A movement faces the paradox that identity is not primordial; it changes as you use it."[18]

This is another way of noting that the present epoch is marked by a

---

[16] Thomas L. Friedman, "Time of the Turtles," *New York Times*, August 15, 1998, p. A27.

[17] "The Rise and Decline of the 'Patriots,'" *Intelligence Report*, No. 102 (summer 2001), p. 6.

[18] Alison Brysk, "Turning Weakness into Strength: The Internationalization of Human Rights," *Latin American Perspectives*, Vol. 23 (spring 1996), p. 50.

pervasive preoccupation with issues of identity, with a restless need for affiliation provoked by the transformative dynamics that pose troubling questions about who one is and where one fits in the emergent epoch. It can even be said that the relentless surge toward multiplying and specifying identities is inherent in the age of fragmegration. As some organizations fragment and others cohere, as some countries, economies, and societies break down while others move toward integration, as the pulls of deterritorialization compete ever more with the ties that bind people to territory, and as some social movements expand transnationally even as some ethnic and religious groups become increasingly exclusive, so do identities proliferate as each of these diverse distant proximities raises powerful concerns about the extent to which one's prime affiliations are spatially near-at-hand or remote. And since relatively few people have the clear-cut identities that come with being Insular Locals or Territorial Globals, such concerns are likely to preoccupy most individuals irrespective of the world with which they feel they have the most affinity.

Stated more generally, the distinctions between Self and Other have become an especially salient feature of people's identities as they acquire more and more Selves and relate to more and more Others. Likewise, as patterns of migration intensify and increasing numbers of people occupy the amorphous space between Friend and Enemy—that of the Stranger[19]— so do the ambiguities that can attach to identity deepen and broaden.

Put differently, increasingly people have to think of themselves in terms of a multiplicity of identities. Except for the Insular Locals and the Territorial Globals, gone are the days when one could define oneself in terms of a singular geographic space. In large part due to dynamic technologies, there has been a "dissolution of self,"[20] a fragmenting of interests, values, and affiliations such that the individual has different identities that can vary as widely as the different interests, values, and affiliations he or she may have. As one analyst puts it, "Small and enduring communities, with a limited cast of significant others, are being replaced by a vast and ever-expanding array of relationships."[21] And as identities proliferate in the emergent epoch, the more difficult it becomes to maintain clarity with respect to them. In earlier epochs,

> If you say who you are, you could say where you came from; broadly speaking, what race you belong to, a nation state of which you are a citizen or subject; you have a class position, an established and relatively secure gender position. You knew where you fitted in the world . . . whereas most of us now live with

[19] Zygmunt Bauman, "Modernity and Ambivalence," in Mike Featherstone (ed.), *Global Culture: Nationalism, Globalization and Modernity* (London: Sage, 1990), pp. 143–69.

[20] Kenneth J. Gergen, *The Saturated Self: Dilemmas of Identity in Contemporary Life* (New York: Basic Books, 1991), p. x.

[21] Ibid., p. xi.

a sense of a much greater plurality, a sense of unfinished character of each of those [roles]. It is not that they have disappeared but they do not stitch us in place, locate us, in the way they did in the past.[22]

For most people, of course, a singular territorial space—"home"—still matters. A minuscule number may see themselves as citizens of the world, but most identify with a neighborhood, city, region, or country (and even the "world" is a territorial conception). Rooted into a particular territorial space as they may be, however, people are increasingly sensitive to the other identities they have evolved through the new relationships they have formed in response to distant proximities. They not only are capable of differentiating among territorial spaces and maintaining an identity with more than one of them—as a leader of the Northern League in Italy put it, "We care about being Lombards first and Europeans second. Italy means nothing to us"[23]—but also appear able to sustain simultaneously the identities that attach to work, professions, social movements, global issues, and the many other aspects of their lives that are undergoing both fragmenting and integrating processes.

This capacity for maintaining multiple identities is a major feature of the fragmegrative era. Social identity theory hypothesizes that such a capacity is difficult to maintain, that different levels of identity tend to be mutually exclusive, that the more people are aware of themselves as individuals, the less aware they are of themselves as members of collectivities, and vice versa. But social identity theory underestimates the impact of the various macro developments discussed in chapter 3—the skill revolution, the organizational explosion, the mobility upheaval, and the electronic technologies that have greatly narrowed the geographic distance between people—all of which have enormously facilitated the shouldering of multiple identities. With the advent of fragmegration, people can use their enlarged skills to develop new priorities among their affiliations, emotionally attach themselves to more than one collective enterprise, move among the several worlds, and imagine themselves as tied to distant others who share their aspirations or fears.

But, it might be argued, such a capacity for multiple identities is an illusion, or at least a luxury enjoyed when times are good and conflicts among the various identities do not arise. After all, the argument might stress, the commitment of the socialist movement to a worldwide labor movement gave way to nationalist orientations with the outbreak of

[22] Stuart Hall, "Old and New Identities, Old and New Ethnicities," in Anthony D. King (ed.), *Culture, Globalization and the World-System: Contemporary Conditions for the Representation of Identity* (Minneapolis: University of Minnesota Press, 1997), pp. 62–63.

[23] Paul Friggerio, quoted in Frank Viviano, "Separatist Party on Rise in Italy," *San Francisco Chronicle*, March 3, 1993, p. 1.

World War I. True enough, but such reversions to a singular territorial identity preceded the skill revolution and the emergence of an epoch in which people are simultaneously exposed to fragmenting and integrating forces, to contradictory dynamics that they now have the skills to manage through adjusting to both forces rather than favoring only one. In short, in an era of fragmegration it is becoming increasingly difficult to think of oneself in constant, fixed ways, and increasingly easy to move from one identity to another—to appreciate that as the distant becomes ever closer, one's identity becomes ever more tied up with diverse global worlds.

To be sure, movement to other worlds induced by new roles and identities can be no less agonizing than that accompanying issue-induced attitudinal change, but it is unlikely to result from sudden jolts in the lives of people. Rather, adaptation to new roles and identities involves learning through repeated experiences that are slow to take hold. The learning may be a source of considerable pain as people struggle to accommodate their new identities with those that have previously marked their lives, but it is the kind of pain that endures rather than getting resolved through a sudden jolt.

CONCLUSION

Despite the conservative incentives to stay in one of the twelve worlds, clearly it is becoming increasingly difficult to do so. The incentives to move back and forth, from one identity to another in response to one issue or another, can be extensive in an epoch pervaded by numerous contradictions and ambiguities through which global and local pressures simultaneously play upon the lives of people. The psychology of fragmegration, this and the previous three chapters suggest, is rooted in uncertainties and nuance, compelling individuals to balance multiplying identities, diverse issues, and organizational affiliations as the worlds in which they live and work become ever more complex and dynamic. In short, there is a correspondence between the mobility upheaval that sustains the movement of people through geographic space and the analytic conception whereby they move intellectually and emotionally among the metaphorical spaces of the twelve worlds that are here conceived to mark the emergent epoch.

This is especially the case for immigrants, whose movements around the world define who they are and can well encourage them to shift from a local to a global world. Indeed, their life and activities are such a special case of vulnerability to distant proximities that they have been omitted from the analysis thus far in order to examine them separately in the next chapter.

CHAPTER EIGHT

Emergent Spaces, New Places, and Old Faces:
Immigrants and the Proliferation of Identities

I was born in Argentina, my entire family is Argentinean and culturally, I have been raised Argentinean. Yet, at age four I moved out of Argentina and only returned on vacations. I grew up in Panama until I was thirteen and then moved to California. So where does that leave me? I speak perfect English and Spanish. Physically, I can pass as Californian, Panamanian or Argentinean. I know many people that are in my same situation. In a sense, we identify with each other. We have created our own territory, imagined, but a territory nonetheless.
                                    —Virginia Barreiro, graduate student[1]

I see myself as a citizen of the world, and someone who is unmistakably American and Chinese. My parents are Chinese but I grew up in a small town in the Midwest. I have no attachment to a place, but I wish I had one. I am a scientist but I like philosophy. I am a social psychologist but I read a lot of anthropology, sociology, mythology, and political science. I am a shifting person of multicolored hues. I can disguise myself very well, and make it very difficult for others to know exactly where I come from. There are probably more people like me now than at any other time in human history.
                                    —James H. Liu, senior lecturer[2]

I feel equally at home dancing with sherpas on the slopes of the Himalayas as I do at dinner parties in Hong Kong. I have never lived in my country of citizenship. I bow to Hindu deities and kneel at the Cross. Air stewardesses greet me by my first name and in my address book Steve Green, the American Ambassador to Singapore, is listed next to Raya Gunung, a rice farmer in Thailand. Who am I? I am a global nomad, a third culture kid. And what's more, I'm not alone. I come from a growing class of upwardly mobile people whose allegiance has shifted from

[1] In the Elliott School of The George Washington University. The quotation is from a paper she wrote for a course on the dynamics of globalization (March 1999).

[2] In social psychology at the Victoria University of Wellington, New Zealand. The quotation is a composite of comments from notes for a paper entitled "The Psychology of Fragmegration."

countries to corporations and who have to think for a minute if you ask them where they're from.

—Mark Nerney, college student[3]

[Woods said it bothers him when people label him as African-American, since he is one-quarter black, one-quarter Thai, one-quarter Chinese, one-eighth white, and one-eighth American Indian.] Growing up, I came up with this name. I'm a Cablinasian.

—Tiger Woods, golfer[4]

THESE EPIGRAPHS personally and eloquently capture the major themes of this chapter. One theme is that an understanding of the links between contemporary culture, identity, and world affairs requires a commitment to the tracing of nuance. The other, more substantive theme is that the previous discussion of movement among the twelve worlds omitted immigrants, refugees, cross-cultural marriages, and other special cases of persons who are a prime source of proliferating identities and whose movement involves self-conscious complexities that can linger across generations. The epigraphs plainly suggest that while people may not knowingly experience their movements among the analytic worlds noted in the last chapter, they are keenly aware of the consequences that attach to immigration, intermarriage, and the other real-life events directly experienced through moving physically among the worlds of geographic space. I shall refer to the many dimensions of this awareness as a "simultaneity of consciousness" that derives from an earlier effort to outline a psychology of fragmegration.[5] Hopefully it is a psychology that has the potential to clarify the macro implications of the growing number of people whose experiences parallel those of Virginia Barreiro, James Liu, Mark Nerney, and Tiger Woods.

THE CONCEPTS OF CULTURE AND IDENTITY

What follows assumes that, whatever the degree to which they shape each other, the micro identities of immigrants, like any identities, are constituent elements of macro cultures. A culture is conceived to consist

[3] In the Elliott School of The George Washington University. The quotation is from a paper he wrote for a course on the dynamics of globalization (December 2000).

[4] http://204.202.128.130/archive/news/Todays_Stories/970423/4_23_97_woods.htm/.

[5] James H. Liu and James N. Rosenau, "The Psychology of Fragmegration: On the Uses of a Simultaneity of Consciousness in the 'New World Order'" (paper presented at the Third Conference of the Asian Association of Social Psychology, Taipei, Taiwan, August 4–7, 1999).

of established habits, values, attitudes, and practices that are widely shared, that have historical roots, and that are differentiated in diverse ways from the characteristics of other cultures. When people are born into or otherwise acquire a set of such cultural habits, values, attitudes, and practices, they have an identity that links them to the culture. Identities, in other words, are embedded in cultures, but they are nonetheless micro phenomena in the sense that it is individuals who internalize, maintain, modify, or abandon a culture's characteristics. As one analyst put it,

> It is in . . . shifting subcultures that the drama . . . between globalization and localization is being played out. Although cultures exist in different social groups, their contents are physically located in different human minds. It is in the minds that cultural residues collect, accommodating and jostling with each other. It is in these mental reservoirs that the various urges for, as well as the human results of, globalization and localization occur. . . . An individual could be a member of his face-to-face community, transborder expatriate community or virtual electronic community. Each of these communities could also contain several subgroups. The contents of a citizen's mind are thus increasingly composed of elements that are not exclusive to a country, ethnic group or religion. Thus no firm separatism is objectively possible within an individual's internal cultural world. . . . A cultural "Lebanization" of the mind occurs, with multiple frames of reference for action, corresponding to each subculture.[6]

It follows that the concept of culture applies to a very diverse array of collectivities. It refers not only to society-wide or ethnic-wide entities but also to the habits, values, attitudes, and practices of whatever larger aggregate a person internalizes. It allows one to speak, say, of the culture of a corporation, an elite stratum, a transnational movement, a city, or an NGO, as well as the more traditional ethnic, religious, or national kinds of culture. More than that, it enables us to treat Virginia Barreiro and James Liu as having identities that attach to mobile, hybrid, and nonterritorial cultures that neither can quite specify but that both feel they share with others. Indeed, it can well be argued that hybridity is increasingly the dominant feature of societal cultures, that the mobility upheaval is resulting in more and more people having identities comparable to that of Tiger Woods.[7]

Some might argue that this broad approach is needlessly stretching the concept of culture, rendering it devoid of any meaningful content and undermining the more fundamental and accepted conceptions of culture. Such reasoning would also lead to the contention that the foregoing formulation treats identities too loosely, that any activity can be viewed as

[6] Susantha Goonatilake, "The Futures of Asian Cultures: Between Localization and Globalization," in UNESCO, *The Futures of Cultures* (Paris: UNESCO Publishing, 1994), p. 72.

[7] Geneva Overholser, "Look at the Face of Tiger Woods and See the Face of America's Future," *International Herald Tribune*, June 22, 2000, p. 9.

deriving from some kind of identity, and that therefore this loose conception needlessly equates identities with roles. My response to this line of thought focuses on the contradictions, ambiguities, and complexities of the emergent epoch. These are so numerous, and their evolution in the future so obscure, that it seems unnecessarily constraining to employ narrow concepts of culture and identity. Faced with a plurality of authorities and an explosion of organizations, surely at least some people will evolve new identities that, in turn, are located in emergent cultures. And if this is so, it is important that the concepts of culture and identity be framed in sufficiently wide-ranging contexts to enable us to back away from "the idea that the world is a collection of nameable groups."[8] Put more strongly, like the notion of culture, "[t]he concept of identity, when it does not refer to individuals but is used to represent a whole, is debasing and dehumanizing, it becomes an all-encompassing magic word that groups individuals under one heading and deprives the unique human being of all originality and creativity, all that is not indelibly impressed in his genes, imposed by his geographical environment or social pressure but is the result of his ability to resist all those influences and balance them with acts of free will and personal invention."[9]

Furthermore, while there is some overlap between identities and roles in the sense that both ascribe behavior and orientations to people, the two are not the same. Roles are largely defined by the expectations of others, whereas identities, being internalized, are defined by the self, by how a person feels and thinks about whatever array of habits, values, attitudes, and practices he or she perceives to be encompassed by each of his or her identities. But the line between external expectations and internalized self-definitions may not be clear-cut. The former can develop into the latter with a fair amount of ease, especially at a time of rapid and pervasive transformations in which the dynamic forces of fragmegration are tearing at cultures and proliferating identities as time and distance collapse, with the result that individuals are compelled or enabled to negotiate their identities as they encounter new ideas, alternative cultures, and transformed situations.[10] "Even at a personal level," in other words, "identity is not altogether internal to an individual but is part of a social process."[11]

---

[8] John D. Kelly, "Time and the Global: Against the Homogeneous, Empty Communities in Contemporary Social Theory," in Birgit Meyer and Peter Geschiere (eds.), *Globalization and Identity: Dialectics of Flow and Closure* (Oxford: Blackwell Publisher, 1999), p. 241.

[9] Mario Vargas Llosa, "Local Cultures and Globalization," in *Tokyo 2000* (New York: Trilateral Commission, 2000), p. 41.

[10] Vanessa Scherrer, "The Notion of Political Identity Negotiation: The Case of Young Activists" (paper presented at the Congress of the International Political Science Association, Quebec City, August 4, 2000).

[11] Craig Calhoun, "The Problem of Identity in Collective Action," in Joan Huber (ed.), *Macro-Micro Links in Sociology* (Newbury Park, Calif.: Sage, 1991), p. 52.

Whether or not they are immigrants, in other words, people are led by present-day circumstances to occupying new roles defined by new rule-setting authorities and, as they do, internalizing the habits, values, attitudes, and practices prescribed by the roles and thereby contributing to the formation of new identities and cultures. As one astute observer has noted, "In real life, identities, like garments, are interchangeable or wearable in combination rather than unique and, as it were, stuck to the body."[12] While the shouldering of multiple identities can be the source of acute tension for some individuals, others have no problem in this regard. As a novelist put it, "In Berlin I don't particularly feel that I'm a Berliner or even a German—I just feel at home. But when I'm in Munich I can't deny the fact that I am indeed from Berlin. In Rome or Paris I'm aware that I'm German. And in America I become a European. I wouldn't want to give up one or more of these identities in favor of another."[13]

The Multiple Flows of Culture

While this chapter focuses mainly on cultural phenomena as they are experienced at the micro level by immigrants, it is useful to stress that cultures are macro phenomena in the sense that any culture is a socially constructed concept, a widely shared set of norms and practices to which people subscribe as sources of their conduct both within and outside the culture. One of the consequences of fragmegrative dynamics, however, is that the coherence and boundaries of cultures, like those of states, have become porous and often frayed as other norms and practices intrude through the circulation of ideas and pictures from abroad, the mobility upheaval, the organizational explosion, the diverse products of a global economy, and the other dynamics enumerated earlier. Many observers view the ongoing diffusion of culture as a one-way process that begins in the United States and the West and then radiates around the rest of the world. For such analysts, globalization is the equivalent of Americanization. But once again this appears to be an oversimplified conception. McDonald's may be thriving in Asia and thousands of other locations around the world,[14] but so are Chinese, Japanese, Vietnamese, and Korean restaurants frequented widely in the United States and Europe, and much the same can be said about the direction of intercultural flows in the fields of medicine, education, and religion. Moreover, there are good indications that aspects of Japanese culture are spreading widely through-

[12] Eric Hobsbawm, "Identity Politics and the Left," *New Left Review*, Vol. 217 (1996), p. 41.

[13] Peter Schneider, "Conquering Europe, Word for Word," *New York Times*, May 1, 2001, p. A27.

[14] George Ritzer, *The McDonaldization of Society: An Investigation into the Changing Character of Contemporary Social Life* (Newbury Park, Calif.: Pine Forge Press, 1993).

out East Asia, even to countries where the elder generations retain their war-induced hostility toward Japan.[15] Or consider children's toys and books: at this writing a Japanese toy, Pokémon, has "enslaved . . . the entire child population of America," and "[t]he British are not far behind the Japanese in the race to seduce America's children," with a "literary sensation," a series by J. K. Rowling, capturing the interest of teenagers and "for younger children yet another British product, the Teletubbies, [being] almost as popular as that quintessentially American programme, 'Sesame Street.'"[16] In short, notwithstanding the worldwide appeal of American movies and music, the dynamics of fragmegration do not spur change in a uniform direction. Westernization may appear to be the dominant direction, but it would be a gross mistake to view its processes as the only source of globalizing dynamics.

Furthermore, there are good reasons to presume that worldwide tastes in clothing, food, and music are not overwhelming and emasculating local customs. On the contrary, fragmegrative dynamics heighten the sensitivities of people to their cultures and identities. As people recognize and experience a greater awareness of the homogenizing processes inherent in globalizing processes, so does their involvement in these processes "trigger a search for fixed orientation points and action frames, as well as determined efforts to affirm old and construct new boundaries."[17] The fact that McDonald's has adapted its menu to the core preferences of host countries[18] is suggestive of how local cultures are rooted in deep-seated habits and a resilience that tend to absorb rather than emulate the lures of the global economy. Indeed, "today, thanks to the weakening of the nation-state, we are seeing forgotten, marginalized, and silenced local cultures reemerging and displaying dynamic signs of life in the great concert of this globalized planet."[19] In short, the adoption of a foreign norm or practice does not necessarily reflect an inroad into a native culture. Consider, for example, how people whose rights are violated seek refuge in the human rights regime so as to preserve some of the basic premises of their own cultures:

[T]he emergence of the global market has assisted the diffusion of human rights, since markets break down traditional social structures and encourage the emergence of assertive temperaments. But while markets do create individ-

[15] Calvin Sims, "Japan Beckons, and East Asia's Youth Fall in Love," *New York Times*, December 5, 1999, p. 3.

[16] "Pokemania v Globophobia," *The Economist*, November 20, 1999, p. 36.

[17] Meyer and Geschiere, "Introduction," in Meyer and Geschiere (eds.), *Globalization and Identity*, p. 2. See also Gianni Riotta, "The Coming Identity War," *Foreign Policy*, No. 120 (September–October 2000), pp. 86–87.

[18] J. L. Watson (ed.), *Golden Arches East: McDonald's in East Asia* (Stanford, Calif.: Stanford University Press, 1997).

[19] Mario Vargas Llosa, "The Culture of Liberty," *Foreign Policy*, No. 122 (January/February 2001), p. 71.

uals, as buyers and sellers of goods and labor, these individuals often want human rights precisely to protect them from the indignities and indecencies of the market. Moreover, the dignity such a person is seeking to protect is not necessarily derived from Western models. The women in Kabul who come to Western human rights agencies seeking their protection from the Taliban militias do not want to cease being Muslim wives and mothers; they want to combine respect for their traditions with certain "universal" prerogatives, like the right to an education or professional health care provided by a woman. . . . Human rights has gone global, but it has also gone local.[20]

That cultural flows are as infused with complexities and nuances as any other dimension of fragmegration is further—and nicely—summarized in this account of their multiple sources and directions:

> There is growing evidence that the consumption of the mass media throughout the world often provokes resistance, irony, selectivity, and, in general, agency. Terrorists modeling themselves on Rambo-like figures (who have themselves generated a host of non-Western counterparts); housewives reading romances and soap operas as part of their efforts to construct their own lives; Muslim family gatherings listening to speeches by Islamic leaders on cassette tapes; domestic servants in South India taking packaged tours to Kashmir; these are all examples of the active way in which media are appropriated by people throughout the world. T-shirts, billboards, and graffiti as well as rap music, street dancing, and slum housing all show that the images of the media are quickly moved into local repertoires of irony, anger, humor, and resistance. . . . It is the imagination, in its collective forms, that creates ideas of neighborhood and nationhood, of moral economies and unjust rule, of higher wages and foreign labor prospects. *The imagination is today a staging ground for action, and not only for escape.*[21]

This last, italicized sentence is worth pondering. For all its defects, fragmegration has fostered circumstances whereby collective actions at the grass roots can be stimuli to change, given the will of publics to converge around and act upon their collective aspirations. Indeed, sensitivity to one's identities can be seen as a powerful fragmegrative dynamic in itself: with local cultures being challenged by globalizing forces, people have become disposed to ask who they are and where they fit, thus giving rise to "[t]he intercontinental spread of identity discourse and identity politics during the last third of the twentieth century."[22]

---

[20] Michael Ignatieff, "Human Rights: The Midlife Crisis," *New York Review of Books*, Vol. 46 (May 20, 1999), pp. 59, 60. For additional insights into the ways in which human rights have gone local as well as global, see chapter 14.

[21] Appadurai, *Modernity at Large*, p. 7 (italics added).

[22] Ulf Hannerz, "Epilogue: On Some Reports from a Free Space," in Meyer and Geschiere (eds.), *Globalization and Identity*, p. 328.

The spread of English as the language of discourse offers an incisive example of the fragmegrative underpinnings of identity politics. Not only is it expected that 'by mid-century half the planet [will] be more or less proficient in English compared to roughly 12 percent now,"[23] but in the business world, "as European banks and corporations burst national boundaries and go global, many are making English the official corporate language."[24] In addition, the pervasiveness of English in Europe is viewed as a means of binding the continent together. Some 70 percent of those surveyed in one European Union poll agreed with the proposition that "everyone should speak English." On the other hand, nearly the same percentage replied that their own language should be protected.[25] And the felt need for language protection can be extremely virulent. A Swiss newspaper, for example, castigated Zurich's education minister, who favored teaching English as the first foreign language, "as the gravedigger of the Swiss identity." Similarly, the leader of the Free Democrats in Germany excoriated the "flood of Anglicisms descending on us from the media, advertising, product description and technology" as a form of "violence not coming from the people, but imposed on them."[26] Then there are the intense conflicts that periodically surface in France and Quebec over the intrusion of English, conflicts that have even led to a recurring concern for "linguistic security" in children's games.[27]

Finally, the salience of identity has been further heightened by the microelectronic sources of fragmegration that have facilitated the stealing of identities.[28] In the United States the use of stolen credit card, social security, and driver's license numbers has led to identity theft being the fastest-growing white-collar crime.[29] And despite his Cablinasian identity, even Tiger Woods has been the victim of identity theft.[30]

---

[23] Gregory Rodrigues, "The Overwhelming Allure of English," *New York Times*, April 7, 2002, Sec. 4 p. 3.

[24] John Tagliabue, "In Europe, Going Global Means, Alas, English," *New York Times*, May 19, 2002, p. 13.

[25] Suzanne Daley, "In Europe, Some Fear National Languages Are Endangered," *New York Times*, April 16, 2001, p. A1.

[26] Wolfgang Gerhardt, quote in ibid., p. A10.

[27] James Brooke, "Pokémon Wins a Battle but Not the Language War," *New York Times*, March 15, 2000, p. A4.

[28] Timothy L. O'Brien, "Officials Worried over a Sharp Rise in Identity Theft," *New York Times*, April 3, 2000, p. A1.

[29] Jennifer 8. Lee, "Fighting Back When Someone Steals Your Name," *New York Times*, April 8, 2001, p. 8. See also Robert O'Harrow Jr., "Identity Thieves Thrive in Information Age," *Washington Post*, May 31, 2001, p. A1.

[30] Dave Anderson, "Sports of the Times: Sometimes a Nickname Has a Price," *New York Times*, May 3, 2001, p. D1.

IMMIGRANTS IN A FRAGMEGRATIVE WORLD

As indicated by the foregoing epigraphs, persons whose lives are marked by prolonged residence in two or more countries are especially subject to the opportunities and vulnerabilities inherent in the contradictory pressures of fragmegration. This would include ex-patriots and mobile jet-setters as well as immigrants, but it is the latter who are on the move in great numbers and seek permanent entry to other countries,[31] who thus most fully confront the challenges of acculturation, and who can therefore be regarded as quintessential cases for a probing of the possible ways in which a simultaneity of consciousness might operate.

Social identity theory is a primary focus of the field of social psychology, and in the last two decades it has witnessed a major theoretical advance in the form of what is called self-categorization theory (SCT).[32] However, despite having provided a framework for integrating a number of social processes such as the dynamics of conformity, attitude polarization, stereotyping, and prejudice, early formulations of SCT posited people as having difficulty valuing both themselves and their collective identities.[33] Such a difficulty runs counter to the nature of fragmegration, which fosters multiple identities and induces people to shift back and forth between different identities in response to shifting circumstances in their lives. Accordingly, reinforced by the various dynamics of fragmegration enumerated in chapter 3, a psychological theory of fragmegration presumes that many people have acquired the capacity for juggling more than one, even many, identities at the same time.

To be sure, this capacity may not obtain for everyone. There are no definitive data on the distribution of the enlarged capacity for multiple identities among people in developed and developing parts of the world,

---

[31] Between 1990 and 1998, for example, nearly 250,000 immigrants from 193 countries and territories moved to live in the Washington, D.C., metropolitan area. Audrey Singer, Samantha Friedman, Ivan Cheung, and Marie Price, "The World in a Zip Code: Greater Washington, D.C., as a New Region of Immigration," *Survey Series* (Washington, D.C.: Brookings Institution, April 2001), p. 1.

[32] J. C. Turner, M. A. Hogg, P. J. Oakes, S. D. Reicher, and M. S. Wetherell, *Rediscovering the Social Group: A Self-Categorization Theory* (New York: Basil Blackwell, 1987).

[33] For subsequent and more nuanced probings of SCT, see Bernd Simon, Giuseppe Pantaleo, and Amélie Mummendey, "Unique Individual or Interchangeable Group Member? The Accentuation of Intragroup Differences versus Similarities as an Indicator of the Individual Self versus the Collective Self," *Journal of Personality and Social Psychology*, Vol. 69, No. 1 (1995), pp. 106–19; and Bernd Simon, Claudia Hastedt, and Burgit Aufderheide, "Self-Categorization Makes Sense: The Role of Meaningful Social Categorization in Minority and Majority Members' Self-Perception," *Journal of Personality and Social Psychology*, Vol. 73, No. 2 (1997), pp. 310–20.

but it is reasonable to presume that such a talent will evolve among immigrants who choose or are compelled to move across countries and cultures. Confronted with an ever-increasing multiplicity of identities inherent in the ever-increasing challenges and obligations fostered by the age of fragmegration, they are the people most likely to maintain a simultaneity of consciousness. Consider, for example, Mexicans who move north: they "learn only in America that they have to have a specific 'identity.' In their home areas, patterns of self-identification are diffuse, permeable and multiple, but in America they are pressurized in all sorts of ways to cultivate and mark their own identity."[34]

A step toward rectifying the polarizing assumption of SCT was subsequently taken with developments in acculturation theory that focused on the tensions between the motivation of immigrants to value their heritage culture versus their host culture. Viewing acculturation processes in the context of these tensions, four separate processes can be specified through a 2 × 2 matrix that differentiates four types of immigrants (table 8.1): those who value both the host and the heritage culture are located in the "integration" quadrant; those who value the host but not the heritage culture are classified in the "assimilation" category; those who value the heritage but not the host culture adhere to a "separation" strategy; and those who value neither are designated as "marginalized."[35] Whatever may be the proportion of people who fall in the integration quadrant, they are immigrants who comfortably identify with their newly adopted culture as well as the one they left behind, and there is considerable evidence that this is the most beneficial acculturation strategy for a variety of immigrants.[36] Contrariwise, the Separationists are likely to be the immigrants most intensely concerned about threats to the security of their culture emanating either from members of the host culture or from fellow immigrants who have assimilationist or integrationist attitudes.

Yet even this more nuanced conception of acculturation appears to fall short of what at least some modern immigrants experience. It leaves no space either for immigrants whose self-categorization does not fall in any of the quadrants or for those who are able to move freely among the quadrants as circumstances may warrant. Where, for example, might peo-

---

[34] Meyer and Geschiere, "Introduction," p. 8.

[35] J. W. Berry, U. Kim, and S. Young, "Acculturation Attitudes in Plural Societies," *Applied Psychology: An International Review*, Vol. 38, No. 2 (1989), pp. 185–206.

[36] J. W. Berry, U. Kim, and P. Boski, "Psychological Acculturation of Immigrants," in Y. Y. Kim and W. B. Gudykunst (eds.), *Cross-Cultural Adaptation* (Newbury Park, Calif.: Sage, 1987), pp. 62–89; and G. Dona and J. W. Berry, "Acculturation Attitudes and Acculturative Stress of Central American Refugees," *International Journal of Psychology*, Vol. 29, No. 1 (1994), pp. 57–70.

TABLE 8.1.
A Model of Immigrant Acculturation

	Devalue Host/ Majority Culture	Value Host/Majority Culture
Devalue Heritage/ Minority Culture	Marginalized	Assimilationist
Value Heritage/ Minority Culture	Separationist	Integrationist

ple like those quoted in the epigraphs locate themselves? Each is a product of too many cultures to fit readily into any of the quadrants; indeed, James Liu says not only that he is "a shifting person of multicolored hues" but also that he knows how to disguise his complex background. Equally important, the fourfold scheme presented in table 8.1 does not make room for the proliferation of identities that has accompanied the emergent epoch. Educated immigrants who move to new host cultures to pursue professional interests may be especially ready to shoulder several identities. Nor need such a readiness be confined to educated professionals: conceivably, as all "people move across national boundaries, they may be less willing to exchange one absolute identity for another, choosing instead to acquire multiple citizenships and multiple identities."[37] It might even be argued, if the epigraphs by Virginia Barreiro, Mark Nerney, and James Liu are any indication, that the rapidity and variety of present-day immigration are generating a long-term trend toward "the creation of a new layer of citizenship above that of the nation—the citizen who does not belong."[38]

In short, spaces need to be opened up in the formulation set forth in table 8.1 to accommodate the growing number of immigrants whose circumstances are hypothesized to be the basis of a widening simultaneity of consciousness. Table 8.2 suggests the existence of these spaces, with the newly created space in the middle representing the greatest fusion of habits, values, attitudes, and practices from disparate cultures leads, so to speak, to a hybridity composed of several identities and cultures.[39] Not

[37] David H. Kaplan, "Territorial Identities and Geographic Scale," in G. H. Herb and D. H. Kaplan, *Nested Identities: Nationalism, Territory, and Scale* (Lanham, Md.: Rowman and Littlefield, 1999), p. 43.

[38] Stephen Castles and Alastair Davidson, *Citizenship and Migration: Globalization and the Politics of Belonging* (New York: Routledge, 2000), p. 157.

[39] I am indebted to James Liu for the formulation underlying the opening up of a new space in table 8.2. See Liu and Rosenau, "The Psychology of Fragmegration."

TABLE 8.2.
Immigrant Acculturation Model with Spaces for Movement

	Devalue Host/ Majority Culture	Value Host/Majority Culture
Devalue Heritage/ Minority Culture	Marginalized	Assimilationist
	Hybrids	
Value Heritage/ Minority Culture	Separationist	Integrationist

only can the authors of the epigraphs be viewed as hybrids in this regard, but the first two also explicate a conviction that many others are in a similar situation and, in effect, crowding into the newly created space.[40] And they may well be right. The world's ever-greater sensitivity to the challenges faced by multicultural societies suggests, given the dynamics of the emergent epoch, that the space created by opening up the 2×2 matrix is increasingly draining immigrants away from the fixed positions represented by the four quadrants in table 8.1.[41] The creation of this space is not, however, analytically arbitrary. On the contrary, "[g]lobalization is not about the absence of or dissolution of boundaries, but about the dramatically reduced fee that time and space impose, and thus the opening up of new spaces and new times within new boundaries that were hitherto inconceivable."[42]

In sum, a nuanced conception of the links between immigrants, their identities, and their cultures requires us to avoid treating them as an

[40] But there is a new cluster of hybrids that the first two epigraphs do not anticipate: illegal migrants who flee war or poverty in their home countries and are then rejected by the countries they seek to enter out of fear of setting a precedent that will lead to an endless flow of "undesirable" persons. "Blocked by laws and regulations from going either forward or back, they are superfluous people, undocumented and unwanted." Seth Mydans, "Caught between Home and Hope," *International Herald Tribune*, November 26, 2001, p. 7.

[41] Of course, there are limits to movement in and out of the spaces represented in tables 8.1 and 8.2. Most notably, adhering to a simultaneity of consciousness is presumably extremely difficult under strong polarizing conditions such as war or other forms of intense intergroup conflict.

[42] Wim van Binsbergen, "Globalization and Virtuality: Analytic Problems Posed by the Contemporary Transformation of African Societies," in Meyer and Geschiere (eds.), *Globalization and Identity*, p. 275.

undifferentiated group. Indeed, in some cases—say, Hispanics in California—it no longer makes sense to cluster them together as a "minority."[43]
Depending on the circumstances of the communities into which they
move and the orientations they bring with them, immigrants can vary
considerably as they adapt to their new circumstances. Of course, although it is not the focus of this chapter, the same can be said of the
cultures into which immigrants move: "The admission of immigrants
with cultural heritages and historical experiences different from those of
their host societies inevitably changes the fabric of these societies and
requires a complex process of mutual adaptation."[44] Some host societies,
for example, have adapted through policies of *differential exclusion* to
incorporate immigrants, allowing them to work in certain jobs but denying them full access to citizenship; others have enacted *assimilation* regulations in which immigrants are required to forgo the characteristics of
their heritage cultures and become indistinguishable from those of the
host culture; and still others adopt *pluralist* policies that grant immigrants full citizenship without having to forfeit those features of their
heritage culture they wish to retain.[45]

IMMIGRANTS IN THE TWELVE WORLDS

Except for the four private worlds, any of the local or global worlds analytically identified in the previous chapters are likely to be meaningful to
both legal and illegal immigrants. By virtue of their movement across
geographic and cultural space—indeed, by definition—all immigrants
seem unlikely to live and think in any of the private worlds. At the very
least they have left one local world for another and, in so doing, often
they may find themselves in one or another of the global worlds. In many
cases, they may be marginalized by people in their new worlds, especially
by Exclusionary Locals who are hostile to their presence. Those with
special skills, on the other hand, may be welcomed and easily assimilate
into their new worlds. In any event, whatever the reasons why they emi-
grate and however they may be received by their host culture, by defini-

---

[43] Susan Sachs, "Redefining Minority," *New York Times*, March 11, 2001, Sec. 4, p. 1.

[44] Douglas Klusmeyer, "Introduction," in T. Alexander Aleinikoff and Douglas
Klusmeyer (eds.), *From Immigrants to Citizens: Membership in a Changing World* (Washington, D.C.: Carnegie Endowment for International Peace, 2000), p. 1.

[45] This threefold formulation is elaborated in the writings of Stephen Castles. See his
"How Nation-States Respond to Immigration and Ethic Diversity," *New Community*, No.
21 (1995), p. 293; and Stephen Castles and Mark Miller, *The Age of Migration: International Population Movements in the Modern World*, 2d ed. (New York: Guilford Books,
1998), pp. 293–308.

tion all immigrants will have firsthand encounters with fragmegrative dynamics and thereby experience simultaneity of consciousness.

Perhaps the most intense and complicated fragmegrative circumstances are those confronted by Insular Locals who are forced to flee their homelands and become immigrants involuntarily. However sympathetic may be their welcome in the country to which they have fled, and no matter the intensity of the experiences which forced them to become refugees, some of these immigrants are likely to be reluctant to become Insular Locals in their newly adopted land, their sense of place being so strong that they long to return to their homeland. Alternatively, they gather in the same neighborhoods and found schools, newspapers, and TV stations based on their native tongues. In effect, they never leave "home," and their Insular Localism continues to dominate their orientations toward the complexities of a fragmegrated world—or at least such orientations are likely to continue to the extent these individuals anticipate an eventual return to their homeland and ghettoize their refugee communities (or see them ghettoized by their resistant hosts). Eventually, however, their ghettos are likely to begin to fray either as new generations educated in the host language and exposed to the new culture succeed those who emigrated or as the latter discover upon visits to their homeland that its lifestyle and other changes are so great that it no longer feels like home. At that point they may begin to abandon the notion of having ties to the land and use their immigrant experience as a basis for becoming Affirmative, Resistant, or Exclusionary Locals or Affirmative, Resistant, or Specialized Globals. Of course, it is also possible that they will have been so traumatized by their fragmegrative encounters that they join the ranks of the Alienated Cynics or the Tuned-Out Passives.[46]

Nor are difficulties of settling in new locales confined only to Insular Globals. Studying abroad or moving to new cultures and jobs can present a number of difficulties for Affirmative Locals and Globals as well. Consider Rasha Shaath, who thrived in her studies at the University of Virginia and anticipated returning to her family's home in Saudi Arabia after graduation to work in journalism: she "frets less about [wearing a] veil than about landing a newspaper job in a country where men and women cannot work together. She fears on some level, the loss of the person she has become. . . . She worries, too, that the critical reflexes she sharpened here may be interpreted as disloyalty back home. 'That can get dangerous, if I allow myself to become too much of an outsider.' Ms. Shaath

---

[46] For compelling insights into how traumatizing the experience of involuntary immigrants can be, see the account of returning Bosnian refugees in Roger Thurow, " 'If You Rebuild Our Houses, You Can't Just Drop Us Back Here,' " *Wall Street Journal*, August 24, 1999, p. 1.

said."[47] Similarly, although Europeans have the right to move freely around the continent, this guarantee is of little help in overcoming the difficulties of moving for many of them: "Locked in by culture, language, and a host of soft barriers like differences in the recognition of professional licensing, trouble transferring pension rights, access to public housing and varying tax codes, few Europeans are actually working outside their own countries in Europe."[48] That the barriers to mobility in Europe are considerable can readily be seen in a comparison of the figures for movement within the European Union and within the United States (which has a common language and culture, as well as none of the soft barriers): only 0.4 percent of Europeans move from country to country within the Union each year, whereas the figure for movement from state to state by Americans in 1998 was 2.4 percent.[49]

Irrespective of the obstacles to within-region movement, the mobility upheaval has not only contributed to the evolution of a preoccupation with identity at the micro level; it has also had a number of other beneficial and detrimental effects at the macro level both for the societies from which immigrants depart and for their new host societies. A main benefit for the societies they leave behind is the money they send home once they get established in their host societies. In a variety of ways such funds often contribute to the processes of development within their home countries: "Worker remittances account for 24 percent of Nicaragua's gross domestic product, 14.5 percent of Uganda's and 7 percent of Bangladesh's."[50] The $10 billion received in remittances from overseas citizens is the second-largest source of foreign exchange for the Philippines. There is a downside, however, as the remittances come from Filipinos with skills that are crucial to the country: "All kinds of people flee. Nurses trained . . . at government expense, leave the under-financed Filipino medical system for well-endowed hospitals in Saudi Arabia and the United States. Teachers migrate to Hong Kong to become maids to wealthy families, where they can earn a starting salary of about $450 a month compared with a teacher's salary of $200 at home. . . . [As one

[47] Quoted in Diana Jean Schemo, "Foreign Graduates Ask, 'What Now?'" *New York Times*, May 23, 2001, p. A10.

[48] Suzanne Daley, "Despite European Unity Efforts, to Most Workers There's No Country Like Home," *New York Times*, May 12, 2001, p. A6.

[49] Ibid.

[50] Moisés Naim, "The Diaspora That Fuels Development," *Financial Times*, June 9, 2002, p. 13. In the case of one community in Bangladesh, "Virtually every family . . . depends on at least one able-bodied man and sometimes a woman working overseas." Somini Sengupta, "Money from Kin Abroad Helps Bengalis Get By," *New York Times*, June 24, 2002, p. A3.

teacher put it,] 'the country is bleeding. We educate these young people and then they go overseas.' "[51]

While the recipient countries may benefit from the skills migrants bring with them, their influx in substantial numbers can also undermine societal coherence. For many persons in the recipient countries the arriving immigrants are "strangers," people with different lifestyles, religions, and commitments that seem capable of undermining the ties that have long bound the communities into which they move. At best the flow of outsiders gives rise to multicultural societies that manage to absorb, even seek, newcomers.[52] At worst, irrespective of whether their acculturation has been assimilationist or integrationist, the flow of immigrants and refugees leads to pervasive resentments, tensions, and outright prejudices in which immigrants are treated—if not legally, then socially—as second-class citizens, as stereotypes incapable of conforming to the community's prevailing norms and responsible for its polarization. In more than a few communities—from East Timor to Oldham in England, from the Ivory Coast to Germany—violence among ethnic groups can be recurrent and vicious. A measure of the potential scope of the problem is readily inferable from the fact that the total number of refugees in the top forty asylum countries in 2000 was 11,497,759.[53]

Nor are outbreaks of ethnic violence the only negative consequences of the mobility upheaval. Perhaps the most noxious consequence is extensive trafficking in people sustained by ruthless smugglers who make false promises of a better life to and demand large fees from (mostly) Insular Locals or Circumstantial Passives. There are numerous horror stories of smugglers pocketing the fees and either forcing many young women into prostitution or abandoning their human cargoes in the desert or in shipping containers without the resources necessary for survival.[54] Human cargo tragedies, moreover, involve "one of those issues full of contradictions that the globalized world inevitably aggravates. . . . [It] is about man and turf, the right to establish a place and defend it from being

[51] Jane Perlez, "Educated Filipinos: Disillusioned at Home, Look Abroad for a Better Life, *New York Times*, April 8, 2002, p. A11.

[52] Indeed, the mobility upheaval that, among other consequences, fosters depopulation and labor shortages has led "a small but growing number of cities" in the United States to embrace "new strategies to attract immigrants to replenish shrinking neighborhoods, fill labor shortages and inject greater ethnic diversity in their communities." Eric Schmitt, "To Fill In Gaps, Shrinking Cities Look Abroad for New Residents," *New York Times*, May 30, 2001, p. A1.

[53] This figure is derived from data presented in Thuy Do, "Statistics: Refugees and Australia's Contribution," in *Refugees and the Myth of the Borderless World* (Canberra: National Library of Australia, 2002), p. 44.

[54] See, for example, "More Trafficking in Teenagers to Feed Sex Industry in Europe," *New York Times*, June 16, 2001, p. A3.

overrun, the right to claim a home versus the right to move and seek a share of what society has to offer."[55]

Another negative consequence is exemplified by elites among the Exclusionary Locals who exploit the presence of immigrants for political advantage, railing against their threats to jobs and lifestyles as a means of generating support and moving up political ladders and thereby enhancing the legitimacy of the right wing in their communities. Jörg Haider of Austria, Pauline Hansen of Australia, Jean Marie Le Pen of France, Angela Merkel of Germany, Pim Fortuyn of the Netherlands (prior to his assassination in 2002), and Patrick Buchanan of the United States are only the most conspicuous Exclusionary or Resistant Locals or Globals to gain momentum through appeals to anti-immigrant sentiment. Indeed, the macro pattern in Europe is one in which "the political landscape is being dramatically redrawn" as the refugee flow moves voters and parties to the right.[56]

The rightward shift in German politics is perhaps especially illustrative of the macro consequences of the mobility upheaval. Propelled by the presence of the highest proportion of immigrants (7.3 million, or 9 percent of the German population) of any European country, the shift has fostered a nationwide preoccupation with the question of what it means to be a German.[57] To be sure, this pervasive debate over national identity has many sources—including issues deriving from the forty-five-year division between the East and West sections of the country[58] and, more recently, a recognition that the Nazi period ended decades ago and thus entitles Germans to feel pride in their subsequent accomplishments as a democracy[59]—but in good measure it also stems from right-wing actions against the numerous Turkish immigrants who entered the country throughout the postwar decades.

[55] Flora Lewis, "After Dover: People Ever Moving and Not Always Welcome," *International Herald Tribune*, June 22, 2000, p. 8.

[56] Alan Cowell, "Europe 'Is Rubbing Its Eyes' at the Ascent of the Right," *New York Times*, May 17, 2002, p. 3A. See also Steven Erlanger, "A Jumpy, Anti-immigrant Europe Is Creeping Rightward," *New York Times*, January 30, 2002, p. A3.

[57] Roger Cohen, "How Open to Immigrants Should Germany Be? An Uneasy Country's Debate Deepens," *New York Times*, May 13, 2001, p. 9.

[58] One former East German, Michael Schindhelm, described the end of the country's division as leading to "this strange loss of roots, of identity, of context—this experience of a cut that forces you to define yourself anew." Roger Cohen, "From Germany's East to West, Conservative Tries to Span Gulf," *New York Times*, June 1, 2001, p. A8.

[59] See Roger Cohen, "To Be German and Proud: Patriotism versus the Past," *New York Times*, January 10, 2001, p. A8; and Roger Cohen, "Schröder Joins Debate, Taking Side of Pride in Germany," *New York Times*, March 20, 2001, p. A11.

CONCLUSIONS: FROM MICRO WORLDS TO MACRO INSTITUTIONS

Clearly, a psychology of fragmegration is rooted in complexities that defy easy summarization. It operates differently for different people, depending on the degree to which their lives are caught up in the vortex of the clash of fragmenting and integrating dynamics. Wherever they may be in that vortex, moreover, these dynamics heighten awareness of identity and challenge immigrants and their hosts alike to unravel the many sources of proliferating identities. The emergent epoch is generating uncertainty among individuals who have to contend with a lack of clarity over the directions in which their preferred cultures are moving. An extreme case of this uncertainty is presently being felt in the former Yugoslavia, where a series of wars has left everyone "stuck with having to reinvent himself, with having to construct new 'imagined communities' from the debris of the old Communist federation."[60] Not surprisingly, moreover, pervasive uncertainty may foster movement in the direction of local worlds: ". . . [W]hat can be described as 'identity crises' . . . is precisely when people in places feel themselves threatened by developments seemingly outside their control that the issues of identification with place and representation of place become more urgent."[61]

But it would be erroneous to view the impetus for an accelerating flow of immigrants as originating only at the micro level of people fleeing political calamities or moving to better their economic circumstances. Some part of the flow also derives from dynamics at the macro level. For instance, faced with aging populations and the advance of the microelectronic revolution in industrial countries, societies and their governments have had to confront growing needs for both skilled and unskilled labor. In Japan, for example, a projected population decline of 17 percent by 2050 will generate the need for an unprecedented ten million immigrants if the current balance between workers and retirees is to be maintained.[62] Indeed, in many ways the demand for immigrants to fill labor needs underlies a classic fragmegrative situation: on the one hand, Affirmative Local elites recruit foreign workers, who are then seen by Exclusionary and Resistant Local activists as overrunning the community. In effect, foreign workers are wanted but not welcome. Macro policies to resolve these kinds of fragmegrative dilemmas usually have a singular outcome: "Efforts to prevent temporary workers from settling more perma-

[60] William Finnegan, "Letter from the Balkans: The Next War," *New Yorker*, September 20, 1999, p. 61.

[61] Richard Meegan, "Local Worlds," in John Allen and Doreen Massey (eds.), *Geographical Worlds* (New York: Oxford University Press, 1995), p. 84.

[62] Leah Platt, "The Working Caste," *The American Prospect*, May 7, 2001, p. 35.

nently—limiting slots to single men and women, rotating recruitment, and restricting options in employment (often to a single employer)— have failed, almost without exception."[63]

Anticipating the analysis of subsequent chapters, it is noteworthy that as huge as the diverse issues spawned by the mobility upheaval are, efforts to address them by macro institutions of the state-centric world have not been very successful. Migration issues are global in scope and scale, but neither regional international organizations nor the United Nations and the International Labor Organization have effectively undertaken their regulation. Rather, the handling of such issues is confined to national and local levels, where the rights and well-being of immigrants and migrants are often constricted or ignored. In 1990, for example, the International Convention on the Protection of the Rights of All Migrant Workers and Members of Their Families was adopted by the General Assembly of the United Nations, but it continues to languish in diplomatic limbo, with "not one person anywhere in the world, in any international organization, in any government, or any civil society group engaged with full-time responsibilities related to promoting this convention. There is simply no one yet taking up on a full-time basis the huge tasks of information distribution, coordination, advocacy, etc., that promoting . . . [ratification] of a major international treaty requires."[64]

The record of inaction on the migrant workers' convention, however, is not necessarily representative of macro responses to micro problems. Like individuals, global norms and institutions vary in the ways they affect the clash of fragmenting and integrating dynamics. Thus, it is to the interplay of other fragmegrative tensions that the inquiry now turns. This shift requires us to raise our analytic eyes from the micro to the macro level and seek to identify how macro collectivities both shape and are responsive to the intentional and unintentional inputs of individuals at the micro level. This shift is accomplished in two stages. The chapters of part II focus on an elaboration of conceptual equipment relevant to micro-macro interactions, while those of part III undertake to analyze several macro issues and the micro inputs that sustain them. In effect, we need to turn from the psychology of fragmegration to the sociology and politics of fragmegration in the hope of developing a social psychology of fragmegration.

---

[63] Ibid., p. 36.
[64] Patrick Taran, director of Migrants Rights International, quoted in ibid., p. 35.

PART TWO

Conceptual Equipment: Retooling the Storehouse

CHAPTER NINE

Normative and Complexity Approaches

> [S]ome of the key issues have become too complicated to distort. They are so complex they don't fit on a bumper sticker at all. You'd need the whole bumper to describe them.
>
> —Thomas L. Friedman[1]

IF A MODICUM of synthesis can be achieved across seemingly incompatible micro and macro phenomena, it is plausible at least to consider the synthesizing potential of two even more incompatible theoretical perspectives. Pondering this potential is imperative because the two perspectives, one stressing normative judgment and the other focusing on empirical complexity, are central to comprehending the dynamics of fragmegration. As the world, its societies and its people, become ever more interdependent, so have its situations and conflicts become increasingly complex, thus posing a seemingly endless array of new circumstances for which long-standing norms may offer little guidance. The expanded war on terrorism, the consequences of the attacks on the United States, the intrusion of NATO forces into Kosovo, the effort to bring former dictators in foreign lands to trial, the challenge of viruses on the Internet, the question of whether there are universal human rights—these are but a few of the numerous situations for which there are few normative or empirical precedents in the emergent fragmegrative epoch.

Thus hesitantly, and ambivalently, students of world affairs have become increasingly sensitive to the inextricable links between their normative perspectives and their empirical observations and theories.[2] Comprehending these links has been a difficult struggle, hindered by a past in which the first few decades after World War II were marked by scientific modes of inquiry that faltered when confronted with the dilemmas posed by nuclear weapons and a tragic and misguided war in Vietnam; then, as the scientific road appeared to be a dead end, many international relations scholars turned to poststructural, postpositivist, and post-anything-

---

[1] "The Water's Edge," *New York Times*, March 3, 2000, p. A23.

[2] See, for example, Paul Wapner and Lester Edwin J. Ruiz, (eds.), *Principled World Politics: The Challenge of Normative International Relations at the Millennium* (Boulder, Colo.: Rowman and Littlefield, 2000).

but-scientific-empiricism approaches that also faltered when faced with the genocidal conflicts that wracked the Balkans and Africa.

The main lesson of this contradictory past now seems obvious. Understanding that can lead to human betterment cannot be expanded unless careful and systematic empirical observations are recorded, but the processes of observation are bound to be shaped by normative concerns. Since the whole story of any set of circumstances can never be told and explained (there is too much detail), there can be no observation without selecting out some circumstances as important and dismissing others as trivial on the basis of ontological and value preferences.[3]

In short, the empirical and normative enterprises need each other. Neither alone can advance our grasp of distant proximities. Neither alone can come to terms with the enormous challenges of an ever more complex and changing world. Neither alone can make a lasting impact on policy-making processes. Subjective judgments may underlie and precede empirical observations, but the judgments take on a fuller meaning only as they are amplified by systematic and reliable data gathered through the application of scientific theory and methods.[4] Anecdotes, single-case illustrations, inferences from experience, and critical assessments are not sufficient for effective normative arguments. They may be insightful, suggestive, and supportive, but they are not nearly so persuasive as findings that systematically depict desirable or noxious patterns that can be pondered by people at the micro level and addressed by government policies or the actions of private organizations at the macro level.

Necessary as subjective and scientific appraisals are to each other, the relationship between them is a delicate and complicated one. Science can be tailored to serve subjective preferences, and the latter can be adjusted to support scientific findings. Accordingly, analysts have to be clear about both the values that underlie their work and the limits to the truth claims permitted by their scientific inquiries. Accomplishing this clarity has been made all the harder by the deepening complexity of world affairs that has accompanied the end of the Cold War, the microelectronic revolution, and the onset of globalization in the economic and cultural realms. These dynamics have posed enormous normative and empirical questions: Are the processes of globalization good or bad for humankind? Do the strides in communication sustained by the Internet and other technologies expand the dominance of the haves over the have-nots? Can viable theories

---

[3] For an elaboration of this point, see James N. Rosenau and Mary Durfee, *Thinking Theory Thoroughly: Coherent Approaches to an Incoherent World*, 2d ed. (Boulder, Colo.: Westview Press, 1999), Chap. 9.

[4] James N. Rosenau, "Normative Challenges in a Turbulent World," *Ethics and International Affairs*, Vol. 6 (1992), pp. 1–19.

be developed with which to evaluate the growing complexities that are rendering the world both more intricate and less stable?

This chapter focuses on the last of these questions. It outlines a fledgling theory—or, more accurately, several basic propositions—that can be used as analysts move beyond globalization and evolve means for probing the complexities and instabilities that mark fragmegrative dynamics. And it is founded, to repeat, on the premise that whatever one's normative premises may be, they are better served if incisive empirical theories of how the world works can be developed and applied. At the same time, what follows also cautions against excessive reliance on the fledgling theory, stressing that it is premature to reach conclusions as to its utility.

FAMILIAR PREMISES AND FLEDGLING THEORY

Although complexity theory is still very much a newcomer in the storehouse of social science tools, many analysts have long shared its underlying propositions (noted later). What is new is the explicitness and integration of these premises into a coherent whole that facilitates inquiry. Heretofore, social scientists have tended to ignore the premises of complexity theory by employing parsimonious models that treat the premises as exogenous conditions, as background factors rather than as endogenous to the course of events. Today, however, the normative and empirical uncertainties that mark world affairs are so widespread that analysts are increasingly prepared to build exogenous factors into their models as endogenous dynamics. In short, while more than a few observers have always been rudimentary complexity theorists, today they are more ready than ever to acknowledge that if the price of relaxing their criteria of parsimony is a greater ability to discern patterns in phenomena that previously seemed too complex to manage analytically, it is a price worth paying.

At the same time, risks attach to the newfound potentials of complexity theory. Although it is little noticed, one can discern a discrepancy between our intellectual progress toward grasping the underlying complexity of human systems and our emotional expectation that advances in complexity theory may somehow point the way to policies that can ameliorate the uncertainties inherent in a fast-changing world. This discrepancy is profoundly causal: the more uncertainty has spread since the end of the Cold War, the more analysts are inclined to seek panaceas for instability, and thus the more have they latched on to recent strides in complexity theory in the hope that it will yield solutions to the intractable problems that beset us. No less important, these links—the uncertainty, the search for panaceas, and the strides in complexity theory—are interactive and still intensifying.

Circumstances are thus in place for an eventual disillusionment with complexity theory. For despite the strides, there are severe limits to the extent to which such theory can generate concrete policies that lessen the uncertainties of a fragmegrated world. And as these limits become increasingly evident subsequent to the present period of euphoria over the theory's potential utility, a reaction against it may well set in and encourage a reversion to simplistic, either-or modes of thought. Such a development would be regrettable. Complexity theory does have insights to offer. It provides a cast of mind that can clarify, that can alert observers to otherwise unrecognized sources of instability, and that can serve as a brake on undue enthusiasm for particular courses of action. But these benefits can be exaggerated and thus disillusioning. Hence a central purpose of this chapter is to offer a layman's appraisal of both the potentials and the limits of complexity theory in clarifying micro-macro interactions that may undermine stable patterns.

UNCERTAINTIES AND RISKS

That a deep sense of uncertainty should pervade world affairs since the end of the Cold War is hardly surprising. The U.S.-Soviet rivalry, for all its tensions and susceptibility to collapsing into nuclear holocaust, infused stability into the course of events that was comprehensible, reliable, and continuous. The enemy was known. The challenges were clear. The dangers seemed obvious. The appropriate responses could readily be calculated. Quite the opposite is the case today, however. If there are enemies to be contested, challenges to meet, dangers to avoid, risks to assume, and responses to be launched, we are far from sure what they are. So uncertainty is the norm and apprehension the mood. The sweet moments when the wall came down in Berlin, apartheid ended in South Africa, and aggression was set back in Kuwait seem like fleeting and remote fantasies as the alleged post–Cold War order has emerged as anything but orderly. Whatever may be the arrangements of the emergent epoch that replace the bipolarity of U.S.-Soviet rivalry, they are at best incipient and ambiguous structures and, at worst, insidious processes marked by fragile governments, financial crises, and wide-reaching terrorist organizations.

But how do we assess a world pervaded with ambiguities? How do we begin to grasp a political space that is continuously shifting, widening and narrowing, simultaneously undergoing erosion with respect to many issues and reinforcement with respect to other issues? How do we trace the new or transformed authorities that occupy the new political spaces created by shifting and porous boundaries? How do we know when macro structures are especially vulnerable to micro inputs from local or global worlds? And most important for present purposes, how do we analyze the ways in which individuals in the various local, global, and private worlds cope with the uncertainties and instabilities that pervade the emergent epoch?

The salience of such questions—and the uncertainty they generate—reflects the conviction that we are deeply immersed in an epochal transformation likely to foster a new worldview about the essential nature of human affairs, a new way of thinking about how global politics unfold. At the center of the emergent worldview lies an understanding that the order that sustains families, communities, countries, and the world through time rests on contradictions, ambiguities, and uncertainties. Where earlier epochs were conceived more in terms of central tendencies and orderly patterns, the present epoch appears to derive its order from contrary trends and episodic patterns. Where the lives of individuals and societies once tended to move along linear and steady trajectories, now the movement seems nonlinear and erratic, with equilibria being momentary and continuously punctuated by sudden accelerations or directional shifts.

Accordingly, tendencies to think in either-or terms have begun to give way to framing challenges as both-and problems. Except perhaps for many Insular Locals and Circumstantial Passives, there is now a widespread understanding that unexpected events are commonplace, that anomalies are normal occurrences, that minor incidents can mushroom into major outcomes, that what was once transitional may now be enduring, and that the complexities of modern life are so deeply rooted as to infuse ordinariness into the surprising development and the anxieties that attach to it.

To understand that the emergent order is rooted in contradictions and ambiguities, of course, is not to lessen the sense of uncertainty regarding where world affairs are headed and how distant events are likely to impinge on personal affairs. Indeed, the more one appreciates the contradictions and accepts the ambiguities, the greater will be the uncertainty one experiences. And the uncertainty is bound to intensify the more one ponders the multiplicity of reasons why the end of the Cold War has been accompanied by pervasive instabilities. Clearly, the absence of a superpower rivalry is not the only source of complexity. Technological dynamics are also major stimulants, and so are the breakdown of trust, the shrinking of distances, the globalization of economies, the explosive proliferation of organizations, the information revolution, the fragmentation of groups, the threat of terrorism, the integration of regions, the surge of democratic practices, the spread of fundamentalism, the moderation of intense rivalries, and the revival of historic animosities. All these dynamics, in turn, provoke further reactions that add to the complexity and heighten the sense that the uncertainty has become an enduring way of life.

Some observers appear to share a recognition that the intellectual tools presently available to probe the pervasive uncertainty underlying our emergent epoch may not be sufficient to the task. More than a few analysts could be cited who appreciate that our conceptual equipment needs to be enhanced and refined, that the disciplinary boundaries that have separated the social sciences from each other and from the hard sciences are no longer clear-cut, and that the route to understanding and sound policy initiatives has to be traversed through interdisciplinary undertakings.[5]

It is perhaps a measure of this gap between the emergent epoch and the conceptual equipment available to comprehend it that our vocabulary for understanding the transformations lags well behind the changes themselves. However messy the world may have been in the waning epoch, at least we had confidence in our tools to analyze it. But today, as the course of events moves beyond globalization, we lack ways of talking about the diminished role of states without at the same time treating them as superior to all the other actors in the global arena. We lack a means for sorting out how major events such as the terrorist demolition of the World Trade Center impact on the processes of globalization. We do not have techniques for analyzing the simultaneity of events such that all their interconnections and feedback loops are identified.

SEARCHING FOR PANACEAS

So it is understandable that elites in the several global and local worlds are vulnerable to searching for analytic panaceas. Aware that they are ensconced in an epoch of contradictions, ambiguities, and uncertainties, and thus increasingly sensitive to the insufficiency of their conceptual equipment, thoughtful observers may be inclined to seek understanding through an overall scheme that seems up to the challenges posed by the emergent epoch. Complexity theory is compelling in this regard. Since "complexity lies somewhere between order and disorder, predictability and surprise,"[6] the very fact that a theoretical lens can be focused on such phenomena with the presumption that they are subject to systematic inquiry, thereby implying that complex systems are patterned and ultimately comprehensible, may encourage undue hope that humankind's problems can be unraveled and effective policies pursued to resolve them.

Stirring accounts of the Santa Fe Institute, where complexity theory was nursed into being through the work of economists, statisticians, computer scientists, mathematicians, biologists, physicists, and political

[5] See, for example, John L. Gaddis, "International Relations Theory and the End of the Cold War," *International Security*, Vol. 17 (winter 1992–93), pp. 5–58.

[6] George Johnson, "Researchers on Complexity Ponder What It's All About," *New York Times*, May 6, 1997, p. C7. See also Symposium, "Beyond Reductionism," *Science*, Vol. 284 (April 2, 1999), pp. 79–109.

scientists in a prolonged and fruitful interdisciplinary collaboration, kindled these hopes.[7] The stories of how Brian Arthur developed the notion of increasing returns in economics; of how John H. Holland developed genetic algorithms that could result in a mathematical theory capable of illuminating a wide range of complex adaptive systems; of how Stuart Kauffman generated computer simulations of abstract, interacting agents that might reveal the inner workings of large, complicated systems such as the United States; of how Per Bak discovered self-organized criticality that allowed for inferences as to how social systems might enter upon critical states that jeopardize their stability; of how Murray Gell-Mann pressed his colleagues to frame the concept of coevolution wherein agents interact to fashion complex webs of interdependence—these stories suggested that progress toward the comprehension of complex systems was bound to pay off. And to add to the sense of panacea, expectations were heightened by the titles these scholars gave to works designed to make their investigations meaningful for nonspecialists. Consider, for example, the implications embedded in Holland's *Hidden Order* and Kauffman's *At Home in the Universe*[8] that creative persistence is worth the effort in the sense that underlying patterns are out there to be discovered.[9]

There are, in short, good reasons to be hopeful: if those on the cutting edge of inquiry can be sure that human affairs rest on knowable foundations, surely there are bases for encouragement that the underpinnings of micro-macro interactions and the other dilemmas of the emergent epoch are susceptible to clarification. Never mind that societies are increasingly less cohesive and boundaries increasingly more porous; never mind that vast numbers of new actors are crowding the world stage; never mind that money moves instantaneously along the information highway and that ideas swirl instantaneously in cyberspace; never mind that the ripple effects of horrific terrorist actions seem endless; and never mind that the feedback loops generated by societal breakdowns, proliferating actors, and boundary-spanning information are greatly intensifying the complexity of life at the outset of a new century—all such transformative dynamics may complicate the task of analysts, but complexity theory tells us that they are not beyond comprehension, that they can be grasped.

I do not say this sarcastically. Rather, I accept the claims made for

---

[7] Roger Lewin, *Complexity: Life at the Edge of Chaos* (New York: Macmillan, 1992); and M. Mitchell Waldrop, *Complexity: The Emerging Science at the Edge of Order and Chaos* (New York: Simon and Schuster, 1992).

[8] John H. Holland, *Hidden Order: How Adaptation Builds Complexity* (Reading, Mass.: Addison-Wesley, 1995); and Stuart Kauffman, *At Home in the Universe: The Search for Laws of Self-Organization and Complexity* (New York: Oxford University Press, 1995).

[9] For a title pointing in the opposite direction, see Kevin Kelley, *Out of Control: The New Biology of Machines, Social Systems, and the Economic World* (New York: Addison-Wesley, 1994).

complexity theory. Despite conceptual and definitional difficulties,[10] it has made enormous strides, and it does have the potential for clarifying and perhaps ultimately ameliorating the human condition. Its progress points to bases for analytically coping with porous boundaries, weakened societies, new actors, fast-moving money and ideas, and elaborate feedback loops. But to stress these strides is not to delineate a time when they will reach fruition, and it is here, in the discrepancy between the theoretical strides and their practical application, that the need to highlight theoretical limits arises.

STRIDES IN COMPLEXITY THEORY

Before specifying the limits of complexity theory, let us first acknowledge the claims made for it. This can be accomplished without resort to mathematical models or sophisticated computer simulations. Few can comprehend the claims in these terms, but if the theoretical strides that have been made are assessed from the perspective of the philosophical foundations of complexity theory, it is possible to identify how the theory can serve the needs of those who are not tooled up in mathematics or computer science but who have a felt need for new conceptual equipment. Four foundations of the theory are sufficient for this purpose. The four are equally important and closely interrelated, but they are briefly outlined separately here to facilitate an assessment of the theory's relevance to the analysis of world affairs and its distant proximities.

The core of complexity theory is the complex adaptive system—not a cluster of unrelated activities but a system; not a simple system but a complex one; and not a static, unchanging set of arrangements but a complex adaptive system. Such a system is distinguished by a set of interrelated parts, each one of which is potentially capable of being an autonomous agent that, through acting autonomously, can impact on the others, and all of which either engage in patterned behavior as they sustain day-to-day routines or break with the routines when new challenges require new responses and new patterns. The interrelationships of the agents are what make the system. The capacity of the agents to break with routines and thus initiate unfamiliar feedback processes is what makes the system complex (since in a simple system all the agents consistently act in prescribed ways). The capacity of the agents to cope collectively with the new challenges is what makes the system adaptive.

Such, then, is the modern urban community, the nation-state, and the fragmegrative global system. As in any complex adaptive system in the natural world, the agents that constitute world affairs are brought to-

---

[10] Johnson, "Researchers on Complexity Ponder What It's All About," p. C7.

TABLE 9.1.
Comparison of Simple and Complex Systems*

Simple Systems	Complex Systems
few agents	many agents
few interactions	many interactions
decomposable	irreducible
closed system	open system
equilibrium	dissipative
static	dynamic
centralized decision making	disaggregated decision making
few feedback loops	many feedback loops
predictable outcomes	surprising outcomes
Examples	Examples
pendulum	immune system
bicycle	genes
engine	molecules in air
Boyle's law	ecosystems
gravitational system	markets

*I am indebted to Neil E. Harrison for this table.

gether into systemic wholes that consist of patterned structures ever subject to transformation as a result of feedback processes from their external environments or from internal stimuli that provoke the agents to break with their established routines. There may have been long periods of stasis in history where, relatively speaking, each period in the life of a human system was like the one before it, but our fragmegrative epoch is one of social systems and their polities undergoing profound transformations that exhibit all the characteristics of complex adaptive systems. Put in micro-macro terms, the advent of the skill revolution and the organizational explosion—those dynamics that have rendered the global stage ever more dense with interacting agents—have contributed enormously to the complexity of world affairs.

Table 9.1 lists some of the key distinctions between simple and complex systems, and here it can be seen that the differences between the two are neither trivial nor minimal. The four basic propositions of complexity theory further highlight the differences and the theory's relevance to the analysis of distant proximities.

Self-Organization and Emergent Properties

The parts or agents of a complex adaptive system, being related to each other sufficiently to form recurrent patterns, do in fact self-organize their patterned behavior into an orderly whole, and as they do so, they begin to acquire new attributes.[11] Nevertheless, even as the emergent properties of a system continue to proliferate and mature, its essential structures remain intact. Through time the new properties of the system may obscure its original contours, but to treat these processes of emergence as forming a new system is to fail to appreciate a prime dynamic of complexity, namely, the continuities embedded in emergence. As one analyst puts it, the life of any system, "at all levels, is not one damn thing after another, but the result of a common fundamental, internal dynamic."[12] Thus, for example, today's NATO is very different from the NATO of 1949 and doubtless is very different from the NATO that may exist in 2009, but its emergent properties have not transformed it into an entirely new organization. Rather, its internal dynamic has allowed it to adapt to change even though it is still in fundamental respects the North Atlantic Treaty Organization.

It follows that there is a close link between the processes of emergence and those that sustain micro-macro interactions. Just as complexity theory posits the self-organization of parts as the emergence of a whole that is larger than the sum of the parts, so do micro-macro interactions render a collectivity more encompassing than and different from its individual members. If several groups of Resistant Globals band together to protest globalization, they may have an impact on the course of events that none of the groups could have accomplished on its own. Accordingly, assuming that self-organizing tendencies occur from the bottom up, the emergence concept is central to both the complexity of collectivities and their micro-macro dynamics.

Adaptation and Coevolution

But there is no magic in the processes whereby systems self-organize and develop emergent properties. In the case of human systems, it is presumed they are composed of learning entities,[13] with the result that the dynamics of emergence are steered, so to speak, by a capacity for adaptation, by the ability of complex systems to keep their essential structures within acceptable limits or, in the case of nonhuman organisms, within

---

[11] As one complexity theorist put it, referring to self-organization as a natural property of complex genetic systems, "There is 'order for free' out there." Stuart Kauffman, quoted in Lewin, *Complexity*, p. 25.

[12] Lewin, *Complexity*, p. 192. For an analysis that focuses specifically on political systems, see Yong Pil Rhee, "Self-Organizing Systems Approach to the Study of Political Change" (paper presented at the World Congress of the International Political Science Association, Quebec City, August 1–5, 2000).

[13] Holland, *Hidden Order*, p. 93.

physiological limits.[14] Human systems face challenges from within and without, and the adaptive task is to maintain an acceptable balance between their internal needs and the external demands. At the same time, in the process of changing as they adapt, systems coevolve with their environments. Neither can evolve in response to change without corresponding adjustments on the part of the other. On the other hand, if a system is unable to adjust to its environment's evolutionary dynamics and thus fails to adapt, it collapses into the environment and becomes extinct. To recur to the NATO example, the organization managed from its inception to coevolve with the Cold War and post–Cold War environments despite internal developments such as the defection of France from its military command in 1967 and external developments such as the demise of the Soviet Union and the superpower rivalry. Indeed, as the environment evolved subsequent to the end of the Cold War, NATO accepted France's decision to rejoin the military command in 1996. The adaptation of NATO stands in sharp contrast to that of its Cold War rival, the Warsaw Pact. It could not coevolve with the international environment and failed to adapt; in effect, it collapsed into the environment so fully that its recurrent patterns are no longer discernible. Likewise, to cite a more recent example, if international economic institutions in the present era fail to adapt to the backlash against them sustained by Resistant Locals and Globals, the future of those institutions will be very problematic indeed.

As the history of France in NATO suggests, the coevolution of systems and their environments is not a straight-line progression. As systems and their environments become ever more complex, feedback loops proliferate and nonlinear dynamics intensify, with the result that it is not necessarily evident how any system evolves from one stage to another. While "no one doubts that a nation-state is more complex than a foraging band," and while the evolution from the latter to the former may include tribal, city-state, and other intermediate forms, the processes of evolution do not follow neat and logical steps.[15] Ever more skillful individuals and ever more numerous organizations contribute an erratic dimension to evolutionary processes. Consequently, systems are unalike and thus subject to local variations, as well as diverse trajectories through time. Equally important, evolution may not occur continuously or evenly. Even the most complex system can maintain long equilibria before undergoing

---

[14] The notion of physiological constraints setting adaptive limits is developed in W. Ross Ashby, *Design for a Brain*, 2d ed. (New York: Wiley, 1960), p. 58, whereas the substitution of acceptable limits in the case of human systems is developed in James N. Rosenau, *The Study of Political Adaptation* (London: Frances Pinter, 1981).

[15] Lewin, *Complexity*, p. 19.

new adaptive transformations, or what complexity theorists call *phase transitions*. Put differently, their progression through time can pass through periods of stasis or extremely slow, infinitesimal changes before lurching into a phase transition, thereby tracing a temporal path referred to as a *punctuated equilibrium*.

Viewed from a micro perspective, it follows that with people today besieged by ubiquitous distant proximities, the necessity of individual adaptation and coevolution is ever present. However, it is far from a simple task to achieve and maintain a balance such that distant proximities are integrated into a person's personal and professional life, not to mention his or her inclinations toward political action. Where the distant event or trend fits in a person's proximate circumstances may require the rethinking of values, the adjustment of attitudes, and the redirection of behavior if successful adaptation is to occur. Deep-seated habits may have to be overcome, and long-standing commitments may have to be modified if individuals are to coevolve with the dynamics of fragmegration. Put differently, with the dynamics of fragmegration having undermined tradition for vast numbers of people, the need to enhance and preserve one's autonomy is correspondingly greater if former traditionalists are to develop complex skills that allow for coevolution with the ever greater complexities sustained by fragmegration. As will be seen in the next chapter, there are sound reasons to believe that most people are slowly acquiring the skills needed for effective and continuing adaptation to the distant proximities that intrude upon their lives.

The Power of Small Events

It follows from the vulnerability of complex adaptive systems to punctuations of their equilibria and tumultuous phase transitions that small, seemingly minor events can give rise to large outcomes, that systems are sensitive at any moment in time to the conditions prevailing at that moment and can thus initiate processes of change that are substantial and dramatic. Examples of this "butterfly effect" abound. It is not difficult to reason, for instance, that the end of the Cold War began with the election of a Polish Pope more than a decade earlier,[16] just as the release of

---

[16] One observer contends that through his June 1979 speeches in Poland, John Paul II restored "to his people a form of freedom and a fearlessness that communism could not touch . . . [and thus] set in motion the human dynamics that eventually led, over a decade, to what we know as the Revolution of 1989." George Weigel, "Pope John Paul II and the Dynamics of History" (e-mail distributed by the Foreign Policy Research Institute, Philadelphia, March 7, 2000), p. 3.

Nelson Mandela from prison was arguably (and in retrospect) an event, a tipping point, that triggered the end of apartheid in South Africa.[17]

It is thus reasonable to presume that the power of small events contributes substantially to the pervasive uncertainties that mark the fragmegrative epoch. With the skills of people heightening their awareness that distant developments can quickly feed back as immediate, close-at-hand experiences, and with a growing sensitivity that seemingly slight developments can initiate powerful feedback mechanisms, modern life can readily appear to be a game of chance in which one's vulnerabilities seem unduly exposed.

Sensitivity to Initial Conditions

Closely related to the power of small events is the premise that even the slightest variation in initial conditions can lead to very different outcomes for a complex adaptive system. This premise can be readily grasped in the case of human systems when the processes of emergence are viewed as passing through a number of irreversible choice points that lead down diverse paths and, thus, to diverse outcomes. This is not to imply, of course, that changes in initial conditions necessarily result in unwanted outcomes such as the outbreak of war. As the example of Mandela demonstrates, the power of an altered initial condition can lead to desirable as well as noxious results.

THE LIMITS OF COMPLEXITY THEORY

Can complexity theory anticipate precisely how a complex adaptive system in world affairs will organize itself and what trajectory its emergence will follow? Can the theory trace exactly how the system will adapt or how it and its environment will coevolve? Can the theory specify what initial conditions will lead to what outcomes? No, it cannot perform any of these tasks. Indeed, it cannot even anticipate whether a large outcome will occur or, if it does, the range within which it might fall. Through computer simulations, for example, it has been shown that even the slightest variation in an initial condition can result in an enormous deviation from what would have otherwise been the outcome. Two simulations of the solar system are illustrative:

---

[17] For an extensive account that traces the end of apartheid back to Mandela's links to South African president F. W. de Klerk while he was still in prison, see Allister Sparks, "The Secret Revolution," *New Yorker*, April 11, 1994, pp. 56–78.

Both simulations used the same mathematical model on the same computer. Both sought to predict the position of the planets some 850,000,000 years in the future. The first and second simulation differed only in that the second simulation moved the starting position of each planet 0.5 millimeters. With such a small change in the initial conditions, [it is reasonable] to expect that the simulations would yield almost identical outcomes.

For all but one of the planets this is exactly what happened. Pluto, however, responded differently. The position of Pluto in the second simulation differed from its position in the first by 4 billion miles. Pluto's resting position is, in this mathematical model, extremely sensitive to the initial conditions.[18]

Applying these results metaphorically to the global system of concern here, it could well be presumed that the Pluto outcome is the prototype in world affairs, that numerous communities and societies could deviate often from their expected trajectories by the social and political equivalent of four billion miles. The variables within human systems at all levels of organizations are so multitudinous, and so susceptible to wide variations when their values shift, that anticipating the movement of planets through space is easy compared with charting the evolution of human systems through time.

In short, there are strict limits within which theorizing based on the premises of complexity theory must be confined. It cannot presently—and is unlikely ever to—provide a method for predicting particular events and specifying the exact shape and nature of developments in the future. As one observer notes, it is a theory "meant for thought experiments rather than for emulation of real systems."[19] Yet such thought experiments are likely to be increasingly powerful. "Supercomputers powerful enough to sift through piles of data that would crush the unaided mind," along with the aforementioned potential of computer chips ten billion times faster than those presently in use, suggest that in the future particular events and developments in the social as well as the physical sciences will be simulated and anticipated with ever-greater precision even if exactitude is not possible.[20]

Consequently, it is when our panacean impulses turn us toward complexity theory for guidance in the framing of exact predictions that the payoffs are least likely to occur and our disillusionment is most likely to intensify. The strides that complexity theorists have made with their mathematical models and computer simulations are still a long way from

---

[18] R. David Smith, "The Inapplicability Principle: What Chaos Means for Social Science," *Behavioral Science*, Vol. 40 (1995), p. 22.

[19] Holland, *Hidden Order*, p. 98.

[20] George Johnson, "All Science Is Computer Science," *New York Times*, March 25, 2001, Sec. 4, p. 1.

amounting to a science that can be relied on for exactitude in charting the course of human affairs that lies ahead. Indeed, to a large extent theorists continue to be confounded by the behavior of complex systems.[21] And while their work has demonstrated the existence of an underlying order, it has also called attention to a variety of ways in which that order can collapse into pervasive disorder. Put differently, while human affairs have both linear and nonlinear dimensions, and while the latter dimensions can range from inoperative to operative or "well behaved,"[22] it is not known when or where the nonlinear dynamics will trigger inexplicable feedback mechanisms. Such unknowns lead complexity theorists to be as interested in patterns of disorder as those of order, an orientation that may run counter to their normative concerns.

THEORIZING WITHIN THE LIMITS

To acknowledge the limits of complexity theory, however, is not to assert that it is of no value for those charged with comprehending world affairs. Far from it: if the search for panaceas is abandoned and replaced with a nuanced approach, it quickly becomes clear that the underlying premises of complexity theory have a great deal to offer as a perspective or worldview with which to assess and anticipate the course of events. Perhaps most notably, they challenge prevailing assumptions that political, economic, and social relationships adhere to patterns traced by linear processes. Complexity theory asserts that it is not the case, as all too many officials and analysts presume, that "we can get a value for the whole by adding up the values of its parts."[23] In the words of one analyst,

> Look out the nearest window. Is there any straight line out there that wasn't man-made? I've been asking the same question of student and professional groups for several years now, and the most common answer is a grin. Occasionally a philosophical person will comment that even the lines that look like straight lines are not straight lines if we look at them through a microscope. But even if we ignore that level of analysis, we are still stuck with the inevitable observation that natural structures are, at their core, nonlinear. If [this] is true, why do social scientists insist on describing human events as if all the rules that make those events occur are based on straight lines?[24]

[21] Dennis Overbye, "Time of Growing Pains for Information Age," *New York Times*, August 7, 2001, p. D3.

[22] For the use of this phrase, see Smith, "The Inapplicability Principle," p. 30.

[23] Holland, *Hidden Order*, p. 15.

[24] Stephen Guastello, *Chaos, Catastrophe, and Human Affairs: Application of Nonlinear Dynamics to Work, Organizations, and Social Evolution* (Mahwah, N.J.: Erlbaum, 1995), p. 1.

To view the world as pervaded with distant proximities is a useful way to ensure that human events are understood as governed by underlying nonlinear dynamics rather than by "rules . . . based on straight lines." The economic realm offers many commonplace situations that exemplify the nonlinear complexities embedded in distant proximities. Local transformations, for instance, are

> as much a part of globalization as the lateral extension of social connections across time and space. Thus whoever studies cities today, in any part of the world, is aware that what happens in a local neighbourhood is likely to be influenced by factors—such as world money and commodity markets—operating at an indefinite distance away from the neighbourhood itself. The outcome is not necessarily, or even usually, a generalized set of changes acting in a uniform direction, but consists of mutually opposed tendencies. The increasing prosperity of an urban area in Singapore might be causally related, via a complicated network of global economic ties, to the impoverishment of a neighbourhood in Pittsburgh whose local products are uncompetitive in world markets.[25]

In short, a complexity perspective acknowledges the nonlinearity of both natural and human systems. It posits human systems as constantly learning, reacting, adapting, and changing even as they persist, as sustaining continuity and change simultaneously. It is a mental set, a cast of mind that does not specify particular outcomes or solutions but that offers guidelines and lever points that can be employed to assess more clearly the specific problems for which comprehension is sought. Equally important, it is a cast of mind that ignores neither the centrality of micro-macro processes nor the role of history. Rather, focusing as it does on initial conditions and the paths that they chart for systems, complexity theory treats the historical context of situations as crucial to understanding.

The first step toward adopting a complexity perspective is to recognize that inevitably we operate with some kind of theory. It is sheer myth to believe that we need merely observe the circumstances of a situation in order to understand them. As noted elsewhere, facts do not speak for themselves; observers give them voice by sorting out those that are relevant from those that are irrelevant, and, in so doing, they bring a theoretical perspective to bear. Theory provides guidelines; it sensitizes observers to alternative possibilities; it highlights where levers might be pulled and influence wielded; it links ends to means and strategies to resources; and perhaps most of all, it infuses context and pattern into a welter of seemingly disarrayed and unrelated phenomena.

---

[25] Anthony Giddens, *The Consequences of Modernity* (Stanford, Calif.: Stanford University Press, 1990), pp. 64–65.

It follows that the inability of complexity theory to make exact predictions is not a serious drawback. Understanding and not prediction is the task of theory. It provides a basis for grasping and anticipating the general patterns within which specific events occur. The weather offers a good example. It cannot be precisely predicted at any moment in time, but

> there are building blocks—fronts, highs and lows, jet streams, and so on—and our overall understanding of changes in weather has been much advanced by theory based on these building blocks. . . . We understand the larger patterns and (many of) their causes, though the detailed trajectory through the space of weather possibilities is perpetually novel. As a result, we can do far better than the old standby: predict that "tomorrow's weather will be like today's" and you stand a 60 percent probability of being correct. A relevant theory for [complex adaptive systems] should do at least as well.[26]

Given the necessity of proceeding from a theoretical standpoint, it ought not be difficult to adopt a complexity perspective even though the virtual simultaneity of cause and effect in a time of fragmegration poses a severe methodological problem noted in chapter 2. As already indicated, many of us have in subtle ways already adopted such a perspective. Even if analysts are not tooled up in computer science and mathematics, the premises of complexity theory and the strides in comprehension they have facilitated are not difficult to grasp. Despite our conceptual insufficiencies, we are not helpless in the face of mounting complexity. As the consequences of dynamic transformations have become more pervasive, so have observers of the global scene become increasingly wiser about the ways of the world, and to a large degree we have become, each of us in our own way, complexity theorists. We not only are getting accustomed to a fragmegrative worldview composed of contradictions, anomalies, and uncertainties but also have learned that situations are multiply caused, that unintended consequences can accompany those that are intended, that seemingly stable situations can topple under the weight of cumulated grievances, that some situations are ripe for accidents waiting to happen, that expectations can be self-fulfilling, that organizational decisions are driven as much by informal as formal rules, that feedback loops can redirect the course of events, that tipping points can transform disparate micro orientations into macro outcomes, and so on through an extensive list of understandings that appear so commonplace as to obscure their origins in the social sciences only a few decades ago.[27] Equally

---

[26] Holland, *Hidden Order*, p. 168.

[27] For an eye-opening sense of how rapidly the social sciences have advanced in recent years, consider that it was only several decades ago that, for the first time, a gifted analyst arrested systematic attention to the dynamics of informal patterns of organizations, an in-

important, we now take for granted that learning occurs in social systems, that systems in crisis are vulnerable to sharp turns of direction precipitated by seemingly trivial incidents, that the difference between times one and two in any situation can often be ascribed to adaptive processes, that the surface appearance of societal tranquillity can mask underlying problems, and that "other things being equal" can be a treacherous phrase if it encourages us to ignore glaring exceptions. In short, we need to rephrase the old adage about history: it is not one damn thing after another so much as it is many damn things simultaneously.

And if we ever slip in our understanding of these subtle lessons, if we ever unknowingly revert to simplistic formulations, complexity theory serves to remind us there are no panaceas. It tells us that there are limits to how much we can comprehend of the complexity that pervades world affairs and that we have to learn to become comfortable living and acting under conditions of uncertainty.

In sum, while it is understandable that we are vulnerable to the appeal of panaceas, this need not be the case. The analytic capacities and concepts of those of us who study world affairs are not so far removed from complexity theorists that we need be in awe of their accomplishments or ready to emulate their methods. Few of us may have the skills or resources to undertake sophisticated computer simulations, but as a philosophical perspective, complexity theory is not out of our reach. None of its premises and concepts is alien to our analytic habits. They sum to a perspective that is consistent with the transformations that appear to be taking the world into unfamiliar realms. Hence, through its explication, the complexity perspective can serve as a guide both to comprehending a fragmegrated world and to theorizing within its limits.

A Normative Approach

No less relevant, to revert to the theme developed at the outset of the chapter, complexity theory can be readily put to the service of normative commitments. Even the most passionate crusaders can enhance their chances of improving the human condition by being aware of the power of small events, the properties of situations that can emerge as they co-evolve with their environments, the capacities for self-organization that can advance or thwart desired goals, and the links between initial conditions and subsequent outcomes. They may have to suspend their subjective impulses while empirically assessing the conditions they seek to pro-

---

sight that is today taken for granted. See Herbert A. Simon, *Administrative Behavior: A Study of Decision-Making Behavior in Administrative Organization* (New York: Macmillan, 1945).

mote, but patience in this regard seems bound to pay off. To suspend norms is not to abandon them. To pursue them in the absence of sound empirical understanding is to undermine the prospects for normative progress. Complexity theory, like any social science perspective, can thus serve to discipline our value concerns and, in so doing, enable us to move closer to realizing them.

The concept of stability offers useful insights into the ways in which subjective concerns can be clarified through complexity theory. Confronted with pervasive uncertainties at every level of community and in every issue arena—with an appreciation that any small event or the initial conditions of any situation can upset normal routines and the prevailing equilibrium—people in all the local, global, and private worlds are likely to yearn for stability and, in so doing, to treat stable conditions as objective realities. But stable equilibria not only consist of highly complex, delicate, and fragile balances; they also are profoundly and thoroughly the focus of normative preferences. One person's stability is another's instability. How, then, to draw distinctions between the two? Can the normative foundations of stability and instability be framed in such a way that they can be distinguished from empirical observations? Are preferences for stability at the micro level of individuals a prerequisite for empirical stability at the macro level of collectivities, and vice versa? Are Affirmative Globals or Locals likely to perceive stability where Resistant Globals or Locals see instability, and vice versa?

To begin to respond to such questions it is important to recognize that stability is a form of change, that the pace at which stable change occurs can vary considerably—from infinitesimal to incremental to abrupt change—and that both individuals and collectivities can undergo any form of change. It follows that what counts is whether the unfolding changes are acceptable or unacceptable at the micro level and thereby contribute to or detract from the coherence of macro collectivities. We can thus distinguish between two dimensions of stability, its value dimension (acceptability) and its analytic dimension (collectivity coherence). And it is here, in the confluence of the two dimensions, that complexity theory serves to clarify normative issues. While the coherence of a collectivity can be empirically assessed in terms of whether it is likely to retain its adaptability, the degree to which its stability is acceptable requires a normative appraisal. If people at the micro level adapt to change and thus accept the emerging properties of their collectivities, or if they maladaptively resist the directions in which change is taking their collectivities, then their normative responses will facilitate or undermine macro coherence.

Complexity theory is especially applicable to the stability of situations because, as collectivities evolve through time, people can differ over the question of whether the pace and direction of the evolutionary processes

TABLE 9.2.
Stability along Two Dimensions

Analytic Dimension	Value Dimension	
	Acceptable	Unacceptable
High Collectivity Coherence	Chinese reforms	Burma
Low Collectivity Coherence	Russia	Apartheid in South Africa

are or are not acceptable. Thus the analytic and value dimensions can be at odds. During the Cold War and not infrequently in subsequent years, for example, coherent systems lacking in basic democratic practices were treated as acceptable, just as democratic systems on the brink of collapse were regarded as unacceptable.

It follows that differentiating between stable and unstable situations in world affairs involves assessing their analytic and value dimensions, with the former focusing on degrees of collectivity coherence and the latter on degrees of acceptability. Table 9.2 presents a 2 × 2 matrix that highlights this distinction between the two dimensions. The entries in the cells are examples drawn from my own values and analytic judgments about contemporary collectivities. Assuming the distinctions between high and low collectivity coherence and between acceptable and unacceptable situations are adequately specified (a task not undertaken here), any assessments can be readily classified in one of the cells, thus providing a first cut at locating what are considered to be the stable and unstable features of the world scene. Second and third cuts are suggested below by identifying four structures of stability and four paces at which situations may or may not change.

The four structures of stability consist of those at the level of individuals (micro stability), those that prevail within collectivities (macro stability), those that persist among both individuals and collectivities (micromacro stability), and those operative among collectivities (macro-macro stability). All four structures have a common quality. They all are based on the premise that stability consists of acceptable changes in which systemic coherence is free of widespread efforts to resist, prevent, or undo them.

And it is here that complexity theory's stress on initial conditions can guide analysis: people can vary in their sensitivity to whether the prevailing stability amounts to an initial condition that may undergo unexpected changes. They have to attach priorities to the analytic and value dimensions of potential changes in the context of each stability structure. Most notably, different consequences can follow when change is viewed as reflecting movement away from an initial condition toward an unknown outcome. Such appraisals are likely to be differentially accepted at the micro level on the one hand and the other three levels on the other hand. More often than not the fear of unknown outcomes will lead ordinary people to view pending changes as unacceptable, but such a reaction at the micro level is unlikely to be matched by ruling elites and governments at the macro and macro-macro levels because the latter tend to accord higher priority to collectivity coherence than to the value dimensions of stability. While publics may not be interested in the acceptability of some distant proximities and thus are not consistently preoccupied with change and stability elsewhere in the world, Territorial Globals and their governmental agencies are charged with being sensitive to low collectivity coherence abroad and thus may be quick to perceive unacceptable stability. From the hegemonic perspective of U.S. officials, for example, the world is pervaded with numerous situations that are viewed as unacceptable and call for efforts to resist, prevent, or undo them.

It follows that whatever may be the pace of change, global stability prevails as long as the change is widely accepted at the micro level of individuals, the macro level of collectivities and their leaders, and the macro-macro level of other collectivities. Again, complexity theory and its focus on adaptation and coevolution become relevant. Global stability is rare because only infrequently are any of the rates of change acceptable to most actors at every level. The advent of global television exemplifies an abrupt change that did not undermine global stability because, with few exceptions, it was widely accepted by people and collectivities everywhere. On the other hand, the abrupt changes that accompany successful revolutions, invasions, and terrorist attacks are likely to be widely accepted at the micro level of the revolutionaries, invaders, and terrorists and the macro level of their collectivities, but at the same time such changes will foster macro-macro instability if other countries view the revolution, invasion, or terrorism as a threat to their coherence and undertake to reverse it. Likewise, infinitesimal or incremental economic growth will be acceptable to those with vested interests in the growth at micro and macro levels, but such change is likely to be unacceptable to the poor (and their spokespersons) who do not participate in the processes of growth. In addition, the more infinitesimal change borders on the absence of change (as may be the case in highly authoritarian regimes that prevent change), the more can stasis be said to prevail, though in all likelihood it will not prevail for long because in the emergent epoch stasis runs counter to the aspirations of people, who will become restless and aspire to at least a modicum of change the more the stasis persists and the less responsive are their society's institutions.

Given this linking of stability to change, it seems reasonable to presume that, on balance, Affirmative Locals and Globals view globalizing processes, irrespective of the pace at which they foster change, as ultimately promoting collectivity coherence and thus as acceptable. Contrariwise, Resistant Globals and Locals are likely to perceive the potential of incoherence embedded in fragmegrative processes and thus, again irrespective of their pace, to judge them as unacceptable. Variability along these lines, of course, is customary in world affairs. Whether the observers are policy makers, journalists, academics, or ordinary citizens in any country, some will view situations as essentially stable while others see them as unstable, depending on the criteria of collectivity coherence through which their assessments are made. The entries in table 9.3 are illustrative in this regard, with me being the observer employing my value and system-coherence criteria to assess acceptable (bold type) or unacceptable (italics) systems or situations on the current world scene.

The foregoing formulation enables us to probe further into the value and analytic dimensions of stability. Table 9.3 makes clear that, irrespective of the pace of change or the structure of stability, some situations are acceptable and some are not, depending on the value and analytic perspectives that different observers bring to bear. Change is considered noxious when it is perceived as undermining the well-being of people and/or the coherence of their collectivities by perpetuating poverty, racial prejudice, and a host of other injustices. On the other hand, most people view change as acceptable when it enlarges the competence of individuals and the coherence of communities, thereby allowing for a coevolution that improves the human condition. Viewed in this way, uncertain situations need not be feared if they involve steady movement toward goals marked by fluctuations within an acceptable range. As indicated earlier, change can be a dynamic form of stability or instability, one that allows for progress on the part of communities and their members or for a deterioration of their circumstances.

Implicit here is the large degree to which stability and change are part and parcel of the aforementioned close links between collectivities at the macro level and individuals at the micro level. Exceptions aside (see later discussion), these links may be symmetrical in the sense that changes at one level can generate comparable changes at other levels. Situations that most people view as expressive of abrupt change are especially conspicuous in this regard: the instability that accompanies unacceptable abrupt change at one level is likely to precipitate parallel changes at other levels. Iraq's abrupt invasion of Kuwait in 1990, for example, disrupted the prevailing macro-macro stability and generated abrupt macro change on the part of the countries that joined to form the thirty-two-nation coalition to reverse the situation. Similarly, incremental and progressive change at one level is likely to be matched by acceptable change at other levels, as is

TABLE 9.3.
Stability and Instability in World Affairs: 1990s Examples (acceptable systems in bold type; unacceptable systems in italics)

	Stability Structures			
Pace of Change	*Micro*	*Macro*	*Macro-Macro*	*Micro-Macro*
Stasis (no change)	*Vigilantes* **Patriotism**	*North Korea* **Japanese culture**	*Arms trade* **U.S.-British relations**	*Burma* **Postwar Bosnia**
Infinitesimal change	*Drug consumption* **Decline of AIDS**	*Colombia* **Iran**	*Middle East* **Decline of populations**	*Northern Ireland* **Human rights**
Incremental change	*Rich-poor gap* **Emergence of Chinese middle class**	*Russia* **Spread of democracy**	*UN financing* **International election monitoring**	*Afghanistan* **European Union**
Abrupt change	*Flight of refugees* **Fall of the Berlin Wall**	*East Timor* **Collapse of the Soviet Union**	*Nuclear proliferation* **End of Cold War**	*World Trade Center collapse* **Apartheid's end in South Africa**

illustrated by, say, those situations in which close links are established between domestic publics and governmental policies over environmental regulations.

But there are important exceptions. The most conspicuous asymmetry occurs when activists are quiescent at the micro level and the silence of the Tuned-Out Passives and Insular Locals is magnified, thus suggesting that publics are oblivious to or unconcerned about distant situations even as their governments may perceive some situations as threatening a diminution of collectivity coherence and act to prevent further deterioration. Similarly, incremental micro changes can, on occasion, foster abrupt macro changes. Consider, for instance, the conclusions of one analyst who studied the micro level in the United States over three decades. He "finally" found that

> societies learn and react differently than individuals. Surprisingly, social learning is often far more abrupt than individual learning. It is more extreme. It is less incremental. Mature adults who encounter new circumstances will usually adjust to them in a slow and moderate fashion. They have learned that cautious

adjustments keep them from making huge mistakes. But for a variety of reasons, societies react less cautiously. They tend to lurch suddenly and abruptly from one extreme to the other.

We have developed a theory to account for the discontinuities. We call it "lurch-and-learn." It holds that a typical pattern of social change starts with a sharp lurch in the opposite direction which is then followed by a complex series of modifications based on trial and error learning. Some of this learning is valid and some of it is false. People do not always draw the right lessons from trial and error learning.

We have found that two factors usually precipitate such lurches: a change in circumstances and a lack of responsiveness to the change on the part of institutions.[28]

COMPLEXITY AND STABILITY AT THE MICRO LEVEL

Given the nature of the emergent epoch, it should be clear that fragmegrative dynamics are assaulting individuals—elites and ordinary people, citizens and aliens, consumers and investors, migrants and workers, rural peasants and computer technicians, the poor and the wealthy, Locals and Globals—at the micro level. For some the assault is destabilizing in the sense that long-standing habits and affiliations are challenged by the emergent properties of their collectivities, while others experience beneficial consequences in the sense that their enhanced skills enable them to adapt to and coevolve with the changes, to shoulder new responsibilities, and to aspire to new accomplishments. In other words, many subtleties accompany the impact of fragmegrative dynamics at the micro level: none of them has singularly stabilizing or destabilizing consequences; all of them can serve both to promote and to undermine the stability of the lives and routines of people. For our purposes, then, it is useful to identify the ways in which the dynamics of the emergent epoch may foster abrupt or incremental changes at the micro level that are sufficiently widespread to feed into the behavior of collectivities at the macro and macro-macro levels. Since most people everywhere experience one or more consequences of the clash between globalizing and localizing forces, their experiences become meaningful as micro instabilities only when they cumulate and result in unintentional or intentional inputs, in collective unease or action to which policy makers must attend.

Perhaps the most destabilizing consequences of fragmegration at the micro level that can cumulate into a powerful collective force are the insecurities that stem from the rapid and bewildering transformations

---

[28] Daniel Yankelovich, "How American Individualism Is Evolving," *The Public Perspective*, February/March 1998, p. 4.

noted earlier. With their worlds turned upside down by the multiple and swift flows of ideas, goods, people, money, crime, drugs, pollution, and terrorism that are part and parcel of the emergent epoch, numerous people undergo an uprooting of their daily routines and feel lost and threatened by the changes. Often they cope with the sense of loss by seeking comfort through religion, by joining labor unions, by supporting protest organizations, by clinging ever more fervently to local mores and norms, and by a host of other means of valuing the local and downplaying the global. When such reactions and fears are aggregated into collective action through the mobilizing efforts of elites, they result in abrupt changes that can roil societies and become salient pockets of instability on the world stage. The Iranian revolution of 1979 is an example of this potential for unstable situations. Secession movements in the former Soviet Union, Indonesia, and elsewhere are also illustrative. In such cases support at the micro level of mass publics can be abruptly generated by leaders, who for various reasons and using diverse techniques are able to tap into people's need for a sense of belonging. Given an epoch marked by a skill revolution, an organizational explosion, and weakened states, it is hardly surprising that micro-macro dynamics underlie a rapid proliferation of secessionist movements.

But abrupt changes at the micro level are not always the result of gifted leaders or demagogues. Sometimes circumstances evolve in such a way that multitudes of individuals react abruptly in the same way without prior provocation by their leaders and, in so doing, create as much instability through unintentional inputs at the macro level as is the case when publics are mobilized. The sudden flight of refugees responding to a shared fear of pending aggression is a frequent instance of unstable situations that evolve swiftly out of uncoordinated micro actions. A sharp collapse of a currency or stock market is another cases in point. As investors and traders read new economic data as portending problems ahead, so will their separate acts of withdrawing investments, selling stock, or trading currencies conduce to macro instabilities.

Nor does the aggregation of individuals in the absence of mobilization by leaders always result in abrupt change. Often the aggregation can occur incrementally as more and more people are induced to move in the same direction with the passage of time. When fearful reactions spread widely through incremental change that eventually cumulates to the point where large numbers of people are in distress and thus potentially mobilizable, they may well evoke governmental responses at the macro level that, in turn, create an unstable situation. The Falun Gong movement in China is a recent instance of incremental micro aggregation in response to a perceived need for spiritual guidance to cope with the complexities of globalization that gave rise to an unstable situation. As Beijing's leaders came to view the movement as a threat to their party's rule and their country's stability, they clamped down on it and risked fulfilling their own prophecy of instability. Much the same can be said about the massacre at Tiananmen Square in 1989. It was precipitated by uncoordinated individual actions that ultimately cumulated in a mass movement that macro leaders felt obliged to suppress.

In sum, there are many routes through which developments can be unacceptable at the micro level of individuals in any of the local or global worlds, thus generating unstable macro or macro-macro consequences. Indeed, it can reasonably be anticipated that in the present era the unease fostered by globalizing dynamics, combined with the skill revolution and the organizational explosion, will increase the prospects for collective action and generate an ever greater number of diverse situations marked by instability. This conclusion renders ever more difficult the task of Territorial Globals charged with being sensitive to patterns that can get out of hand and foster low-collectivity coherence elsewhere in the world. It means that their analytic antennae must be as geared to the grass roots as to the more easily comprehended threats that may evolve at the macro level of governments and societies. And to the extent that macro leaders ignore, underestimate, or otherwise misread the complexity through which micro circumstances may foster unwanted collective actions, then to that extent they will initiate feedback processes that perpetuate instability and limit stability at both the micro and macro levels.

CONCLUSION

The widening interdependence of publics, economies, societies, and polities generated by the collapse of time and space has heightened the possibility of instabilities in one part of the world spreading quickly to other parts. Terrorists emulate each other; currency collapses cascade quickly across national boundaries; secessionist movements are contagious; environmental, human rights, and labor groups join protests against the policies of the IMF, the World Bank, and the WTO; increasing numbers of states can be classified as "messy," as "too big to fail; too messy to work."[29] Such patterns cumulatively suggest an expanding number of pockets of instability on a global scale.

Yet generation after generation has managed to cope with the complexities they are compelled to confront. And the present generation is no exception. For all the problems and uncertainties that mark the emergent epoch, countertrends can also be noted. Most people have adapted to the changes, and most collectivities remain coherent in the context of

---

[29] Thomas L. Friedman, "What a Mess!" *New York Times*, October 3, 2000, p. A31.

increasingly democratic practices. And while there are numerous unstable situations in every region of the world, the evolving bifurcation of the global stage and the sheer number of actors that clamber upon it increasingly make it difficult for a few collectivities to dominate the others. Vulnerabilities to terrorism are likely to continue for the foreseeable future, but terrorists cannot dominate; they can only wreak havoc. And when they do, it turns out that salience attaches less to the unacceptable instability they foster and more to the restored, resilient, and acceptable set of stable conditions that subsequently emerge.

In sum, as the course of events becomes ever more complex, so do normative challenges become ever more numerous and ubiquitous. With history now a matter of many damn things simultaneously, the task of sorting out subjective preferences becomes increasingly urgent and difficult.

CHAPTER TEN

The Skill Revolution

When [1989] was over, the people had changed the course of history.

—News item[1]

If there is one broad general trend observable at this critical juncture of world history, it must surely be the awakening of the people, the common man, from rich and poor nations alike, who are now clamoring and positioning themselves to have more say in the determination of their livelihoods and well being, and demanding more transparency in the execution of the affairs of state.

—Bichai Rattakul[2]

For governments and big companies, the telecoms revolution will be unsettling, because it will put more power into the homes and on to the desks of ordinary people. Voters and customers alike will find it easier to make comparisons, acquire information, by-pass gatekeepers, cross borders.

—The Economist[3]

Here, I am a name on a page; there, I am a web-site address; elsewhere I am a national insurance number in a government computer. My relationship to modern society—my social identity—has become unglued from the contexts, communities and expectations that once circumscribed my (and your) knowledge of who I am and how I live. Today, I am responsible and liable for my own identity. No longer bound by external reference points, my identity is a moving projection through the complex social and institutional contours of a globalized cultural system. In this world, . . . each person is required to steer his or her own individual course between the threats and the promises of modern society.

—Martin O'Brien[4]

---

[1] "Special Report," *Newsweek*, December 25, 1989, p. 19.

[2] Speaker of the Thailand House of Representatives, as quoted in Barbara Crosette, "At a U.N. 'Summit,' Lawmakers Urge Stronger Legislative Bodies," *New York Times*, September 2, 2000, p. A3.

[3] September 30, 1995, p. 16.

[4] "The Sociology of Anthony Giddens: An Introduction," in Anthony Giddens and

> [T]he perceptions of ordinary citizens are more to be trusted
> than the pretensions of national leaders and of the bureaucracies
> who serve them.
>
> —Susan Strange[5]

WHILE IT IS NOT always self-evident how local and global developments get linked, it is clear, as stressed earlier, that individuals are key variables of the emergent epoch, that they need extensive skills to negotiate the identities, construct the scenarios, make the judgments, and refine the imagination needed to cope with the complexities of fragmegration that intrude ever more closely upon their concerns. No less important, the need for skills is also pressing at the macro level. As information technologies become increasingly relevant to the routines of collectivities, so has the need increased for personnel trained to operate effectively in the functioning of economies, societies, and polities. Thus both micro and macro imperatives underlie processes whereby most people in the world can be hypothesized to have enlarged their competence in recent decades. Their multiple identities have become more manageable. Their scenarios have become lengthier and more elaborate. Their judgments have become sharper and more incisive. Their imaginations have become more wide-ranging and less inhibited. Their training is more extensive than ever before.

To be sure, such trends are as old as human history, but the acceleration of distant proximities spawned by the fragmegrative epoch has heightened the need for adaptive skills. The pace of acceleration may vary widely among different groups, but it is doubtful whether the skills of any group have remained constant or declined. And not only is the skill revolution worldwide in scope; it is also unfolding at all levels of society, from the rich to the poor, from elites to ordinary persons, from the Circumstantial Passives to the Insular Locals to the Affirmative Globals. Stated more emphatically, acceleration is the hallmark of our time, and thus arguably the pace of skill acquisition today has expanded at a faster rate than was the case in prior epochs.

It follows that a probe of the micro-macro dynamics that sustain fragmegration requires amplification of the hypothesis that the talents of in-

---

Christopher Pierson, *Conversations with Anthony Giddens: Making Sense of Modernity* (Cambridge, Mass.: Polity Press, 1998), pp. 18–19.

[5] *The Retreat of the State: The Diffusion of Power in the World Economy* (Cambridge: Cambridge University Press, 1996), p. 3.

dividuals are—through the skill revolution—making an ever-greater contribution to public affairs as a consequence of either their individual actions or their collective inputs into macro collectivities. It is a controversial issue, as will be seen, and thus necessitates elaboration of the circumstances and competencies through which people have acquired a central place on the world stage.

CONCEPTUAL PROBLEMS

The conceptual foundations of the skill revolution are not self-evident. Distinguishing among analytic, emotional, and imaginative skills is not an easy task. For example, at least twenty types of intelligence, both cognitive and emotional, have been identified as relevant to how people lead their lives.[6] Differentiating among these diverse means of reaching understanding is obviously a huge conceptual challenge. Do people in the local, global, and private worlds systematically differ in the kinds of intelligence they have? Are their skills the equivalent of learning, wisdom, and knowledge? Do their skills cumulate with experience and result in empowerment? Are the skills enhanced by computer technologies dehumanizing and alienating as well as enlarging and enriching? Is it conceivable that people with little information can be as skillful as those with extensive information? Are skills transferable from one issue area to another? Are analytic and emotional skills compatible, or are the former more suited to technical matters and the latter more relevant to identity issues? Is there a point beyond which information overload fosters a diminution of skill levels? Do all peoples have a modicum of learning skills that enable them to adapt to new circumstances, or are they equally likely to fall back on stereotypes and simplistic either-or generalizations? Do situational factors—such as fluctuations between periods of global tension and tranquillity—determine whether people resort to simplistic or complex patterns of thought? Or are analytic and emotional skills embedded in people's character and thus independent of prevailing situations?

This is not the place to respond to all these questions. Some of them are clarified in the ensuing discussion, but mainly they are raised here only to highlight the complexity of analyzing the skill revolution. Rather than being put off by the difficulties associated with the concept, however, I take an open-ended approach here by conceiving of skills as enlarged through information, observation, and/or experience, and thus as always subject to change. This approach is open-ended in the sense that

---

[6] D. Goleman, *Emotional Intelligence* (New York: Bantam Books, 1995), p. 38. See also Steven L. Gordon, "Micro-sociological Theories of Emotion," in H. J. Helle and S. N. Eisenstadt (eds.), *Micro-sociological Theory* (Beverly Hills, Calif.: Sage, 1985), pp. 133–47; and Neta C. Crawford, "The Passion of World Politics: Propositions on Emotion and Emotional Relationships," *International Security*, Vol. 24 (spring 2000), pp. 116–56.

it does not posit a fixed baseline for human capacities. No assumption is made, in contrast to some sociologists, that "cognition is limited to a few relatively uncomplex operations [such that] people cannot follow a chain of thought very many steps, either forward to its consequences or back to its premises."[7] Such an assumption posits people as deficient in framing scenarios, but the perspective employed here allows for learning, adaptation, and growth as means through which people cope with the complexity of present-day situations.

Emotional and analytic skills are conceived as interactive and cumulative. "In a very real sense we have two minds, one that thinks and one that feels," and taken together, "[t]hese two fundamental ways of knowing interact to construct our mental life. One, the rational mind, is the mode of comprehension of which we are typically conscious: more prominent in awareness, thoughtful, able to ponder and reflect. But alongside that there is another system of knowing: impulsive and powerful, if sometimes illogical—the emotional mind."[8] There is no reason not to assume both minds are also active and interactive in the way people respond to world affairs. Where the rational mind analyzes the logical implications of distant events and the circuitous routes through which they can culminate in one's home and pocketbook, the emotional mind further shrinks the faraway into the close-at-hand[9] and renders "distant proximities" into features of daily life.

A Multidimensional Phenomenon

Diverse talents constitute what is meant here by skills. These range from advanced learning to street smarts, from reflective to judgmental capacities, from technical training to native intelligence, and from experiential wisdom to intellectual curiosity. In short, the skill revolution is not one-dimensional. Its various dimensions can be summarized as consisting of analytic, emotional, and imaginative skills, each of which has its own dynamics even as each also contributes to the expansion of the others.[10] Analytic skills involve the ability to trace the links out of which cause-and-effect chains are fashioned. The causal chains are ever more complex, circuitous, and rapid in the present era of instant communications, thereby

[7] R. Collins, "On the Microfoundations of Macrosociology," *American Journal of Sociology*, Vol. 86 (1981), p. 992.

[8] Goleman, *Emotional Intelligence*, p. 8.

[9] J. LeDoux, *The Emotional Brain: The Mysterious Underpinnings of Emotional Life* (New York: Simon and Schuster, 1996), Chap. 9.

[10] Some analysts posit "ingenuity" as another dimension of the skill revolution, but the analytic and imaginative dimensions developed here subsume its focus on an ability "to solve practical social and technical problems." See Thomas Homer-Dixon, "The Ingenuity Gap: Can Poor Countries Adapt to Resource Scarcity?" *Population and Development Review*, Vol. 21 (September 1995), pp. 587–612.

necessitating a greater readiness and sensitivity to tracking how situations unfold. Expanded emotional skills refer to a supplementing of analytic talents with heightened inclinations to assess situations as good or bad, as welcoming or threatening, capacities that have also been expanded as a consequence of the world shrinking and impinging ever more closely on daily routines. Being and feeling more competent, individuals are more aware of their values with respect to issues on the global agenda. At least some of those who might have responded "no opinion" when completing public affairs questionnaires in previous eras are today more likely to render judgments on whether a proposed policy or prior action is or was desirable or noxious.[11] Scenes of genocide, accounts of riots, reports of corruption, and the many other situations laden with heavy ethical or normative implications and depicted by the mass media have enriched the sensitivities of people and heightened their emotional skills.

Perhaps the least-appreciated dimension of the skill revolution involves the way in which the dynamics of the fragmegrative era have freed up people's imaginations—their capacity to envision alternative futures, lifestyles, and circumstances for themselves, their families, and their cherished organizations. Their electronic connections, their travel, their friends and family abroad, their ethnic ties, and their professional contacts all serve to stimulate notions of different—and often preferred—ways of living. However the stimuli are provided—whether by global television, soap operas, or letters from relatives working as maids in Hong Kong, cousins who find employment in Saudi Arabia, or children who marry foreign spouses—the materials for wide-ranging imaginative musings are abundantly available. The learning embedded in messages sent home is less directly experiential for the recipients than are the encounters reported by their authors, but it can nevertheless be a major contributor to the more worldly skills of those who do not travel. It may even be that the letters and phone calls from relatives abroad can be as much a window on the norms and practices of distant places as those offered on the television screen. These stimuli are especially relevant for peoples in developing countries whose circumstances previously limited contacts with other cultures and alternative lifestyles. Indeed, from the perspective of those who have long been hemmed in by the realities of life on or below the poverty line, the freeing up of their imaginative capacities is among the most powerful forces at work in the age of fragmegration. Such individuals are better able to visualize the benefits and

---

[11] I recently undertook to test this hypothesis by compiling data on the percentage of "no opinion" responses in U.S. public opinion polls from the 1930s to the present. While slight traces of a decline in these percentages were discernible, for a number of reasons the data were not sufficiently reliable to justify a claim the hypothesis was upheld.

drawbacks of life in distant places and thus draw on skills they did not previously have. The imagination sharpens generational differences, divides families, undermines cultural affinities, and otherwise disturbs the routines and relations of individuals and communities.[12] Stated more generally, "The single most underestimated force in international affairs today is what happens—thanks to globalization—when we all increasingly know how everyone else lives. People everywhere start to demand the same things, and when they can't get them, they get frustrated."[13]

It is important to stress that the skill revolution does not refer only to levels of information or intelligence. While it is doubtless the case that the more training, information, and intelligence a person has, the more skillful he or she is likely to be, this linkage involves more than a one-to-one correlation. One can think of numerous persons who are well-informed and highly intelligent but who use these capacities in less than skillful ways. Contrariwise, there is more than a little evidence that people with scant education and limited intelligence handle situations wisely, sensibly, and with aplomb. The Oxford Ph.D. and the Asian peasant may have vastly different degrees of sagacity and knowledge, but they may also be equally capable of grasping the underlying dynamics of situations, anticipating their outcomes, and imagining alternative resolutions. Indeed, it is not inconceivable that in some situations the street smarts of less educated people will prove more insightful than those of their well-educated counterparts. A compelling illustration in this regard is provided by the work of C K Janu, who is illiterate, has no political ideology, was born of poverty, and had the experience of working as a domestic and daily-wage laborer since she was seven in Kerala, India. But today she is the leader of a movement on behalf of land reform for Kerala's "tribals," who constitute barely 1 percent of the state's total population. In effect, against all odds, she "has come to dominate public life in Kerala by sheer determination and huge will power." Indeed, she leaves no doubt as to the source of her considerable skills: "Experience is my guide."[14] Another example in this regard is that of elderly Korean women whom the Japanese used as "comfort women" for their troops in World War II and who seek acknowledgment of and compensation for their mistreat-

[12] The relevance of the imagination to the dynamics of change is compellingly developed in Arjun Appadurai, *Modernity at Large: Cultural Dimensions of Globalization* (Minneapolis: University of Minnesota Press, 1996). See also Marion O'Callaghan, "Continuities in Imagination," in Jan Nederveen Pieterse and Bhikhu Parekh (eds.), *The Decolonization of Imagination: Culture, Knowledge and Power* (London: Zed Books, 1995), pp. 22–42.

[13] Thomas L. Friedman, "Three Movies and a Funeral," *New York Times*, June 16, 2000, p. A31.

[14] Mukundan C. Menon, "C K Janu, Experience Is My Guide," http://www.infochangeindia.org/changemakers9.jsp.

ment: apparently they are fully aware of the different legal consequences that flow from the distinction between an expression of "regret" and an apology on the part of the Japanese government. Likewise, experience is teaching persons in rural areas of China to question and challenge the residency rules that treat them as illegal migrants when they move to cities to improve their standard of living: they have "become increasingly aware of the discrimination and increasingly vocal about their rights."[15]

Similarly, birth control education and television followed by word-of-mouth communication are assessed to be major reasons why fertility rates in India, Brazil, and other countries of the developing world are falling at much quicker rates than had been expected. The education is enabling women in rural villages to take control of their reproductive lives, and television programs depicting small and happy families are providing incentives to restrict the number of children they have. In addition, according to Gita Sen, an Indian economist, the fertility decline "seems to start in one village and then spread to other places around that area. Attitudes are changing and people are watching what their neighbors are doing."[16] The director of the UN population division, Joseph Chamie, interpreted these patterns in a micro-macro context: "A woman in a village making a decision to have one or two or at most three children is a small decision in itself, but when these get compounded by millions and millions and millions of women in India and Brazil and Egypt, it has global consequences."[17]

Put differently, whether they are grounded in experience or intelligence, skills are needed to convert information into applicable and usable understanding. No matter how plentiful it may be, information is not useful unless it can be organized into knowledge relevant to its user. It follows that people do not need detailed information in order to grasp the nature and potential of situations or the range within which the situations may evolve. What counts is their working knowledge, their understanding of the rules of the game at work in any situation, of how individuals, groups, and nations are likely to confront new situations and manage long-standing ones. Many observers tend toward apoplexy when confronted with findings depicting the proportion of people who do not know the name of the capital of Pakistan or have not heard of the World Trade Organization, but it is an apoplexy that rests on the premise that

---

[15] Elizabeth Rosenthal, "China Eases Rules Binding People to Birth Regions," *New York Times*, October 23, 2001, p. A6.

[16] Quoted in Barbara Crossette, "Population Estimates Fall as Poor Women Assert Control," *New York Times*, March 10, 2002, p. 3. In India the overall fertility rate has declined from 2.1 children per woman to 1.85 children, which portends roughly 85 million fewer people in India by 2050 and 686 million fewer by 2150.

[17] Quoted in ibid.

only with precise information can people reason their way through to a keen grasp of current situations.[18] It may well be sufficient to know that a coup d'état in South Asia, or anywhere else, results in developments that culminate in one's pocketbook or living room without having specific information about who initiated the coup or what country it occurred in. Likewise, it is sufficient to recognize that tariff rules imposed by an international organization that one's country is about to join will have consequences for the price at which one can sell one's products without knowing either the name of the organization or the specific rules it is obliged to follow. In short, there is no necessary correspondence between the working knowledge and the levels of information one brings to situations, and it is the expansion of working knowledge, analytic as well as imaginative, experiential as well as intellectual, emotional as well as historical, that lies at the heart of the skill revolution and enables people everywhere to partake of it.

An insightful example of the operation of working knowledge is provided by an experiment conducted in the early 1970s with samples of chess players and non–chess players. Each sample was exposed to a screen on which was flashed for five seconds the same chessboard and then asked to re-create what they saw. The chess players, having working knowledge of the game, had no trouble with the assignment, but the non–chess players, not knowing the rules of the game, were helpless. They could not re-create what they observed. More telling, the chess players were then subdivided into two groups, one of which was shown a chessboard with pieces arrayed from a game, while the other was confronted with a chessboard with the pieces arrayed at random. While the former again had no trouble re-creating what they saw in five seconds, the latter were as helpless as the non–chess players. Confronted with an unfamiliar situation, with a situation for which their working knowledge was not appropriate, they could not cope.[19] And so it is with all the situations that arise in the lives of people everywhere in the world. Increasingly the distant situations are familiar proximities; increasingly the underlying rules on which their development unfolds correspond to earlier circumstances, and thus increasingly the working knowledge of people expands, whatever their levels of information and education.

In other words, to note that individuals have become increasingly skillful in relating themselves to world affairs is not to say that they are necessarily more informed about them. What is involved is reasoning ability in

---

[18] See, for example, Richard Craig, "Don't Know Much about History," *New York Times*, December 8, 1997, p. A23.

[19] William G. Chase and Herbert A. Simon, "Perception in Chess," *Cognitive Psychology*, Vol. 4 (1973), pp. 55–81.

the case of analytic skills, self-consciousness in the case of emotional skills, unrestrained thinking in the case of imaginative skills, and self-reflection in the case of skills acquired experientially, and none of these is dependent on the level of information possessed. One may be able to reason better or to be more self-aware and freer to think creatively the more informed one is; but such skills can thrive and deepen whatever the extent of the information available. A general understanding of the major contradictions and uncertainties that predominate in our fragmegrative epoch, as distinguished from detailed facts about particular situations, is sufficient to construct the scenarios that trace distant developments back into proximate circumstances and that are thus expressive of analytic skills. Likewise, a general understanding along these lines plus a sensitivity to one's values and the priority among them are sufficient to the nourishment of emotional skills. As for the imagination, it too can thrive in the absence of extensive information. It can, that is, as long as periodic inputs, be they remote or personal, are experienced that provoke speculation or reflection about alternative ways of living.

Viewed in this way, it is hardly surprising that when people have been accorded the right to vote for the first time, they may not be familiar with the details of democratic processes, but experience tells them they have been afforded a new opportunity to enhance their well-being. Consequently, they turn out in droves despite a steaming hot sun and long line in order to cast their ballot. Such has been the pattern in every newly independent country in recent years. In East Timor, for example, more than 90 percent of the 425,000 eligible voters participated in that country's first balloting for an assembly to frame a new constitution.[20]

In short, working knowledge, unlike information and intellectual erudition, is acquired through experience, through observing one's self or others handling or failing to handle the diverse situations that arise every day. Experiential knowledge is more likely than other forms of knowledge to leave residues of understanding. Neither great intelligence nor a backlog of information is required for experiential knowledge to cumulate. That which is experienced or observed firsthand is not easily forgotten. It lingers, and as it does, it builds upon itself. The commonalties and discrepancies of situations get merged in the senses and understandings of individuals, with the result that their working knowledge springs from an expanding base on which they can draw.

This is not to overlook the skills of those with advanced education or technical competence or other specialists. Such persons are, of course, central to the viability of societies, scientific progress, and economic de-

[20] Seth Mydans, "Timorese Vote in Prelude to Nationhood," *New York Times*, August 31, 2001, p. A8.

velopment. Businesses, governments, advocacy groups, and, indeed, organizations of all kinds are consistently on the lookout for personnel with honed skills in order to enrich their human capital.[21] For decades after World War II, numerous individuals with technical skills moved from the developing to the developed world in order to improve their circumstances, creating thereby what came to be called a "brain drain" for the less developed countries. More recently, however, many of these highly skilled persons are returning to their original homes, a process that has appropriately been called a "brain circulation" and that has substantially contributed to growth in Shanghai, Bangalore, and other locales in the developing world.[22] The skill revolution, in short, knows no boundaries. It is unfolding at every level, among elites as well as ordinary people.

A MULTIPLICITY OF SOURCES

Of the many sources that have given rise to the skill revolution, perhaps the most powerful and certainly the most controversial are the various electronic technologies that have developed so rapidly in the last few decades. While a fuller exploration of the relevance of these technologies to micro-macro dynamics is undertaken in the next chapter, here the focus is on their impact as a source of the skill revolution. One of these technologies is global television—a one-to-many technology that, for better or worse, reaches into most homes throughout the world. On the one hand, the ideas and pictures it conveys often provide new perspectives on the practices, problems, and cultures of places to which people would not otherwise be exposed. In this sense TV serves to provoke analyses, evoke emotions, and expand imaginations in ways and to an extent that have no parallel in prior history. People experience the diminution of time and distance by seeing the actions and reactions, the conflicts and collaborations, the sights and sounds—indeed, the whole range of past and present human experiences—that unfold elsewhere in the world. Thus there are good reasons to argue that their working knowledge has been substantially advanced by the cumulative impact through which aerials, cables, and satellite dishes depict diverse situations on a global scale.

On the other hand, there are at least two reasons why television is controversial as a stimulus to working knowledge. First, as a one-to-many technology, it can be pervaded with the biases of the few who control the

---

[21] Nicholas Bennett, "How to Add People Power to the Balance Sheet," *Financial Times*, December 5, 2001, p. 12.

[22] See, for example, AnnaLee Saxenian, *Local and Global Networks of Immigrant Professionals in Silicon Valley* (San Francisco: Public Policy Institute of California, 2002).

content and themes of the ideas and pictures that appear on the screens.[23] The producers of programs often have hidden agendas they seek to advance through the analytic, emotional, and imaginative capacities they tap; in some instances, in closed societies, their agendas are quite overt and explicit, thus posing the question of whether television contributes to working knowledge that elevates and enlarges the skills of viewers. But the degree to which those who control the media also control their audiences can be exaggerated. The outputs of the mass media still have to pass through the screens of education and experience through which people filter the media messages, and such screens are no less powerful as filters than the hidden agendas conveyed by the mass media. Second, it has been elaborately and forcefully argued that television is a narcotic, that instead of expanding working knowledge it paralyzes and overwhelms those exposed to it, thus becoming a habit that leads to endless hours of viewing that precludes the acquisition of skills and involvement in community life.[24] Once again, however, this negative consequence of television needs to be seen as limited by the diverse other sources through which people experience their daily lives and respond to world affairs.

In short, while there is no controversy over the fact that more and more people in all parts of the world are plugging into its television fare, the question of whether their skills are thereby enlarged is open to considerable debate. My own (optimistic) view is that, on balance, global television contributes substantially to working knowledge everywhere despite the singular control of information exercised by the broadcasters, the quality of programs, and the addictive, unthinking habits its audiences may acquire. For all its faults, global television provides insights into alternative lifestyles that, however distorted the portrayal of them may be, would not otherwise be available to hundreds of millions of people. More than that, the accelerated and continuous flow of words, pictures, and statistics from remote places to local sites highlights the prevalence of distant proximities. From high in the Andes to the lowlands of Bangladesh, from the rural areas of Greece to the crowded cities of China, skylines have been pervaded by satellite dishes and antennae that enable people to receive accounts and images of events to which their

[23] In Guatemala, for instance, the four main television stations are owned by the same person, Angel Gonzales, who "has used these stations to play a major role in determining the outcome of elections, squelch criticism of the government and further the interests of congenial politicians." Tina Rosenberg, "The Monochromatic Media of Latin America," *New York Times*, May 7, 2001, p. A20.

[24] For a cogent analysis of how the electronic revolution, and especially television, may be undermining ties to the community, see Robert D. Putnam, *Bowling Alone: The Collapse and Revival of American Community* (New York: Simon and Schuster, 2000).

great-grandparents never had access. While there is a widespread tendency to filter out unwanted information and to receive only what is compatible with one's preferences, there is always a residue that enlarges the recipient's grasp of how the world works. In the words of one analyst, "It is often said that we are entering the information age. This coming period could equally be called the age of learning: The sheer quantity of learning taking place in the world is already many times greater than in the past."[25]

Less controversial are the one-to-one and many-to-many technologies that have also advanced rapidly in years. Fax machines, wireless phones, computers, and most important perhaps, the Internet, have served to shrink time and distance, to so extensively span the world that people can now interact and network in ways likely expand to their working knowledge. To be sure, these technologies are not as readily available as television, with sizable portions of the world still inadequately wired. Indeed, it can be argued that the one-to-one and many-to-many technologies are available only to the elites and educated throughout the world. Yet as their costs come down, so are these technologies increasingly likely to facilitate the expansion of the skill revolution among ordinary folk as well as elites.

Another source of skill expansion is the aforementioned organizational explosion whereby new organizations and associations are being formed at an astounding rate throughout the world. The steep, upward trend line traced by their proliferation reflects the advent of human rights and environmental challenges as global issues, but the explosion of voluntary organizations is by no means confined to just a few issues. Rather, it is occurring at all levels of community in all walks of life, suggesting that increasingly people are recognizing the virtues of coming together for a common purpose, a recognition that can be inferred to reflect an expansion of analytic, emotional, and imaginative skills, as well as the ways in which the new microelectronic technologies have greatly facilitated interactions among people separated by wide geographic distances.

No less relevant as a source of the skill revolution is the growing complexity people confront as a result of living in or near large urban areas. As noted earlier, they have to learn to adapt to the new complexities—to the water shortages, the massive traffic jams, the paralyzing strikes, the pervasiveness of crime, the electrical brownouts, the calamities of erratic weather, the continuing threat of terrorism, and the shift from traditional agricultural and industrial jobs to those of the information society—and it seems reasonable to presume that this experiential learning has honed

[25] S. Papert, *The Children's Machine: Rethinking School in the Age of the Computer* (New York: Basic Books, 1993), p. vii.

their skills in coping with the contradictions and uncertainties that unfold within and beyond their urban communities. Indeed, as the third epigraph to this chapter indicates, the learning and adaptation required by the deepening and all-encompassing complexities of modern life are inescapable necessities.

Equally important, as indicated elsewhere, more and more people all over the world are receiving more and more education at all levels, primary, secondary, university, vocational, and long-distance learning through the Internet,[26] thereby acquiring skills that were not available to their forebears.[27] A survey conducted by the Organization for Economic Cooperation and Development found that on average its twenty-four member countries "increased the amount spent on building their knowledge economies by 3.4 percent annually during the 1990s."[28] And to this source of expanded skills must be added those acquired as a consequence of the mobility upheaval through which people are moving around the world on a vast scale.[29] Whatever the reasons for the travels, people are bound to ponder the implications of the variety of practices and folkways that sustain communities around the world. Thus it is not unreasonable to conclude that if the greater skills refined by electronic contacts are viewed as supplemented by the impact of education and travel, as well as the complexities of urban life, the power of the skill revolution becomes almost limitless.

Finally, and to expand on a point made earlier, a significant contribution to the skill revolution originates in the changing nature of work and the aforementioned need of macro collectivities for highly trained personnel who can master and manage the new and diverse information technologies.[30] From the innumerable companies that provide employees in-house training to cope with complex new computerized tasks to gov-

[26] United Nations University, "Virtual University: Transforming the Way We Learn," *Advanced Perspectives*, No. 5 (spring 2000), pp. 1–3.

[27] In Uganda the link between education and skills is formally recognized through a constitutional regulation that "its president and all members of Parliament meet a strict educational requirement before they take office [by earning an advanced-level certificate]. No degree, no office." Marc Lacey, "Ugandan, Seeking Higher Office, Submits to Higher Education," *New York Times*, August 30, 2001, p. A9.

[28] These data are broken down by country and reported in "Bucks for Brains," *Foreign Policy*, No. 127 (November/December 2001), p. 19.

[29] For data on travel patterns, see the discussion of the mobility upheaval in chapter 3. For impressive data on the expansion of education that depict growth patterns at several levels of education for virtually every country in the world, see Rosenau, *Turbulence in World Politics*, pp. 356, 358–60.

[30] Robert B. Reich, *The Work of Nations* (New York: Knopf, 1991); and Jeremy Rifkin, *The End of Work: The Decline of the Global Labor Force and the Dawn of the Post-market Era* (New York: Putnam's, 1996).

ernments that adopt programs designed to upgrade the workforce,[31] from immigration policies that privilege highly skilled workers to those who favor low-skill workers to replace those that have been retrained for more advanced technical jobs,[32] from athletic teams that scour the world for tall, strong, or agile talent[33] to universities that recruit accomplished students to fill out their programs, collectivities engage in continuous efforts to upgrade their personnel. In some instances, moreover, the search is for Affirmative Globals, for "experienced globetrotters," people with "global skills" who are "definitely seen as a hot ticket."[34]

It should also be noted that the worldwide scale of the skill revolution does not carry the implication that people everywhere are becoming equally skillful. For it is certainly the case that the learning capacities of individuals vary considerably, as does their access to the electronic media—much of Africa, for example, is not wired to connect to the Internet or global television—and that consequently opportunities for the advancement of skills can differ substantially. Rather, the skill revolution is worldwide in the sense that even as the analytically, emotionally, and imaginatively rich get richer, so do those who are poor in these respects get richer. Moreover, the recent advent of wireless phones has the potential of narrowing the skill gap between the rich and poor in nontrivial ways because it can enable the latter to leapfrog their way into the information age more quickly than was the case for the former.[35] As has often been remarked, in other words, a rising tide lifts all ships, the rowboats as well as the oceangoing liners.

Nor is there an implication that the skill revolution is generating a worldwide value convergence around, say, democracy or capitalism. The presumption is, rather, that individuals and officials are differently, if not more, skilled in terms of their own culture. This is the case for Latin American peasants relative to their great-grandparents, just as Parisian sophisticates, Islamic fundamentalists, and all other groups have advanced their world-linking skills beyond those of their forebears even as a preponderance of them have retained the core premises of their particular cultures and beliefs.

But, it might be asked, what about the impact of globalization? Has it

---

[31] James Glanz, "Trolling for Brains in International Waters," *New York Times*, April 1, 2001, Sec. 4, p. 3.

[32] "Bridging Europe's Skills Gap," *The Economist*, March 31, 2001, pp. 55–56.

[33] Mike Wise, "Scouting the World to Fill a Tall Order," *New York Times*, March 11, 2001, Sec. 8, p. 3.

[34] Melinda Ligos, "Overseas as a Career Move," *Globe and Mail*, October 24, 2000, p. B14.

[35] Cf. J. P. Singh, *Leapfrogging Development: The Political Economy of Telecommunications Restructuring* (Albany: State University of New York Press, 1999).

not made inroads into local cultures such that the more skillful people become, the more they begin to shed earlier habits and attitudes in favor of the cosmopolitan perspectives that accompany globalized economies and television's distant images? Put more bluntly, has the skill revolution facilitated an Americanization that undermines the practices of native cultures? The questions are apt, and they probe at the heart of fragmegrative dynamics. But, as previously noted, the habits of local cultures are normally so ingrained that they tend to absorb and redefine, rather than get replaced by, the lures of globalization. And while much of the flow of influence accompanying the dynamics of globalization originates in the United States, the networks of influence are not by any means sustained exclusively by the United States. Japanization, Indianization, and Islamization—among others—are also operative.

Some might argue that there is nothing new about the skill revolution, that the history of the human brain across millennia is one of ever-greater capacity, empathy, and creativity. Such an argument is, of course, well taken. Social biologists have demonstrated that the cognitive and evaluative capacities of the brain have expanded continuously since the formation of human societies.[36] From the perspective of accelerated time, however, the skill revolution can be viewed as a new set of phenomena. As previously noted, the pace of learning today is probably expanding at a much faster rate than was the case in prior epochs. Pictures, words, and ideas are transmitted more rapidly than in the past, transportation facilities move people around the world more swiftly than ever, education and teaching materials allow for quicker adaptation by students than previously, and the computer gives virtuously instantaneous feedback when mistakes are made—all these dynamics have contributed to the expansion of world-linking skill levels in recent decades at a rate that is difficult to calculate but that is surely greater than in earlier eras. Indeed, cognitive scientists have demonstrated that slow changes in *inherited* skills have undergone acceleration to a new level as a consequence of skills *acquired* through the various technological and educational dynamics already noted.[37] Previous generations may well have been more skillful at, say, building fireplaces and other necessities of daily survival than are present-day populations, but the latter have exceeded the former in acquiring the working knowledge that enables them to link the course of distant events to their proximate circumstances.

---

[36] Edmund S. Ferguson, "Biological Memory Systems and the Human Species," *Journal of Social Biological Structures*, Vol. 11 (1988), p. 411. See also Gina Kolata, "Studies Find Brain Grows New Cells," *New York Times*, March 17, 1998, p. B9.

[37] S. Veenema, and H. Gardner, "Multimedia and Multiple Intelligences," *The American Prospect*, No. 28 (November–December 1996), pp. 69–76.

A CONTROVERSIAL HYPOTHESIS

While identifying dynamics that justify positing a skill revolution hypothesis is considerably easier than providing convincing evidence of its validity, both the dynamics and the evidence are bound to be controversial. The hypothesis is so closely linked to our view of ourselves and the human condition, to our optimistic or pessimistic natures, that people tend to react strongly against any grand claim which, on balance, asserts that ordinary persons, from urban sophisticates to rural peasants, are increasingly competent. "Look at the declining test scores of schoolchildren," say the pessimists. "Or consider how readily adults join rowdy mobs; or adhere to the dictates of autocrats; or yield to emotional appeals of advertisers; or lose themselves in front of television screens"—to cite but a few of the many anecdotal bases for rejecting the hypothesis and arguing that mass and educational media are "dumbing down" their audiences and creating "dumbocracies."[38] No, retort the optimists, think about the worldwide trend toward more and more education; or the ever-greater number of persons who are increasingly able to roam the World Wide Web; or the learning that accompanies the movement of people around the world; or the capacity of most individuals to shoulder multiple identities and adapt to increasingly complex urban environments; or the worldwide trend toward democracy and voter turnout,[39] even among the very poor;[40] or the impressive evidence that the central media trend is not a dumbing down but a "clevering up"[41]—to mention some of the main arguments on behalf of the optimistic perspective. To a large extent, in other words, our view of human capacities and their openness to change, along with any evidence in support of one or another perspective, is shaped by our temperaments, by our fundamental conceptions of who we and others are and who we and others can be.

Since both the optimistic and the pessimistic line of reasoning can seem persuasive, it follows that if the skill revolution hypothesis is sound, as is argued here, it does not necessarily trace a clear-cut and steep up-

[38] Ivo Mosely (ed.), *Dumbing Down: Culture, Politics, and the Mass Media* (Bowling Green, Ohio: Imprint Academic, 2000).

[39] Between 1945 and 1990, turnout around the world increased steadily from 61 percent in the 1940s to 68 percent in the 1980s and then dipped to 64 percent after 1990. Most people vote in most countries: of the 163 countries that held elections in the 1990s, 125 had a turnout of over 50 percent of the voting-age population. Institute for Democracy and Electoral Assistance, *Voter Turnout from 1945 to 1997: A Global Report on Political Participation* (Stockholm, 1997).

[40] Celia W. Dugger, "India's Poorest Are Becoming Its Loudest," *New York Times*, April 25, 1999, Sec. 4, p. 3.

[41] Madeleine Bunting, "Special Report: Are We Dumbing Down?" *The Guardian*, November 13, 2000, p. 21.

ward trend. Many of the skills involved are acquired incrementally and selectively, thus forming a gentle upward slope that at moments can be jagged as new data on the poor performance of students and their lessening interest in books are released[42] and reinforce some people to revert to generalized, simple, and stereotypical notions of how publics are becoming less rather than more skillful.[43]

Any effort to probe the hypothesis, in short, requires nuance and the avoidance of sweeping conclusions. Yet even if the reasoning and evidence in support of the hypothesis is carefully set forth, the controversy over its validity is unlikely to be resolved. Some observers, those prone to skepticism, doubt, or cynicism, are bound to reject even the most solid evidence that the skills of people are expanding. The premises embedded in the hypothesis are too central to the values people hold dear to enable those with pessimistic worldviews to accept the notion that the competence of individuals everywhere is on the rise. And since the evidence noted here is, at best, only partially systematic, it is unlikely to be persuasive for some readers. But hopefully they will at least momentarily suspend their skepticism and ponder whether there may be a germ of truth in the hypothesis.

Despite its controversial foundations, however, two overall statements about the hypothesis do seem justifiable: first, it is an important proposition. It matters whether or not the world's populations are increasingly competent in terms of their analytic, emotional, and imaginative skills. If the trend line traces a gentle upward slope in the working knowledge of

---

[42] Just as the discrepancy between journalistic accounts of airplanes that crash greatly exceed those of planes that arrive safely, so do stories about poor student performance seem to greatly outnumber those that depict increasing learning skills. See, for example, this sample of news accounts over a brief period: Jodi Wilgoren, "Students Show Few Gains in Reading Skills," *New York Times*, September 6, 2000, p. A14; Diana Jean Schemo, "Students in U.S. Do Not Keep Up in Global Tests," *New York Times*, December 6, 2000, p. A1; Tamar Lewin, "Children's Computer Use Grows, but Gaps Persist, Study Says," *New York Times*, January 22, 2001, p. A11; Cherry Norton and Adam Nathan, "Computer-Mad Generation Has a Memory Crash," *Sunday Times* (London), February 6, 2001, p. 1; Kate Zernike, "Gap between Best and Worst Widens on U.S. Reading Test," *New York Times*, April 7, 2001, p. A1; Kate Zernike, "Parents Hungry for ABC's Find Schools Don't Add Up," *New York Times*, April 28, 2001, p. A1; and Linton Weeks, "The No-Book Report: Skim It and Weep," *Washington Post*, May 14, 2001, p. C1.

[43] For an extensive analysis contending that the Internet has fostered a decline in skills, see Deborah C. Sawyer, "The Pied Piper Goes Electronic," *The Futurist*, February 1999, pp. 42–46. For optimistic perspectives, see Kathryn C. Montgomery, "Children in the Digital Age," *The American Prospect*, No. 27 (July–August 1996), pp. 69–74; and Robert J. Samuelson, "Test Scores Don't Tell the Whole Story," *St. Petersburg Times*, March 12, 1998, p. 18A. A viewpoint somewhere between the optimistic and pessimistic approaches can be found in George Johnson, "Tests Show Nobody's Smart about Intelligence," *New York Times*, March 1, 1998, Sec. 4, p. 1.

individuals, then governments can tap into a pool of increasingly proficient people and become more effective and democratic, just as economies are likely to become more productive and cultures more inclusive and creative. Alternatively, if the line remains even or is in decline, then the prospects of leaders and publics confronting their problems and surmounting their challenges are not encouraging.

Second, it can reasonably be argued that the trend line is an upward one and that the skill revolution is central to the processes whereby people in all parts of the world appear to have a greater sense of empowerment. As previously noted, substantial evidence indicates that the ranks of activists are swelling among both Affirmative and Resistant Locals and Globals as more and more people voice in one or another fashion their convictions about an ever-wider range of issues on the agendas of their local or global worlds. Whether their voices are expressed through such intentional micro inputs as street protests or through diverse and uncoordinated unintentional inputs experienced by elites, the volume and intensity of voices appear greatly in excess of exits into any of the private worlds.[44] Indeed, unintentional micro inputs that foster unexpected macro outcomes can foster pride and a "euphoric feeling of empowerment" within an entire population.[45]

Skeptics might argue that the apparent trend toward protests across the world is not so much the consequence of the skill revolution fostering micro-level empowerment as it is the availability of more effective mobilizing tools in the hands of macro leaders, but few would dispute the presence of the trend in the Philippines, Indonesia, the European Union, Serbia, Mexico, and China—to mention only the most recent instances in which the relevance of voice seems considerably greater than that of exit. People may be experiencing uncertainty over where their lives are headed, and they may have a greater sense of remoteness from the centers of decision, but they nonetheless seem ready to act on their convictions. And once it is conceded that the empowerment of people is on the rise, it becomes hard to deny that expanded skills are at work. Empowerment has its roots in enlarged analytic capacities, in deeper commitments, in an enhanced imagination as well as in networking tech-

---

[44] See, for example, Albert O. Hirschman, *Exit, Voice, and Loyalty* (Cambridge, Mass.: Harvard University Press, 1970); Harlan Cleveland, "The Age of People Power," *The Futurist* (January–February 1992), pp. 14–18; Peter Ackerman and Jack DuVall, *A Force More Powerful: A Century of Nonviolent Conflict* (New York: St. Martin's Press, 2000); and Peter Ackerman and Jack DuVall, "Count on People Power," *Philadelphia Inquirer*, February 17, 2001.

[45] Mexico after the 2000 election that ended the decades-long rule of the PRI is illustrative in this regard. Ginger Thompson, "Strong Feelings of Pride over Orderly Balloting," *New York Times*, July 4, 2000, p. A7.

nologies that facilitate concerted action, and in a greater sense of personal autonomy that often leads to an alteration of the links between elites and ordinary individuals.[46] People could not have a greater capacity for collective action unless they also evolve a greater readiness to defy authority by participating in such actions, and this readiness can be traced in good part to the skill revolution.

WHY A REVOLUTION?

If it is the case, as previously suggested, that people acquire working knowledge incrementally, on what grounds can this process be labeled a "revolution"? Such a label implies a huge change, even a parametric reversal, and clearly the expansion of skills is not of such a quantitative scope. In part the answer to the question lies in the large qualitative consequences that can follow from incremental changes that unfold on a worldwide scale with respect to the competence of publics. These may well involve parametric transformations, or at least even a gentle upward slope can significantly affect the way in which people respond to events that impinge on their lives. Partly, too, such a label involves a measure of poetic license: the skill hypothesis is so counterintuitive relative to the way many people think about such matters that referring to enlarged competencies as a skill revolution arrests attention to the potential importance of this development.

Further justification for the label lies in the large degree to which the pace of the skill revolution, incremental as it may be, has accelerated. With the Internet and many other recent technological innovations having collapsed time and distance, the learning curve has of necessity steepened for most people. It may still be only a gentle slope, but its angle of growth seems likely to be much less infinitesimal than was the case in earlier eras.[47]

It is important to stress that the skill revolution is more than a single tributary of the larger stream of change known as the knowledge "explo-

[46] For an interesting analysis of how the links between elites and nonelites may be undergoing alteration, see Henrik P. Bang, "Excellent Ordinarity: Connecting Elites with a Politics of the Ordinary" (paper presented at the XVIII World Congress of the International Political Science Association, Quebec City, August 2, 2000).

[47] Although conceived more narrowly than is the case here, the "skill revolution" label is not new. Both Heinz Eulau, in his presidential address to the American Political Science Association, and Harold Lasswell used it to refer to the increased specialization of occupations that accompanied industrial development. See Harold D. Lasswell, "Skill Politics and Skill Revolution," in H. D. Lasswell, *The Analysis of Political Behavior: An Empirical Approach* (New York: Oxford University Press, 1948), pp. 133–45; and Heinz Eulau, "Skill Revolution and Consultative Commonwealth," *American Political Science Review*, Vol. 67 (1973), pp. 169–91.

sion."[48] Exemplified by the fact that the processing power of computers doubles roughly every eighteen months, the knowledge explosion tends to be equated with technology and the ways in which societies apply the knowledge that is generated in industrial and academic laboratories. The trend toward service-based economies, for example, is seen as a major consequence of the knowledge explosion. But here the focus is on individuals and not on economies or technologies, on how individuals have become increasingly competent. To be sure, some part of that increase can be traced to the efforts of collectivities to enlarge their pool of trained personnel, but it bears repeating that the increase derives from a multiplicity of sources in addition to advances in technical skills and the knowledge revolution.

THE PROBLEM OF EVIDENCE

To depict the expansion of skills as revolutionary is not, of course, to demonstrate that such processes are at work in the world today. Skeptics and pessimists can well argue that the case for the skill revolution set forth here is founded on anecdotes and inferential evidence. They can cite innumerable examples and some trend lines depicting cases and situations that appear to suggest narrowed horizons and lessened skills and that thus seem to offset and negate the impact of the various sources enumerated in this chapter. Indeed, so many factors underlie the capabilities of publics—from situational determinants to the adequacy of educational institutions, from the competence of political leadership to cultural precepts, from technological advances to the impact of fragmegrative dynamics, to mention only a few of the more salient factors— that skeptics can quickly assert that the skill hypothesis is substantively flawed and methodologically questionable. As noted, for example, some point to abundant indicators that television is not so much expanding the competencies of publics as it is constricting the ability of people to think through problems and weakening their readiness to undertake civic engagement.[49] Even more telling, despite the abundance of anecdotal materials, skeptics can readily stress the lack of systematic evidence descriptive of the skill revolution.

But the skeptical reasoning can also be misleading. In compiling im-

---

[48] A cogent and wide-ranging discussion of the knowledge explosion can be found in Paul R. Ehrlich, Gary Wolff, Gretchen C. Daily, Jennifer B. Hughes, Scott Daily, Michael Dalton, and Lawrence Goulder, "Knowledge and the Environment," *Ecological Economics*, Vol. 30 (1999), pp. 267–84.

[49] R. D. Putnam, "Tuning In, Tuning Out: The Strange Disappearance of Social Capital in America," *Political Science and Politics*, Vol. 28 (1995), pp. 664–83; and Neil Postman, *Amusing Ourselves to Death* (New York: Viking Press, 1986).

pressionistic indicators that negate the skill hypothesis, the critics may well commit the same errors for which they criticize the proponents of the hypothesis. Their skepticism can obscure the growing number of activists in the various local and global worlds. It can be so centered on the United States that it ignores the many unstable areas of the world in which people have been compelled by circumstances to hone their skills. It can all too easily dismiss voluminous anecdotal materials reflective of enlarged skills and, in so doing, downplay their cumulative implications across time. In other words, approached with an optimistic temperament, the proliferation of activists, the unstable situations that command attention, and a plethora of skillfully managed anecdotal incidents can be viewed as delicate links in a causal chain that may be difficult to prove but that is manifestly evident. If one suspends doubt and rigorous criteria of evidence, the plentiful anecdotes, along with the data on expanding education, travel, and electronic technologies, suggest that the links in the causal chain affirm the ongoing presence of a skill revolution. In short, even though systematic evidence gathered for the exclusive purpose of assessing the evolution of skill levels across time may be in short supply, it is possible to marshal inferential evidence in support of the hypothesis.

Furthermore, at least two systematic studies that measure changes in skill across time and culture have been undertaken, and both of them offer findings consistent with the skill hypothesis. One involves a major investigation of IQ scores across more than six decades and twenty countries. It concluded, "People are getting smarter. Researchers who study intelligence say scores around the world have been increasing so fast that a high proportion of people regarded as normal at the turn of the century would be considered way below average by today's tests."[50] To be sure, even though they have subjected a large body of data to intensive and sophisticated analysis, specialists differ considerably over the meaning of IQ; over what the tests measure; over what the decadal increase in scores across so many countries signifies; over whether the scores reflect genetic sources, altered dietary habits, more education, altered family patterns, evolving lifestyles, greater competence, or still other, unrecognized factors.[51] For all the argumentation and causal ambiguity, however, not a

[50] Trish Hall, "I.Q. Scores Are Up, and Psychologists Wonder Why," *New York Times*, February 24, 1998, p. B11. For a full analysis of how and why IQ scores have risen in every technologically advanced country, see Ulric Neisser (ed.), *The Rising Curve: Long-Term Gains in IQ and Related Measures* (Washington, D.C.: American Psychological Association, 1998).

[51] See Ulric Neisser, "Rising Scores on Intelligence Tests," *American Scientist*, Vol. 85 (September–October 1997), pp. 440–47; James R. Flynn, "Searching for Justice: The Discovery of IQ Gains over Time," *American Psychologist*, Vol. 54 (January 1999), pp. 5–20; and William T. Dickens and James R. Flynn, "Heritability Estimates versus Large Environ-

single investigator disputes the finding that IQ scores have been rising at a steady rate for decades in various parts of the world. Nor do they quarrel with the finding—implied here in the previous discussion of working knowledge—that the greatest gains have occurred not in content-related and fact-based tests such as vocabulary, arithmetic, or general information but in problem-solving and visual abstraction subtests. Indeed, the rise in vocabulary, arithmetic, or general information skills is much flatter than is the case for problem-solving and visual abstraction skills.

The other systematic inquiry sought to test the skill revolution hypothesis directly, using a seven-point scale for scoring the integrative complexity of recorded statements by elites in Canada, Mexico, and the United States. All told, 907 statements made by seven types of actors were compared across three cultures and three issue areas separated by sixty or seventy years. Twenty-eight across-epoch comparisons were subjected to statistical analysis, twenty-two of which favored the skill revolution hypothesis, four of which were in the opposite direction and indicated that skills had undergone regression, and two of which involved such minor differences as to suggest no change in skills across time. Calculated in terms of mean scores, the twenty-two favorable comparisons increased within a range of 9 to 14 percentage points. An overall comparison of all the actors in all the issue areas revealed an 11 percent increase in the mean integrative complexity scores from the earlier to the later epochs.[52]

What, it might be asked, do the statistically significant central tendencies of the findings portend for the links between people at the micro level and their collectivities at the macro level? What does an increase of 9 to 14 percentage points suggest with respect to either intentional or unintentional micro inputs that shape the conduct of world affairs by macro governmental and nongovernmental organizations? And even if such a shift has the potential for transforming global structures, is the trend toward increased analytic and emotional skills likely to continue and further roil the waters of world politics? Or are there reasons to anticipate that the learning curve will soon level off at a new equilibrium? One's answers to such questions depend on the credence one attaches to the findings and, if they are accepted as reflecting a skill revolution, on the dynamics one considers to be at work as both sources and effects of the revolution continuing to unfold.

---

mental Effects: The IQ Paradox Resolved," *Psychological Review*, Vol. 108, No. 2 (2001), pp. 346–69.

[52] James N. Rosenau and W. Michael Fagen, "Increasingly Skillful Citizens: A New Dynamism in World Politics?" *International Studies Quarterly*, Vol. 41 (December 1997), pp. 655–86.

Having set out to generate systematic data relevant to the increased-skill hypothesis on the grounds that the capacities of people constitute a new dynamism in world affairs, my inclination is to discern considerable portent in the findings and view them as affirming the innumerable anecdotal materials reflective of the skill revolution. All the reasons for anticipating a continuing expansion of skills are still very much at work. The Internet, global television, educational institutions, communications networks, and the many other sources of micro change continue to expand, and there is no basis for concluding that these trends will diminish. To be sure, the systematic inquiry is limited by its focus exclusively on elites. Conceivably a study of ordinary people would yield more ambiguous findings. Yet, changes of 9 to 14 percent are not trivial. They may well reflect a growth rate sustained by a satellite-ringed, fiber-optic wired world and, equally crucial, by a continuing trend in which everywhere people are increasingly committed to a democratic, free-market ideology.

On the other hand, not only will expanded skills link individuals in the several local and global worlds ever more securely to distant events, but so may they foster the fragmentation of communities by intensifying the readiness of people to become Alienated Cynics or Tuned-out Passives or otherwise engage in collective actions that express distrust of public institutions and amount to pressure for satisfaction of their private demands.[53] Even the distrust, however, is marked by increased skill levels, with more and more people able to make clear distinctions between their support for regime principles, regime performances, regime institutions, and political actors.[54] In short, inexorable as the skill revolution is likely to be, and despite an upwardly sloping trend line, it may well amount to a mixed blessing, one that can topple authoritarian governments and paralyze democratic systems alike.[55]

In sum, numerous dynamics are at work in the present, fragmegrative era that seem bound to elevate the skill levels of people everywhere. In the words of one observer, "Whether it is to enhance existing skills, or

---

[53] Cf. Ronald Inglehart, "Postmaterial Values and the Erosion of Institutional Authority," in Joseph S. Nye Jr., Philip D. Zelikow, and David C. King (eds.), *Why People Don't Trust Government* (Cambridge, Mass.: Harvard University Press, 1997).

[54] Pippa Norris, "Introduction: The Growth of Critical Citizens?" in Pippa Norris (ed.), *Critical Citizens: Global Support for Democratic Government* (New York: Oxford University Press, 1999), pp. 1–27.

[55] For an example of downside of the skill revolution, see the extensive account of the remarkable analytic and organizational skills of the terrorists who planned and executed the September 11, 2001, attacks on the United States in Don van Natta Jr. and Kate Zernike, "Hijackers' Meticulous Strategy of Brains, Muscle and Practice," *New York Times*, November 4, 2001, p. 1.

master new ones, continuing education and continuing to learn are now permanent features of our lives."[56] As a result,

> Far from dumbing down, most of us are cleverer than our grandparents and great-grandparents. Millions of women are far better educated than previous generations could have dreamt, and their mental skills are far more developed by participation in the labour market. We know of a much wider range of information than our predecessors: far more people have a familiarity, albeit sometimes cursory, with thousands of subjects, from Attenborough's explanation of how birds fly to Palm Beach ballot papers. This "clevering up" is a hugely significant development: the vital prerequisite for the 21st-century knowledge economy. Our brains are being retooled to suit an information age. A premium is put on mental speed and flexibility. Thinking fast, and absorbing and adapting to new information continually is what is demanded. We are expected to juggle different mental tasks at the same time to an extent which would have made our great-grandmothers dizzy. We are all developing, in varying degrees, the ability to process huge amounts of information (skim-reading) and select what is significant and what can be trusted. The demands made on our brains are growing exponentially.[57]

No less important, all the sources of the skill revolution are interactive, with each reinforcing the impact of the others. Whether people cling to their traditional ways or undergo transformation to modern ways, the foregoing discussion suggests that there are powerful reasons to presume their horizons have been expanded and their ability to cope with ever-greater complexity has been augmented. One of these reasons, the advent of new communications technologies, is amplified and further assessed in the next chapter.

[56] Harold McGraw III, "The Global Information Revolution: Opportunities and Obstacles," *Vital Speeches of the Day* (Los Angeles: July 14, 2000), p. 657.
[57] Bunting, "Special Report: Are We Dumbing Down?" p. 21.

CHAPTER ELEVEN

The Information Revolution: Both Powerful and Neutral

Terms like *communications* revolution and *information* revolution actually don't go far enough in explaining the transition at hand. There is more at stake than just being able to send messages more quickly or having access to a supercharged digital library. What [the long-term effects] suggest is a potentially momentous transfer of power from large institutions to individuals. The real change set in motion by the Internet may, in fact, be a control revolution, a vast transformation in who governs information, experience, and resources. Increasingly, it seems that *we* will. . . . [There is a] palpable sense of deciding for yourself, as opposed to having some larger, impersonal *them* deciding for you. . . . It is a time of diminishing stature for many authority figures: legislators and other public officials, news professionals, commercial middlemen, educators. Hierarchies are coming undone. Gatekeepers are being bypassed. Power is devolving down to "end users."

—Andrew L. Shapiro[1]

Perhaps hand-held gadgets will offer the kind of power over the rest of our experience that the remote control gives us over TV: the power to edit and jump—instant access, fluid montage, snippets and shards. For better or worse.

—James Gleick[2]

IN ASSESSING the several major factors that are carrying the world beyond globalization, there is a strong temptation to treat new technologies as the prime transformative dynamic. But it is a temptation that must be resisted unless one is willing to become a technological determinist and trace all developments back to the introduction of innovative electronic and transportation technologies. As one who confines the meaning of causation

---

[1] *The Control Revolution: How the Internet Is Putting Individuals in Charge and Changing the World We Know* (New York: Public Affairs, 1999), p. 10 (italics in the original).

[2] "Theories of Connectivity," *New York Times Magazine*, April 22, 2001, p. 112.

to human agency, I am unwilling to revert to technological (or any other) form of determinism. Yes, it is certainly the case that recent technological innovations have had enormous consequences (as this chapter's epigraphs indicate), that they have collapsed time and space and thus added substantially to the complexities that mark our era. Perhaps most notably, they are the prime source of distant proximities. The electronic mechanisms render close-at-hand what once was remote and, in so doing, transform the linear into the nonlinear and the sequential into the simultaneous.

But such consequences reek of complexity and of the need to guard against the simplistic conclusions to which determinisms are heir. Clearly, if we are to begin to grasp the meaning and potentials of the information revolution, once again we need to be sensitive to nuance. I have tried to highlight this need in the title of the chapter, in characterizing the information revolution as both powerful and neutral. Surely, some would argue, anything that is powerful must be value laden and thus cannot be neutral, that the word *revolution* suggests power, that power in human hands suggests purpose, and that by their very nature purposes are anything but neutral. Thus, such a line of reasoning would conclude, to speak of the information revolution as powerful but neutral is not to trace nuance; it is to be profoundly erroneous!

No, I contend, it is nuance and not error if one treats the revolution in terms of the technologies that facilitate the simultaneity of distant proximities and the rapid spread of information rather than in terms of the information itself. Information is perforce subjective and anything but neutral. It can be skewed and designed to distort. This is not the case, however, with information technologies. They are inherently neutral because they do not in themselves tilt in the direction of any particular values—neither toward good or bad, nor toward left or right, nor toward open or closed systems. They are neutral in the sense that their tilt is provided by people—by those in local and global worlds who affirm or resist globalization and, in so doing, employ information technologies to advance their perspectives. It is people and their collectivities that employ the technologies to infuse values into information. For better or worse, it is individuals and organizations that introduce information into political arenas and thereby render it good or bad. The technologies enable authoritarians as well as democrats to skew their information and speed up its spread in whatever way they see fit. The neutrality premise thus compels us to focus on human agency and how it does or does not make use of information technologies.

This is not to imply, of course, that consequences do not follow from the power of information technologies and the degree to which information technologies are available. On the contrary, these technologies facilitate human choice. Through the Internet people can now make choices in a vast global market, in the political realm, in the types of entertainment they enjoy; and there are endless other ways in which the power of choice is undergoing disaggregation down to the individual level. Clearly, then, the new information technologies facilitate or constrain the exercise of human agency. They set the context—limit or expand the range—within which ends and means are framed, alternatives pondered, and choices made. But to establish the context and range within which choices are made is not to determine the choices. The technologies are simply equipment, inanimate hardware, gadgetry, but as such, they are both powerful and neutral. They permit the pursuit of values, but they do not determine what values are sought. And no less important, the cost of these technologies has steadily declined, enabling ordinary people in the local, global, and private worlds to purchase and use them.[3]

By treating information technologies as neutral, we cast them as background conditions and not as immediate stimuli to action—as second-order dynamics that influence, contextualize, assist, permit, or inhibit courses of action but not as first-order dynamics that change, transform, foster, impose, or shape courses of action. The distinction between the two types of dynamics is important; it differentiates between the operation of structures and that of agents. Put more forcefully, the distinction prevents the analyst from mistaking second-order for first-order dynamics, from treating information technologies as an unseen hand that somehow gets people, groups, or communities to pursue goals and undertake actions without awareness of why they do so and, accordingly, without taking responsibility for their conduct.

A good illustration of the dangers of positing information technologies as first-order causal dynamics is evident in the adaptation of vertical business organizations in the 1980s to the horizontal flexibility required by the globalization of national economies. When diverse enterprises first seized upon the new technologies, they treated them as labor-saving devices and as means to control labor rather than as mechanisms for organizational adaptation. The result was an aggravation of their vertical bureaucratic rigidities. It was only after they made the necessary organizational changes in order to keep abreast of their operational environments that the information technologies "extraordinarily enhanced" the success of their enterprises.[4] For all practical purposes, in other words,

---

[3] Presently, for example, "a phone call from Hong Kong to the U.S. costs pennies a minute; and an e-mail message, which might attach a long spreadsheet or a document, is almost free." Harry Harding, "The Complex Impact of Information Technologies on International Affairs" (paper presented to the "Conference on Information Technology and Telecommunications in the Arab World: Digital Divide in an Integrated World," sponsored by the International Economic Forum, Cairo, May 27–29, 2002), p. 1.

[4] Manuel Castells, *The Information Age: The Rise of the Network Society* (Oxford: Blackwell, 1996), Vol. 1, p. 169.

the primary cause of the improving performance of enterprises was not the information revolution but the restructuring of businesses away from hierarchical and toward network forms of organization. Information technologies did not facilitate enterprise growth until after the restructuring was put in place.

The neutrality of the information revolution is also evident in the many ways it has served both desired values and noxious purposes. Just as the Internet and the cellular phone have been instrumental in enabling Specialized Globals such as environmental or human rights activists to mobilize support,[5] for example, so has the Internet been used by Alienated Illegals such as "Islamic terrorist groups . . . quick to discover the power of the Internet, and particularly e-mail, to propagate ideas of holy war. In some cases, according to U.S. investigators, the Internet has been used to send coded instructions from bin Laden's headquarters in Afghanistan to agents in his al Queda network in the field."[6] Nor should the role played by hackers be overlooked. Their efforts to disrupt or otherwise undermine organizations can be both extensive and consequential.[7] And some of the negative consequences of the Internet are subtle and not easily traced. For example, some fear that it encourages faddism in science.[8] Still others offer evidence that the Internet encourages extremism through a process known as *group polarization* that results when "like-minded people in an isolated group reinforce one another's views, which then harden into more extreme positions."[9] In the words of one observer's general conclusion about the downside of new information technologies,

[5] An account of the successful campaign waged through the Internet to get PepsiCo to cease its business operations in Burma is illustrative in this regard: see Tiffany Danitz and Warren P. Strobel, *Networking Dissent: Cyber Activists Use the Internet to Promote Democracy in Burma* (Washington, D.C.: Virtual Diplomacy Series No. 3, United States Institute of Peace, February 2000). Similarly, the role of cellular phones is depicted in the downfall of Philippine president Joseph Estrada during a National Public Radio interview with Eric Weiner (Morning Edition, November 29, 2000).

[6] Michael Dobbs, "Online Agitators Breaching Barriers in Mideast," *Washington Post*, October 24, 2002, p. A10.

[7] Surveys in both the United States and Europe revealed that some 60 percent of various corporate, governmental, and other collectivities experienced security breaches of their computers. Philip Manchester, "Security: The Dilemma of Where to Draw the Line," *Financial Times*, June 7, 2000, p. vii. See also "Chinese Hackers Invade 2 Official U.S. Web Sites," *New York Times*, April 29, 2001, p. 6; Matt Richtel, "Nike Web Site Is Taken Over by Protesters," *New York Times*, June 22, 2000, p. C2; and Thomas L. Friedman, "Hacker Lesson: Wired Citizens Need Government," *International Herald Tribune*, February 16, 2000, p. 6.

[8] James Glanz, "The Web as Dictator of Scientific Fashion," *New York Times*, June 19, 2001, p. D1.

[9] Alexander Stille, "Adding Up the Costs of Cyberdemocracy," *New York Times*, June 2, 2001, p. A15.

"[I]n some ways, global satellite TV and Internet access have actually made the world a less understanding, less tolerant place."[10]

Nor does the notion of technology as neutral ignore the convertibility of information into knowledge and, thus, into power. More accurately, technologies facilitate the exercise of what has been called "soft power," a concept that differentiates information technologies from the conventional dimensions of material power such as oil production, troops in uniform, military hardware, and agricultural production.[11] Yet despite the innumerable ways in which soft power can be used, it is nonetheless the case that the information technologies on which it is based are neutral. To repeat, what counts is how officials and governments generate and employ the technologies and how publics interpret the information and knowledge that comes their way.

Needless to say, as such, as conditions with which humans must cope, information technologies are crucial dimensions of the political scene. As they change, so do the contexts in which choices are made. As new technologies are developed, so is the range of plausible choices altered. Among other things, for example, technological innovations pose the question of how the range of choice is expanded by the availability of information for those who are, so to speak, informationally rich and how it is narrowed for those who are informationally poor—and, indeed, how the discrepancies between the rich and the poor configure the context within which the two perceive each other and interact.

Students of world affairs have mostly neglected these contextual factors, a neglect this chapter seeks to highlight by addressing four main ways in which information technologies are part of the context within which world affairs unfold. More specifically, it undertakes to explore (1) how the technologies have contributed to an alteration of the skills of individuals; (2) how they may be affecting the circumstances whereby the gap between the informationally rich and poor is undergoing transformation; (3) how they may be changing the conditions under which individuals and groups interact; and (4) how they may be contributing to the evolution of new global structures.

---

[10] George Packer, "When Here Sees There," *New York Times Magazine*, April 21, 2002, p. 13.

[11] See, for example, Joseph S. Nye Jr. and William A. Owens, "America's Information Edge," *Foreign Affairs*, Vol. 75 (March/April 1996), pp. 20–36; Richard Rosecrance, "The Rise of the Virtual State," *Foreign Affairs*, Vol. 75 (July/August 1996), pp. 45–61; Ryan Henry and C. Edward Peartree (eds.), *The Information Revolution and International Security* (Washington, D.C.: CSIS Press, 1998); and Martin C. Libicki, "Information War, Information Peace," *Journal of International Affairs*, Vol. 51 (spring 1998), pp. 411–28.

THE SKILL REVOLUTION

As stressed in the previous chapter, there are good reasons to presume that the skills of today's person-in-the-street are different than those of his or her predecessor. Global television, the Internet, the fax machine, fiber-optic cable, e-mail, the computer, and, most recently, the mobile phone that links one's e-mail and computer are among the dynamics that have enabled individuals to alter their skills in such a way as to adapt more effectively to the demands of an ever more complex world.

Some have argued that people tend to adapt to the information age by turning away from the realm of ideas and politics, by joining the ranks of the Tuned-out Passives or the Alienated Cynics. However, quite the opposite proved to be the case in a survey of Americans who, through extensive use of at least four of five information technologies, were classified as "Connected" or "Superconnected" to the digital world:[12]

> Despite the national lament that technology undermines literacy, Connected Americans are . . . more likely to spend time reading books than any other segment of the population broken down in this survey. Seventy percent of the Connected say they spend 1 to 10 hours reading a book during a typical week; another 16 percent read for 11 to 20 hours a week. Far from being distracted by the technology, Digital Citizens appear startlingly close to the Jeffersonian ideal—they are informed, outspoken, participatory, passionate about freedom, proud of their culture, and committed to the free nation in which it has evolved.[13]

Furthermore, the dynamics of change fueling the skill revolution are likely to accelerate as increasingly computer-literate generations of children and adolescents move into adulthood. For example, it is portentous, or at least noteworthy, that a 1999 survey of young people between age thirteen and seventeen in the United States resulted in 63 percent who reported using a computer at home (compared with 45 percent in 1994) and 42 percent who said they have e-mail addresses.[14] To be sure, many young people turn to their computers to play video-type games,[15] but presumably such a tendency will attenuate as they age, or at least be

[12] The Superconnected were those in the survey of 1,444 randomly selected Americans who exchange e-mail at least three days a week and use a laptop, a cell phone, a beeper, and a home computer, whereas the Connected were those who exchange e-mail three days a week and use three of the four other technologies. Jon Katz, "The Digital Citizen," *Wired*, December 1997, p. 71.

[13] Ibid., p. 72

[14] Carey Goldberg and Marjorie Connelly, "Fear and Violence Have Declined among Teen-Agers, Poll Shows," *New York Times*, October 20, 1999, p. A1.

[15] Jennifer 8. Lee, "In China, Web Revolution Means Games," *New York Times*, June 30, 2000, p. G1.

supplemented by more serious uses of the Internet. The findings of the 1999 survey suggest that the ranks of the Superconnected and Connected are likely to swell with the passage of time and the advent of new generations, thus adding to the ways in which the skill revolution is a powerful source of change in world affairs.

There are, however, personal and psychological costs of being extensively wired to the world. Information technologies provide Superconnecteds with control over their worlds, but such individuals also risk losing control because they have to respond to endless messages from those with whom they are connected.[16] In other words, even as "wireless devices are instruments of liberation" and "lend an unprecedented degree of flexibility to the workday," so can they be extremely limiting: despite the liberation and flexibility, "whatever line people have drawn between work and leisure, between office and home, is growing thinner than ever as a sense of obligation to stay connected to work at all hours continues to grow."[17]

While the acceleration rate of the skill revolution elsewhere in the world may not match or exceed the rate in the United States, it is important to stress that the changing skills of people everywhere matter, that their ever-greater connectivity alters the playing field on which politics unfolds. As previously noted, newly acquired analytic, emotional, and imaginative skills have enabled both Locals and Globals to join and participate in organizations appropriate to their interests and thereby to know when, where, and how to engage in collective action. Put differently, the various information technologies, and especially the Internet, have stimulated a greater sense of political efficacy on the part of individuals, perhaps especially the Resistant Locals and Globals whose involvement and activity in the political arena have been heightened and extended by their electronic contacts.[18] As will be seen, moreover, these individuals' enhanced public affairs skills have also contributed to a major transformation of the global structures that are emerging as instruments of governance in the age of fragmegration.

Bridging the Information Gap

There is little question that the benefits of the information revolution have been fully enjoyed by only a small proportion of the world's popula-

[16] Arlie Russell Hochschild, *The Time Bind: When Work Becomes Home and Home Becomes Work* (New York: Metropolitan Books, 1997).

[17] Katie Hafner, "For the Well Connected, All the World's an Office," *New York Times*, March 30, 2000, p. E1.

[18] See, for example, Leslie Wayne, "On Web, Voters Reinvent Grass-Roots Activism," *New York Times*, May 21, 2000, p. 22.

tion and that the gap between those who are rich and poor with respect to their access to information is huge.[19] For example, while North America and Western Europe cornered, respectively, 43.5 and 28.3 percent of the world information technology market in 1995, the comparable figures for Latin America on the one hand and Eastern Europe, the Middle East, and Africa on the other were 2.0 and 2.6 percent. Put even more starkly, while in 1995 the numbers of personal computers per one thousand people residing in low-income and lower-middle-income economies were 1.6 and 10.0, the comparable figures for those in newly industrialized economies (NIEs) and high-income economies were 114.8 and 199.3. Or consider Internet users per one thousand people in 1996: for the former two types of economies the numbers were 0.01 and 0.7, respectively, whereas the numbers in the latter two types of economies were 12.9 and 111.0.[20] Then there are the overall figures that reveal 88 percent of the world's Internet users live in industrial countries, whereas only 0.3 percent live in the world's poorest countries.[21]

Notwithstanding the importance of these huge digital gaps between the informationally rich and poor—gaps both within and between countries that provide the rich with advantages and opportunities not available to the poor[22]—such data tell only part of the story. Most notably, they do not depict the trend line that readily allows for the assertion that not only the informationally rich but also the informationally poor are getting richer. The gap remains huge and may well be widening, but in a variety of ways the information revolution is also unfolding in the developing world, and along several dimensions the gap may begin to narrow in the years ahead. This potential shrinking of the gap stems from several sources. One is the enormous decline in the costs of information technologies, a decline that is brilliantly suggested by the fact that, for diverse reasons, "computing power per dollar invested has risen by a factor of 10,000 over the past 20 years" and that the "cost of voice transmission circuits has fallen by a factor of 10,000 over those same 20 years."[23] Another potential source of a narrowing of the gap involves the capacity of developing countries to "leapfrog the industrial countries by going straight

[19] For a cogent discussion of the information gap, see Jason P. Abbott, "The Internet and the Digital Divide: Representational Space or Representation of Space?" (paper presented at the annual conference of the British International Studies Association, Bradford, December 2000).

[20] World Development Report, *Knowledge for Development, 1998/99* (New York Oxford University Press for the World Bank, 1999), p. 63.

[21] "U.N. Fears Divisive Impact of the Internet," *New York Times*, July 29, 2000, p. A16.

[22] For an instance of the gap in the United States, see Steve Lohr, "A Nation Ponders Its Growing Digital Divide," *New York Times*, October 26, 1996, p. D5.

[23] World Development Report, *Knowledge for Development, 1998/99*, p. 57.

from underdeveloped networks to fully digitized networks, bypassing the traditional analog technology that still forms the backbone of the system in most industrial countries."[24] Likewise, while most of the developing world has yet to be wired, its peoples can get mobile phones and do not have to wait for the installation of fixed lines. It is noteworthy, for instance, that the

> number of cellular phones per fixed line is already as high in some low- and middle-income economies as in some industrialized countries; some developing countries with low density in both traditional telephone service and cellular phones have recently invested in cellular technology at a very fast rate. . . . The Philippines, a country with low telephone density (only 2.5 main lines per 100 people), has a higher ratio of mobile phone subscribers to main lines than Japan, the United Kingdom, the United States, or several other industrial countries with densities of more than 50 main lines per 100 people.[25]

Put differently, not long ago it was conventional to regret that development in Africa lagged because the continent was not wired. But now this lag is less portentous because communications in and to much of Africa are on the verge of becoming wireless.[26] In other words,

> The wireless revolution is ending the dictatorship of place in . . . profound way[s]. . . . In the past, one of the biggest disadvantages of being born in the poor world was that you were isolated from modern communications—and hence locked into the local economy. But mobile phones are great levelers, spreading the latest tools of communication to areas where traditional phone companies could not reach. The phone ladies of Bangladesh are going around with mobile phones that would turn heads in Hollywood restaurants, and enabling their customers to plug themselves into the global economy.[27]

Of course, despite the commitment of heads of state and other political leaders to narrow the digital divide,[28] the rise in the trend line in developing countries is nevertheless confined mostly to their elite and educated populations. Once the Internet was introduced into Kuwait in 1992, for example, scientists, scholars, and students came on-line in increasing numbers. Within six years their ranks increased to some forty-five thousand, many of whom are younger people who hang out in any of

---

[24] Ibid.

[25] Ibid. See also Simon Romero, "A Cell Phone Surge among World's Poor," *New York Times*, December 19, 2000, p. C1.

[26] By 2002 in Kenya, for example, there are "already double the number of mobile phones as there are fixed lines." Mark Turner, "Leap of Faith in an Untested Market," *Financial Times*, February 13, 2002, p. 14.

[27] "A Survey of Telecommunications: The World in Your Pocket," *The Economist*, Vol. 353 (October 9, 1999), p. 36.

[28] Ricardo Lagos, Thabo Mbeki, and Goran Persson, "We Will Harness Information Technology for the Have-Nots," *International Herald Tribune*, July 13, 2000, p. 6.

seven Internet cafés in Kuwait City, where they escape the heat and at the same time use the Internet for chatting, dating, or otherwise reinforcing their local culture.[29] The information revolution has also reached the small villages of the Middle East: in the case of Al Karaka, Egypt, there was electricity and only one telephone in the 1970s, but less than two decades later all its houses had electricity and "there are also 20 telephones and more than 55 television sets."[30]

Nor are authoritarian countries able to hold back the information revolution. China, for example, has some eighty million households receiving cable TV[31] and seventeen million Internet accounts, many of which are shared by several users, and it would appear that these numbers grow continually,[32] thus posing a potential for mass organization that is an anathema to the Chinese leadership.[33] Likewise, Iran has an estimated thirty thousand people with Internet accounts even as it also seeks to control the flow of information to and among them.[34] Whether such controls can ever be adequately established, however, is questionable.

In sum, while there are billions of persons who do not have access to the Internet, their numbers are dwindling as more and more people and organizations everywhere are coming on-line. To recast a commonplace metaphor, to focus on those who lack access may be to see the glass as nineteen-twentieths empty, but the trend line is in the direction of it being increasingly more than one-twentieth full.[35]

INTERACTIVE CONTEXTS

Perhaps the single most important consequence of the newer information technologies—and the consequence that justifies a continuing reference to the "information revolution"—concerns their impact on the modes

[29] Deborah L. Wheeler, "Global Culture or Culture Clash: New Information Technologies in the Islamic World—A View from Kuwait," *Communications Research*, Vol. 25 (August 1998), pp. 359–76.

[30] William E. Schmidt, "The Villages of Egypt Relish the Fruits of Peace," *New York Times*, September 24, 1993, p. A4.

[31] Leslie Chang, "China Changes Course on Competition," *Wall Street Journal*, October 27, 2000, p. A15.

[32] Leslie Chang, "Internet Attracts Numbers in China, but Not Spenders," *Wall Street Journal*, July 28, 2000, p. A13.

[33] See Craig S. Smith, "The Wired Age: China Arrives at a Moment of Truth," *New York Times*, April 1, 2001, Sec. 4, p. A1; Barbara Crossette, "The Internet Changes Dictatorship's Rules," *New York Times*, August 1, 1999, Sec. 4., p. 1; and Erik Eckholm, "A Trial Will Test China's Grip on the Internet," *New York Times*, November 16, 1998, p. A8.

[34] Neil MacFarquhar, "With Mixed Feelings, Iran Tiptoes to the Internet," *New York Times*, October 8, 1996, p. A4.

[35] For a discussion of the problems associated with raising the volume of the glass, see Wayne Arnold, "Cell Phones for the World's Poor," *New York Times*, January 19, 2001, p. C1.

through which individuals and organizations interact. Until the advent of the most recent technologies, especially e-mail and the Internet, the vast proportion of these interactions were hierarchical, both within organizations and across organizations engaged in similar pursuits. The former hierarchies tended to be formally established, with ranks and positions that allowed for top-down flows of authority and policy directives, whereas the across-organization hierarchies were also marked by top-down arrangements but were more in the nature of, so to speak, pecking orders—informal but widely shared rankings of prestige, influence, and power. The horizontal networks that the newer technologies permit, however, have supplemented both the formal and the informal hierarchies. As a consequence of the capacities for networking facilitated by the newer information technologies, a veritable explosion of organizations and associations marks the present era. As noted in chapter 3, the organizational explosion is so vast that fully tracing and documenting it is virtually impossible. At every level of community in every part of the world, new organizations are continuously being formed that are preponderantly sustained by network rather than hierarchical structures.[36]

A measure of the growth of transnational networks is readily evident in the estimate that the ranks of transnational NGOs have risen from six thousand in 1990 to more than twenty-six thousand in 1999.[37] Equally impressive, a measure of the capabilities and effectiveness of networked organizations is provided by the events surrounding the 1999 WTO meeting in Seattle, where some "1,500 NGOs signed an anti-WTO protest declaration set up online," a phenomenon called an "NGO swarm" that can undermine IGOs precisely because it has no "central leadership or command structure; it is multi-headed, impossible to decapitate."[38]

Note that hierarchies are being supplemented and not replaced by networks. To stress that the network has become a central form of human organization is not to imply that hierarchies are headed for extinction. There will always be a need for hierarchy, for authority to be arrayed in such a way that decisional conflicts can be resolved and policies adopted by higher authorities when consensual agreements prove unachievable at lower levels in any type of organization. The present period of dynamic transformations is likely to be one in which many hierarchies are flattened, perhaps even disrupted, but such a pattern is not the equivalent of anticipating the demise of hierarchical structures.[39]

---

[36] Lester M. Salamon, "The Global Associational Revolution: The Rise of the Third Sector on the World Scene," *Foreign Affairs*, Vol. 73 (July/August 1994), pp. 109–22.

[37] *The Economist*, December 11, 1999, p. 21.

[38] Ibid.

[39] For an analysis that stresses the limits of networks and the necessity of hierarchies, see

This is not to imply that horizontal networks are new forms of organization. The networks that flow from horizontal communication have long been features of human endeavor. Such interactions have always been possible, say, by steamship and letters during most of the nineteenth century and by telephone during the first half of the twentieth century. But these earlier technologies were available only to elites. Others could not afford them. Today, however, not only are horizontal exchanges rendered virtually simultaneous by the information revolution, but their cost has been greatly reduced. As a result, horizontal networking is no longer confined to the wealthy and the powerful. Now it is available to ordinary folk who have access to the Internet. Stated in terms of the new technologies, "The growth of a vast new information infrastructure including not only the Internet, but also cable, cellular, and satellite systems, etc., [has shifted] the balance . . . from one-to-many broadcast media (e.g., traditional radio and television) to many-to-many interactive media. A huge increase in global interconnectivity is resulting from the ease of entry and access in many nations, and the growing interest of so many actors in using the new infrastructure for all manner of interactions."[40]

The networking potential that flows from the easy availability of information technologies is perhaps especially conspicuous in the United States. For not only has Internet usage in the United States more than doubled in recent years,[41] but 9 percent of respondents in the aforementioned survey of the usage of diverse information technologies were classified as either "Connected" or "Superconnected" to public affairs.[42] That this high-usage stratum of the public is capable of extensive networking can be readily deduced from a central finding of the survey:

> The Internet, it turns out, is not a breeding ground for disconnection, fragmentation, paranoia, and apathy. Digital Citizens [the Connected and the Superconnected] are not alienated, either from other people or from civic institutions. Nor are they ignorant of our system's inner workings, or indifferent to the social and political issues our society must confront. Instead, the online world encompasses many of the most informed and participatory citizens we have ever had or are likely to have.[43]

Francis Fukuyama, "Social Networks and Digital Networks" (paper presented at the Workshop on the Future of the Internet, Palo Alto, May 6, 1996).

[40] David Ronfeldt and John Arquilla, "What If There Is a Revolution in Diplomatic Affairs?" (paper presented at the annual meeting of the International Studies Association, Washington, D.C., February 17, 1999), p. 4.

[41] Rajiv Chandrasekaran, "Politics Finding a Home on the 'Net,'" *Washington Post*, November 22, 1996, p. A4.

[42] Katz, "The Digital Citizen," p. 71.

[43] Ibid.

Clearly, then, the significance of virtually free access to the Internet by ever-greater numbers of people can hardly be overestimated. Already it has facilitated the formation and sustenance of networks among like-minded people who in earlier, pre-Internet times could never have converged. The result has been the aforementioned organizational explosion, a vast proliferation of associations—from environmental to human rights activists, from small groups of protesters to large social movements, from specialized interest associations to elite advocacy networks, from business alliances to interagency governmental committees, and so on across all the realms of human activity wherein goals are sought. This weblike explosion of organizations has occurred in territorial space as well as cyberspace, but the opening up of the latter has served as a primary stimulus to associational proliferation in the former. Indeed, the trend toward network forms of organization "is so strong that, projected into the future, it augurs major transformations in how societies are organized—if not societies as a whole, then at least parts of their governments, economies, and especially their civil societies."[44] Not least among these transformations are the ways in which information technologies have facilitated the formation of networks that narrow the gap between rural and urban areas of societies,[45] rendering it all the more difficult for Insular Locals and Tuned-Out Passives to avoid distant proximities.

Stated differently, the information revolution has fostered a relationship revolution: "Along every conceivable dimension—from the intimate to the institutional—digital media force both individuals and organizations to redefine what kind of relationships create value."[46] Both in large networks and in small-group interactions, people in the local and global worlds are increasingly involved in diverse and proliferating relationships, a trend that is probably altering not only their interpersonal skills but also their views of themselves and their links to macro collectivities. The consequences of their immersion in rapidly expanding relationships may also be enormous for micro-macro interactions. One observer, for example, speculates that movement within the local and global worlds may eventually accelerate in such a way as to reduce intergroup tensions: notwithstanding

[44] David Ronfeldt, "Tribes, Institutions, Markets, Networks: A Framework about Societal Evolution" (Santa Monica: RAND, 1996), p. 1. For a skeptical view of the potential of networks, and especially the Internet, see Deborah C. Sawyer, "The Pied Piper Goes Electronic," *The Futurist*, February 1999, pp. 42–46.

[45] Jay E. Gillette, "The Information Renaissance: Toward an End to Rural Information Colonialism," *Pacific Telecommunications Review*, Vol. 18 (December 1976), pp. 29–37.

[46] Michael Schrage, "The Relationship Revolution," *Merrill Lynch Forum* (http://www.ml.com/woml/forum/relation.htm), p. 3.

a lessening of one's sense of a coherent or fundamental self and a resulting vulnerability to group allegiance, the long-term effects may be different. With expanding associations, interdependencies, and commitments, the tendency toward singular group allegiance may abate. At a minimum, individual commitments to groups are likely to be shortened. Individuals may enthusiastically join a group, actively participate, donate time and resources, then move on. This kind of temporally situated commitment has already been evidenced in the political sphere, with election-dependent party allegiances now commonplace. "Temporary ecstasies" are also apparent in the deterioration of brand loyalty and in the rapidly shifting terrains of celebrity worship, team loyalty, and spiritual allegiance. And in the realm of identity politics, an increasingly common complaint is that an identity commanded by a political standpoint inadequately represents the complex lives of the participants.[47]

This line of reasoning can lead to radically different outcomes. On the one hand, "If the trajectory is extended with individuals multiply engaged, we may approach the point where intense or lethal conflict between groups will recede. There will be little enthusiasm for harsh attacks on other groups, because members of groups on the offensive will share membership, allegiances, or interdependencies with those under attack." On the other hand, if a

> slow erosion of belief in an integral and basic self [occurs], and if the return to the group ultimately proves futile, then our traditional concepts of the fundamental building blocks of society will be thrown into doubt. Neither the self nor the group will command ultimate significance in our deliberations and practices. . . . [T]he door is thus opened for the creative construction of alternatives to these traditional but tired concepts. One of the most fascinating alternatives on the cultural horizon represents a shift toward the relational—that is, turning away from the concepts of self and group in favor of such concepts as interdependence, conjoint construction of meaning, mutually interacting entities, and systemic process.[48]

Information technologies are posited as central to this relational revolution:

> Particularly relevant is the development of chat rooms, bulletin boards, e-mail lists, and other Internet features that facilitate bodiless relationships. On the Internet identities can be put forward that may not be linked in any specific way to the concrete existence of the participants, and these cyber-identities may carry on active and engaging relationships. Most significant is that these relationships proceed not on the basis of "real selves" (integral minds in physi-

---

[47] Kenneth J. Gergen, "The Self in the Age of Information," *Washington Quarterly*, Vol. 23 (winter 2000), p. 211.
[48] Ibid.

cal bodies), but on the basis of positionings within conversations or the discursive flow. Further, it is only the coordinated functioning of these discursive formations that enables "community" to be achieved. In effect, community has no geographic locus outside the web of discourse. Here we approach pure relatedness, without self or community in the traditional sense.[49]

A more immediate and macro consequence of the network trend is occurring in the military field. A stunning example is evident in the ways the new information technologies have facilitated innovative networking undertaken by the U.S. Marine Corps. In an exercise conducted on the California coast and called "Urban Warrior," a unit of marines composed of all ranks from generals to privates launched an "invasion," with the lower-ranked personnel that "hit the beaches" all carrying hand-held computers that linked them to all the others in the unit and collectively provided all concerned with a picture of how the "battle" was unfolding. In effect, they operated as a network in which rank and hierarchy were irrelevant, an arrangement that the Marine Corps plans to apply on a larger scale in the future.[50]

The networking facilitated by information technologies has also enabled protestors to concert their efforts through boycotts. Because of U.S. support for Israel, for example, such an action was undertaken in the Arab world with not a little success: "With word spread via the Internet, mosque sermons, fliers and even mobile phone messages, the boycott seems to be slowly gathering force, especially against consumer products."[51]

While it is hardly possible to overstate the extent to which the Internet underlies macro trends toward networking in government, business, and military organizations, the relevance of these trends to the world of voluntary associations and nongovernmental organizations may be even more profound. In effect, the information revolution has facilitated a substantial change in what is called "civil society," that domain of the private sector where people have not had the equipment or financial resources to widen their contacts and solidify their collaborative efforts that have long been available to governments, corporations, and armies. As NGOs and the advocacy networks they sustain proliferate and cross-fertilize at stunning rates,[52] it has become increasingly possible to inform, coordinate,

---

[49] Ibid.

[50] Joel Garreau, "Point Men for a Revolution: Can the Marines Survive a Shift from Hierarchies to Networks?" *Washington Post*, March 6, 1999, p. 1.

[51] Neil MacFarquhar, "An Anti-American Boycott Is Growing in the Arab world," *New York Times*, May 10, 2002, p. A1.

[52] See chapter 3 for data on the proliferation of advocacy networks. For an instance of cross-fertilization in which a dissident movement in Japan gained momentum by explicitly

and mobilize individuals in all parts of the world who have common goals to which they are willing to devote time and energy. Put more forcefully, the proliferation of advocacy networks is altering the landscape of world affairs and having substantial consequences for the course of events. Whether or not a global civil society will ever evolve, it is certainly the case that transnational networks of private persons have become pervasive and central actors on the global stage.[53] In sum,

> Our exploration of emergent social structures across domains of human activity and experience leads to an overarching conclusion: as a historical trend, dominant functions and processes in the information age are increasingly organized around networks. Networks constitute the new social morphology of our societies, and the diffusion of networking logic substantially modifies the operation and outcomes in processes of production experience, power, and culture. While the networking form of social organization has existed in other times and spaces, the new information technology paradigm provides the material basis for its pervasive expansion throughout the entire social structure.[54]

New Global Structures

With people in both developed and developing countries becoming more skillful in relating to public affairs, with organizations proliferating at an eye-catching rate, it is not surprising that information technologies have contributed to transformations in historic global structures. As noted in chapter 3, as the global arena becomes ever more dense with actors and networks, the traditional world of anarchical states has been supplemented by a second world of world politics composed of diverse nongovernmental, transnational, and subnational actors. Despite its diversity and cross-purposes, this "multi-centric" world is seen as having a modicum of coherence such that it coexists with the state-centric world and, in effect, has given rise to the aforementioned bifurcation of global structures in which the two coexisting worlds are conceived as sometimes cooperating and often conflicting but at all times interacting.

Needless to say, this interaction between the worlds has been greatly facilitated by the new information technologies. The more the technologies advance, the more do they open up both governments and NGOs to the influence of their members, to bottom-up and horizontal processes

---

using the Internet to imitate a similar movement in South Korea, see Howard W. French, "Lone Voice No Longer, Japan Gadfly Catches On," *New York Times*, June 18, 2000, p. 5.

[53] See, for example, Margaret E. Keck and Kathryn Sikkink, *Activists Beyond Borders: Advocacy Networks in International Politics* (Ithaca, N.Y.: Cornell University Press, 1998).

[54] Castells, *The Rise of the Network Society*, Vol. 1, p. 469.

that have greatly complicated the tasks of governance on a global scale.[55] For national governments these changes—and the vast proliferation of interconnections they have fostered—have confounded the traditional practices of diplomacy and the long-standing premises of national security, thereby necessitating a rethinking of how to pursue goals in relation to the demands of both other states and the innumerable collectivities in the multicentric world.[56] For NGOs the increased connectivity has provided opportunities as well as challenges as they seek to network and build coalitions with like-minded actors and contest the coalitions that stand in the way of their goals.[57]

In short, the bifurcation of global structures has led to a vast decentralization of authority in which global governance becomes less state-centric and more the sum of crazy-quilt patterns between unalike, dispersed, overlapping, and contradictory collectivities seeking to maintain their coherence and advance their goals. More than that, the interconnection of these patterns "is likely to deepen and become the defining characteristic of the 21st Century. The information revolution is what makes this possible; it provides the capability and opportunity to circuitize the globe in ways and to degrees that have never been seen before. This is likely to be a messy, complicated process, rife with ambivalent, contradictory, and paradoxical effects."[58]

The information revolution may be neutral in the sense that it permits the application of diverse and competing values, but clearly it underlies extensive consequences in every realm of global affairs. And since there is no end in sight to the development of new information technologies, the ramifications of their impact are yet to be fully experienced as people and their collectivities seek to keep abreast of the dynamic transformations that are altering the human condition.

---

[55] Michael Peter Smith and Luis Eduardo Guarnizo (eds.), *Transnationalism from Below* (New Brunswick, N.J.: Transaction, 1998).

[56] See Richard H. Solomon, Walter B. Wriston, and George P. Schultz, *Keynote Addresses from the Virtual Diplomacy Conference* (Washington, D.C.: U.S. Institute of Peace, 1997); and Center for Strategic and International Affairs, *Reinventing Diplomacy in the Information Age* (Washington, D.C., 1998).

[57] See, for example, Julie Fisher, "International Networking: The Role of Southern NGOs," in David L. Cooperrider and Jane E. Dutton (eds.), *Organizational Dimensions of Global Change: No Limits to Cooperation* (Thousand Oaks, Calif.: Sage, 1999), pp. 210–34.

[58] Ronfeldt and Arquilla, "What If There Is a Revolution in Diplomatic Affairs?" pp. 19–20.

CHAPTER TWELVE

Structures of Authority:
In Crisis or in Place?

> Around the world the crises pile up, and the collage of
> headlines does not make a pretty picture. In Kosovo, babies die
> of cold on hillsides where mothers have fled to save their lives.
> In Sierra Leone, madmen posing as a rebel army cut off the
> hands of teen-aged boys and trap families in their homes to
> torch them. Angolans shoot down relief planes. A defiant
> Saddam Hussein watches the United Nations drift helplessly
> without a policy. Haiti spirals back into chaos. And the chief
> judge of an international tribunal is stopped cold at Serbia's
> border when she tries to investigate crimes against humanity in
> Kosovo.
> Who's in charge here?
>
> —News item[1]

As IMPLIED by this epigraph, the dynamics of fragmegration have led to numerous authority structures in various parts of the world being overtaken by crises, some of which are so thoroughgoing as to amount to vacuums of authority. Nor are countries the only systems vulnerable to crisis. The futile debate over the "new world order" proclaimed more than a decade ago, the failure of the Kyoto Protocol on Climate Change, and the more recent spate of remedies proposed to prevent another Asian financial crisis suggest the search for effective institutions of authority has also been intense and largely unsuccessful at supranational levels. More than that, while practitioners may unknowingly stumble upon and develop fledgling institutions, scholars are likely to continue pondering the meaning of the world's many authority crises until such time that they link them more fully to the profound transformations at work in the world. This is especially the case, it seems to me, where research agendas are still rooted deeply in the premise that the world is crisscrossed by boundaries that divide the international from the domestic and that accord to nation-states the role of presiding over these boundaries. Such a conception of world affairs is, I am convinced, profoundly flawed. As one

---

[1] Barbara Crosette, "Lost Horizon," *New York Times*, January 24, 1999, Sec. 4, p. 1.

observer put it in the context of a particular issue area, "[C]onventional approaches to authority . . . are utterly deficient in the face of both transnational societal pressures and efforts to address global environmental problems."[2] Accordingly, given profound transformations in the institutions, structures, and processes that sustain economic, political, and social life today, authority is clearly among the conceptual tools that need clarification and specification if analysis is to move meaningfully beyond globalization and address how micro-macro interactions contribute to the changing dynamics of fragmegration. Indeed, if the manner in which people cope with the distant proximities that make up their worlds is to be securely grasped, it is crucial that the authority crises that affect every level of community be elaborated. The purpose of this chapter is first to highlight the nature of authority structures and then to indicate ways in which they may enter into different forms of crisis. The possible emergence of new spheres of authority (SOAs) is addressed in the next chapter.

AUTHORITY

Influence, power, and authority are concepts that share a common quality. They all are relational rather than possessional. Language usage often results in treating influence, power, or authority as possessed by an individual or agency, but this is a misleading conception because it leads analysts to look for the influence, power, or authority as it may be manifested in the attributes of the individuals or agencies said to be endowed with such capacities. Such a search is bound to fail because the measure of influence, power, or authority at work in a situation is to be found in the extent to which those toward whom such efforts are directed comply with the directives—that is, in the relationship between the wielders and targets of the influence, power, or authority. In the words of one astute analyst, authority "can only be determined on the basis of outcomes."[3] To be sure, compliance will depend in part on the possessions of those who issue the directives, but these possessions become meaningful only as they are assessed and interpreted by the persons or collectivities whose compliance is sought. More than that, the resulting delicate and complex relationships are sustained or subverted not only by the goals and capabilities of the conflicting parties but also by the perceptions that they

[2] Karen Litfin, "Environment, Wealth, and Authority: Global Climate Change and Emerging Modes of Legitimation," *International Studies Review*, Vol. 2, No. 2 (summer 2000), p. 121.

[3] Susan Strange, *The Retreat of the State* (Cambridge: Cambridge University Press, 1996), p. 91.

have of each other and their own capabilities. Put differently, such relationships are shaped by underlying (and often unrecognized) bargaining processes between those who exercise influence, power, or authority and those toward whom their actions are directed.

How, then, to distinguish authority relations from those based on power and influence? While there can be some overlap of the authority, power, and influence at work in any relationship—in the sense that any of the three may be more effective if it is supported by either or both of the other two—there are important ways in which they differ. Most notably, the compliance evoked by authority is a direct and voluntary response to a stimulus, whereas influence can operate circuitously as well as through direct stimuli, and power tends to obscure the voluntarism of the compliance because it may be backed up by the threat or use of coercion. Actors who achieve compliance through pointing a gun or some other method that does not derive from the formal right to engage in such actions are exercising power rather than authority. Authority is often backed up by the fear of coercive power, but power that forces compliance cannot serve as the basis of an authority structure and, indeed, in all likelihood cannot long sustain the compliance (which is why dictators tend to hold elections: they are a means to achieve legitimacy even if they are rigged and the dictator wins virtually 100 percent of the vote).

In short, the more authorities have to resort to the threat or use of force, the less voluntaristic is the compliance and the weaker is their authority. To be sure, voluntary compliance can occur for various reasons, from a fear of reprisal to a respect for expertise, from a recognition that the authorities have a right to rule to a habit founded on this recognition. But whatever the reason, the compliance is voluntary in the sense that it stems from habitual decisions made by the complying individuals. At times it may seem that they have no choice, but that is only because the legitimacy of the authority is well established or because it is hard to imagine individuals choosing to go to jail or giving their life in the face of the authority's demands. Yet some persons, such as those among the Resistant Locals and Globals committed to nonviolent protests against the IMF and World Bank, do choose not to comply despite the risk of jail and the seeming absence of choice.

It follows that authority relations are to a large degree founded on an unthinking readiness to comply with directives, on a habit of consent under certain circumstances, on a legitimacy that has been accorded the authorities by those toward whom their compliance efforts are directed. Structures of authority may be founded on traditional norms or, more frequently, on formally established legal enactments, be they a constitution, a law, a court decision, bylaws, or any other authority-granting mechanism that conveys legitimacy upon the roles or offices occupied by the authorities.[4] But formal mechanisms are no guarantee that authority can be effectively exercised. Authority relationships must also draw upon habits of compliance, and these are not easily constructed or sustained, since they evolve only through repeated reinforcement. When compliance habits become frayed or fail to evolve with the continued intrusion of distant proximities, an authority structure is bound to be weak and tenuous. Such structures can collapse quickly if the underlying tendencies toward habitual compliance are undermined by circumstances—such as economic crises or outlandish policy initiatives—that deviate sharply from the long-standing terms of an authority relationship. And since unthinking habits are founded on repeated experience, it takes a prolonged period of time for authority structures to evolve or to recover once they have deteriorated.

The Compliance-Defiance Continuum

It would be a mistake, of course, to conceptualize authority in black-and-white terms. Rather, any authority relationship is best viewed as located somewhere along a continuum that stretches from habit at one extreme to defiance at the other. Habitual compliance is the purest expression of authority relationships, but obviously there are gradations in the degree to which the compliance may be forthcoming. If automatic acquiescence is the purest extreme on the continuum, then reluctant and hesitant compliance would be located near the other, noncompliant extreme, with periodic and spasmodic compliance falling between the two extremes. It follows that the more circumstances move away from the compliance extreme and toward the center of the continuum, the more do processes of persuasion and bargaining sustain the authority relationship, just as the more a situation is located at the noncompliant extreme, the more is power evoked to reinforce the relationship.

Historically, or at least for the last several hundred years, the authority of states has been supreme. Aside from revolutionary times or intense factional conflict, wherever states are recognized as having the legitimacy to govern within their borders, their domestic directives have superseded those of any other collectivities and achieved the compliance of their publics. Moreover, enduring sequences of micro-macro interactions eventually culminate in the authority of states being specified in constitutions, bylaws, legislative enactments, and judicial decisions, which collectively outline the rules of the game whereby politics and governance within a

---

[4] For an interesting discussion of the links between legitimacy and compliance, see Timothy Dunne and Nicholas J. Wheeler, "Closing the Compliance Gap: Pluralist and Solidarist Readings of International Legitimacy" (paper presented at the annual meeting of the International Studies Association, Toronto, March 18–22, 1997).

state's jurisdiction are conducted and thereby serve as constant reinforcements for compliance habits.

The formal rules of the game that states adopt, supplemented by the accumulation of historical experience, endow their authority with tradition as time passes. A combination of moral sanctions, constitutional legitimacy, heroic legends, and superior knowledge bases, the traditional foundations of a state's authority underlie the readiness of its citizens to comply habitually with its directives. Their unthinking acceptance of their government's policies is unthinking precisely because its actions are backed by the weight of its practices, laws, and institutions that have become, in effect, traditions. As will be seen, it is also precisely the breakdown of these traditions and their replacement by performance criteria of legitimacy that have led to widespread crises of authority in the state-centric world, to a "normative change related to the recognition that entities other than the state have the right to act authoritatively within a domestic context. . . . The rules of domestic order no longer exclusively involve the state, but rather include global institutions, NGOs, and sub-state actors as legitimate and authoritative entities."[5]

To repeat, however, the key to the effectiveness of an authority structure lies not in its formal documents but in the readiness of those toward whom authority is directed to comply with the rules and policies promulgated by the authorities. Formal authority is vacuous if it does not evoke compliance, whereas informal authority not backed by formal documentation can be stable and effective if its exercise produces compliance. This is especially so in the multi-centric world where hierarchy is often less important than nonlinear feedback processes as the basis for coherence among those who make and implement decisions. Where hierarchy is minimal, as is the case for numerous collectivities in the multi-centric world, compliance derives more from shared aspirations and practices than from traditional obligations or coercive threats that foster an unthinking acceptance of directives.

The available conceptual equipment offers little guidance with respect to tracing and evaluating authority structures that lie outside the reach of governments and states.[6] We are inclined to fall back on the simple notion that the authority of actors in the multi-centric world is rooted in compliance habits that have emerged in response to repeated experience with directives emanating from centers of leadership in that world. Sim-

---

[5] Ann Mason, "Colombian State Failure: Global Restructuring and the Erosion of Domestic Authority" (paper presented at the annual meeting of the International Studies Association, New Orleans, March 23–27, 2002).

[6] For an exception, see A. Claire Cutler, Virginia Haufler, and Tony Porter (eds.), *Private Authority and International Affairs* (Albany: State University of New York Press, 1999).

ple as this premise may be, however, it is essentially misleading. Not only is the authority of NGOs, social movements, epistemic communities, corporate alliances, and other collectivities in the multi-centric world founded as much on informal as formal sources of legitimacy, but it is also the case that the relationships that sustain such collectivities are embedded in horizontal networks as well as vertical hierarchies. Indeed, as previously implied, networks are probably more central to the daily routines and successes of NGOs than any hierarchical structures they manage to fashion.[7] Numerous NGOs were founded in one country and subsequently formed coalitions and alliances with like-minded groups in other countries.[8]

Some might argue that authority is to be found only in hierarchical systems, that horizontal systems are based on cooperation rather than authority, that cooperation can readily cease, whereas hierarchical authority relationships are enduring. But such an argument—what one observer calls the extreme case[9]—is a throwback to state-centric ways of thinking in which traditional lines of command are seen as the basis of coherence and forward movement.

How, then, to account for the operation of authority relationships in a world increasingly pervaded by organizations sustained through horizontal networks? Clearly, the concept of authority has to be extended to locate such organizations on the compliance-defiance continuum. Here

[7] Network forms of organization have become increasingly adopted by a wide variety of associations, corporations, governmental agencies, and so forth, as the microelectronic revolution spreads across the whole spectrum of collective endeavor. Diverse examples are provided in W. Mitchell Waldrop, "The Trillion-Dollar Vision of Dee Hocks," *Fast Company*, October–November 1996, pp. 75–86. For the underlying rationale of network organizations, see Dee W. Hocks, *Birth of the Chaordic Age* (San Francisco: Berrett-Koehler, 1999).

[8] In Asia, for example, the Asian NGO Coalition for Agrarian Reform and Rural Development provides a network for dialogue among South Asian, Southeast Asian, and northern NGOs. David C. Korten, *Getting to the 21st Century: Voluntary Action and the Global Agenda* (West Hartford, Conn.: Kumarian Press, 1990), pp. 93, 94. Many other examples of NGO coalitions are cited in Thomas Princen and Matthias Finger, "Introduction," in T. Princen and M. Finger (eds.), *Environmental NGOs in World Politics: Linking the Local and the Global* (London: Routledge, 1994), pp. 2–4. For an assessment of the roles they play, see Jane G. Covey, "Accountability and Effectiveness in NGO Policy Alliances," in Michael Edwards and David Hulme (eds.), *Beyond the Magic Bullet: NGO Performance and Accountability in the Post–Cold War World* (West Hartford, Conn.: Kumarian Press, 1996), Chap. 15.

[9] "I see no reason to conclude that the extreme cases are predominant in most social systems. There are numerous situations in which subjects left to their own calculations in the absence of any organized sanctions nevertheless exhibit high levels of compliance." Oran R. Young, *Compliance and Public Authority: A Theory with International Applications* (Baltimore: Johns Hopkins University Press, 1979), pp. 31–32.

the concept is reformulated to allow for patterns of compliance in the multicentric world that become habitual through processes wherein initial phases of bargaining through horizontal interactions become so recurrent and patterned that people and organizations in horizontal networks comply with requests as well as directives. Repeated and unthinking compliance with requests is not the same as responses marked by bargaining and cooperation. Whether they occur in horizontal networks or hierarchical structures, such responses fall in the middle of the compliance-defiance continuum and thus result from calculations, from assessments as to how to achieve goals, from thinking through situations, whereas habitual responses to requests are grounded in an acknowledgment as to the location of authority in the relationship and thus do not require calculations to initiate or sustain the responses.

To equate requests with directives is not to play with words or to redefine meanings to suit a particular perspective; rather, it is to emphasize that the compliance continuum is the key to authority relationships. Whether requests or directives serve as the initial stimuli that evoke compliance, the more habitual the responses become, the more can it be said that an authority structure has been established. Viewed in this way (i.e., applying the habitual compliance test), networked organizations can be integrated into the storehouse of conceptual equipment with which to probe the underpinnings of the multi-centric world.

Locating authority structures along the compliance-defiance continuum serves well the task of tracing authority in a fragmegrated world. The continuum allows for movement back and forth as particular authority structures change in response to the complex adaptation of collectivities in diverse situations. Moreover, it provides a context that can be applied equally to states and collectivities as diverse as crime syndicates, nonprofit organizations, multinational corporations, coalitions of the willing, issue regimes, and so on. Many sovereign states can exercise both the formal and the informal authority that enables them to achieve compliance in their domains, but the authority structures of an ever-greater number of states are fragile and in crisis as developments undermine the habitual readiness of their citizens to comply. Likewise, other types of collectivities are located at various points along the compliance continuum, with a few (such as the European Union) having successfully created both formal and informal authority that can be effectively exercised, while some (such as Greenpeace) have developed informal authority that relies on requests rooted in moral persuasion to evoke compliance on the part of their members, and still others (such as crime syndicates) use threats, coercion, and other techniques located toward the defiance extreme of the continuum to generate compliance. In short, wherever the persistence of collectivities is based on networked relations, they have authority structures that in one way or another enable them to mobilize and give direction to their memberships on behalf of their policies.

The Transformation of Authority Structures

Habitual compliance also helps explain why the world scene is presently marked by pervasive authority crises.[10] For not only are states experiencing a diminution of their traditional authority—as corruption undermines their moral authority, as internal conflicts and pressures toward decentralization undermine their constitutional legitimacy, as prolonged periods of peace abroad and industrialization at home subvert their heroic legends, and as the Internet challenges their superior knowledge bases—but the same process is corroding all social institutions rooted in traditional modes of conduct, from the family to the church, from the local community to the trade union, from the military establishment to the corporation.[11] In effect, with individuals more autonomous, more skillful, and more sensitive to the distant proximities in which they are ensconced, historical criteria of legitimacy are being replaced by performance criteria, and, as a consequence, fewer and fewer patterns of habitual compliance seem to sustain the life of communities.[12] Rather, the trend is toward more self-conscious assessments as to when and where compliance is appropriate, a trend that in turn fosters increasing challenges to established authorities and enlarges the ranks of the Resistant Locals and Globals.[13]

Most collectivities in the multi-centric world are beneficiaries of this

[10] For an elaboration of the pervasiveness of authority crises, see James N. Rosenau, *Turbulence in World Politics: A Theory of Continuity and Change* (Princeton, N.J.: Princeton University Press, 1990), pp. 186–91.

[11] A 2001 survey of twenty thousand citizens in twenty countries conducted by Environics International yielded findings indicating "a rejection of traditional authority in favor of a growing allegiance to organizations based on values," with 65 percent reporting they trusted NGOs to work in the best interests of society while the comparable figure for national governments was only 45 percent ("Poll Findings Suggest Trouble Ahead for the Globalization Agenda," www.EnvironicsInternational.com), p. 3.

[12] An elaboration of the shift from traditional to performance criteria of legitimacy is developed in Rosenau, *Turbulence in World Politics*, pp. 380–81. While citizens can intuitively react to the performance of collectivities, the task of analysts is not so simple. On the contrary, "assessing NGO performance is a difficult and messy business" (Edwards and Hulme, "Introduction," in *Beyond the Magic Bullet*, p. 4). For an extended analysis of the problem of evaluating performances, see Alan F. Fowler, "Assessing NGO Performance: Difficulties, Dilemmas, and a Way Ahead," in Edwards and Hulme (eds.), *Beyond the Magic Bullet*, Chap. 13.

[13] For an interesting history of how the decline of traditional criteria of authority in the United States has led to an increasing readiness to defy authorities, see Jeffrey Rosen, "In Lieu of Manners," *New Times Magazine*, February 4, 2001, pp. 46–51.

shift in the criteria of legitimacy. For the shift has accompanied the decentralization and fragmentation of long-standing institutions, which in turn have fostered the organizational explosion that enhances a trend toward single-issue concerns and organizations and their subsequent regrouping into the networks and alliances of which NGOs are increasingly composed. And as this restructuring of organizational life progresses and becomes increasingly entrenched on a global scale, so may new habits of compliance begin to develop that are appropriate both to the decentralized and fragmented nature of global politics and to the tasks undertaken in the multi-centric world.

This evolution of new criteria of legitimacy has contributed substantially to the aforementioned "pluralism of authority."[14] It is a pluralism in which, as responsibility

> shifts away from the state or is actively shed on the state's own initiative[, i]t is not taken over by another agent. . . . [Instead i]t dissipates; it splits into a plethora of localized or partial policies pursued by localized or partial (mostly one issue) agencies. With that vanishes the modern state's tendency to precipitate and draw upon itself almost all social protest. . . . Under the postmodern condition grievances which in the past would cumulate into a collective political process and address themselves to the state, stay diffuse and translate into self-reflexivity of the agents, stimulating further dissipation of policies and the autonomy of postmodern agencies (if they do cumulate for a time in the form of a one-issue pressure group, they bring together agents too heterogeneous in other respects to prevent the dissolution of the formation once the desired progress in the issue in question has been achieved . . .).[15]

It must quickly be noted, however, that while collectivities in the multi-centric world may be beneficiaries of the change from traditional to performance criteria of legitimacy, this is not to presume that they are filling the gaps left by the authority crises of states. Although the authority of states subjected to terrorist attacks may be temporarily reinvigorated by such attacks, it is otherwise likely that the diminution of state authority throughout the world has led not only to a shift of authority to other collectivities but also to vacuums of authority, to situations in such disarray as to be lacking any centers of authority. Indeed, given the way in which fragmegrating dynamics are highlighting self-interests at the expense of community interests, possibly the central tendency is toward individuals and their households being the sole repositories of authority. Some Affirmative Globals exhibit tendencies in this direction, as do their

[14] Zygmunt Bauman, "A Sociological Theory of Postmodernity," in Peter Beilharz, Gillian Robinson, and John Rundell (eds.), *Between Totalitarianism and Postmodernity: A Thesis Eleven Reader* (Cambridge, Mass.: MIT Press, 1992), p. 160.

[15] Ibid., pp. 156–57.

counterparts among the Resistant Locals and Globals.[16] What follows suggests that the devolution of authority to individuals and households can be exaggerated, that several forms of authority persist at more macro levels and enable collectivities to rely on habitual compliance as they frame their policies and move toward their goals; but the trend toward self-interest is surely manifest in many parts of the world, and its implications for the loci of authority ought not be dismissed.

Two Realms of Authority

Before turning to the several types of authority that can generate compliance, it is useful to note the links between the authority that the leaders of collectivities exercise with respect to their members, what can be labeled *internal authority*, and that which they direct toward individuals or organizations elsewhere in the world, what can be referred to as *external authority*. Collectivities vary along both dimensions: internal authority can vary from those with memberships that are habitually compliant to those that are more erratically organized, just as the external authority of both types can vary from collectivities that are able to evoke compliance widely around the world to those that are weak in this respect. Normally the two forms of authority reinforce each other in the sense that the degree of internal authority exercised by a collectivity tends to enhance its external authority, and vice versa.

Such interactions, however, have little bearing on the dearth of transparency and democracy in the multi-centric world. To conclude that the authority of actors in the multi-centric world may become increasingly solidified and extensive is not to imply a trend in which their internal authority is also becoming more open and accountable. That problem may or may not be ameliorated as they acquire more authority, but nothing in the foregoing formulation offers any clue as to the likelihood of movement toward a solution of the accountability problem.

TYPES OF AUTHORITY

Although organizations in the multi-centric world vary greatly in their size, resources, goals, interests, and capacity to evoke habitual compliance, there are only a limited number of ways in which they can exercise either internal or external authority. Lacking the weight of long-standing traditions, they can draw on five sources of habitual compliance: moral

---

[16] For an example of these tendencies in a single country, see Seth Mydans, "Thailand's Annual Water War Mirrors a Wild Era," *New York Times*, April 15, 2001, p. 8.

authority, knowledge authority, reputational authority, issue-specific authority, and what might be called affiliative authority. There is some overlap among these types, but they are sufficiently different to be considered separately.

Moral Authority

Organizations dedicated to alleviating torture, famine, and other forms of suffering are especially capable of generating habitual compliance. Neither people nor collectivities nor governments can readily resist appeals for support and money on behalf of the downtrodden, the exploited, or those victimized by nature's disasters. More accurately, when such appeals are successfully made, it is because they are "portrayed as humanitarian, apolitical and representative of the best in motivations"[17] and thus backed by the moral authority that attaches high value to human dignity, freedom, and well-being. Some of the subjects of their exercise of authority—be they individuals giving money, groups offering services, or governments providing relief supplies—may waffle, need further persuasion, or be entirely unresponsive; but others are so sensitive to moral authority that they do not hesitate to comply with the requests. Such a pattern was evidenced by the donor community in Rwanda and other African situations, by human rights groups that sponsored the disinvestment campaign against apartheid in South Africa, and by the fund-raising efforts of such NGOs as Amnesty International, Médicins sans Frontièrs, CARE, and Oxfam. Indeed, habitual compliance to moral authority has become so thoroughgoing in the United States (and perhaps elsewhere) that some people now permit their donations to such organizations to be deducted automatically (and electronically) from their bank accounts every month.

While the moral authority of human rights and refugee organizations has expanded, however, the same cannot be said of governments. Torn by scandals, pervaded with corruption, buffeted by policy failures, many national governments appear to have lost all or most of any moral authority they may once have had, both with respect to each other and in relation to their publics.[18] They still have authority they can exercise, but its effectiveness derives from sources other than high-minded appeals to

[17] Abdul Mohammed, "Responses of Non-governmental Organizations to Conflict Situations," in Thomas G. Weiss (ed.), *Humanitarian Emergencies and Military Help in Africa* (London: Macmillan, 1990), p. 101.

[18] A compelling discussion of this point is presented in Ronnie D. Lipschutz, *After Authority: War, Peace, and Global Politics in the 21st Century* (Albany: State University of New York Press, 2000), Chap. 7.

values associated with human dignity and decency. Accordingly, as one analyst put it, "In this situation the human rights NGOs have to be the conscience of the world, as one government will often be reluctant to make accusations against another because of political alliances, commercial interests or fear of the 'pot calling the kettle black.'"[19]

Knowledge Authority

Scientific associations and epistemic communities are clear-cut examples of how collectivities in the multi-centric world can use their knowledge to create authority that evokes habitual compliance. Their expertise on medical, biological, and ecological issues is so scarce and specialized that private groups and governments are often ready to comply with their recommendations about such issues. More accurately, if scientific communities can make pronouncements with a united voice on issues relevant to their expertise, then the world is poised to comply automatically with the policy implications of their advice. This is, of course, a big "if," as often such issues are divisive among the specialists, a circumstance that is likely to detract from the authority of their knowledge.[20]

While national governments tend to have access to more information and knowledge than counterparts in the multi-centric world, again it can be said that their authority in this regard has eroded. As previously indicated, one of the reasons for this erosion are the microelectronic technologies that have provided NGOs with access to a wide base of information and knowledge that is not so far removed from that available to governments. But an equally important reason is that the mushrooming of cynicism toward governments has tended to render any pronouncements they make—no matter how solid the evidence or how advanced the expertise they offer may be—objects of suspicion and ridicule.[21] The rejection by some Resistant Locals and Globals of IMF and World Bank data indicating policy shifts in the direction of addressing the grievances of protesters is illustrative in this regard.

[19] John Sankey, "Conclusions," in Peter Willetts (ed.), *"The Conscience of the World": The Influence of Non-governmental Organizations in the U.N. System* (Washington, D.C.: Brookings Institution, 1996), p. 273.

[20] For a cogent analysis of the limits of the authoritative nature of scientific expertise, as illustrated by the case of the 1987 Montreal Protocol on Substances That Deplete the Ozone Layer, see Karen T. Liftin, *Ozone Discourses: Science and Politics in Global Environmental Cooperation* (New York: Columbia University Press, 1994), pp. 5–7.

[21] Satellite reconnaissance data may be an exception in this regard. Suspicion is hard to maintain in the face of photographic data depicting, say, Iraqi weapons facilities or Bosnian burial sites that prove accurate when subsequently checked on the ground. For a discussion of the role of proof in global affairs, see Rosenau, *Turbulence in World Politics*, pp. 198–209, 425–29.

Reputational Authority

Closely linked to moral and knowledge authority is the kind of authority that derives from a reputation for integrity and competence. A good illustration is the authority of credit-rating agencies. Their capacity to evoke habitual compliance is rooted in the impeccable reputation they build up for fairness and thoroughness, a reputation that appears to be so authoritative that defying it entails undue risks.[22] Consider, for example, this assessment of one such agency:

> Moody's is the credit rating agency that signals the electronic herd of global investors where to plunk down their money, by telling them which countries' bonds are blue-chip and which are junk. That makes Moody's one powerful agency. In fact, you could almost say that we live again in a two-superpower world. There is the U.S. and there is Moody's. The U.S. can destroy a country by leveling it with bombs; Moody's can destroy a country by downgrading its bonds.[23]

Following this reasoning as to the authority governments can exercise through the knowledge they proffer, they surely fall far short of achieving habitual compliance when it comes to their reputational authority. The lack of trust and cynicism toward politics and governments today makes it very difficult for them to evoke compliance on the basis of a reputation for equity and evenhandedness. And for many governments it may well be that this form of authority has eroded beyond repair.

Issue-Specific Authority

Some NGOs have established themselves so predominantly in an issue arena that more often than not their authority evokes habitual compliance on the part of those toward whom it is directed. In addition to any moral claim, special knowledge, or reputation that may sustain their authority, their actions are backed by the history and nature of the specific issues on which they focus—that is, by the weight of the path-dependent processes that led to the differentiation of their issue arena. The issues must have worldwide appeal and be based on concerns that lie beyond the aegis of governments. Sports offer an excellent illustration in this regard, particularly the International Olympic Committee (IOC) and the quadrennial games over which it exercises authority. The IOC has not

---

[22] See, for example, Timothy J. Sinclair, "Passing Judgment: Credit Rating Processes as Regulatory Mechanisms of Governance in the Emerging World Order," *Review of International Political Economy*," Vol. 1 (April 1994), pp. 133–59.

[23] Thomas L. Friedman, "Don't Mess with Moody's," *New York Times*, February 22, 1995, p. A19.

been free of politics, and in recent years its leadership has been caught up in corruption scandals, but the tendency on the part of both athletes and governments is to comply with the IOC's rulings. It might be argued that the issue-specific authority of the IOC had its origins in the moral authority inherent in the ideals of amateur athletics as an activity where talent and sportsmanship predominate. While such an argument may have once carried weight, its foundations were undercut when the amateur rule was abandoned in 1992. Furthermore, because the Olympics are organized by country delegations, thus giving rise to nationalistic preoccupations, rather than concern for the athletes, the IOC's authority can hardly be regarded as a consequence of moral considerations. In the words of one analyst, "The Olympic movement has been forced to define its health in terms of the growth and size of its organizations rather than in terms of its ideals. The ideals have been made secondary but have been used as the primary justification for its existence."[24]

Has there been a loss in the issue-specific authority of governments? Probably not in the case of those issues, such as agriculture, finance, and immigration, where the regulatory capacities of governments remain effective. Of course, the trend toward deregulation and smaller government has doubtlessly reduced the scope of their issue-specific authority, but compared with their loss of other forms of authority, that which attaches to issues that remain within the purview of governments would appear to be still capable of evoking habitual compliance.

Affiliative Authority

Collectivities that serve the emotional needs of ethnic minorities, diasporas, and other groups with deep cultural roots can often evoke more than a little habitual compliance when they make requests of the groups they represent. Whether it be Jewish organizations in the United States responding to requests for funds from counterparts in Israel, Armenians in Los Angeles heeding requests from their homeland for supplies and manpower to cope with earthquakes, or Chinese in Southeast Asia being asked by the Chinese government to contribute their wealth or technological know-how or otherwise help the country's development, habitual compliance usually occurs quickly through the authority inherent in shared affiliations.[25] Indeed, common cultural or religious roots combined with a sense of being a beleaguered minority are perhaps the most

[24] Richard Espy, *The Politics of the Olympic Games, with an Epilogue, 1976–1980* (Berkeley and Los Angeles: University of California Press, 1981), p. 171.

[25] For an insightful analysis of the authority that attaches to affiliations, see Joel Kotkin, *Tribes: How Race, Religion, and Identity Determine Success in the New Global Economy* (New York: Random House, 1993).

effective source of authority on which any collectivity in the multi-centric world can draw.

But quite the opposite conclusion obtains with respect to many national governments. The focus of skepticism and cynicism, wracked with internal divisions, and lacking a clear-cut external enemy, a number of governments cannot rely on loyalty to their country to achieve compliance with their policies. The problems that many governments have in collecting taxes or maintaining the personnel of their armed forces at full strength are illustrative in this regard. Stated differently, as individuals become increasingly engulfed by distant proximities, as the values of multiculturalism become increasingly ascendant throughout the world, the authority of states is likely to be weakened, with their capacity to sustain broad consensuses around shared goals diminished and their ability to concert the energies of citizens in support of policies reduced. Indeed, it is with respect to the breakdown of national consensuses and the subsequent diminution of national loyalties that governments may have incurred the greatest loss of authority. As Hegel once put it, "[N]othing assures the atrophy and corruption of the various organizations and structures of a state more than prolonged periods of peace. War with other countries generates that spirit of national unity which is indispensable for the health and stability of the state as an *organism which transcends and holds together its individual components*."[26]

AUTHORITY CRISES

The compliance-defiance continuum also facilitates the analysis of different types of authority crises. If it is the case, as has been suggested, that many authority structures are founded on unthinking habitual processes that link those who preside over them and those who are subject to their directives, the question arises as to what dynamics sustain such structures. Two stand out: one concerns the degree to which a community's authority structures maintain their viability and stability, while the other focuses on the degree to which the individuals who constitute the community are free to pursue their interests and values without the intervention of the authorities. The two dynamics are inextricably linked. History has repeatedly recorded the difficulty of achieving and sustaining a balance between the needs of the community and those of individuals. Indeed, it could be argued that authority crises are pervasive in history precisely because few societies have managed to institutionalize this delicate balance such that

---

[26] Quoted in G. Dale Thomas, "Historical Uses of Civil Society and the Global Civil Society Debate" (paper presented at the annual meeting of the International Studies Association, Toronto, March 18–22, 1997); italics in original.

their members are content with the freedoms they enjoy without undermining social stability.

It follows that relations between authorities and their followers at the habitual extreme of the compliance continuum are recurrent and stable, while at the noncompliant extreme the performance of the authorities and/or the consent of their followers is problematic and unstable. The more a particular authority structure moves toward the noncompliant extreme, and the longer its patterns of interaction are ensconced in unstable circumstances, the more is such a structure likely to move from compliance to defiance, from being in place to being in crisis.[27] Given the continuities and inertia that normally sustain social systems, only under special circumstances do substantial moves toward the defiance extreme occur; but once events or trends jar an authority structure out of a stable state, the movement can build momentum as support for it widens, rumors spread, antagonisms accelerate, and alienation cumulates.

Thus it would be erroneous to conclude that each time the authorities are negatively rated in an opinion poll or are otherwise denounced for their actions that the structure collapses into crisis. To repeat, the reference here is to recurrent patterns of interaction, to institutionalized mechanisms for exercising authority, to habitual modes of complying with directives. Particular polls or events can reflect movement on the continuum, but it is only when the patterns persist that a specific development becomes a tipping point and reflects a shift along the continuum rather than a mere fluctuation.[28] The increasing regularity of street protests outside board

[27] It is useful to stress again that this conception of authority structures and the crises they can undergo is not confined to states and governments. It is equally applicable to families, communities, corporations, and social institutions such as churches, universities and nongovernmental organizations. Indeed, wherever organizations persist, they have authority structures that enable them to mobilize and give direction to their memberships on behalf of their policies or that are insufficient to achieve the decisive actions needed to adapt to changing circumstances. For an extended analysis of how various structures in a society can fluctuate along the compliance-noncompliance continuum, see Neil Nevitte, *The Decline of Deference: Canadian Value Change in Cross-National Perspective* (Peterborough, Canada: Broadview Press, 1996). For an imaginative formulation of how an authority crisis might come to conventional schools and result in "a reversal of power from the days when teachers held it all," see Caryn James, "Excuse Me, Class, While I Go Slit My Wrists," *New York Times*, October 23, 2000, p. 3.

[28] That such a shift is occurring can be readily discerned in systematic data sets. For example, one involving twenty-one countries surveyed during the 1980s found that in seventeen of them "emphasis on more respect for authority became less widespread," while another poll across twenty countries in 2001 uncovered "a startling rejection of traditional authority across many of the countries surveyed." For the first finding, see Ronald Inglehart, "Postmaterialist Values and the Erosion of Institutional Authority," in Joseph S. Nye Jr., Philip D. Zelikow, and David C. King (eds.), *Why People Don't Trust Government* (Cambridge, Mass.: Harvard University Press, 1997), p. 222; the second is set forth in "Poll Findings Suggest Trouble Ahead for the Globalization Agenda," p. 1.

meetings of the IMF and World Bank is a recent instance of this shift, with the Battle of Seattle having been the tipping point.

But the tendencies toward noncompliance are not confined to street protesters. As implied in chapter 3, except for periods of severe crisis such as war, terrorism, and economic collapse, the authority of states has waned enough to suggest that loyalties are undergoing reshuffling and patriotism has become problematic for more than a few people. Traces of these attitudinal shifts can be discerned in the increasing difficulties states are encountering in recruiting military personnel, generating tax revenues, and converging around shared understandings of the meaning of national flags and anthems.[29] More specifically, the proliferation of distant proximities—of boundaries and traditions becoming less meaningful— has encouraged people in several of the local, global, and private worlds to alter the relative balance of their personal and national commitments. As one observer put it, "Loyalties to tribe and race and communities both virtual and vital, not to mention ardor for mergers and startups and global networking, have apparently crowded out love of nation."[30] These tendencies may be especially the case for three of the private worlds—the Alienated Cynics, Tuned-Out Passives, and Alienated Illegals—where the essential pattern is one of turning away from the political arena. Likewise, it would appear that in resisting globalization some activists among the Resistant Locals and Globals are rethinking the priorities they attach to their various identities and affiliations. In the same manner but for different reasons, elite Affirmative Globals, whose commitments to globalization have become increasingly extensive, appear correspondingly ready to be less moved by patriotism, to value interdependence and multilateralism over independence and nationalism.[31] Either ensconced in gated communities or traveling widely abroad, such elites tend to be isolated from patriotic norms and, instead, interact more with each other than with their fellow citizens. It will be recalled that those who attend meetings of the World Economic Forum are conceived to have evolved a "Davos culture" that sets them apart and amounts to, as it were, "a yuppie internationale."[32]

[29] See, for example, Steven Lee Myers, "Military Reserves Are Falling Short in Finding Recruits," New York Times, March 28, 2000, p. A1; David Cay Johnston, "Calling Income Tax Illegal, Businesses Are Refusing to Pay," New York Times, November 19, 2000, p. 1; Lizette Alvarez, "Amendment to Ban Flag Burning Falls Short in Senate by 4 Votes," New York Times, March 30, 2000, p. A18; and Patrick E. Tyler, "Soviet Hymn Is Back, Creating Much Discord," New York Times, December 6, 2000, p. A1.

[30] David M. Kennedy, "The Truest Measure of Patriotism," New York Times, July 4, 2000, p. A13.

[31] William Safire, "The New Patriotism," New York Times, July 2, 2001, p. A19.

[32] See chapter 5 for details on the Davos culture. The quotation is from Peter L. Berger, "Four Faces of Global Culture," The National Interest, No. 49 (fall 1997), p. 24.

In short, uniformity does not exist at the noncompliant extreme of the authority continuum. Just as five types of authority can serve as sources of compliance, so can several types of authority crises be delineated. Depending on the degree of consensus among the authorities and the degree to which their citizens or members are unwilling to comply with their directives, authority crises can take very different forms. For analytic purposes, distinctions can be drawn among four basic types.[33] *Decisional crises* occur when the holders of authority are so divided among themselves over how to address the challenges they face that stalemate and paralysis set in. New policies appropriate to coping with internal or external challenges do not get adopted because the authorities cannot agree on either the causes of or the solutions to their problems.[34]

When the policies of the authorities are unacceptable to major segments of those who fall within their jurisdiction, either of two other forms of crisis can develop, with one founded on noncompliance through passivity and the other based on active defiance. The former, which can be labeled passive crises, ensue when the subjects of authority (citizens of polities or members of organizations) are so alienated as to withhold the support necessary to decisiveness on the part of the authorities (e.g., when widespread nonpayment of taxes prevails in a society, when Insular Locals refuse to affirm new political institutions,[35] when transferred authority fosters "uncertain loyalties and little sense of patriotism,"[36] or when members of an ethnic minority are so distressed by events they feel the law does not apply to them).[37] On the other hand *opposition crises* evolve when citizenries become so antagonistic to their authorities that they resort to collective actions such as frequent public rallies or daily street marches. Depending on whether or not such situations collapse into the widespread use of armed force, a further distinction can be drawn between *nonviolent* and *violent* opposition crises. The distinction between the "velvet revolution" in Czechoslovakia in 1989 and the up-

---

[33] For a typology that delineates seven types of crises in "disrupted states," see Amin Saikal, "Dimensions of State Disruption and International Responses" (unpublished manuscript, no date).

[34] See, for example, Suzanne Daley, "Who Decides? The Question Is Bedeviling Europe Again," *New York Times*, December 7, 2000, p. A1.

[35] Roger Cohen, "Danish Voters Say No to Euro; A Blow to Unity," *New York Times*, September 29, 2000, p. A1.

[36] In a poll conducted four years after the British handed Hong Kong over to the Chinese, only 28 percent of the Hong Kong respondents were found to see themselves as Chinese, whereas some two-thirds described themselves as "Hong Kong Chinese" or "Hong Kong people." Rahul Jacob, "Hong Kong's Uncertain Loyalties," *Financial Times*, June 30, 2001.

[37] Rick Bragg, "Stand over Elián Highlights a Virtual Secession of Miami," *New York Times*, April 1, 2000, p. A1.

heaval in China's Tiananmen Square six months earlier is illustrative in this regard. On occasion, even Circumstantial Passives can become so angry about their plight that they resort to whatever form of nonviolent opposition they can. Angry farmers in rural China, for example, have been provoked into protest marches over taxes and administrative fees, just as in far western China a Muslim minority protests through a "million little acts of personal defiance . . . like wearing Islamic dress, refusing to speak Chinese or setting your watch to local time."[38] In sum, authority crises do not necessarily involve violent confrontations, albeit such incidents stand out as the most extreme form of defiance at the noncompliance end of the continuum.

The different kinds of crisis can endure for different lengths of time and eventually result in different outcomes. Decisional and passive crises are susceptible to lasting across generations, depending on how deepseated are the issues that divide the authorities and foster passivity among publics. The more divisive they are, the less room there is for the kind of accommodations that are needed to resolve decisional stalemates and reactivate publics. And the duration of such crises can be further extended by the fact that it may take a while before enough instances of decisional paralysis or passive resistance cumulate to make clear to officials and publics alike that either the authorities are stalemated or the compliance habits of people have waned to the point where they cannot be readily evoked.

Opposition crises, on the other hand, can be short-lived. The struggles against colonialism and apartheid lasted for decades, and so have student protests in South Korea, but the onset of the fragmegrative epoch usually renders the circumstances underlying opposition crises too explosive to allow for a continual avoidance of resolution. Instead, they are likely to escalate into a toppling of the authorities, or lead to major structural concessions by the authorities, or spur a violent squashing of the resistance. Put differently, today opposition crises erupt when long-term global dynamics and short-term immediate circumstances interact in such a way that any unexpected development—an instance of police brutality, a collapsed financial scheme, an arrest of a dissident, a negation of electoral results, a leader's funeral, or a suicidal terrorist's truck bombing—can serve as a tipping point and trigger collective actions seeking to bring about basic changes.

In short, the fragmegrative dynamics of the emergent epoch conduce to opposition crises when authority structures gather momentum toward

[38] Craig S. Smith, "Chinese Farmers Rebel against Bureaucracy," *New York Times*, September 17, 2000, p. 1; and Elizabeth Rosenthal, "Defiant Chinese Muslims Keep Their Own Time," *New York Times*, November 19, 2000, p. 3.

the defiance extreme of the compliance-defiance continuum. With citizenries more skillful and more capable of knowing when to engage in collective action, with a recent worldwide history of street protests on a wide variety of issues, and with the bifurcation of global structures offering ever-greater avenues for expressing antagonism and making demands, it seems likely that if decisional and passive crises persist without any signs of resolution, they will undergo transformation into opposition crises. Some civic cultures may be able to sustain the former for generations, but the greater likelihood in this era of fragmegration is that few civic cultures will be able to withstand domestic and/or foreign pressures to resolve the stalemates of decisional and passive crises through active opposition. The recurring protest marches that contributed to the collapse of Milosevic's Yugoslavia are a case in point.

In a fragmegrative world, moreover, opposition crises are often subject to contagion effects. Through global television, publics in restless countries may observe upheavals elsewhere in the world and subsequently emulate them. The fall of communist regimes in Eastern Europe in 1989–90 is illustrative in this regard, but an even more recent instance of the contagion potential of opposition crises occurred in the Ivory Coast, where a popular uprising ended a dictatorship because, as one student put it, the regime made the mistake of letting "us watch scenes from Belgrade."[39]

The ever-increasing frequency of crises within both governmental and nongovernmental authority structures suggests that the fragmegrative dynamics of the emergent epoch are generating significant transformations in the nature of such structures. Or at least the pervasiveness of the various types of crises highlights a need to reconceptualize authority less in terms of structures and more as encompassing spheres of activity. A formulation along this line is developed in the next chapter.

---

[39] Norimitsu Onishi, "Popular Uprising Ends Junta Rule over Ivory Coast," *New York Times*, October 26, 2000, p. A1.

CHAPTER THIRTEEN

Spheres of Authority

In the next century I believe most states will begin to change from cultlike entities charged with emotion into far simpler and more civilized entities, into less powerful and more rational administrative units that will represent only one of the many complex and multileveled ways in which our planetary society is organized.

—Václav Havel[1]

These processes of globalization challenge us to reconceptualize the social world in which we live. Centralization and hierarchization of power within states and through states in the international system are steadily replaced by the pluralization of power among political, economic, cultural, and social actors, groups, and communities within states, between states, and across states. We move into a plurilateral world of diffused and decentralized power, into a world characterized by a variety of loci of power and cross-cutting and intersecting power networks.

—Roland Axtmann[2]

You can expect to see crises of misgovernment in many countries as political promises are deflated and governments run out of credit and institutional support. Ultimately, new institutional forms will have to emerge that are capable of preserving freedom in the new technological conditions, while at the same time giving expression and life to the common interests that individuals share.

—James Dale Davidson and Lord William Rees-Mogg[3]

[1] "Kosovo and the End of the Nation-State," *New York Review of Books*, Vol. 46 (June 10, 1999), pp. 4–6.

[2] "Collective Identity and the Democratic Nation-State in the Age of Globalization," in Ann Cvetkovich and Douglas Kellner (eds.), *Articulating the Global and the Local: Globalization and Cultural Studies* (Boulder, Colo.: Westview Press, 1997), p. 51.

[3] *The Sovereign Individual: Mastering the Transition to the Information Age* (New York: Touchstone, 1999), p. 333.

THE WEAKENING of states stressed in earlier chapters suggests that the central institution of modern society may no longer be suitable as the organizing focus of inquiry. Informal and noninstitutional forms of authority (spheres) may emerge at least to supplement, if not to replace, the long-established formal and institutionalized structures of authority. If this is the case, rather than dividing up the world in terms of clear-cut boundaries that separate the domestic from the international, we need to view it as consisting of indeterminate and shifting cones of fragmegration (see figure 2.4) that weave between the local and the global. Put in terms of ongoing research agendas, there is a need to move beyond thinking as students of international relations and to begin viewing inquiry as devoted to the study of how authority evolves, persists, or erodes in global affairs. Such a reorientation makes it easier to remove the state from the center of our concerns and allows for unfettered probings of the relations that link the local and the global, the regional and the provincial, the social and the political, the private and the public, the multinational corporation and the nongovernmental organization, the social movement and its disparate supporters, and a host of other connections that tend to be obscured by the imposition of state-based conceptions. Put in an even more general way, political inquiry needs to approach contestation as unfolding in decentralized, often nebulous institutional contexts.

Such an orientation might not be difficult: other disciplines have accomplished it. Anthropologists, for example, "have now acquired the habit of contrasting the local and the global, and tend to take for granted that the local is to the global more or less as continuity is to change."[4] Yet it is a measure of the degree to which specialists in world affairs are entrapped in state-based models that once again I need to record the caveat that this is not to anticipate the demise of the state as a political entity. It ought to be unnecessary to make this disclaimer, but states are so deeply ensconced in our paradigms that I feel compelled to stress what I am not arguing. The state and conventional authority structures will surely be around for the foreseeable future and I am not asserting or implying otherwise. Rather, I think it is probable, as hinted at previously, that spheres of authority other than states designed to cope with the links and overlaps between localizing and globalizing dynamics will evolve and render the global stage ever more dense. Some of the actors who preside over the SOAs will prove to be rivals of states, while others will become their partners, but in either event SOAs—or whatever they come to be labeled[5]—seem likely to move to the center of world affairs. Indeed,

[4] Ulf Hannerz, *Transnational Connections: Culture, People, Places* (London: Routledge, 1996), p. 19.

[5] One possibility is that of "political complex," a label that is conceived to "refer to the

traces of such moves can already be discerned, with respect to the Internet, biotechnology, the international mineral industry, voluntary standards set by the International Standards Organization (ISO) in industrial production, and rating agencies in the financial community serving as the foci of inquiry into what is called "private" authority.[6]

Some of these SOAs may be partially founded on territoriality, but none are fully grounded in the same kind of geographic space that has marked the nation-state era. Rather, the boundaries of the bargaining agents, the SOAs, are defined by those entities to which people accord salience and thereby attach their loyalties. Thus an SOA can be an issue regime, a professional society, an epistemic community, a neighborhood, a network of the like-minded, a truth commission, a corporation, business subscribers to codes of conduct (e.g., the Sullivan principles), a social movement, a local or provincial government, a diaspora, a regional association, a loose confederation of NGOs, a transnational advocacy group, a paramilitary force, a credit-rating agency, a strategic partnership, a transnational network, a terrorist organization, and so on across all the diverse collectivities that have become sources of decisional authority in the ever more complex multi-centric world. To be sure, while many states manage to cling to sufficient authority to be viewed as legitimate by their own populations, the advent of SOAs with their own emerging brand of legitimacy in the multi-centric world has reduced the number of states that have the kind of unqualified authority granted their counterparts in the past.

The possibility of potential actors with authority that parallels that of states can be summarized with a broad generalization that again highlights a central premise of this inquiry: namely, we have become so accustomed to assuming states are *the* terminal political collectivity of social systems that we lack any inclination to view the transformative dynamics presently at work in the world as the first traces of new terminal entities that may emerge in the future. More than that, we are so accustomed to

---

multitude of forms of lasting or temporary coalitions of actors, aiming at influence and control over more or less extended issues of relevance for a group or everybody this issue may affect by virtue of interest or impact. A political complex . . . is not predefined by geographical range, means of organization, formality of access to the decision-making process, forms of action, duration, or formal legitimation." Petra Dobner, "After Constitutionalism? State Transformation, Deconstitutionalization, and the Rise of 'Political Complexes'" (paper presented at the ninety-sixth annual meeting of the American Political Science Association, Washington, D.C., August 30–September 2, 2000), pp. 15–16.

[6] A. Claire Cutler, Virginia Haufler, and Tony Porter (eds.), *Private Authority and International Affairs* (Albany: State University of New York Press, 1999). For a similar but less extensive probe of the authority concept, see Gary Marks and Liesbet Hooghe, "Optimality and Authority: A Critique of Neoclassical Theory," *Journal of Common Market Studies*, Vol. 38 (December 2000), pp. 795–816.

the state as a provider of stability and order that we presume any other terminal entity will perforce be marked by instability and disorder. In short, we do not treat terminal entities as problematic, as susceptible to change and evolution, all of which stifles our imaginations and curbs our talents. We need to dare to be counterintuitive, to heed the wisdom expressed by Václav Havel in the foregoing epigraph.

Free of the shackles of state-based models—or what I have elsewhere referred to as the states-are-forever habit[7]—it becomes all the more clear that the crises of states, along with the organizational explosion, mobility upheaval, skill revolution, and other sources of fragmegration, have created spaces for new SOAs to evolve. If it is the case that globalizing dynamics involve "processes whereby social relations acquire relatively placeless, distanceless and borderless qualities,"[8] then it is reasonable to presume that circumstances are ripe for the advent of a plethora of new and/or expanded SOAs in the multi-centric world. In the words of the second epigraph to this chapter, they are ripe for the onset of "a plurilateral world of diffused and decentralized power . . . characterized by a variety of loci of power and cross-cutting and intersecting power networks."

Some of the new SOAs are likely to encompass Alienated Cynics who share the same grievances over established governments in which they have lost confidence. Others will doubtless consist of Alienated Illegals who join together to protect themselves against what they perceive to be encroaching systems that seek to terminate their activities. Exclusionary locals are also likely to form SOAs embracing one or another ethnic group. Likewise, each new issue that becomes salient on the global agenda is likely to generate an SOA among Resistant Locals and Globals that addresses their common concerns. To the extent Affirmative Locals and Globals feel threatened by the advent of new SOAs opposed to issues dear to them, so will they be inclined to counter with new SOAs of their own. To be sure, established SOAs may be the prime beneficiaries of the readiness of people in the various worlds to shift their traditional allegiances away from governments, but the number of new entities that draw people from the various local, global, and private worlds seems likely to proliferate as the complexity of the emergent epoch deepens. Little wonder, then, that the density of the global stage is likely to deepen with the passage of time.

But the proliferation of diverse SOAs raises some important questions:

---

[7] James N. Rosenau, "Aging Agendas and Ambiguous Anomalies: Tensions and Contradictions of an Emergent Epoch," in Stephanie Lawson (ed.), *The New Agenda for International Relations* (Cambridge: Polity Press, 2002), pp. 19–34.

[8] Jan Aart Scholte, "Globalization and Modernity" (paper presented at the annual meeting of the International Studies Association, San Diego, April 15–20, 1996), p. 15.

How are both individuals and societies going to adapt to the new and vastly increased pluralism? How can they manage the distant proximities that pull simultaneously toward the local and the global? Will issue-oriented groups be able to keep their essential structures intact and move toward their goals in the face of dynamic changes that have given birth to the fragmegrative epoch?[9] In a decentralizing global system undergoing processes wherein authority is continuously undermined and relocated, how can publics be mobilized and problems addressed? Is it possible, as some contend, that global markets "increase the incentives and wherewithal for organizing" new social contracts because they liberate "social, political, and cultural intentions from spatial constraints, and from economic domination"?[10] If the ability of states to control the flow of ideas, money, goods, pollution, crime, and people across their boundaries has diminished, will the new SOAs be able to generate the authority and power necessary to fill the gaps vacated by states, or is the world headed for ever-greater disarray? That is, will the resources, commitments, and orientations commanded by new SOAs be sufficient to render them effective as macro agents? And no matter how effective they may be, how will the power conflicts among autonomous SOAs be resolved?

Doubtless many scenarios encompassing answers to these questions may unfold. A recurring clash revolves around the capacity of states to use their taxing powers to exercise control over NGOs. Canada, for example, refused to recognize the Greenpeace Environmental Foundation as a charity. On the other hand, Greenpeace receives "the blessing of most of Europe's left-wing governments" inasmuch as its "politicians abhor confrontation with pressure groups and try to appease them as much as possible."[11] In effect, there is considerable variability in the readiness of governments to focus their taxing powers on SOAs.

Another pervasive set of scenarios pit SOAs in the multi-centric world against each other. While such conflicts can often be intense and enduring, there is more than a little evidence that the power conflicts among the SOAs may be resolved even in the absence of effective central authorities. Consider the conflicts between multinational corporations and the advocacy groups composed of Resistant Locals and Globals who oppose their policies. The former may have thousands of employees, huge budgets, and immense resources, while the latter may consist of only a few

[9] For a discussion of the essential structures that collectivities need to keep intact in order to persist, see James N. Rosenau, *The Study of Political Adaptation* (London: Frances Pinter, 1981).

[10] Judith R. Blau, *Social Contracts and Economic Markets* (New York: Plenum Press, 1993), p. 97.

[11] Roger Bate, "Canada Leaves Greenpeace Red-Faced . . . ," *Wall Street Journal,* July 22, 1999, p. 10.

individuals who operate on shoestring budgets. Yet this power equation can be highly misleading. It ignores moral issues and what I call the politics of shame. The activities and successes of Global Witness, a small NGO that employs fourteen persons with an annual budget of $800,000, is illustrative in this respect. It led a network of NGOs in a power struggle with De Beers, the global diamond giant with a payroll of twenty thousand people in some twenty countries that annually sells diamonds worth billions of dollars. By using the politics of shame and activating a network of like-minded NGOs, Global Witness succeeded in getting De Beers to reverse its strategy of marketing diamonds mined in areas that foster insurrection and exploitation. Indeed, De Beers began to cast itself as the champion of a cleaned-up world diamond trade. Nor was De Beers alone in succumbing to the politics of shame: BP Amoco, Nike, and Royal/Dutch Shell are also among corporations that revised their public posture on labor rights and the environment.[12] Indeed, a measure of the efficacy of the politics of shame is readily observable in a regular survey of business executives that probes what they consider to be their greatest risks. Usually they have responded by citing fire or other interruptions of business operations, but in 2001 "loss of reputation" headed their list of concerns.[13]

Furthermore, as the successes of SOAs accumulate, so do the virtues of coordination among them accelerate. Aside from the relative minority prone to violence, many SOAs perceive considerable advantages flowing from concerting their efforts around diverse issues. In November 2000, for instance, 263 consumer advocacy groups formed Consumer International to press international financial institutions for "social justice and consumer protection in the global markets."[14] Partly in response to the politics of shame and an unwillingness to yield the high moral ground to NGOs exclusively, eight months later some fifty corporations joined with NGOs to sign a UN-sponsored Global Compact committed to promoting high standards in human rights, the environment, and labor practices on the part of transnational corporations.[15]

To be sure, possessed of greater resources than advocacy groups, corporations are capable of co-opting their adversaries in the multi-centric world. Yet, as an executive of an international mining corporation ob-

---

[12] Alan Cowell, "Advocates Gain Ground in a Globalized Era," *New York Times*, December 18, 2000, p. C19.

[13] Vanessa Holder, "Campaigners Learn Lesson of Business Advantage," *Financial Times*, July 24, 2001, p. 4.

[14] Cowell, "Advocates Gain Ground in a Globalized Era," p. C20.

[15] Kofi A. Annan, "A Deal with Business to Support Universal Values," *International Herald Tribune*, July 26, 2000, p. 8; and Joseph Kahn, "Multinationals Sign U.N. Pact on Rights and Environment," *New York Times*, July 27, 2000, p. A3.

served, "It's not such an unequal power relationship. You can be an $8 billion company or whatever, but in the court of public opinion the non-governmental organizations start with more credibility than businesses."[16]

These accounts of power conflicts and coordination within the multi-centric world pose further questions: Is fragmegration manageable and governable? Given tendencies toward the global and the local that are deeply embedded in both macro systems and micro individuals, how are the tensions between them likely to play out in the future? Are the instances of coordination among SOAs in the multi-centric world typical? I shall return to these questions of governability in the last two chapters, but here it is useful to ponder whether the tensions among SOAs, and between them and states, are likely to unfold as dialectical processes, or whether their evolution will be characterized more by cyclical patterns.

A logical case can be made for a cyclical future. One can reasonably speculate that prolonged periods in which globalizing forces are predominant foster localizing reactions that predominate until the pendulum swings back to the ascendancy of globalizing dynamics. Conceivably, for example, the Battle of Seattle and subsequent skirmishes reflect a return to the predominance of localizing forces. Likewise, possibly the fallout of the Asian financial crisis, cascading as it subsequently did through Russia and Brazil, laid the foundation for reversions back in localizing directions, with some states resurrecting barriers to trade and investment to ward off the negative consequences of globalization. But such explanations have always seemed too simple. The cascading Asian crisis did lead Malaysia in a localizing direction, and others may do the same in future crises, but on balance the dynamics underlying fragmegrative tendencies seem much too numerous and diverse to result in unchanging and repetitive cycles. It is equally logical to presume that the complexity of fragmegrative dynamics will foster new transformations, that new syntheses will be generated as globalizing theses foster localizing antitheses. But what might be the nature of the new syntheses? If dialectical processes are at work, in other words, where might they be taking the world? For a long time the answer to these questions proved elusive and led me reluctantly to concede that history may be repetitive—a conclusion with which I have never been comfortable[17]—and that fragmegrative processes are essentially cyclical.

But this reluctant conclusion did not override my nagging sense that history is not so elegant as to be cyclical, that new syntheses reflective of dialectical processes may well unfold. To make a long story short, eventu-

---

[16] Cowell, "Advocates Gain Ground in a Globalized Era," p. C20.

[17] See the discussion of historical break points in James N. Rosenau, *Turbulence in World Politics*, pp. 72–73.

ally the nagging sense won out when further reflection began to focus on the question of why most states, communities, governments, NGOs, and a host of other sociopolitical systems have changed rather than failed to adapt to the challenges posed by fragmegrative dynamics. At this point the outlines of a plausible answer evolved: namely, as indicated by the formation of Consumer International and the UN's Global Compact, the disruptive power of fragmegration highlights the large degree to which the glue that holds collectivities together is also undergoing transformation—changes so profound as to encourage the framing of new social contracts that can generate more effective forms of systemic coherence.[18]

NEW SOCIAL CONTRACTS?

And it is here, in the framing and promotion of new social contracts, that clues to the governability of fragmegration can be found: for in crucial ways it is in the evolution of new spheres of authority, or the modification of old ones, composed as they are of interacting international and domestic actors and institutions, that the nature and direction of the new social contracts will be shaped and solidified. Otherwise, in the absence of interactions that help form contracts for new SOAs founded on values that enable people to manage their distant proximities and thus make it possible for collectivities to remain intact and move toward their goals, it is reasonable to anticipate that the world is indeed headed for ever greater disarray—for circumstances in which, in effect, there are no social contracts.

But what kinds of new social contracts are likely to evolve under epochal conditions that can no longer sustain those that developed out of the Treaty of Westphalia and the American and French Revolutions centuries ago? What might be the bases of new social contracts? Leaving aside the fact that contracts involving aggregates of people cannot be simply imposed from the top, or at least that they must resonate broadly with the affected publics, on what values might the new contracts rest such that localizing and globalizing forces can be reconciled and the ten-

[18] Although the conception of new social contracts developed here is not to be found elsewhere, pieces of it can be found in the following formulations: Greg Hill, "Reason and Will in Contemporary Social Contract Theory," *Political Research Quarterly*, Vol. 48 (March 1995), pp. 101–16; Thomas Fleiner, "Nation State and Autonomy for Ethnic Communities," *Peace and the Sciences*, December 1994, pp. 1–10; G. M. Tamas, "A Disquisition on Civil Society," *Social Research*, Vol. 61 (summer 1994), pp. 205–22; Bryan S. Turner, "Outline of a Theory of Human Rights," *Sociology*, Vol. 27 (August 1993), pp. 489–512; Philip J. Frankenfeld, "Technological Citizenship: A Normative Framework for Risk Studies," *Science, Technology and Human Values*, Vol. 17 (autumn 1992), pp. 459–84; and Manfred Henningsen, "Democracy: The Future of a Western Political Formation," *Alternatives*, Vol. 14 (July 1989), pp. 327–42.

sions between them ameliorated? What, then, might be the essential terms of the new contracts? And, no less important, who shall be the parties to the new contracts?

Before addressing these questions, it is important to stress that to expect that new social contracts will accompany the emergent epoch is not to express a commitment to values that espouse civil society. Rather, the expectation stems from an empirical formulation that focuses on the evolution of such contracts. New social contracts are conceived to be in the offing because of the many dynamic transformations altering the authority structures that have long undergirded the expiring epoch and our understanding of it.

Clearly, full answers to the foregoing questions require a separate and lengthy treatise. But an outline of tentative answers sufficient for present purposes can be proposed on the basis of the following assumptions:

1. With a continuing collapse of time and space as bases for community, the main clauses of the new social contracts will involve SOAs that derive their legitimacy from sources other than territoriality.
    a. Rather than being defined exclusively by spatial boundaries, social contracts in the emergent epoch will be configured by ethnoscapes, ideoscapes, mediascapes, financescapes, technoscapes, and identiscapes.
2. Since the conditions underlying the emergent epoch are global in scope, the new social contracts will have many dimensions in common, albeit regional, structural, and issue variations are likely.
    a. The main structural variation will differentiate SOAs founded on voluntary membership (NGOs and, to some degree, states) and those based on financial incentives (corporations).
3. By a social contract is meant a set of agreements that specifies the benefits received by those who sign on to it and the obligations that people in the SOA shoulder in return, obligations that detail how they should conduct themselves, their relations with each other, and their relations with other SOAs.
4. The agreements constituting the new social contracts will consist of inarticulate and informal premises as well as explicit and formal ones.
5. Since social contracts are partly sustained by habit, some time will elapse before new ones evolve into shared values and agreements and the old ones incrementally slip away through processes that are barely noticeable.
6. Lacking the impulses to coherence that derive from the history associated with territorial boundaries, the core premises of the new contracts will revolve around the nature, limits, and direction of authority—the glue that holds people together and enables them to make collective decisions that are effective and enduring.
7. Given the nature of fragmegration, the meaning of citizenship in the new

social contracts will be quite different from the one built into the old contracts.

8. The failure of some new social contracts to become institutionalized, or of others to break down and atrophy, ought not be viewed as indicating that numerous new contracts will not be successfully concluded.

9. Nor should the task of outlining possible social contracts be deterred by those situations in the world marked by intense antagonisms that may collapse into violence.

    a. Such situations are surely of central concern, but they are by no means the only fragmegrative dynamics and thus cannot be allowed to divert attention from typical circumstances that are unlikely to deteriorate into some form of war.

CONTRACTING PARTIES

The question of those who are likely to be the major parties to any new social contract is perhaps the easiest to handle. The historic contracts between states and their individuals and publics have eroded as the territorial state has weakened and the publics have become more skillful, their organizations more numerous, their boundary-spanning activities more extensive, and their coalescence in cyberspace more secure. Clearly, then, the new social contracts must involve more than two parties—with the result that the state will no longer be the only collective agent that strikes a bargain with individuals. Clearly, SOAs may frame contracts with states, with other SOAs, or with individuals. Clearly, the many collective agents cannot be exclusively founded on territoriality. And no less clear, since the concept of a citizen has long been associated with membership in a state, the individuals who are parties to the new social contracts can no longer be regarded simply as citizens. Rather, fragmegration has given rise to a normative change in the meaning of citizenship such that we need to conceive of the individuals who are parties to the new social contracts in terms that reflect the widening or narrowing allegiances and identities fostered by fragmegrative processes.

Let us examine briefly the nature of the three types of parties to the new social contracts. In the case of individuals, the tensions they experience between the tugs of globalizing and localizing dynamics have led either to a multiplicity of new allegiances for those caught up in globalizing processes or to a consolidation of old allegiances and identities for those inclined to retreat to more localized boundaries. Since in both cases the individuals redraw the boundaries within which their affiliations are sustained as they move back and forth between and among the several local and global worlds outlined in chapters 4 and 5, it seems appropriate to designate them as *adaptable citizens*, a term that maintains the relevance of states but allows for the legitimation of new, nonterritorial allegiances and identities. Indeed, fragmegration has so fully highlighted the salience of identiscapes—those horizons that individuals have come to value as a composite of the ethnoscapes, technoscapes, mediascapes, and ideoscapes through which they have reconfigured their identities in a fragmegrative world—that SOAs have increasingly sanctioned and thereby legitimated the adaptable citizen. Put differently, with states no longer capable of providing adaptable citizens with protection from a liberalized and globalized marketplace, they have agreed, implicitly or otherwise, to recognize their members' need, even their right, to affiliate with other SOAs. The result is a new compromise in which adaptable citizens accept globalization and/or its localizing alternatives in exchange for the state's willingness to allow them to seek protection and assistance from other authorities. In effect, traditional citizenship no longer precludes allegiances to other authorities that supersede those to the state. The new social contracts embody the value that alternative affiliations are legitimate for every individual.

The same line of reasoning leads to a recasting of the notion of embedded liberalism. Given the vulnerabilities of individuals everywhere to the liberal international trade order, one can reasonably argue that fragmegration and the adaptable citizen have contributed to the demise of embedded liberalism. As the scholar who identified this social contract put it, "What is needed—for the sake of America and the world—is a new embedded liberalism compromise, a new formula for combining the twin desires of international and domestic stability, one that is appropriate for an international context in which the organization of production and exchange have become globalized, and a domestic context in which past modalities of state intervention lack efficacy or legitimacy."[19]

Put differently, if the nation-state is viewed as having always been an imagined community, a political entity that exists by virtue of the fact that its citizens believe it to exist and thus abide by its institutions, regulations, and policies,[20] the emergent epoch is one in which communities are being reimagined.[21] The multiple dynamics of the fragmegrative ep-

---

[19] John Gerard Ruggie, "Globalization and the Embedded Liberalism Compromise: The End of an Era?" (Cologne: Lecture Series on Economic Globalization and National Democracy, Max Plank Institute for the Study of Societies, Working Paper 97/1, January 1997), p. 11. Ruggie has subsequently attempted to outline a new embedded liberalism compromise in "Taking Embedded Liberalism Global: The Corporate Connection" (paper presented at the "Workshop on Global Governance: Towards a New Grand Compromise," (Canadian Congress of the Social Sciences and Humanities, Toronto, May 29, 2002).

[20] Cf. Benedict Anderson, *Imagined Communities: Reflections on the Origin and Spread of Nationalism*, rev. ed. (New York: Verso, 1991).

[21] See James N. Rosenau, "Material and Imagined Communities in Globalized Space," in

och combine to allow people to envision themselves as citizens with multiple allegiances to new structures may be short-lived, as when issues move off the global agenda and the SOAs they encompass cease to exist, but effective authority is embedded in their activities as long as the reasons for their existence endure.

The population of collectivities that make up the multi-centric world, in other words, undergoes continual growth and shifts in its composition as new needs arise and traditional practices are superseded. Examples of SOAs stemming from new needs are the cybernation,[22] the trend toward the self-regulation of industries,[23] the Internet Corporation for Assigned Names and Numbers (ICANN),[24] and the vigilante group.[25] Examples of traditional practices becoming obsolete and being replaced by newly formed SOAs can be found in the banking and accounting industries. Aware of a growing reputation for being havens of illicit money, members of the banking industry framed a code of conduct whereby banks would be required to have their offshore subsidiaries cease the practice of accepting laundered deposits by organized crime and corrupt political leaders.[26] Similarly, under pressure from investors to replace diverse country rules with a single set of global rules, the accounting industry created a new International Accounting Standards Board designed to coordinate standards on a worldwide basis.[27] In the words of a special adviser to the

---

Donald H. McMillen (ed.), *Globalization and Regional Communities: Geoeconomic, Sociocultural and Security Implications for Australia* (Toowomba, Australia: USQ Press, 1997), pp. 24–40; and the various essays in Daniele Archibugi, David Held, and Martin Kohler (eds.), *Re-imagining Political Community* (Cambridge: Polity Press, 1998).

[22] John Markoff, "Rebel Outpost on the Fringes of Cyberspace," *New York Times*, June 4, 2000, p. 14.

[23] See Virginia Haufler, *A Public Role for the Private Sector: Industry Self-Regulation in a Global Economy* (Washington, D.C.: Carnegie Endowment for International Peace, 2001).

[24] The ICANN is "an international organization entirely constituted by representatives from the international private sector in a pure, bottom-up manner. National governments are only granted advisory status and have no direct influence on the body's working. In this respect, ICANN exemplifies an amazing novelty in international affairs: A private international organization that acts on behalf of the public trust, but stands outside of government control and is responsible for the management of a crucial global public good, that is the unique Internet addresses (IP-numbers)." Marc Hollister, "Global Internet Governance and the Rise of the Private Sector," *Swiss Political Science Review* at http://www.ib.ethz.ch/spsr/debat net/art-2-4/html.

[25] For an instance of when "the law has had to make a pact with vigilantism," see Patti Waldmeir, "Vigilantes Patrol the Web: Citizens Are Being Increasingly Called on to Become User Police to Combat Fraud in the Online World," *Financial Times*, July 19, 2001, p. 12.

[26] Elizabeth Olson, "A New Push to Combat Dirty Money," *New York Times*, October 25, 2000, p. W1.

[27] Michael Peel, "Big Win Hangs in the Balance for Accountants," *Financial Times*, June 6, 2000, p. 19; and Floyd Norris, "Fewer Borders for Global Accounting," *New York Times*, January 26, 2001, p. C1.

World Bank, "What's wrong is that auditing and accounting rules are national in origin while today capital is global in origin. The inconsistency is causing trouble in the investor community."[28] Since diverse fields of endeavor face the same local-global discrepancy, presumably the proliferation of SOAs will continue as more and more lines of work are pressed to evolve common standards for all their practitioners.

The organizational decentralization on which many SOAs are founded stems from at least two important sources. First, in order to generate and command allegiance, SOAs have an incentive to develop decentralized authority that permits more proximate links to their members, as well as opportunities to evoke their participation. Such close-at-hand contact with existing and prospective members can heighten their loyalties and strengthen the moral authority of an SOA. Second, the decentralized structures of many SOAs can serve their need to avoid confrontations with states. In the case of multinational corporations, for example, locating managers in one state and production facilities in another (such as the Maquilladores factories in Mexico) not only serves to increase profits due to lower wage rates but also may deny striking laborers an office building in front of which to strike; in addition, the workers and their government have little recourse against an authority (the corporation) protected by another government. Similarly, in the case of voluntary NGOs that are global in scope such as the International Red Cross or Amnesty International, their decentralization enables them to better command loyalty and maintain their legitimacy.[29] That is, by establishing a decentralized niche, SOAs are better able to survive in a world where territorial authorities still retain some capacity to enforce compliance. Moreover, the decentralized organizational structures of SOAs fit well with several of the key terms of the new social contracts outlined later in this chapter.

Of course, decentralization can give rise to both negative and positive consequences. There are more than a few conditions, for example, in which fiscal decentralization can result in unwanted outcomes for both states and SOAs.[30] Likewise, decentralization can follow when SOAs become so factionalized that they break up and the factions go their sepa-

---

[28] Ira Millstein, quoted in Norris, "Fewer Borders for Global Accounting," p. C1.

[29] It should be noted, however, that even as organizations such as the Red Cross decentralize their operations, so do they cope with the competition for funding through informal partnerships with SOAs that have overlapping interests. A global partnership between the International Red Cross and the Royal and SunAlliance insurance group, for example, has proved beneficial to both partners in a number of diverse ways. Alison Maitland, "Relationship Taps into Each Other's Skills," *Financial Times*, June 2, 2000, p. iii.

[30] Vito Tanzi, "Pitfalls on the Road to Fiscal Decentralization," *Global Policy Program* (Washington, D.C.: Carnegie Endowment for International Peace, No. 19, April 2001).

rate ways. Indeed, in the case of the Episcopal Church a factional separation occurred in response to a prior alliance with the Lutheran Church.[31]

Given a skill revolution that is enabling individuals to become increasingly adept at managing multiple identities and loyalties, in the early stages of the evolution of new SOAs there is likely to be considerable overlap among them, with the result that initially their boundaries may be obscure and the scope of their authority may be ambiguous. Nor is there any certainty that eventually the boundaries of SOAs will evolve such that the overlaps are eliminated and SOAs become the focus of ultimate loyalties, much as the nation-state has long been the terminal community insofar as loyalties are concerned. Indeed, it is exactly because of the nature of the complexities underlying the emergent epoch that the notion of terminal loyalties has to be treated as highly problematic. Although states have enjoyed such a status, it would be erroneous to view them as evidence that their successors will become terminal entities. On the contrary, given the extent to which SOAs are founded on nonterritorial sources of legitimacy, the greater likelihood is that some overlaps will endure and that people will be responsive to one of their SOAs under certain conditions and to others of them under different circumstances.

Is this to say that global structures are likely to resemble those of the medieval era? In important respects such a conclusion is warranted, but along one crucial dimension it is erroneous. Observers who anticipate neomedieval arrangements perceive close similarities between the decentralized structures of authority and the vast array of political entities that mark the fragmegrative epoch on the one hand and those that prevailed prior to the onset of the interstate system in the medieval period.[32] In the sense that individuals in the latter era did not have ultimate loyalties, but rather shared their fealties between the overlapping authority of monarchical and ecclesiastical structures, the comparison holds up inasmuch as individuals in the fragmegrative epoch may also replace their ultimate loyalty to their state with multiple allegiances to numerous SOAs. Once again, in other words, people will have to learn to balance diverse and sometimes conflicting commitments in the absence of a terminal state. But the structures of the two eras differ in one significant way: in the medieval period the overlapping patterns of authority were largely top-down structures,[33] whereas in the emergent epoch the patterns are likely

---

[31] Laurie Goodstein, "Episcopalians Inaugurate Alliance with Lutherans," *New York Times,* January 7, 2001, p. 12; and Gustav Niebuhr, "Episcopal Dissidents Find African Inspiration," *New York Times,* March 6, 2001, p. A10.

[32] See, for example, Hedley Bull, *The Anarchical Society: A Study of Order in World Politics* (New York: Columbia University Press, 1977), p. 238.

[33] I am indebted to Robert W. Cox for noting that bottom-up movements were not lacking in medieval Europe. The friars, for example, churned up conflict in ecclesiastical authority structures. Personal communication, March 1, 1999.

to evolve out of bottom-up processes. It is the difference, in effect, between institutions that shared "subjects" and SOAs sustained by the affiliation of adaptable citizens.

Nor are the new social contracts necessarily confined to individuals on the one hand and SOAs on the other. The dynamics of fragmegration also encourage contracts between SOAs and states—that is, contracts that span the bifurcated worlds of state-centric and multi-centric collective actors. Indeed, more than a few SOAs, especially those involved in emergency relief and development assistance, receive their funding from national governments or international organizations, resulting in private-public partnerships that serve the goals of all parties in a variety of ways and, in effect, add to the plethora of SOAs that crowd the global stage.[34]

But do social contracts evolve only between collectivities that engage in socially approved activities? What about other SOAs that engage in illicit behavior? Are organizations such as money-laundering banks, arms dealers, mercenary soldiers, the Cali Cartel, or the Mafia likely to be parties to contracts that form SOAs? While states may recognize the right of adaptable citizens to engage in contractual arrangements with other SOAs, would the boss of a Colombian drug cartel countenance a member's multiple affiliations and loyalties? The core of an answer to such questions lies in the notion that SOAs are essentially neutral from an analytic point of view. Whether they operate to improve or undermine the human condition is immaterial from the perspective of fragmegrative tensions. What counts is the existence and location of collective authority and not whether it is exercised under desirable or undesirable auspices.

Core Norms

Assuming a multiplicity of new social contracts between diverse SOAs and the individuals responsive to them, is there a core set of norms on which the bargaining that leads to all the contracts might be founded? While each SOA will doubtless have clauses in its contract that are unique to its circumstances, there are at least two clusters of norms that come to mind as essential. One follows from the foregoing discussion and involves an appreciation that no SOA has exclusive authority with respect to those individuals within its purview. In a fragmegrated world people have too many identities and affiliations to accord any SOA the sole legitimacy to make decisions on their behalf. Rather, recognizing that they cannot be responsive to the directives of all the SOAs to which they owe allegiance, their contracts are likely to require them to accept

[34] For a succinct analysis of the pluses and minuses of proliferating private-public partnerships, see "NGOs: Sins of the Secular Missionaries," *The Economist*, January 29, 2000, pp. 25–27.

that their various SOAs might issue contradictory directives and that they are obliged to frame a set of priorities for responding to them. Second, faced with contradictory directives, people are likely to feel obliged by their contracts to be open to dialogue across—as well as within—the various SOAs relevant to their circumstances. The agenda for such dialogues is likely to consist precisely of those contradictory issues that span their SOAs—such as when it is appropriate to accept or resist compromise among the issues, or under what conditions it is acceptable to move out of the purview of one SOA in favor of another.

These core norms give rise to two obvious questions. One concerns the readiness of states to embrace the norm that does not posit them as holders of exclusive authority, and the other focuses on the readiness of individuals to take on the responsibilities inherent in this norm. Both questions can be readily answered. In the case of states, they have to begin to abandon, or at least ignore, the long-standing precepts of sovereignty that assert, in effect, that states can compel obedience to their authority while SOAs do not possess a right to compel compliance. Indeed, the essence of the SOAs is that they derive their legitimacy from the voluntary and conditional participation of individuals who can revoke their consent at any time.

In effect, the changing norms inherent in fragmegrative tensions have so delimited the legitimate exercise of state power that the differences between the authority of states and other SOAs have become increasingly blurred. It might even be argued that other SOAs have proliferated precisely for this reason, that the emergent epoch enables adaptable citizens to subscribe to the social contracts of several SOAs voluntarily and to revoke their consent to authority at any time.[35] Put in still another way, the changing norms attached to legitimacy have facilitated new SOAs, some of which may expand their membership rolls because skilled citizens increasingly seek protection from the adverse effects of globalization when states fail to provide it.

As for the question of whether individuals will be amenable to adopting and living by the new contracts, conceivably the long-standing impulse to have a highest loyalty will prevent many people from abiding by a contract in which no SOA is accorded exclusive claims on those within its purview. And if this is the case, it can be argued, surely there will be no basis for accepting an obligation to engage in dialogues that redefine where the boundaries of SOAs are drawn. If the need for a terminal entity to which to attach the highest loyalty is strong, how can it be

---

[35] Cf. James S. Fishkin, "Toward a New Social Contract," *Noûs*, Vol. 24, No. 2 (1990), pp. 217–26.

expected that the new contracts will attract sufficient signatories to be meaningful?

While this line of reasoning can hardly be discounted, it may be exaggerated. It fails to allow for the power and urgency of the underlying currents sustaining the emergent epoch. The disarray that is likely to attend the dispersion of authority under pervasive fragmegrative conditions may well serve to encourage an appreciation of the foregoing core norms on which the new social contracts are founded. To be sure, compliance with established authority is rooted in habit-driven behavior, and people are thus likely to be slow in acknowledging the need for new social contracts and then agreeing to their terms; but at the same time most people are capable of learning and adapting when conditions change, so that in the long run it is possible to conceive of a readiness to negotiate new contracts that are not founded on an exclusive acquiescence to the authority of states. Already a dialogue and literature on the idea of a global civil society have evolved that are deep and broad enough to suggest movement in the direction of some kind of new contractual foundations.[36] As one astute observer put it, "It makes no more sense to try to grasp the identity of many nonstate actors without understanding their involvement in global civil society than it does to think of states without paying attention to their connection to international society."[37]

Stated in another way, "authority cannot always be equated with domination." It can be founded on "freely exercised reason, in which fundamentally equal individuals reach collective decisions through rational deliberations that are open to all."[38] Accordingly, as noted in the previous chapter, authority exercised through requests rooted in moral persuasion may be as effective as that based on directives or commands. Many NGOs are a case in point: they "are free to manage their own affairs." Consequently,

> they obtain a high degree of compliance with their internal rules and operating procedures. From the point of view of individual members, such compliance only makes sense. It is rational to abide by the rules, standards, and codes of

[36] See, for example, Ronnie D. Lipschutz, with Judith Mayer, *Global Civil Society and Global Environmental Governance* (Albany: State University of New York Press, 1966); Paul Wapner, "Governance in Civil Society," in Oran R. Young (ed.), *Global Governance: Drawing Insights from the Environmental Experience* (Cambridge, Mass.: MIT Press, 1997), pp. 65–84; and Ann M. Florini (ed.), *The Third Force: The Rise of Transnational Civil Society* (Washington, D.C.: Carnegie Endownment for International Peace, 2000).

[37] Oran R. Young, *Governance in World Affairs* (Ithaca, N.Y.: Cornell University Press, 1999), p. 10.

[38] John Boli, "World Authority Structures and Legitimations," in John Boli and George M. Thomas (eds.), *Constructing World Culture: International Nongovernmental Organizations since 1875* (Stanford, Calif.: Stanford University Press, 1999), p. 273.

ethics of the groups to which they belong because such prescriptions have been established by noncoercive procedures established and controlled by the members themselves. [Likewise, international NGOs] are constructed in accordance with the rational-voluntarism model, and their members find it rational, even natural, to comply with the authority they exercise. Explicitly or implicitly, members see themselves as parties to a genuine social contract, where membership signifies both willingness to accept the authority structure and authorization to attempt to influence or reshape that structure.[39]

In sum, given the uncertainty that pervades the age of fragmegration, there are ample incentives to seek, or at least to accept, new contracts that might do better in channeling, stabilizing, or even reducing the instabilities of life than do their state-bound predecessors.

Specific Terms

While it is clearly difficult to generalize about the essential terms that the new social contracts will contain, some eight can be derived from the core norms set forth here. To some extent, these reflect the paradoxical nature of fragmegrative tensions in the sense that they stipulate the privatization of many state functions, as well as new state obligations beyond their borders.

1. ORGANIZATIONAL DEVOLUTION

Partly to allow for the expression of localizing impulses and partly because of an assumption that greater efficiency may be achieved by reducing the sphere within which authority is exercised, a key term of new social contracts is likely to highlight the legitimacy of SOAs limiting the scope of their activities. The trend toward states privatizing many of the protections they once provided citizens is illustrative in this regard, as are the decentralization of multinational corporations, the trend toward autonomy on the part of indigenous peoples, and the operation of the principle of subsidiarity in the European Union. To some extent, of course, the inclusion of this term in the contract reflects an aversion to big government, but in some cases it may also stem from efforts to reduce the distance between organizations and their memberships.

2. OPEN MEMBERSHIP

Inasmuch as SOAs can be founded on any number of different issues and aspirations, a crucial term in their contracts is likely to specify that membership in them is open to all persons who are concerned about the issues or qualified to share in the aspirations. Signs of the evolution of

[39] Ibid., p. 279.

norms along this line can be discerned in the increased protection—and, in some cases, citizenship—now being offered by some states to resident aliens. Needless to say, the development of this norm has also been stimulated by the mobility upheaval and the globalizing processes whereby NGOs and other SOAs seek to enlarge the size and expertise of their memberships by admitting or recruiting persons from all regions of the world. At the same time, this term of the contract is likely to be highly controversial in the sense that it runs counter to localizing impulses. Virtually by definition, Exclusionary Locals are likely to limit the size of their membership.

3. HUMANITARIAN PROTECTIONS

Although surely not yet a term in many present social contracts, there are clear indications that increasingly basic human rights will be included as a contractual term in the SOAs of the emergent epoch. The commitment of, say, feminist, handicapped, ethnic, and indigenous groups to enlarging their sphere of authority so as to protect the well-being of people who may qualify for membership in their ranks points to the potential of these values for codification in the new social contracts. Much the same can be said about the ways in which the international community has circumscribed the prerogatives of state sovereignty and framed new rules for foreign intervention to protect individuals in "rogue" states. Norms that uphold the rights of people everywhere to protection can also be seen as promoting the globalization of personhood as a value. Just as the label "citizen" designated new rights and protections that "subjects" did not enjoy in medieval times, so does the emergence of such labels as "transborder citizens," "netizens," "global villagers," and "cybernations" in the age of fragmegration highlight the evolution of new conceptions of individuals and their relationship to authorities. Indeed, one observer posits individuals as trapped in their consumer and societal roles, as not being their own "personal Subjects," a formulation that leads to an exploration of "the desire of individuals to become the actors in their lives, or to become Subjects."[40]

4. SHARED EXPERTISE

Perhaps more relevant to virtual SOAs in cyberspace than to tangible ones in the state-centric or multi-centric worlds, new social contracts may well include a term that specifies the obligation to share knowledge and expertise. A virtual community that originated in the San Francisco area, for example, has a social contract governing the relationships among its

[40] Alain Touraine, *Can We Live Together? Equality and Difference*, trans. David Macey (Stanford, Calif.: Stanford University Press, 2000), p. 290–91 (quotation p. 291).

members that includes a rule that nobody is anonymous, and another that expresses an expectation in which members will share the expertise and information they possess with other individuals in the community.[41] Indeed, this commitment to dialogue is widespread among the SOAs in cyberspace, and to a large extent similar contractual terms can be found in more than a few professional societies. To be sure, the issue of intellectual property rights confounds this dimension of the new social contracts, but it is nonetheless the case that many NGOs, such as Médecins sans Frontières, Greenpeace, and Amnesty International, conjoin political lobbying activities with informational and educational campaigns and, in so doing, reflect an obligation to share socially beneficial knowledge.

5. SELF-REFLEXIVITY

Although it is still far from global in scope, it seems likely that increasingly another important term of new social contracts will revolve around the value SOAs accord to the need for self-reflexivity—that is, for a keen awareness on the part of members and SOAs of their place in the more encompassing worlds to which they are responsive—as a quality shared by their members. As one observer sees it, SOAs add to their legitimacy by engaging in political practices that stress self-reflexivity, by which is meant "they must be subjected to continuing critical examination through unmanipulated debate."[42] Given the ways in which the skill revolution has heightened the sensitivity of adaptable citizens to the complexities of their affiliations, self-reflexivity is accelerating as an empirical process and as a norm. Even corporations have participated in this acceleration, as indicated by their readiness "to develop new codes of conduct that set standards for their behavior on issues that top the international agenda."[43]

6. EGALITARIANISM

This is one term in new social contracts that may never become full-blown and pervasive. The growing disparities exacerbated by globalization between the financially rich and poor, not to mention between the informationally rich and poor, indicate it may not be incorporated in social contracts for a long time, if ever. On the other hand, since the new contracts are conceived to be in the nature of syntheses generated by localizing antitheses responding to globalizing theses, conceivably a greater degree of egalitarianism will eventually be embedded in the syn-

[41] Kurt Mills, "Cybernations: The Internet, Virtual Reality, and Self-Determination" (paper presented at the annual meeting of the International Studies Association, Minneapolis, March 17–21, 1998), p. 5.

[42] Fishkin, "Toward a New Social Contract," p. 221.

[43] Haufler, *A Public Role for the Private Sector*, p. 1.

theses and become a major clause of the new contracts, albeit such a development may still lie far in the future. Conceivably, the collapse of time and space makes it increasingly possible to form SOAs that sustain, even presuppose, an equality of rights heretofore unimaginable. How? By new electronic and transportation technologies that not only foster greatly increased social and geographic mobility but also undermine prior social contracts—as one observer puts it, the old "social norms lose their hold on people because people spend a larger proportion of their life with strangers who are not enforcing the norms with the same efficacy."[44]

7. TERRITORIALITY

Since the fragmegrative epoch is marked by the diminution of the salience of long-standing geographic boundaries, it becomes feasible for a term in social contracts to evolve that allows for the formation and maintenance of large voluntary communities, from social movements to issue regimes, that are founded on metaconventions of cooperation and that specifically exclude territoriality as a basis for organizational structures. In effect, it becomes plausible "to think of space-free social contracting."[45]

8. ACCOUNTABILITY

A central problem for most SOAs is that of rendering the exercise of authority accountable to their members. While there is a discernible trend toward the transparency of their procedures, many SOAs lack formal mechanisms through which their memberships can hold their leaders accountable for their conduct. So it may very well be that, like the clause on egalitarianism, this term of the contract may encounter obstacles that inhibit its development and never evolve into one that specifies formal structures. On the other hand, all the previous seven terms may contribute, in one way or another, to informal mechanisms of accountability for nonprofit SOAs. Stated most succinctly, the necessity of such an SOA maintaining loyalty and authority among a fluid, voluntarist membership of adaptable citizens requires its leaders to act in such a way as not to incline its members to give up their commitment and affiliation. In terms of the exit, voice, and loyalty conception of organizational affiliations,[46] the ease of an adaptable citizen's exit places a premium on a SOA's ability to facilitate voice. The accountability of many SOAs and their ability to command loyalties and achieve compliance arise precisely because they are voluntary organizations and always vulnerable to mass exits. An SOA

---

[44] Jon Elster, *Nuts and Bolts for the Social Sciences* (New York: Cambridge University Press, 1989), p. 162.
[45] Blau, *Social Contracts and Economic Markets*, p. 105.
[46] Cf. Albert O. Hirschman, *Exit, Voice, and Loyalty* (Cambridge, Mass.: Harvard University Press, 1970).

that is not accountable to its membership, shareholders, workers, or other stakeholders is likely to falter and possibly cease to exist under the dense competitive conditions that mark the multicentric world.

CONCLUSION

From the perspective of a new century, the foregoing outline of possible social contracts generated by fragmegrative dynamics may seem idealistic and unrealistic. After all, it can readily be argued, the new contracts have no clauses that hint at how new institutional contexts will evolve to reconcile fragmegrative tensions or otherwise assure the effectiveness of SOAs in wielding their authority and achieving compliance. Nor are there any clauses that allow for the handling of those trouble spots in the world where localizing dynamics have fostered violence and resistance to new sources of authority. On the contrary, there are good reasons to presume that the emergent epoch will be as marred by difficult and intractable trouble spots as the expiring epoch has been; indeed, such situations may never allow syntheses between globalizing theses and localizing antitheses. And surely it is also the case that any new contracts will be slow to develop and that the habits necessary to support them may require generations to become fully implanted.

But such a line of reasoning ignores the transformative dynamics at work in the world and presumes that the future is bound to emulate the past. In this sense it is equally reasonable to presume that the uncertainties inherent in the multiplicity of fragmegrative tensions are so pervasive that any number of plausible futures may unfold. Viewed in this way, it may not be idealistic to conclude that the acceleration of the organizational explosion, the skill revolution, and the mobility upheaval render the probability of new institutional contexts expressive of new social contracts evolving no less than the likelihood of the old contracts perpetuating a state-dominated world. The answer to the who's-in-charge-here question posed in the epigraph of chapter 12 may well prove to be that, given a continual disaggregation of authority, many collectivities will be in charge. Or perhaps the question should be rephrased: Who is not in charge here?

PART THREE

Issues, Processes, and Structures as Distant Proximities

THROUGHOUT the preceding chapters, frequent reference has been made to the global stage being crowded with agents and the global agenda being crowded with macro issues the agents seek to highlight and re-solve. As perceived by the diverse agents, all the issues consist of distant proximities, of situations that can have consequences for people in the several local, global, and private worlds. Tracing these consequences for all the issues on the global agenda, and how micro agents shape the structures and resolutions of the various issues, is a staggering task that cannot be undertaken here. There are too many issues. One recent and reputable inquiry, for example, includes chapters on sixteen major issues presently roiling world affairs.[1] Confronted with such a long agenda, it seems preferable to probe for the micro-macro links intensely in a few of them rather than attempt to be extensive and only cursorily examine all of them.

Accordingly, the chapters that follow are limited to five issues that are sufficiently diverse in structure to suggest how any issue might be as-sessed in terms of its micro-macro dynamics. And even this narrowing of the scope of the macro inquiry is limited. Given the complexity of each issue, the five chapters only begin to identify the sources, outcomes, and ramifications of the issues on which they focus. Indeed, each issue has been the subject of a large literature that, regrettably, does not explicitly employ a micro-macro framework. Hopefully, however, the ensuing anal-ysis is sufficient to point the way to further and deeper investigations into the micro-macro dynamics that sustain issues on the global agenda.

---

[1] P. J. Simmons and Chantal de Jonge Oudraat (eds.), *Managing Global Issues: Lessons Learned* (Washington, D.C.: Carnegie Endowment for International Peace, 2001).

CHAPTER FOURTEEN

Progress toward Human Rights

> [T]ransnational human rights pressures and policies, including
> the activities of advocacy networks, have made a very significant
> difference in bringing about improvements in human rights
> practices in diverse countries around the world.
> —Thomas Risse and Stephen C. Ropp[1]

> [A] human rights perspective, focusing as it does on enhancing
> human agency, draws attention to the importance of unblocking
> individual agency as a motor for economic development.
> —Michael Ignatieff[2]

THESE EPIGRAPHS pose a number of questions about the twelve worlds
conceptualized in earlier chapters. Do human rights issues foster individual agency in any of the four private worlds? Are they distant proximities
for Insular Locals? Do Affirmative, Exclusionary, or Resistant Locals care
about such matters? Is the violation of the rights of individuals abroad
preoccupying for Resistant Globals or for Specialized Globals? Are Affirmative Globals who focus on the benefits of macro economic globalization able to extend their concerns to the well-being of people at the
micro level? Under what circumstances, if any, might Territorial Globals
be inclined to respond to distant proximities that involve human degradation? Does the same cluster of values encompass diverse issues such as
ethnic cleansing, torture, exploitative poverty, and trafficking in women,
or does the relevance of each issue vary among the twelve micro worlds?
Are there, in short, systematic connections among the panoply of human
rights concerns and residence in any of the twelve worlds? And equally
important, when are such issues likely to provoke either collective actions
or widely shared orientations that culminate in unintentional micro inputs?
    While a full response to such questions would require a separate trea-
tise, light can be shed on them, first, by noting several broad tendencies

---

[1] "International Human Rights Norms and Domestic Change," in Thomas Risse, Stephen C. Ropp, and Kathryn Sikkink (eds.), *The Power of Human Rights: International
Norms and Domestic Change* (Cambridge: Cambridge University Press, 1999), p. 275.
[2] "Dignity and Agency," in *Human Rights as Politics and Idolatry* (Princeton, N.J.:
Princeton University Press, 2001), p. 166.

among the several worlds even though exceptions to them may be numerous and, second, by probing the distinctive features of human rights as an issue area. Perhaps the generalization with the fewest exceptions is that intentional micro inputs—collective actions—on behalf of individual rights in distant places are likely to be largely the concern of elites and activists with global orientations, especially those Specialized Globals for whom human rights are the primary distant proximities that continuously engage their attention and energy. These are the people who initiate or respond to the mobilizing efforts of Amnesty International, CARE, Save the Children, and other NGOs concerned with one or another aspect of human rights. Some Territorial and Affirmative Globals may also be especially sensitive to human rights issues,[3] the former because their official responsibilities encompass human rights and the latter because their global orientations are not confined to macro economic dynamics. The more cosmopolitan elites and activists among the Affirmative Globals are, in other words, the more are they likely to be parties to intentional micro inputs. As for the contribution of ordinary people to unintentional micro inputs, the ensuing discussion identifies some features of the human rights regime that can arrest wide attention and create the conditions where elites cannot ignore the drift of public sentiments they perceive to be at work.

Another generalization that can be safely advanced concerns the Insular Locals who, like those in the various private worlds, are unlikely to be attentive to distant human rights issues. Their narrow horizons, their lack of concern with any processes that render distant events highly proximate, militate against their becoming preoccupied with how individuals are treated outside their own community. Violations of the rights of others within their community may be of great concern, and conceivably such inward-looking orientations can expand when situations abroad turn so ugly as to intrude upon their horizons. More often than not, however, their predispositions to accord primacy to their own geographic space and to ignore far-off violations of human rights are likely to prevail.

Finally, it is reasonable to presume that many Exclusionary Locals and some Resistant Locals and Globals are ready to violate, or at least to deny, the rights of immigrants whose arrival and presence are seen as undermining their communities and threatening their jobs. The electoral campaigns and policies designed to minimize or halt the flow of immigrants pursued by extreme right-wing politicians in more than a few countries exemplify intentional micro inputs along these lines, while the electoral support they receive and the prejudices and acts of vandalism to

---

[3] It should be noted that a minority of Affirmative Globals, such as oil company executives, are insensitive to human rights, that they are notorious for having violated the well-being of indigenous peoples.

which immigrants are subjected poignantly illustrate unintentional micro inputs that have helped elevate human rights issues to the top of the global agenda.

In sum, whatever may be their reasons, those who would deny human rights do so on the basis of the identity of those whose rights they seek to abrogate. Accordingly, human rights are another dimension of the questions about identity raised in chapter 8. Hence this and the following chapter are extensions of earlier ones in the sense that they seek to trace the impact of fragmegrative dynamics on the identities embraced by the human rights regime at the outset of the twenty-first century. Two questions drive the analysis: In what ways do human rights issues sustain micro-macro interactions? In what ways does fragmegration inhibit and enhance the various struggles for human rights?

It will be noted that in the last question the word *and* rather than *or* is used as the basis for probing alternative impacts of fragmegrative dynamics. For the consequences of these dynamics are multiple. They encourage efforts both to advance and to violate human rights. Both types of efforts are analyzed here, while an extreme version of the latter, what I call *systemic hatred*, is analyzed in chapter 15.

HUMAN RIGHTS AS AN ISSUE AREA

Although the issues encompassed by the human rights regime are enormously diverse—as varied as there are cultures and subcultures in the world—and although the various issues did not climb high onto the global agenda until after World War II, they are marked by sufficient commonalties to justify clustering them together in an issue area and thereby differentiating them from other kinds of issues. One common characteristic is the large extent to which the various human rights issues can foster overly simplified forms of analysis. Their moral dimensions are so compelling that often they obscure the larger empirical contexts in which the norms, principles, rules, institutions, and procedures of the human rights regime are violated, implemented, expanded, or contracted. The temptation to rush to judgment is powerful and yet dangerous. It tends to treat complex situations as elementary, as lacking nuance, as too urgent to pause in the interest of explicating the theoretical perspectives underlying the judgments. But explication of underlying premises is important. It infuses meaning into the empirical arguments and moral conclusions around which human rights issues are contested. In the absence of explication, arguments can lead nowhere, and judgments can be ill informed. And explication is always possible because observers, whether they know it or not, inevitably bring theoretical lenses to bear in the process of assessing those aspects of human rights issues they view as important and dismissing those they regard as trivial. If they do not do so, if they do not indicate the underlying premises through which they differentiate the central from the peripheral, their claims as to what is appropriate and reprehensible about any given human rights question can be neither validated nor persuasive.

A second common quality of human rights issues—and perhaps the one that most sustains micro-macro sequences—is that in any context, whether Asian or Western, legal or moral, universal or particularistic, human rights situations focus on the well-being of individuals as either singular persons or group members. Environmental issues share a preoccupation with nature, economic issues converge on the flow of goods and money, diplomatic issues center on the interaction of states and nations; but only human rights issues locate the well-being of discrete people at the core of their concerns. Such issues revolve around the fact or potential of bodily harm to individuals or socioeconomic and political harm to their collectivities, characteristics that are so immediately imaginable that violations of the rights of persons and groups have the power to rise quickly to the top of political agendas. When people suffer individual or collective harm imposed systematically by any organized source, such actions are bound to arouse the sensibilities of others, especially when the bodily harm to individuals is on a mass, genocidal scale. This ever-present intimacy that pervades human rights issues helps to explain why protest groups so readily form, why some organizations persist beyond their successful protests, why some governments are sensitive to criticism of their conduct in this regard, why other governments go out of their way to hide or justify their violations of individual rights, and why people insist that their culture's conception of human rights is no less justifiable than that of any other culture.

In short, however they may be defined, the rights of persons and groups are distinguished by the singular quality of striking at the heart of individual experience, and in so doing, they occupy a moral ground to which no other issue area can lay claim. And as the complexity of modern urban and transnational life deepens, the more salient does this moral ground become.

Another distinguishing feature of the issue area is the high degree to which violations of human rights are organized and systematic. Unlike most cases of crime or corruption,[4] those involving violated human rights do not occur as isolated events undertaken for idiosyncratic reasons.[5]

---

[4] For a discussion of corruption as an issue area, see chapter 16.

[5] Technically, incidents of both crime and corruption deprive their victims of human rights, but they are not normally located in the human rights issue area precisely because they tend to derive from idiosyncratic rather than systematic sources. To be sure, some

Rather, whatever specific actions their perpetrators may take, they derive from some set of presumptions that justify depriving others of their security or their economic, cultural, or political rights. These presumptions are organized and systematic in the sense that seemingly isolated events may stem from the same deeply embedded cultural, historical, or economic prejudices that perpetrators believe absolve them of any wrongdoing (as was the case for so long of mistreatment of African-Americans in the United States), or they may underlie organized campaigns to deprive whole classes of people of their rights (as was the case of the Holocaust in Germany and ethnic cleansing in Yugoslavia).

In other words, the human rights issue area tends to be distinguished by a lack of ambiguity and uncertainty. Particular individuals who violate the rights of others may be anonymous, but the sources of their actions are likely to be clear-cut and explicit. There may be disagreements over who are the perpetrators and who are the victims and how the former should be held to account for their actions, but except for the oppression of women in some Islamic cultures and limitations on political rights in many Asian countries, there is no uncertainty that such actions are unacceptable.

Still another dimension of the human rights issue area is its pervasiveness and salience. In a shrinking world crisscrossed by endless flows of information, people everywhere—with the possible exception of Insular Locals and Circumstantial Passives—have become aware of such issues. While some observers argue that this awareness is universal and amounts to a "remarkable international normative consensus on the list of rights,"[6] others acknowledge the universality of the awareness but contend that it encompasses conflicting conceptions of what constitutes human rights and their violation. Despite such differences, however, there can be no gainsaying that rights issues have become a matter of widespread concern, as if the conscience of humankind has at long last found a shared focus. More than that, it is a retrospective as well as a current focus. Increasingly, the misdeeds of human rights violators no longer pass from humankind's conscience once they leave the world stage: as two former South Korean prime ministers, several members of the Argentine military, and General Pinochet painfully discovered, their retirement from office did not remove them from the danger of retribution.[7] Indeed, an explanation of why and how past as well as present human rights issues have

---

crime is sustained by organizations, but a preponderance of criminal actions throughout the world are undertaken by individuals who bear no organizational relation to each other.

[6] Jack Donnelly, *Universal Human Rights in Theory and Practice* (Ithaca, N.Y.: Cornell University Press, 1989), p. 23.

[7] Bruce Broomhall, "Criminal Justice on a Global Scale," *New York Times*, June 13, 2001, p. A31.

only lately risen to the top of local, national, transnational, and global agendas—what one observer summarizes as the "unprecedented global diffusion of the idea of rights"[8]—is inherent in the ensuing effort to assess the impact of fragmegrative dynamics.

THE IMPACT OF FRAGMEGRATION

The various dynamics depicted in the previous chapters serve as a useful means of evaluating the human rights regime. Taken together their impacts are mutually reinforcing, but each contributes differently to the various ways in which rights are protected and violated. Each involves different processes relevant to the human condition, but collectively they constitute a powerful force for both good and bad insofar as human rights are concerned.

The Skill Revolution

In the case of the skill revolution, its analytic dimension has inhibited the rights violators by enabling people everywhere to more clearly assess the violations and how they affect their victims. Its emotional dimension has served to strengthen judgments about the immorality of violations. Its imaginative dimension has facilitated understanding of the implications of violations for the conduct of public affairs. As a result of these enlarged skills, those groups and organizations that seek to mobilize people to contest human rights violations can draw upon a degree of empathy and commitment that is widespread and intense. Distant as the violations may be, they can quickly become proximate. It was hardly a random occurrence, for example, that journalistic accounts and televised scenes of ethnic cleansing in Kosovo evoked deep, energetic, and persistent responses from numerous Affirmative Locals and Globals who supported NATO's efforts to hold Yugoslavia accountable for its actions. Although halting and much too late, similar responses eventually developed with respect to the Rwandan genocide.

On the other hand, those who perpetrate human rights violations can be enhanced as well as inhibited by the skill revolution. For just as those who abhor rights violations are more easily mobilized, so are those, especially Exclusionary Locals, who subscribe to value systems that justify the violations. Their newly acquired skills enable them to respond more effectively to mobilizers who appeal to their antirights prejudices. It is worth recalling that a major consequence of the skill revolution is the

[8] Anthony G. McGrew, "Human Rights in a Global Age: Coming to Terms with Globalization," in Tony Evans (ed.), *Human Rights Fifty Years On: A Reappraisal* (Manchester: Manchester University Press, 1998), p. 194.

growing capacity of people everywhere to know when, where, and how to engage in collective action, a capacity that can be just as easily put to the service of opposing as supporting what are regarded as human rights violations. The Chilean crowds protesting and praising the detention of General Pinochet in England for human rights violations in earlier decades are illustrative of how the skill revolution can have contradictory consequences and empower both champions and violators of civil rights.

Bifurcated Global Structures

The transformation of the macro parameter has been especially consequential as an inhibitor of actors inclined to violate human rights. Most notably, the processes of bifurcation that culminated in the multi-centric world have facilitated the formation of numerous groups and networks that coordinate their resources and energies in the struggle to contest states and other collectivities that deprive their citizens or members of their rights. The successful efforts of numerous NGOs and some states to oppose apartheid in South Africa exemplify the kind of powerful pressures that can be generated in the multi-centric world to contest the actions of governments dedicated to subjugating the rights of oppressed peoples.[9] Although the form of pressure was different, a similar outcome was achieved in Argentina, led by weekly marches on the part of mothers seeking to account for their "disappeared" children.[10] Indeed, it can readily be argued that such successes in advancing human rights are quintessential examples of how both intentional and unintentional micro inputs can be traced as sources of macro patterns.

The advent of the multi-centric world has also contributed to rendering violations of human rights more visible. Numerous organizations in that world—such as Amnesty International and Human Rights Watch—highlight violations by governments in ways that other states cannot readily emulate without breaking long-standing diplomatic protocols. Nor are governments the only collectivities whose practices are tracked by human rights NGOs. The work of the Southern Poverty Law Center, which calls attention to the activities of private hate groups and militia organizations in the United States, is illustrative of the increasing degree to which transparency has come to mark the human rights issue area. Indeed, given the diverse ways in which the bifurcation of global structures have facilitated the exposure of individuals and groups who systematically deprive others of their rights, it is difficult to identify ways in

[9] Audie Klotz, *Norms in International Relations: The Struggle against Apartheid* (Ithaca, N.Y.: Cornell University Press, 1999).

[10] Alison Brysk, *The Politics of Human Rights in Argentina: Protest, Change and Democratization* (Stanford, Calif.: Stanford University Press, 1993).

which the transformation of the macro parameter has enhanced the efforts of the violators.

No less important, the bifurcation of global structures has tended to weaken the capacity of states to resist external pressures on behalf of human rights. The focus of numerous and unrelenting pressures from the multi-centric world, those states that have long histories of assaulting the rights of their citizens are less able to hide behind the precedents of sovereignty to engage in such practices, while those states long committed to the protection of human rights experience the same pressures as bases for ignoring the sovereignty of the violating states and intervening in their affairs so as to bring violations to an end. A number of dynamics account for the surge of what have come to be called *humanitarian interventions* in recent years, but the bifurcation of global structures and the relative loss of capabilities that this has meant for states are surely a prime source of such interventions.

Whatever form the pressures generated in the multi-centric world may take, the channels through which they flow can vary from situation to situation. While in some instances they are brought to bear directly on the rights violators, perhaps even more frequently they are exercised indirectly through pressing sympathetic agencies of governments who, in turn, employ their diverse resources to press the violators. Since governments still retain considerable clout, close cooperation between them and NGOs is the most effective mechanism for highlighting and rectifying human rights situations.[11] Such cooperation is not easily achieved, however. Within both governments and the multi-centric world, different, even contradictory, perspectives often prevail over how—even whether— to address particular human rights situations. United States' policy toward human rights in China is a quintessential example in this regard. On the one hand, various human rights organizations and some members of Congress, as well as some agencies of the executive branch, argue for pressing the Chinese government hard to abandon its policies toward individual rights and collective action; at the same time, many business organizations and the Commerce Department seek to preserve investment opportunities in China by minimizing pressure for the amelioration of human rights. Yet despite the difficulties of achieving cooperation across the bifurcated structures of the global system, it is nonetheless the case that increasing coordination among like-minded human rights organizations within the multi-centric world has served to alert governments to human rights violations and resulted in policies designed to end them.

---

[11] For an elaborate and cogent discussion of the various stages through which interactions over human rights issues can unfold between the state-centric and the multi-centric world, see Risse, Ropp, and Sikkink (eds.), *The Power of Human Rights*.

Authority Crises

The proliferation of authority crises at every level of community and in every part of the world cuts both ways in terms of enhancing or inhibiting those who violate human rights. On the one hand, it enhances the violators by providing them with a line of reasoning that justifies their actions and enlarges the support proffered by their followers: such actions are defended on the grounds that challenges which move authority structures toward crisis undermine social stability and thus necessitate the curbing of rights. On the other hand, authority crises can be inhibiting in the sense that the bases of support for violations may shrink and opportunities may be created for individuals and groups to organize counteractions on behalf of those whose rights are denied. Put more forcefully, more than a few authority crises arise precisely because the violated and their supporters become so agitated that they resort to vigorous, even violent, protests over the continuing deprivation of rights. The struggle for civil rights in the United States and against apartheid in South Africa are obvious examples of authority crises precipitated by the emergence of performance criteria of legitimacy that have accompanied the onset of a fragmegrative epoch.

In sum, if it is assumed that norms upholding human rights are spreading throughout the world—and the case for this assumption is a strong one[12]—the pervasiveness of authority crises at every level of community can readily be viewed as accelerating the struggles to defend and advance the rights of individuals and groups. Under conditions of stasis or even stability, the inclination of communities to "rock the boat" by altering the prevailing formal and informal arrangements that sustain relationships and rights within them is not likely to be very intense. But when, for whatever reasons, authority is being questioned and contested, uncertainties are introduced into a community, and openings to press for the rights of its members are thereby created. Neither the amelioration nor the abrogation of human rights is ever a subdued or quiescent matter, with the result that the commotion attending authority crises fosters the elevation of rights issues to higher levels on the community's agenda.

Microelectronic Technologies

On balance, the many new technologies that have collapsed time and space serve to accelerate struggles on behalf of human rights more than

---

[12] See, for example, the various essays in ibid. For the counterassumption that the human rights movement "may have reached the limits of its effectiveness" and is thus "in trouble," see David Rieff, "The Precarious Triumph of Human Rights," *New York Times Magazine*, August 8, 1999, pp. 36–41.

they have undermined them. Perhaps most notably, all the new micro-electronic technologies, each in its own way, enable individuals and collectivities in both state-centric and multi-centric worlds to coordinate more extensively and respond more rapidly to any actors who may undertake to violate their rights. Examples abound. The way in which Commander Marcos utilized the Internet to mobilize worldwide support for the Zapatistas in Mexico is a classic case, as was the way in which fax machines and global television helped (at least briefly) the student protests in Tiananmen Square in 1989.

Of course, as stressed in chapter 11, technologies are essentially neutral. What counts is how they are applied in the political arena. They can be used to thwart human rights as well as to advance them. Thus those who deprive people of rights can serve their purposes by drawing on the same instruments of rapid communication to inform, arouse, activate, and link their followers. Just as Amnesty International, for example, can use the Internet to generate a letter-writing campaign on the part of its members, so can militia forces, racist organizations, terrorists, and crime syndicates employ the same means to keep their members up-to-date on the weaponry, threats, and enemies central to their preoccupations.

Yet, to repeat, the various microelectronic technologies have been more consequential for the human rights movement than for its opponents. Indeed, it could well be argued that it is precisely because of the ease with which ideas and pictures can move around the world today that human rights issues have climbed close to the top of the global agenda and are a widely shared focus of humankind's conscience. In effect, the age of fragmegration has provided those who champion human rights, however defined, with powerful tools for moving toward their goals. Often these tools are not sufficient to moderate successfully or terminate the activities of organizations, cultures, and states that suppress individual and group rights, but nonetheless the struggle for human rights has not been previously so well equipped to carry forward. Many of the dynamics of fragmegration have noxious consequences, but the provision of an extensive, elaborate, and rapid-fire communications system for the human rights regime is surely among the salutary features of the transformations at work in world affairs.

Furthermore, and hardly less important, this communications system has contributed to processes of emulation and isomorphism that have indirectly extended the scope of the human rights regime. It is no accident, for example, that indigenous peoples have successfully begun to emulate the techniques of other human rights groups,[13] with the acquisi-

---

[13] A compelling analysis along these lines can be found in Alison Brysk, *From Tribal Village to Global Village: Indian Rights and International Relations in Latin America* (Stanford, Calif.: Stanford University Press, 2000).

tion of their own territory in Canada by the Inuit people being perhaps a prime example in this regard.[14] To be sure, the success of the Inuits resulted from hard organizational work and a vigorous advocacy network, but the rapidity of their success—from an isolated minority to a full-fledged autonomous province in roughly fifteen years—can readily be interpreted as a measure of how the new microelectronic technologies have widely and quickly cascaded from one part of the world to another the bases for emulating the values, aspirations, and practices of human rights activists.

In sum, the new media of communications, and especially the Internet, are major factors underlying the transnationalization of the human rights regime. Long-standing national boundaries are no longer barriers to cooperation among like-minded people and groups devoted to exposing and contesting rights violations.

The Organizational Explosion and the Spread of Networks

Given the huge proliferation of associations, it is hardly surprising that the movement of human rights issues toward the top of the global agenda has been accompanied by a mushrooming of new organizations devoted to protecting and enhancing the rights of people: "There are now over 200 U.S. NGOs associated with human rights issues, a similar number in the UK and across Europe, and expanding numbers of such organizations within the developing world."[15] Indeed, between 1981 and 1990 the number of human rights groups in Latin America rose from 220 to over 550.[16] This array of organizations is not in itself the prime source of support for the human rights regime, since the latter also includes the agencies of national governments and international organizations,[17] but the regime's growth and solidification are clear-cut indications of the extent to which the dynamics of fragmegration have accelerated the salience of the many values that attach to the concept of human rights.

[14] Nunavut came into being as a territory for the Inuit people on April 1, 1999. See Martin O'Malley, "Nunavut: Canada's Nw Territory" (CBC News Online-Indepth: Nunavut; http://CBCnews.CBC.CA/news/indepth/nanuvut/home.html).

[15] David Held, Anthony McGrew, David Goldblat, and Jonathan Perraton, *Global Transformations: Politics, Economics and Culture* (Stanford, Calif.: Stanford University Press, 1999), p. 67. During a visit to Kathmandu in 1999, I was informed by the president of the Human Rights Organization of Nepal, Kapil Shrestha, that in but a few years the number of human rights organizations in Nepal had risen from fifteen to forty.

[16] Margaret E. Keck and Kathryn Sikkink, *Activists beyond Borders: Advocacy Networks in International Politics* (Ithaca, N.Y.: Cornell University Press, 1998), p. 92.

[17] Michele Waslin, "Who Are the Regime Takers? An Analysis of the International Human Rights Regime" (paper presented at the annual meeting of the American Political Science Association, Boston, September 3–6, 1998).

As suggested in chapter 3, a major feature of the organizational explosion involves the evolution of horizontal networks that sustain ties both within and among NGOs. The vertical, hierarchical forms of earlier eras have neither disappeared nor been superseded, but the advent of networked organizations facilitated by the Internet and other recent technological innovations has added considerably to the number, capabilities, and effectiveness of NGOs in the multi-centric world. In the words of one observer, "Human rights groups, often linking through the Internet, have gained more leverage than ever against the governments that have elbowed them out of the spotlight in the past."[18]

In short, the explosive advent of networked organizations has enabled like-minded NGOs to reach across boundaries and pool their resources, share their information, exchange their personnel, and otherwise coordinate their efforts. To be sure, their activities are not entirely harmonious. In the words of one observer, "The NGOs make up a large amorphous movement, but many of its components are middle-aged and office-bound; their energies are dissipated in interagency competition for money and publicity."[19] Still, since the goals of different human rights NGOs tend to be overlapping, their networks are not confined exclusively to intense rivalries; they are also marked by cooperative endeavors to monitor, if not to deter, the practices of those who violate human rights. Indeed, by working together, the NGOs serve as a monitoring network that exposes human rights violations, and the Internet has enabled them to become a transnational advocacy network with considerable influence.[20] Perhaps they have yet to swarm as effectively around human rights situations as others did at the WTO meeting in Seattle, but the recent acceleration in the evolution of the human rights regime (see later discussion) can at least partly be traced to earlier swarms that converged on IGO meetings in Vienna and Beijing. Such collective endeavors have rendered the issue area much more transparent, just as the pressures on human rights violators have often yielded at least a modicum of the desired outcomes. As previously noted, today it is exceedingly more difficult for violators to hide their misdeeds than was the case prior to the coherence of the transnational advocacy networks.[21] Put differently, the

---

[18] Barbara Crosette, "Global Look at Racism Hits Many Sore Points," *New York Times*, March 4, 2001, p. 8.

[19] Michael Ignatieff, "Human Rights: The Midlife Crisis," *New York Review of Books*, Vol. 46 (May 20, 1999), p. 60.

[20] Keck and Sikkink, *Activists beyond Borders*, p. 119.

[21] The Argentine military personnel provide a good case in point. In the late 1970s they tried to hide their violations of human rights by pushing their opponents out of airplanes over the open seas. It was not long, however, before a coordinated effort by the human rights activists circulated word that something was amiss, that people were disappearing,

processes bifurcating global structures into two interactive, sometimes cooperative and often competitive worlds of world politics have moved at a greatly quickened pace since the organizational explosion turned in horizontal directions. Viewed with hindsight, the responsiveness of the state-centric world on human rights issues to its multi-centric counterpart is readily explicable.

The Mobility Upheaval

In important ways the mobility upheaval has intensified the struggle for human rights. Or at least one of its main dimensions, the migration of large numbers of people from southern countries into northern countries, has led to considerable prejudice and, in some cases, violence on the part of Exclusionary Locals and some Resistant Globals in the host countries. Whatever the reasons for the migrations—and there are many—the migrants are seen by more than a few of the long-standing citizens of the host countries as threats, as low-wage or specialized competitors for jobs, as conveyors of alien cultures, as strangers who need to be controlled, if not removed. As previously noted, right-wing politicians are especially antagonistic to the swelling number of immigrants in their midst and willing to argue for policies that would violate the rights of immigrants. Indeed, in several developed countries they have conducted campaigns founded on anti-immigrant appeals and generated more than trivial electoral support. And the more unemployment and other economic difficulties pervade countries that are host to large numbers of immigrants, the more are the rights of the latter likely to be jeopardized. Indeed, although no singular figures have gained worldwide prominence as anti-immigration politicians, the issue has also surfaced in Belgium[22] and in the traditionally liberal politics of Denmark[23] and Norway.[24]

While the negative consequences for human rights of the mobility upheaval can hardly be overstated and can seem insurmountable, there are also ways in which greater mobility has fostered positive consequences. Most notably, the vast movements of people have contributed to a worldwide preoccupation with identity, with a sense of ethnic, religious,

---

with the result that eventually the military junta was brought down and some of its members tried and jailed. For close accounts of these developments, see ibid., pp. 103–10; and Brysk, *The Politics of Human Rights in Argentina.*

[22] Barry James, "Belgian Stance on Austria Reflects Worry over 'Haiderization' at Home," *International Herald Tribune*, March 6, 2000, p. 2.

[23] John Vinocur, "Danes Struggle to Deal with Populist Instincts," *International Herald Tribune*, February 24, 2000, p. 1.

[24] Alan Cowell, "Black Youth Dies, and Norway Looks Inward," *New York Times*, January 3, 2002, p. A1.

cultural, gender, or other common roots that has enabled people to aggregate themselves into groups and press collectively for recognition of their rights at all levels of community. Examples abound. Facilitated by the new microelectronic technologies and the organizational explosion as well as by the mobility upheaval, women, indigenous people, the handicapped, and homosexuals are among those who have become sufficiently aware of their shared interests and identities to establish transborder political movements that national governments and international organizations cannot ignore.

In sum, the worldwide surge toward identity politics has been both a boon and a detriment to the human rights movement. On the one hand, it has given many people a new or renewed sense of themselves, an uplifting integrity and dignity that had not existed before and that is consistent with the goals of those who espouse human rights. On the other hand, a keener sense of identity can mean that those who do not share in it are outsiders, strangers who may not be trustworthy, whose rights are questionable, and who can easily be redefined as threats to the insiders' way of life. For every group that has found strength in a greater sense of common identity, there is a Yugoslavian internecine disaster waiting to happen or currently unfolding.[25]

The Globalization of National Economies

The emergence of a global economy has also had both positive and negative consequences for human rights. Perhaps most notably, the increased mobility of capital renders workers' rights more vulnerable in both developed and developing countries. Economic globalization also may have widened and intensified the gap between the rich and the poor both within and among countries.[26] If one is inclined to view these economic deprivations generated by the global economy as an assault on human rights (as many observers do), or if one is disposed to view the global economy as producing like-minded consumers who have little choice about the commodities and values they hold dear (as more than a few observers do), then clearly those who initiate and sustain these economic dynamics can be treated as actors who undermine human rights in significant ways. By the same token, to the extent that the same dynamics raise standards of living, reduce the unfairness in the system, and lessen the rich-poor gap (as seemed to be the case in Asia during the several years

[25] Tamara Cofman Wittes, "Mass Refugee Flows: What Challenges for State Sovereignty?" (paper presented at the annual meeting of the International Studies Association, Toronto, March 18–23, 1997).

[26] For an elaboration of this point, see chapter 17.

prior to the financial crisis in that region), then to that extent they brighten and accelerate the processes favoring human rights.

Weakened States and Narrowed Sovereignty

The diminished capacities and sovereignty of states fostered by fragmegration have had major consequences for the human rights issue area. The most conspicuous indicator in this respect is the shifting norms that have resulted in humanitarian interventions into the domestic affairs of countries on behalf of oppressed minorities, but there are a number of other ways in which fragmegrative dynamics have strengthened the struggle for human rights. In a world of weaker states the various microelectronic technologies can more readily focus the bright glare of publicity on states' transgressions of the rights of their citizens; rights-upholding states can brighten this glare by listing the rights-insensitive records of other states; transnational human rights advocacy groups can more easily mobilize support; rights victims and their pleas for help can more immediately and widely be heard in far-off places; people fleeing economic and political policies that undermine their rights can more surely cross borders and find refuge elsewhere; alternative cultural conceptions of rights can be more effectively challenged and defended; actors in the multi-centric world can more extensively press counterparts in the state-centric world to convene (say, in Vienna or Beijing) and debate resolutions and policies favoring those deprived of their rights; and so on across all the dimensions of state capabilities that have previously been relatively impervious to pressures on behalf of human rights.

IDENTIFYING HUMAN RIGHTS ACTORS AND THEIR OPPONENTS

Much of the literature on human rights tends to treat states as the prime culprits. But the approach developed here suggests a multiplicity of violators. Some states are surely sources of human rights deprivations, but so are leaders who arouse ethnic or racial hatreds, private associations that contribute to or sustain cultures of prejudice, terrorist organizations that attach no value to human life, multinational corporations that suppress peaceful protests,[27] militia groups that derive their coherence from a loathing of foreigners, rebel movements that treat their goals as justifying any means to achieve them, and so on across a wide range of individual and collective actors for whom the rights of people are not a high priority.

[27] See, for example, Human Rights Watch, *The Enron Corporation: Complicity in Human Rights Violations* (London: Human Rights Watch, 1999).

Much the same can be said about the actors who seek to protect and expand human rights. These can include the United Nations through its Commission on Human Rights; states that are committed to enhancing the well-being of individuals; NGOs that contest those who violate human rights and that seek to mobilize support for their efforts; publics that are outraged by cases in which rights have been brutally negated; like-minded elites who launch advertising campaigns on behalf of groups that have been deprived of their rights; individuals with heroic pasts as victims of prejudice and injustice; public officials who are moved to isolate, undermine, or otherwise contain the most obstreperous actors who voice or act out their prejudices; and so on across a vast array of individual and collective actors for whom rights issues are especially salient. The human rights issue area, in short, has become dense with actors on the various sides of any situation in which people are regarded as having been deprived of their well-being.

The Human Rights Regime and the Challenge of Systemic Hatred

With NATO forces having belatedly taken a stand against ethnic cleansing in Kosovo, it seems clear that among the most powerful consequences of a fragmegrative world are those that have fostered greater local, national, and transnational sensitivities to human rights. In the decades since the adoption of the Universal Declaration of Human Rights in 1948, the regime that has evolved through various treaties, advocacy networks, situational outcomes, and policy pronouncements can be readily discerned even though it encompasses contradictory and conflictual elements. To be sure, these contradictions and conflicting perspectives are serious and portend the possibility, even the expectation, that the moral consensus that has undergirded the regime since 1948 will continue to splinter as localizing definitions of rights fracture the globalizing notion that such rights are universal.[28] Nonetheless, "this does not mean the end of the human rights movement, but its belated coming of age, its recognition that we live in a plural world of cultures which have a right to equal consideration in the argument about what we can and cannot, should and should not do to other human beings."[29]

Moreover, recent years have been marked by enough evolution of the norms, principles, rules, institutions, and procedures constituting the human rights regime to suggest that some of its core will survive the debate and splintering that lie ahead.[30] The fall of the junta in Argentina, the

---

[28] Ignatieff, "Human Rights," p. 62.
[29] Ibid.
[30] For indications of the depth of the debate, see Symposium, "Human Rights in Times

detention of General Pinochet in London, the Khmer Rouge trials in Cambodia, and the indictment of selected persons in Bosnia and Serbia as war criminals—not to mention China's "vigorous" struggle to avoid being listed as a human rights violator by the United Nations[31]—are clear indicators that the regime and the international law supporting it retain a measure of coherence. Indeed, whatever the wisdom of NATO's resort to bombing on behalf of the Kosovars, the forcefulness of the military campaign has in all likelihood permanently altered the meaning of sovereignty and the readiness of governments to assault the rights of their own people. The world's intrusion into the domestic affairs of countries that undertake such assaults may be inconsistent and variable, as a comparison of its actions in Yugoslavia, Chechnya, and several situations in Africa clearly demonstrate, but the principle that sovereignty is inviolable has been narrowed.[32]

Put differently, the human rights regime has been both the victor over and the victim of human rights violators in a world of accelerating fragmegration. Perhaps its prime antagonist is systemic hatred, those micro values and macro arrangements that are group-wide or society-wide, that feed on themselves, and that are thus highly resistant, even immune, to efforts to protect and advance the rights of both the haters and the hated caught up in a spiral of loathing. It is in systemic hatred that the human rights regime, the principles of sovereignty, and the effectiveness of states and SOAs have been most severely tested in recent years. Table 14.1 suggests some ways in which systemic hatred in groups and societies is both sustained and constrained by the dynamics of fragmegration (the rows) in four domains of human rights (the columns).[33] The next chapter elaborates on the entries in some of the cells of the table in an attempt to analyze the underpinnings of systemic hatred and the problem of designing SOAs capable of reversing the spiral of loathing. In so doing, it offers further insight into the limits of the human rights regime.

---

of Conflict: Humanitarian Intervention," *Human Rights Dialogue*, Series 2, No. 3) (winter 2001), pp. 1–24; Barbara Crossette, "Canada Tries to Define Line between Human and National Rights," *New York Times*, September 14, 2000, p. 11; and Richard Bernstein, "To Butt In or Not in Human Rights: The Gap Narrows," *New York Times*, August 4, 2001, pp. A15, A17.

[31] Elizabeth Olson, "China Tries to Fend Off U.N. Censure over Rights," *New York Times*, March 21, 1999, p. 9.

[32] Judith Miller, "Sovereignty Isn't So Sacred Anymore," *New York Times*, April 18, 1999, Sec. 4, p. 4; and Barbara Crossette, "Long-Range Justice Raises Fears for Sovereignty," *New York Times*, July 1, 2001, p. 8. For a perspective that posits the scope of sovereignty as not having narrowed, that views human rights as having challenged sovereign rights since the Vienna settlement following the Napoleonic Wars, see Stephen D. Krasner, "Sovereignty," *Foreign Policy*, No. 122 (January–February 2001), p. 22.

[33] I am indebted to Kathryn Sikkink for the idea to construct table 14.1.

TABLE 14.1.
The Impact of Fragmegration on the Perpetuation of Systemic Hatred (SH) in Four Domains of Human Rights

	Types of Rights			
Aspects of Global Change	Security Rights	Economic Rights	Cultural Rights	Political Rights
Skill revolution	both sustains and constrains SH through increased sensitivity of individuals and groups to their needs and wants	empowers individuals to participate in boycotts and protests designed to lessen foreign support for SH	sustains SH through greater awareness of and commitment to long-standing identities	sustains SH through increased capacity of individuals to engage in collective action
Authority crises	constrain SH by highlighting rights violations; sustain SH by deepening animosities	constrain SH by heightening sensitivities to the scarcity of jobs	sustain SH by increasing consciousness of cultural differences among groups	undermine competence of external agents to rebuild states pervaded with SH
Bifurcation of global structures	allows for diverse pressures on the parties to SH to reconcile their differences	provides opportunities for relief agencies to help rebuild the economies of SH-torn societies	sustains SH by encouraging the identity preoccupations of the parties to it	facilitates efforts of vigilante groups to sustain SH; hampers efforts to rebuild SH-torn societies

TABLE 14.1. (*continued*)

Organizational explosion	constrains SH by facilitating proliferation of human rights organizations	fosters innovative mechanisms designed to rebuild war- and SH-torn economies	sustains SH through the proliferation and strengthening of diaspora	constrains SH through disaggregation of authority
Mobility upheaval	facilitates separation of parties to the SH	facilitates transfer of resources to SH- and war-torn societies	constrains SH through dispersal of minorities	enhances SH by contributing to greater awareness of minority rights
Microelectronic technologies	sustain SH by facilitating networking within the contesting groups	empower crime syndicates to launder money and otherwise feed off the disarray embedded in SH	sustain SH by facilitating perpetuation of awareness of cultural differences	sustain SH by enabling opposing groups to mobilize more effectively
Weakening of Territoriality, states, and sovereignty	renders aid from abroad more difficult; hinders efforts to reconcile differences on part of parties to SH	lessens ability to provide needed aid for infrastructure reconstruction	sustains SH by dampening efforts of outside parties to encourage reconciliation	strengthens prejudices on which SH rests; limits ability of outside states to mediate among haters and hated

CHAPTER FIFTEEN

Retreat from Human Rights:
The Challenge of Systemic Hatred

> Outside the tents is the rain and the mud. Inside is the brewing hatred. Hamit Beqiri, a big, robust man and father of two, was taken captive by Serbian soldiers, he said. They made him and 30 other men build fortifications against NATO air raids. He escaped by bribing three of the guards with most of his life savings.
>
> "Are Serbs good people?" he asked his 5-year-old son, Egzon.
>
> The boy was confused. "Yes," he said.
>
> "Who stole our money, burned our house and took our car?" the father asked impatiently.
>
> This time Egzon was in tune. "The filthy Serbs," he said.
>
> "And what should you do if you meet a Serb like Slobodan Milosevic?"
>
> "I will kill him," the little boy said.
>
> —News story[1]

THIS EXCHANGE across generations poignantly sums up the enormity of the task of advancing human rights, moderating intense ethnic conflicts, and rebuilding war-torn societies. The exchange affirms that once the core fabric of a community breaks down, it collapses rapidly, and identities steeped in hatred remain embedded as they pass from one generation to the next. The epigraph, in other words, cuts to the core of the proposition that it is much easier to tear down a community than to restore it to a prior harmony. Tearing down can occur in response to a single, searing experience; building up can require decades or even centuries as the single, searing experience gets passed on from parents to children time and time again. Put in micro-macro terms, Exclusionary Locals can be irreconcilably stubborn, and when this trait is grounded in hatred, they tend to be so persuaded of the righteousness of their hatred that they can be very effective in socializing their children into their perspec-

[1] Barry Bearak, "In a Sea of Tents, Life Goes On and Hatred Festers," *New York Times*, April 28, 1999, p. A15.

tives. Cast in terms of the title of this and the previous chapter, Exclusionary Locals hinder progress toward human rights and facilitate retreat from them.

To be sure, identities sustained by hatred are not genetic. They have to be created and renewed. That is, they have to be learned, and if that is so, then presumably they can also be unlearned. But the persistence of enmities across decades and centuries suggests that time may not heal, that hatred can become a self-reinforcing habit, that unlearning or relearning may never occur as the learned hatred reaches deep into a community's culture and becomes central to its way of life. It is thus risky, even misguided, to assume deep-seated enmities will eventually dissipate. It has even been noted that, "in many conflicts, the passing of the [hate] agenda from one generation to another is accompanied by increasing radicalism."[2] The recent histories of Ireland, Cyprus, Armenia, Yugoslavia, Rwanda, Palestine, and a host of other communities highlight the dangers of taking the eventual restoration of communities for granted. Conceivably wishful thinking rather than sound analysis underlay the reasoning of an observer of the persistent and violent clashes between Israel and the Palestinians who commented, "One can assume that this can indeed go on for a long time, . . . [but] it can't go on forever."[3]

SYSTEMIC HATRED

While hatred is passed along person by person and family by family, it can be viewed as systemic in the sense that its roots are widely shared within a culture, community, or society as the consequence of common historical experiences. The perpetuation of stories about—and embedded hostility generated by—the common experience is what renders hatred systemic rather than simply personal. Part and parcel of systemic hatred, moreover, is the evolution of institutions that support and reinforce the hatred, according it legitimacy and righteousness that are sustained by official policies as well as by word of mouth. As a result, the hatred can come to be felt so intensely that it feeds on itself and encompasses all those who are part of the culture, community, or society. And as the hatred spreads and becomes deeply rooted as a systemic trait, the more vulnerable does it become to justifying a resort to violence. States and governments maintain police establishments to cope with personal violence on a case-by-case basis, but police efforts are to no avail wherever systemic hatred is concerned. On the contrary, as members of the culture and community,

[2] Alan Cowell, "When Parents Leave a Bequest of Hatred," *New York Times*, June 23, 2002, Sec. 4, p. 1.

[3] Joseph Alpher, a strategic analyst in Israel, quoted in Clyde Haberman, "In Jerusalem, Making Targets of Each Other's Symbols," *New York Times*, August 12, 2001, p. 8.

the police are likely to subscribe to the hatred and contribute to its perpetuation. In short, many Exclusionary Locals thrive on systemic hatred, and systemic hatred thrives on Exclusionary Locals. Not all persons with exclusionary orientations buy into the hatred system, of course, but those who do are likely to draw on deep, even endless, wells of hatred. It follows that systemic hatred poses a challenge for other communities that are not part of the hatred system and that care, perhaps for diverse reasons, about the harm the system is causing its members, its neighbors, and the world in general.

While recent events in Yugoslavia, Rwanda, and Afghanistan point to ethnic groups as having the kind of common experiences that foster systemic hatreds, it is important to stress that ethnicity is not the only basis for such cultures. Religion, language, race, and political ideology have also served as prime sources of systemic hatred, and, with the possible exception of political ideology, more often than not these sources operate as reinforcements for the lines of cleavage. Members of an ethnic group, for example, tend to speak the same language and adhere to the same religion. Obviously, the greater the convergence of common sources, the greater is the intensity of any systemic hatred likely to be. This is not to imply, of course, that any groups astride the fault lines of cleavage are destined to become hatred systems. History records innumerable groups delineated by ethnicity, religion, race, language, or ideology that avoid the transformations that give rise to systemic hatreds. Just as malevolent leaders, insecure elites, compliant media, and stagnant economies can precipitate and sustain systemic hatreds, so can enlightened leadership, open political parties, educational reforms, independent media, and productive economies prevent a culture from being enveloped by hatreds.

Interestingly, and importantly, hatred systems tend to be the products of intrastate and not interstate wars. The enmities generated during interstate wars, while vicious and intense, do not endure for as long subsequent to the end of hostilities as do enmities involving combatants within the same state. One needs only compare the life span of hatreds generated by World War II with those resulting from conflicts within, say, Yugoslavia and Ireland to grasp this difference between interstate and intrastate wars. Whereas intense Western hatreds toward the Germans and Japanese did not endure for more than a few years after the war and, indeed, were replaced by alliances, hatreds in Yugoslavia have continued for centuries, and those in Ireland go back a number of decades. Or consider the history of East Timor in Indonesia, where systemic hatred long existed between the East Timorese aspiring to independence and Indonesians who favored maintenance of the country's integration. In 1999 the hatred reached a peak. As the leader of the pro-integration militia, Enrico Guterres, put it, "As from today I order . . . a cleansing of the traitors of integration: capture them and kill them. It's going to be a civil war."[4]

In short, apparently the experience of living close together within the same borders and sharing parts of the same cultures and histories can conduce to much more deep-seated and long-lasting animosities than is the case for conflicts in which the combatants have little in common other than the immediate issues over which their conflicts have arisen.[5] In other words, intrastate wars involve neighbors as the enemy, whereas in interstate wars the enemy consists of strangers, and it is much easier to overcome antagonisms toward and disentangle from a distant stranger than a close-at-hand neighbor. It follows that the rebuilding of a war-torn society, whatever may have been the bases for the war, is far more difficult than rebuilding a postwar international system, whatever may have been the reasons for its collapse into war.

WHAT IS A WAR-TORN SOCIETY?

But several conceptual issues need to be faced before examining the challenge of systemic hatred. What is meant by a war-torn society? Are the United States, France, Russia, China, and Iran former war-torn societies because each experienced a system-transforming revolution that witnessed neighbors at war with each other and that culminated with victors and vanquished? Or should we concentrate more on the current period in which societies without a long and established history of prior coherence are torn by wars that do not fit the model of a revolution, that have no clear-cut winners and losers, and that evoke extensive participation on the part of the international community? My answer is essentially arbitrary. What follows focuses on the current period because, as has already been stressed, world affairs are in numerous ways very different from what they were when the great revolutions unfolded. The earlier period may have lessons for the present period—such as the realization that, with the possible exception of Iran, the war-torn societies that experienced major

---

[4] Quoted in Seth Mydans, "With Peace Accord at Hand, East Timor's War Deepens," *New York Times*, April 26, 1999, p. A3.

[5] The reference here is to a central tendency. There are, of course, exceptions, with the eventual dissipation of the hatred that accompanied the U.S. Civil War being illustrative of an intrastate conflict that does not conform to the overall pattern, and with the continuing antagonisms that separate Greece and Turkey or India and Pakistan exemplifying interstate wars that contributed to systemic hatreds of an enduring nature. For an extensive elaboration of the central tendency, see James N. Rosenau, "Internal War as an International Event," in James N. Rosenau (ed.), *International Aspects of Civil Strife* (Princeton, N.J.: Princeton University Press, 1964), pp. 45–91.

revolutions did in fact get rebuilt and systemic hatreds did get over-come—but this is not the place for such a wide-ranging exploration.

What Does Rebuilding Entail?

Then there is the conceptual question of what is meant by a rebuilt soci-ety. Presumably there are various stages through which the rebuilding process passes, and presumably each stage has outcomes that can qualify as a form of rebuilding. Which stages should our conceptualization focus on? How do we know a rebuilt society when we see one? The question is daunting. Given the intensity and breadth of systemic hatred, the task of rebuilding a community or society that has been wracked by virulence and destroyed by violence can seem insurmountable. Clearly, a return to the status quo ante in which deep-seated enmities are somehow restored to quiescence and a modicum of harmony somehow achieved is unlikely to occur in the medium term, let alone the short run. One can imagine a restless and uneasy peace being established, one that is always on the edge of collapse, but quick regression to prewar circumstances seems more a fantasy than a meaningful potential. But what, then, is meant by "rebuild-ing" in the context of war-torn conditions? Assuming the status quo ante is unrealistic and also presuming that any rebuilding scheme will involve outside forces to maintain order and supply resources to help in recon-structing the physical damage, does rebuilding consist of providing the material means to reconstruct roads, housing, hospitals, and other key dimensions of infrastructure and hoping that with restored cities and vil-lages daily life will return to a semblance of normalcy? Does it mean the provision of personnel to train and counsel underskilled and depressed survivors of the conflict, as well as the restoration of material infrastruc-tures? Does rebuilding also extend into the economic and legal realms and entail the development of a reliable banking and payment system, laws to enforce contracts, and a new currency arrangement? Does it extend to the resuscitation of educational and medical systems, the training of specialists along the huge range of diverse occupations on which modern commu-nities must rely? Does a public service system have to be put in place? Does rebuilding involve the imposition of democratic institutions if none existed before? Or is rebuilding to be accomplished in terms of whatever values and practices the local populations subscribe to? And when, and under what conditions, can a community be said to have been rebuilt? When, that is, can outsiders who aided in the rebuilding safely return home without fear that their work will be overcome by another round of systemic hatred?

There are, obviously, no easy answers to such questions. To simply answer yes, of course, is to beg the question of how to implement all the varied dimensions of the rebuilding process, especially since the foregoing lists only a small sample of the dimensions that may be required. As a minimum, successful implementation within a reasonable time frame will depend partly on the degree and scope of the commitment to rebuilding brought in from abroad, just as the readiness and ability of local publics to overcome their conflict-induced lethargy will also determine the pace at which progress is achieved. And perhaps most important, a great deal will turn on the extent to which educational reforms, media attention, and committed leadership foster a live-and-let-live attitude that replaces suspicion and anger as the basis for interaction among the previously warring factions.

Difficult as the rebuilding of war-torn societies seems bound to be, the world is not lacking in experience in this regard. Quite aside from what can be learned from the rebuilding successes that ensued after the great revolutions of earlier periods—conceivably, for example, there are lessons to be learned from the fact that the United States did eventually move beyond the systemic hatred generated by its civil war—the United Nations, the UNDP, governmental aid agencies, humanitarian NGOs, and a variety of other organizations have evolved more than a little experience rebuilding societies, experience that is the subject of a large literature and that can surely be put to good use in future situations. In addition, numerous sources can be consulted which probe the dynamics of internal community and societal conflicts. So the knowledge necessary to the task would seem to be available. More problematic is the will to use and apply the knowledge and the amenability of systemic hatred to attenuation even if the will to overcome it is high. One mechanism that could be used for this purpose is partition—that is, separating those who constitute the culture of hatred from the objects of their abhorrence. Another is to employ forms of authority that can contain, contest, and progressively dismantle the institutions of hatred, disrupting the self-reinforcing channels through which the hatred gets transmitted from generation to generation. It matters, in other words, what political structures are put in place as the rebuilding effort is undertaken. Should it be assumed that the structure is the state, and, presuming the state also fell victim to the deterioration of the war-torn society, is it necessary therefore to also rebuild the state? Or, given the weaknesses of states set forth in prior chapters, is state rebuilding bound to fail in the face of unrelenting systemic hatred? Might there be other mechanisms for concentrating the authority necessary to carry off the rebuilding process?

THE STATE AND OTHER REBUILDING MECHANISMS

These last questions may seem absurd. There is no alternative to the state, most observers would respond; it has to be the vehicle for exercising authority and generating compliance with the directives necessary to sustain the rebuilding process. There are no other political mechanisms that can reconstruct or replace a system that has been so destroyed by systemic hatred as to have disappeared into its environment and become barely recognizable.

Yet just as the concept of rebuilding a war-torn society needs to be more precisely formulated, so does it seem appropriate to reiterate that the present-day state may not be capable of initiating, sustaining, and controlling an appropriate rebuilding process. For no less entrenched than the habits of hatred are those that attach to the concept of the state. As previously indicated, the widely shared beliefs what states represent, what they can accomplish, and what they can prevent are profoundly habitual. People simply presume that the terminal entity for loyalties, policy decisions, and moral authority is, for better or worse, the state. This presumption is so deeply ingrained in the culture of modernity that it is not treated as problematic. Those familiar with history know that the state is of relatively recent origin, that for millennia it was preceded by other terminal entities; but even history-minded observers seem unable to envision a future world in which states are not the terminal entity. Thus, with the state deeply ensconced as a cast of mind, as an organizing premise, the initial—indeed, the only—response to the collapse of states due to war, internal strife, or other calamities is to rebuild them. No matter if a state is teetering on extinction, it is viewed as worth propping up rather than permitting the disorder that might result if its various subgroups go their own way.

Examples of the state-preserving orientations abound. One was evident in NATO's aspiration to prevent Serbs from leaving Kosovo and thereby maintaining a semblance of multiculturality. Another is discernible in the effort to prevent the breakup of Macedonia. Still another occurred at the end of the Gulf War in 1991: it was terminated out of fear that Iraq would break into factions and create an intolerable instability in the region. Rarely do voices get heard that say, in effect, "Okay, let the fragmenting forces lead to partition. Why try to force the two highly antagonistic groups to live together?"[6]

The state-preserving habit opposes partition and favors forcing antagonistic groups to remain together on the grounds that a rebuilt society and state will lead to degrees of stability and progress such that the antagonisms and hatreds will give way as conditions improve, as if hatred derives from rational calculations as to what is in the best interest of those who hate. To be sure, if the resources are available, the material destruction

[6] For an exception in this regard, see John J. Mearsheimer and Steven Van Evera, "Redraw the Map, Stop the Killing," *New York Times*, April 19, 1999, p. A23.

accompanying war can be cleared away and roads, bridges, homes, and factories rebuilt. But the logic of hatred is not readily amenable to alteration by the advent of new infrastructures. Nor is it necessarily susceptible to reduction by the presence of outsiders who can keep hateful enemies from acting out their animosities. It may be as much wishful thinking as sound analysis to presume that a firm, humane, and prolonged external intervention can diminish hate. Richard Holbrooke, an experienced practitioner on the Yugoslav scene, may well have been farfetched when he asserted, "I believe firmly and have stated repeatedly in public and private that Albanians and Serbs will not be able to live together in peace in Kosovo until they have had a period of time with international security forces to keep them from tearing each other to pieces."[7]

Another indicator of the strength of the state as a deeply entrenched habit is the recurring spectacle of many subgroups around the world pressing for the establishment of states of their own. It would seem that the diverse pressures for statehood validate the state as the terminal entity. Even as leaders of established states welcome these validations of their basic premises, moreover, so do they often seek to preserve their interstate system by resisting any pressures that might lead to the evolution of new types of terminal entities. Consequently, when an internal war ravages a society and leads to a collapse of its state, the unquestioned impulse in the halls of government everywhere is to "rebuild" the state. Fragmentation along ethnic, economic, political, and cultural lines is considered such a dire threat to global stability that rebuilding the state is, to repeat, considered preferable to letting the fragmenting dynamics unfold in whatever ways history may dictate. It is as if the poverty, pain, and violence that accompany the rebuilding process are but temporary conditions and bound to be less costly than the price of not undertaking the effort to rebuild.

Of course, permitting fragmentation to unfold through partition is no guarantee that enmities can be consigned to the dustbins of history. Much depends on the conditions under which partition occurs. If it is forced, the enmities endure but become international in scope, as happened subsequent to the partition of India and Pakistan and as continues to mark the history of Palestine and Israel.[8] If it is voluntary, enmities can

---

[7] Philip Shenon, "Holbrooke Defends Dealings with Milosevic but Admits Administration Errors," *New York Times*, June 25, 1999, p. A13.

[8] A measure of the depth of systemic hatred in the Palestinian-Israeli situation is provided by this observation of Ibrahim Titi, whose son, a suicide bomber, blew himself up near an ice cream parlor and killed and wounded several Israelis: "I would hope my son would be a nuclear bomb, not a normal bomb, to destroy everything. If we are not able to live, we don't want others [the Israelis] to live. We can either live together or die together." Mo-

decline, as appears to have occurred with partition of the Czechs and Slovaks. If it is neither forced nor voluntary, as is the case of Serbs leaving Kosovo out of fear of vengeance, it seems likely that a decline in violence will follow even though the enmities are unlikely to diminish as the hatreds that initiated the split continue to be passed from generation to generation. There are certain circumstances, in other words, where permitting fragmenting dynamics to unfold may result in more rather than less stability.

Paradoxically, aspirations to statehood and state-preserving habits persist undaunted in the face of a growing controversy among thoughtful observers over the future of the state. On the one hand, as suggested in previous chapters, a growing consensus can be discerned that posits states as progressively losing more than a little control over their well-being both at home and abroad. Some analysts regard the diminution of control as a "retreat,"[9] others argue that the range of its competencies has been narrowed substantially,[10] and still others go so far as to foresee its imminent demise.[11] On the other hand, dissenting voices call for retrieving the state as an analytic focus,[12] and some even contend that the state is stronger than ever.[13] This paradox is less perplexing, however, when it is appreciated that the statehood and state-preserving habits are embedded in the orientations of politicians, activists, and mass publics, whereas the conceptual controversy has ensued for some time among academics and attentive publics, with more than a few also locked into the states-are-forever habit.[14]

If one presumes, as I do, that, while established states are not about to depart from the global stage, their capacities are becoming weaker, the tasks of rebuilding war-torn states are rendered all the more difficult. Troubling questions arise: If even the most historically successful states have become less able to frame goals, move toward them, resolve internal

hammed Daraghmeh, "A Palestinian Father's Wish," *National Post* [Canada], May 29, 2002.

[9] Susan Strange, *The Retreat of the State: The Diffusion of Power in the World Economy* (Cambridge: Cambridge University Press, 1996). See also J. C. Scott, *Seeing Like a State: How Certain Schemes to Improve the Human Condition Have Failed* (New Haven, Conn.: Yale University Press, 1998).

[10] James N. Rosenau, *Along the Domestic-Foreign Frontier: Exploring Governance in a Turbulent World* (Cambridge: Cambridge University Press, 1997).

[11] Kenichi Ohmae, *The End of the Nation-State* (New York: Free Press, 1995).

[12] Peter B. Evans, Dietrich Rueschemeyer, and Theda Skocpol (eds.), *Bringing the State Back In* (Cambridge: Cambridge University Press, 1985).

[13] See, for example, G. John Ikenberry, "The Myth of Post–Cold War Chaos," *Foreign Affairs*, Vol. 75 (May/June 1996), pp. 79–91.

[14] P. Boniface, "The Proliferation of States," *Washington Quarterly*, Vol. 21 (summer 1998), pp. 111–27.

conflicts, or otherwise address their problems, if proliferating organizations, increasingly skilled citizens, and highly mobile populations undermine the capacity of states to control the movement of goods, ideas, drugs, and crime across their borders and render them ever-more paralyzed and mired in stalemate, how can a rebuilt state be expected to bring systemic hatreds under control? How can a political system that has emerged from a long, dark night in which systemic hatred prevailed ever see a daylight in which sufficient civility prevails among the previously antagonistic segments of the population for stable and effective governance to prevail?

I am tempted to assert that it cannot be done. At the very best a very uneasy truce between the hostile groups might be established, but it would constantly teeter on the edge of collapse, with any of a multitude of minor incidents being capable of pushing it over the precipice. Sure, peacekeepers from elsewhere could sustain the truce, but sustaining the truce is a far cry from moving toward stable and effective governance. And sure, across time there might be some education and healing that would lessen the intensity of the hatreds, but that would require several generations of peacekeepers if this chapter's epigraph is treated as a metaphor for the problem.

But, some might argue, if a gifted leader who grasped the depth and breadth of the systemic hatred and had the personality not to be drawn into its maelstrom led the rebuilding process, perhaps steady progress toward more humane governance could be realized. After all, it could be reasoned, if Hitler and Milosevic had unique and charismatic qualities that enabled them to exploit historical memories and turn them into widespread and virulent prejudice, surely it ought to be possible for leaders with comparable qualities but decent values to undermine systemic hatreds and turn them in constructive directions. An example here might be Nelson Mandela, who both understood what his country needed to begin to heal and had the patience and wisdom to rise above the hatred system.

While competent leadership may be a necessary prerequisite to rebuilding a war-torn society and polity, it is certainly not a sufficient basis for doing so. An individual leader, a Mandela, can initiate the rebuilding process, and he or she may even succeed in readying able successors for the task, but the process is a long-term one. It is bound to extend beyond the life span of a single individual and the following generation of leaders. Besides, while Mandela offers a compelling case for the notion that leadership can help bridge the hatred gap that separates groups, the combination of his long prison term and his conciliatory personality accorded him a degree of informal authority that is not likely to be emulated. Furthermore, it is probably premature to conclude that systemic hatred is nearing an end in South Africa. There is already evidence that the post-Mandela years are marked by tumult and extensive hostilities across racial lines.

Even more important, leadership requires followership, a readiness of publics to go along with, rather than resist or divert, the directives of their leaders. No single leader, not even a Mandela, can substantially diminish systemic hatreds unless followers are open to accepting his or her espoused values. At best, then, gifted leadership is only one dimension of the process whereby the rebuilding of war-torn societies moves steadily forward.

But if states are too weak and gifted leaders too limited and scarce to meet the challenge of systemic hatred, what mechanisms of governance, if any, can be employed to diminish its virulent consequences and eventually bring it to an end? Is systemic hatred a problem without a solution?

This last question may be as deceptive as it is depressing. It is depressing because, as indicated previously, it would not be difficult to make a case for answering it in the affirmative; but the question is also deceptive because the human spirit is such that an affirmative answer would in any event be ignored. Even granting the pervasive weaknesses of the modern state and the pervasive scarcity of creative leadership, the evolving norm that posits systemic hatred as everyone's problem has spread sufficiently for organizations, publics, and people around the world to seek additional, if not alternative, mechanisms for making a dent in those situations where societies have been torn apart and seek to move beyond the antagonisms that tore them up. In effect, it is no longer morally or politically acceptable for the world to stand aside while systemic hatred exacts its horrendous toll. The problem may never go away, but neither will efforts to cope with and diminish it.

My own estimate is that such situations will continue to be addressed in the future, and many may be avoided, contained, and/or eliminated through a process whereby the loci of authority undergo continuous dispersion. Some might be inclined to view the continuous devolution of authority away from states as amounting to the emergence of civil society. But this concept carries so much baggage and is the focus of so many different formulations that I prefer to speak of the world stage as simply becoming ever more dense with collective actors, with SOAs. As indicated in chapter 13, the population of SOAs includes a wide range of collectivities that have little in common other than being repositories of authority that evoke compliance on the part of others.

It follows that as authority gets decentralized across the world, so may the density of the global stage undermine the foundations of systemic hatred. Put differently, the dynamics of fragmegration may be leading to the negotiation of new identities that are filling the social and psychological spaces vacated by weakening states and fragmenting societies, spaces that may have the capacity to siphon off the fears and memories that serve as the sustenance of systemic hatred. Indeed, one new SOA, the truth commission in South Africa, was designed precisely to enable that torn society to confront the consequences of deep and pervasive hatred and, in so doing, to move on to identities where animosities are less intense.

In sum, the probability of systemic hatreds ever being superseded by systemic decencies is slim. Still, the will to employ mechanisms that may moderate the intensity of systemic hatreds is strong, and the ingenuity needed to develop the mechanisms is not in short supply. Efforts to contain systemic hatreds will not lack for institutional and coordinated ways of undermining their perpetuation. Young Egzon's grandchildren may be a little less ready to kill.

CHAPTER SIXTEEN

Corruption as a Global Issue

Corruption = Monopoly + Discretion − Accountability[1]

LIKE HUMAN RIGHTS violations, incidents of corruption can activate and enrage large numbers of ordinary people in all the local and global worlds; even the Tuned-Out Passives can be stirred whenever it seems clear that government officials are on the take and putting corrupt practices ahead of their official responsibilities. Indeed, few would quarrel with the proposition that issues of corruption are a prime source of the long-term, worldwide trend toward public distrust of political institutions.

Corruption issues are also similar to those of human rights in the sense that both are rooted in orientations at the micro level. Just as bodily harm and individual degradation are so personal as to accord universality to human rights issues, so are people everywhere familiar with, and some often participate firsthand in, the illegal purchase of influence. While they may not be familiar with the equation in this chapter's epigraph, people know that the scale and level of corruption range widely, from small bribes of low-level bureaucrats (petty corruption) to distortions of large procurements and major policy decisions (grand corruption).[2] Many individuals even engage in petty bribery and defend their participation in such transactions as necessary to greasing the wheels of organizations and evoking desired outcomes. One does not have to be an activist or live in a global world to understand that money gets exchanged for favors on the part of public officials at all levels of government.[3]

Parts of this chapter are adapted from an article coauthored with Hongying Wang entitled "Transparency International and Corruption as an Issue of Global Governance," *Global Governance*, Vol. 7 (January 2001), pp. 25–49.

[1] Robert Klitgaard, *Controlling Corruption* (Berkeley and Los Angeles: University of California Press, 1988), p. 75.

[2] Kimberly Ann Elliott, "Corruption as an International Policy Problem: Overview and Recommendations," in Kimberly Ann Elliott (ed.), *Corruption and the Global Economy* (Washington, D.C.: Institute for International Economics, 1997), pp. 178–79.

[3] Most analysts accept this widespread understanding and make no attempt to elaborate the various dimensions of corruption. While some conceive of corrupt transactions occurring between corrupters and corruptees in the private sector, most emphasize that corruption involves public officials. A few observers, on the other hand, undertake extensive definitional efforts. See Michael Johnston, "The Search for Definitions: The Vitality of Politics

On the other hand, there are striking differences between human rights and corruption issues. Aside from the fact that human rights issues are widely seen as founded on worthy values while those involving corruption are widely considered as expressive of despicable values, the former are the focus of continuing activities on the part of numerous NGOs and advocacy groups, whereas the latter tend not to generate widespread organized and continuous activities. Rather, while many people and activists in the local and global worlds are aware of corruption, and while there are isolated incidents of local organizations forming to contest corrupt practices,[4] the participation of ordinary individuals within the various local and global worlds in popular outbursts against corrupt practices tends to be sporadic and associated with other grievances that people have against their leaderships. The uprisings that led to the ouster of Marcos and Estrada in the Philippines and Suharto and Wahid in Indonesia, for example, amounted to mass upheavals based on a wide diversity of complaints, of which grand corruption was a major but hardly the only grievance. Much the same can be said about pervasive anticorruption uprisings in China.

Other distinctive features of corruption as an issue area help explain why it does not galvanize sustained organizational activities. First, corruption is *covert*. Parties to bribery at both the giving and the receiving end extend themselves to keep their transactions hidden from others. That such practices exist may be widely surmised or known, but the specific acts of corruption are founded on secrecy and vehemently denied when evidence of them is alleged. Second, corruption often involves *collusion* between the relevant parties. Unlike instances of human rights abuse and environmental pollution, wherein one side is victimized, the practices of corruption benefit all concerned. All those involved have reasons to maintain their collusion and keep it secret. Third, corrupt practices are committed by widely *dispersed* actors rather than by large collectivities. Unlike the targets of those who rail against violations of human

---

and the Issue of Corruption," *International Social Science Journal*, Vol. 149 (September 1996), pp. 321–36. An example of an extensive definitional effort is provided by one analyst who sought to design a "culturally neutral" definition: "corruption is any attempt, whether successful or not, to persuade someone in a position of responsibility to make a decision or recommendation on any grounds other than the intrinsic merits of the case with a view to the advantage or advancement of him- or herself or another person or group to which he or she is linked through personal commitment, obligation, or employment, or individual, professional, or group loyalty." A. W. Cragg, "Business, Globalization, and the Logic and Ethics of Corruption," *International Journal*, Vol. 53 (autumn 1998), p. 651.

[4] Thailand and Youngstown, Ohio, are examples of such developments at the local level. See Michael Vatikiotis, "Power to the People," *Far Eastern Economic Review*, July 9, 1998), pp. 18–19; and Francis X. Clines, "Field Trip to Sicily Helps Youngstown Face Latest Indictment," *New York Times*, May 12, 2001, p. A8.

rights or the environment, those who seek to expose corruption must focus on particular individuals whose dispersion within a system is never clear or concentrated. In effect, corrupt practices tend to be proximate concerns and not distant proximities, thereby limiting the scope of any effort to mobilize opposition to them. Fourth, corruption is a relatively recent entry high on the global agenda. "'A half decade ago, one didn't speak of corruption—it was considered offensive.' People are talking now"[5]

Given these characteristics, it is not surprising that corruption issues are not conducive to forming a social movement, which involves mass mobilization and sustained mass participation, or to a transnational activist network based on linkages with grassroot organizations. The success of activist networks is based on campaigns with "short and clear" causal chains that galvanize support by images of bodily damage, especially to the vulnerable members of the population.[6] But corruption issues do not lend themselves to such campaigns. The covert nature of corruption, the collusion involved, and the absence of any obvious and sensational victims make it hard to demonstrate the causal chains of corruption and to pinpoint its consequences. Thus it is extremely difficult to mobilize mass support to focus solely on the fight against corruption. While people are aware and resentful of corruption, they are not readily responsive to calls for collective action against it.

Furthermore, the covert and dispersed nature of corruption exacerbates the difficulty of measuring any progress in its reduction. It is thus hard for potential participants to know that they have made a difference; and yet this knowledge is the lifeblood of any social movement. In the corruption issue area the logic of large-scale collective action breaks down.

Accordingly, corruption is essentially a micro issue area, perhaps more so than any other on the global agenda. Its consequences are macro in scope, and some macro collectivities seek to reduce its impact, but the actions that sustain corrupt practices are widely dispersed at the micro level, which is a primary reason they are so difficult to contest. As will be seen, with the exception of upheavals such as those in the Philippines and Indonesia, only through the involvement of elites among the Affirmative and Territorial Globals in the press, political parties, international organizations, and one worldwide NGO do corrupt practices get framed and addressed as micro-macro interactions.

---

[5] Tim Weiner, "U.N. Takes Swing at Crooks Who Steal Aid for the Poor," *New York Times*, May 19, 2002, p. A10. The quotation is by Ruth Jacoby, the Swedish ambassador to the United Nations.

[6] Margaret E. Keck and Kathryn Sikkink, *Activists beyond Borders: Advocacy Networks in International Politics* (Ithaca, N.Y.: Cornell University Press, 1997), pp. 27, 204–5.

The Corruption Eruption

Of course, neither corruption nor efforts to contest it are new. Yet, while corruption issues do not lend themselves readily to grassroot activities, in recent years they have undergone a dramatic ascendance on the global agenda—what one analyst calls the "corruption eruption."[7] Consider, for example, its growing salience suggested by the results of a Lexis-Nexis keyword search of the *New York Times Index* for the average number of annual entries on corruption during each of the six-year periods starting in 1969. These data are presented in table 16.1, where it is evident that sensitivities to corruption issues have indeed peaked in the most recent period.[8]

Growing media attention reflects and reinforces increased public awareness of the corruption issue and appears to foster a growing consensus against corruption.[9] People in the local and global worlds, as well as all but the Circumstantial Passives in the private worlds, are not only more aware of corruption issues but also more judgmental with respect to it. With few exceptions, these judgments are all in the direction of viewing corruption as detrimental, "as one of the world's greatest scourges."[10]

The evidence is compelling. In the first place, as noted, the long-standing taboo precluding public criticism of corruption has begun to crumble. A recent example is the enormous success of a Kiswahili song that denounces corruption in Kenya.[11] Another is the scandal—and its worldwide repercussions—involving the International Olympic Committee decision to grant the 2002 winter games to Salt Lake City. This scandal is especially indicative of the pervasive preoccupation with corruption inasmuch as such practices involving the IOC had not previously captured worldwide attention even though they were not new. Indeed, the IOC had been virtually a world government unto itself, with authority and autonomy that had not been seriously challenged.[12] Still another recent

[7] Moisés Naím, "The Corruption Eruption," *Brown Journal of World Affairs*, Vol. 2 (summer 1995), pp. 245–61.

[8] For comparable data and findings based on the *Financial Times* and the *Economist*, see Patrick Glynn, Stephen J. Kobrin, and Moisés Naím, "The Globalization of Corruption," in Elliott (ed.), *Corruption and the Global Economy*, p. 21.

[9] Media and public agendas are highly correlated, with the former tending to shape the latter. Cf. John W. Dearing and Everett M. Rogers, *Agenda Setting* (Thousand Oaks, Calif.: Sage, 1996), Chap. 1.

[10] Fred Hiatt, "Corruption Is Finally Getting the Attention It Needs," *International Herald Tribune*, February 25, 1999, p. 9.

[11] Marc Lacey, "A Song about Corruption Takes Kenya by Storm," *New York Times*, September 6, 2001, p. A4.

[12] Volker Rittberger and Henning Boekle, "The International Olympic Committee: A World Government of Sport?" *Law and State*, Vol. 56 (1997), pp. 24–53.

TABLE 16.1.
Average Annual Entries on Corruption in the *New York Times Index* for Recent Six-Year Periods

Years	Index Entries
1969–1974	357
1975–1980	245
1981–1986	302
1987–1992	402
1993–1998	578

scandal resulted in the mass resignation of the commissioners of the European Commission. This was precipitated by a highly critical self-study by the commission in response to widespread criticism, which was subsequently interpreted as evidence of growing tendencies toward democracy in the European Union.[13]

Second, the normative changes that have brought corruption near the top of the global agenda are also evident in the politics of many countries. Heightened public awareness and abhorrence in the various local and global worlds have served to politicize corruption. In a growing number of countries, political oppositions have used corruption issues to attack the sitting government. And both Affirmative and Resistant Locals have been responsive:

> In less than a half-decade, the worldwide backlash against corruption has swept like a firestorm across the global political landscape. Governments have fallen. Longtime ruling parties have been hounded from office. Presidents, prime ministers, parliamentarians, and once mighty corporate chieftains have been grilled by prosecutors and herded into the docket. Italy, France, Japan, South Korea, India, Mexico, Colombia, Brazil, South Africa: no region, and hardly any country, has been immune.[14]

Third, at the international level, clusters of Specialized Globals have formed around the issue to sustain the normative tide against corruption in a variety of ways. The International Anti-Corruption Conference (IACC), first convened in 1983, was originally a forum for cooperation in international law enforcement. It has subsequently become increasingly focused on fighting corruption. In 1997 the eighth conference, composed of "over 1,000 citizens drawn from 93 countries," convened in Peru and adopted the Lima Declaration, a document that consisted of more than

---

[13] See E. J. Dionne Jr., "Score One for the Media Snoops," *Washington Post*, March 26, 1999, p. A33, and Marie Geoghegan-Quinn, "Discredited Musketeers Were Right to Fall on Their Swords," *Irish Times*, March 20, 1999, p. 14.

[14] Glynn, Kobrin, and Naím, "The Globalization of Corruption," p. 7.

forty clauses specifying actions to be taken. The declaration was billed as representing "the global community's first attempt to articulate a broad strategy for the combating of corruption, at the international and national levels, in all sectors and with the participation and cooperation of all walks of life."[15] In 1999 the ninth conference convened in Durban, South Africa, with sixteen hundred participants from 135 countries. The delegates declared corruption to be "one of the most debilitating legacies of the twentieth century" and reiterated their commitment to fighting it.[16]

The momentum—also designated as "a gathering posse"[17]—favoring efforts to curb corruption on a global scale has also swept through international economic organizations. While the World Bank, the International Monetary Fund, and the World Trade Organization used to be silent on the issue, they, too, have lately undergone change. James Wolfensohn, president of the World Bank, has made prevention of corruption a cornerstone of his speeches at each year's annual meeting.[18] In 1997 the World Bank produced an anticorruption initiative, which laid down new guidelines for granting of project funds, including spot audits on projects.[19] Two years later Wolfensohn reiterated his commitment to anticorruption policies in a memorandum to the board, management, and staff of the World Bank Group:

> While building an effective government framework is difficult, it will become impossible if there is corruption, which is the single most corrosive aspect of development and must be fought systematically at all levels. Particularly it must start with a vigorous commitment from the leadership to fight corruption on all levels, with initiative both to prevent it from happening and a system for finding and punishing wrongdoers where corruption exists. The lead must come from the top and efforts must be persistent and unyielding.[20]

Likewise, Michel Camdessus, former chairman of the IMF, has been outspoken on the corruption issue.[21] The WTO has launched talks on

[15] "The Lima Declaration," reproduced in *Combating Corruption: Are Lasting Solutions Emerging?* (Berlin: Transparency International, Annual Report 1998), pp. 163–68.

[16] Reported on Transparency International's official Web site at http://www.transparency.de/iacc/durban—commitment.html.

[17] John Brademas and Fritz Heimann, "Tackling International Corruption: No Longer Taboo," *Foreign Affairs*, Vol. 77 (September/October 1998), p. 20.

[18] Ibid.

[19] However, Wolfensohn was careful to point out that "it would be quite wrong of us to come in like the police." See Trevor Royle, "Corruption Pays Its Way throughout the World," *Scotland on Sunday*, May 4, 1997, p. 21.

[20] James D. Wolfensohn, "A Proposal for a Comprehensive Development Framework (A Discussion Draft)" (unpublished manuscript, January 21, 1999), p. 10.

[21] Lee Siew Hua, "Who's Who in the Graft League," *Straits Times* (Singapore), September 24, 1998, p. 12.

354 • Chapter Sixteen

proposals to combat bribery by increasing transparency in public procurement.[22] The United Nations General Assembly, the European Union, the G-7, the Inter-American, European, and Asian Development Banks, the Asia-Pacific Economic Cooperation Forum, the Global Coalition for Africa, the Organization of American States, the International Chamber of Commerce, the World Economic Forum, the Open Society Institute, and the Interparliamentary Union have similarly contributed to the accelerating momentum. In 1997 the Organization for Economic Cooperation and Development (OECD) adopted an antibribery convention that was signed by its twenty-nine member countries and five other countries. The convention entered into force in February 1999. As of that date, nineteen nations had ratified the antibribery pact.

In short, in the last several years corruption issues have increasingly become distant proximities and thus the basis of a new global issue area, characterized by surging micro-macro interactions on the part of Affirmative as well as Resistant Globals that have heightened public awareness and fostered the emergence of worldwide norms. Several structural changes are likely to have contributed to this development and thus help to explain how some issues manage to become at least rudimentary global norms and climb high on the world's agenda.

Structural Changes

One plausible explanation for the rise of corruption as a global issue is that corrupt practices have actually increased, thus provoking a greater sensitivity to them and a greater readiness to condemn them. Of course, given the covert nature of corruption, there is no easy and reliable way to determine if this is indeed the case. It is almost impossible to track petty corruption that "greases" the working of bureaucracies (and is measured, say, by transactions of a few hundred dollars).[23] On the other hand, according to anecdotal evidence, "grand" corruption (measured on the scale of thousands and millions of dollars) appears to have increased.[24]

The World Bank's chief procurement officer, for instance, contends that "economic development brings more money into play," and, as a

[22] John Mason and Guy de Jonquieres, "Goodbye Mr. 10%," *Financial Times*, July 22, 1997, p. 15.

[23] Some even argue that petty corruption is not corruption at all: such " '. . . payments, which are made to get people to do or speed up what they should be doing anyway,' get you 'what you're legally entitled to, not subverting the integrity of decision-making at somebody else's expense.' Even the US Foreign Corrupt Practices Act (1997) permits these facilitating payments." The subquotation is from Jeremy Pope, in Anita van de Vliet, "Corruption Check," *Corporate Location*, November/December 1995, p. 22.

[24] Susan Rose-Ackerman, "Democracy and 'Grand' Corruption," *International Social Science Journal*, Vol. 48 (September 1996), pp. 365–80.

consequence, "corruption has been going up geometrically over the past 10 years."[25] The bank estimates that at least $80 billion is paid as bribes in international business transactions every year (compared with legitimate investments of about $180 billion).[26] The U.S. Security and Exchange Commission's enforcement director asserts that, despite his country's Foreign Corrupt Practices Act (FCPA), bribery by U.S. firms of foreign officials "may be surfacing as a significant problem for the first time in 20 years."[27] One observer notes that, "though 'commissions' or kickbacks of 5 percent used to be common in international business, requests for payments of 10–15 percent of contract value are on the rise, with some recent reports of demands for commissions of 20–30 percent."[28] Another cites businesspeople as reporting that the going rate for bribes has soared, such that "'Mr. 10 percent' has ballooned into 'Mr. 30 percent' in many countries."[29] Similarly, "Italian business people, imprisoned for corruption in the clean-up that started in Milan in 1992, blamed extortion by politicians for the error of their ways and pointed out that an average 7 percent kickback fee in the '70s had grown to 20 percent in the greedy '90s."[30]

In short, corruption appears to have become systemic. More than a few elites among the Affirmative and Specialized Globals seem to consider it a justifiable and appropriate proclivity even as counterparts in the same worlds contest their activities.

Another reason why corrupt practices may be increasing can be found in the processes of economic reform in countries such as China and Russia, which used to have planned economies but have now turned to mixed economies. Under these circumstances the combination of market mechanisms and government intervention has provided unprecedented incentives and opportunities for corruption.[31] Recent economic booms in

[25] Michelle Celarier, "The Search for the Smoking Gun," *Euromoney*, September 1996, p. 50.

[26] Ben Richardson, "SAR Wanted to Act on Corrupt Behavior of Businessmen Abroad," *South China Morning Post*, January 31, 1999, p. 1.

[27] William McLucas, quoted in Neil Roland, "U.S. Firm May Feel Need to Bribe Overseas" (Commission Appeal, March 6, 1997), p. B4.

[28] Frank Vogl, "Laying Corruption to Rest," *Economic Reform Today*, (July 18, 1993).

[29] This remark was made by Michael Wiehen of TI and quoted in John Mason and Guy de Jonquie'res, "Goodbye, Mr. 10%," p. 15.

[30] van de Vliet, "Corruption Check," p. 22.

[31] On China, for example, see Julia Kwong, *The Political Economy of Corruption in China* (Armonk, N.Y.: M. E. Sharpe, 1997); Barbara N. Sands, "Decentralizing an Economy: The Role of Bureaucratic corruption in China's Economic Reforms," *Public Choice*, Vol. 65 (April 1990), pp. 85–91; and Melanie Manion, "Corruption by Design: Bribery in Chinese Enterprise Licensing," *Journal of Law, Economics, and Organization*, Vol. 12 (April 1996), pp. 167–95. On Russia, see Britta Hillstrom, "Effects of Corruption on Democracies in

other emerging markets, such as those of Mexico, Brazil, Indonesia, and Malaysia, have occurred without adequate regulation and thus also fostered increasing business-related corruption.[32] In the words of a Thai observer,

> When you start to change the formal structure of government—from an authoritarian system to elections, parties and parliaments—many of the old institutions of centralized power, and many of the accompanying attitudes, remain unchanged. The new elected politicians start out by opposing the old corrupt, bad habits of dictators and all-powerful bureaucrats. But before too long, they discover the profits to be made from collusion. All of our big corruption scandals of the last few years have had one factor in common: cooperation between politicians and senior bureaucrats. It's a very powerful combination.[33]

Other sources of possible increases in corruption derive from the nature of economic globalization. As growing numbers of Affirmative Globals with companies from northern industrialized countries expand their operations into developing countries, where the monitoring and regulative framework tends to be less developed, they are subjected to greater temptations to engage in practices not allowed at home. The digitalization of international finance and the proliferation of strategic business alliances accompanying globalization may also underlie corrupt practices: it is technically much easier than ever before to launder and dispose of the gains harvested through such practices.[34]

The changes in international political structures also may have contributed to the newly gained salience of corruption on the global agenda. In the first place, the collapse of the Soviet Union and the emergence of democratic institutions have voided the strategic rationale for the United States and other Western nations to back corrupt governments. Govern-

---

Asia, Latin America, and Russia," *Woodrow Wilson Center Report*, Vol. 8 (December 1996), pp. 3–40; Federico Varese, "The Transition to the Market and Corruption in Post-Soviet Russia," *Political Studies*, Vol. 45, No. 3 (1997), pp. 579–96; and Steven Lee Solnick, *Stealing the State: Control and Collapse in Soviet Institutions* (Cambridge, Mass.: Harvard University Press, 1998).

[32] The recent economic growth in Malaysia has its flip side. The boom has necessitated an increase in administration, which beefs up the amount of corruption as well as its scale. See Sharon Nelson, "Towards More Open Dealings," *New Straits Times*, May 1, 1997, p. 9. On Latin America, see Juigi Manzetti and Charles H. Blake, "Market Reforms and Corruption in Latin America: New Means for Old Ways," *Review of International Political Economy*, Vol. 3 (winter 1996), pp. 662–97.

[33] Pasuk Phongpaichit, "Corruption, Democracy and Civil Society" (speech presented at the International Conference on Corruption, Democracy and Development, Bangkok, September 18–19, 2000).

[34] Glynn, Kobrin, and Naím, "The Globalization of Corruption," p. 14.

ments in the north are more willing to challenge former allies in the developing world on grounds ranging from human rights to corruption.

Second, the failure of socialism has led to market capitalism on a global scale. Getting the state out of the economy seems to be the order of the day. The fight against corruption by reducing government discretion and enhancing the role of market competition is part of the zeitgeist of economic liberalization. International economic organizations, such as the World Bank and the IMF, used to tolerate corruption because they saw the state as agents of development, and state intervention in the economy inevitably led to corruption.[35] But with the advance of the private sector in economic development, international economic organizations are less hesitant to oppose corruption.

Finally, the rising tide of political liberalization and democratization means more and more media freedom in countries around the world. In this new and more tolerant political atmosphere, Affirmative and Resistant Globals in the press have been able to investigate and report on corruption with unprecedented freedom.

TRANSPARENCY INTERNATIONAL

But issues do not automatically rise to the top of the global agenda. Even though changes on the world scene may render issues conducive to elevation as core concerns, their ascendance and the formation of norms around them require agents to nurse them into being and then to sustain their salience. While the rise of the corruption issue can be attributed to the work of many actors—elites in the press, political parties, and international organizations, for example—one group of elites, composed mainly of Affirmative Globals, stands out as the prime, if not the only, transnational advocacy network that is solely dedicated to the fight against corruption, namely, Transparency International (TI), a transnational network founded in 1993. During TI's first eight years, the world witnessed a dramatic rise in the salience of corruption issues. While TI has not been the source of this change, it has been an important agent of the increased salience.[36]

[35] According to one model, industrial policy promotes both corruption and investment. Corruption is higher in countries pursuing active industrial policy. See Alberto Ades and Rafael Di Tella, "National Champions and Corruption: Some Unpleasant Interventionist Arithmetic," *Economic Journal*, Vol. 107, No. 443 (July 1997), pp. 1023–42. Studies show that in Indonesia bureaucrats have siphoned off one-third of the World Bank loans. Kastorius Sinaga, "WB Loans Graft Needs to Be Curbed," *Jakarta Post*, August 12, 1997, p. 4.

[36] For a firsthand assessment of TI, see Fredrik Galtung, "A Global Network to Curb Corruption: The Experience of Transparency International," in Ann M. Florini (ed.), *The*

Mission, Organization, and Activities

TI defines its mission succinctly: "To curb corruption by mobilizing a global coalition to promote and strengthen international and national integrity systems."[37] TI seeks to do so by encouraging governments to establish and implement effective laws, policies, and anticorruption programs. Its focus has been on increasing the transparency and accountability of government operations, especially government procurements, and changing the public's moral and ethical attitude. Lately it has also turned to research on petty corruption at the micro level, as well as to promoting reforms of substantive programs and government structures. These include measures that minimize the discretionary power of public officials, strengthen autonomous oversight mechanisms, reduce conflict of interests, and increase public supervision of the government.

Organizationally, TI consists of elites among the Affirmative Globals who manage an international secretariat in Berlin and an ever-expanding number of national chapters (either established or in formation)—from some fifty in 1995 to more than one hundred in 2000. The central governing body of TI is the board of directors, which is elected by representatives of the national chapters at the annual meeting. Members of the board include lawyers, consultants, business executives, and former government officials from a number of countries. TI also has an advisory council of prominent Affirmative Globals from different parts of the world.

Each component of TI plays an active role in accomplishing the mission of fighting corruption. The national chapters are composed of individuals who, in effect, have become Specialized Globals as they pledge to abide by and work for the principles of TI. Accredited by the board of directors and supported by the international secretariat, they engage in anticorruption activities in their respective home countries. A major part of their work is to raise public awareness of the problems posed by corruption. They inform the public on the scale and damage of corruption through survey research, workshops and conferences, educational programs, mass media, and the Internet, as well as newsletters and bulletins.

In addition, they try to influence the attitude and behavior of government officials and businesses at the center of corrupt practices. TI national chapters everywhere seek to engage governments and companies in the fight against corruption, but their emphasis varies. The national chapters in developing countries often focus on alerting governments to the costs of corruption for national economic development and on getting TI's principles of transparency and accountability incorporated into laws

---

Third Force: The Rise of Transnational Civil Society (Washington, D.C.: Carnegie Endowment for International Peace, 2000), pp. 17–47.

[37] "Mission Statement," in *Combating Corruption*, Report, p. 9.

and regulations. The national chapters in developed countries, on the other hand, concentrate on lobbying governments to endorse and ratify international agreements aimed at controlling corruption. They also try to persuade and assist companies to free themselves from corrupt business practices.

As part of TI's holistic approach to corruption, the national chapters also actively engage in building networks and coalitions. Although the national chapters are independent, are self-financed, and develop their own programs, they stay in close touch with one another. They often assist with the launching of national chapters in developing countries and provide the latter with information and expertise. Some also form regional chapters to enhance regional cooperation, and others enter alliances with churches and human rights organizations whose goals overlap those of TI.

Besides the national chapters, TI's board of directors, advisory council, and the international secretariat actively engage in the effort to promote transparency and to change public attitudes toward corruption. Members of the board of directors and advisory council lend their support to the national chapters by visiting their countries and participating in their events. In addition, they have been particularly effective in publicizing TI and its positions in a number of highly visible ways, including speaking at national and international forums, participating in media events, writing for journalistic as well as scholarly publications, and seeking dialogues with national and international leaders.

The international secretariat has been especially important as a center for the worldwide fight against corruption. First, it is a vital source of information and support for national and regional chapters. It sends delegations to help with the launching of national chapters. It provides national chapters with information and other types of assistance with their ongoing programs. Second, the international secretariat prepares and updates the TI Source Book, which is published in many languages and continuously updated with practical steps that can be followed to contest corruption. Third, the international secretariat maintains a database that serves as an international information source on corruption, good governance, and economic crimes. The database contains about fifteen thousand documents, ranging from short newspaper pieces to voluminous reports. Providing such information is a major component of TI's strategy to change attitudes toward corruption. Finally, the international secretariat promotes publicity for TI by publishing annual reports, newsletters, and other publications, as well as by interacting with the media. It also maintains contact with Local Affirmatives in the general public by answering inquiries and maintaining a Web site.

Perhaps the most visible undertaking of TI is its Corruption Perception Index (CPI), issued annually since 1995, which ranks countries in terms of their perceived degree of corruption. As TI is careful to point out, the CPI is not an objective measurement of corruption in different countries.[38] Rather, it is based on a number of respected polls and is, in effect, a poll of polls. It reflects the perceptions and opinions of Affirmative Globals working with multinational corporations and international institutions.[39]

But TI's use of research methodologies is not confined to the CPI. On the grounds that two parties are necessary to any act of corruption, and in response to criticism of the one-sided bias of the Corruption Perception Index by developing societies—which have routinely been perceived as the most corrupt—TI initiated a "bribe payers' index" in 1999, which ranks countries in terms of the perceived extent to which their companies are likely to pay or offer bribes in order to win or retain contracts. In the 2002 survey, which listed twenty-one industrial countries and was based on interviews with 839 business experts, Russian and Chinese companies were seen as the most flagrant bribe payers, with Taiwan and South Korea not far behind. In TI's view, however, the "more surprising" finding "was the perception that anti-bribery laws in the United States and other industrial nations were apparently not deterring bribe-payers from multinational companies based in the West and Japan."[40]

In addition, TI also undertakes surveys at the micro level. The Kenya Urban Bribery Index, for example, "represents the first attempt in Africa to quantify the extent of bribery in a country that is synonymous with systematic graft." Based on twelve hundred interviews conducted in Kenya's urban areas, the survey found that "the cost of rampant petty corruption was 'many times bigger' than that of top-level scams." Using rankings based on six criteria, it also found that "the police emerged as the most corrupt institution in Kenya, followed by the ministry of public works and the immigration department. Foreign embassies and international institutions also came high in the league, in terms of size of bribe requested."[41]

Strategies

Thus far TI appears to have been very successful. Jeremy Pope, its executive director, recalls that "in the early 1990s, the topic of corruption was

---

[38] See, for example, Tan Sai Siong, "Corruption Perceptions Index Should Carry Health Warning," *Strait Times* (Singapore), June 8, 1996.

[39] For a discussion of the sources and interpretation of data presented in CPI, see Transparency International, *The Fight against Corruption*, Chap. 6.

[40] Barbara Crossette, "Russia and China Called Top Business Bribers," *New York Times*, May 17, 2002, p. A8.

[41] Mark Turner, "Bribery Drives Up the Cost of Living in Kenya," *Financial Times*, January 19–20, 2002, p. 7.

simply not addressed in polite company."[42] In 1998, TI's chairman, Peter Eigen, took note of the worldwide momentum toward greater sensitivity to corruption issues by stressing TI's growth: "If today our movement seems at times to be just a trifle breathless, it is because we have traveled such a long distance in such a short space of time. . . . Quite suddenly, from being a very small office we have acquired a critical mass."[43] TI's budgetary income increased from $582,441.39 in 1995 to $1,114,834.26 in 1997.[44] TI's effectiveness owes much to its various strategies.

1. FRAMING THE ISSUE

TI has been careful in its framing of the corruption issue. First, it relates the fight against corruption to a number of issues already well established on the global agenda. TI's official mission statement portrays opposition to corruption as humanitarian, democratic, ethical, and practical.[45] In the words of a member of TI-USA, "We are talking about more than scandals. . . . Corruption has become a crosscutting issue with the potential to dissipate the dividends of the end of the Cold War: (1) the consolidation of democracy, political stability and respect for the rule of law; (2) effective development; and (3) the expansion of open, competitive markets."[46] Similarly, according to another active member in the TI circle, corruption "is no longer seen as principally an ethical issue, subject to the vagaries of cultural relativism. Increasingly, it has become an economic development issue, a competitiveness issue and an issue of political accountability."[47]

TI varies its emphasis on different aspects of corruption to maximize support from different actors. It sought start-up funding from the World Bank by arguing that the bank should address the corruption problem because it was a *fiduciary* issue (the bank has a duty to its funders to ensure proper application of loan moneys). It is also an *economic* issue (corruption distorts project selection and decisions thereafter) and a *legal* issue (if the World Bank lends money knowing it was being stolen by the borrowing government, then debts to the successor to that government

---

[42] Personal correspondence, April 14, 1999.

[43] Peter Eigen, "Sustainable Strategies in Fighting Corruption: An Overview," in *Combating Corruption*, pp. 12, 15.

[44] These figures can be found in *Combating Corruption*, pp. 118–19.

[45] TI home page, www.transparency.de.

[46] Nancy Zucker Boswell, "Building Effective Anticorruption Regimes: A Public-Private Sector Partnership," *Proceedings of the Annual Meeting of the American Society of International Law* (Washington, D.C.: April 10, 1997), pp. 151–72.

[47] R. Michael Gadbaw, "International Anticorruption Initiatives: Today's Fad or Tomorrow's New World?" *Proceedings of the Annual Meeting of the American Society of International Law* (Washington, D.C., April 10, 1997), pp. 151–72.

may be void for illegality).[48] Framing the issue of corruption this way rather than simply as an ethical and moral problem makes it easier to generate support from international economic organizations.

In its dialogues with state governments, TI stresses the fight against corruption as part of economic development. After the Cold War, in the absence of pressing security threats, governments everywhere are more dependent than ever on delivering economic growth to shore up their legitimacy. Citing scholarly research on the subject, TI argues that corruption is a major stumbling block for economic development in developing countries.[49] The success of TI and others in framing corruption as a development issue is remarkable, given that not long ago many economists argued that corruption could actually facilitate economic development.[50] It was reasoned that corrupt practices promote the provision of public goods by reducing delays and avoiding burdensome regulations and taxes.[51] They offer incentives for bureaucrats to accede to market-oriented reforms.[52] They may improve allocative efficiency.[53] Corruption not only serves the interest of the agents but may be beneficial to the principal as well.[54] In recent years, however, as the scale of corruption increased everywhere in the world, more and more economists have come to argue the opposite view that corruption inhibits development.[55]

[48] Personal correspondence with TI official, April 1999.

[49] TI 1997 report, pp. 10–11. An oft-cited article is Shang-jin Wei, "How Taxing Is Corruption on International Investors?" (Cambridge: Kennedy School of Government, Harvard University, February 25, 1997). Controlling for other factors, Wei finds that corruption tends to discourage foreign direct investment by, in effect, acting as a tax on foreign business. From Singapore to Mexico, the marginal tax rate on foreign investment is raised by 20 percent. According to Peter Eigen, there is a tendency for countries with rampant corruption to face difficulties in sustaining economic development "because very often the wrong projects are chosen, not the ones which give the best price and best product. Very often funds are not made available to schools, hospitals and other services which are important to create a healthy and prosperous society." Kang Siew Li, "KL's Anti-graft Laws Lauded," *Business Times*, Malaysia, September 17, 1998.

[50] See Shahid M. Alam, "Anatomy of Corruption: An Approach to the Political Economy of Development," *American Journal of Economics and Sociology*, Vol. 48 (October 1989), pp. 441–56.

[51] Tyler Cowen, Amihai Glazer, and Henry McMillan, "Rent Seeking Can Promote the Provision of Public Goods," *Economics and Politics*, Vol. 6 (July 1994), pp. 131–45.

[52] Basu and Li, "Corruption and Reform."

[53] Francis T. Liu, "Three Aspects of Corruption," *Contemporary Economic Policy*, Vol. 14 (July 1996), pp. 26–29.

[54] Trond E. Olsen and Gaute Trosvik, "Collusion and Renegotiation in Hierarchies: A Case of Beneficial Corruption," *International Economic Review*, Vol. 39 (May 1998), pp. 413–38.

[55] See Oluwole Owoye and Ibrahim Bendardaf, "The Macroeconomic Analysis of the Effects of Corruption on Economic Growth of Developing Economies," *Rivista Internazionale de Scienze Economiche e Commerciali*, Vol. 43 (January–March 1996), pp. 191–

TI's position is firmly in this camp. The Asian economic recession in the aftermath of the financial crisis of 1997 added to the credibility of the argument that corruption is bad for economic development. Most analysts blamed the crisis on "crony capitalism," of which corruption is a major aspect.

2. THE POLITICS OF SHAME

TI's annual publication of the CPI generates a great deal of media coverage, which brings public attention to the issue of corruption as well as TI itself. Governments around the world are sensitive to their standing on the CPI. Understandably, governments of countries that are ranked low (meaning perceived to be corrupt) are critical of TI. For instance, in 1998, Cameroon was ranked the lowest on the CPI, and that country's government issued a statement vehemently condemning TI.[56] On the other hand, whether they like it or not, governments all over the world pay attention to their ranking.

3. CO-OPTATION

The politics of shame aside, most of the time TI works with, rather than against, powerful actors. First, TI specifies its mission as one of gradually changing national and international systems so that they become more transparent and less conducive to corruption. It stays away from exposing specific cases of corruption. The national chapters are urged to observe TI's guiding principles of noninvestigative work and independence from government, commercial, and partisan political interests. Thus TI tends not to be seen as threatening any government, company, or individual.

The national chapters cooperate with national governments. As Tunku Aziz, chairman of TI-Malaysia points out, "It is in fact more beneficial if we use persuasion and present ourselves as an ally, rather than if we force confrontation."[57] The same is true of TI's approach to international organizations. It has patiently lobbied major international economic organizations to incorporate the corruption issue in their missions. TI played an

---

211; Paolo Mauro, "Corruption and Growth," *Quarterly Journal of Economics*, Vol. 110 (August 1995), pp. 681–712; and M. Shahid Alam, "Anatomy of Corruption: An Approach to the Political Economy of Underdevelopment," *American Journal of Economics and Sociology*, Vol. 48 (October 1989), pp. 441–56.

[56] "The Cameroon government condemns strongly the arrogance of certain bodies that are in the pay of neo-colonial clusters of people at work to impede the progress of our countries instead of supporting efforts and sacrifices made by our people"; quoted in Barbara Crossette, "Europe Dominates Survey's Top 10 Least-Corrupt-Countries List," *New York Times*, October 4, 1998, p. 5.

[57] Quoted in Sharon Nelson, "Towards More Open Dealings," *New Straits Times*, May 1, 1997, p. 9.

important role in helping the OECD adopt the 1997 antibribery convention. Since then various national chapters have been pushing for their governments to ratify the convention. Having been instrumental in pushing the World Bank and IMF to take a stand against corruption, TI is now working hard on lobbying the WTO to do the same. Its co-optation approach also consists of dialogues with "the enemy." In order to win over corporations that have an appalling record in bribery, TI has conscientiously resisted the temptation to denounce their conduct to the press.[58]

4. POLITICAL SENSITIVITY

TI has been very careful to appear neutral and noninterventionist. All the national chapters are autonomous. They are financially and institutionally independent. TI has been especially sensitive to developing countries' suspicion and hostility toward foreign imposition. Many in the developing world are resentful of Western portrayals of corruption as a problem of developing countries. In the words of Prime Minister Mahathir of Malaysia, "We can't take bribes unless you offer them."[59] In response, TI's chairman, Peter Eigen issued a warning against focusing on corruption in the developing world: "Corruption is perceived to be greatest there, but I urge the public to recognize that a large share of the corruption is the explicit product of multinational corporations, headquartered in the leading industrialized countries, using massive bribery and kickbacks to buy contracts in the developing world and the countries in transition."[60]

5. INSTITUTIONAL INNOVATION

TI's success is related to its ability to provide innovative institutional mechanisms that facilitate the fight against corruption. For instance, as TI has found out, a major source of resistance to the movement against corruption comes from the North. While it is in the interest of many of the companies from the North not to have to pay bribes, they are afraid that if they refuse to do so, they will lose contracts and jobs to their competitors.[61] This is a typical case of prisoner's dilemma. TI's "islands of integrity" model offers a useful solution to this dilemma. The model is designed to help governments and companies in a single market with a limited number of competitors to refrain from corruption.[62] It requires all

[58] Personal correspondence with TI official, April 1999.

[59] Quoted in Trevor Royle, "Corruption Pays Its Way throughout the World," p. 21.

[60] Quoted in Roger Boyes, "Britain Moves Higher in Bribery League," *The Times*, August 1, 1997.

[61] "Eigen Fights the Corruption Monster," *New Straits Times* (Malaysia), September 9, 1997, p. 1.

[62] The level of corruption differs among different economic sectors. George Moody-

applicants for a public tender and the government that issues to sign a pact, which obliges all competitors to refrain from corrupt practices. If the agreement is violated, the violators are subject to sanctions, such as loss of contract, liability for damages (to the government and the competing bidders), and forfeiture of the bid security. Companies that engage in corruption can also be barred from future government business.[63] A related method with which the national chapters hope to influence government and business behaviors is to accredit government agencies and companies that refrain from corrupt practices.

6. NETWORKING

TI cooperates and networks with other international forums and organizations, whose primary mission is other than that of fighting corruption, but who make useful allies. As previously noted, TI has also established ties with a number of other IGOs and NGOs. The aforementioned IACC, which has convened every two years since 1983, established a council to coordinate the conferences in 1996, with TI as its secretariat. TI's principal task is to provide advice and assistance to the host of each IACC conference. Most significantly, TI has supported and assisted the OECD with its efforts to curb international corruption, particularly the OECD antibribery convention of December 1997. Through its affiliation with these other organizations, TI has been able to further its reach and influence in the world.

CONCLUSIONS

It is useful to end this chapter with a few words of caution. First, successful as TI has been in promoting normative change in opposition to corruption, its future is far from clear. It is one thing to raise awareness of and sentiment against corruption, but quite another to reduce the practice of corruption. While many companies are drafting codes of conduct

---

Stuart, chairman of TI-UK, ranks industries by the extent to which he estimates they are prone to bribery—aircraft and defense, major industrial goods, major civil works, supplies and consultancy. See Michael Prest, "$40bn Business Best by Bribes and Kickbacks," *The Observer*, October 22, 1995, p. 1. Defense sales are ideal for grand corruption because of their size and secrecy. George Moody-Stuart, "Scope for Corruption in Arms Trade," *The Times*, February 26, 1996. In many countries, construction projects tend to be where corruption concentrates. For instance, according to official reports, 63 percent of the more than 100,000 cases of corruption in recent years have taken place in the construction sector (see China News Service, March 6, 1999).

[63] For more details on this model, see Transparency International, *The Fight against Corruption*, Chap. 4.

and setting up hot lines that offer employees advice on ethical questions,[64] more than a few of them continue to play the bribery game. Indeed, for all their complaints about the constraints imposed by the FCPA, American foreign investors do not seem to behave much differently from their counterparts abroad,[65] or at least they turn out to be no more or less inclined to do business in corrupt countries than anyone else.[66] The Council on Hemispheric Affairs, for example, criticizes the United States for not vigorously applying FCPA: "Between 1994 and 1996, the Justice Department investigated only 11 cases and did not prosecute a single one. It is estimated that during this period there may have been hundreds, if not thousands, of instances of US business executives corrupting Latin American officials."[67] TI's islands-of-integrity model addresses this problem on a limited scale, but the piecemeal approach may fall short of freeing companies from the fear that in complying with the new norms they would lose business to competitors who continue to pay bribes.[68] More time needs to pass before it will be possible to draw any firm conclusions about the prospects for the global contest against corruption,. It may prove easier to elevate an issue to the top of the global agenda than it is to resolve the issue and get it off the agenda.

Second, idea and organizational entrepreneurs among the Affirmative Globals are important, as indicated by the case of TI. Yet it would be misleading not to point out that these entrepreneurs' cause has a better chance of success if it does not contradict the interests of powerful actors. TI's success results in part from powerful supporters, particularly U.S.-based multinational corporations,[69] which are concerned that multinational corporations abroad have a "competitive edge on them because the foreign multinationals can pay bribes."[70] The FCPA prohibits American companies from doing so and criminalizes bribery abroad. For years, American companies have complained that they have lost business to less scrupulous competitors from Europe and elsewhere. According to the U.S. Department of Commerce, American companies lost more than one hundred international contracts, valued at $45 billion, in 1994 and 1995

[64] Kerene Witcher, "A Bribe or Tip? A Dilemma," *Asian Wall Street Journal*, September 15, 1997, p. A1.

[65] Shang-Jin Wei, "How Taxing Is Corruption on International Investors?"

[66] Stephanie Flanders, "Clear Thinking on Corruption," *Financial Times*, June 23, 1997, p. 10.

[67] Nancy Dunne, "US Presses Drive against Business Bribery," *Financial Times*, February 24, 1999, p. 7.

[68] Mason and Jonquieres, "Goodbye Mr. 10%," p. 15.

[69] A review of TI's financial supporters reveals the importance of corporate donors, especially American multinational corporations. Twenty-nine of the 73 corporate donors are American companies. See TI's home page at www.transparency.de.

[70] Vogl, "Laying Corruption to Rest."

as a result of bribery.[71] The Treasury estimates that U.S. corporations lose $30 billion in contracts every year because of their inability to pay bribes.[72] Nor are U.S. companies the only ones that suffer from corrupt practices. International executives name corruption as one of the biggest obstacle to doing business in less developed countries. A poll of Danish business-men overseas revealed 74 percent had paid bribes to win contracts. The problem is widespread and can account for up to 30 percent of a proj-ect's cost.[73]

Third, a question implicitly addressed in the foregoing needs to be asked directly: Does it matter if an issue has moved high on the global agenda? What impacts may follow from the growing awareness of and emerging norms against corruption globally? While it is still too early to provide any conclusive answer, in all probability the salience of corrup-tion as a major global issue impacts differently on different actors. Ordi-nary individuals experience the issue as very bothersome. The impact on companies is regulative rather than constitutive, and the impact on gov-ernments is both regulative and constitutive. For private companies that are competitive, the preference has always been a level playing field. Once corruption becomes a worldwide issue, it is easier for companies to get out of the trap of corruption. For private companies that lack compet-itiveness, corruption is an important—and sometimes the only—way to gain business opportunities. For them, the impact of the new global envi-ronment makes it difficult and costly to engage in corruption.

For governments, on the other hand, the advent of corruption on the global agenda is likely to have a significant impact on both their prefer-ences and their behavior. Given heightened public awareness of corrup-tion as an obstacle to economic development, and given the increasingly vocal expression of concern about its detrimental consequences by Affir-mative Globals in the international business community and international organizations, governments are likely to reconsider their attitude toward corruption. Whereas many of them used to be tolerant of corruption, they are now likely to see corrupt practices as hurting their interests, and thus they may actively crack down. In short, TI would appear to have contributed substantially to making governments reconceptualize the costs and benefits of corruption and to take the issue seriously. As the chairman of TI-Malaysia observed about his country, people have to "se-riously consider the urgent need to develop a national code of business

---

[71] Michael Hershman, "A Blow against Bribery," *Financial Times*, February 23, 1998, p. 14.

[72] Martin Dyckman, "Taking a Reading on Corruption around the World," *St. Petersburg Times*, October 11, 1998, p. 3D.

[73] Ben Richardson and David Murphy, "Graft Battle Begins at Home," *South China Morning Post*, January 31, 1999, p. 3.

ethics to regulate business transactions . . . and to combat extortion and bribery. . . . The globalization of our economy means one thing, that is the rules are no longer ours to lay down. We either play by the new global rules which demand greater transparency and accountability than we were used to in the past, or remain spectators."[74]

This conclusion anticipates the next two chapters. The first of these focuses on the issues posed by the economics of fragmegration; the second probes those that are relevant to transparency, accountability, and other challenges to the governance of fragmegration.

[74] Tunku Aziz, quoted in Desmond Ngiam, "Call for Greater Transparency in Financial Sector," *New Straits Times*, April 2, 1998, p. 19.

CHAPTER SEVENTEEN

Prosperity and Poverty

> [W]hat can your nation do for you that a good credit card cannot do?
>
> —Ulf Hannerz[1]

> The world may be moving inexorably toward one of those tragic moments that will lead future historians to ask, why was nothing done in time? Were the economic and policy elites unaware of the profound disruption that economic and technological change were causing working men and women? What prevented them from taking the steps necessary to prevent a global crisis?
>
> —Ethan Kapstein[2]

> Because business enterprises have outgrown political institutions at the local, national, and supranational levels, national leaders are exerting less and less control over economic issues. As a result the world faces an authority crisis without precedent in modern times.
>
> —Richard J. Barnet and John Cavanagh[3]

THERE is an explicit reason why this chapter on the economic dimensions of fragmegration comes near the end of the volume. All too often globalization and resistance to it are conceived as driven by material and economic concerns. While such dynamics are certainly central and powerful determinants of fragmegration, they are not the only determinants. As indicated throughout the previous chapters, a number of other factors are also operative. Thus, in the interest of maintaining a broad perspective on fragmegrative processes, their economic aspects have not previously been the focus of the analysis. Here, however, economic dynamics are explored for their fragmegrative content.

Such an exploration is especially propitious at this writing. The downturn of the global economy that began in 2000 and continued unabated

---

[1] *Transnational Connections: Culture, People, Places* (London: Routledge, 1996), p. 88.

[2] "Workers and the World Economy," *Foreign Affairs* (Vol. 75 (May/June 1996), p. 18.

[3] *Global Dreams: Imperial Corporations and the New World Order* (New York Simon and Schuster, 1994), p. 422.

into 2001, only to be further intensified after the collapse of New York's World Trade Center on September 11 of that year, has highlighted the micro underpinnings of the macro processes that sustain the expansion or contraction of money, trade, productivity, and consumption. Be they workers, consumers, investors, or voters, the salience of individuals has increased greatly as stock prices decline, job layoffs proliferate, buyers postpone purchases, inventories grow, and currencies fluctuate. In periods when globalization fosters growth and integration the relevance of people tends to be taken for granted, but awareness of their attitudes, confidence, and conduct heightens when hard times set in and globalization generates protests and fragmentation. Under these circumstances, for example, activists among the Resistant Locals and Globals find it easier to mobilize support, and corporate executives are more readily "seen as individually culpable rather than agents of a global system."[4] In short, as the second epigraph implies, economic downturns make it increasingly difficult to ignore the differences between winners and losers, between those who have gained from the world's turn toward free-market economies and those who have lost out, between those in the affirmative and resistant worlds, between the prosperous and the poverty-stricken, between those who use credit cards and those who do not.

PROSPERITY

There is no better indicator of fragmegration than the pervasive and often growing gap between the world's rich and poor. It is a gap of long duration, but in the present period it has widened as the production and distribution of wealth have reached unprecedented heights. In the long run the information revolution may enhance the skills and well-being of the poor, but the access of the well-off to the Internet and other microelectronic technologies has further broadened the gap between them and those below the poverty line.

Any analysis of the economic dimensions of fragmegration must be careful about the labels and words used to describe the gap. As will be seen, for instance, the rich-poor gap is not the equivalent of the distinction between capital and labor, and it is the gap that underlies the effort here to compare the distinctions between prosperity and poverty.

Highly consistent with the micro-macro approach of this book, recent "microdata" research undertaken by economists has uncovered major findings that suggest the rich-poor gap—the distinction between winners

---

[4] Stephen J. Kobrin, "'Our Resistance Is as Global as Your Oppression': Multinational Corporations, the Protest Movement and the Future of Global Governance" (paper presented at the annual meeting of the International Studies Association, Chicago, February 2001), p. 3.

and losers—derives in good part not from macro structures and processes but from the choices that individuals and collectivities make with respect to the global economy. Those who choose to connect to the global economy tend to prosper in comparison with those who choose not to link up with it: both American and foreign "firms, workers, and communities that commit to all sorts of global linkages prosper relative to comparable counterparts that do not. Among other benefits, their market prospects and rewards usually grow more rapidly and more stably over time. As a result, they gradually replace more insular firms, workers, and communities and are subject to less volatility (contrary to the impression that globalization breeds unpredictability)."[5] And just as the focus on micro phenomena undertaken here has led to delineating people in terms of their orientations toward local, global, and private worlds, so has the microdata research of economists

> generated new terminology. *Globally committed*, *globally engaged*, and *globally integrated* are the terms we use to describe plants, workers, and communities that are linked to the global economy through some combination of exports, imports, investments, and technology transfer. We sometimes label those that are not linked globally in any way *insular* or *domestically focused*. Those that are linked in some ways, but not others, we sometimes call *narrow* (or *opportunistic* or *one-way*) globalizers, as opposed to *deep* or *broadly engaged* globalizers. The old language . . . describes its subjects as exporters, importers, investors, and so on, implicitly assuming that they are one or another of these things more or less exclusively. That language and those categories are increasingly irrelevant to a world in which *any* type of global engagement pays off.[6]

Credit Cards: The Production and Distribution of Wealth

Following the startling question posed in the first epigraph to this chapter, it is surely arguable that the credit cards of individuals are symbolic of the prosperity that has spread into various pockets around the world. Leaving aside whether they can do more for the daily routines and satisfactions of people than their nation, credit and debit cards enable people to spend and consume with ease at any time and most every place. What began as an American practice is now worldwide in scope. Such a pattern can readily be discerned in the fact that whereas two-thirds of Visa cards were held in the United States in 1983, fewer than half were in 1993. It is also plainly evident in the pattern for Mastercard, which in 1998 announced expansion of its ATM network to Antarctica, the seventh conti-

---

[5] Howard Lewis III and J. David Richardson, *Why Global Commitment Really Matters!* (Washington, D.C.: Institute for International Economics, October 2001), p. 35.
[6] Ibid., p. 15 (italics in the original).

nent on which such facilities are available, facilities that grew by 5,000 every month and, all told, now provide more than 650 million cardholders with instant access to cash at more than 350,000 ATMs in over one hundred countries and territories. Similarly, cash can be obtained through Visa's 160,000 ATMs around the world. As of March 1997, Visa had issued 546 million debit cards worldwide that could be used through 20,600 member financial institutions at 13 million acceptance locations. In the United States alone the number of credit cards increased from 157 million to 331 million between 1984 and 1993. The average American cardholder carries nine different cards, with the result that there are more than a billion credit cards of all types in the United States.[7] Roughly 4.7 million people used credit cards to purchase something on the World Wide Web in June 1997, but six months later this figure rose to 10 million.

While vast numbers of people in the developing world do not have credit cards, and while the consequences of the cards' wide availability are both positive and negative—they enhance consumption, increase debt, and reduce savings, as well as foster forms of behavior that are especially noxious[8]—the data summarized in the previous paragraph highlight the plausibility of treating these plastic artifacts of our epoch as a metaphor for the large degree to which the global economy affects the lives of people everywhere. More precisely, credit cards can be used as a metaphor to represent two major dynamics sustained by the age of fragmegration. One is their impact on the production and distribution of wealth, and the other involves the spread and growing uniformity of consumer tastes. In addition, credit cards are another indicator that speaks to the micro dimensions of the global economy. If the upside of economic globalization focuses on its macro processes, the millions of credit cards serve as a reminder of the degree to which prosperity has also been widespread among individuals in local as well as global worlds.

Few would quarrel with the proposition that the processes whereby national economies have been globalized constitute one of the most powerful forces at work in the emergent epoch. As one analyst concludes after examining extensive data, "No matter how many different numbers are presented or how frequently one hears them, the growth of international economic activity in the past thirty years remains staggering."[9] These growth processes are a major source of fragmegration because the

[7] *The Futurist*, Vol. 29 (September–October 1995), p. 54.

[8] Fraud, invasions of privacy, and credit-card delinquency are among the less salutary consequences. See George Ritzer, *Expressing America: A Critique of the Global Credit Card Society* (Thousand Oaks, Calif.: Sage, 1995).

[9] Geoffrey Garrett, "The Causes of Globalization" (paper presented at the Conference on Development and the Nation-State in the Cross-Currents of Globalization and Decentralization, St. Louis, April 8, 2000), p. 8.

production and distribution of wealth, the neoliberal economic policies that have turned many state controls over to markets, are applauded by their beneficiaries and deplored either by those who have not benefited from the growth or by those activists who empathize with the losers and protest on their behalf.

The issues posed by the winners-losers dichotomy derived from the economics of fragmegration are numerous. To a large extent their origins can be traced to the fact that while not long ago economies were organized on a national scale, today most (though, of course, not all) of the world's producers, consumers, traders, investors, public officials, workers, and many other relevant actors tend to conduct themselves in terms of global rather than national markets. The world's some 60,000 multinational corporations, for example, now decentralize their operations through more than 450,000 subsidiaries in diverse countries,[10] thereby sustaining the acceleration of a flow of foreign direct investment (FDI) across borders in multiple directions. Currency transactions move around the world's financial centers in milliseconds, just as producers move or build their plants where labor costs are cheapest, develop products to cater to regional and local tastes far removed from corporate headquarters, and disperse their research, advertising, accounting, and legal staffs to service corporate needs in far-flung markets.

Since it is thus virtually impossible for any national or local community to be self-contained and independent of the global economy, these processes are bound to impact positively or adversely on the lives of people everywhere. Those who benefit from the integrative forces unleashed by economic globalization are likely to resist any efforts to constrain the lowering of barriers to trade and investment, whereas those who view themselves as suffering from the freeing up of trade and investment are likely to support policies that raise such barriers. Yet the differences between winners and losers are not as clear-cut as they may seem. Some winners fear the excesses of capitalism and warn that wealth will be diminished unless regulatory policies are adopted to protect against the excesses,[11] just as workers are divided by whether or not their jobs are enhanced or threatened by productivity abroad. Thus some in the labor force are winners and others are losers, thereby adding further to the complexity of fragmegrative dynamics. Much the same can be said about business executives and politicians whose careers are either advanced or

[10] Jessica T. Matthews, "Foreword," in Virginia Haufler, *A Public Role for the Private Sector: Industry Self-Regulation in a Global Economy* (Washington, D.C.: Carnegie Endowment for International Peace, 2001), p. vii.

[11] See, for example, George Soros, "The Capitalist Threat," *Atlantic Monthly*, February 1997, pp. 45–58, and Joseph E. Stiglitz, *Globalization and Its Discontents* (New York: W.W. Norton, 2002).

hindered by the globalization of economies. For the executive whose foreign supplies are vulnerable to instabilities in the supplying countries, or for city mayors eager to get foreign companies to build plants in their communities, distant events are very much a part of close-at-hand circumstances. Examples of this sort can be multiplied many times over once salience is accorded to a fragmegrative perspective.

Harsh criticisms of the International Monetary Fund, the World Bank, and the World Trade Organization are an especially persistent theme of Resistant Locals and Globals who reject the dominant neoliberal assumptions of their Affirmative counterparts that worldwide economic deregulation is to be desired, that capital flows should be freed from national or transnational controls and markets thereby allowed to flourish. The former view the policies of international economic institutions designed to reduce inflation and curb inefficiencies as ill-founded, as hurting the poor and favoring the wealthy, as oblivious to poverty and the rich-poor gap, as part of the problem rather than as bases for solutions to the dislocations that periodically beset the developing regions of the world. More than that, the critics argue that these institutions are not accountable to those whose lives they so profoundly effect. The IMF, for example, is viewed as having "awesome power," as "a surrogate government in financial matters . . . [that] is insinuated into the inner sanctums of nearly 75 developing country governments around the world—countries with a combined population of some 1.4 billion."[12] The translation of these critical concerns into street protests in Seattle and elsewhere is thus a logical extension of proliferating fragmegrative tensions and, as indicated later, an extension that may have more than symbolic consequences.

But these concerns are not confined to international economic institutions. Multinational corporations are also a salient preoccupation of Resistant Locals and Globals. The corporations not only are seen as prime culprits in sustaining and widening the rich-poor gap but also are faulted for promoting environmental degradation and cultural homogeneity without regard for values other than those to be found in their profit and loss statements. The lack of transparency in the manner by which corporations make their decisions is another key entry in the litany of complaints against them. Yet it remains to be seen whether opponents of globalizing dynamics are powerful and united enough to serve as a match for the Affirmative Globals who collectively wield the levers of power on behalf of an ever-freer market that is subject to only a modicum of controls. Although the Battle of Seattle and subsequent skirmishes suggest that the issues dividing the diverse groups opposed to globalizing pro-

[12] Jeffrey Sachs, "The IMF and the Asian Flu," *The American Prospect*, No. 37 (March–April 1998), pp. 16–17.

cesses can be bridged, worldwide economic deregulation and the global market's universal reach may be too ascendant, too much a perceived source of growing prosperity, to be derailed.

Still, there remain persistent difficulties in generating a widespread consensus on how rules governing the global economy ought to be framed and who should make the decisions required to do the framing, with the result that the present free-enterprise structures of the global economy may well endure and continue to foster fragmegrative processes. Evidence for this likelihood is suggested by a meeting of world finance leaders from twenty-two countries that ended without significant agreement on how to cope with the situation.[13]

To be sure, a severe, prolonged worldwide economic recession might create the conditions for a moderation of the present fragmegrative balance, but it is highly unlikely that any such a recession will undermine the dynamics of fragmegration; rather, it will only lead to a new set of winners and losers who form a new fragmegrative balance. While there are indications (see later discussion) that some measure of moderation will result from a continuing series of street protests when the boards of international economic institutions convene, it is also the case that such changes may prove to be more rhetorical than actual.

In sum, the more the economic dynamics of fragmegration have accelerated, the more intense have been the conflicts between the winners and losers, with the former insisting that in the long run all will benefit from the wealth being created and the latter claiming, often through collective action in the streets, that the creation of wealth is highly selective. To rephrase an oft-used metaphor, the winners argue that a rising tide raises all ships, oceangoing liners and rowboats alike, while the losers assert the rowboats are likely to be capsized by the swift and strong currents of the rising tide. Of course, the winners are not free of controversy. Among other issues, they argue over the pace at which the barriers to trade should be lowered and whether the losers should be made to fend for themselves or provided a safety net by governments until their ships begin to rise with the tide.

Credit Cards: The Production of Consumers

Before looking more closely at the poverty side of the fragmegrative balance, it is worth noting that credit cards are also symbolic of the large degree to which economic globalization has led to the production of

[13] See, for example, David E. Sanger, "Economic Leaders Differ in Strategy on Halting Crisis," *New York Times*, October 4, 1998, p. 1; and Sanger, "Meeting of World Finance Leaders Ends with No Grand Strategy but Many Ideas," *New York Times*, October 8, 1998, p. A6.

consumers, to people with the means to redefine their wants as needs and then go out to fulfill their needs at malls and other shopping outlets. This dynamic leads to the widening and consolidating of consumer tastes. Today credit cards make it possible for the winners to make frequent and expensive purchases, thereby spreading consumerism on a global scale and also, through the merchandising of the same goods throughout the world, encouraging the development of uniform tastes among people everywhere. From McDonald's hamburgers to Nike footwear, from Disney movies to Chicago Bulls caps, from MTV to Michael Jackson, from wireless phones to computerized toys—to cite only a few of the many tangible and intangible items that are now available virtually everywhere—the dynamism of consumerism appears to be creating, for better or worse, a seemingly prosperous world culture. The phrase "for better or worse" is crucial because it bespeaks fragmegration: even as people everywhere generate demand for the same products, their consumption of the products is viewed by many as an unhealthy universalism that erodes local cultures and practices.[14] Indeed, in some countries the products of the global culture are seen as such a direct threat to long-standing religious, linguistic, and ethnic traditions that extensive efforts are made to prevent the intrusion of the products. Just as France, for example, attempts to keep the French language free of the "impurities" of English, so do fundamentalist regimes like that in Iran seek to control inputs from abroad that are seen as degrading and undermining the premises and practices of Islam. In the largest sense, in other words, the tendencies toward the homogenization of cultural tastes are a major source of the fragmegration that has come to dominate the emergent epoch.

Yet, while there is no question that the prosperity associated with global consumerism can do harm to local cultures, its dynamics are more complex than they appear at first glance. Consumers are also products of the skill revolution, and as buyers become more aware of alternative goods available in the global market, more sensitive to their own preferences, and more able to imagine alternative lifestyles, they have expanded and refined their tastes. McDonald's is illustrative in this regard. As indicated in chapter 4, its impact has been as much one of localization as of globalization.

POVERTY[15]

People below the poverty line—mostly the three hundred million Circumstantial Passives who are unemployed or underemployed and fall

---

[14] See, for example, Helena Norberg-Hodge, "The March of the Monoculture," *The Ecologist*, Vol. 29 (May–June 1999), pp. 194–97.

[15] Parts of this section are drawn from James N. Rosenau and Mary Durfee, "Playing Catch-Up: IR Theory and Poverty," *Millennium*, Vol. 25, No. 3 (1996), pp. 521–45.

short of a subsistence wage level calculated at one dollar a day[16]—can hardly be regarded as consumers in the sense of having been produced by economic globalization. Their consumption needs are shaped by the requirements of survival and not by corporate advertisers or mall displays. Their range of choice is thus confined by price and not by taste.

Since the predicaments of Circumstantial Passives are as old as human history, the pressures to address the poverty dilemma did not begin in Seattle. They simply moved to the streets in that northwestern U.S. city. The plight of the poor and the growing ranks of losers have long been a matter of dispute among economists, sociologists, public officials, pundits, and IGO and NGO leaders. But nothing resembling a consensus on the definition, meaning, sources, and consequences of poverty has ever evolved. Instead, a bewildering array of interpretations, contradictions, accusations, and affirmations mark the debate in corporate boardrooms, newspaper columns, academic journals, governmental arenas, and diplomatic circles. Resistant Globals argue that the excesses of capitalism sustained by corporations and the opening up of markets through globalization are the prime cause of poverty, while their Affirmative counterparts contend that the ranks of losers were swollen before the advent of present-day globalizing dynamics and that in fact the poor have been beneficiaries of reduced trade barriers and lessened governmental controls.[17] During the 1997–98 Asian financial crisis, for instance, Resistant Globals ascribed the situation to flawed IMF policies, to which Affirmative Globals vigorously responded that the IMF followed exactly the right policies.[18] And the latter are not hesitant to cite empirical data in support of their position: arguing that "the best weapon against poverty is not less globalization but more of it," Affirmative Globals point to a World Bank study that

> divided developing countries into two groups: a club of 24 globalizers that have doubled their ratio of trade to GNP over the past two decades and a residual group that on average trades less than it did 20 years ago. In the globalizing club, which is home to 3 billion people, income per person grew by an impressive 5 percent a year during the 1990s. In the non-globalizing group, comprising 2 billion people, average incomes *fell* by nearly 1 percent a year over the same period.[19]

[16] Christopher S. Wren, "World Needs to Add 500 Million Jobs in 10 Years, Report Says," *New York Times*, January 25, 2001, p. A13.

[17] For a thorough and balanced analysis of the debate between the Resistant and Affirmative Globals that concludes favoring the latter, see the separate section of *The Economist*, "Globalization and Its Critics," September 29, 2001, pp. 1–30.

[18] See Joseph E. Stiglitz, "The Insider: What I Learned of the World Economic Crisis," *New Republic*, April 17, 2000, and a letter to the editor in a subsequent issue by Rudi Dornbusch.

[19] Editorial, "Trade and Poverty," *Washington Post*, November 8, 2001, p. A30 (italics in the original).

Such arguments about the proper role of international economic institutions have been summarized in terms of three different (but overlapping) schools of thought: enthusiasts, tacticians, and skeptics.[20] Some of the skeptics also insist that the problems originate in domestic policy-making organizations and not in the policies of international economic institutions. What is needed, some contend, is less porous safety nets, while others posit the need for time to elapse so that the benefits of open markets can trickle down deeper into the ranks of the poor.[21]

In contrast to economists, however, international relations analysts who theorize about world affairs have had virtually nothing to offer on the subject of poverty. To be sure, Western textbooks, journals, and monographs occasionally cite the links between poverty, on the one hand, and starvation, food production, population trends, or the North-South gap, on the other. Yet such analyses are predominantly empirical descriptions of depressing statistics and are not set forth in a theoretical context. It is as if poverty is so self-evident—so obviously a case of "the poor will always be with us"—that it does not warrant a niche in the pantheon of theory. Notwithstanding the fact that poverty respects no borders, spreads as jobs diminish, tugs at moral sensibilities, affects a billion people, induces citizens to riot, and generates action by numerous international organizations, no school of IR theory has yet to tackle the realities and fears of substandard living conditions. Some theoretical attention has been paid to macro poverty—the underdevelopment of some developing countries[22]—but attention has not been devoted to micro poverty, to the plight and inequality of Circumstantial Passives living in squalor. This lack of attention is even more glaring in the light of other current problems involving people at the micro level, such as human rights and sustainable development, that have recently climbed high on the global agenda and are increasingly the focus of theoretical inquiries.[23]

---

[20] Michael Edwards, "Enthusiasts, Tacticians and Skeptics: The World Bank, Civil Society and Social Capital," *Kettering Review*, spring 2000.

[21] For a succinct summary of nuanced perspectives articulated by Resistant Globals who accept the goal of integrating economies around the world but outline ways of achieving the goal through other than mechanisms for promoting free trade, see Louis Uchitelle, "Challenging the Dogmas of Free Trade," *New York Times*, February 9, 2002, p. A15.

[22] See, for example, Stephan Haggard (ed.), *The International Political Economy and the Developing Countries* (Bookfield, Vt.: Edward Elgar, 1994); Zaven N. Davidian, *Economic Disparities among Nations: A Threat to Survival in a Globalized World* (New York: Oxford University Press, 1994); and Mitchell A. Seligson and John T. Passe-Smith (eds.), *Development and Underdevelopment: The Political Economy of Inequality* (Boulder, Colo.: Lynne Rienner, 1993).

[23] The human rights issues that occupy a high place on the global agenda underscore the lack of concern for micro poverty on the part of Western theorists. Observers elsewhere see human rights as having two main components—social-economic and political rights—but in the West only questions of political freedom enjoy legitimacy as a global issue. Social-

Nor has the surge of interest in the dynamics of globalization or the renewed preoccupation with the underpinnings of international political economy led to extensive consideration of where micro poverty phenomena fit in the processes of world politics.[24] To the extent that the collective roles played by underdeveloped countries in the world arena are probed, they are usually cast in the context of the problems that international debt poses for order and stability.[25] To be sure, references to poverty are occasionally made, but these fall far short of systematic discussions grounded in explicit theory.[26]

Accounting for the Paucity of Theoretical Attention

Documenting the paucity of theoretical concern for micro poverty is easy. A search of recent volumes of major IR journals published in the United

---

economic rights, which include a freedom from poverty, are not part of Western discourse and thus have yet to climb to the higher rungs of the human rights agenda. For a contrast of Asian and Western views on human rights, see Daniel A. Bell, *East Meets West* (Princeton, N.J.: Princeton University Press, 1999).

[24] None of these recent books on globalization, for example, includes "poverty" as an item in its index: Barrie Axford, *The Global System: Economics, Politics and Culture* (New York: St. Martin's Press, 1995); Mike Featherstone, Scott Lash, and Roland Robertson (eds.), *Global Modernities* (London: Sage, 1995); Philip Gummett (ed.), *Globalization and Public Policy* (Cheltenham: Edward Elgar, 1996); David Held, Anthony McGrew, David Goldblatt, and Jonathan Perraton, *Global Transformations: Politics, Economics and Culture* (Stanford, Calif.: Stanford University Press, 1999); Paul Hirst and Grahame Thompson, *Globalization in Question: The International Economy and the Possibilities of Governance* (Cambridge, Mass.: Polity Press, 1996); Roland Robertson, *Globalization: Social Theory and Global Culture* (London: Sage, 1992); Martin Shaw, *Global Society and International Relations* (Cambridge, Mass.: Polity Press, 1994); and Leslie Sklair, *Sociology of the Global System*, 2d ed. (Baltimore: Johns Hopkins University Press, 1995). As for international political economy, neither a major compilation of essays on regime theory nor two major collections of readings—totaling fifty-three selections—on the subject include index entries with the heading of "poverty": see Stephen D. Krasner (ed.), *International Regimes* (Ithaca, N.Y.: Cornell University Press, 1983); George T. Crane and Abla Amawi (eds.), *The Theoretical Evolution of International Political Economy: A Reader* (New York: Oxford University Press, 1991); and Jeffrey A. Frieden and David A. Lake (eds.), *International Political Economy: Perspectives on Global Power and Wealth*, 3d ed. (New York: St. Martin's Press, 1995).

[25] See, for example, Ethan B. Kapstein, *Governing the Global Economy: International Finance and the State* (Cambridge, Mass.: Harvard University Press, 1994); and Stephan Haggard and Robert R. Kaufman (eds.), *The Politics of Economic Adjustment: International Constraints, Distributive Conflicts, and the State* (Princeton, N.J.: Princeton University Press, 1992). For an exception in this regard, see Joan M. Nelson, "Poverty, Equity, and the Politics of Adjustment," in Haggard and Kaufman (eds.), *The Politics of Economic Adjustment*, pp. 221–69.

[26] Illustrations of this point can be found in Robert Boyer and Daniel Drache (eds.), *States against Markets: The Limits of Globalization* (London: Routledge, 1996), p. 391; and James H. Mittelman (ed.), *Globalization: Critical Reflections* (Boulder, Colo.: Lynne Rienner, 1996), pp. 18, 219–20.

States yielded no articles that concentrate directly and fully on the subject.[27] While journals and books in the fields of comparative politics, development economics, and feminist theory are marked by a recurrent interest in various dimensions of poverty, this pattern only makes the absence of similar foci in the IR literature all the more glaring.[28]

Why is IR theory so mute about a pervasive global phenomenon? Are poverty phenomena so inextricably woven into the domestic fabric of societies that IR theorists properly ignore them? Explanations abound. One set involves cultural variables: conceivably some of the inattention derives from the fact that, at least historically, most IR theorists have focused on the problem of war and, in addition, they have come from industrial countries where poverty appeared to be waning. These circumstances produced a theoretical lacuna: out of sight, out of mind.[29] Similarly, Affirmative Globals tend to reason that the spread of the liberal economic order would make poverty less and less a problem. They conceive of technological change not only as expanding the market for goods and finances all over the world, bringing wealth to everyone, but also as shifting power from the center to the periphery, thus further integrating the world economy and helping to solve the distribution-of-wealth problem.[30]

An intellectual explanation can also be cited as a source of the silence: the voluminous literature produced by the numerous social scientists who do focus on poverty as a cause or consequence of intrasocietal processes lacks formulations that might provide guidance for IR theorists. This literature is summarized in a huge compendium of the corpus of theories and findings generated by inquiries into both micro and macro poverty

[27] Five years (1991–95) of *International Organization, International Security, International Studies Quarterly*, and *World Politics* were examined.

[28] See, for example, Irma Adelman, "A Poverty-Focused Approach to Development Policy," in John P. Lewis and Valeriana Kallab (eds.), *Development Strategies Reconsidered* (New Brunswick, N.J.: Transaction, 1986), pp. 49–65; William J. Dixon and Bruce E. Moon, "Domestic Political Conflict and Basic Needs Outcomes: An Empirical Assessment," *Comparative Political Studies*, Vol. 22, No. 2 (1989), pp. 178–98; Paul Streeten, Shaid Javed Burki, Mahbub Ul Haq, Norman Hicks, and Frances Stewart, *First Things First: Meeting Basic Human Needs in the Developing Countries* (New York: Oxford University Press, 1981); and Joycelin Massiah (ed.), *Women in Developing Economies: Making Visible the Invisible* (New York: Berg/UNESCO, 1993).

[29] For an incisive analysis that elaborates on how theoretical lacunae can derive from the circumstances in which theorists conduct their inquiries, see Karl Mannheim, *Ideology and Utopia: An Introduction to the Sociology of Knowledge* (New York: Harcourt, Brace, 1949), especially pp. 239–61.

[30] Robert Gilpin, *U.S. Power and the Multinational Corporation* (New York: Basic Books, 1975), p. 42. For a contrary perspective, see Alex Duncan, "Aid Effectiveness in Raising Adaptive Capacity in the Low-Income Countries," in Lewis and Kallab (eds.), *Development Strategies Reconsidered*, pp. 129–52.

phenomena in every part of the world, but it offers little by way of encouragement for IR specialists.[31] Rather, only disheartening conclusions are available: those who do study poverty widely agree that research has been "long on measurements, but short on explanations and theories,"[32] that "we are far from having reached a stage where we could postulate a general theory,"[33] that "poverty research up till now has contributed little by way of new or original ideas and theories,"[34] that "there is no uniform definition of poverty or agreement on its most precise form of measurement,"[35] and that, indeed, "it would be folly to globalize the concept of poverty because it cannot mean the same thing to every country or region, let alone the world itself."[36] Stated more specifically, "Everyone knows that being poor in the United States means something different from being poor in India; the same is true of America in the 1960s compared with the 1930s or some other decade. . . . The state of poverty is thus a continuum rather than a point on an absolute scale."[37]

There is also a normative explanation for the theoretical silence. Experience suggests that "the great problem in poverty research is that explanations imply a policy or direction,"[38] a reality that may well dissuade many IR theorists, inasmuch as many of them believe in stepping back from the policy world in order to comprehend the empirical world more fully.[39] It follows that what has been concluded with respect to colleagues who probe intra-societal poverty phenomena can be said with equal force about IR theorists:

> It is not an unreasonable hypothesis that poverty researchers feel more frustrated and lonely than do researchers in most other fields. It takes courage to live with the complexity of a poverty definition and the lack of an adequate theoretical framework. . . . It takes courage to break down stereotypes of poverty when communicating research results to policymakers who already have

[31] Else Oyen, S. M. Miller, and Syed Abdus Samad (eds.), *Poverty: A Global Review—Handbook on International Poverty Research* (Oslo: Scandinavian University Press, 1996).

[32] Francis Wilson, "Drawing Together Some Regional Perspectives on Poverty," in Oyen, Miller, and Samad (eds.), *Poverty: A Global Review*, p. 20.

[33] Ibid., p. 24.

[34] Syed Abdus Samad, "The Present Situation in Poverty Research," in Oyen, Miller, and Samad (eds.), *Poverty: A Global Review*, p. 35.

[35] Ibid., p. 34.

[36] Ibid., p. 37.

[37] Charles A. Valentine, *Culture and Poverty: Critique and Counterproposals* (Chicago: University of Chicago Press, 1968), pp. 12–13.

[38] S. M. Miller, "The Great Chain of Poverty Explanations," in Oyen, Miller, and Samad (eds.), *Poverty: A Global Review*, p. 571.

[39] See, for example, Alexander L. George, *Bridging the Gap: Theory and Practice in Foreign Policy* (Washington, D.C.: United States Institute of Peace Press, 1993), p. 3.

their embodied images of poverty. It takes courage to insist on an academic approach to poverty understanding when the call for action is closing in.[40]

In all probability, however, the bulk of the explanation for the paucity of poverty inquiries lies in a disciplinary explanation, namely, the long-standing habit of most IR theorists to express and define ideas and concepts in terms of their relationship to states and the vertical boundaries that divide them and their consequent inability to see the world in terms of horizontal boundaries that separate the poor and rich within and among states. Whatever variant of realism or liberalism to which they may be committed, theorists have focused on the world of states and the ways in which their members, individually and collectively, frame external policies, exercise power, maintain stability, build institutions, respond to crises, and pursue a host of other goals that have little direct bearing on daily life within societies.[41] As a result, despite the huge scale of substandard living conditions and the even more pervasive fears of being overtaken by them, IR theorizing has tended to ignore both the conditions and the fears because the extant theories direct attention elsewhere, particularly toward the capabilities of states and the control they exert in the international arena. Even those theorists who accord relevance to the domestic sources of foreign policy have largely ignored poverty phenomena.[42] This is because, it would seem, the plight of the poor has not been a preoccupation of foreign policy elites and other Territorial Globals, inasmuch as those at or below the poverty line have not been mobilized into a decisive political force to which policy makers must be sensitive.

Put differently, IR theorists, like everyone else, see what their norms condition them to look at and find, excluding other aspects of the world such as transnational poverty and the new class of global knowledge elites. (Thus the terrorist attack on the World Trade Centers can be seen as an attack on the United States, but it can also be viewed as an attack

[40] Else Oyen, "Poverty Research Rethought," in Oyen, Miller, and Samad (eds.), *Poverty: A Global Review*, p. 4. That some have the "courage to insist on an academic approach" can readily be seen in Amartya Sen, *Poverty and Famine: An Essay on Entitlement and Deprivation* (Oxford: Clarendon Press, 1981).

[41] See the various essays in Robert O. Keohane (ed.), *Neorealism and Its Critics* (New York: Columbia University Press, 1986); and David A. Baldwin (ed.), *Neorealism and Neoliberalism: The Contemporary Debate* (New York: Columbia University Press, 1993).

[42] For example, "poverty" does not appear as an entry in the indexes of any of these recent theoretical books concerned with foreign policy: Peter B. Evans, Harold K. Jacobson, and Robert D. Putnam (eds.), *Double-Edged Diplomacy: International Bargaining and Domestic Politics* (Berkeley and Los Angeles: University of California Press, 1993); Robert O. Keohane and Helen V. Milner (eds.), *Internationalization and Domestic Politics* (Cambridge: Cambridge University Press, 1996); and Robert O. Keohane and Elinor Ostrom (eds.), *Local Commons and Global Interdependence: Heterogeneity and Cooperation in Two Domains* (Thousand Oaks, Calif.: Sage, 1995).

on the new elite in the sense that the victims included young knowledge specialists from all over the world.) Perhaps no less relevant, at least a few IR scholars are members of what might be called a "statist moral community," and, as such, they tend to think and write in ways they hope will influence national policy makers, secure them government appointments, and increase the sales of their textbooks.

In sum, no variant of either realism or liberalism in IR theory has made substantial room for the recognition of domestic poverty conditions as sources of significant international repercussions. Only when poverty phenomena can be shown to have international effects—circumstances that may, as the ensuing analysis suggests, increasingly be the case in the near future—are they likely to be picked up by the lenses of IR theorists.

Is this to imply that empirical IR theory has tended to follow, rather than anticipate, the issues that surface in the empirical world? Yes, it is. Our theories have been so narrowly state-oriented that they are modified or extended only when the concerns of states shift and expand. The inequalities and low standards of living that attach to poverty, however defined, can be found everywhere in the world and are thus global phenomena. While this fact has thus far been inconsequential insofar as IR theory is concerned, its salience may well increase if developed states and their international economic institutions continue to face variants of the problems of joblessness and economic insecurity and if, as seems likely, street protests over IMF, World Bank, and WTO policies continue as recurring features of the world scene.[43]

Poverty through Fragmegrative Lenses

Although prior iterations of the fragmegrative approach to IR theory have not substantially addressed the dilemmas of worldwide poverty,[44] some aspects of this approach lend themselves readily to refocusing on such problems. By not locating states and their systems at the center of the theory, and instead according equal attention to individuals and their skills at the micro level, to the organizational explosion and NGOs at the micro-macro level, and to the bifurcation of the global system into state-

---

[43] While the likelihood of the protests continuing is considerable, the form they take may differ since the terrorist attacks on the United States. "I don't think we are going to be in the spotlight as much as before," the director of the Ruckus Society, John Sellers, was quoted as saying. "There's a strong concern about marches since September 11. What would happen if 10,000 people turned out for a peaceful march and then 4 of them burned a flag?" Leslie Wayne, "For Trade Protesters, 'Slower, Sadder Songs,'" *New York Times,* October 28, 2001, Sec. 3, p. 1.

[44] Of the two main prior iterations, my *Turbulence in World Politics* (1990) and *Along the Domestic-Foreign Frontier* (1997), the former lists only three entries in its index under poverty, while the latter's index contains but one entry.

centric and multi-centric worlds, a fragmegrative perspective makes ample conceptual room for a focus on poverty. No less important, given the centrality of technological innovations and especially the networking potential of the communications revolution, global awareness of poverty conditions and the sensitivity of the poor to their unequal circumstances are likely to undergo continuous reinforcement until remedial institutions are put in place that enable people to move above the poverty line.

The Likelihood of a Surge in Theoretical Attention

Notwithstanding the regretful conclusion that IR theories tend to follow rather than anticipate the course of events, it is quite likely that poverty phenomena will soon become central preoccupations of the theory enterprise. Several reasons underlie this expectation. One is recent events: the globalization backlash sustained by Resistant Globals who organized advocacy NGOs and other networks of activists that began in Seattle in November 1999 and then moved to the streets of some fifteen other cities around the world whenever representatives of international economic institutions gathered;[45] the fallout of the Asian financial crisis that began in 1997; high levels of unemployment and continued fears of futher downsizing;[46] the surfacing of open debate on whether globalization promotes or combats poverty;[47] a growing appreciation of the close links between strong democratic institutions and the creation of more winners than losers;[48] and a host of other recent developments have converged to heighten sensitivities to the growing gap between the rich and poor. As a result, jobs and poverty are moving swiftly toward the top of political

[45] For a map that locates the fifteen cities, see John Micklethwait and Adrian Wooldridge, "The Globalization Backlash," *FP/Foreign Policy*, No. 126 (September/October 2001), p. 17.

[46] It is noteworthy, for instance, that widespread labor protests and strikes in South Korea against a new law that makes it easier for companies to dismiss workers were rooted in a felt need to "[take] a stand against the global economic forces that brought investment and prosperity to low-wage Korea and now threaten to take it elsewhere." See Andrew Pollack, "Thriving, South Koreans Strive to Keep It That Way," *New York Times*, January 17, 1997, p. Al.

[47] Myriad contributions to the debate have flowed from the communications media. The following are only a small sample of the various lines of argument: Thomas Friedman, "1 Davos, 3 Seattles," *New York Times*, February 1, 2000, p. A25; Paul Krugman, "Bash the IMF for the Right Reasons," *International Herald Tribune*, March 11–12, 2000, p. 8; Judith Miller, "Globalization Widens Rich-Poor Gap, U.N. Report Says," *New York Times*, July 13, 1999, p. A8; Joseph S. Nye Jr., "Look Again, Globalization Isn't Bad for the Poor," *International Herald Tribune*, April 13, 2000, p. 8.

[48] *New York Times*, June 24, 2001, Sec. 4, p. 1.

agendas in the state-centric and multi-centric worlds.[49] In the multi-centric world, for example, an NGO, the Microcredit Summit Campaign, has stimulated a plethora of worldwide microcredit programs that have granted loans, some as small as forty dollars, to help some twenty million poor people with no credit history start businesses.[50] In addition, there are more than a few signs that officials of governments and international organizations have heard at least part of the messages conveyed by the street protests. As previously noted, some fifty multinational corporations and twelve labor associations responded to UN leadership and signed a Global Compact in which they agreed to support human rights, permit free trade unions, eliminate child labor, and desist from polluting the environment.[51] No less telling perhaps, and in the same spirit, wealthy countries have forgiven the debts of twenty-two poor countries.[52] Likewise, lately the IMF, the World Bank, and the G-8, among other collectivities in the state-centric world, have focused on poverty issues in ways that suggest their leaderships are sensitive to the concerns expressed by the protests. Or at least they have been persuaded that while they may have long been attentive to poverty issues, the problem is one of perceptions as well as economics. As one editorial noted, the street protesters may have been misguided, but their restlessness needs to be heeded:

> In one sense, these outbursts [of protest] are irrelevant. Unlike the Vietnam war protests a generation ago, they lack any obvious purpose but simply express an incoherent jumble of demands espoused by a motley of organizations. Often, their positions are self-contradictory: many of the nostrums trotted out in the name of helping developing countries would simply impoverish them further.
>
> The protests also achieve little, other than publicity. Demonstrators' claims to have torpedoed the WTO's Seattle meeting, and plans for a Multilateral Agreement on Investment two years earlier, are nonsense. Both were sunk by deadlock at the negotiating table. Nor has noisy arm-waving against capitalism and market-based policies so far stemmed their worldwide advance.
>
> But such cavils miss an important point. Many protesters may be muddle-headed and represent only themselves. But they are also storm warnings of a

---

[49] Michael H. Cosgrove, *The Cost of Winning: Global Development Policies and Broken Social Contracts* (New Brunswick, N.J.: Transaction, 1996).

[50] Ginger Thompson, "Small Loans Help Millions of World's Poorest, Coalition Says," *New York Times*, October 8, 2001, p. A3.

[51] Joseph Kahn, "Multinationals Sign U.N. Pact on Rights and Environment," *New York Times*, July 27, 2000, p. A1. See also Christopher S. Wren, "The U.N. Offers 87 Remedies to Help Poor Nations Develop," *New York Times*, February 4, 2001, p. 6.

[52] Joseph Kahn, "Rich Nations Will Forgive Debts of 22 of the Poorest," *New York Times*, December 23, 2000, p. A6.

wider reaction—mainly in the industrialized world—to deeper social and political shifts, which governments ignore at their peril.[53]

Whether intensified sensitivities to the deeper needs underlying the restless protests can be translated into productive policies that ameliorate poverty remains to be seen.[54] In any event, whether poverty is defined in objective or subjective terms, and irrespective of whether new policies lead to its decrease, the reality and threat of its spread on a global scale seem likely to pose a severe challenge to theorists who have long felt they had no reason to accommodate such phenomena in their formulations.[55]

In addition to the recent flow of events, two more long-term reasons explain why IR theorists can no longer ignore poverty issues. One is that the developing world, having been familiarized through global television with the much better living conditions of the developed world, has been sensitized to the inequities and has thus moved them ever higher on the global agenda.[56] Consequently, "what may be termed a revolution has taken place with regard to the political and moral significance of this issue, and this change has made the immense gap between the rich Northern half of the globe and the largely impoverished Southern half a new and explosive issue."[57]

Secondly, and no less important, poverty issues are no longer the exclusive preserve of developing societies that have yet to raise their standards of living to acceptable levels. While pockets of abject poverty, homelessness, and borderline subsistence levels have always been part of the world's social landscape, now such problems are spreading into the developed world at increasing rates that neither politicians nor the private sector can continue to treat as peripheral.[58] Due to the accelerating dynamics spawned by the worldwide turn to open markets late in the 1970s, the processes of globalization have expanded the ranks of the unemployed, widened the gap between the rich and the poor,[59] enlarged the gulf between those with and without a university education, ex-

---

[53] *Financial Times*, April 23, 2000.

[54] See, for example, John Burgess, "Accent on Poverty Battle Suggests a Shift at IMF," *International Herald Tribune*, April 19, 2000, p. 1.

[55] An indication that IR theorists are becoming sensitive to the challenges posed by poverty issues is evident in the convening of a panel on "Poverty and Inequality: Global and Regional Perspectives" at the annual meeting of the International Studies Association (Chicago, February 24, 2001).

[56] See, for example, B. Ramesh Babu (ed.), *Changing Global Political/Ideological Context and Afro-Asia: Strategies for Development* (New Delhi: South Asia Publishers, 1996).

[57] Robert Gilpin, *The Political Economy of International Relations* (Princeton, N.J.: Princeton University Press, 1987), p. 263.

[58] See, for example, William Julius Wilson, *When Work Disappears: The World of the New Urban Poor* (New York: Knopf, 1996).

[59] Signs that the gap began to narrow in the 1990s, at least in the United States, are reported in Lewis and Richardson, *Why Global Commitment Really Matters!*, pp. 53–55.

ploited women in the workforce, ghettoized urban centers, spurred the flow of immigrants, and otherwise generated pervasive fears of marginalization on the part of people in every walk of life.[60] Furthermore, the developed world has witnessed a transformation of the subjective as well as the objective underpinnings of poverty conditions: even those with jobs in the North now fear a future in which their earning capacities, if not their jobs, will be decimated.[61] In short, there are winners and losers everywhere.

Perhaps most important for present purposes, the growing salience of poverty is now rooted deep in international processes.[62] Fostered by fragmegrative dynamics, the elements of the poverty continuum—from meeting basic needs to addressing economic insecurities—are not amenable to resolution simply through the domestic policies of governments. Each country will have to address its jobs problem in terms of its own particular situation, to be sure, but the repercussions of the problem seem likely to pose challenges for the institutions and practices of both the state-centric and multi-centric worlds. Consequently, theorists can no longer ignore poverty-related phenomena, not so much because their consciences have somehow been triggered in ways they never were before but because such phenomena have become inextricably enmeshed in the emergent structures of world affairs.[63] "What in America was once called the battle between Wall Street and Main Street has now become global."[64]

The intrusion of poverty and jobs issues into world affairs occurs in a variety of ways. Innovative information technologies have led to the replacement of individuals by machines in manufacturing production.[65] The globalization of trade and investment has undermined and altered the labor markets of advanced industrial countries, with workers in the North being replaced by counterparts elsewhere whose wages are considerably

---

[60] For a cogent analysis in which these negative dimensions of globalization are assessed, see Michael A. Cohen, Blair A. Ruble, Joseph S. Tulchin, and Allison M. Garland (eds.), *Preparing for the Urban Future: Global Pressures and Local Forces* (Washington, D.C.: Woodrow Wilson Center Press, 1996), passim.

[61] See Jeremy Rifkin, *The End of Work: The Decline of the Global Labor Force and the Dawn of the Post-market Era* (New York: Putnam's, 1995).

[62] In the words of one analyst, "The universal concern over the distribution of wealth is truly a novel issue in world politics; scant prior interest in the subject is to be found in diplomatic histories." Gilpin, *The Political Economy of International Relations*, p. 264.

[63] For good examples of this newfound need to focus on poverty, see the various articles in the symposium "Globalism and the World's Poor," *The American Prospect* (Winter 2002, special supplement); and Arie M. Kakowics, "The Dark Side of the Moon: Globalization and Poverty as a Global Process" (paper presented at the annual meeting of the International Studies Association, Chicago, February 24, 2001).

[64] Kapstein, "Workers and the World Economy," p. 29.

[65] See, for example, John Eatwell (ed.), *Global Unemployment: Loss of Jobs in the '90s* (London: M. E. Sharpe, 1996), passim, and Jeremy Rifkin, *The End of Work: The Decline of the Labor Force and the Dawn of the Post-market Era* (New York: Putnam, 1995).

lower.[66] The globalization of national economies, reinforced by the policies of the World Bank and the IMF, has weakened governments, with the result that "[j]ust when working people most need the nation-state as a buffer from the world economy, it is abandoning them."[67] Demographic trends continue to enlarge the ranks of the world's poor. Massive migrations have swollen pockets of poverty and discontent in the developing world.[68] All these factors, and many others that could be cited, have combined to leave a trail of disaffected workers: "[T]he sudden exposure to the 'vagaries' of the market . . . [has] left the greater mass of the populations involved in a state of shock designated by sociologists as anomie, a loss of all sense of identity and direction, a breakdown of the normative structure."[69] Some analysts, moreover, contend that even if this state of shock is not immediately evident, concern about unemployment represents an underlying discontent that may be unfolding: "Even though we cannot see the visible signs of a great revolution which might change the present world order to one that is more humane, equitable and sustainable, we can hear countless underground rumbles all over the world which presage a global transformation."[70]

In short, the jobs and poverty issues have the explosive potential to significantly rearrange the ways in which the world conducts its affairs. Increasingly, analysts are rereading Karl Polanyi's 1944 classic, *The Great Transformation*, as a basis for warning that the "double movement," which he saw as culminating in the horrors of war and fascism of the twentieth century, may be unfolding again with equally disastrous consequences for the twenty-first century.[71] Noting that "[n]ineteenth century

[66] See, for example, Richard Stubbs and Geoffrey Underhill (eds.), *Political Economy and the Changing Global Order* (New York: St. Martin's Press, 1994), passim.

[67] Kapstein, "Workers and the World Economy," p. 16. See also the special issue, "The Globalisation of Liberalism?" *Millennium*, Vol. 24, No. 3 (1995), especially John Gerard Ruggie, "At Home Abroad, Abroad at Home: International Liberalization and Domestic Stability in the New World Economy," pp. 507–26.

[68] Doris M. Meissner, Robert D. Hormats, Antonio Garrigues Walker, and Shijuro Ogata, *International Migration Challenges in a New Era* (New York: Trilateral Commission, 1993).

[69] Kees van der Pijl, "The Second Glorious Revolution: Globalizing Elites and Historical Change," in Björn Hettne (ed.), *International Political Economy: Understanding Global Disorder* (London: Zed Books, 1995), p. 101.

[70] Yoshikazu Sakamoto, "Democratization, Social Movements and World Order," in Hettne (ed.), *International Political Economy*, p. 142.

[71] Karl Polanyi, *The Great Transformation* (New York: Rinehart, 1944). Examples of reliance on Polanyi's analysis can be found in Kapstein, "Workers and the World Economy," pp. 19–20; Stephen Gill, "Theorizing the Interregnum: The Double Movement and Global Poilitics in the 1990s," in Hettne (ed.), *International Political Economy*, pp. 66–67; and Robert W. Cox with Timothy J. Sinclair, *Approaches to World Order* (Cambridge: Cambridge University Press, 1996), pp. 31–32, 527–28. For a journalistic account in which it is

civilization . . . disintegrated as the result of . . . the self-regulating market,"[72] Polanyi reasoned that the first movement began in the previous century when fervor for wide-open capitalism, untrammeled by governmental control, led to grave economic crises. This, in turn, gave rise to a second movement founded on brutal authoritarian government that first disciplined the weakest in national societies, then disciplined all of society, and ultimately gave rise to the onset of world war. As indicated by the questions and assertions set forth in the last two epigraphs that open this chapter, there are reasons to wonder whether the street protests against international economic institutions that mark the turn into the twenty-first century—not to mention the terrorist attack on the center of American capitalism—are forerunners of another second movement.

Viewed from this perspective, the economic boom and prosperity that have accelerated in recent decades are comparable to the first movement of more than a century ago. To ponder this possible comparison, however, is to ruminate about political and not economic matters—about whether the world is capable of developing effective institutions through which to manage the course of events in the present era of fragmegration. The next chapter directly confronts the prospects for governance in our fragmegrative epoch.

---

argued, in effect, that the world is already moving into the second stage of the double movement, see Robert D. Kaplan, *The Ends of the Earth: A Journey at the Dawn of the 21st Century* (New York: Random House, 1996).

[72] Polanyi, *The Great Transformation*, p. 249.

CHAPTER EIGHTEEN

Governance in Fragmegrative Space

> So dominant in contemporary consciousness is the assumption
> that authority must be centralized that scholars are just
> beginning to grapple with how decentralized authority might
> be understood. . . . [T]he question of how to think about a
> world that is becoming "domesticated" but not centralized,
> about a world after "anarchy," is one of the most important
> questions today facing not only students of international
> relations but of political theory as well.
>
> —Alexander Wendt[1]

WE LIVE in a messy world. There are far too many people who survive on
or below the poverty line. There are far too many societies paralyzed by
division. There is too much violence within and between countries. In
many places there is too little water and too many overly populated,
pollution-ridden cities. And, most conspicuously, there is all too little
effective governance capable of ameliorating, if not resolving, these and
numerous other problems that crowd high on the global agenda. Indeed,
as distant proximities become ever less distant and ever more proximate,
so do the problems of governance become ever more acute. Hardly less
troubling, our generation lacks—as this chapter's epigraph implies—the
orientations necessary to sound assessments of how the authority of governance can be brought to bear on the challenges posed by the prevailing
disarray. Consequently, as implied in the preceding chapters, the dynamics of fragmegration, and perhaps especially the complexities inherent
in the extensive disaggregation of authority it has fostered, pose the question of whether governance on a global scale can be achieved in the
emergent epoch.

To be sure, a vast and ever-growing literature on global governance
has evolved in recent years, and much of it is imaginative and constructive,[2] suggesting that a variety of steering mechanisms and institutions

---

[1] *Social Theory of International Politics* (Cambridge: Cambridge University Press, 1999),
p. 308.

[2] See, for example, David Held, *Democracy and the Global Order: From the Modern State
to Cosmopolitan Governance* (Cambridge, Mass.: Polity Press, 1995); Jon Pierre (ed.), *Debating Governance: Authority, Steering and Democracy* (Oxford: Oxford University Press,

have come into being as instruments of governance. But while some of the literature does allow for disaggregated authority, it suffers from three major limitations: it does not focus on the tensions between localizing and globalizing forces and thus ignores the dynamics of fragmegration; second, it presumes that the primacy of states and that of their international institutions are the principal vehicles of governance on a global scale; and third, for these reasons it does not accord centrality to micro-macro processes.

It would be a mistake, however, to correct for these limitations by exploring the governance of fragmegration without reference to states and the international organizations they have fashioned to govern the course of events. If the times call for governance of a nonlinear world composed of endless feedback loops, contradictions, ambiguities, and uncertainties, then obviously states and the interactions of their governments need to be included in the exploration along with diverse, nongovernmental SOAs and micro-macro processes. If the previous chapters are essentially accurate in depicting profound and deep-seated changes that are transforming the processes and structures of individual and collective life at the present moment in history, this does not mean that global governance, which is founded on a commitment to promoting a world that is at the same time peaceful, democratic, and orderly, and the governance of fragmegration, which focuses on resolving tensions between localizing and globalizing dynamics, should be treated as mutually exclusive undertakings. Instead, it seems imperative to view global governance and the governance of fragmegration as inextricably interrelated and possibly mutually reinforcing. While the types of conflict with which the two forms of governance are concerned differ somewhat, each seeks to minimize conflict and advance human well-being both within and across the borders that divide countries, cultures, and economies.

Accordingly, what is needed is a conception of governance that allows for the interplay of all the fragmegrative dynamics set forth in the previous chapters and that does not shrink from the possibility that present generations, having matured in a world of states and fixed boundaries, may lack the experience—and possibly the political will—to cope with the many tensions, ambiguities, and contradictions to which fluid bound-

---

2000); Martin Hewson and Timothy J. Sinclair (eds.), *Approaches to Global Governance Theory* (Albany: State University of New York Press, 1999), pp. 287–301; Raimo Väyrynen (ed.), *Globalization and Global Governance* (Lanhan, Md.: Rowman and Littlefield, 1999); Oran Young, *International Governance: Protecting the Environment in a Stateless Society* (Ithaca, N.Y.: Cornell University Press, 1994); University of Victoria, *"Rethinking Governance" Handbook: An Inventory of Ideas to Enhance Accountability, Participation, and Transparency* (Victoria: Centre for Global Studies, 2001); and Heikki Patomaki, *Democratising Globalisation: The Leverage of the Tobin Tax* (London: Zed Books, 2001).

aries and diverse opposing forces give rise. Indeed, the governance of fragmegration must be conceived in broad enough terms to allow for Ashby's "Law of Requisite Variety," which asserts that for a system to survive it must be as complex as its environment.[3] The achievement of such a level of complexity in the present era requires learning and adaptation, else the global system will eventually collapse as a coherent whole. It remains to be seen whether the skill revolution, the organizational explosion, the mobility upheaval, and the other sources of transformation are powerful enough to foster the requisite learning, or whether the understanding and political will of elites and publics are insufficient to the tasks of adaptation.

Despite the enormous complexity that marks the emergent epoch, several of its features that underlie the potential for governance on a global scale are readily discernible. One is that the goals and interests of the individuals and collectivities on the global stage are so numerous, diverse, and disaggregated that a hierarchical global structure with a single mechanism for governance is not going to evolve in the foreseeable future. No hegemon, nor any cluster of like-minded powerful rule systems, nor the United Nations, is likely to evolve exclusive jurisdiction over the tasks of global governance. Some steering mechanisms may have wider scope for influencing the course of events than do others, but none is likely ever to be capable of alone dominating the processes of governance. A second characteristic of the current scene is that progress toward more effective governance must perforce be halting and accomplished in small increments, given the huge degree to which authority has been decentralized at every level of community. A third characteristic concerns the pervasiveness of authority crises in every part of the world, a pattern that seems bound to accelerate if Affirmative Locals and Globals persist in pursuing policies that can degrade the environment or promote poverty, or if system-wide circumstances such as a deep global recession lead individuals to greatly enlarge the ranks of the Resistant and Exclusionary Locals and join in collective actions designed to deter progress toward resolving global problems. In short, an overview suggests that the prospects for effective governance on a worldwide scale are highly problematic, that progress in this respect may take decades, and that the probability of evolution toward a harmonious and progressive global order may not be any greater than the chance of deterioration toward a tension-filled and retrogressive disorder.

[3] Ross Ashby, "Variety, Constraint, and the Law of Requisite Variety," in Walter Buckley (ed.), *Modern Systems Research for the Behavioral Scientist: A Sourcebook* (Chicago: Aldine, 1968), pp. 129–36.

The Proliferation of Governance

To meet the requirements of a broad conception, governance is here regarded as sustained by rule systems that serve as steering mechanisms through which leaders and collectivities frame and move toward their goals.[4] In the state-centric world some of the rule systems are presided over by states and their governments, while international institutions and regimes maintain others. In the multi-centric world numerous steering mechanisms are to be found in NGOs, and still others consist of informal SOAs that may never develop formal structures.

With the wide dispersion of authority at every level of community, in other words, recent decades have witnessed a vast expansion of rule systems and steering mechanisms. Nor is there a lack of variety in the extant systems of governance. On the contrary, as indicated in earlier chapters, the era of fragmegration is both fostering and sustaining a world marked by a proliferation of all kinds of governance. And the organizational explosion is not confined to nongovernmental entities. New forms of government have been developed, and old ones have either added new layers or transferred their authority downward to subnational levels or upward to supranational levels. The result is an ever-widening realm in which governance is undertaken and implemented, a development that suggests the world may indeed be adapting to the ever-greater complexity of community, national, regional, and global life.

But how to probe the number and diversity of rule systems such that the governance of fragmegration can be assessed? And assuming that assessment is possible, what are the probabilities that the emergent disaggregated, diverse global system can achieve effective governance? In a world where groups and countries are simultaneously fragmenting and integrating, where the two contrary forces are pervasive, interactive, and feed on each other, are the resulting tensions subject to governance? Can mechanisms be developed that steer the tensions in constructive directions? If collapsed distance, time, and sequentiality are taken seriously, can they serve as stimuli to a renewal of creative thought about what governance may mean in the twenty-first century?

Except for the last, these questions serve as the focus of this chapter, but the answers to them are far from clear. My response to the last ques-

---

[4] This conception of the nature of governance is elaborated in James N. Rosenau, "Governance in the 21st Century," *Global Governance*, Vol. 1 (1995), pp. 13–43; and Rosenau, "Governance, Order, and Change in World Politics," in J. N. Rosenau and E. O. Czempiel (eds.), *Governance without Government: Order and Change in World Politics* (Cambridge: Cambridge University Press, 1992), Chap. 1.

tion, however, is an unqualified yes. It is an unqualified response in the sense that the transformations at work in the world are so profound that a thoughtful observer cannot but experience a sense of renewal, an impulse to think afresh about how control might be achieved over the contradictions and changes that mark our emergent epoch.

But the task of thinking afresh involves more than sensitivity to profound transformations. A broad conception of governance also requires breaking out of the conceptual jails in which we have long been ensconced.[5] To do so it is useful to start at the beginning and treat politics and governance as social processes that transcend state and societal boundaries so thoroughly as to necessitate the invention of new wheels. What is needed are conveyances with many wheels that sometimes roll harmoniously in the same direction, that sometimes move crazily in contradictory directions, and that often lurch fitfully as some wheels turn while others are stationary. This is a metaphorical way of again asserting that, as the differences, overlaps, and contradictions that mark collectivities on the global stage have become ever more pervasive, rethinking is needed that allows for the possibility of new terminal entities emerging that serve as the focus of the most salient loyalties and affiliations of groups and individuals in the same ways states have.

One way to develop a broad conception that encompasses the micro-macro underpinnings of both global governance and the governance of fragmegration and allows for the vast proliferation of rule systems is to frame a typology that sorts out and juxtaposes the diverse horizontal and hierarchical actors and processes through which authority is exercised. While the greater number and variety of governance entities suggests that parsimonious classification may be unachievable, more than a few observers have undertaken to develop an appropriate typology. Two of these are illustrative of the difficulties involved. One is based on the movement of issues and labeled the "governance ladder."[6] The other differentiates five alternative models of state-society interactions in governance through "a continuum ranging from the most dominated by the State and those in which the State plays the least role and indeed one in which there is argued to be governance without government."[7]

---

[5] Elsewhere I have elaborated at length on why we thrive entrapped in conceptual jails of our own making. See James N. Rosenau, *Turbulence in World Politics: Change and Continuity in World Politics* (Princeton, N.J.: Princeton University Press, 1990), Chap. 2.

[6] In an agenda for the Workshop on Globalization and the Comprehensive Governance of Water, sponsored by the Commission on Economic, Environmental, and Social Policy of the World Conservation Union (Gland, Switzerland, May 26, 2000).

[7] B. Guy Peters and Jon Pierre, "Is There a Governance Theory?" (paper presented at the XVIII Congress of the International Political Science Association, Quebec City, August 1–5, 2000), p. 4.

The Governance Ladder and the State-Society Continuum

The governance ladder focuses on the movement of issues up and down the various rungs as they arrest the attention of officials and publics, thereby becoming governance issues. Issues that first generate widespread awareness at local levels get onto the ladder at the bottom rungs, while those that originate at the global level occupy the top rungs, just as those that get onto political agendas at the national level perch on the middle rungs. Some issues remain on the same rung throughout; some start at the bottom and move to the top; and some start at the top and percolate down. Such a scheme has been cogently framed with reference to environmental issues:

> If climate change has been introduced so-to-speak at a global level and is slowly moving down the governance ladder, biodiversity, on the other hand, . . . has mainly been introduced at a national level and is currently moving both upwards and downwards. Water . . . is clearly characterized by a bottom-up approach: awareness that it constitutes a governance issue has emerged first at a local level, tied as it is to livelihoods, and is currently moving to the national and the global levels. We propose here to use the term of comprehensive governance in order to account for the fact that governance occurs at all levels (from local to global), involves all stakeholders, and links at least the three issues together, i.e., water, biodiversity, and climate change.[8]

The state-society continuum is less hierarchical. At one extreme is the Etatist model based on "the assumption that government is the principal actor for all aspects of governance and can control the manner in which the society is permitted to be involved, if it is at all." Next to it on the continuum is the Liberal-Democratic model, which "accepts the role of the state as the principal actor in governance," but which allows for other actors competing to influence the state. There follows the State-Centric model, which "remains at the center of the process, but institutionalizes its relationships with social actors." The fourth is the Dutch Governance School that "depends heavily upon the role of social networks in governing, with the state being merely one among many actors involved in the process." Finally, at the other extreme of the continuum is the Governance without Government model, which argues that "the state has lost its capacity to govern and is at best an arena within which private actors play out their own governance arrangement."[9]

---

[8] Agenda for the Workshop on Globalization and the Comprehensive Governance of Water, p. 1.

[9] Peters and Pierre, "Is There a Governance Theory?" pp. 4–5.

Mobius-Web Governance

Useful as such typologies may be, however, they do not adequately serve the need of analyzing the governance of fragmegration. With the exception of one extreme of the state-society continuum, both typologies differentiate governance undertaken within the state-centric system and do not extend the typology to the multi-centric system. And with the exception of links to livelihoods and stakeholders at the bottom rung of the governance ladder, neither typology explicitly includes micro-macro interactions as relevant to any form of governance.

Hence, a somewhat more elaborate conception needs to be framed if account is to be taken of micro-macro interactions as well as the diversity, the horizontality, the complexity, and the sheer number of SOAs that now mark the global stage and contribute to governance in both state-centric and multi-centric worlds. I have sought to meet this need through a more elaborate scheme that identifies six types of governance systems that, taken together, span the several dimensions of fragmegration that require the exercise of effective authority. The six types are set forth in table 18.1, with the distinctions between them being drawn in terms of the degree to which authority is formally established, the directions in which it may flow, and the eight kinds of actors principally involved in sustaining the flow. Since all six types have been analyzed elsewhere,[10] there is no need to probe each of them in this chapter. Rather, here the focus is on only one of them, what I call the *mobius-web* model of global governance.[11] If the mobius-web form does not presently subsume the other five, it is so fully expressive of the complexities of the emergent epoch that in the long run, if not the medium term, it is likely to encompass the other five. The underlying central tendency, in other words, is conceived to be one in which the mobius-web form is probably the end state toward which all other types of global governance are evolving.

Mobius-web governance is rooted in the impetus to employ rule systems that steer issues through both hierarchical and networked interac-

---

[10] This sixfold typology can be found in James N. Rosenau, "The Governance of Fragmegration: Neither a World Republic nor a Global Interstate System," *Studia Diplomatica*, Vol. 53, No. 5 (2000), pp. 15–39; and Rosenau, "Governance in a New Global Order," in David Held and Anthony McGrew (eds.), *Governing the Global Polity* (Cambridge, Mass.: Polity Press, 2002), pp. 70–86.

[11] For another formulation that employs the mobius metaphor to assess the porosity of boundaries, see Didier Bigo, "The Mobius Ribbon of Internal and External Security(ies)," in Mathias Albert, David Jacobson, and Yosef Lapid (eds.), *Identities, Borders, Orders: Rethinking International Relations Theory* (Minneapolis: University of Minnesota Press, 2001), pp. 91–116.

TABLE 18.1.
Six Types of Global Governance

	Processes (type of collectivities involved in each form of governance)	
Structures	Unidirectional (vertical or horizontal)	Multidirectional (vertical and horizontal)
Formal	**Top-Down Governance** (*governments, TNCs, IGOs*)	**Network Governance** (*governments, IGOs, NGOs, INGOs—e.g., business alliances*)
Informal	**Bottom-Up Governance** (*mass publics, NGOs, INGOs*)	**Side-by-Side Governance** (*NGO and INGO, governments*)
Mixed formal and informal	**Market Governance** (*governments, IGOs, elites, markets, mass publics, TNCs*)	**Mobius-Web Governance** (*governments, elites, mass publics, TNCs, IGOs, NGOs, INGOs*)

Note: TNC (Transnational Corporation); INGO (International Nongovernmental Organization)

tions across levels of aggregation that may encompass all the diverse collectivities and individuals who participate in the processes of governance. These interactions constitute a hybrid structure in which the dynamics of governance are so intricate and overlapping among the several levels as to form a singular, weblike process that, like a mobius, neither begins nor culminates at any level or at any point in time. Mobius-web governance does not culminate with the passage of a law or compliance with its regulations. Rather, it is operative as long as the issues subjected to governance continue to be of concern.

The complexity of mobius-web governance suggests that fragmegrative dynamics pose perhaps the most difficult of all the challenges that face those who undertake to exercise authority. The difficulties are rooted in the nature of either the fragmenting forces that lead groups to resist the integrating forces they feel impinge on their well-being or the integrating forces that foster a sense of exclusion on the part of people and collectivities left out of the integrative process. The resistances tend to be deeply rooted in one or another kind of commitment to local practices, habits, and traditions, while resentments over exclusion tend to derive from aspirations for a better standard of living and other perquisites that may flow from integration.

Neither the resistant nor the resentful groups are readily amenable to the directives that stem from hierarchical authority. The governance of fragmegration, therefore, also requires authority that is dispersed and decentralized, that flows as much horizontally as vertically through participatory channels. Recent conflicts in Chechnya and Sri Lanka are extreme examples of how steering mechanisms founded on vertical authority do not result in effective governance, whereas the subsidiarity principle that has strengthened the European Union is illustrative of how various forms of horizontal authority can minimize, if not overcome, resistances to integration.

It follows that in mobius-web governance the relevant actors are closely linked, with the result that the relevant agencies are prone to cross the private-public divide by mobilizing mass publics as well as elites on behalf of the values at stake. The environmental issue area is illustrative. It encompasses intricate networks of actors at subnational, national, transnational, and international levels who interact in such diverse ways as to render fruitless any attempt to tease out the direction of causal processes. That is, IGOs and most states have often yielded to the pressures of NGOs and INGOs on issues pertaining to the environment and cooperatively formed both formal and informal networks through which the spreading norms get translated into mechanisms of governance.[12] Indeed, mobius-web governance may be marked by a cumulative sequencing in which the pressures generated by bottom-up governance give rise to top-down and side-by-side governance that, in turn, becomes a vast network encompassing all levels of governance and diverse flows of authority. One analyst disputes this possibility and, instead, estimates that in the course of these complex sequences the governance of issues will become more formalized under IGOs and states, thereby "eating into the realms of the INGOs/NGOs."[13]

Equally illustrative of mobius-web governance was the response to the challenges created by the terrorist attacks on the World Trade Center. The war on terrorism subsequently launched by the U.S. government; the anti-terrorist coalition of states it formed; the central role of protests by Islamic fundamentalists in Pakistan and elsewhere in the Middle East; the continued defiance of Osama bin Laden and his Al Qaeda network; the intensified recognition of the rich-poor gap as a negative consequence of globalization; the involvement and coordination of national police forces; the anxieties that mushroomed in American society over fears of anthrax, smallpox, nuclear, and other mass terrorist attacks; and

---

[12] David John Frank, Ann Hironaka, John W. Meyer, Evan Schofer, and Nancy Brandon Tuma, "The Rationalization and Organization of Nature in World Culture," in Boli and Thomas (eds.), *Constructing World Culture*, Chap. 3.

[13] John Boli, personal correspondence, April 30, 1999.

the redirection of the antiglobalization protests into an antiwar move-ment are only the more conspicuous aspects of the mobius-web govern-ance with which the world reacted to the situation created by the attacks of September 11, 2001.

Mobius-web governance is not lacking in overlaps among the other types of governance outlined in table 18.1. Given the diversity of new forms of horizontal governance, however, the notion of authority being exercised horizontally as well as vertically through mobius webs brings a modicum of order to the subject even as it highlights the complexity of our fragmegrative epoch.

CONCLUSIONS

Of course, typologies are only aides in organizing thought. In themselves they do not in any way come close to answering the questions that need to be clarified: Will the weakening of states, the proliferation of rule sys-tems, the disaggregation of authority, the clash between globalization and its opponents, the advent of mass terrorism, and the greater density of the global stage enhance or diminish the effectiveness of the overall system of governance on a global scale? While doubtless there will be pockets of ineffectiveness and breakdown, will the emergent system, on balance, make for more humane and sensitive governance? Are the ten-sions and conflicts fostered by the deleterious aspects of fragmegration likely to prove ungovernable?

It is not difficult to frame pessimistic answers to such questions. The gap between globalization's winners and losers persists as the skills of both groups continue to enlarge and their organizations continue to pro-liferate. And even if nonzero-sum solutions to fragmegrative dynamics do evolve, progress along such lines is likely to be so slow and intermittent as not to keep pace with the many tensions to which uncertainty is heir. The age of fragmegration, it can reasonably be concluded, will endure as far as one can see into the decades ahead.

On the other hand, upbeat responses to the foregoing questions strike me as plausible if one is able to look beyond the prevailing uncertainty. In the first place, sensitivity to the rich-poor gap and its deleterious poten-tial is widening. The gulf between the Affirmative Globals and Locals on the one hand and their Resistant counterparts on the other may have narrowed as the realization of mutual interdependence has deepened since the hints of apocalypse were heightened by the mother of all distant proximities on September 11, 2001.

Second, more than a little truth attaches to the aphorism that there is safety in numbers. The more crowded the global stage gets with steering mechanisms, the less can any one of them, or any coalition of them, dominate the course of events, and the more will all of them have to be sensitive to how sheer numbers limit their influence. Every rule system, in other words, will be hemmed in by all the others, thus conducing to a growing awareness of the virtues of cooperation and the need to contain the worst effects of deleterious fragmegration.

Third, there is a consciousness of and intelligence about the processes of globalization that is spreading widely to every corner of the earth. What has been called "reflexivity"[14] and what I call the *globalization of globalization*[15] is accelerating at an extraordinary rate—from the halls of academe and government to the boardrooms of corporations, from the streets of urban cities to the rural homes of China (where the impact of the WTO is an intense preoccupation), people in all walks of life have begun to appreciate their interdependence with others as time and distance shrink. For some, maybe even many, the rush into a globalized world may be regrettable, but with perhaps only the Insular Locals and the Circumstantial Passives oblivious to the dynamics of change, there is likely to be a growing understanding of the necessity to confront the challenges of fragmegration and an openness to new ways of meeting them. Put more positively, there is substantial evidence that good minds in government, academe, journalism, and the business community in all parts of the world are turning, each in their own way, to the task of addressing and constructively answering the questions raised here. It is difficult to recall another period in history when so many thoughtful people concentrated their talents on the human condition from a worldwide perspective.

Fourth, the advent of networks and the flow of horizontal communications appear to have enlarged the local and global worlds, thereby bringing many more people into the political arena. The conditions for the emergence of a series of global consensuses never existed quite to the extent that they do today. The skills of individuals and the orientations of the organizations they support are increasingly conducive to convergence around shared values.

Fifth, as consensuses form, widen, and compete, so will expansion occur in the realm of governance. Increasingly, it seems clear, multilevel governance will be the dominant mode through which NGOs, communities, governments, regions, and the world attempt to exert a modicum of control over their affairs.

[14] Anthony Giddens and Christopher Pierson, *Conversations with Anthony Giddens: Making Sense of Modernity* (Cambridge, Mass.: Polity Press, 1998), pp. 115–17.

[15] For a discussion of how concerns about globalization are spreading on a global scale, see James N. Rosenau, "The Globalization of Globalization," in Michael Brecher and Frank Harvey (eds.), *Millennium Reflections on International Studies* (Ann Arbor: University of Michigan Press, 2002), pp. 271–90.

None of this is to suggest, however, that nirvana lies ahead. Surely it does not. Surely distant circumstances will become ever more proximate. Surely fragmegration will be with us for a long time, and surely many of its tensions will intensify. But inclinations to incorporate new, horizontal forms of authority into the panoply of governance mechanisms are not lacking, and that is not a trivial conclusion.

PART FOUR

Postscript

A Transformed Observer in a Transforming World: Confessions of a Pre-Postmodernist

> When the mind is forced to repudiate the immediate past, the intellectual community splits in two. On one side stands the majority, the great mass, who cling to established ideas; on the other side, the scant few who venture forth alone, the minority of alert souls who glimpse, somewhere in the distance, a zone never seen, a skin never touched. These amazing sights inspire them to gesture in ways that most people can make little sense of, for the sluggish majority has not yet climbed to the heights from which terra incognita can be discerned. Thus, the forward-moving few are doomed to be misunderstood. They must face the dangers of the unconquered lands that lie ahead and at the same time endure harassment from those who lag behind. While creating the new, they must defend themselves against the old.
>
> —José Ortega y Gasset[1]

MOST OF US who labor in the ivory tower do our best to be detached, to advance the knowledge-building process without skewing our data and interpretations. Yet, it is self-deceptive to believe that one can be fully objective about the materials one probes. In the absence of perfect information (a permanent condition with which we must all contend), we can never tell the whole story about a situation, country, political system, or any other phenomena we seek to explain. Perforce we must select some of their aspects as important and dismiss others as trivial, and our bases for making these selections stem from our values and prior experiences, as well as our expertise. The only way distortions derived from these built-in biases, premises, or understandings can be minimized is by making them as explicit as possible. Explication is the key to knowledge building. It enables others to assess our conclusions because they can retrace the steps we took to arrive at them.

So while it may well be an ego trip that leads me to focus on myself in

---

[1] Quoted in Oded Balaban, *Politics and Ideology: A Philosophical Approach* (Aldershot, United Kingdom: Ashgate, 1995), p. xiv.

this concluding chapter, it also stems from strong intellectual convictions. By tracing salient experiences, I hope to provide the reader with a sense of how I arrived at my intellectual preoccupation with micro-macro inter-actions and the concepts of distant proximities and fragmegration as a result of a wavering intellectual journey that has undergone at least one major transformation.

The Scholar as an Adaptive System

Like the nations, bureaucracies, and officials they study, students of world politics are beset by tensions between long-standing habits and new learnings. They pride themselves on being open to new stimuli, but they are also prone to engage in habit-driven behavior that leads them to cast their inquiries into molds that have worked for them before.[2]

At least such is the case with me. In many ways I am the quintessential habit-driven actor, always ready to let variables vary but, with one major exception elaborated later, resistant to tampering with an analytic per-spective that consistently yielded insights in the past. The ensuing pages are no exception. I am so accustomed to forcing myself up the ladder of abstraction by asking about anything I observe in world politics, "Of what is *this* an instance?" that I cannot help wondering what larger pat-tern my career and scholarship might exemplify. Likewise, I am so accus-tomed to treating collective actors as adaptive systems that seek to main-tain a balance between internal requirements and external demands[3] that I cannot even undertake an autobiographical assessment without positing myself as an adaptive actor who has tried, across a long professional ca-reer, to accommodate the internal drives stemming from my personal orientations and the external pressures emanating from the larger envi-ronment of world affairs.

Viewing myself through these lenses has not been easy. It is one thing to note, as an observer, that scholars are subject to the same tensions between internal and external demands as beset macro collectivities; but it is quite another to confront, as an actor, the task of looking back over a career and acknowledging how these tensions may have shaped one's commitments and research. One's personal tensions and history invite distortion and rationalization, whereas those of macro collectivities can be approached with a reasonable degree of detachment. Furthermore, getting a proper perspective on myself adapting to new opportunities and limitations has proven difficult because the assumption that turning points

---

[2] For an elaboration of the concept of habit-driven actors, see James N. Rosenau, "Be-fore Cooperation: Hegemons, Regimes, and Habit-Driven Actors in World Politics," *Inter-national Organization*, Vol. 40 (autumn 1986), pp. 849–94.

[3] James N. Rosenau, *The Study of Political Adaptation* (London: Frances Pinter, 1981).

in one's intellectual development are largely responses to climactic moments in world affairs does not apply in my case, compelling me to search for understanding in less coherent and more intimate causal dynamics.

The essential lines of my intellectual development seem, retrospectively, less a product of war (hot and cold) and more a consequence of two personal traits that have shaped both the central themes and the major transformation that mark my inquiries over several decades. One of the traits is captured by this chapter's epigraph. Viewed negatively, my tendency to "venture forth alone," as Ortega puts it, could be interpreted as a need to be different, to be always in the minority, to contest the prevailing perspectives regardless of their content. Viewed positively, it is a trait that has led to research and writing that anticipated new forms and directions of inquiry that others eventually found useful. During the first decades of my career I was among the handful of practitioners who initiated and sustained the so-called behavioral revolution in the study of international politics and foreign policy. Involved here was a commitment to proceeding scientifically in the analysis of empirical materials—that is, to framing hypotheses and theories that were tested with quantified data and verified with statistical tests of significance. In the early years the notions of science and quantification were an anathema to many in the international field, and those of us who had moved down this path were subjected to considerable criticism, even ridicule, for daring to believe that human affairs are patterned and that these patterns could be uncovered through scientific methods. By the end of the 1970s, however, the underlying premises of the behavioral revolution came to be widely shared (even if they were not so labeled), and it was roughly at that time that the major transformation in my intellectual journey occurred. The transformation had extensive intellectual roots, but it could also be interpreted as another instance of my need to be different and contest the prevailing perspectives. The transformation involved relaxing the scientific criteria of parsimony and their dependence on quantitative analysis in favor of an interpretive approach that allowed for scientific methods but at the same time seemed more appropriate to the changes that were rendering world affairs ever-more turbulent and complex. So again I am in a minority and have had to endure criticism, even ridicule, for having offered inquiries that lack scientific discipline and that do not readily conform to the premises of any of the prevailing paradigms in the field. The preceding chapters are the latest iteration of this quirky approach.

The second personal trait that underlies my work has never been so fully expressed as it is in this book, though its presence can be traced throughout both my "science" years and the subsequent "relaxed-science" years. Some would label this trait as a commitment to methodological individualism, to locating the individual at the substantive center of my analytic universe, but I prefer to see it as an extension of the empirical commitment embedded in my behavioral period. One can usefully conceptualize and trace the conduct of systems, of large aggregates of people, but one can only observe empirically individuals and infer how their attitudes and actions collectively contribute to, sustain, or undermine the aggregates or systems under examination. Put differently, just as I cannot separate my inquiries from who I am, so do I have difficulty divorcing collectivities, institutions, states, regimes, organizations, and any other macro entities from the people who constitute them. Thus it is that my first professional article was a personal account of the challenge of completing a dissertation;[4] thus it is that I have previously turned on three other occasions to autobiography to account for my research;[5] thus it is that my pre-theory of foreign policy that helped found the subfield of comparative foreign policy posits the characteristics of individuals and the roles they occupy as two of the five prime variables underlying how countries conduct themselves abroad;[6] thus it is that I authored a play that focuses on the tensions between personal and professional life;[7] and thus it is that micro-macro interactions are the organizing focus of this book, with four chapters devoted to different kinds of individuals and their movement among the worlds I have constructed to try to grasp their links to a fragmegrative epoch.

A TRANSFORMED OBSERVER IN A TRANSFORMING WORLD

For a long time I was reluctant to acknowledge that my commitment to a quantitative, parsimonious form of science had undergone a significant transformation that began early in the 1980s. Indeed, I did not just avoid attempting to explain it to others; I also shunned an effort to clarify it for

---

[4] James N. Rosenau, "The Birth of a Political Scientist," *PROD*, Vol. 3 (January 1960), pp. 19–21.

[5] James N. Rosenau, "The Scholar as an Adaptive System," in J. Kruzel and J. N. Rosenau (eds.), *Journeys through World Politics: Autobiographic Reflections of Thirty-four Academic Travelers* (Lexington, Mass.: Lexington Books, 1989); Rosenau, "Confessions of a Pre-postmodernist: Or Can an Old-Timer Change Course?" in Neil L. Waters (ed.), *Beyond the Area Studies War: Toward a New International Studies* (Hanover, N.H.: University Press of New England, 2000), pp. 181–89; and Rosenau, "A Transformed Observer in a Transformed World," *Studia Diplomatica*, Vol. 52, Nos. 1–2 (1999), pp. 5–14. The last two of these articles serve as the basis for much of this chapter.

[6] James N. Rosenau, "Pre-theories and Theories of Foreign Policy," in R. B. Farrell (ed.), *Approaches to Comparative and International Politics* (Evanston, Ill.: Northwestern University Press, 1966), pp. 27–92.

[7] James N. Rosenau, *Kwangju: An Escalatory Spree* (produced at the Odyssey Theater, Los Angeles, November–December 1991).

myself. Then, during a lecture in Belgium in 1999, a student asked directly why I had made such a seemingly abrupt shift.[8]

As I recall it, the question was, in effect, "Tell us about Rosenau versus Rosenau. What happened to you? Back in the sixties and the seventies you did a lot of work on the scientific study of foreign policy, which you no longer do. What happened to you?" The questioner may not have said it in quite this way, but that is the way it felt because it is the case, as noted earlier, that the early years of my career were devoted to an aspiration to study foreign policy scientifically, to generate well-founded empirical studies of foreign policy, and to engineer basic breakthroughs in the study of foreign affairs. And surely it is the case that I no longer do that. But if this shift is confusing to those who do not know me, so has it also been confusing to me, which may be why I have never undertaken to explain it. While the explanation has been elusive, one thing is clear: I do know that I did not desert the study of foreign policy; I still believe in what we undertook in those early years and the conceptual framework, or pre-theory, we employed using a database called Comparative Research on the Events of Nations (CREON) designed to test key elements of the pre-theory. Indeed, that work continues today.[9] So I think it is fair to say that rather than abandoning the comparative study of foreign policy, I moved away from pursuing it. But the question remains: Why?

In addition to the personal traits just identified, one intellectual reason stands out. As the seventies moved into the eighties and the eighties into the nineties, national states seemed increasingly less competent to frame and move toward their goals. Indeed, it is reasonable to assert, as several of the preceding chapters do, that states have become quite unable to control major flows across their borders. They cannot control the flow of ideas (China is trying but failing). As we know from the Asian financial crisis, they are unable to control the flow of money; nor can they control this flow collectively: despite subsequent efforts to build international institutions through which control could be exercised, little progress has been made in that direction. They are unable to control the flow of drugs. They are unable to control the flow of crime. (I learned in Brussels that to a large extent the Belgian government has lost control of Antwerp to criminal elements.) And the question of whether they can control the flow of terrorists remains problematic. The more it became apparent that states were losing much of the control that my training had taught me

[8] At the "Seminar on After the Cold War: Theoretical and Methodological Challenges," Facultes Universitaires Catholiques de Mons, February 26, 1999. What follows in this section of the chapter is an edited version of the transcription of that lecture.

[9] See, for example, Margaret G. Hermann and Bengt Sundelius (eds.), *Comparative Foreign Policy Analysis: Theories and Methods* (Englewood Cliffs, N.J.: Prentice-Hall, forthcoming).

they had, the more I was inclined to move away from my original preoccupation with the comparative study of foreign policy and toward trying to understand what seemed to me to be the transformation of the international system and the emergence of a new epoch.

This paradigmatic shift had its origins in a file I call my "anomaly file." I am a close daily reader of the *New York Times*, and every time I came upon an item with which my training could not cope, an item that just didn't make sense, I would clip it and put it in my anomaly file. As the seventies came to an end and the eighties unfolded, my anomaly file grew so large that at some point it seemed to me the time had come to go back to the drawing board and rethink the nature of world politics. There seemed to be so much that was anomalous in terms of my training, my teaching, and my scientific inquiries into foreign policy. For example, one day I was reading the paper, and I came upon an item that said that the Hotline (that Cold War telephone through which the Kremlin and the White House were linked after the Cuban Missile Crisis) had been sold. I scratched my head and exclaimed to myself, the Hotline was sold! Yes, it was sold to the Swiss! What is going on here? The question led the clipping directly to the anomaly file.

And as the file grew and grew, an entirely new model of world politics began to emerge and dominate my thinking. The result was what I consider my most important book, *Turbulence in World Politics: A Theory of Change and Continuity*.[10] So I now speak of my *turbulence model*, or what I also call my *post-international model*, because with states increasingly less competent and their role in world politics increasingly less preeminent, it seemed clear that the world had moved into a "post" condition,[11] that it had moved beyond being international, that the boundaries between domestic and foreign affairs have become porous, that what is domestic is also foreign and what is foreign is also domestic. Yet, in our profession we continue to draw that line between the domestic and the foreign: we do so in our courses, in our models, and in our writing, as if the distinction is sacrosanct. But I am finding the distinction increasingly anomalous, increasingly irrelevant, and increasingly less powerful as a way to organize our understanding of the world. Thus I now tend to avoid the word *international* and refer instead to *world affairs*. For example, I now give a course entitled "The Dynamics of Globalization" and no

---

[10] James N. Rosenau, *Turbulence in World Politics: A Theory of Change and Continuity* (Princeton: Princeton University Press, 1990).

[11] As indicated by the fragmegrative theme that pervades this book, and as made even more explicit elsewhere, I now think it is possible to assert that the world has moved beyond a "post" condition. See James N. Rosenau, "Beyond Postinternationalism," in Heidi H. Hobbs (ed.), *Pondering Postinternationalism: A Paradigm for the Twenty-first Century* (Albany: State University of New York Press, 2000), pp. 219–37.

longer give courses with the word *international* in the title. Avoidance of such terminology is a deep-seated commitment. My 1997 book elaborates on this at some length, stressing that what is foreign is domestic, that what is domestic is foreign, and that as a result a frontier has been created where the two converge, interact, overlap, and sometimes merge.[12] That book's essential argument is that it is on the frontier between the domestic and the foreign (and I think it is a very wide frontier, perhaps the whole world) where the interesting issues and institutions of politics are to be found.

If I had my way and could organize curricula around the world, I would urge the designing of courses that work along the frontier where the domestic and foreign overlap so fully as to have become synthesized. I suspect few agree with this perspective, but that is who I am intellectually at this time.

The more I ransacked my anomaly file for new perspectives, the more I became preoccupied with the "Of what is this an instance?" question. The key word in the question is *this*, which refers to anything you observe, whether it is in personal life, university life, national life, European life, or global life. For this reason I consider it the most important and powerful question one can ask. It stirs the mind and fosters big thoughts. It is a powerful question because it drives you up what I call the ladder of abstraction. It compels you to look for a larger category into which to put that which you observe. And that, of course, is the route to theory.

I say to my students it does not matter if you are eighteen years old and you have just entered college, you bring to bear some notions with which to answer that question with respect to any aspect of world affairs you confront. There is no right answer to the question; there can be as many answers as there are different levels of analysis. I once wrote a paper on the fiftieth Anniversary of the United Nations. I began by asking, "Of what is the fiftieth anniversary of the United Nations an instance?"—a question that generated twenty-three answers. To be sure, any paper that explores twenty-three answers is bound to be tedious,[13] but it illustrates the point that the question offers a way of forcing oneself to be theoretical.

To assert that the interesting questions of politics are located at the higher rungs of the ladder of abstraction and not at the lower rungs is, of

[12] *Along the Domestic-Foreign Frontier: Exploring Governance in a Turbulent World* (Cambridge: Cambridge University Press, 1997).

[13] The paper was later published under the title "Powerful Tendencies, Enduring Tensions, and Glaring Contradictions: The United Nations in a Turbulent Era," in Albert J. Paolini, Anthony P. Jarvis, and Christian Reus-Smit (eds.), *Between Sovereignty and Global Governance: The United Nations, the State and Civil Society* (New York: St. Martin's Press, 1998), pp. 252–73.

course, only one person's perspective. Others may have different perspectives on what engages the mind and makes it reach. Some may be stimulated by descending the ladder and roaming around hard empirical materials, and that is no less valid a perspective than moving high on the ladder for theoretical insight. While my approach does not downplay the empirical data or the appropriate methodologies to be found toward the lower rungs on the ladder, for me it is not until one moves up the ladder that the mind comes alive, that one begins to generate an understanding that will endure beyond the immediate moment.

Let me illustrate by noting a couple of the theoretical premises that all of us, in one way or another, bring to bear whenever we engage in observation. As indicated in chapter 2, one is that we all proceed from certain premises about the nature of change, the relevance of history, its repetitiveness, continuities, and transformations. As professional students, we should be able to meaningfully distinguish between slow, evolutionary, and break-point change. Was the end of the Cold War a sharp breakpoint in history, or was it simply one more stage in an evolving process? If viewed from the perspective of December 1989, it seemed like a sharp, break-point change; in the context of circumstances more than a decade later, it seems more like a logical step in an evolving world situation.

Likewise, we all have some notion of the adaptability of human systems, the capacity of collectivities to adapt to change, challenges, threats, and opportunities. Needless to say, analysts differ on such matters. In one form or another, for example, I have often been asked, "Hey Rosenau, what's new? What you describe could have been said about the seventeenth century." My response to the question is that the world has entered a new epoch, that a lot has changed, and that there is more transformation at work than we appreciate. To those who skeptically ask, "What's new?" my response is, "You have a different assumption about the nature of change and history than I do. Where you tend to see continuity, I tend to see change." I used to drive a former colleague apoplectic by arguing that in many ways our contrary approaches stemmed from a temperamental difference. For him history involves objective realities. "What do you mean calling this temperamental!" he would say, raising his voice. "You're demeaning us!" My view is that inescapably we are always linked into that which we study, and since our temperaments are inherent in whom we are, our notions of change and history are in part temperamental. The same is true of the adaptability of human systems. Some of us see collectivities as retreating to the local when challenged from abroad; others of us regard human systems as adaptable and capable of coping with challenges.

The location of causation in human affairs is another assumption that we all bring to bear, in one form or another, on any problem we study.

The literature on this assumption involves the distinction between agency and structure—whether things unfold as they do because of human agency, be it individual or collective, or whether they unfold because of large macro structures that, in effect, dictate what humans do, be they collectivities or individuals. Again analysts may differ substantially with respect to the agent-structure distinction. But such differences matter less than whether they are made explicit so that they can be evaluated. Years ago I made up a word that many of my students still recall. In order to stress the need to be explicit, which is at the heart of science, the word I made up is *checkableupable*. One has to be checkableupable so that the influence of one's concepts, values, and methodologies underlying one's findings and interpretations can be assessed. And it is my commitment to checkableupableness that has led to the inclusion of this chapter here at the end of this book. I hope it will enable the reader to go back and account for some of the observations that seemed perplexing during the first reading.

These several presumptions add up to an initial premise, one that is the basis of my anomaly file and one about which I feel very strongly, namely, that people and communities at every level are undergoing transformations that are profound, pervasive, and consequential. I argue that these transformations are so profound that presently we are not fully aware of their implications and their nature. Sometime late in the twenty-first century people will look back to our time and say, "Oh, that is when the lifestyle and the institutions we have today began. They began back late in the twentieth century." My *Turbulence in World Politics* and all my subsequent writings are rooted in the proposition that these transformations continue to unfold.

I should add that even as these transformations unfold, so do resistances to them develop; that even as globalization proceeds apace, so is it the case that in various parts of the world and in various institutions at various levels of community, localizing tendencies evolve as the implications and processes of globalization come to be appreciated. As previously indicated, this reasoning about the continuing, pervasive, and dominant tensions between such contradictory forces underlies the conviction that analysis must go beyond globalization and focus on fragmegrative dynamics. I like the notion of fragmegration because it captures in one expression these tensions. It continuously reminds us that integrative and fragmenting forces are endlessly interactive and that they are causally linked. It is also a grating word; it is bothersome; and it is uncomfortable. I don't mind that it's annoying because that way we remember it better and remain in touch with its polar opposites. Indeed, my visit to Belgium led me to the conclusion that it is among the richest laboratories for probing the dynamics of fragmegration. It is the headquarters of the European Union, where the goal is to integrate the practices, laws, and standards of diverse countries, and it is also the site of such strong fragmenting impulses that it may be led to break into two countries in the decades ahead.

The anomaly file, it is clear, opened my eyes experientially as well as intellectually. One travels outside the ivory tower only to find that it is not nearly as removed from ongoing developments in the world as is so often alleged.

CONFRONTING POSTMODERNISM

While it was not until 1999 that I was compelled to confront why my intellectual identity had changed during the 1980s, the evolution of postpositivist, postmodern, and allied perspectives in the study of international relations during the 1990s posed new and important challenges to my hard-won commitment to the turbulence model. The challenges took a concrete form when I was asked to react to the utility of the new approaches in a conference paper. That paper serves as the basis for the remainder of this chapter,[14] and it is founded on an underlying ambivalence. On the one hand, as a sympathetic veteran of shifting perspectives, I can readily grasp the sense of isolation shared by the early postmodernists as a consequence of their divergence from the field's prevailing paradigms—that feeling of being under siege for sensing what others fail to see, that recognition, to quote one of them, "of the extraordinary lengths to which one must go to challenge a given structure of intelligibility, to intervene in resident meanings by bringing what is silent and unglimpsed into focus, is an essential step towards opening up possibilities for a politics and ethics of discourse"[15]—but on the other hand the newer approaches seemed far removed from both my early science and my later relaxed-science empirical orientations. Most of all, the new approaches posed a series of troubling questions: What does the proliferation of postmodern, poststructuralist, postpositivist, and post-or-neo-anything-that-is-a-long-standing-approach-to-the-field signify? Intellectual ferment? A growing wisdom? A sense that deep understanding is not possible? A need for polarities? A generational transformation? A political move? A fragmenting world? Questions such as these are worth probing, but here I can only hint at the answers by addressing a persistent bewilder-

---

[14] For a published version of the paper, see Rosenau, "Confessions of a Pre-postmodernist."

[15] Michael J. Shapiro, quoted in Roland Bleiker, *Retracing and Redrawing the Boundaries of Events: Postmodern Interferences with International Theory* (Copenhagen: Danish Institute of International Affairs, No. 17, Working Papers, 1997), p. 2.

ment over why the lines between newer and older schools of IR thought are drawn so tightly and, alternatively, why so few efforts are made to achieve synthesis among them.

Nor is my bewilderment new or naive.[16] It has plagued me across five decades of IR teaching and research. The content of the competitive schools has changed substantially, but the lack of efforts at synthesis is hardly less conspicuous. Unaffected by mushrooming complexity, unawed by transformative dynamics, unwilling to concede we may be in error, and ever ready to denigrate other approaches, most of us either remain ensconced in our own paradigmatic world or slug away at other worlds. For an old-timer who was a vigorous participant in earlier slugfests, the time has come to resort to bridge-building, to seek to span the gulfs that divide us.

It might be asked why efforts should be made to bridge theoretical and methodological differences between the older and newer schools. Is it merely a wishy-washy, idealistic aspiration to minimize needless tensions and conflicts? Or are there sound substantive reasons to undertake synthesizing efforts? Conceding ontological and epistemological differences can be inherently contradictory—not to mention an idealistic preference for cooperation and an emotional distaste for energy wasted on sustained tensions—and may underlie my response to these questions, I nevertheless believe that a good, substantive case can be made for bridge-building. The case is founded on the premise that knowledge-building is a consensual process, that understanding derives from shared, intersubjective agreements as to how the world works, and that therefore seemingly conflictual approaches can benefit from converging with each other, or at least from remaining open to, rather than condemning, alternative theories, methodologies, and findings. None of us has a corner on ultimate truth. All of us undertake inquiries with a point of view, with values and agendas that we may not fully appreciate are operative. So we ought to be appreciative of alternative perspectives that highlight how our analyses may suffer from exaggerated and unrecognized premises and procedures. Put more specifically, surely those who articulate the newer perspectives can draw on the insights and findings of their predecessors even as they tailor them to their own inquiries and methodologies. Likewise, surely those who employ the older perspectives can profit from pondering the interpretations and critiques of the newer approaches even as they maintain their theoretical and methodological premises.

---

[16] See, for example, James N. Rosenau, *Of Bridges and Boundaries* (Research Monograph No. 27, Center of International Studies, Princeton University, 1967).

SOME CREDENTIALS

Aside from the alleged perspective that goes with being an old-timer, I view myself as loaded down with credentials that attach some legitimacy to this effort at synthesis. The main credential—but not the only one—derives from having been an early warrior in the battle to establish behavioral and quantitative perspectives as legitimate approaches to the study of IR. As implied earlier, it does not require much effort to recall either the unqualified convictions and enthusiasm with which we waged that struggle in the 1950s or the thoroughgoing obstinacy and ridicule with which our arguments were dismissed by early realists. We were, or at least we felt we were, a small band of renegades who dared to question the prevailing wisdom that states predominated in an anarchical world and that they did so by seeking to maximize their power.

As we became more articulate in advancing our case and carrying out studies that supported it, so did we evoke more articulate and intense criticism and ridicule[17]—an escalatory process that seemed to acquire greater momentum with each publication and each counterreaction. Indeed, we had to devote considerable energy to defending our flanks and answering the more extreme of the criticisms,[18] a process that doubtless led us to be insular and aggressive, to convene conferences and read journals in which we quoted each other and avoided open interaction with other than like-minded colleagues. And the more we fed off each other, the more sharply did we draw the lines that divided us from our critics and the more did we become convinced that we had discovered the royal road to "truth" that had eluded others. That royal road was paved with expectations in which the application of scientific methods would enable us to uncover quantified patterns that would demonstrate how the underpinnings of world politics functioned or, in my case, how and why different countries pursued different foreign policies on the basis of their size, their degree of economic development, and their form of political accountability.[19] To be sure, we acknowledged, there were exceptions and anomalies—or, in statistical terms, outliers—but we did not attach much

---

[17] See, for example, Hedley Bull, "The Case for a Classical Approach," in Klaus Knorr and James N. Rosenau (eds.), *Contending Approaches to International Politics* (Princeton, N.J.: Princeton University Press, 1969), pp. 20–38.

[18] An insightful example is provided in Robert C. North, "Research Pluralism and the International Elephant," in Knorr and Rosenau (eds.), *Contending Approaches to International Politics*, pp. 218–42.

[19] James N. Rosenau, "Pre-theories and Theories of Foreign Policy," in R. B. Farrell (ed.), *Approaches to Comparative and International Politics* (Evanston, Ill.: Northwestern University Press, 1966), pp. 27–92.

importance to them as long as the central tendencies embedded in large bodies of data were unmistakable in their direction.

As hinted at earlier, these were heady times, imbued with a spirit of righteousness and adventure. There was satisfaction, even exhilaration, to be had in feeling we were fighting the good fight—the fight for "truth," for understanding founded on the secure footings of a rigorous methodology, for systematic inquiry rather than intuitive and unsubstantiated observations. Moreover, there was a sense of triumph in pointing out how the traditional approaches yielded findings that were questionable because they could be interpreted in so many ways.

Partly because we were successful and began to be defined as the mainstream, partly because our claims for the virtues of a scientific approach proved to be premature as our inquiries raised as many questions as they answered, and partly because new schools of IR research evolved that seem to hold greater promise than did ours, by the mid-1970s our élan began to wane, and instead of affirming their scientific commitments, some of those in our ranks began to deny they ever were "behavioralists"—as if the word represented an outmoded and far-fetched approach to the study of world politics. In some quarters, especially those that began to turn to postmodern perspectives, the notion of "behavioralism" or "positivism" came to be used pejoratively. I do not recall any of those in our ranks referring to themselves as "positivists"—in fact, I had never heard the term until I was accused of being one—but for the critics there seemed to be a special pride in insisting they were postpositivists or poststructuralists, as if such a label indicated they had cleansed the impurities from their inquiries and had moved on to become serious scholars free of the silliness of science. Indeed, I have the impression that many of those who saw themselves as postpositivists latched on to postmodernism or poststructuralism because they seemed to offer a philosophical perspective, an intellectual structure and rationale, that infused substance into their rejection of behavioral approaches. In short, postpositivists and poststructuralists became as rigid and ideological with respect to behavioralists as we had been in our rejection of Morgenthau and other versions of realism. And in neither paradigmatic transition were voices heard that sought to bridge the differences and achieve syntheses. Reinforced by the publication of Kuhn's persuasive argument that paradigms are all-encompassing and mutually exclusive,[20] we saw no need to reach out across the paradigmatic divides for greater understanding.

---

[20] Thomas S. Kuhn, *The Structure of Scientific Revolutions*, 2d ed. (Chicago: University of Chicago Press, 1970).

A CAVEAT

Looking back on my participation in the early debates and the writings I contributed to them, I find comfort in a perspective I articulated that more than offsets the subsequent postpositivist, poststructural, and postmodern criticisms. The latter fault those committed to scientific inquiry for claiming objectivity when in fact they have hidden political agendas and are endlessly making what the postmodernists call political moves. Indeed, as I understand their paradigm, it is a central tenet of postmodernism that all observations, even those consisting of statistically affirmed quantified patterns, are rooted in values and thus can never claim objectivity. The trouble with behavioralism, positivism, and science, the argument would appear to be, is that the findings uncovered can never tell the whole story, that inevitably they rest on value premises that are pervaded with silences not revealed by their patterns, and that therefore it is profoundly deceptive to contend that "truths" have been uncovered even by the most careful and systematic of inquiries. From postmodern and poststructural perspectives, scientists deceive themselves as well as their audiences when they cast their results in the language of established facts.

There is truth in this line of reasoning—except in my case it does not hold. As noted in previous chapters, in the very earliest of my works and consistently thereafter, I reiterated the caveat that it was not possible to engage in objective analysis, that we practice a value-explicit and not a value-free science, that the scientist has the obligation to explicate the value, conceptual, and methodological bases of his or her analysis. Time and again I stressed that the core of science involved explicitness so that the reader could check up on whether the purported findings held up in the context of other values, concepts, or methodologies. If others concluded that a set of findings did check out, then they could join a consensus in support of the understandings thereby generated; if their checkableupableness resulted in a rejection of the findings, then no consensus would form around the findings, and they would probably disappear into an ever-widening dustbin of failed inquiries. Thus, I argued, did knowledge evolve: it consists of an ever-evolving series of competitive consensuses that are not objective but intersubjective in nature.

I have never come upon objective results, and I never will; the postmodernists and poststructuralists are right: such results do not and cannot exist. And they are also right in arguing that the prevailing consensuses may overlook matters of concern, silences to which attention needs to be paid. But they are wrong, I would argue, in claiming that those committed to scientific inquiry presume they can uncover objective truths. Our early enthusiasm for behavioralism may have conveyed such a presumption, but it was not long before our subsequent "truth" claims were couched in probabilistic terms that acknowledged the intersubjective nature of any conclusions derived from systematic analyses. To repeat, be they in the hard or soft sciences, the best that scientists can do is uncover findings that are the focus of widespread consensuses.

TOWARD SYNTHESIS

This caveat, I would argue now with the hindsight of an old-timer, has the makings of a workable synthesis that can bridge some of the paradigmatic divides. If it is the case that most or all versions of postmodernism and poststructuralism presume that interpretations are inevitably subjective and reflective of the values and/or goals of those who offer them, then that is not far removed from the position of those who view science and scientific methods as rooted in intersubjectivity. Scientists care more than postmodernists or poststructuralists about establishing widespread agreement among observers about the nature of what they study, but they acknowledge that their findings do not exist prior to their interpretation of them and that the widespread agreements can dissipate as new findings refute them and observers flock to the new findings and form a consensual interpretation of them. "Wait a minute," a postmodernist or poststructuralist might respond. "We don't care about consensuses. Every interpretation is unique to the interpreter, and it doesn't much matter if different interpreters come to similar conclusions." Even if this response is accurate—and I doubt that it is, as one can readily cite convergences among postmodernists and poststructuralists—it skirts the essential point that both scientists and their opponents share a view that interpretation derives from subjective sources that channel observations. That scientists aspire to broadening support for their interpretations, while postmodernists and poststructuralists imply they have no such aspirations, does not alter the conclusion that all three schools of thought allow for the intrusion of personal biases, values, and convictions. Nor is the conclusion undermined by the commitment of scientists to an elaborate methodology for checking out their findings while such a methodology tends to be an anathema to postmodernists and poststructuralists who believe that "checkableupableness" can never fully explicate the interpretations hidden in the methods of science.

ON THE NATURE OF PRE-POSTMODERNISM

It is precisely the commitment to moving from subjective to intersubjective understanding through a methodology that allows consensuses to form that prevents my crossing the line into the world of postpositivists, poststructuralists, and postmodernists. I have changed course in the sense that I share their view that science's preoccupation with parsimony narrows the field within which they can engage in observations; as already indicated, since the early 1980s I have argued the time has come to relax the strictures of parsimony. And I also agree that the silenced voices need to be heard, that some scientists are unmindful of the need for explicitness and thus deceive themselves into viewing their findings as objective reality, and that some of them also have implicit political agendas that guide their inquiries. Still, to concede these points is not to negate my view of science as an explicit, consensus-building enterprise. It is merely to acknowledge that some scientists fit the postmodernist and poststructuralist stereotype of modernist procedures. Even though the shoe fits some practitioners, however, it remains the case that at their core the scientific methodologies of the modernist, the critical discourse methodologies of the postpositivist, and the deconstructionist methodologies of the postmodernist are essentially identical insofar as they share a readiness to proceed explicitly as they probe whatever problems of world politics they deem significant.

To be a pre-postmodernist or a pre-poststructuralist, then, is to straddle the two schools of thought and to discern a mechanism for synthesizing them. It is to acknowledge that many of the charges against modernism, behavioralism, and positivism are not without merit, but it is also to retain a commitment to empirical inquiry that is founded on explicitness. This is the unifying mechanism. While the several approaches may differ on the virtues of empiricism, intersubjectivity, and the relevance of power, they share a deep-seated belief in checkableupableness. Admittedly, this does not mean they will accept each other's knowledge that checks out, and thus they may never subscribe to the same consensuses, but each arrives at its interpretations through a shared commitment to explication, and therein lies the basis for pre-postmodernism and/or pre-poststructuralism: they are empirical enterprises committed to a relaxed view of scientific methods and a readiness to concede that values shape the questions asked by investigators and the answers they offer subsequent to their analyses.

In sum, age has led to moderation. My story is that of a transition from a feisty behavioralist certain his was the only way to a bridge-builder ready to acknowledge that any intellectual endeavor may have merit. What I do not know is whether one can get to the latter outcome without experiencing the earlier feistiness. In a deep sense this book is an effort to contribute to narrowing the gap between the two perspectives. The complexities of fragmegration and the many sources that sustain it are too great to espouse approaches that do not allow for subtle nuances.

Author Index

Subject Index